ENCYCLOPEDIA OF INDIAN PHILOSOPHIES

ENCYCLOPEDIA OF INDIAN PHILOSOPHIES
General Editor: Karl H. Potter

VOLUMES ALREADY PUBLISHED

I. **Bibliography [Sections I and II] (1995)**—Ed. *Karl H. Potter*

II. **Indian Metaphysics and Epistemology**: The Tradition of Nyāya Vaiśeṣika up to Gaṅgeśa (1977)—Ed. *Karl H. Potter*

III. **Advaita Vedānta up to Śaṁkara and His Pupils (1981)** —Ed. *Karl H. Potter*

IV. **Sāṁkhya:** A Dualist Tradition in Indian Philosophy (1987) —Eds. *Gerald James Larson & Ram Shankar Bhattacharyya*

V. **The Philosophy of the Grammarians (1990)**—Eds. *H.G. Coward & K. Kunjunni Raja*

VI. **Indian Philosophical Analysis:** Nyāya-Vaiśeṣika from Gaṅgeśa to Raghunātha Śiromaṇi (1993)—Eds. *Karl H. Potter & Sibjiban Bhattacharyya*

VII. **Abhidharma Buddhism with to 150 A.D. (1996)**—Eds. *Karl H. Potter*, with *Robert E. Buswell Jr., Padmanabh S. Jaini & Noble Ross Reat*

VIII. **Buddhist Philosophy from 100 to 350 A.D. (1999)** —Ed. *Karl H. Potter*

IX. **Buddhist Philosophy from 350 to 600 A.D. (2003)** —Ed. *Karl H. Potter*

X. **Jain Philosophy [Part I] (2007)**—Eds. *Dalsukh Malvania & Jayendra Soni*

XI. **Advaita Vedānta from 800 to 1200 A.D. (2006)**—Ed. *Karl H. Potter*

XII. **Yoga: India's Philosophy of Meditation (2008)**—Eds. *Gerald J. Larson & Rama Shankar Bhattacharyya*

XIII. **Nyāya-Vaiśeṣika Philosophy from 1515 to 1660 A.D. (2010)** —Eds. *Sibjiban Bhattacharyya & Karl H. Potter*

XIV. **Jain Philosophy [Part II]**—Eds. *Karl H. Potter & Piotr Balcerowicz*

XV. **Bhedabheda and Dvaitādvaita Philosophy**—Eds. *M.M. Agrawal & Karl H. Potter*

VOLUMES UNDER PREPARATION

Buddhist Philosophy from 600 to 750 A.D.—Ed. *Eli Franco*

Buddhist Philosophy from 750 to 1300 A.D.—Ed. *Karl H. Potter*

Kaśmīr Śaiva Philosophy—Ed. *Navjivan Rastogi*

Viśiṣṭādvaita Vedānta Philosophy–Eds. *Stephen H. Phillips & M. Narasimhachary*

Advaita Vedānta from 1200 A.D. to the present—Ed. *Godavarisa Misra*

Pūrvamīmāṁsā Philosophy—Eds. *K.T. Pandurangi & Karl H. Potter*

Acintyabhedābheda Philosophy—Ed. *Srivatsa Goswami*

Dvaita Vedānta Philosophy—Ed. *Sarothaman*

Cārvāka Philosophy—Ed. *Eli Franco*

Śuddhādvaita Vedānta Philosophy—Eds. *Sharad Aniruddha Goswami & Shyam Manoharaji Goswami*

Vīraśaiva Philosophy—Eds. *N.G. Mahadevappa*

Collective Glossary-Index—Ed. *Karl H. Potter*

ENCYCLOPEDIA OF INDIAN PHILOSOPHIES

VOLUME XII

Yoga: India's Philosophy of Meditation

Edited by
GERALD JAMES LARSON
RAM SHANKAR BHATTACHARYA

MOTILAL BANARSIDASS PUBLISHERS
PRIVATE LIMITED • DELHI

2nd Reprint : Delhi, 2016
First Edition: 2008

ISBN: 978-81-208-3349-4 (Vol. XII)
ISBN: 978-81-208-0307-7 (Set)

Also Available at:
MOTILAL BANARSIDASS
41 U.A. Bungalow Road, Jawahar Nagar, Delhi 110 007
8 Mahalaxmi Chamber, 22 Bhulabhai Desai Road, Mumbai 400 026
203 Royapettah High Road, Mylapore, Chennai 600 004
236, 9th Main III Block, Jayanagar, Bengaluru 560 011
8 Camac Street, Kolkata 700 017
Ashok Rajpath, Patna 800 004
Chowk, Varanasi 221 001

MLBD Cataloging-in-Publication Data
Encyclopedia of Indian Philosophy Vol. XII
Yoga: Indian's Philosophy of Maditation by G.J. Larson and R.S. Bhattacharya
Includes bibliography and Glossary-Index
ISBN : 978-81-208-3349-4
I. Encyclopedia II. Philosophy III. Yoga IV. Yogasūtras V. Patañjali
VI. Larson, Gerald James VII. Bhattacharya, Ram Shankar

Printed in India

By Nice Printing Press,
A-33/3A, Site 4, Sahibabad Industrial Area, Ghaziabad, U.P.
and published by JP Jain for Motilal Banarsidass Publishers (P) Ltd.
41 U.A. Bungalow Road, Jawahar Nagar, Delhi-110 007

CONTRIBUTORS

Govardhan Bhatt
Jyotirmoyee Bhattacharya
Ram Shankar Bhattacharya
Tuvia Gelblum
Autumn Jacobsen
Gerald James Larson
K. N. Misra
R. N. Mukerji
Karl H. Potter
N. S. S. Raman
T. S. Rukmani
Anima Sen Gupta
Dolgobinda Shastri

ABBREVIATIONS

E = the edition being used here
ET = edited and translated
n.d. = no date
passim = here and there
T = the translation being used here
VKS = Vivaraṇakāra Śaṃkara
YB = Vyāsa's *Yogabhāṣya*
YS = Patañjali's *Yogasūtras*

CONTENTS

PART TWO: SUMMARIES OF WORKS

TEXTS: Pātañjala Yoga Traditions

IN MEMORIAM

Dr. Ram Shankar Bhattacarya (1927-1996)

My first visit to India was in 1968 as a post-doctoral research scholar in the old College of Indology (now the Department of Ancient History and Culture) at Banaras Hindu University, Varanasi. I had studied classical Sanskrit (and other South Asian languages) for some five years at Columbia University in New York City and had completed my Ph.D. degree with a dissertation on Sāṃkhya philosophy. Even though my western education was finished, I very much wanted to read with a traditional pandit. A. K. Narain, Principal of the College of Indology in those days, arranged for me to meet a certain Ram Shankar Bhattacharya who was working in the research division of the Sanskrit university (Sampūrṇānanda Saṃskṛta Viśvavidyālaya) in downtown Varanasi.

After a brief meeting, Dr. Bhattacharya and I agreed to read Sanskrit together every morning at his residence in the Sonarpura district (in Varanasi). I was evidently his first foreign student, since it became clear that he was as uncomfortable with me as I was with him. Nevertheless, we persevered and eventually began to make significant progress. At first he felt insulted when I would ask a question. He expected me simply to listen as he expounded various Sanskrit passages, unscrambling compounds in Sanskrit and giving cross-references to related texts. As a young Ph.D., however, I was not about to spend a year as a passive student, and so I began to interrupt him with questions, usually about Sanskrit compounds, but eventually about the interpretation of the meaning of the texts that we were reading. Simple questions and answers quickly turned into more detailed discussions, then from time to time into rather heated exchanges, and finally, on some occasions into raging debates. In short, we were becoming friends, and a collaboration began to unfold that was to continue for nearly three decades until his unexpected death in June of 1996.

I recall many wonderful occasions during our interactions through the years, including meeting his new bride, the distinguished Dr. Jyotirmoyee Bhattacharya (*ācārya* and Ph.D. in *Jyotiṣa* and one of the chief astrologers in Varanasi); taking food together for the first time when Dr. Bhattacharya determined that the pollution entailed by eating with a *mleccha* was worth the risk for the sake of our growing friendship; touring around Varanasi to visit the various Durgās during the time of Durgā Pūjā; and getting to know the young nieces that Dr. and Mrs. Bhattacharya had agreed to raise from earliest childhood because of the untimely death of their mother (Mrs. Bhattacharya's sister-in-law).

One anecdote in particular is worth recounting by way of illustrating the sort of person Dr. Bhattacharya was. In the early months of our reading together, he inquired one day about the books that Americans use to learn Sanskrit. I told him about Lanman's *Sanskrit Reader,* the various first-year Sanskrit books available at that time, W. D. Whitney's *Sanskrit Grammar* (the basic reference grammar, still widely used even though dated) and, of course, M. Monier-Williams's *Sanskrit-English Dictionary*. He then asked if he could borrow Whitney's grammar, and I immediately handed over my copy of Whitney. When I came the next day for our reading session, Dr. Bhattacharya informed me that he had stayed up all night reading Whitney's grammar. He commented: "This fellow, Whitney--his explanations are not very good, but his collection of passages is very helpful!" I then described for him the now-dated tradition of American empirical linguistics, but I was impressed that he had understood what was at issue in a single reading.

Ram Shankar Bhattacharya was born September 18, 1927 in the village of Bhattapara in what is now West Bengal. Both his father and grandfather were well-known Sanskritists. He received the status of "Śāstri" in Pāṇinian grammar (First Class

First) from the Government Sanskrit College (later to become the Sanskrit University) in Varanasi in 1951, and the status of "Ācārya" in Pāṇinian Grammar from the same institution in 1954. He took an M.A. in Sanskrit from Agra University in 1957, a Ph.D. in 1962 with a thesis entitled "A Critical Study of the Vedic Data in the Purāṇas" (published in Hindi by the Hindi Sahitya Sammelan in 1963). He also received a D.Litt. (1969) with a thesis entitled "A Critical Study of the Principles Underlying the Structure and Arrangement of the Pāṇinian Sūtras" (unpublished).

Through his long career as scholar and teacher, he worked as a resident scholar in the research division of Sampūrṇānanda Sanskrit University, as one of the directors of the Purāṇa project of the Maharaja of Banaras and as editor of the journal *Purāṇa*. He had numerous advanced students, both Indian and foreign, who worked with him on an individual tutorial basis. His main areas of scholarly interest were Sanskrit grammar, Sāṃkhya and Yoga philosophical texts, and Purāṇic studies. He was the author of over thirty volumes of editions, translations, annotated texts and critical studies in Sanskrit, Hindi, Bengali and English. His most important studies, especially with reference to the present volume, include the following: (1) his edition *Pātañjalayogadarśanam*, with the *Bhāṣya* of Vyāsa and the *Tattvavaiśāradī* of Vācaspatimiśra, in Sanskrit with Introduction and Notes (Varanasi: Bharatiya Vidya Prakashana, 1963); (2) his edition of *Pātañjalayogasūtram* with *Rājamārtaṇḍa* of Bhojadeva, in Sanskrit with Introduction in Hindi and accompanied with a Hindi commentary, *Vyākhyā,* by A. D. Sinha (Varanasi: Bharatiya Vidya Prakashana, 1963); (3) his edition of *Sāṃkhyasāra* of Vijñānabhikṣu, in Sanskrit with Introduction and Notes (Varanasi: Bharatiya Vidya Prakashana, 1965); (4) his edition of *Sāṃkhyatattvakaumudī* with the *Sāṃkhyakārikā*, in Sanskrit with Introduction and Notes in Hindi (Delhi: Motilal Banarsidass, 1965, 1967, 1976); (5) his edition *Sāṃkhyadarśanam* with *Tattvasamāsasūtra* and the *Ṭīkā* of Bhāvaganeśa, in Sanskrit with Introduction and Notes

(Varanasi: Bharatiya Vidya Prakashana, 1968); (6) his original work, *An Introduction to the Yogasūtra* (Varanasi: Bharatiya Vidya Prakashana, 1985); (7) his co-edited edition with Gerald J. Larson, *Sāṃkhya: A Dualist Tradition in Indian Philosophy* (Princeton University Press, 1987, and Delhi: Motilal Banarsidass, 1987) (Volume IV of the Encyclopedia of Indian Philosohies, general editor Karl H. Potter); (8) his edition and translation of *Yogasārasaṃgraha* of Vijñānabhikṣu, in Sanskrit with translations in Hindi and English (Varanasi: Bharatiya Vidya Prakashana, 1989); (9) his edition of *Sāṃkhyadarśanam* with *Sāṃkhyasūtras* and *Bhāṣya* of Vijñānabhikṣu, in Sanskrit with Hindi commentary, *Vyākhyā* (Varanasi: Bharatiya Vidya Prakashana, 1994); and (10) his edition of *Sāṃkhyasūtra* with the *Vṛtti* of Aniruddha, in Sanskrit with Introduction and Notes (Varanasi: Bharatiya Vidya Prakashana, n.d.).

In addition to these volumes that are of immediate relevance to this volume, Ram Shankar Bhattacharya also published some four volumes of studies on the *Purāṇas* (Agni, Vāmana, Kūrma and Garuḍa), four volumes of studies on Pāṇinian grammar, and some studies of the works of the Yogin Hariharānanda Āraṇya (whom he considered to be his guru, and for whose Ashrama in Madhupur, Bihar, he served as a member of the Board of Directors). He was also the author of numerous scholarly articles on grammar, Indian philosophy, and Purāṇic studies.

While his scholarly work ranged widely in Sanskrit literature, philosophy and grammar, it was always clear to me that his first love was the Yoga philosophy of Patañjali together with the great *Bhā*ṣya attributed to Vyāsa. It is especially appropriate, therefore, that this volume of the Encyclopedia of Indian Philosophies be dedicated to this very special human being, Ram Shankar Bhattacharya, tenacious scholar, engaging colleague, and truly authentic *jñāna-yogin*.

Gerald James Larson

PREFACE

There has been a long period of time between the publication of the Sāṃkhya volume of the Encyclopedia of Indian Philosophies (*Sāṃkhya: A Dualist Tradition in Indian Philosophy*, Volume IV) in 1987 and this sequel on Yoga. Nevertheless, in our view, the two volumes are best used in tandem, since Pātañjala Yoga as a philosophical tradition is unintelligible without the Sāṃkhya ontology and epistemology. As may be recalled from our earlier Sāṃkhya volume, we are inclined to go even further and to claim that Yoga as a philosophical tradition is a particular form of Sāṃkhya, namely Pātañjala-Sāṃkhya. The expression "...as a philosophical tradition," of course, is a fundamental caveat, and this will be discussed at some length in the Introduction. It will be shown that although Yoga and Sāṃkhya are by no means identical and that there are significant differences in the classical formulation of each system, the family resemblance is so striking that it is impossible to discuss one system apart from the other.

I deeply regret that Dr. Ram Shankar Bhattacharya's untimely death kept him from composing the Introduction to this Volume on Yoga. He very much wanted to do the Introduction, since he viewed the philosophy of Yoga as an area of his primary scholarly interest through the years. His great erudition is to be found in his many critical editions of the Sanskrit texts of Yoga in the medium of Sanskrit. Also he wrote at least a brief summary of his views on Yoga in the medium of English in his book, *An Introduction to the Yogasūtra*, already mentioned above in the foregoing In Memoriam.

Two additional acknowledgments are also necessary. First, varieties of Yoga have become popular throughout the world, and this volume on Yoga of the Encyclopedia of Indian Philosophies, if for no other reason than providing a summary overview, should at least touch upon these popular traditions. I would like to thank Ms. Autumn Jacobsen, a doctoral student in Religious Studies at the University of California at Santa Barbara, who wrote the final portion of the Introduction to this Volume, namely the section entitled "Contemporary Yoga Traditions".

Second, thanks to Richa Pauranik Clements, my doctoral student at Indiana University, Bloomington, who assisted me in the editing of many of the summaries.

The bibliography on Yoga, of course, is vast, and we had to make difficult decisions about what to include and what not to include, both in terms of primary and secondary works. We hope that our selection, if not exhaustive, is at least representative of the most important texts. Also, it should be noted that we have divided the texts into two main groups, the Pātañjala Yoga texts and what we have called "The Haṭha Yoga System and Other Satellite Traditions of Yoga". The dating of texts in the later centuries, of course, is nearly an impossible task, and it should be recognized that our attempts at dating are almost all only rough approximations.

Gerald James Larson
Santa Barbara, California
August 2007

PART ONE

INTRODUCTION TO THE PHILOSOPHY OF YOGA

INTRODUCTION TO THE PHILOSOPHY OF YOGA

Gerald James Larson

The History and Literature of Yoga

The History of Yoga: Preliminary Remarks

Yoga in the region of South Asia is much more than a philosophical tradition, but it is at least a philosophical tradition; and one primary goal of this volume is to clarify in what sense yoga can be considered one of the philosophies of India. A second goal of the volume is to determine with some care the boundary lines between Yoga as a philosophy and Yoga as one or another tradition of experimental or experiential practice (whether ritualistic, devotional, meditative, therapeutic, alchemical or magical). Yet a further goal of the volume is to address the issue of the manner in which one can separate the experimental or experiential claims of Yoga from the philosophical claims. Finally, an important goal of the volume is to clarify the meaning of the term "*yoga*", and to indicate the manner in which the term will be used in this volume. Let me begin this Introduction, then, by offering some comments about each of these goals.

(1) Regarding the first goal, the Sanskrit textual tradition clearly identifies Yoga as one of the philosophies of India. It is usually referred to as Pātañjalayogaśāstra or Pātañjalayogadarśana ("the learned tradition of Yoga in the lineage or school belonging to Patañjali") or simply Pātañjala Yoga as set forth in the *Yogasūtra* (hereafter, YS), compiled by a certain Patañjali in the early centuries of the Common Era (ca. 350-450). The *sūtra* collection itself (called simply *sūtrapāṭha*) is a compilation of 195 *sūtras* in four chapters or *pādas* containing 51, 55, 55 and 34 *sūtras* respectively. Some of these *sūtras*, it should be noted, may well be much older than the first centuries of the Common Era when they were incorporated into what we now know as the YS. The YS has an accompanying commentary or *Bhāṣya*, attributed to a certain Vyāsa, and likewise to be dated somewhere in the fourth or fifth century of the Common Era

(ca. 350-450). The YS and the Vyāsa *Bhāṣya* are almost always taken together for purposes of interpretation, mainly because the *sūtras* themselves are exceedingly difficult to decipher without some sort of commentary.

Some of the more important commentators on the YS, who comment on the YS in the light of the Vyāsa *Bhāṣya*, are Vācaspatimiśra (ca. 9th or 10th century), Bhojarāja (11th century), Vijñānabhikṣu (16th century), Bhāvāgaṇeśa (16th century), Rāmānanda Sarasvatī (16th century), Nārāyaṇatīrtha (17th century), Nāgojibhaṭṭa (18th century), Hariharānanda Āraṇya (20th century), et al.* Some claim that even the famous Advaita Vedānta philosopher Śaṃkara (ca. 8th century) has commented on the YS and the Vyāsa *Bhāṣya* in a text entitled *Pātañjalayogaśāstravivaraṇa*, although this attribution has not been accepted by all in the field. It would seem to be the case, however, that even if not correctly attributed to Śaṃkara himself, this commentary is closely related in style and language to one of the followers of Śaṃkara. If the commentary is by Śaṃkara himself, then it is an early interpretation of the YS. If the commentary is by a later follower of Śaṃkara, it may be as late as the fourteenth century.

In any case, there is clearly an identifiable Yoga philosophy from the time of the YS up through the twentieth century. It should also be noted at the outset that Yoga as one of the philosophies of India with an identifiable Sanskrit textual

---

*It should be noted that Bhoja's commentary does not directly comment on the Vyāsa *Bhāṣya*, claiming to be an original commentary on the *sūtras*. In fact, however, the commentary is dependent throughout on the Vyāsa *Bhāṣya*.

heritage is closely related to a companion system of philosophy--in Sanskrit, a *samānatantra* (common tradition)--known as the Sāṃkhya philosophy. It is not identical to the Sāṃkhya philosophy insofar as it moves beyond the purely theoretical claims of Sāṃkhya in order to explore the empirical techniques and strategies, or perhaps better the experiential implementation of the theoretical insights of Sāṃkhya. Moreover, Yoga philosophy as set forth in the YS and the Vyāsa *Bhāṣya* appears to be a more sophisticated version of the Sāṃkhya philosophy, based upon interactions with Buddhist philosophizing in the first centuries of the Common Era, as will be discussed in the sequel. Without exception, however, the Sanskrit textual tradition on the YS from the time of Vyāsa's *Bhāṣya* up through the twentieth century recognizes that Yoga philosophy is closely related to the Sāṃkhya philosophy. The Vyāsa *Bhāṣya* identifies itself in each of its four sections of commentary on the YS as a "*sāṃkhyapravacana*", that is, "an explication or explanation of Sāṃkhya". Frequently the two systems are simply referred to together as the tradition of Sāṃkhyayoga. In this regard, both Sāṃkhya and Yoga, whether as distinct philosophical traditions or as a common tradition, have been profoundly influential, not only in Hindu, Buddhist, and Jaina religio-philosophical environments but in almost all dimensions of South Asian cultural life, including medicine, law, language, literature, and art.

(2) Regarding the second purpose of this volume, that is, an attempt to clarify the boundaries between Yoga as a philosophy and Yoga as one or another experimental or experiential practice, Mircea Eliade commented long ago, "the *yogadarśana* is not solely a 'system of philosophy'; it sets its mark, so to speak, on a very considerable number of pan-Indian practices, beliefs, and aspirations. Yoga is present everywhere--no less in the oral tradition of India than in the ancient Sanskrit and vernacular literatures. Naturally, this protean Yoga does not always resemble the 'classic' system of Patañjali; rather, we find it in the form of traditional clichés to which, during the

course of the centuries, an increasing number of 'popular' beliefs and practices has been added. To such a degree is this true that Yoga has ended by becoming a characteristic dimension of Indian spirituality."*

On the one hand, there appears to be Yoga as a "system of philosophy", and, on the other hand, there appears to be Yoga as a "characteristic dimension of Indian spirituality". Unfortunately, however, such a neat dichotomy, though perhaps heuristically helpful as a starting point, does not take us very far, for there are considerable problems on either side of the dichotomy. On the philosophical side, it is not fully clear how the Pātañjala Yoga of the YS relates to the classical Sāṃkhya philosophy of Īśvarakṛṣṇa's *Sāṃkhyakārikās* and other traditions of Sāṃkhya such as those of Vārṣagaṇya and Vindhyavāsin. Nor is it fully clear if there was a philosophical Yoga prior to the compilation of the YS and the formulation of the classical Sāṃkhya system. Furthermore, it is not yet clear how the Pātañjala Yoga relates to Buddhist philosophy in the first centuries of the Common Era. The influence of Buddhist thought on the YS and the influence of some notions of Yoga (and Sāṃkhya) on Buddhist thought are undeniable. Similarly, influences of Yoga (and Sāṃkhya) on Jaina thought and on early Vedānta are likewise undeniable. In this regard, it can be plausibly argued that until these relations between Yoga, Sāṃkhya, Buddhist thought, Jaina thought and Vedānta have been clarified it will not be possible to write a cogent history of early Indian philosophy. On the "Indian spirituality" side, it is not sufficiently clear how one should use the term "Yoga" for the congeries of experimental practices and ascetic exercises that appear to go back to time immemorial in the South Asian

---

*In this regard, see Eliade 1958. p. 101.

region. The most recent research indicates that there were a variety of experimental ascetic traditions in ancient South Asian history and culture.* These traditions can be traced not only to Vedic contexts (the Vedic sacrificial texts and the speculative Upaniṣads); some can possibly be traced to Indus Valley environments and even to archaic traditions of Central Asian Shamanic traditions.** How these ancient traditions of practice related to one another and how they came to be identified in some sense as kinds of Yoga is yet to be properly understood.

Likewise there are gaps in our understanding of how the tradition of the YS relates to other traditions of Yoga that run parallel to philosophical Yoga from the early centuries of the Common Era through the medieval and modern periods. There is, for example, the Yoga of the *Bhagavadgītā* and the *Mokṣadharma* portions of the epic *Mahābhārata*.[2] There is the Yoga of the later post-Vedic *Yoga Upaniṣads*.[3] There is the Pāśupata tradition (early centuries of the Common Era) of the

---

*Perhaps the best recent discussion is Bronkhorst 1993. Bronkhorst, utilizing the important work of J. F. Sprockhoff, Patrick Olivelle, et al., who have written extensively on the history of asceticism in South Asia, comprehensively lays out the great variety of ascetic traditions, both Vedic and non-Vedic, in ancient India.

**I have discussed the history of pre-Yoga or proto-Yoga in Larson 1981, pp. 813-817. I have also discussed the history of proto-Yoga traditions in connection with the history of pre-classical Sāṃkhya in Gerald J. Larson 1979; second edition, pp. 75-134. Perhaps the best comprehensive discussions of these ancient proto-Yoga traditions is to be found in Feuerstein 2002, pp. 121-280, and in Feuerstein 1990, *passim*. Feuerstein has written a number of other works on Yoga which are useful reference guides. While his views regarding the philosophy of Yoga and his interpretation of the significance of classical Yoga diverge considerably from mine, his solid work with the original texts over many years is to be taken seriously, in my judgment, for anyone working in the field of Yoga studies.

early Śaiva heritage and the Hiraṇyagarbha ("Golden Germ") tradition as found in the *Ahirbudhnya Saṃhitā* (fourth century of the Common Era) of the Pāñcarātra Vaiṣṇava heritage.[4] Furthermore, there are the later Nātha Yoga and Haṭha Yoga traditions of Mātsyendranātha and Gorakṣanātha (ca. 1000 CE and later); the medieval Siddha traditions (both Hindu and Buddhist); the Aghorīpanth; the Kaula cults; and the many other varieties of later so-called Tantric Yoga traditions.[5] All of these are clearly different from the Pātañjala Yoga, but all freely use the term Yoga for their systems of practice and experimentation. Clearly the boundaries need to be drawn among these various traditions.

(3) This, then, brings us to the third goal of this volume, namely determining whether one can separate the experimental and/or experiential claims of Yoga from the philosophical claims. For the most part, scholarship on Yoga has tended to develop in two distinct directions. First, there are the standard philosophical and philological treatments of Yoga. These include the work of scholars such as Surendranath Dasgupta, Ram Shankar Bhattacharya, M. Hiriyanna, Paul Deussen, H. Jacobi, J. W. Hauer, E. Frauwallner, T. S. Rukmani, A. Wezler, J. Bronkhorst, Stephen H. Phillips et al. This is largely the treatment of Yoga as found in traditional Indology. Second, there are the social anthropological treatments of Yoga which are much more interested in the practical, experiential side of Yoga.These include the work of such scholars as Mircea Eliade, Jean Filliozat, Heinrich Zimmer, Corrado Pensa, A. Janacek, A. Padoux, H. Coward, Georg Feuerstein, Frits Staal, C. Chapple, Ian Whicher, David G. White, et al. These sorts of studies come primarily from the history of religions, religious studies, social anthropological studies and those interested in the practice of Yoga. Some have attempted to work on both sides of the interpretive street, for example, the comprehensive work of Feuerstein. Typical, however, is the tendency to focus on the one side to the exclusion of the other. In this regard Eliade's wonderful but unbalanced *Yoga: Immortality and Freedom* is a

striking example of this tendency. Eliade gives about forty pages to Yoga philosophy (in his Chapter I: "The Doctrines of Yoga", pp. 3-46) but then over four hundred pages to what is perhaps best characterized as massive motif research in the anthropology of South Asia. The problem, of course, is that almost anything or everything related to spiritual practice becomes subsumed under the category of "Yoga," or as Eliade himself puts it, there is a "protean Yoga" or a "baroque" Yoga that comes to be a "characteristic dimension of Indian spirituality".[6] From a certain perspective, of course, this is perfectly true in the sense that all sorts of experimental/experiential spiritual traditions in India claim the name "Yoga". From the perspective of assessing the manner in which experimental/experiential practice is an inextricable component of the Yoga philosophy of the YS, however, more precise theoretical analysis is clearly needed.[7]

One possible way of accomplishing a more precise theoretical analysis is to look more closely at the philosophical relevance of the second and third Books (*pādas*) of the YS itself. These are the Books called the "Sādhana Pāda" (the "Practice" Portion) and the "Vibhūti Pāda" (the "Extraordinary Cognitive Capacities" Portion), portions which are seldom taken seriously in presenting the philosophy of Yoga. The theoretical task is to show how these practices and the resulting "extraordinary cognitive capacities" are integral to accomplishing the ultimate goal of Yoga. The ultimate goal of Yoga philosophy, of course, is set forth in *sūtra* I.2 and I.51 in terms of *yogaś cittavṛtti-nirodhaḥ,* "the cessation of the transformations of ordinary awareness" (YS I.2), and in terms of attaining a "content-less altered state of awareness" (*asamprajñātasamādhi* or *nirbīja samādhi*) (YS I.51), which is "spiritual liberation" (*kaivalya*). If it thus can be made clear how the experimental practices and experiences of the second and third Books of the YS relate to the philosophical goal of Yoga, it then becomes possible to distinguish Yoga *sensus strictus*.

Many of the later peripheral and tangential traditions

appear to represent popular extensions, which sometimes have degenerated into pointless superstition and aberrant psychological behavior. Unfortunately , some of this peripheral and tangential material has found its way into contemporary New Age spiritual practices. New Age bookshelves continue to be filled with the most incredible nonsense that passes itself off as Yoga, ranging from so-called Yoga massage books to *au courant* techniques for new and improved tantric orgasms. Few serious attempts have been made to sort out the remarkable insights of Yoga practice, including the "extraordinary capacities" (*siddhi* or *vibhūti*) from questionable claims that have tended to make Yoga a laughing-stock among serious people. In this regard, it can be plausibly argued that until these matters are sorted out in a responsible discourse, there will be no persuasive way of appropriating the valuable insights of Yogic practice for such fields as philosophy of mind, cognitive, psychology, and bio-medical research.

(4) Finally, let me comment about the term "*yoga*" itself and its correct usage. YS I.1 states: "Herein begins an inquiry into disciplined meditation (*yoga*) based upon past tradition" (*atha yogānuśāsanam*). The Vyāsa *Bhāṣya* in its opening lines literally comments: "Yoga is concentration" (*yogaḥ samādhiḥ*), and Vācaspatimiśra in his commentary points out that Vyāsa's expression "Yoga is concentration" has to do with the etymology of the word "*yoga*". There are two roots "*yuj*" in the Sanskrit grammarian Pāṇini's list of verbal roots as set forth in a text known as the *Dhātupāṭha*, namely (1) *Dhātupāṭha* IV.68: "*yuj samādhau*" and (2) *Dhātupāṭha* VII.7: "*yujir yoge*".[8] The latter root means "yoke" or "join" and indeed is cognate with our English "yoke". The former root "*yuj*" means "in the sense of *samādhi*" (*samādhau*, locative case). In other words, both Vyāsa and Vācaspatimiśra are pointing out that Yoga in this context of Pātañjala Yoga does not mean "*yuj*" in the sense of "yoke" or "join", but rather "*yuj*" in the sense of *samādhi* or concentration. Put another way, the term "Yoga" in the tradition of the YS and its principal commentaries is seldom used in the sense of "yoke",

"join" or "union" as it is sometimes claimed in popular accounts of Yoga. The term refers, rather, to concentration and is most easily understood in the YS and its commentaries simply as "disciplined meditation" in regard to the various states of awareness.

Considerably more about this will be discussed in the sequel, but let me comment a bit further about this issue here at the outset of the Introduction, since this discussion of the meaning of the word is closely related to determining the subject-matter of this Volume. The Vyāsa *Bhāṣya* in its opening lines commenting on YS I.1 further states that "*samādhi*" refers to all levels of mental life (*sārvabhauma*), suggesting in other words that "*yoga*" as "*samādhi*" refers to all possible states of awareness, whether ordinary or extraordinary. Next, the Vyāsa *Bhāṣya* mentions five states of awareness, some of which are ordinary and some extraordinary. They are as follows: (a) distracted (*kṣipta*, an ordinary level of awareness that is largely dominated by (the *guṇa) rajas*); (b) sluggish (*mūḍha*, an ordinary level of awareness that is largely dominated by (the *guṇa) tamas*); (c) partially distracted (*vikṣipta*, an ordinary level of awareness that is largely dominated, again, by *rajas*, but has some influence of (the *guṇa) sattva*); (d) one-pointed (*ekāgra*, a highly-disciplined state of awareness that largely consists of *sattva* with some *rajas*); and (e) suppressed (*niruddha*, an altered state of pure *sattva* in which the other two *guṇas* are inoperative). The Vyāsa *Bhāṣya* then concludes its opening comment by saying that "*yoga*" properly understood refers only to the fourth and fifth levels, that is, to the one-pointed *yoga*, which is equivalent to the various levels of "altered states of awareness with some sort of content" (i.e. content-filled concentration, *samprajñāta-samādhi*), and to the suppressed, which is equivalent to the final goal of Yoga praxis, namely an altered state of awareness that is content-less (content-free concentration, *asamprajñāta-samādhi*).

A reasonable conclusion, therefore, would be that the term "*yoga*" has two distinct uses, one general and the other specific, both of which relate to the idea of Yoga as states of awareness. There is, first, Yoga as a general term to be translated as "disciplined meditation" that focuses on any of the many levels of ordinary awareness. In this general sense, the term "*yoga*" may well encompass disciplined work in any number of areas, including law, medicine, art, ritual, language, and so forth. There is, second, Yoga as that specific system of thought (*śāstra*) that has for its focus the analysis, understanding and cultivation of those altered states of awareness that lead one to the experience of spiritual liberation. It is Yoga as a philosophy in this specific sense, that is, as Pātañjala Yoga, that is the focus of this volume of the Encyclopedia of Indian Philosophies. Perhaps needless to say, in order to clarify Yoga in this specific sense, it will be necessary to range widely from time to time into the areas of more general usage, but it is useful at the outset to make clear the primary focus of our undertaking.

Historiography on Yoga

In any attempt to describe the history of Yoga as a philosophy one immediately encounters in the scholarly literature two extreme positions that render the work of historical reconstruction extremely difficult, if not impossible. The first position represented in the work of J. W. Hauer, Georg Feuerstein, Mircea Eliade et al., is what I am inclined to call the "Yoga is everywhere" point of view. This orientation finds Yoga in archaic folk traditions, the Indus Valley Civilization, the Vedic and Upaniṣadic heritage, the Buddhist and Jaina traditions, the epic traditions (especially the *Bhagavadgītā* and the *Mokṣadharma* of the *Mahābhārata*), the theistic traditions of the Śaivas and Vaiṣṇavas, and later Tantric traditions. In other words, Yoga is an ancient system of spiritual practice that goes back to time immemorial in the South Asian and Central Asian region. There is a primordial or pure Ur-Yoga that resembles something like the perennial philosophy that has found one of its first manifestations in the mystical traditions of South Asia. This point of view downplays the connection of

Yoga with Sāṃkhya. To be sure, there is a recognition by those who follow this approach that Yoga is classified as a *samāna-tantra* ("common tradition") with Sāṃkhya. It is usually asserted, however, that the connection with Sāṃkhya was artificial and largely forced upon Yoga by later commentators, beginning with Vyāsa, most of whom were not really practicing *yogins*. Hauer's comment is illustrative in this regard: "The commentaries subsequent to Vyāsa, even already Vyāsa himself, instead of presenting the genuine philosophy of Yoga often foist on Yoga the philosophy of Sāṃkhya."[9]

The other position, represented by Johannes Bronkhorst, Eric Frauwallner et al., is what I am inclined to call the "Yoga is nowhere" point of view. This sort of orientation argues that Yoga as a coherent philosophical position is found nowhere until it becomes associated with Sāṃkhya or Vedānta or Nyāya-Vaiśeṣika or any philosophical position whatever. The reference to "Yoga followers" in *Nyāyasūtra* I.1.29, for example, according to Bronkhorst is really a reference to Naiyāyikas.[10] Likewise, the reference to Kauṭilya's *Arthaśāstra* I.2.10, "*sāṃkhyaṃ yogo lokāyataṃ cety ānvikṣikī*", usually taken to mean that there were three traditions of "logical thinking" in the early period, namely Sāṃkhya, Yoga and Lokāyata, is not a reference to Pātañjala-yogaśāstra. It really refers to Nyāya-Vaiśeṣika.[11] According to Bronkhorst, there is no clear reference to a Yoga system of philosophy until the time of Śaṃkara's *Brahmasūtrabhāṣya* at II.1.3, which refers to a Sāṃkhya *smṛti* and a Yoga *smṛti*, with the latter referring to Pātañjalayogaśāstra. Illustrative of this "Yoga is nowhere" position is Bronkhorst's conclusion: "If the above expositions are correct, we must conclude that there never was a separate Yoga philosophy. This is saying more than that the 'Yoga philosophy' is closely related with Sāṃkhya, or even an old school of the latter. It entails that the early history of the Yoga school of Sāṃkhya cannot be written, not because there is not sufficient material available, as Frauwallner maintains, but simply because it has no early history and can have none. It seems justified in conclusion to repeat

Frauwallner's observation that the spiritual discipline yoga does not belong to any particular philosophical system, but may, or may not, get connected with a variety of philosophies, depending on the circumstances."[12]

One obvious problem with these two extremes of "Yoga is everywhere" and "Yoga is nowhere" is that Yoga itself as an historical tradition of intellectual learning, or what the tradition calls a *śāstra*, gets lost in the special pleading. In the first case, Yoga becomes a mystical gnosis that somehow floats in and out of the history of spiritual practice in South Asia. In the second case, Yoga becomes whatever one wants it to be. If one is a Naiyāyika, there can be a Nyāya Yoga. If one is a Vedāntin there can be a Vedānta Yoga. If one is a Tantric, there can be a Tantric Yoga, and so forth.

Another problem with these two extremes is their obsession with distancing their interpretive perspectives from the dualism of the Sāṃkhya philosophy in their treatments of Yoga. In the case of the "Yoga is everywhere" point of view, it is perhaps not too difficult to venture a guess as to the reason for the instinctive dislike of the linkage with Sāṃkhya. It is admittedly difficult to argue that the so-called "mystical gnosis" of Yoga, which is marketed as India's great contribution to the perennial philosophy, is closely tied to a dualistic philosophizing that accepts the reality of an intelligible material world and shows little or no interest in traditional religiosity of any kind. There are, of course, numerous other intellectual difficulties with the Sāṃkhya position, but finally it is the very idea of a thoroughgoing eccentric dualism that appears to be the major sticking point.

In the case of the "Yoga is nowhere" point of view, it is somewhat more difficult to find an adequate explanation for the instinctive dislike of the linkage with Sāṃkhya. Partly it is the obviously composite nature of Yoga, both in terms of philosophical articulation as well as literary format, that troubles many scholars. Clearly the YS is a compilation from a variety of sources. There is an apparent lack of unity and coherence in the *sūtrapāṭha* (that is, the actual *sūtras* themselves) that has troubled interpreters since the time of Deussen. More than that, there are deep philosophical suspicions. To be sure, Yoga's ontology and epistemology are clearly derived from Sāṃkhya, but there appear to be profound influences from Buddhist philosophy as well. Most of all there is an eccentric theology of God (*īśvara*) which is absent in Sāṃkhya and not typical of any other theology in the South Asian region. Finally, all sorts of strange traditions claim the name "Yoga" in South Asia and in the absence of sufficient evidence to the contrary, perhaps the best approach is to say that Yoga has no distinctive place in any philosophical tradition in South Asia. It is India's intellectual chameleon!

Early "*sāṃkhya*" and "*yoga*"

The main problem with these extremes, however, is that they fail to take seriously the dense and complex historical process by means of which the Pātañjalayogaśāstra has developed. As I have commented elsewhere in several earlier publications, it is important to be clear about what we mean when we use the term "philosophy" in the South Asian context.[13] Many Indologists and Buddhologists become involved in an anachronism or an equivocation with respect to the word "philosophy". One reads, for example, about the "philosophy" of the Vedas and Upaniṣads, or the "philosophy" of the *Bhagavadgītā*, or the "philosophy" of the epics. There is hardly any "philosophy" in any of these texts beyond the most elementary speculative intuitions. Most serious researchers are fully aware, of course, of the fundamental difference between speculative intuitions in environments of received authority, on the one hand, and systematic reflection that seeks overall coherence and persuasive presentation on the other. The former, that is, speculative intuitions in environments of received authority, are as old or older than the Vedic tradition itself, but "philosophy" in any significant sense of the notion is largely absent. The latter, however, that is, systematic reflections that seek overall coherence and persuasive presentation, is much more recent, and may legitimately be called "philosophy". Interestingly, the terms "*sāṃkhya*" and "*yoga*" appear to be crucial in tracing the latter from the former. That is to say, there are a number of contexts in which *sāṃkhya* and *yoga* appear to mean little more than "speculative intuition of a cognitive sort" (*sāṃkhya*) and "speculative intuition of a conative sort" (*yoga*). The important work of Franklin Edgerton is well-known in this regard, and Edgerton is undoubtedly correct when he suggests that it is a fundamental error in historical judgment to assume the existence of a Sāṃkhya system or a Yoga system whenever one finds the terms *sāṃkhya* and *yoga* in such texts as *Kaṭha Upaniṣad, Śvetāśvatara Upaniṣad, Maitrāyaṇī Upaniṣad, Mokṣadharma, Bhagavadgītā, Carakasaṃhitā, Suśrutasaṃhitā, Buddhacarita,* and so forth.[14] To be sure, these are the textual environments from which the later Pātañjalayogaśāstra and the technical Sāṃkhya system will be fashioned.[15] One might well call such textual environments "proto"-Yoga contexts or "pre-philosophical" Yoga traditions (as well as "proto"-Sāṃkhya" or "pre-philosophical" Sāṃkhya contexts), but the focus must be on pluralistic and diffuse speculations.

The more recent work of John Brockington and Peter Schreiner has largely confirmed Edgerton's point.[16] Brockington comments as follows about the early speculative trends in the epics: "The available evidence points rather to a number of separate and tentative beginnings, some of which proved blind alleys and others of which lead somewhere, but often only after interacting with other patterns of thought and being profoundly modified in the process. They are indeed 'beginnings' rather than anything that could be termed a 'school'', and it is probably misguided to associate them with particular teachers".[17]

Schreiner's conclusion is roughly the same with the important further claim, however, that the Yoga passages in the epic definitely appear to be older, or as Schreiner puts it, "In terms of the *Textgeschichte* and *Redaktiongeschichte* of the

M(ahā)Bh(ārata) it is evident that 'Yoga' is closer to the raw material out of which the epic has been formed...'Sāṃkhya' has certain characteristics of a 'metatext' term...Sāṃkhya passages enclose or precede, but also succeed Yoga passages. Thus the criterion of redactional priority has not yielded unambiguous results and needs more detailed analysis. Nevertheless, when seen in the light of other criteria, I venture to hypothetically interpret the redactional position of the Sāṃkhya passages as indicative of the fact that Sāṃkhya was the newcomer in the epic compendium; the redactors wanted to convey authority and orthodoxy to that newcomer by putting it on a par with Yoga as the better known and more generally accepted paradigm of a *mokṣadharma*, a doctrine and method to reach salvific liberation".[18]

Schreiner's tentative conclusion confirms a similar observation that I offered many years ago regarding the relation between Sāṃkhya and Yoga in such environments as the epics, the *Gītā*, the middle Upaniṣads, and so forth. "Given this undifferentiated *yoga* tradition, the frequent refrain in the later texts of this second period--i.e. in the *Mokṣadharma* and the *Gītā*--that Sāṃkhya and Yoga are one must be viewed in a somewhat new way. Rather than interpreting such passages as attempts to synthesize an older Sāṃkhya and Yoga, the passages probably reflect precisely the opposite. They represent attempts to deny a process of differentiation which is beginning to occur in later times.[19]

In other words, the various diffuse "*yoga*" passages probably represent the context from which a particular technical tradition, namely the Sāṃkhya, is beginning to emerge. In any case, in all of these environments the terms *sāṃkhya* and *yoga* do not refer to philosophical positions in the sense of systematic reflection that seeks overall coherence and persuasive presentation. They refer, rather, to spiritual methodologies "innocent of metaphysics" (*vierge de métaphysique*), to use La Vallée Poussin's idiom.[20] It is very likely the case that early Buddhist, Jaina and Ājīvika traditions were very much in the same mold. J. A. B. Van Buitenen has put the matter well: "There must have existed scores of more or less isolated little centres where parallel doctrines were being evolved out of a common source. Occasional meetings at pilgrimages and festivals, reports from other and remote *āśramas* brought by wandering ascetics, polemical encounters with other preachers must have resulted in a laborious process of partial renovation and conservation, more precise definitions of doctrines and eclecticism, re-adjustments of terminology, etc. At this stage to credit these little centers with the name 'schools' is to do them too much, or too little honor...Most of the process must elude us necessarily, but we stand a better chance of recovering the little that is left by allowing for the greatest diversity rather than the greatest uniformity of doctrine".[21]

Sāṃkhya and Yoga as Systems of Thought

Put directly, then, it must be said that the "Yoga is everywhere" perspective is untenable in the light of the historical evidence. There simply is no primordial or pure Ur-Yoga upon which the Sāṃkhya philosophy was "foisted" or to which it was "falsely attributed". Quite the contrary, instead of a single primordial Ur-Yoga, there appears to have been a great plurality of diffuse speculative and/or ascetic traditions and the absence of technical formulations prior to the last two centuries or so before the Common Era and the first centuries of the Common Era.

If the "Yoga is everywhere" perspective is untenable, the "Yoga is nowhere" position hardly fares better. There can be no serious doubt that a "Pātañjalayogaśāstra" emerges as a technical philosophical system in the first centuries of the Common Era (ca. 200 CE through 500 CE). This is a period that sometimes coincides historically with the consolidations in north India accomplished by the great Kaniṣka (ca. 100 CE) in the northwest and the imperial Guptas (ca. 320-550) on the Ganges River basin and the Gangetic plain. The various technical traditions of Indian philosophy (Hindu, Buddhist and

Jaina) are all beginning to take shape in this period, each one centering around a founding figure and a collection of utterances (*sūtras*) or verses (*kārikās*). Vaiśeṣika, Nyāya, Mīmāṃsā, Vedānta, Jaina, and Yoga traditions all develop *sūtra* collections in this sense, with the respective "founding" or lineage figures of Kaṇāda, Gautama, Jaimini, Bādarāyaṇa, Umāsvāti and Patañjali.[22] Sāṃkhya, Mādhyamika and Vedānta have primarily *kārikā* collections, with the respective "founding" figures of Īśvarakṛṣṇa, Nāgārjuna and Gauḍapāda. The term "*sūtra*" means "string" or "cord" and refers to abbreviated aphorisms composed or compiled by teachers for purposes of teaching a particular subject matter. Most teaching was done orally, and the compilations of *sūtras* became the vehicle for memorizing the contours of a subject. The term "*kārikā*" means simply a concise "verse" and like the "*sūtra*" is primarily a vehicle for teaching a particular subject matter. Followers of these various traditions, or successors in the line of transmission (*guruparamparā* or "the sequence of teachers") would then write elaborate commentaries and sub-commentaries on the original *sūtras* or *kārikās*, and over the centuries a huge technical commentary tradition developed for each of the systems. What distinguishes technical philosophizing in these early centuries of the Common Era from older traditions of speculations are the following: (a) a concern for specifying at the outset the means of knowing (*pramāṇa*)--such as perception, inference, reliable authority and so forth--of a particular school and for defending those means; (b) a concern to define terms precisely and technically; (c) a concern that arguments be formed in a correct manner; (d) a fair accounting of the views of other schools together with a polemical attack on those views; and (e) an attempt to present a consistent and clear overall system of thought.

Sāṃkhya, "*ṣaṣṭitantra*", Vārṣagaṇya and Īśvarakṛṣṇa

Among these systematic traditions of philosophical reflection that were getting started in the first centuries of the

Common Era, Sāṃkhya philosophy was probably the oldest tradition to begin to take systematic shape.[23] It stretched back in its pre-classical forms to the first century of the Common Era and to some extent to one or two centuries prior to the Common Era. It was known as the tradition of "*ṣaṣṭitantra*" ("the science of sixty topics"), which may have been the name of a text or simply an older name of the tradition, and its principal exponents were Vārṣagaṇya and Vindhyavāsin.[24] The original founders or teachers of the Sāṃkhya, namely Kapila, Āsuri and Pañcaśikha, are known by name only or by a few fragments that are either unintelligible or wrongly attributed.[25] Regarding Vārṣagaṇya and Vindhyavāsin, however, even though there are likewise only fragments that are available, it is possible partially to reconstruct a reasonably coherent account of their interpretations of Sāṃkhya. Vārṣagaṇya worked in the first centuries (ca. 100-200) of the Common Era, and "the followers of Vārṣagaṇya" (in Sanskrit, the *vārṣagaṇāḥ*) included such figures as Īśvarakṛṣṇa and a certain Vindhyavāsin (or Vindhyavāsa). Īśvarakṛṣṇa's *Sāṃkhyakārikā* is the only extant text of the school from this early period. It was composed probably in the fourth century (ca. 300-350) of the Common Era, and it is evidently just what it claims to be, namely a simple in-house or school-book summary (see *Sāṃhyakārikā* 52) of the "*ṣaṣṭitantra*", probably reflecting for the most part the tradition of Vārṣagaṇya.[26]

Sāṃkhya and Vindhyavāsin

The situation with Vindhyavāsin, however, is interestingly different. It appears that Vindhyavāsin re-interpreted or revised the old Sāṃkhya philosophy, most likely because of his polemical contact with Buddhist philosophizing that was developing in the first centuries of the Common Era, especially regarding the Sarvāstivāda and Sautrāntika traditions as found in the Abhidharma philosophy of the *Mahāvibhāṣā*.[27] This was likewise the period in which the Mādhyamika and Yogācāra schools of Mahāyāna Buddhist philosophy were taking shape.

There was the important work of Nāgārjuna in his *Mūlamadhyamakakārikā*, a basic text of the Mādhyamika school, and there was the work of the great Buddhist thinker Vasubandhu (ca. 350-400) in his *Abhidharmakośa* and *Bhāṣya*. Vasubandhu's work reflects the impressive systematic scope and polemical issues in early Buddhist philosophizing, traceable back to the *Mahāvibhāṣā* tradition of the Sarvāstivādins and Sautrāntikas from about the middle to the second half of the second century CE.[28] Vasubandhu, of course is also a crucial figure in terms of the development of the Yogācāra orientation in Mahāyāna Buddhist thought.

Vindhyavāsin and Vasubandhu

According to Chinese textual evidence, specifically Paramārtha's famous "Life of Vasubandhu", Vindhyavāsin, the Sāṃkhya teacher, became involved in a bitter intellectual debate with Buddhamitra, one of the teachers of Vasubandhu. Evidently Vindhyavāsin was the winner of the debate, and when Vasubandhu learned about the humiliation of his teacher, he became enraged. He then wrote a scathing critique of Sāṃkhya.[29] The details of the debate need not concern us, nor need we be bothered by the exaggerations regarding the money involved. What is probably authentic is the memory of a vigorous, even vicious, exchange between Vindhyavāsin, an aggressive Sāṃkhyan innovator of the late fourth century, and the Buddhist philosopher Vasubandhu. Moreover, it may well be the case that the innovations that Vindhyavāsin introduces in his reinterpretation of the old Sāṃkhya of Vārṣagaṇya, as well as the appearance of Buddhist terminology for the first time into the "Sāṃkhyapravacana" (the "explanation of Sāṃkhya"), are reflected in what we now call the "Pātañjala-yogaśāstra", namely the YS and the Vyāsa *Bhāṣya*..

Vindhyavāsin and Vedavyāsa

Erich Frauwallner and Pulinbehari Chakravarti have both suggested a strong connection between Vindhyavāsin and the

Vyāsa *Bhāṣya* on the YS, and more recently Ashok Aklujkar has articulated a similar claim.[30] Admittedly, the claim has yet to be conclusively proved and is largely speculative, as indeed most historical claims about this early period are. There are some indications, however, that the author of the Vyāsa *Bhāṣya* may really have been Vindhyavāsin. As Aklujkar points out, scholars have always recognized that the legendary Vyāsa or Vedavyāsa, supposed author of the *Mahābhārata* and the *Purāṇas*, cannot seriously be considered to be the author of the *Bhāṣya* on the YS. Most traditional ascriptions claim that the author of the *Bhāṣya* is none other than Patañjali himself, the compiler of the YS, which would imply that the *Bhāṣya* is, therefore, a *svopajñabhāṣya* or "self-commentary". This view seems to have been held by such later writers as Śrīdhara (in his *Nyāyakandalī*), Abhinavagupta (in his *Abhinavabhāratī*) and Malliṣeṇa (in his *Syādvādamañjarī*). Furthermore, according to Aklujkar, Vādirājasūri in his *Nyāyaviniścayavivaraṇa*, quotes some passages from the *Bhāṣya* on the YS and ascribes them to Vindhyavāsin. The other traditional ascription, of course, is the verse by Vācaspatimiśra in the opening of his *Tattvavaiśāradī* wherein he says the following: "*natvā patañjalam ṛṣiṃ vedavyāsena bhāṣite...bhāṣye vyākhyā vidhīyate*" ("having done obeisance to the *ṛṣi*, Patañjali, a comment is set forth (by me) with respect to the *Bhāṣya* composed by Vedavyāsa"). "*Vedavyāsena bhāṣite*" could easily have been misread for "*Vindhyavāsena bhāṣite*", and, as Aklujkar suggests, it may well prove to be the case that when a critical edition of the *Tattvavaiśāradī* is finally prepared, the reading may well be corrected to "*Vindhyavāsena*".*

Be that as it may, what is reasonably plausible given the current state of the evidence is that Vindhyavāsin reinterpreted

---

*Certainly if one writes out the two expressions, "*vedavyāsena*" and "*vindhyavāsena*" in Devanāgarī script, it becomes immediately apparent that such a transcriptional error could easily have occurred.

the old Sāṃkhya and that his reinterpretation occurred most likely as a result of his encounter with the Buddhists. More than that, Vindhyavāsin's reinterpretation appears to be closely related to what we now know as the "Pātañjalayogaśāstra" of the YS and the so-called Vyāsa *Bhāṣya*. As A. B. Keith argued many years ago, the appearance of Īśvarakṛṣṇa's *Sāṃkhyakārikā* as a systematic formulation and summary of the old Sāṃkhya of Vārṣagaṇya's "*Ṣaṣṭitantra*" may have occasioned the compilation of a systematic Yoga philosophy in keeping with Vindhyavāsin's reinterpretation of Sāṃkhya.[31]

In terms of chronology, the sequence would then be something like the following. Vārṣagaṇya (ca. first or second century CE, or roughly in the time of Kaniṣka) fashions a systematic account of the older "*Ṣaṣṭitantra*". Īśvarakṛṣṇa some time later in the fourth century (ca. 300-350 or roughly in the imperial Gupta period) summarizes the views of "the followers of Vārṣagaṇya" in his *Sāṃkhyakārikā*. In the meantime, however, the old Sāṃkhya has come up against the vigorous critique of Vasubandhu and his colleagues in the Buddhist school in Ayodhyā and been reworked and revised in the reinterpretation of Vindhyavāsin. This, then, becomes the occasion for the compilation of a systematic Yoga that reflects the philosophical issues being debated in this new intellectual milieu. This new philosophical Yoga is, indeed, a "*sāṃkhya-pravacana*" (an "explanation of Sāṃkhya") but not an explanation of the old Sāṃkhya but, rather, a new related system (reflecting a common tradition) in polemical encounter with the emerging Buddhist philosophy of the period.

Admittedly, this sort of historical reconstruction reverses many of the common assumptions about the history of Yoga and about the significance of the philosophy of Yoga, as was briefly mentioned earlier. The traditional historical perspective regarding Yoga is that it is either a set of ascetic practices that reflects an Ur-philosophy that goes back to primordial time (which I called earlier the "Yoga is everywhere" view), or that Yoga is a set of ascetic practices that has no particular philosophical orientation whatever, Yoga having been taken over by any number of philosophical perspectives (which I called earlier the "Yoga is nowhere" view, or Yoga as India's intellectual chameleon). Both views, I think, are mistaken and anachronistic. Contrary to the former view, the evidence suggests that the so-called Ur-Yoga is nothing more than a congeries of ascetic traditions that have almost no intellectual coherence whatever prior to the first centuries of the Common Era. Contrary to the latter view, Yoga is much more than a set of practices upon which one might foist any number of philosophical views, whether Sāṃkhya or whatever. Yoga, rather, is a specific intellectual and learned tradition that arises out of an older Sāṃkhya environment but is a new philosophical tradition in direct polemical dialogue with the Abhidharma Buddhist philosophizing occurring approximately in the time of the great Vasubandhu.

Yoga, Sāṃkhya and Buddhist Thought

Let me develop this new historical perspective somewhat further by way of clarifying the relation between Yoga, Sāṃkhya and Buddhist thought.[32] It has been recognized since Deussen and Dasgupta that there are many Buddhist terms in the YS. Especially the *sūtras* in Book Four have often been cited as being under heavy Buddhist influence, since it appears that in *sūtras* 16-21 of Book Four the compiler of the YS is responding to the consciousness-only notions of Yogācāra Buddhist thought. Beginning with Dasgupta and coming down to Frauwallner, many scholars have therefore dismissed Book Four as a later appendage or interpolation. The problem of Buddhist terminology, however, cannot be so easily swept away, for, as Louis de la Vallée Poussin demonstrated years ago, the presence of Buddhist terminology in the YS is found not only in Book Four but extensively in the first three Books as well. La Vallée Poussin has cited well over a hundred terms or notions that appear to be common to both the YS (in the *sūtras* themselves) and Buddhist philosophy. Some fifty of these La

Vallée Poussin traces to discussions in the *Abhidharmakośa* and *Bhāṣya*, that is, to Sarvāstivāda, Sautrāntika and early Yogācāra contexts. I have listed these elsewhere in detail. Here I shall list only some of the more important notions that appear in all four Books of the YS. They are as follows: *śraddhā, vīrya, smṛti, samādhi, prajñā, ṛtambharā, bīja, vāsanā, kleśa, āśaya, nirodha, dharma, lakṣaṇa, avasthā, bhūmi, dharmamegha, samāpatti, pratipakṣabhāvanā*, and so forth.[33] La Vallée Poussin himself is somewhat cautious about the significance of this terminology in terms of understanding the relations between Pātañjalayoga-śāstra and Abhidharma Buddhist thought. He sees his listing as adding "some new pieces of information" (*quelques renseignements nouveaux*) to the on-going task of constructing a more accurate intellectual history.

My own puzzlement has to do with the opposite problem, that is, how this terminology that is common to the YS and Buddhist Abhidharma relates to the old Sāṃkhya philosophy. What is striking is that all of these common terms used in the YS and Buddhist textual environments are totally absent in Sāṃkhya textual environments. If one thinks, for example, of the terminology of "the system of sixty topics" (*ṣaṣṭitantra*); there is no overlap even of a single technical term.[34] The only parallel, often cited, is to the five "misconceptions" (*viparyaya*) of the *ṣaṣṭitantra* (*tamas, moha, mahāmoha, tāmisra* and *andhatāmisra*). According to Vācaspatimiśra and others, the "misconceptions" are equivalent to the "afflictions" (*kleśa*) of Book Two (the so-called *kriyāyoga* portion of the YS and the first part of the *yogāṅga* portion), namely *avidyā, asmitā, rāga, dveṣa,* and *abhiniveśa*.

Yoga as a Hybrid System of Thought

Conceptually, of course, one can show numerous parallels among all of these technical terms in Sāṃkhya, Yoga and Buddhist (largely Abhidharma) thought. The evidence seems clear, however, that there are at least three distinct tradition-complexes operating in the YS: (1) one or more Sāṃkhya traditions, (2) one or more Buddhist traditions, and (3) an emerging philosophical Yoga tradition that is compiling various older ascetic and religious strands of speculation. This suggests the rather obvious conclusion that the YS represents a hybrid formulation, a conflation, of old Sāṃkhya philosophy, early Buddhist philosophy and an attempt to codify older meditation traditions coming from the last two centuries BCE and the first centuries CE.

The first stream in the Yoga conflation, the old Sāṃkhya philosophy or *ṣaṣṭitantra*, might well be characterized as "discernment philosophy". Its focus is on *adhyavasāya* or "reflective discernment" by the intellect (*buddhi*) and on "*vyaktāvyaktajñavijñānā*" (*Sāṃkhyakārikā* II) or, in other words, the "reflective discernment of *prakṛti* and *puruṣa*". The principal means of knowing is *anumāna* or inferential reasoning. Its ontology is an eccentric dualism of primordial materiality and content-less consciousness. Its epistemology is a critical realism, based upon its assertion of *prakṛti* as composed of the three *guṇas* (*triguṇa*), and its philosophy of mind is physicalist or materialist, that is to say, there is no mind/body or thought/extension dualism in Sāṃkhya.[35]

The second stream in the Yoga conflation, the old Buddhist philosophy, might well be characterized as "*nirodhasamādhi*" philosophy. Its focus is on meditation and the pursuit of altered states of awareness. The principal means of knowing is *pratyakṣa* or perception. Its ontology is pluralist, and its epistemology is naive realist (Sarvāstivāda) or representationist (as, for example, Sautrāntika and the later Yogācāra). In terms of its philosophy of mind, it is also physicalist or materialist in the sense that it like Sāṃkhya also affords no special status to the "private life of the mind". Unlike Sāṃkhya (and the later Vedānta), however, it rigorously rejects any notion of substantive transcendence.[36]

The third stream in the Yoga conflation, a codification of older traditions of ascetic meditation, brings together various strands, including at least what has ben identified as the *kriyā*-

yoga sections of Book Two (YS II.1-27), the *yogāṅga* sections of Books II and III (YS II.28-III.55), some *karma-yoga* sections in Book Four (YS IV.7-13), and various *sūtras* having to do with the issue of God (*īśvara-praṇidhāna*) (YS I.23-28, II.1, II.32 and II.45). All of these will be discussed in greater detail in the sequel when we deal with the composition of the YS. Suffice it to say at this point that many of these strands come probably from contexts such as the *Mokṣadharma* and *Bhagavadgītā* portions of the epic, some passages from the early *Purāṇas*, the so-called middle verse Upaniṣads (*Kathā, Śvetāśvata, Maitrī* and so forth), and from oral traditions of regional teachers and any number of local *āśramas*.[37]

To identify these streams, however, is not to say that Yoga philosophy is nothing more than a combination of Sāṃkhya, Buddhist thought and older meditation traditions. Yoga appears to represent, rather, an updating of the old Sāṃkhya, an attempt to bring the old Sāṃkhya philosophy into conversation with many of the issues that were developing in the more technical traditions of Indian philosophizing occurring in the fourth and fifth centuries (300-500 CE). One is tempted to use the expression "neo-Sāṃkhya" because of its close association with the work of Vindhyavāsin. Also, it is clearly an explanation of Sāṃkhya. At the same time, however, it differs in a number of significant respects from the old Sāṃkhya of Vārṣagaṇya's "*ṣaṣṭitantra*" and Īśvarakṛṣṇa's *Sāṃkhyakārikā*. Hence, it is probably best simply to retain what the Indian philosophical tradition itself claims, namely that Yoga is a distinct system of thought which is to be construed as a "common tradition" with Sāṃkhya.

Yoga and Sāṃkhya: The Important Differences

I shall be discussing the philosophy of Yoga in greater detail in the sequel. Nevertheless, it is important already at this point in the discussion to articulate the salient differences between Yoga and Sāṃkhya by way of completing this sketch of the intellectual history of Yoga as a distinct system of Indian philosophy. Conventional textbook accounts of Yoga have been less than adequate in this regard. These accounts usually focus only on two main differences. First, whereas Sāṃkhya represents the theoretical basis for meditation, Yoga represents the practical implementation or praxis. Second, whereas Sāṃkhya is non-theistic, Yoga incorporates the notion of God by way of accommodation to popular and/or religious sentiment. Both claims are partially correct, but much more needs to be said about both claims. Moreover, a number of other salient differences require mentioning. Altogether there are six salient differences between the older Sāṃkhya and the newly emerging Yoga philosophy.

(a) First, whereas Sāṃkhya speaks of intellect *(buddhi)*, ego *(ahaṃkāra)* and mind *(manas)* as three distinct faculties that make up the *antaḥkaraṇa* or "internal organ", Yoga philosophy reduces the three to one all-pervasive *citta* or "awareness" (or "mind-stuff", to use J. H. Woods' idiom (YS I.2, 30, 33, 37; II.54; III.1, 9, 11, 12, 19, 34, 38; IV.4, 5, 15, 16, 17, 18, 21, 23, 26). The "thirteen-fold instrument" *(trayodaśa-karaṇa)* of Sāṃkhya, consisting of intellect, ego, mind, the five sense-organs and the five action-organs, becomes, then, for Yoga only an eleven-fold instrument, or even more simply, the all-pervasive mind-stuff itself. The term "*citta*", of course, appears variously in the ancient literature, both Brahmanical and Buddhist, but it is hard to avoid the parallel with discussions of "*citta*" in Sautrāntika and Vijñānavāda Buddhist contexts in particular. The Yoga view, however, stresses the objectivity, materiality or non-sentience of *citta*, thus making *citta* almost synonymous with *prakṛti* (YS IV.19). Moreover, *citta* becomes largely a pre-individual or pre-personal notion of cognitive functioning. Personal identity comes into play in the cognitive framework as an affliction (YS II.3), and specifically the affliction known as egoity (lit., "I-am-ness", *asmitā*) (YS II.3 and II.6). A pure content-less consciousness (*puruṣa* or *citiśakti*) is needed in order to render *citta* capable of functioning and being aware of itself. Yoga's notion of awareness, in other words, differs from Sāṃkhya and Buddhist (as well as from the later Vedānta) notions of awareness.

(b) Second, whereas Sāṃkhya speaks of the thirteen-fold instrument wrapped, as it were, in the five subtle elements, as the eighteen-fold "subtle body" (*sūkṣmaśarīra*) that transmigrates at death to a new rebirth body, the simpler and more sophisticated Yoga view is that if awareness (*citta*) is all-pervasive, at the moment of death there is an immediate transference to a new embodiment, hence obviating the need for a subtle body (YS II.13; IV.10). Here again the parallel with Buddhist (and Jaina) discussions is obvious. The Theravādins (and classical Jaina thought) like the Yoga philosophy argue that there is no need for an intermediate existence (*antarābhava*) or subtle body, and the Sarvāstivādins and other Buddhist schools argue for some sort of intermediate existence or subtle body. Interestingly, on this point, the *Abhidharmakośa* and *Bhāṣya* position comes out closer to the older Sāṃkhya view of a need for a subtle body in contrast to the Yoga view which appears to relate to the Theravāda (and Jaina) rejection of a subtle body.[38]

(c) Third, whereas the Sāṃkhya deals with what can be called the phenomenology of experience in terms of the fifty components of the so-called "intellectual creation" (*pratyaya-sarga*), consisting of five misconceptions, twenty-eight incapacities, nine contentments and eight attainments, which, together with the ten "basic principles" (*mūlikārtha*) make up the group of sixty (*ṣaṣṭi*) components of "the science of sixty" (*ṣaṣṭitantra*), Yoga greatly simplifies the description of phenomenal experience in terms of the "transformations of ordinary awareness", the *citta-vṛttis*, namely knowing, error, constructing, sleeping and remembering (*pramāṇa, viparyaya, vikalpa, nidrā* and *smṛti*). Clearly the Yoga idiom is a more sophisticated philosophical account. The Yoga discussion closely mirrors the classical Indian discussions of theory of knowledge, theory of error, theory of language and meaning, theory of states of awareness and theory of memory that are to be found in the various technical schools of Indian philosophy (Hindu, Buddhist and Jaina).*

(d) Fourth, whereas Sāṃkhya deals with the issue of time and transformation solely in terms of a rather simple theory of transformation of the *guṇas* (*guṇapariṇāma*), Yoga philosophy offers a sophisticated account of time and transformation in terms of a theory of momentariness (*kṣaṇa*, YS IV.33) and a theory of the three perspectives on change and transformation (YS III.13-14), namely change in "characteristic form" (*dharma*), change in "temporal variation" (*lakṣaṇa*) and change in temporal "age" or "condition" (*avasthā*) (YS III.13). Change in *dharma* is the change of characteristic form, that is, a lump of clay becoming a pot. Change in *lakṣaṇa* is the change in temporal variation from past to present and finally to future, that is, a lump of clay becoming a pot and finally breaking up into pieces. Change in *avasthā* is the change in any object's condition as it grows old, that is, the pot as young or newly made, the pot in its intermediate condition, and the pot as it becomes old. As is well known, the Buddhists (Sarvāstivādins, Sautrāntikas and Vijñānavādins) all debated the problem of change in almost precisely the same terms. Whereas the Buddhists debated about these possibilities (and others as well), the Yoga philosophy accepts all three explanatory modes. Yoga then relates the three to its theory of the "*dharmin*" (YS III.14) or, in other words, the Sāṃkhya theory of causation (*satkāryavāda*) and its notion of a substance (*prakṛti*) abiding over time. Sāṃkhya philosophy thereby is updated with a

*It should perhaps be noted here that Oberhammer thinks that the *pratyayasarga* of Sāṃkhya has to do largely with the Sāṃkhya theory of meditation. My view is somewhat different. In my view, the *pratyayasarga* of Saṃkhya has to do with the Sāṃkhya interpretation of ordinary experience. Its parallel in Yoga philosophy is the notion of the *cittavṛttis*, the "transformations of ordinary awareness". See the chapter "Die Sāṃkhyistische Meditation" in Oberhammer 1977, pp. 17-56.

sophisticated theory of change and transformation within the developing idiom of classical discussions of change and transformation.

(e) Fifth, whereas Sāṃkhya refrains from mentioning God and is considered for the most part (at least in its systematic formulations) to be non-theistic in the sense that God is really not necessary given the overall metaphysical account of *puruṣa* and *prakṛti*, Yoga develops an interesting theory or theology of God. On one level, Yoga follows the Sāṃkhya orientation in that God is not a creator but rather one among the plurality of *puruṣas* (YS I.23-24). Also, if God is a *puruṣa,* God can neither be personal nor any kind of cosmic absolute. On another level, the Yoga theory of God appears to hold back from reducing God to a phenomenal *ādividvān* ("primal knower") on analogy with, for example, a Buddha or a Jina or a Kapila or any other sort of *avatāra*-figure (YS I.24-25).* The Yoga God is untouched (*aparāmṛṣṭa*) and, hence, uninvolved in the transactions of afflictions, action, and the karmic ripening of traces (YS I.24). Hence, God in Yoga becomes an impersonal, acosmic, detached presence whose inherent contentlessness can only show itself as what it is not.** What it is not, of course, is "perfect *sattva*"

---

*This is the case, I should hasten to point out, according to the commentaries of Vyāsa and Vācaspatimiśra. In some of the later commentaries (for example, Vijñānabhikṣu et al.) the Yoga notion of *īśvara* is not properly understood or, alternatively, is reinterpreted in the direction of conventional *bhakti*.

**Both the Vyāsa *Bhāṣya* and Vācaspatimiśra understand the implications of an *īśvara* that transcends the usual conceptions of a creator or any kind of personal god. Also, of course, *īśvara* in Yoga cannot enter ordinary life or become "incarnate" as *avatāra* because of being "untouched" by any of the processes (*kleśa, karman, vipāka* and so forth) that would permit embodiment of some sort. The notion of *praṇidhāna* is indeed, therefore, a "unique kind of *bhakti*" (say Vyāsa and Vācaspati), along the lines of a profound meditation on divinity as radical transcendence beyond all conceptualization. Other (*prakṛṣṭasattva* or *prakṛṣṭacittasattva*) with *rajas* and *tamas* completely inhibited, the beginningless (*anādi*) "eternal excellence" (*śāśvatika utkarṣaḥ*) whose presence allows all things to be. The term *praṇidhāna* is not *bhakti* or devotional theism in any conventional sense. It is, rather, a role (*adhikāra*) of content-less consciousness. It is, to be sure, a "unique sort of *bhakti*" (*bhaktiviśeṣa*) as Vyāsa and Vācaspatimiśra put it (YS I.23), but it is *bhakti* that is a deep meditation on the nature of transcendence, not any sort of devotional theism. Moreover, since *īśvara* is not personal in any meaningful sense of that term, *īśvarapraṇidhāna* (YS I.23, II.1, II.32 and II.45) can only be a deep longing for transcendence. As will be discussed in the sequel, the reason for the introduction of this sort of *īśvara* in Yoga is to deal with an important cosmological question from the older Sāṃkhya. Instead of the standard Sāṃkhya account of a primordial equilibrium of *triguṇa* that is disturbed by the presence of *puruṣa*, the Yoga interpretation suggests a beginningless (*anādi*) or "eternal excellence" (*śāśvatika utkarṣaḥ*) alongside of or in the presence of content-less consciousness (*puruṣa*), a "perfect *sattva*" that is always present as a kind of role (*adhikāra*) that abides throughout the cosmic cycles of *pralaya* and *mahāpralaya*.

(f) Finally, sixth and perhaps most important, Sāṃkhya had developed its soteriology largely in terms of the simple "discernment" of the difference between *puruṣa* and *prakṛti* (*vyaktāvyaktajñavijñānāt*), arguing for its ultimate principles of *puruṣa* and *prakṛti* on the basis of inferences largely of the "general correlation" (*sāmānyatodṛṣṭa*) type. These are inferences arguing to what is imperceptible in principle on the

---

commentaries, perhaps especially the so-called Śaṃkara commentary (*Pātañjalayogaśāstravivaraṇa*) and Vijñānabhikṣu's *Yogavārttika* appear to miss this point entirely and speak in terms of traditional *bhakti*. Likewise, most modern interpreters of Yoga, both in India and the West, have misunderstood the unique notion of *īśvara* in Yoga.

basis of certain features of what is perceptible.[39] The problem of liberation for Sāṃkhya is primarily, therefore, an intellectual or fundamental philosophical issue and can be resolved through inferential reasoning or philosophical reflection. Such reflection involves meditation, of course, but the process of meditation required in order to achieve reflective discernment is largely presupposed. Yoga fully accepts the Sāṃkhya focus on the reflective discernment of the difference between *puruṣa* and *prakṛti* (YS II.17-21, IV.14-23), but Yoga's principal concern is with the purposeful strategies, both physical and psychological, to be employed in order to achieve the requisite reflective discernment. Hence Yoga's focus is primarily on concentrated states of awareness that ultimately issue in reflective discernment--hence, the very etymology of the term "*yoga*": "*yogaḥ samādhiḥ*". Yoga develops a sophisticated and detailed theory of awareness based upon "altered states of awareness" (one-pointed and suppressed) of the intentional or content-filled (*samprajñāta*) types and the non-intentional or content-free (*asamprajñāta*) types. The former types are those types which have content or, in other words, are about something. The latter types are those types which have no content or are content-less, "without seed" (*nirbīja*).* Many interpreters of

---

*I am using the terms "intentional" and "non-intentional" in the sense that these terms are used in contemporary philosophy of mind. The "intentionality of consciousness", or perhaps better in an Indian context, the "intentionality of awareness" refers to the idea that mental states are for the most part "about" something. That is, they have some sort of content, whether that content be an object or a state of mind. "Non-intentionality" refers to states of mind that have no content in this sense or, in other words, are content-less. For a clear discussion of this issues, see Searle 2004, the section entitled "The Structure of Intentionality", pp. 166ff. Let me hasten to add that I am not suggesting that Indian philosophy generally discussed states of mind in the sense of contemporary philosophical discussions of the intentionality of consciousness.

Yoga have misunderstood this important distinction and have, therefore, wrongly concluded that there are two (or more) types of Yoga patched together in the YS. They have overlooked, in other words, the philosophical issue involved, that is, the difference between intentional and non-intentional awareness.* In any case, one might well argue that the YS in its entirety is best read as an attempt to describe and analyze states of awareness which need to be cultivated in order to achieve clarity regarding the relation between awareness (*cittatattva*) and consciousness (*puruṣa* or *citiśakti*). Put into the idiom of contemporary philosophy, Yoga philosophy is a fascinating inquiry in that branch of philosophy known as philosophy of mind.

Chronology of Yoga Philosophy--Principal Texts up through Vijñānabhikṣu

The historical overview presented thus far may be charted as follows:

The modern discussion, however, is a useful interpretive perspective, in my view, for attempting to understand this important distinction in Yoga philosophy.

*Frauwallner, for example, argues for a basic distinction between what he calls the "eight-limbed Yoga" (of YS II and III) (*der Weg des achtgliedrigen Yoga*) and the Yoga of the cessation of cognitive functioning (*der Weg der Unterdrückung der Geistestätigkeit*) (YS I), in Frauwallner 1, p. 438, and see pp. 408-445 for the full discussion. Oberhammer (pp. 124ff.) follows Frauwallner in this regard. For a thoughtful yet appreciative critique of both Frauwallner and Oberhammer see Feuerstein 1979, pp. 79-86. It should perhaps also be mentioned that Oberhammer discusses the "structure of Sāṃkhya meditation" in terms of the *pratyayasarga* of the *Sāṃkhyakārikā*, see pp. 17-55.

500-200 BCE - "middle" Upaniṣads, epic passages, *Bhagavadgītā*, *śramaṇa-yati* traditions, Vedic and non-Vedic asceticism (= "*sāṃkhya*"-cum-"*yoga*") ("vierge de métaphysique")

200 BCE-100 "Ṣaṣṭitantra" Buddhist *Abhidharma*

100 - 200 Vārṣagaṇya Sarvāstivāda/*Mahāvibhāṣā*

200 - 300 "*vārṣagaṇaḥ*" Sautrāntika

350 - 400 Īśvarakṛṣṇa's *Sāṃkhyakārikā*

350- 400 Vindhyavāsin Vasubandhu, *Abhidharmakośa*

350 - 400 *Yogasūtrapāṭha* and Vyāsa's *Bhāṣya*

500 - 600 Gauḍapāda, *Māṇḍūkyakārikās**

700(?) Śaṃkara the Advaitin**,

---

*I include Gauḍapāda's *Kārikās* both as an early text of Vedānta influenced by Yoga as well as Buddhist thought. See Nakamura, Part Two (New Delhi: Motilal Banarsidass, 2004 reprint of multi-volume work, 1950-1956), Part VI, pp. 211-389.

**For ongoing debate about the authenticity of Śaṃkara's *Pātañjalayogaśāstravivaraṇa* see, of course, Leggett 1990 and Rukmani 2001. The former accepts the authenticity of the text; the latter does not. See in addition Hacker, pp. 119-148, and Wezler's four studies, namely Wezler 1983, Wezler 1984a, Wezler 1984b and Wezler 1984c. Finally, see Halbfass, Appendix, "Notes on the *Yogasūtrabhāṣyavivaraṇa*", pp. 107 ff. One must conclude regretfully that the problem of the authenticity of the text has not yet been satisfactorily resolved. The text, in any case, is an Advaitin commentary on the YS.

Pātañjalayogaśāstravivaraṇa

850-950 Vācaspatimiśra, *Tattvavaiśāradī*

1050 Bhojadeva or Bhojarāja, *Rājamārtanda*

1050 al-Bīrūnī, *Kitāb Pātañjala*

1050 Sāyaṇa Mādhava, *Sarvadarśanasaṃgraha*

1550-1600 Rāmānanda Sarasvatī, *Maṇiprabhā*

1550 Vijñānabhikṣu, *Yogavārttika*

Composition of the YS and the Identity of Patañjali

There has been no more vexing pair of problems in the history of Yoga scholarship than the matter of the composition of the YS itself and the identity of the compiler, Patañjali. For nearly a century debates have unfolded regarding the disparate strands of the *sūtras* themselves and the proliferation of Patañjalis. Both debates have generated interesting books and articles, but no consensus has emerged regarding either problem. My own inclination, therefore, in the absence of persuasive evidence to the contrary, is to go with the testimony of tradition itself whenever possible. In this regard, it is fair to say that the tradition itself appears to present the following claims:

(1) Yoga is a learned scientific tradition concerning the

Even if it is authentically a work of Śaṃkara, it is not sufficient evidence to claim that Śaṃkara was a follower of Yoga as a young man, *pace* Hacker et al. If it is a fourteenth century work, between the work of Vācaspatimiśra (ca. ninth or tenth century) and Vijñānabhikṣu (sixteenth century), as Rukmani thinks, it is only one more interesting Vedāntin work in a long series of Vedāntin interpretations of Yoga.

study of mind (*citta, manas*) and is related to two other learned scientific traditions, namely the study of language (*śabda*) and the study of medicine (*cikitsā*).

(2) All three learned traditions appear to be connected with the name "Patañjali" and in each instance with a particular text, namely the YS of Patañjali in the case of the study of mind, the *Mahābhāṣya* of Patañjali in the case of the study of language, and the *Carakapratisaṃskṛta* of Patañjali in the case of the study of medicine.

Note that tradition recognizes Patañjali as someone who worked and was interested in all three areas of learning but was not the major figure in each. Regarding the study of mind, Hiraṇyagarbha is said to have been the original figure.[40] Regarding the study of language, Pāṇini is said to have been the major figure. Regarding the study of medicine, Caraka was the major figure.

Three traditional verses are often cited to establish this linkage between the three sciences. The first is one of the opening verses of Bhojadeva's commentary on the YS, the *Rājamārtaṇḍa* (ca. eleventh century), which J. H. Woods translates as follows: "Victory to the luminous words of that illustrious sovereign, [Bhoja] Raṇaraṅgamalla, who by creating his Grammar, by writing his comment on the Pātañjalan [treatise, the YS], and by producing [a work] on medicine called *Rājamṛgāṅka* has--like Patañjali--removed defilement from our speech and minds and bodies.[**] The name "Patañjali", of course, in the verse is "protector or lord of serpents" (*phaṇibhṛtaṃ bhartrā*), or, better, "lord of the protectors of serpents").

---

[*]Woods, p. xiii. The text runs as follows:

śabdānāṃ anuśāsanaṃ vididhatā pātañjale kurvatā
vṛttiṃ rājamṛgāṅkam api vyātanvata vaidyake /
vāk-ceto-vapuṣāṃ malaḥ phaṇībhṛtāṃ bhārtrā iva yena
uddhṛtas tasya śrī-raṇaraṅgāmalla-nṛpater vāco
jayanty ujjvalāḥ //

The second verse often cited is from Cakrapāṇi (ca. eleventh century), the medical commentator, and may be tra translated as follows: "Reverence to the Lord of serpents, the slayer of the faults of mind, speech and body by way of the three treatises, the *Pātañjalayogaśāstra* (YS), the *Mahābhāṣya* and the *Carakapratisaṃskṛta*".*

There is, third, a stanza cited in Śivarāma's commentary on the *Vāsavadattā* (ca. eighteenth century), which may be translated "I am bowing down with raised hands in reverence Patañjali, best among *munis*, who removed the impurity of the mind by means of Yoga, (the impurity) of words by grammar (*pada*) (and) moreover, (the impurity) of the body by means of medicine (*vaidyaka*)"**

There is also another eighteenth century verse from the *Pātañjālacarita* that attests to Patañjali's work in medicine and Yoga, which may be translated "Patañjali, the *muni*, having composed *sūtras* and then *vārttikas* on the *yogaśāstra* and the medical *śāstra*, came forth to rescue this world."

---

*In Sanskrit:
Pātañjala-Mahābhāṣya-Carakapratisaṃṣkṛṭaiḥ
mano-vāk-kāya-ḍoṣāṇāṃ ḥantre'hipataye namaḥ

**In Sanskrit:
Yogena cittasya, padena vācāṃ
malaṃ śarīraṣya tu vaidyakena
yo 'pākarot, tāṃ pravaraṃ munīṇāṃ
patañjaliṃ pṛāñjalir ānato 'smi

Woods dismisses the significance of these verses inasmuch as they are all quite late, the earliest (the verse of Bhojadeva) being from the eleventh century. In fact, however, the tradition of linking the three sciences of the study of Yoga, the study of language and the study of medicine is considerably older than Woods realized. The linkage is already mentioned in Canto I of Bhartṛhari's *Vākyapadīya* (I.147), which can be dated roughly from the middle to the latter part of the fifth century (ca. 450 or a bit later). "What impurities there are whose contents relate to the body, speech and intellect, the impurities of them (are overcome) by the *śāstras* of medicine, language and study pertaining to the self (*adhyātma* or Yoga)."*

Admittedly, " Patañjali" is not used in the verse nor is the term "*yoga*" used. The important point, however, is that there is clearly a linkage between the three areas of learning. Aklujkar has offered the following comment in support of linking the verse with the tradition of the identity of the Patañjalis. "First, we need to ask ourselves what probability is there that a relatively widespread pattern would reflect itself in Bhartṛhari's verse (even to the extent of having the words "*kāya*", "*vāc*" and "*mala*" in common) and Patañjali, who is associated with that pattern, would still not be intended. The probability would seem to be very low. Secondly, in Bhartṛhari's works as well as in the YB [the Vyāsa *Bhāṣya*], which we can now think of as a pre-Bhartṛhari work, there are signs of a rather special concern with pointing out the relatedness of grammar, Yoga and medicine as branches of learning or text traditions."[41] The former comment of Aklujkar is not especially persuasive, since it presupposes that the tradition of relating the three sciences was a "widespread pattern", which, of course, is precisely at issue. His latter comment, however, is much more suggestive.

***Kāyavāgbuddhiviṣayā ye māḷāḥ ṣamavasthitaḥ*
cikitsālakṣaṇādhyātmaśāṣṭrais teṣāṃ viśūḍḍhayaḥ

The other argument that Woods gives against the identity of the two Patañjalis has to do with what appears to be a different understanding of the notion of "substance" (*dravya*) in the YS (and Vyāsa's *Bhāṣya*) and Patañjali's *Mahābhāṣya*.[42] Woods' evidence and arguments are more than a little ambiguous regarding this issue, but, in any case, the matter has been researched in much greater detail by Albrecht Wezler and with a much different (albeit still ambiguous) conclusion.[43] Wezler argues that the evidence suggests that Patañjali of the *Mahābhāṣya* was familiar with the basics of Sāṃkhya and Yoga philosophy. Likewise, Surendranath Dasgupta long ago argued that Woods' argument about the notion of "substance" is not at all persuasive and that Patañjali, the grammarian, was familiar with the basics of Sāṃkhya and Yoga. Wezler's research can now be said to document Dasgupta's observations. Dasgupta also points out that the grammarian's theory of *sphoṭa* is present both in the *Mahābhāṣya* and in Yoga. Furthermore, Dasgupta adds that "...unlike any other work they both begin their works in a similar manner (*atha yogānuśāsanam* and *atha śabdānuśāsanam*)--"now begins the compilation of the instructions on Yoga" (*Yogasūtra*) and "now begins the compilation of the instructions of words" (*Mahābhāṣya*).[44]

It should perhaps also be noted that the name "Patañjali" is not a common one in the Indian tradition and, hence, the possible identity of the two Patañjalis cannot be explained away by way of mistaken references in the ancient texts--as, for example, the attribution of all sorts of views to Kapila, Pañcaśikha and other ancient sages. Ram Shankar Bhattacharya points out that "Patañjali" is a *gotra* name, not in the technical sense of Sanskrit grammar, but in the sense of *laukika gotra*, that is, family names as enumerated in works like the *Dharmaśāstra* and the *Kalpasūtras*.[45] The name "Patañjali" nowhere appears in the Vedic literature nor in the *Mahābhārata* nor in the passages on *gotra-pravaras* in standard works. It is evidently a late *gotra* name appearing for the first time in a *gotra*-list in the *Matsyapurāṇa*.[46] Various etymologies have been given for the name, perhaps the most common being "*patantaḥ añjalayaḥ yasmai*, for whom the hands are folded as a mark of reverence".* Moreover, the name "Patañjali" appears to be related to *nāgas* or *sarpas*.[47]

By way of summary, the arguments for accepting the identity of the two Patañjalis include the following:

(1) There are references, admittedly late, to a single Patañjali who worked in three *śāstra*-traditions: the study of mind, the study of language and the study of medicine.

(2) There is the much older reference in the *Vākyapadīya*

---

*Dasgupta, HIP, p. 230. RSB 1985 rejects this and other etymologies as basically unsound. Often the derivation of the name is related to "*patat*" or "*patita*", "falling or fallen on the ground", and "*añjali*" (the hands making a sign of reverence), and early along the name became associated with the *nāga* cult. Ram Shankar Bhattacharya comments as follows: "The most striking factor in the life of Patañjali–the grammarian as well as the Yogin–is his connection with *nāgāṣ* oṛ *sarpas*...Patañjali was called Ādīśeṣa (the primal serpent)...Ahipati (lord of serpents) was used by Cakrapāṇi...and the word "*phaṇibhṛt*" (protector of serpents) by Bhoja...It is interesting to note in this connection that according to *Viṣṇudharmottara* (which is generally assigned to 500-600 C.E.) the author of the *Yogasūtra* waṣ coṇsiḍered to be the same as an incarnation of the lord of snakes. In the later Yogic tradition a highly exalted place has been given to Ananta. A Yogin is required to bow down to Ananta, the lord of snakes, before taking up his daily exercises...The first benedictory verse of the *Vyāsabhāṣya* (which is evidently an interpolation) contains a salutation to the god Ahīśa possessing a hood with many mouths. All these positively show that the connection of Patañjali with snakes has an age-old tradition behind it." (RSB 1985), pp. 91-92)

One other point by RSB 1985 is worth mentioning, namely that the later legendary accounts of the life of Patañjali indicate that he was born under the Āśleṣā asterism, whose superintending deity is the snake (RSB 1985, p. 93). This may go a long way in understanding the association with *nāgas* and *sarpas*.

(from the fifth century) that the three *śāstras* of mind, language and medicine are frequently linked together with some of the important notions of Sāṃkhya and Yoga.

(3) The author of the *Mahābhāṣya* was familiar with some of the important notions in Sāṃkhya and Yoga.

(4) Both Patañjali of the *Mahābhāṣya* and of Yoga seem to accept the *sphoṭavāda* notion of the grammarians.

(5) Both the *Mahābhāṣya* and the YS begin with the same sort of opening *sūtra*.

(6) The name "Patañjali" is a unique and recent *gotra*-name, not easily lending itself to the sorts of confusions typical of reference to ancient sages going back to Vedic and epic times.

The arguments for not accepting the identity of the two Patañjalis include the following.

(1) The late references to the identity of the two Patañjalis are just that, namely late, and not to be taken seriously as guides to what was going on centuries earlier.

(2) The reference in the *Vākyapadīya,* while admittedly showing a linkage to the three related *śāstras* already in the fifth century, makes no reference at all to Patañjali.

(3) That the author of the *Mahābhāṣya* is familiar with some of the notions of Sāṃkhya and Yoga provides no basis whatsoever for identifying the two Patañjalis.

(4) The *sphoṭa* doctrine in Patañjali, the grammarian, is different from the later *sphoṭavāda* doctrine of Bhartṛhari, and more than that, there is no specific reference to the term "*sphoṭa*" either in the YS or the Vyāsa *Bhāṣya*. The term "*sphoṭa*" is mentioned in the context of Yoga for the first time in the commentary by Vācaspatimiśra (ca. ninth or tenth centuries), and even there it is not clear that Vācaspatimiśra is referring to Bhartṛhari's *sphoṭavāda*. The term "*sphoṭa*" is also used in the commentary of Bhojadeva (ca. eleventh century) and, of course, in more recent discussions.

(5) That the opening *sūtras* of the two texts are similar cannot be taken seriously as showing the identity of the two

Patañjalis.

(6) Similarity of name, no matter how unusual the name, is hardly evidence for identity.

(7) Most telling, perhaps, there appears to be a serious anachronism if one identifies the Patañjali of the *Mahābhāṣya*, coming from the second BCE (ca. 150 BCE), with the author of the *Pātañjalayogaśāstra* (YS) of the fourth or early fifth century CE. If one wishes to push the *sūtras* themselves, that is, the *sūtrapāṭha*, back to the second century BCE, it would seem to require eliminating many of the *sūtras* as later interpolations, including almost all of Book Four and additional *sūtras* as well in Books One, Two and Three.

Ram Shankar Bhattacharya develops all of the arguments against the identity of the two Patañjalis in some detail and asserts, finally, that in his opinion there were two Patañjalis, Patañjali the grammarian and Patañjali the Yogin. He also, however, makes the following observation:"...we want to inform our readers that we find no harm if the identity of the grammarian Patañjali and the Yogin Patañjali is proved undoubtedly. We simply assert that the aforesaid arguments are incapable of proving the identity of these two teachers".[48]

I concur with Ram Shankar Bhattacharya that the identity of the two Patañjalis has not been proved, but I think it may be premature to posit two separate Patañjalis. In my view, Sāṃkhya and Yoga were possibly in the process of being systematically formulated in the last century or two BCE, to be sure not, as I have argued above, in the full systematic form that emerges in the first centuries CE. It could possibly be the case, however, that early attempts at systematizing Yoga (and Sāṃkhya) were of interest to Patañjali, the grammarian, just as he was interested in systematizing the study of language and possibly the study of medicine. The tradition, in other words, may be reflecting an authentic memory. The task, then, is how to resolve the issues of anachronism.

As J. F. Staal has noted, there has been a tendency in modern scholarship to dissect the Yoga texts to such an extent that the subject-matter of Yoga itself has been overlooked.[49] This process of excessive dissection began already at the beginning of the twentieth century in the work of Paul Deussen (1845-1919) and Richard von Garbe (1857-1927).[50] Deussen was one of the first to dissect the YS into its component layers. Garbe did much the same for the *Bhagavadgītā*. The trend continued with Surendranath Dasgupta's solution to the problem of the *sūtras* having to do with later Buddhist thought in the YS by simply eliminating Book Four of YS as a later interpolation! J. W. Hauer (1881-1962) offered his final dissection in 1958. Erich Frauwallner published his views of the dissection in 1953, followed by Oberhammer in 1965 and 1977. The most recent contribution (and by far the most reasonable) has been that of Georg Feuerstein in 1979. With Feuerstein it can rightly be said that Humpty Dumpty has finally been put back together again.[51] (Lest my comment be taken as being overly flippant in such a scholarly context, let me hasten to add that all of us who work in Indological studies stand on the shoulders of giants such as Deussen, Garbe, Dasgupta, Frauwallner et al.)

Deussen's analysis became the basic pattern upon which many of the later analyses developed. He focused primarily on the *sūtras* themselves, apart from the commentaries, and argued that the YS is a patchwork compilation. Deussen divided the YS as follows:

First Text: I.1-16, ordinary awareness and cessation;

Second Text: I.17-51, altered awareness (*samādhi*) with support (*samprajñāta-*) and without support (*asamprajñāta-samādhi*).

Third Text: II.1-27, meditation practice (*kriyāyoga*) for removal of afflictions (*kleśas*);

Fourth Text: II.29-III.55, eight-limbed Yoga (*aṣṭaṅga-yoga*);

"Nachtragteile" (addenda or appendices),

IV.1-6, individual minds (*nirmāṇacitta*),

IV.7-13, action (*karman*) and subliminal traces (*vāsanā*)

IV.14-23, reality (*vastu*), mind (*citta*) and self (*puruṣa*)and

IV.24-33 (not including IV.16), final release (*kaivalya*).[52]

For Deussen the YS is a haphazard compilation, the strands and fragments of which cannot be put into a cogent historical sequence.

J. W. Hauer, following Deussen's model, suggests the following divisions in the YS.

YS I.1--opening *sūtra*;

I.2-I.22--the "cessation" (*nirodha*) text;

I.23-I.51--the "devotion to God" (*īśvarapraṇidhāna*) text;

II.1-II.27--the "meditation practice" (*kriyāyoga*) text;

II.28-III.55--the "eight-limbed Yoga" (*aṣṭāṅgayoga*) text;

IV.2-IV.34--the "individual mind" (*nirmāṇacitta*) text.[53]

Hauer, unlike Deussen, sorts out the "*īśvarapraṇidhāna*" text as a separate section on theistic Yoga which he traces to old Rudra-Śiva-Viṣṇu religious traditions. Also, he argues that the "eight-limbed Yoga text" is the oldest text in the compilation and can be possibly attributed to Patañjali, the grammarian. Furthermore, he suggests that Book Four (*sūtras* 2-34) is a distinct "individual mind" text, and not simply a series of addenda. Finally, he argues that the "cessation" (*nirodha*) text is the latest of the layers and was probably contributed by the final editor when the YS was given its final form some time in the fourth century.[54]

Erich Frauwallner suggests that the YS can be divided into two main traditions. There is, first, the "way of the eight-limbed Yoga" (*der Weg des auchtgliedrigen Yoga*) which focuses on achieving mental alertness and clarity. This tradition is to be found in Books Two and Three of the YS. Second, there is the "way of suppression of mental functioning" (*der Weg der Unterdrückung des Geistestätigkeit*) which can be found in Book One of the YS.[55] Frauwallner, like Dasgupta before him, dismisses Book Four as a later addition. Oberhammer, as noted earlier, largely follows Frauwallner's division.

Finally, the most detailed and cogent analysis of the YS (the *sūtrapāṭha*) can be found in the work of Georg

Feuerstein.[56] His primary method has been to assume a basic homogeneity in the text overall, rather than a basic heterogeneity as Deussen et al. have assumed. Says Feuerstein, "Past scholars, on the whole, proceeded from the assumption that the *Yogasūtra* cannot possibly be a single homogeneous textual entity owing to its apparent disorganization. In the following I shall commence from the opposite end as it were by presupposing the perfect homogeneity of the text. In other words, I shall look for points which seem to contradict, or at least seriously challenge, this basic working hypothesis. In this way I hope to avoid the fallacy common to all attempts of textual criticism so far, namely to cut more and more slices from the cake until it simply vanishes out of sight and nothing but disconnected fragments--quite meaningless in themselves--are left behind."[57]

Feuerstein then proceeds to carry through a careful analysis of the terminology and various sequences of *sūtras* in the YS. His conclusion is that the text overall is a single compilation that centers primarily around the notion of "meditation practice" (*kriyāyoga*). Book One of the YS (the *Samādhi Pāda*, I.1-I.51) is an Introduction, or simply what Feuerstein calls Part I, of *kriyāyoga*. Book Two of the YS (the *Sādhana Pāda*, II.1-II.27) is a continuation, and, more than that, the main text of Part I of *kriyāyoga*. Part II of *kriyāyoga* picks up again in Book Three (the *Vibhūti Pāda*) from III.3 or 4 and runs through most of Book Four (the *Kaivalya Pāda*). This leaves out, of course, YS II.28-III.3 or 4, the so-called "eight-limbed Yoga" (the *yogāṅga* portion). Feuerstein sees this "eight-limbed Yoga" portion as a separate insert or long quotation in the YS. Put simply, the YS is basically a text about *kriyāyoga* with a long insert or quotation of an "eight-limbed Yoga" portion. Feuerstein also suggests that the YS has some later interpolations or fragments, for example, IV.1 and III.55.

Whether one agrees or disagrees with these various analyses of the composition of the YS, they all at least have the merit of having identified important themes in the YS.

Feuerstein's analysis is the most meritorious, in my view, because it puts the text back together again. Unfortunately, however, one has to admit that no overall consensus has emerged in all of these attempts regarding the YS as a whole, with the possible exception of Feuerstein's analysis, although it is doubtful that most researchers would concede that the YS overall centers on *kriyāyoga*. The one area of consensus that is possibly of some importance is that all researchers seem to agree that the so-called *yogāṅga* portion, the "eight-limbed Yoga", is a distinct unit. There is disagreement as to the full extent of the "eight-limbed Yoga" portion, that is, whether it extends from YS II.28-III.5 (or thereabouts) or if it extends throughout Book Three, but all seem to agree that the *yogāṅga* portion is an identifiable unit.

The reason for the lack of consensus regarding the YS as a whole is not hard to find. The reason is clearly insufficient evidence. Especially if one only works with the *sūtras* themselves, the task of finding various layers will always be arbitrary. The *sūtras* themselves, I am inclined to argue, are simply impossible to interpret without the commentaries. Moreover, even with the Vyāsa *Bhāṣya*, the YS is difficult to decipher, especially in regard to explanations in the later portions of Book Three and some sections of Book Four. It is only with Vācaspatimiśra's *Tattvavaiśāradī* that one comes upon a genuine *śāstra*-text that sets forth a plausible interpretation of the YS in its entirety. It is this text-complex, therefore, that, in my judgment, is fundamental. In other words, the YS, the Vyāsa *Bhāṣya* and the *Tattvavaiśāradi* of Vācaspatimiśra taken together provide the core textual evidence for *Pātañjalayoga-śāstra*. Later commentaries are all dependent on this core evidence. Bhojadeva's *Rājamārtaṇḍa* (eleventh century) and Rāmānanda Sarasvatī's *Maṇiprabhā* (sixteenth century) offer hardly anything original beyond Vyāsa and Vācaspatimiśra. Vijñānabhikṣu's *Yogavārttika* (sixteenth century), of course, is a major work, but it too is heavily dependent upon Vyāsa and Vācaspatimiśra and gives a strong *bhedābheda* Vedānta overlay that is frequently misleading, especially regarding the notion of God. Likewise the *Pātañjalayogaśāstravivaraṇa*, attributed to Śaṃkara, quite apart from the issue of its authenticity, is misleading in its comments about God.

By taking together what I am calling the core textual evidence for interpreting the YS, namely the *sūtrapāṭha,* the Vyāsa *Bhāṣya,* and the *Tattvavaiśāradī,* the vulgate or traditionally received text of the *sūtrapāṭha* is quite straightforward in its basic structure as follows:

Book One, acording to Vyāsa and Vācaspatimiśra, entitled "*Samādhi Pāda*" and including 51 *sūtras,* deals with the descriptions of the levels of awareness that are especially appropriate to *yoga* proper, that is, one-pointed or content-filled awareness and suppressed or content-free awareness and the means for attaining these levels of awareness: "practice" (*abhyāsa*) and "renunciation" (*vairāgya*).[58]

Book Two, according to Vyāsa and Vācaspatimiśra, entitled "*Sādhana Pāda*" and including 55 *sūtras,* deals with those practical exercises needed to train those who have not yet reached the levels of awareness described in Book One, and includes both the *kriyā-yoga* exercises and the first five of the eight *yogāṅga* exercises.[59]

Book Three, according to Vyāsa and Vācaspatimiśra, entitled "*Vibhūti Pāda*" and including 55 *sūtras,* sets forth the results that are attained when the means pursued in the second Book lead to the concentrated states that have been described in the first Book. These attainments arise through the exercises involving the final three of the eight *yogāṅga* exercises: *dhāraṇā, dhyāna* and *samādhi* practiced togeth er as *saṃyama.*[60]

Finally, Book Four, according to Vyāsa and Vācaspatimiśra, entitled "*Kaivalya Pāda*" describes the final goal of Yoga,

spiritual liberation (*kaivalya*), a condition that goes beyond the content-filled awarenesses of the third Book and brings the *yogin* to the condition of content-free or seedless concentration or, in other words, liberation.[61]

If the YS, the Vyāsa *Bhāṣya* and Vācaspatimiśra's *Tattvavaiśāradī* make up the obvious core textual base for understanding Yoga, why has so much scholarly effort been expended in interpreting the YS solely in terms of the *sūtras* alone? The only plausible answer appears to be the reluctance of the scholarly tradition, both in India and Europe, to accept the claim of both Vyāsa and Vācaspatimiśra that *Pātañjalayoga-śāstra* has a clear foundation in Sāṃkhya philosophy. The claim that Sāṃkhya has been "foisted upon" or "wrongly attributed" to Yoga or the claim that Vyāsa and Vācaspatimiśra were not "really" practicing *yogins* appear to be based upon no evidence whatever and, I would suggest, should finally now be put to rest. Likewise, the claim that Yoga has no philosophical basis and can be utilized by any system of thought is, again, totally inaccurate in view of the core textual evidence of Vyāsa and Vācaspatiimiśra.

Concluding Comments on the History of Yoga

This, then, brings me to the concluding comments I wish to make about the history of Yoga philosophy. I have argued that Yoga philosophy is closely related to the old Sāṃkhya of the first centuries of the Common Era, the Sāṃkhya of the "*ṣaṣṭitantra*", Vārṣagaṇya and his followers, as summarized in Īśvarakṛṣṇa's *Sāṃkhyakārikās*. Yoga philosophy, however, is an updated and revised Sāṃkhya, most likely revised as a result of polemical interaction with Abhidharma Buddhist traditions in the third and fourth centuries. Especially important in this regard are the polemical interactions between the Sāṃkhya thinker Vindhyavāsin and the Buddhist Vasubandhu. This revised Sāṃkhya of Vindhyavāsin appears to be reflected in the Yoga philosophy of the YS. As has been suggested by some, the so-called Vyāsa *Bhāṣya* could even possibly have been composed by Vindhyavāsin, although this latter identity has not yet been established.

In compiling the YS in its present form I am inclined to

think that the editor (Vindhyavāsin?) deliberately composed or included the opening *sūtra (atha yogānuśāsanam)* in full awareness of an earlier textual tradition that began in a similar fashion, that is, Patañjali's *Mahābhāṣya* and its opening *sūtra: atha śābdānuśāsanam*. The compiler of the YS was also fully aware that most *paṇḍitas* of the time would not fail to see the linkage. Moreover, it is not implausible to believe, as Hauer suspected, that the "eight-limbed Yoga" (*yogāṅga*) portion of the YS may be a set of *sūtras* traceable back to the time of Patañjali, the grammarian, a set of *sūtras* that may have even been compiled by the grammarian. In Hauer's view, the *yogāṅga* portion of the YS includes II.28-III.55. I am inclined to limit the *yogāṅga* portion only to 33 *sūtras*, II.28 through YS III.5. The first *sūtra* (II.28) in the group sets forth a program of meditation to be followed: "After the [eight] limbs of Yoga have been followed, and when the impurities have been destroyed, there will arise the light of knowledge leading up to the realization of the discrimination [between *puruṣa* and *prakṛti*]".[62] Thereafter each "limb" or *aṅga* is specifically defined (II.29-III.3), *yama, niyama, āsana, prāṇāyāma, pratyāhāra, dhāraṇā, dhyāna* and *samādhi*. The *yogin* is then enjoined (YS. III.4) to practice the final three members of the eight-limbed sequence, that is, *dhāraṇā, dhyāna* and *samādhi*, together as *saṃyama*. Finally, when this has been mastered (YS III.5, *taj-jayāt*) the full brilliance of insight (*prajñā*) occurs.

If this is a plausible historical reconstruction, then the appearance of the compilation of the YS as we now know it would have represented in its time, ca. the fourth century CE, not simply a renovated or revised Sāṃkhya as a companion philosophical system. It would have represented as well a new scientific tradition having to do with the study of the mind. Unlike the older diffuse religious traditions of meditation (whether Brahmanical, Hindu, Buddhist or Jaina), this new Yoga was being introduced as a *śāstra* on analogy with the study of language and the study of medicine. Hence, the connection with the name "Patañjali", a name which undoubtedly would have resonated favorably among serious scholars in the study of language and the study of medicine. All three *śāstras* are after all empirically based, and all three *śāstras* proceed with ongoing experimentation in their respective areas.

To be sure, all three areas of learning (medicine, language and mind) had their origins in older ritualistic and religious contexts. Interest in medicine, for example, undoubtedly had its origins in the many incantations, potions and herbs of one kind or another and all sorts of ascetic exercises (*tapas*) for the sake of curing bodily ailments. Such concerns are traceable back to the time of the *Atharvaveda* and such progenitors as the physician of the gods, Dhanvantari.[63] Interest in language likewise had its origins in the utterances of the Vedas, the chants and hymns utilized in the ritual sacrifice and such progenitors as the "Lord of Speech" (Bṛhaspati or Vāc, Ṛg Veda X.71 or Brahmaṇaspati, Ṛg Veda X.72).[64] The same is true, of course, in regard to the study of mind. One reads, for example, about the "golden germ" (Hiraṇyagarbha) in Ṛg Veda I.121 who turns out to be at the end of the hymn Prajāpati, the Lord of Creatures.[65] Elsewhere, especially in epic contexts, Hiraṇyagarbha is said to be the "first-born" of the manifest creation as intellect (*buddhi*) or *mahat* (the great one), and, according to the *Yogiyājñavalkyasmṛti*, as quoted by Vācaspatimiśra at YS I.1, the original propounder of Yoga.

By linking the new Yoga *śāstra* with the name of Patañjali, I think that the compiler of the YS is indicating that even though the tradition might well be traced to ancient times,[66] and even to the divine figure, Hiraṇyagarbha, a new intellectual turn is occurring.[67] The inquiry into Yoga is a new role that should not be construed in the older manner of scriptural exegesis along the lines, for example, of the *Brahmasūtras* and their interpretation. It is more like the traditions of grammar and medicine, the results of the study of which are to be judged by whether they work or not. If the techniques work, they should be pursued. If the techniques fail to work, they should be abandoned no matter what the religious heritage may be. In essence this is the argument set forth by Vācaspatimiśra in his introduction and comment on YS I.1.[68]

The Philosophy of Pātañjala Yoga

The Philosophy of Yoga: Some Preliminary Methodological Remarks

Before discussing the contours of the philosophy of Pātañjala Yoga, it is important to make clear two methodological assumptions from which I shall be working. Both have been implicit already in my remarks about the history of Yoga. It is important now, however, to make these assumptions explicit.

(1) First, let me offer a brief methodological remark about relevant textual sources. As I indicated in the final discussions of the history of Yoga, it is not possible, in my judgment, to discuss the philosophy of Yoga solely based upon the YS itself without consulting relevant commentaries. Nor is it possible, in my judgment, to discuss the philosophy of Yoga utilizing only the so-called Vyāsa *Bhāṣya*. The YS itself is full of cryptic *sūtras* and technical notions that often make little or no sense apart from commentators who explain what is being talked about or what is at issue. Likewise the Vyāsa *Bhāṣya*, while providing a great deal more by way of explanation, seldom gets beyond what might be called random notations about the meaning of the YS itself. It is only with the commentary of Vācaspatimiśra, the *Tattvavaiśāradī* ("Clarity regarding the Truth" [of Yoga as set forth in Vyāsa's *Bhāṣya*]) that we come upon a text that is truly a *śāstra*-text in terms of laying out a cogent, detailed interpretation of each *sūtra* from the perspective of the compilation as a whole.* To be sure, Vācaspatimiśra was a Vedāntin and, thus, not himself an adherent of Yoga philosophy. His work, however, in the various philosophical

*In his opening verse, Vācaspatimiśra indicates that he has written a "*vyākhyā*", that is, an "explanation" or "gloss" on the Vyāsa *Bhāṣya*: "*...vedavyāsena bhāsite...bhāṣye vyākhyā vidhīyate*".

traditions is highly regarded by almost all interpreters and can be taken seriously as reflecting authentic knowledge in depth about the various systems of Indian thought in his time. The same cannot always be said of the other commentaries. The others are for the most part dependent upon the YS, the Vyāsa *Bhāṣya* and the *Tattvavaiśāradī*, and while they may disagree on this or that point or add various comments along the way, they are of secondary importance in interpreting the philosophy of Yoga. This is especially true, in my view, regarding the work of Vijñānabhikṣu, both because of his much later date and because of his aggressive stance as an ideological Vedāntin (of the *bhedābheda* variety). I am also reluctant to rely on the *Pātañjalayogaśāstravivaraṇa*, attributed to Śaṃkara. Its authenticity has not yet been persuasively established, and if T. S. Rukmani is correct, its date may be as late as the fourteenth century.** In my interpretation of the philosophy of Yoga, therefore, I have relied primarily on what I would call the "core textual complex", that is, the YS itself, the Vyāsa *Bhāṣya* and Vācaspatimiśra's *Tattvavaiśāradī*.. I have, of course, also referred when appropriate to other commentaries, but what I am calling the "core textual complex" is my primary interpretive

---

**T. S. Rukmaṇi's views suggesting that the text is not an original text by Śaṃkara may be found in Appendix I and Appendix II of Volume II of her translation, op. cit., pp. 212-222. Trevor Leggett's arguments in favor of Śaṃkara's authorship may be found on pp. 17-48, especially pp. 39-48 of his translation, op. cit.. The strongest arguments against the ascription of this work to Śaṃkara are, first, that Śaṃkara ordinarily never composed commentaries on commentaries, and, second, that he never appears to have composed texts on systems other than Advaita Vedānta. The latter, it seems to me, is a compelling point, and I am inclined not to see the text as a composition of Śaṃkara the Advaitin. That Śaṃkara composed the text when a young man and not yet an Advaitin appears to be only a speculative reflection without, as far as I am aware, any supporting evidence.

focus. For those, for example, J. W. Hauer et al., who think that Sāṃkhya philosophy has been "foisted on" or "wrongly attributed to" Yoga and who dismiss Vyāsa and Vācapatimiśra as unreliable because they were not practicing Yogins, I can only say that I respectfully disagree for the reasons stated.

(2) Second, I wish to make clear that, in my view, the philosophy of Yoga is best discussed from the perspective of that branch of contemporary philosophy known as the philosophy of mind.* From that perspective, Yoga can be characterized as a form of dualism, but it is a most unusual form of dualism. Likewise, in terms of the philosophy of mind, Yoga can also be characterized as a form of materialism, but again, it is a most unusual form of materialism. Finally, Yoga

---

*Philosophy of mind as a field within philosophy concerns itself with issues relating to the operation of the mind, including such matters as consciousness, unconsciousness, perception, action, thought, feeling, emotions, reflection, memory and so forth. Standard views within philosophy of mind include dualism, materialism, behaviorism, functionalism, computationalism, eliminativism and epiphenomenalism. In terms of identifying and naming the various dualist and materialist positions, I have found the following discussions helpful: (1) Karl R. Popper's analysis and criticism of radical materialism, panpsychism, epiphenomenalism and identity theory in Popper/Eccles, pp. 51-99; (2) John C. Eccles's discussion of radical materialism, panpsychism, epiphenomanalism, identity theory and duality interactionism in Eccles/Robinson, pp. 25-45; and (3) Paul Churchland's discussion of substance dualism, simple dualism, property dualism (epiphenomenalist, interactionist, and elemental), reductive materialism, functionalism, and eliminative materialism in Churchland 1979, pp. 107-116 and Churchland 1988, pp. 6-49. Other important works in philosophy of mind include (in alphabetical order, as listed in the Bibliography to be found near the end of the present volume) the following: Chalmers, Dennett, Gregory, Priest, Putnam, Rorty, especially the essay "Non-reductive physicalism", Searle 1984, Searle 2004, and Smith 1984.

introduces the notion of God and is, thus, in some sense a form of theism, but as is the case with its dualism and its materialism, Yoga's theism is a most unusual form of theism. In an article I wrote for *Philosophy East and West* many years ago, entitled "An eccentric ghost in the machine", I suggested that the dualism in Yoga (and Sāṃkhya) undercuts the conventional notions of dualism to such an extent that it is best characterized as a materialism.[69] I also argued, however, that Yoga likewise undercuts our usual notions of materialism, and I would add now that it also undercuts most of our usual notions of theism. It would appear, then, that Yoga is not simply an "eccentric" dualism, but also an "eccentric" materialism and an "eccentric" theism. Moreover, in the idiom of most discussions within contemporary philosophy of mind, the proper term to be used is the term "eliminative" rather than "eccentric". That is to say, when an explanation or analysis cannot be reduced to any standard or conventional explanation or analysis, it is usually characterized as an "eliminative" position. It is, in other words, a totally new perspective or analysis, which "eliminates" older ways of explaining or analyzing. In what follows, therefore, I shall be arguing that the philosophy of Yoga is an "eliminative dualism", an "eliminative materialism", and, finally, an "eliminative theism".[70] Put very simply, Yoga can be characterized as an "eliminative dualism" in the sense that it denies the conventional interpretations of dualism while still maintaining a dualist position. Yoga can be characterized as an "eliminative materialism" in the sense that it denies that there are such things as mental states as they are conventionally described and that the notion of a person who has conventional mental states is a fundamentally mistaken belief. And Yoga can be characterized as an "eliminative theism" in the sense that though it denies that there is a personal, creator God in the sense of conventional *bhakti* or devotional theology, a theistic viewpoint may still be maintained.

I have two reasons for selecting the philosophy of mind as an interpretive framework for discussing Yoga. Primarily, of course, since this is a series focusing on the philosophies of India for philosophers who may have only a limited knowledge of non-western philosophy, the idiom or discourse of philosophy of mind may provide a helpful interpretive framework for understanding the philosophical claims and significance of Yoga. Secondly, in my judgment, too much has been written about Yoga in terms of mystical experience, gnostic understanding and paranormal experiences. As a result, research on Yoga has largely been the province of the religious seeker. To be sure, Yoga has an important spiritual dimension, and what I am calling "extraordinary cognitive capacities" have a significant role to play in understanding Yoga. Nevertheless, what is equally important in Yoga is its potential philosophical and scientific significance for understanding the functioning of the body and the mind. Yoga is, after all, one of the oldest experimental, empirically based research programs regarding mind-body interaction known to the human species, and it deserves to be taken seriously as an important chapter in the quest for human understanding. Put directly, it is long overdue to de-mystify and de-mythologize Yoga in order to bring it into conversation with the many contemporary inquiries having to do with the nature of mind and consciousness.

The Philosophy of Yoga: An Introductory Overview

Perhaps the best way to introduce the philosophy of Yoga is to set forth at the outset the first three *sūtras* of the YS together with the Vyāsa *Bhāṣya* on each *sūtra*. The passages are reasonably brief and have the merit of providing a quick overview of the entire system.

YS I.1. "Herein begins an inquiry into disciplined meditation (*yoga*) based upon past tradition (*atha yoga-anuśāsanam*)."

Bhāṣya: "The expression 'an inquiry into disciplined meditation based upon past tradition' is to be understood as indicating that *śāstra* (a learned inquiry) is being undertaken. (The term) '*yoga*' is (etymologically related to the notion of) a concentration (*samādhi*). And the concept of a concentration pertains to all levels of concentration. There are five levels of concentration, namely distracted, depressed, partially focused, one-pointed and content-less. Among these, [the first two are useless levels of awareness in terms of making progress in Yoga as disciplined meditation, and] even when the mind is partially focused, there is still lacking that meditative discipline requisite for doing Yoga in the proper sense (*yogapakṣa*). When, however, the mind becomes one-pointed, the resulting state of awareness illumines an object as it really is (*sadbhūta*), destroys the afflictions, loosens the bonds of karma, and begins to turn the attention towards suppression and is known as that kind of awareness which has a content [or has intentionality] (*samprajñāta*). And these intentional awarenesses, which have empirical content (*vitarka*), rational content (*vicāra*), aesthetic content (*ānanda*), and subjective content (*asmitā*), will be discussed in detail here. Moreover, when all contents of awareness have ceased, then there is a state of awareness known as content-free awareness (*asamprajñātasamādhi*)."

"The compiler of the YS [now] introduces the second *sūtra* in order to define the term '*yoga*'."

YS I.2. "Disciplined meditation (*yoga*) involves the cessation of the functioning of ordinary awareness (*yogaś citta-vṛttinirodhaḥ*)."

Bhāṣya: "Since the word 'all' in the sense of 'all of the functioning' is not mentioned, even intentional states of awareness referred to as 'one-pointed' are to be included in the definition of '*yoga*' properly so-called."

"Now, the mind, since its functioning includes rational reflecting (*prakhyā*), spontaneous activity (*pravṛtti*), and a continuing urge to become involved with objects (*sthiti*), is said to be constituted by the three constituent processes (*triguṇa*) (of primordial materiality)"--[that is to say, mind is a material or physical entity. J. H. Woods, the first accurate translator of the core texts of the Yoga system, translated "*citta*" as "mind-stuff"].[71] "Mind or ordinary awareness, when in its mode of rational reflecting known as *cittasattva*, but when also influenced equally by the urge to activity (*rajas*) and the urge towards involvement with objects (*tamas*), becomes attracted to the world of ordinary objects and the powers of that world. That same mind or *cittasattva*, when overpowered by the urge towards involvement with objects in the world (*tamas*), becomes easily turned towards unconventional conduct, ignorance, impulsiveness, and weakness. That same mind or *cittasattva*, when the cover of delusion is removed, and there is an illumination of awareness on all sides with just a trace of worldly activity (*rajas*) remaining, becomes turned towards proper conduct, intelligent understanding, balanced emotion and healthful vitality. The same mind or *cittasattva*, turned away from even a trace of the urge towards activity, firmly established in its purely *sattva* condition of rational reflecting, solely given over to the realization of the difference between the material mind (*cittasattva*) and *puruṣa*, becomes turned towards the meditative state known as *dharmamegha* ('*dharma*-cloud' realization). Yogins refer to that state of awareness as the (supreme or ultimate) 'reflection' (*prasaṃkhyāna*).[72] On the one hand, therefore, there is *puruṣa*, which is unchanging and does not mix with anything else, has objects presented to it and is eternal--on the other hand, opposite from that, is this realization of discrimination (*vivekakhyāti*) whose essence is the *guṇa sattva* ."

"Next, when the mind has become indifferent to that realization of discrimination, it renounces or turns away even from that discriminative realization. At that point, it tends towards a condition of [abiding only in the residual] predispositions (traces, *saṃskāras*) [or what is referred to elsewhere as "*saṃskāraśeṣa*", the condition of simply abiding in one's own latent predispositions that continue to operate until their own inherent momentum has ceased--like, for example, the potter's wheel continues to turn until it exhausts its own momentum, even after the potter has completed the task of making a pot, see YS I.18]. That is a state of concentration that is content-less. Therein nothing at all is known--it is a state of awareness without content (*asamprajñāta*)."

"Hence, this definition of Yoga in terms of the cessation of the functioning of ordinary awareness is twofold, namely certain intentional states of awareness with content and non-intentional states of awareness without content."

"[One might then well ask:] In that state of mind when no objects are being experienced, what is the nature of pure content-less consciousness (*puruṣa*), whose essence is [ordinarily] to illumine the objects provided by the intellect?."

YS I.3. "Then there is the condition of the seer (*draṣṭṛ*) in its own inherent form (*tadā draṣṭuḥ svarūpe 'vasthānaṃ*)."

Bhāṣya: "At that time pure content-less consciousness is based on its inherent form as it is in spiritual liberation. Moreover, when the mind is functioning as ordinary awareness, pure content-less consciousness continues always to be in its own inherent form, even though it appears not to be."

From these three brief opening *sūtras* with their accompanying commentary, it becomes immediately apparent, even to a casual reader, that there is an unusual assertion of what looks like some sort of materialist position as well as what looks like some sort of dualist position.

The Materialism of Yoga

Regarding the materialist perspective, mind and its ordinary functions (*cittavṛtti*) are said to be made up of three *guṇas*, namely rational ordering (*sattva*), spontaneous activity (*rajas*) and determinate objectification (*tamas*). Mind, in other words, is part of a tripartite material energy continuum that encompasses all of manifest reality. Here, of course, Yoga is simply setting forth its appropriation of the older Sāṃkhya formulation of primordial materiality and its tripartite constituent processes of *sattva, rajas* and *tamas*.[73] The dynamic or continually changing (*pariṇāma*) tripartite material process, which actually constitutes or is primordial materiality, may be described either with reference to objectivity or with reference to subjectivity because, according to Sāṃkhya and Yoga, the tripartite process underlies both sorts of descriptions.

From an objective perspective, the tripartite process is a continuing flow of material energy that is capable of spontaneous activity, rational ordering and determinate objectification. Primal material energy can activate or externalize itself (*rajas*) in a manner that is transparent or intelligible (*sattva*) and substantial or determinate (*tamas*), and all manifestations of primary material energy are, therefore, purposeful (*rajas*), coherent (*sattva*), and objective (*tamas*).

From a subjective perspective, Sāṃkhya and Yoga describe the tripartite process as a continuing flow of experience that is capable of pre-reflective spontaneous desiring or longing (*rajas*), reflective discerning or discriminating (*sattva*), and a continuing awareness of an opaque, enveloping world (*tamas*). The continuing flow of experience actively seeks continuing gratification (*rajas*), reflectively discerns (or learns) the intelligible dimensions within the flow of experience (*sattva*), and continually encounters contents within experience that are opaque and oppressive (*tamas*).

Moreover, the quest for gratification (*rajas*) is frequently frustrated (*duḥkha/rajas*) and, although there are occasional times of reflective discernment (including aesthetic apprehension) that bring satisfaction (*sukha/sattva*), there are also moments when experience is completely overwhelmed by the sheer plenitude of the world (*moha/tamas*). In everyday ordinary life, therefore, experience tends to vacillate between the discomforting failure to attain gratification, occasional moments of reflective comprehension that bring a sense of comfort and tranquility, and moments of confused uncertainty.

Philosophy (*jijñāsā* or the "desire to know") begins, then for both Sāṃkhya and Yoga, as a result of the experience of failure and frustration and represents a desire to overcome that frustration. Crucial to realize is that the constituents of tripartite process presuppose one another and make up a single material energy continuum. There can be no gratification unless there is something external to be appropriated; there can be no reflective discerning in the absence of discernibles; and there can be no confused uncertainty in the absence of a living being or entity seeking discernment of some sort.

More than this, however, there is the recognition that the subjective dilemma of the flow of experience is the obverse side of the inherent objective dilemma of material energy itself (*prakṛti*). That is to say, for Sāṃkhya and Yoga there is no polarity or bifurcation of subjective and objective within the tripartite process, no ontological distinction between "mind" and "matter" or "thought" and "extension". The subjective flow of experience is simply another way of describing the objective primal material energy that unfolds in a continuing tripartite process of spontaneous activity, rational ordering and determinate formulation. The tripartite process of material energy (*mūlaprakṛti*) is, in other words, a sort of philosophical Klein bottle or Möbius strip in which the usual distinctions of subjective/objective, mind/body, thought/extension simply do not apply. Therefore, the subjective dilemma of frustration is an inherent objective dilemma of the material world itself.

Thus far, mind and its ordinary functions are being described solely in terms of a process materialism or dual-aspect materialism, and the only differences between the Sāṃkhya description of materialism and the Yoga description of materialism have to do with the technical terminology employed. Sāṃkhya describes its materialism in terms of "primordial materiality" (*mūlaprakṛti*) made up of the three *guṇas sattva, rajas* and *tamas* described just above. The dynamic *guṇas* mutually interact with one another and are inseparable from one another. One *guṇa* may become totally dominant, but at no point can the material system be without all three of its *guṇaṣ*.

Because of the respective dominance and subordination of the *guṇas* in the process of dynamic transformation (*pariṇāma*), the manifest world shows itself in a sequential series of emergent principles (*tattva*), beginning with intellect/will (*buddhi*) largely made up of *sattva*. Emerging from *buddhi* is the ego-sense (*ahaṃkāra*), made up of *sattva* and *rajas*. Mind (*manas*), the five sense-organs, and the five action-organs largely make up the *sattva*-dimension of the ego-sense. A set of five subtle elements (*tanmātra*) make up the *tamas*-dimension of the ego-sense, and the subtle elements in turn generate a set of five gross elements (*mahābhūta*), also made up of *tamas*. The first three emergents, intellect, ego-sense and mind are referred to as the "internal organ" or *antaḥkaraṇa*. When the threefold internal organ is combined with the five sense-organs and the five action-organs, the aggregate is referred to as the "thirteenfold instrument" (*trayodaśakaraṇa*) and also as the "essential core" (*liṅga*) of a living being. Finally, when the thirteenfold instrument or essential core is combined with the five subtle elements, the aggregate is known as the eighteen-fold subtle body (*liṅgaśarīra* or *sūkṣmaśarīra*). The subtle body generates and then, as it were, becomes nested in a gross body (*sthūlaśarīra*) made up of the five gross elements, *ākāśa*, air, fire, water and earth. The entire manifest world, "from Brahmā down to a blade of grass" (see *Sāṃkhyakārikā* LIV) is a single material continuum.

The Sāṃkhya materialism, it should perhaps be noted, is what might be called a "top-down" materialism rather than a "bottom-up" materialism. Or, put somewhat differently, the Sāṃkhya materialism is, as mentioned earlier, a dual-aspect materialism or a materialist form of panpsychism. In other words, traditional materialism is usually thought of in terms of atoms or other sorts of components that combine together and eventually generate higher-order forms, for example, ancient Greek materialism. The Sāṃkhya materialism reverses this usual picture and poses, instead, the notion of a subtle material energy (*prakṛti*) that is at the outset exceedingly translucent (*sattva*) but gradually becomes increasingly reified as its own inherent capacities (*rajas* and *tamas*) appear in the various manifest *tattvas*. The Sāṃkhya and Yoga theory of manifestation (*satkāryavāda*) in which *prakṛti* unfolds from the "top down", as it were, and in which all material effects are already included in a primordial material cause, differs interestingly from the two other dominant paradigms in Indian philosophy. The other two theories are the "bottom up" atomism of Vaiśeṣika (and Nyāya) and the Buddhist theory of substance-less temporal moments (*dharma, kṣaṇikavāda*) in which effects are different from their cause (*asatkāryavāda*).[74]

Yoga philosophy accepts the Sāṃkhya materialist framework but utilizes a different terminology. Instead of speaking in terms of the threefold internal organ functioning in terms of reflective discernment (*adhyavasāya*), self-awareness (*abhimāna*) and thinking (*saṃkalpaka*), it combines the three into one composite term, *citta* (awareness) or, to use Woods' idiom, "mind-stuff". Moreover, the older Sāṃkhya threefold cognitive functions of reflective discernment, self-awareness and thinking, are expanded by Yoga into the fivefold functions of ordinary awareness (*cittavṛtti*), which are said to be both afflicted and unafflicted (YS I.5). The fivefold functions are correct awareness, error, conceptual construction, sleep and memory (YS I.2-11).

The functions of ordinary awareness are set forth in YS I. 5-11, and the afflictions which, as it were, clog the functions, are spelled out in YS II. 3-9. They may be described together in the following manner. Correct awareness arises through the exercise of the three instruments of knowledge, perception, inference and reliable authority (YS I.7), and these three are characterized in the same manner as in Sāṃkhya.[75]

Error is incorrect awareness based on the misapprehension of something as other than what it is (YS I.8). This arises primarily through the afflictions, which include ignorance (*avidyā*), personal identity (*asmitā*), attachment (*rāga*), aversion (*dveṣa*) and clinging to conventional life (*abhiniveśa*). (YS II.3-9). The first of the five afflictions, ignorance, is the principal affliction, and is the foundation for the other four whether these other four be dormant, declining, inhibited or fully active (YS II.4). Ignorance involves the mistaken apprehension of what is changeless, pure, satisfactory and conscious in what is not changeless, pure, frustrating and conscious (YS II.5). Personal identity involves the error of thinking that one's individual awareness is the same as one's consciousness (YS II.6). Attachment relates to pleasure (YS II.7). Aversion relates to frustration (YS II.8). Clinging to conventional life involves relishing one's own continuing life, characteristic of all living things (YS II.9).

Conceptual or verbal construction relates to the distinctions that arise from the nature of language and the problems of meaning that arise when language operates apart from its purely denotative function (YS I.9).

Sleep is the awareness of absence [and not the absence of awareness] (YS I.10).

Finally, memory is the retention of the contents of what has previously been experienced (YS I.11).

What is striking about this analysis of cognition is the implicit skepticism about the reliability of ordinary awareness. To be sure, correct awareness, the first kind of ordinary awareness, is possible, but only after most of the ordinary modes of self-understanding have been overcome--hence, of course, the basic definition of Yoga as "the cessation of the functioning of ordinary awareness." It is in this sense that the term "eliminative" may be usefully employed by way of understanding what Yoga philosophy is claiming. That is, while correct awareness is ultimately possible via the path of disciplined meditation (*yoga*), correct awareness can only arise after having largely "eliminated" most of our ordinary apprehensions about the world and ourselves, which are hopelessly confused and for the most part incorrigible. Correct awareness is, as it were, undercut by a profound misunderstanding or fundamental ignorance that leads one to mistake one thing for another regarding the nature of what is immutable, the nature of purity or beauty, the nature of genuine happiness, and the nature of authentic consciousness. These basic confusions then lead to flawed self-understanding which in turn generates attachment to pleasure, anger or hatred because of delayed gratification, and a tenacious clinging to one's own life, or, if you will, a clinging to one's own ignorance. Likewise, while the symbolic importance of conceptualization and verbalization, the third function of ordinary awareness, is fundamental for communication and discursive thought and hence certainly not the same as the afflictions of error, nevertheless, language by its very nature sometimes leads to positing assertions that have no basis in reality. Or, again, the usual interpretation of sleeping, the fourth function of ordinary awareness, as the awareness of absence is often misconstrued as absence of awareness. Finally, the fifth function of ordinary awareness, memory, becomes a kind of storehouse for retaining what has been previously experienced.

Moreover, these functions of ordinary awareness encompass more than one life and more than one life form. They refer to all forms of life. In other words, the fluctuation of ordinary awareness is not a humanistic notion, or perhaps somewhat more accurately, not primarily a humanistic notion. It refers to the entire range of life forms from the highest levels of the gods down through the levels of the smallest embodied forms (YS I.40). The functioning or fluctuations of awareness produce traces (*saṃskāra*) and subconscious impressions (*vāsanā*) that are remembered and stored in the field of becoming (*kṣetra, saṃsāra*) (YS I.5 and Vyāsa's *Bhāṣya* with Vācaspatimiśra's gloss).* The traces become predispositions that in turn influence the manner in which new functions of ordinary awareness will develop. In other words, a "wheel"

*Whereas the term "*saṃskāra*" appears to mean the inherent impulse that triggers the recurrence of a memory trace from within, the term "*vāsanā*" appears to refer to the memory trace itself. In what I am calling the "core textual complex", howver, that is, the YS, the Vyāsa *Bhāṣya* and Vācaspatimiśra's *Tattvavaiśāradi*, these terms frequently overlap and are often used synonymously with one another.

(*cakra*) of becoming occurs (YS I.5, with Vyāsa's *Bhāṣya*). The fluctuations generate traces that then become predispositions that in turn influence upcoming fluctuations whether in this life or in rebirth.

As Vyāsa explains, "The fluctuations of ordinary awareness, distorted by the afflictions, become the field for the heaping up of the store of karmic tendencies...Predispositions in keeping with the functions of ordinary awareness are produced, and subsequent fluctuations of ordinary awareness are produced by predispositions. Thus, there is a continuously turning wheel of fluctuations and traces. This process continues to recur by means of its own momentum, or until the process itself goes into reabsorption (*pralaya*)."[76] Actions and their traces reach uition or "ripening" (*vipāka*) at various moments in a particular embodiment or in some future embodiment (YS II.12).* In general, actions produced by the functions of ordinary awareness in any particular embodiment gather together at the conclusion of that given embodiment, that is, at the moment of death or dissolution of a given life form (YS II.13). The *citta* then immediately manifests itself in a new embodiment whose form of life (*jāti*), length of life (*āyus*) and quality of experience (*bhoga*) is programmed by and compatible with the previous rebirth (YS II.13). (As noted earlier, Sāṃkhya's account of the process of rebirth is different, relying on the notion of a subtle body to carry the "thirteen-fold instrument" from the deceased body to the next embodiment.)

As mentioned above, the functioning of ordinary awareness is not totally afflicted. There is the possibility of correct

---

*The standard account in most texts refers to three kinds of karma: (1) *prārabdha*, or ripening currently taking place, (2) *vartamāna* or *āgāṃikaṛṃa*, the new actions taking place that will come to fruition in the future, and (3) *sañcita*,the total stored or accumulated karma from the past. The latter would be the store of action made up of *samskāras* and *vāsanās*.

awareness, but this can only occur when the basic afflictions have been overcome. Such an overcoming, however, is no minor undertaking. Required is a complete reorientation of ordinary awareness. The means for accomplishing this is said to be twofold (YS I.12), practice and renunciation (YS I.12).

Practice is steady effort in disciplined meditation (*yoga*) that is continuous over a long period of time in order to attain a condition of stability in which the mind can attain a peaceful flow without its ordinary distorting functions (YS I.13-14 and Vyāsa *Bhāṣya*). All of Book Two and the first five *sūtras* of Book Three, on both *kriyāyoga*, II.1-27 as well as *yogāṇga* or *aṣṭāṅga-yoga*, II.27-III.5, concern the relevant Yogic activities requisite for practice, according to Vyāsa and Vācaspatimiśra. The remainder of Book Three, again according to Vyāsa and Vācaspatimiśra, having to do with the "comprehensive reflections" (*saṃyama*), refer to the relevant one-pointed content-filled states of awareness that result from pursuing ongoing practice.

Renunciation means turning away from ordinary everyday life as well as from conventional religion (YS I.15). Moreover, there is an ultimate renunciation (*paravairāgya*) which entails turning away from the realm of materiality in its entirety. This means, of course, turning away from any and all intentional functions of awareness, gaining a state of pure *cittasattva* in which *rajas* and *tamas* have been completely suppressed. The requisite reorientation, in other words, involves the elimination or cessation of our usual understanding of mental states, or put in the idiom of eliminative materialism, the denial that our usual understanding of ourselves is a corrigible possibility. The afflictions are so much a part of what ordinary subjectivity means that the very notion of ordinary subjectivity must be eliminated from the explanatory corpus.

The Dualism of Yoga

By re-interpreting the notion of mind and its functions in terms of a tripartite material energy continuum (*prakṛti* as *triguṇa*), one might well conclude, as I have been suggesting thus far, that Yoga philosophy, finally, is simply an eliminative materialism. Oddly enough, however, Yoga (as well as Sāṃkhya) makes an additional puzzling claim that undercuts the materialist orientation and introduces, instead, an unusual form of dualism. Having succeeded in bringing about the cessation or "elimination" of the functioning of ordinary awareness, instead of coming upon the cessation of experience, one rather comes upon the source of experience. That source of experience is described as "consciousness" (*citiśakti, draṣṭṛ, puruṣa*) and is said to be absolutely distinct from "awareness". I use the word "puzzling" because it is difficult to grasp what could possibly be intended by making a distinction between "awareness" and "consciousness".

YS I.2 simply states "Disciplined meditation (*yoga*) involves the cessation of the functioning of ordinary awareness." This is immediately followed by I.3, "Then there is the condition of the seer in its own inherent form." Let me quote again the passage in the Vyāsa *Bhāṣya* which mentions this distinction between "awareness" and "consciousness". "That same mind or *citta-sattva*, turned away from even a trace of the urge towards activity (*rajas*), firmly established in its purely *sattva* condition of rational reflecting, solely given over to the realization of the difference between the material mind and *puruṣa* (*sattva-puruṣānyatākhyātimātra*), becomes turned towards the meditative state known as *dharmamegha* ("*dharma*"-cloud realization). Yogins refer to that state of awareness as the (supreme or ultimate) "reflection" (*prasaṃkhyāna*). On the one hand, therefore, there is pure consciousness (*citiśakti*), which is unchanging (*apariṇāminī*) and does not mix with anything else (*apratisaṃkramā*), has objects presented to it (*darśita-viṣayā*) and is eternal (*ananta*)--on the other hand, opposite from that, is this realization of discrimination (*vivekakhyāti*) whose essence is the *guṇa sattva* (or *cittasattva*)."[77]

The term "consciousness" in English is perhaps the best term for this unique notion of *citiśakti* or *puruṣa*. The English term is derived from the Latin "*scire*", "to know", with the prefix "*con*", meaning "along with" or "together with"". The term "*conscire*", suggests, then, that there is something present along with what is known. The term "awareness" is the best translation for *citta*, since "an awareness" refers primarily to one's experiencing. The term "awareness" is from Anglo-Saxon "*gewaer*" and German "*gewahr*" and refers to what is noticed, discerned, or caught sight of. Consciousness (*citiśakti, puruṣa*) is always present simply as a bare witness (*sākṣin*), whereas the functioning of ordinary awareness (*citta, cittasattva, cittavṛtti, prakṛti*) involves the transactions of the subject-object world of everyday experience.

The realm of awareness is the realm in which there are objects (*grāhya*), both gross and subtle, to be encountered, sense-capacities (*grahaṇa*) for apprehending the objects, both gross and subtle, and subjects (*grahītṛ*) who apprehend the world (YS I.41). Awareness, then, is always intentional in the sense that life in the world is always "about" something, whether believing, desiring, hoping, or acting. It is the realm in which language functions, and it is the realm in which the beginningless wheel of becoming turns for all embodied life forms. Consciousness, on the other hand, in its fundamental nature is understood to be non-intentional, a bare, content-less presence which is neither subject nor object in terms of the intentionality of awareness. To be sure, objects, subjects and the apprehending that links up objects and subjects are shown or appear in consciousness, but consciousness only illumines or reveals all of these as being not consciousness. Consciousness because it is content-less and non-intentional can only show itself as what it is not. Hence, it appears as if it were the intentional contents (*grāhya, grahaṇa* and *grahītṛ*) of ordinary awareness, and these contents in turn appear as if they are conscious (*Sāṃkhyakārikā* XX). In other words, a double negation takes place with consciousness appearing as what it is not, and awareness appearing as what it is not.

Yet it is crucial to understand that both

principles(consciousness (*citiśakti)* and awareness *(citta)*) can only be what they are by appearing as what they are not. That is, *citta* becomes aware of itself by means of the presence of what it appears not to be. Similarly, *citiśakti* is able to become a witness and to see what it is only by means of the presence of what it appears not to be. In Sanskrit the term "*adhikāra*", "role" refers to the notion of authority, prerogative, competence and the right to do or function in a certain fashion. One might well say, therefore, that it is the role of *citiśakti* to appear as what it is not and to be a simple, content-less witness. It is the role of *citta* to make the tripartite material energy continuum appear as what it is not, that is, to make it appear as if it were conscious. More than that, however, it is the role of *citta* to provide the intentional awareness (*vivekakhyāti*) that this double negation must be undone (*viyoga*). Only then is embodied life able to recognize what, in fact, has always been true, that there is a spiritual liberation that is as near to embodiment as embodiment itself inasmuch as it makes the awareness of embodiment and its transcendent freedom possible.

Yoga accepts the Sāṃkhya analysis of the reasons for the introduction of the notion of consciousness (*Sāṃkhyakārikā* XVII) which can be briefly summarized as follows. (a) Combinations (*triguṇa* and its interacting processes) exist for the sake of something other than themselves. (b) This something other cannot be within the combination. It must be separate, in other words, from the realm of the *guṇas*. (c) There must be some sort of controlling principle. (d) There must be an enjoyer of some sort. Finally, (e) there is an urge among all embodied creatures for freedom or release. All of these arguments amount to one basic claim, namely that the very notion of tripartite process itself becomes unintelligible in the absence of a distinct principle of sentience. In other words, tripartite process, although a powerful intellectual synthesis or conceptualization, cannot stand alone in and of itself, for even the awareness of the concept presupposes a ground or basis, or perhaps better, a "medium" through which and for which the concept becomes meaningful. Otherwise what appeared to be a uniform, rational, and meaningful world would finally show itself as an endless mechanical process in which the transactions of ordinary experience would amount to little more than occasional pleasurable respites within an endlessly recurring bondage. Or, putting the matter another way, one would come upon the remarkable paradox that an apparently uniform, rational and meaningful world is finally pointless.

Yoga also accepts the Sāṃkhya claim that the notion of content-less consciousness requires that it be understood pluralistically. That is to say, because consciousness is a content-less, non-intentional presence incapable of performing any activity it therefore cannot know or intuit itself. The presence of content-less consciousness can only be intuited by *cittasattva* in its reflective discerning and in an intuition that awareness (*citta*) in itself is not consciousness, that is, "*sattvapuruṣānyatākhyāti*" (see above, Vyāsa *Bhāṣya*). Because the varieties of awarenesses (*citta*) encompass all manifest embodied life forms in their various trajectories and circumstances (*nirmāṇacittāni*, YS IV.4) in accordance with the varied manifestations of tripartite process, content-less consciousness can only be disclosed pluralistically (cf. *Sāṃkhyakārikā* 18). Yoga and Sāṃkhya, therefore, reject the old cosmic *ātman* of the Upaniṣads and argue instead that content-less consciousness accompanies every particular embodied life form.

Obviously, since consciousness is not an intentional object that can be counted, the notion of a plurality of *puruṣas* or *citiśaktis* must be construed in a peculiar sense. Perhaps the most interesting attempt to deal with this peculiar notion of "plurality" is to be found in the work of K. C. Bhattacharya, who argues that the plurality of *puruṣas* implies the absolute uniqueness of each *puruṣa*. Says K. C. Bhattacharya, "It [the plurality of *puruṣas* as a general notion] is an abstraction in the sense that it cannot be represented like a universal or a substance as really or apparently comprising individuals (or modes) under it, being intelligible only as the *svarūpa* (or the character of being itself) of the individual. The subject is manifest as what has no character (*nirdharmaka*), but this characterlessness is itself taken as its character of self-manifestness...Selfhood is this necessary universality of a singular, being universal only if uniqueness or the unique-in-general is universal. Unique-in-general means *any* unique, not *all* uniques. 'All A is B' indeed means '*any* A is B' but 'any A is B' need not mean 'all A is B", for even the distributive *all* has an implied collective character. As applied to the object, any and all may be regarded as equivalents but not as applied to the subject. In point of being, each self is absolute...In point of being, each self is known in *buddhi* [*citta*] as having with it a community of selves."[78] The Yoga view, it would seem, is that non-intentional consciousness (*citiśakti, puruṣa*) is the warrant for the absolute unique significance of every embodied life form.

The dualism of Yoga, then, is interestingly different from what might be called garden-variety dualisms. The difference between the typical dualist claim and a standard materialist claim has to do with whether mental states can plausibly be reduced or explained or interpreted in terms of physical states. The typical dualist wishes to maintain that finally it is implausible to argue that capacities such as the creative use of language, the processes of logic and reasoning, the intrinsic qualities of sensations, feelings and emotions, and the semantic significance of beliefs and desires and other intentional states, can ever be adequately explained in purely physicalist or materialist terms. The typical materialist maintains, to the contrary, that a purely materialist account is not only possible, but indeed, quite likely correct. As Paul Churchland has put it, "...the important point about the standard evolutionary story is that the human species and all of its features are the wholly physical outcome of a purely physical process."[79]

Yoga (as well as Sāṃkhya), to be sure, is a dualism but not

in the sense of any of the standard accounts of dualism, including substance dualism, epiphenomenalist dualism, interactionist property dualism, or elementary property dualism. Given any of these standard positions, Yoga comes out on the side of materialism. That is, Yoga would agree with the materialist claim that language, logic, reasoning, the *qualia* of immediate experience, the semantic significance of beliefs, desires and other intentional states are all best explained in physicalist or materialist terms, that is, in terms of its theory of *triguṇa*. Yoga, however, also argues for a non-intentional consciousness that is ontologically distinct from the mind-body realm of *citta* and the *cittavṛttis*. In other words, Yoga also finally rejects a purely materialist account.

In this regard, Paul Churchland comments about a version of dualism that is possible but has never seriously been argued, at least in western philosophy. Churchland suggests that there is a possible dualist position "...that to my knowledge has never been cited before, but it is real just the same. Specifically, the P-theory [that is, the notion of mental states or the 'Person-theory', or, in the idiom of Yoga, 'the functioning of ordinary awareness' (*cittavṛtti*)] might prove to be replaceable by some more general theory...but to be irreducible to that more general theory. The ontology of the P-theory would thus be eliminated in favour of the ontology of the more general theory that displaced it. We might call this possibility 'eliminative dualism'!"[80] Yoga, I would argue, is precisely this sort of dualism! Whether the theory of *triguṇa* is a plausible account of mental states or whether the concept of a pluralistic content-less consciousness is a plausible notion, are matters, of course, requiring much further critical discussion. I am inclined to think, however, that the manner in which Yoga philosophy poses the problem of dualism is worth further consideration in contemporary discussions within the philosophy of mind.

The Theism of Yoga

If the materialism and dualism of Yoga are eccentric and

puzzling, the theism of Yoga is even more anomalous. God (*īśvara*) in Yoga philosophy is neither a creator, nor is God personal. God, rather, is said to be a "specific" one among the plurality of *puruṣas*. In order to understand what Yoga intends with respect to its notion of God, it is necessary to understand the cosmology with which the Yoga system operates and the various kinds of sentient beings that populate the world. The details of the cosmology and the many technical names employed need not be delineated in full, since the cosmology is an archaic one that has little more than archival interest in terms of the overall philosophical meaning of Yoga. For the most part, the Yoga cosmology is typical of most Purāṇic cosmologies. Some aspects of the Yoga cosmology must be discussed, however, for the sake of understanding the particular sense in which Yoga uses the notion of God and the important role the notion plays in the overall system.

Relevant for understanding the theism of Yoga is the psychological cosmology summarized in the Vyāsa *Bhāṣya* on YS III.26. The *sūtra* is part of YS III, the Vibhūti Pāda, which concerns the "extraordinary capacities" attained by *yogins* when they have achieved advanced levels of yogic awareeness through the practice of "comprehensive reflection" (*saṃyama*). The *sūtra* itself reads, "When the sun [or perhaps better, the '*sūryadvāra*', the 'solar-entrance', according to the Vyāsa *Bhāṣya*, in the region of the navel or heart] becomes the focus for comprehensive reflection (*saṃyama*), knowledge of (various) universes becomes possible (*bhuvanajñānaṃ sūrye saṃyamāt*).* The Vyāsa *Bhāṣya* then provides a summary description of these

---

*Ram Shankar Bhattacharya points out that the references to the sun, moon, pole star (*dhruva*), and so forth in YS III.26-34 refer to places in the body of the *yogin* as well as to phenomena in the external world. In other words, the "extraordinary psychic capacities" in these *sūtras* relate to correlations between macrocosm-microcosm in on-going Yogic meditation. See RSB 1985, p 137.

universes. Altogether there are seven worlds enclosed within the cosmic egg (*brahmāṇḍa*). From the top down, they are as follows: *satyaloka*--the "world of truth"--the highest or seventh level; *tapoloka*--the "world of discipline or asceticism"--the sixth level; *janaloka*--the "world of living beings"--the fifth level (these first three taken together make up the *brahmaloka*, populated by the high gods and extraordinary beings of the world belonging to the "creator", Brahmā); *maharloka*--the "world of Prajāpati"--the fourth level; *mahendraloka*--the "world of Indra"--the third level (these levels, that is, the third and fourth, together with the fifth, sixth and seventh, all make up the realms of "heaven" (*svar*); *antarikṣaloka*--the "world of the intermediate regions" from the pole-star (Dhruva) down through the stars and planets up to the summit of Meru--the second level; and finally *bhūrloka*, the "world of earth"--the first level, which in turn is divided into three segments: *vasumatī* (our "earth") with its seven continents, including Jambudvīpa, its mountains, and its various oceans; *pātālas*--the "nether" regions--seven in all, in descending order from Pātāla to Talātala, Vitala, Sutala, Atala, Rasātala, and ending with Mahātala--and, finally, *narakas*--the "hells"--again, seven in all, in descending order from Andhatāmisra ("darkness") through Kālāsūtra (air), Mahāraurava (wind), Raurava (fire), Ambarīṣa (water), Mahākāla (earth), and ending with the lowest "hell", Avīci.

Throughout these various worlds are all sorts of deities and creatures working out their karmic trajectories through ongoing cycles of manifestation or coming forth (*pravṛtti*) and withdrawal (*nivṛtti, pralaya* and *mahāpralaya*). This is the case with Brahmā and his world-egg (*brahmāṇḍa*) as well. That is, the so-called "creator", Brahmā or Hiraṇyagarbha, and the world-egg undergo periodic manifestation and withdrawal as well. Put somewhat differently, the worlds, whether in manifestation or withdrawal, are subject to a beginningless (*anādi*) process (*pariṇāma*) of time or becoming (*bhava*). Precisely how the cycles unfold is determined by the trajectories of the various species of beings that have been self-constructed by the afflictions, actions, ripenings and resulting traces (*vāsanās*, *āśayas*, *saṃskāras*) of their own behavior or functioning.

The Vyāsa *Bhāṣya* concludes its comment on YS III.26 by pointing out that two sorts of beings are outside of the world-egg, namely the disembodied ones (*videhas*) and those dissolved in *prakṛti* (*prakṛtilayas*). The former, that is, the "disembodied" ones, are those beings (primarily certain gods (*deva*) as well as *yogins*) who have attained a temporary reprieve from ordinary becoming because of having conquered attachment to gross objects and sense -organs (YS I.19 with Vyāsa *Bhāṣya* and Vācaspatimiśra's *Tattvavaiśāradī*). They have attained a temporary spiritual liberation and content-less concentration. The latter, that is, the "dissolved in *prakṛti*" ones, are those beings or *yogins* who have attained an even longer but still temporary reprieve from ordinary becoming because of having conquered attachment to mind, ego and intellect. They have become dissolved (*laya*) in unmanifest *prakṛti*, which also brings with it a temporary spiritual liberation and content-less states of awareness. Both sorts, however, are still predisposed towards one or another of the *tattvas* of *prakṛti* and, thus, implicated in a yearning for becoming. In other words, both sorts are still predisposed to the vicissitudes of time. Vācaspatimiśra (in his comment on YS I.19 and 20 and in his comment on YS III.26) explains that the disembodied ones hearken back in time by their yearning for objects and sense capacities, while those dissolved in *prakṛti* have a yearning or inclination for future becoming. Both sorts of beings, whether gods or *yogins*, because of the inclination towards becoming will fall back eventually into the temporal realm of the world-egg. Both these two kinds of beings are highly achieved gods and *yogins* whose awareness is temporarily in reprieve from becoming but who will eventually undergo further involvement in becoming.

In addition to the inclination towards becoming (*bhava-*

pratyaya) there is, of course, another and correct means (*upāyapratyaya*) for attaining permanent spiritual liberation. This is referred to in YS I.20: "Among others [that is, those *yogins* who follow the proper path of Yoga], their path involves the practice of faith, energy, mindfulness, the cultivation of altered states of awareness and insight" (*śraddhāvīryasmṛti-samādhiprajñāpūrvaka itareṣām*). We already know, of course, from YS I.12-16, that the correct means (*upāya*) for bringing about the cessation of the functioning of ordinary awareness involves both ongoing practice and renunciation. We also know that practice and renunciation lead to the attainment, first, of altered states of awareness (*samādhi*) with contents (*samprajñāta*) (YS I.17) and then to seedless (*nirbīja*) or content-less concentration (YS I.18). In addition, of course, the correct means involves following the *kriyāyoga* and the "eight-limbed" Yoga as set forth in YS II.1-III.5. Moreover, among those Yogins who follow the correct path to permanent spiritual liberation, there are nine varieties (YS I.21-22), based upon the levels of commitment to practice and renunciation. Some practices are mild, some middling and some intense (YS I.22). Likewise some patterns of renunciation are mild, some middling and some intense (YS I.21). Perhaps reasonably enough, the *yogins* whose practices and patterns of renunciation are intense are coming ever closer to the realization of permanent spiritual liberation (YS I.21).

Altogether, then, the sorts of beings that make up the beginningless world of becoming include the myriad of living beings within the world-egg of Brahmā as well as those caught up in the nether worlds and hells. Then there are the disembodied ones and those dissolved in *prakṛti*, temporarily in reprieve from becoming but destined to re-enter the realm of becoming when their own predispositions ripen. Furthermore, there are those *yogins* who have attained true *kaivalya* or permanent spiritual liberation by the correct path of yogic praxis.

What is distinctive about God in Yoga is that God is none

of these. God, rather, is a "particular or unique consciousness among consciousnesses, untouched by afflictions, actions, ripenings and long-term karmic predispositions" (YS I.24). In God the pinnacle of omniscience (*sarvajñabīja*) has been attained [of what truly is and or what can possibly be known](YS I.25). God is the teacher of all preceding teachers inasmuch as God is not limited by time (YS I.26). The sacred syllable *oṃ* denotes God (YS I.27). Repetition of the sacred syllable and meditation on the object of the expression (namely God) should be practiced in order to achieve *samādhi*) (YS I.28).

If, according to Yoga, God is not touched by afflictions, actions, the consequences of actions, and the resulting traces and/or predispositions, then obviously God cannot be a creator in any meaningful sense, nor can God be personal in any intelligible sense. "What" or "who", then, is God? God as consciousness cannot be a thing or entity, and because consciousness (*puruṣa* and *īśvara* as a particular *puruṣa*) is content-less, it can only appear as what it is not. What distinguishes God can only be what consciousness, untouched by afflictions, actions, consequences and predispositions, appears not to be. What appears not to be in such an environment can only be "perfect *sattva*" (*prakṛṣṭasattva* or *prakṛṣṭacittasattva*) in which *rajas* and *tamas*, though present, are inoperative (and see Vyāsa *Bhāṣya* on YS I.24). The environment of "perfect *cittasattva*", in turn, which pure consciousness appears not to be, functions by way of making possible a non-intentional awareness of the presence of pure consciousness, as being distinct from itself. God, then, is the "eternal excellence" (*śāśvatika utkarṣa*) of the presence of "perfect *sattva*" and content-less consciousness (see Vyāsa *Bhāṣya* and *Tattvavaiśāradī* on YS I.24).

God's "office" or "role" (*adhikāra*) can only be to appear as what it is not. Or, to put the matter somewhat differently, the capacity of consciousness (*citiśakti*) can only be to illumine what is distinct from itself. Thus, it is in this sense that the YS, the Vyāsa *Bhāṣya* and the *Tattvavaiśāradī* use the terms "profound longing" (*praṇidhāna*), "inclination" (*āvarjita*), "unique sort of devotion" (*bhaktiviśeṣa*) and a "moving towards" (*anugraha*). These terms are apparently conceptual constructions (*vikalpa*) or symbolic portrayals for the purpose of highlighting the inherent tendency within each of the two ultimate *tattvas* (*puruṣa* and *prakṛti*). That is, it is the inherent tendency of *puruṣa* to appear as what it is not, thereby illuminating the presence of "perfect *sattva*", and it is the inherent tendency of "perfect *sattva*" to appear as what it is not, thereby illuminating the presence of pure consciousness. This "eternal excellence" of God is beginningless and is always present throughout the ongoing cycles of manifestation and dissolution. In each subsequent unfolding world period, God is present as the exemplum of permanent spiritual liberation, and there is always also the inherent longing within *cittasattva* for complete freedom. In other words, there is always an inherent urge in *cittasattva* to break free from the afflictions and karmic bonds of "ordinary awareness".

The Vyāsa *Bhāṣya* (YS I.24) then poses the question as to whether there is some sort of proof or warrant for the "eternal excellence" of such a God. The answer is that the proof is to be found in the *śāstra*. According to Vācaspatimiśra, "*śāstra*" means *śruti, smṛti, itihāsa* and *purāṇa*. But what, then is the proof or warrant for the validity of the *śāstra*?, asks the Vyāsa *Bhāṣya*. The answer is that the warrant is "perfect *sattva*" (*prakṛṣṭa-sattva*). The truth in *śāstra*, in other words, is the content illuminated by *cittasattva* when *rajas* and *tamas* have become inoperative. God is the "eternal excellence" in which pure consciousness and "perfect *sattva*" are present in one another, a dyadic substantive transcendence in which the "pinnacle of omniscience" (*niratiśayaṃ sarvajñabījam*) has been attained (YS I.25).

God for Yoga, then, serves both as a regulative idea and as an ontological argument. God is a regulative idea in the sense that even at the height or pinnacle of what can be known, God always has a body distinct from pure consciousness, namely perfect *sattva*. Even when the entire manifest world dissolves in the *mahāpralaya*, God as the "seed of the omniscient" continues to abide inasmuch as God is the "eternal excellence" which must always be! God for Yoga also is established by an interesting ontological argument in the sense that that "than which nothing greater can be conceived", namely pure, content-less consciousness, can only reveal itself in the eternal presence of "perfect *sattva*". In this sense, God for Yoga is a mediating position between the theology of Advaita Vedānta and the "theology" of Buddhist thought. In Vedānta, *cittasattva* dissolves as an ontological principle in *māyā*, and there is finally only Brahman. In Buddhist thought, *citta* as temporal becoming is ultimate, and beyond *citta* there is no substantive transcendence.*

It should perhaps also be noted that God in Yoga, therefore, cannot be reduced to any identifiable personal deity or highly accomplished *yogin*, be he Śiva, Viṣṇu, a Buddha, a Jina or Tīrthaṅkara or a figure such as Kapila. To be sure God as the "eternal excellence" or exemplum of the presence of *puruṣa* and *citisattva* in any and all realms of becoming is the "teacher" of all of these (YS I.26), but God cannot be identified with any one of them without compromising God's transcendence of temporal becoming (*kālena anavacchedāt*) (YS I.26). For followers of Sāṃkhya and Yoga, of course, Kapila is the "primal knower" (*ādividvān*) but, says Vācaspatimiśra (on YS I.25), the "primal knower" can never equal the "eternal excellence" of God. Likewise, the particular kind of *bhakti* (*bhaktiviśeṣa*, the

*This is already clear in Aśvaghoṣa's verse (69) in Chapter XII of the *Buddhacarita* when the future Buddha comments about the Yoga described in that work. Says the future Buddha, "I have listened to this doctrine of yours, which grows more subtle and auspicious in its successive stages, but I consider it not to lead to final beatitude, since the field-knower is not abandoned." (Johnston, p. 178)

Vyāsa *Bhāṣya* at I.23-24, II.1, II.32 and II.45) can only be a turning toward God by way of dedicating all one's actions towards the goal of the "eternal excellence" that God embodies. That "eternal excellence", of course, is *puruṣa* and "perfect *sattva*" (*prakṛti*) eternally present to one another, and thus God's token or representation can only be the sacred syllable *auṃ* (YS I.27). Access to God can only occur through continuous meditation on that token symbol, which is God's intentional content (YS I.28).

Finally, let me offer a brief comment about the placement of YS I.23 ("Or, from devotion or deep longing for God" (*īśvara-praṇidhānād vā*) in the *sūtrapāṭha* and the referent of the word "or" (*vā*). The immediately preceding *sūtras* (YS I.21-22) refer to the nine kinds of *yogins* who practice with the greatest intensity. According to the Vyāsa *Bhāṣya* and Vācaspatimiṣra, therefore, the *sūtra* "Or, from devotion or deep longing for God" is an alternative practice in addition to "great intensity". In other words, the word "or" (*vā*) in YS I.23 follows naturally from YS I.21-22. Both J. W. Hauer in *Der Yoga* and Ram Shankar Bhattacharya in *An Introduction to the Yogasūtra* have challenged this traditional view.[81] Both have argued, mainly on the basis of the use of the ablative case in YS I.23, that the word "or" should be construed with an earlier *sūtra* that is also in the ablative case. They suggest, therefore, that a more correct reading is to take YS I.23 as following upon YS I.12 which reads, "The cessation of them [that is, the *cittavṛttis*)] is accomplished through (or from) practice and renunciation" (*abhyāsavairāgyābhyāṃ tan-nirodhaḥ*). This requires construing the ambiguous dual ending "*bhyāṃ*" as an ablative ending. In other words, "devotion or deep longing for God" is to be understood as an alternative method for achieving cessation of the functioning of ordinary awareness, in addition to, or over and above, "practice" and "renunciation".

My own view in this matter differs from both the traditional view and the alternative suggested by Hauer and RSB. On the one hand, I am inclined to agree with Hauer and RSB that one should look for an earlier *sūtra* with an ablative ending, but in my view there is no need to go back as far as YS I.12. Also, in my view, "devotion or deep longing for God" is in no way a substitute for "practice" and "renunciation" in Yoga philosophy. To make "devotion or deep longing for God" an alternative to "practice" and "renunciation" is to give much too strong a role for the theism of Yoga in the cultivation of Yogic *samādhis*. A much more natural, and in my view rather obvious, reading is to take "or" in YS I.23 as an additional option with respect to YS I.17, "Concentrations having content [*samprajñātasamādhi* or, in other words, *ekāgra* or "one-pointed" or "intentional concentrations"] are those derived from meditating on empirical awareness (*vitarka*), rational awareness (*vicāra*), aesthetic awareness (*ānanda*) and self-awareness (*asmitā*)". The needed ablative in YS I.17 is to be found in the compound "from the pursuit of empirical, rational, aesthetic and self-awarenesses (*vitarkavicārānandāsmitānugamāt)*. Then, it seems to me, YS I.23 ("Or, from devotion or deep longing for God") makes perfectly good sense as one more way of attaining content-filled concentration, and the content of this particular concentration would have to be, of course, *praṇava* or *oṃ*.

Concentration (*samādhi*)

As already mentioned at the outset, the Vyāsa *Bhāṣya* on YS I.1 explains the term "*yoga*" by saying simply "Yoga is concentration". That is, disciplined meditation has to do with concentration, and although there are all sorts of concentration only two sorts are especially relevant for Yoga, namely "one-pointed" or content-filled awareness and "restricted" or "content-less" awareness. One-pointed awarenesses are *sattva*-awarenesses in which only a trace of *rajas* is still operative, and content-less states of awareness are *sattva*-states of *citta* in which *rajas* and *tamas* are completely inoperative (Vyāsa *Bhāṣya* on YS I.2). Other states of awareness, for example "distracted" (*kṣipta*), "depressed" (*mūḍha*), and "partially focussed" (*vikṣipta*) are not discussed, since they are not conducive to progress with respect to Yoga in its proper sense (*yogapakṣa*).

These one-pointed and content-less states of awareness become possible after the afflictions have been weakened or diminished through following the various stages of yogic meditation. These stages are outlined in Book Two of the YS and the first five *sūtras* of Book Three, and include the "Yoga of Action" (*kriyāyoga*) (YS II.1-27) and the eightfold "limbs of Yoga" (*yogāṅga*) (YS II.28 through III.5). The remainder of Book Three is given over to describing the extraordinary cognitive capacities that become possible through the systematic practice of comprehensive meditation (YS III.6 through III.55).*

Regarding one-pointed awarenesses, according to Vyāsa on YS I.1 and I.17 there are basically four varieties, namely what, in my view, can be characterized simply as empirical awareness (*vitarka*), rational awareness (*vicāra*), aesthetic or "sensate" awareness (*ānanda*) and self-awareness (*asmitā*).* The Vyāsa

---

*As mentioned earlier, I am inclined to follow Vyāsa and Vācaspatimiśra by way of explaining the manner in which Books One, Two and Three are related to one another. Book Four, according to Vācaspatimiśra, takes up the issue of "spiritual liberation" or "isolation" (*kaivalya*) along with miscellaneous matters that have arisen along the way. In other words, Book Four discusses liberation along with some final summary discussions. This is a straightforward account of the four parts of the YS which makes reasonably good sense. In my view, so long as one recognizes that some *sūtras* have been interpolated here and there throughout the YS and that some of the *sūtras* may be considerably older than the final redaction of the text that we now have, there is hardly any reason to engage in an elaborate reconstruction of the *sūtrapāṭha* as in Hauer et al.

*I use the terms "aesthetic" and "sensate" in the Sāṃkhya sense of "mere sensing" (*ālocanamātra*) meaning the experience of a "*quale*" or the "*qualia*" of experience without intellectual

Bhāṣya on YS I.17 characterizes these types of awarenesses as follows:** "Empirical awareness (*vitarka*) has to do with the experience of gross contents (*vitarkaś cittasya ālambane sthūla ābhogaḥ*). Rational awareness (*vicāra*) has to do with subtle

---

elaboration.

**The manner in which *samādhi* is discussed in the classical Yoga texts bears comparison with the framework of Buddhist meditation. The terms used, for example, *samādhi, samāpatti, vitarka, vicāra* and so forth are the same, but they appear to be used in somewhat differing ways. The four levels of Buddhist *dhyāna* appear to be parallel with the four levels of "one-pointed" *samādhi* in Yoga. The Buddhist sequence, however, has to do with the hierarchical levels of awareness rather than with objects within awareness. The first Buddhist *dhyāna* is made up of empirical awareness (*vitarka*), reflective awareness (*vicāra*), rapture (*prīti*), happiness (*sukha*) and "one-pointed awareness" (*ekāgratācitta*). The second *dhyāna* eliminates *vitarka* and *vicāra*. The third eliminates *prīti*, and the fourth eliminates *sukha*, leaving only *ekāgratācitta*. The four *samāpattis* of the Buddhists also differ from the Yoga sequence. Whereas for Yoga *samādhi* is the awareness itself and the *samāpatti* is the content of the awareness, for the Buddhists the *samāpattis* include the sequence "endless space", "endless consciousness", "nothing at all", and "neither awareness nor nonawareness". Supposedly, according to Aśvaghoṣa's *Buddhacarita* (Canto XII.45-71) the *Sāmaññaphala-sutta* and the *Poṭṭhapāda-sutta* of the *Dīgha-nikāya*, and various passages in Buddhaghosa's *Visuddhimagga*, the Buddha learned about *samādhi* and *samāpatti* from Yoga teachers. Prima facie, however, the Yoga analysis in the YS is considerably more systematic and precise than the usual Buddhist sequence and appears to indicate a much later intellectual milieu. One probable explanation is that there were older traditions of yogic meditation that are reflected in the Buddhist texts but that these were re-worked or updated in classical Pātañjala Yoga. For accounts of the Buddhist sequences of meditation, see Conze, pp. 113-118, and Gimello, pp. 182-183. Still well worth reading is the excellent Introduction to Johnston, pp. xiii-xcviii, especially pp. lx-lxii.

contents (*sūkṣmo vicāraḥ*). Aesthetic (or "sensate") awareness (*ānanda*) has to do with the joy (*hlāda*) of sensuous awareness or the sheer sensing (or the act of cognizing) of contents (*ānando hlāda iti*). Self-awareness (*asmitā*) has to do with the feeling of being one with one's self (*ekātmikā saṃvid asmitā*). The first, that is, empirical awareness, encompasses all four levels of awareness. The second, rational awareness, is without (*vikala*) empirical awareness. The third, aesthetic awareness, is without empirical or rational awareness. The fourth, that is, self-awareness, is just self-awareness alone without the other three. All these concentrated states of awareness have contents (*sālambanaḥ*)." Furthermore, as I have suggested in the previous section, there is also an additional and/or optional sort of one-pointed awareness, and that is what might be called "divine awareness" (*īśvarapraṇidhāna*, or literally, a "deep longing for God") (YS I.23). That is to say, in addition to meditating on an empirical object, a rational object, an aesthetic object, or simply on oneself, one might also meditate on the yogic *īśvara*.

All of these one-pointed awarenesses are intentional in the sense that they are "about" something or, in other words, have some sort of specific content (*samprajñātasamādhi* or *sabīja-samādhi*). The first two varieties of one-pointed awareness, that is, *vitarka* and *vicāra*, are concerned respectively with gross and subtle contents. Empirical awareness (*vitarka*) concerns the everyday realm of ordinary or gross experience, or, in other words, the realm of what Sāṃkhya called the *mahābhūtas*. Rational awareness (*vicāra*) concerns the subtle realm of ideas and conceptualizations that inform ordinary experience, or what Gaspar Koelman has aptly called the "objective universals" within experience, or what Sāṃkhya calls the "subtle elements" (*tanmātras*).* The third variety of one-pointed awareness has

---

*See Koelman, pp. 74, 89, 90, 114, 115. Koelman recognizes that the "subtle" realm of "ideas" in Sāṃkhya and Yoga is an

to do with the processes or instrumentalities of sensing (*grahaṇa*), including cognizing (including thinking and willing, or believing and desiring), hearing (including the language capacity or verbalizing), touching (feeling), seeing, tasting, and smelling. Finally, the fourth variety of one-pointed awareness has to do with self-awareness or the ordinary subject of awareness (*grahītṛ*).

The four varieties of one-pointed awareness encompass three distinct levels of experience. (1) First, there is the level of object or contents (*grāhya*), which itself breaks into two sub-levels, gross-empirical (*vitarka* and/or *sthūla, mahābhūta*), and subtle-rational (*vicāra* and/or *sūkṣma, tanmātra*). (2) Second, there is the level of processes or instrumentalities of cognizing and sensing (*ānanda* and/or *grahaṇa*). (3) Finally, there is the level of self-awareness (*asmitā* and/or *grahītṛ*). The concluding *sūtras* of Book I (YS I.41-51), then, specify the nature of these various levels of yogic awareness.

Important to recognize in this sort of analysis is the overlapping of notions because of the peculiar materialist orientation of Yoga (and Sāṃkhya). That is, all three levels of experience (*grāhya, grahaṇa* and *grahītṛ*) are contents of *citta* and are, therefore, material processes within primordial materialilty (*mūlaprakṛti*). The term "*grāhya*" in this context means "content" and includes gross empirical objects (*sthūla-grāhya, mahābhūtas*) and subtle (objective universal) or rational objects (*sukṣmagrāhya, tanmātras*). The term "*grahaṇa*" in this context means the organs of sensing (*indriya)* and

---

objective, material realm, hence his apt expression "objective universal". In other words, *citta* or "mind-stuff" encompasses or is co-extensive with the entire realm of materiality from the subtlest level, pure *cittasattva* or *buddhisattva,* down through the subtle forms (*tanmātras*) ("objective univerals") of ordinary everyday experience that eventually become the concrete, gross object-world of every day life (*mahābhūtas*). For a full discussion, see Larson-Bhattacharya 1987, pp. 65-73.

cognizing (*manas/citta*), but these instrumentalities are themselves also "contents" (*grāhya*) as well. That is, they too are types of subtle contents and can be the focus for meditation. Finally, the term "*grahītṛ*" in this context means ordinary self-awareness or subjective apprehension, but it, too, is also a type of subtle content (*grāhya*) and can be a focus for meditation.

Ordinary self-awareness (*asmitā* and/or *grahītṛ*) or what would ordinarily be called "subjective awareness" is, according to this analysis, a type of content. It is illumined by consciousness (*puruṣa* or *citiśakti*), but ordinary subjectivity or self-awareness is a material process distinct from non-intentional consciousness. The same must be said about the process of sensing (*grahaṇa*), that is to say, ordinary cognizing, hearing, touching, seeing, tasting and smelling. Each of these, of course, has a gross objective base as brain (or, in this ancient context, the heart region),* ear, skin, eye, tongue and nose, but the actual functioning or "sensing" capacity (*indriya*) must be distiguished from the gross organ and is itself a subtle content (*grāhya*). As is perhaps obvious, dementia, deafness, paralysis, blindness, and the inability to taste or smell are clear evidence that the sensing capacity (*grahaṇa*) must be clearly distinguished from the gross organ. The gross organ is an empirical object made up of a collocation of gross elements (*mahābhūtas*). The ear or eye, for example, according to this analysis, would be a certain form of "earth" (*pṛthivī*), a gross element which itself is a combination that includes space (or, as we might say in modern times, space-time), air, light and liquidity. The ear or eye, furthermore, would be the seat of a certain type of "sensing", hearing in the case of the ear, seeing in the case of the eye, and so forth, which capacities would themselves be "subtle" contents (*grāhya*). These are understood

*In ancient Indian thought generally, the "seat" of cognition is considered to be in the "heart" region rather than the region of the head or brain.

to be subtle elements (*tanmātra*) that enable the gross ear or eye to function. Ordinary awareness or, in other words, *citta* therefore encompasses the gross empirical world of everyday experience (*mahābhūtas*), the subtle elements that inform ordinary experience (*tanmātras*), the subtle capacities of sensing and acting (*buddhendriyas* and *karmendriyas*) that link the object-world with the cognizing world of desiring or intending (*manas*), self-awareness (*ahaṃkāra*) and believing (*buddhi*). There are, then, gross and subtle contents (*grāhya*), the processes and instrumentalities of sensing and cognizing (*grahaṇa*), and the resulting self-awareness (*asmitā, grahītṛ*) that arises.

What the *yogin* must come to understand in ongoing meditative flow is that sensing and cognizing as well as subjective awareness are themselves subtle contents or material entities within the framework of *citta* or "mind-stuff" and are to be clearly distinguished (*viveka-khyāti*) from consciousness. When the *yogin* achieves such a realization, he has attained "truth-bearing insight" ("*ṛtambharā tatra prajñā*", YS I.48), and this insight is a special cognitive experience that transcends both scriptural knowledge (*śruta, āgama*) and inferential knowledge (*anumāna*) (YS I.49). This insight is also called the "*dharma*-cloud meditative flow" (*dharmameghadhyaṇa*) and the "supreme" or "ultimate", "reflection" (*prasaṃkhyāna*) (the Vyāsa *Bhāṣya* on YS I.2 as well as YS IV.28).* When this special cognitive experience occurs, there arises, then, a strong predisposition (*saṃskāra*) that leads towards spiritual liberation (*nirodha, kaivalya*) and that counteracts all other predispositions (YS I.50, YS III.6, and the Vyāsa *Bhāṣya* on YS I.2). Finally, when the *yogin* turns away even from that predisposition or in other words from even that special

---

*All three terms, "*ṛtambharā prajñā*", "*dharma-megha*" and "*prasaṃkhyāna*" are undoubtedly "technical terms" (*saṃjñā*-words) or "code"-words for the highest level of cognitive skill. That is, their eymological or literal sense is not intended.

cognitive experience, inasmuch as all ordinary awareness has been overcome (*sarvanirodha)*, the *yogin* passes into "objectless" or "seedless" concentration. In other words, the *yogin*'s non-intentional "perfect *sattva*" (*prakṛṣṭasattva*) rests in the presence of pure, content-less consciousness, which is identical with the achievement of "isolation" or spiritual liberation (*kaivalya*), that is, the quiescent co-presence of "perfect *sattva*" (*prakṛṣṭasattva*) and *citiśakti* (YS I.51).

Before leaving the discussion of concentrated states of awareness it is important to offer an interpretation of the relation between the term "*samādhi*" and the term "*samāpatti*". Furthermore, it is important to offer an interpretation of the various levels of "*samādhi*" or "*samāpatti*" and to indicate whether there are six or eight levels of one-pointed awareness. Commentators, both ancient and modern, have offered varied interpretations of both of these issues, and the difference between Vācaspatimiśra and Vijñānabhikṣu regarding the latter issues, that is, the number of levels, whether six or eight, has been especially salient.

My own inclination, as I have stated on more than one occasion, is to follow the Vyāsa *Bhāṣya* with Vācaspatimiśra's *Tattvavaiśāradī* as the "core textual complex" for understanding Pātañjala Yoga. Admittedly in these matters, there is not a little ambiguity in Vyāsa and Vācaspatimiśra, mainly because the *sūtrapāṭha* in YS I.41-47 is not exactly a model of clarity. Overall, however, it is possible in my view to offer an interpretation of these matters that is fairly straightforward and reasonable.

Regarding the first issue of the difference between "*samādhi*" and "*samāpatti*", the terms are often used synonymously in the texts, but there is a distinction implied between the state of concentrated awareness itself (*samādhi*) and the content entertained in that state of awareness (*samāpatti*). The term "*samādhi*" is from the root "*dhā*" together with the adverbial particles "*sam*" plus "*ā*" meaning "to put, place or hold together" or, in English, to "con-centrate" (from

Latin, "cum" plus "centrum", meaning "to center along with"). The term "*samāpatti*" is from the root "*pad*", together with the adverbial particles "*sam*" plus "*ā*" meaning "to come together, to meet or to encounter". The terms are obviously close but not identical. It is the difference between "concentration" and that upon which the concentration is directed or focused. One-pointed awareness, unlike the largely multiple, distracted and confused awarenesses of everyday life, is a highly concentrated or focused awareness, and that "one point" upon which the awareness is focused becomes, then, the unique and single object of its engrossment (*samāpatti*). "Content-less" or "seedless" awareness, in contrast, is a highly concentrated or focused awareness without a determinate content. The "content-less" awareness, in other words, is a non-intentional awareness.

The possible varieties of one-pointed concentration that bring about engrossment (*samāpatti*) with certain contents are set forth in YS I.41. "(When the *citta* [of the *yogin*] has been sufficiently cleansed of its dysfunctional functioning (*kṣīṇa-vṛtti*) (and becomes) like a transparent jewel, there arises an encounter or engrossment with (gross and subtle objects) (*grāhya*), the process of cognizing (*grahaṇa*), and the subject of cognizing (*grahītṛ*). (The *citta*) then shows forth or highlights (*añjanatā*) the true nature of those contents." Just as collyrium (*añjanatā*) highlights the eyes, so the *yogin*'s cleansed awareness shows forth the true nature of the contents exhibited in the one-pointed awareness, and, as has been discussed, there are four types or levels of awareness to be exhibited: *vitarka, vicāra, ānanda* and *asmitā* (YS I.17).

Each of these in turn may be construction-filled (*savikalpa)* or construction-free *(nirvikalpa)*. That is, each type of "one-pointed" awareness may be accompanied by "verbal or conceptual construction" (*vikalpa*) and hence accessible to linguistic description, inferential reasoning and so forth, or be free from such constructions and, hence, permitting an immediate or direct apprehension of a content. Thus *vitarka* can be "*savitarka*" (that is, *savikalpavitarka*) or "*nirvitarka*" (that is, *nirvikalpavitarka*). The terms "*savitarka*" and "*nirvitarka*" can then be applied (in Sanskrit) either to the masculine term "*samādhi*", hence giving rise to the expressions "*savitarka-samādhi* and "*nirvitarkasamādhi*", or to the feminine term "*samāpatti*", giving rise to the expressions "*savitarkasamāpatti*" and "*nirvitarkasamāpatti*". Likewise, there can be a *savicāra-samādhi* (or *savicārasamāpatti*) and a *nirvicārasamādhi* (or *savicārasamāpatti*), a *sānandasamādhi* (or *samāpatti*) and a *nirānandasamādhi* (or *samāpatti*), and, finally, a *sāsmitā-samādhi* (or *samāpatti*) and a *nirasmitāsamādhi* or *samāpatti*). Altogether, then, there are eight levels of concentration and/or eight types of engrossments. Here, it should be noted, I am following the interpretation of Vācaspatimiśra, who comments as follows (under YS I.43). "The first four *samāpattis* (that is, *savitarka, nirvitarka, savicāra* and *nirvicāra*), referring to gross and subtle contents (*grāhya*), are obviously determinate by reason of having a specific "seed" (content). But the condition of having a specific content also applies to the *samāpattis* pertaining to "sensing" and/or "cognizing" (*grahaṇa*) and subjective apprehension (*grahītṛ*) inasmuch as the distinction between *vikalpa* and *avikalpa* [or, in other words, *savikalpa* and *nirvikalpa*] equally applies to them. Thus, there are four *samāpattis* that pertain to gross and subtle contents (*grāhya*) and four that pertain to the contents related to "sensing"/"cognizing" (*grahaṇa*) and subjective apprehension (*grahītṛ*)--(altogether, then) eight (*samādhis* and *samāpattis*) are recognized as established."*

**tataś ca catasraḥ samāpattayo grāhyaviṣayāḥ sabījatayā niyamyante. sabījatā tu aniyatā grahītṛgrahaṇagocarāyām api samāpattau vikalpāvikalpabhedena aniṣiddhāvyavatiṣṭhate. tena grāhye catasraḥ samāpattayo grahītṛgrahaṇayoś ca catāsra ity aṣṭau siddhā bhavanti iti.* (RSB on YS, p. 46).

Vijñānabhikṣu thoroughly disagrees with Vācaspatimiśra regarding the number of levels of *samāpatti*. See the discussion

The first type of "one-pointed" awareness, namely empirical awareness (*vitarka*), encompassing the gross manifest world, thus has two subdivisions. There is a lower level of empirical awarenesses in which objects (*artha*), language (*śabda*) and meanings or ideas (*pratyaya*) are mixed together in single constructive or verbalized cognitions (*śabdārthajñāna-vikalpa*). This, of course, is the level of ordinary, everyday experience, and it is known as *savitarka-samāpatti* or *-samādhi* (YS I.42). Since it is a one-pointed awareness, of course, it is a highly focused or disciplined empirical awareness. Perhaps, to use

---

in Rukmani 1981 under YS I.46, pp. 238-242, and especially p. 143. Instead of eight levels, Vijñānabhikṣu argues for six levels, namely *savitarka, nirvitarka, savicāra, nirvicāra, ānanda* and *asmitā* based on his reading of YS I.42, 43 and 44. Simply put, there is neither a *nirānanda* nor a *nirasmitā samādhi* or *samāpatti*. In my view, Vijñānabhikṣu has misunderstood Yoga (and Sāṃkhya) philosophy at this point. The reason for his misunderstanding has to do primarily with his orientation to Vedānta philosophical notions and his failure to appreciate the Sāṃkhya perspective. For Vijñānabhikṣu it is inconceivable that there could be a "*nirānanda-samādhi*, since he understands "*ānanda*" in the Vedānta sense of an ultimate aspect of Brahman. Likewise, he cannot conceive of self-awareness (*asmitā*) on this highest level of *samādhi* apart from the Vedānta notion of *ātman*. If one understands "*ānanda*", however, in the Yoga (and Sāṃkhya) sense of "*karaṇa*", "*indriya*", and "*manas*", and if one understands "self-awareness" along the lines of "*ahaṃkāra*", and if one understands all of these notions as subtle material components of *citta*, then the notions of "*nirānanda*" and "*nirasmitā*" become plausible concepts. Likewise, he misunderstands the notion of "*indriya*" or sense-organ in Yoga and Sāṃkhya. He fails to see the difference between the gross physical organ, on the one hand, and its dynamic function as a capacity on the other.

Along the same lines, it must be said that Vijñānabhikṣu misunderstands the notion of *īśvara* in Yoga. He brings in a great variety of devotional *bhakti* and Vedāntic cosmological notions that go beyond the precise and limited notion of *īśvara* as set forth in Pātañjala Yoga proper (YS I.23-28).

some modern examples, it is not unlike the focused excellence of a competent engineer, a highly trained athlete or a professional musician whose contents of meditation might be respectively a specific project-design, a particular game-strategy or the performance of a piece of music.* There is also, however, a higher level of empirical awareness in which memory no longer operates and, hence, a level in which the constructed or verbalized cognitions of everyday experience, involving language, learning and inferential reasoning, are no longer needed. This is a level in which the *yogin* experiences the empirical object in and of itself "as if" (*iva*) separate from the verbal or conceptual constructions and self-awareness, and it is known as *nirvitarka samāpatti* (or *nirvitarka-samādhi*) (YS I.43). To follow through with the illustrations of a competent engineer, a highly trained athlete or a professional musician, this is a level of awareness in which the engineer becomes totally engrossed in the design *qua* design. Or, the highly trained athlete becomes totally engrossed in a game-move (for example, a specific play-move in a soccer match). Or, the musician becomes totally engrossed in the music itself. The one meditating becomes detached from everything except the meditation-object itself. Of course, this is not meant literally. Hence, the use in Sanskrit of "as if" (*iva*). In other words, in the *nirvitarkasamāpatti* the *yogin* or meditator is completely focused on the object "as if" the cognitive process involved or the meditator's subjective presence were not present.

The second type of "one-pointed" awareness, namely, *vicāra*, likewise has two subdivisions, *savicārasamāpatti* and

---

*In both the popular and scholarly literature of Yoga, in my opinion, there is a tendency to write about *samādhis* in terms of obscure mystical states. The original intent of the classical texts, however, is to speak about levels of awareness that are clear, distinct and precise characterizations of what is truly real! In other words, the original intent is quite the opposite of the obscure and mystical.

nirvicārasamāpatti (or simply *savicārasamādhi* and *nirvicāra-samādhi*) (YS I.44). I have used the expression "rational awareness" for these levels since they relate to the cognitive functioning of the organism. In Yoga (and Sāṃkhya) these functions are discussed in terms of subtle objects (*tanmātras* or what Koelman has helpfully called the "objective universals" of sounds, tangibles, color-forms, tastes and smells). The sense- and action-organs and the faculties of mind, ego and will are also subtle objects or "objective universals" in this sense. Taken together, these subtle objects or contents make up what in Sāṃkhya is called the eighteenfold "subtle body" (*liṅgaśarīra*), which includes the five subtle elements, the five sense-organs, the five action-organs, and the threefold internal organ (*antaḥkaraṇa*) of mind, ego and intellect/will (or simply the *citta*). Put another way, and again using the idiom of Sāṃkhya, the cognitive core of the organism is the thirteen-fold instrument made up of *buddhi, ahaṃkāra, manas,* the five sense-organs and the five action-organs. This cognitive core has its subtle material basis in the five *tanmātras* thereby altogether becoming the "eighteen-fold" subtle body. When these subtle entities make up the contents of "one-pointed" awareness, the levels of *savicārā samāpatti* and *nirvicārā samāpatti* have been attained. The former (*savicāra*) arise in awareness initially in spatial, temporal and causal contexts in which verbalized constructions involving language, learning and inferential reasoning are functioning (Vyāsa *Bhāṣya* on YS I.44). That is, the *savicārā samāpatti* on a lower level is *savikalpa*. The latter or *nirvicārā samāpatti* awareness arises when the spatial, temporal, causal and linguistic/inferential framework is transcended (*nirvikalpa*), and the pure "rational object" is apprehended in and of itself, "as if" devoid of the cognizing process and subjective presence. There is a total engrossment in the abstract subtle contents. Again, to use some modern illustrations, the *savicārā samāpatti* would not be unlike the contents experienced in the awareness of a mathematical physicist, a pure mathematician, a music theorist or a professional philosopher. The *nirvicārā samāpatti* would be a total engrossment in the subtle object contemplated "as if" the cognitive process itself and one's own subjective presence had been eliminated.

The third and fourth types of "one-pointed" awareness, namely *ānanda* and *asmitā*, can also be interpreted, following Vācaspatimiśra, in terms of *savikalpa* and *nirvikalpa*. The difference, of course, is that these latter awarenesses of *ānanda* and *asmitā*, instead of being experienced as contents, have to do with the dynamic processes or functioning of the various cognitive faculties. Put in Husserlian terms, *ānanda* and *asmitā* have to do with the "noetic" processes of "sensing"/"cognizing", rather than with the gross and subtle objects (the noematic contents). From a certain perspective, of course, cognizing capacities, for example, hearing, seeing, thinking, and so forth, can be understood to be subtle contents (*noema*) that can be contemplated and which are, thus, *grāhya*. They can be construed as subtle faculties. They, then, are to be encompassed under *savicārā*- and/or *nirvicārā samāpatti*.

From another perspective, however, cognizing capacities can be understood to be dynamic "noetic" processes (*grahaṇa*), and these dynamic processes can themselves become the focus for meditation. There is a reflexive turning back whereby the cognizing processes themselves become the focus, and this is known as the *ānanda* or blissful awareness. Undoubtedly, the terms "bliss" (*ānanda*) and "joy" (*hlāda*) (YS I.17) are used for this level of awareness, since there is no determinate content beyond the affective (aesthetic) feeling of sensing/cognizing itself. It is evidently a kind of sublime abiding in which the content or "seed" (*bīja*) is the blissful abiding itself. Such aesthetic or "sensate" affective feelings may be described (*savikalpa*) as *sānandā samāpatti*. The *nirānandā samāpatti* counterpart would then be something like an affectless abiding in which only an indescribable (*nirvikalpa*) intentional flow of awareness itself (*grahaṇa*) is the "seed" (*bīja*"). The only modern illustrations that come to mind regarding *sānanda* and *nirānanda* awarenesses are those from the highest levels of science and art.* When a disciplined mathematician, for example, comes upon a new proof and describes it as "elegant", or when a disciplined connoisseur hears a great performance of music or sees a great painting and describes the experience as "noble" or "sublime", these could be cases, in my view, of *sānandā* awareness. All such experiences involve objects, of course, but the true focus is the blissful apprehension of "elegance" or "nobility". More than that, however, there are also those moments of what might be called the sheer act of "sensing" or "cognizing" apart from any affect or feeling, a sheer "sensing' or "cognizing" that often follows as a kind of "after-taste" to the apprehension of "elegance" or "nobility". Such awarenesses could possibly be examples of *nirānanda samāpatti.*

The fourth and final type of "one-pointed" awareness has self-awareness (*asmitā*) or subjective apprehension as its "seed". This level like the *ānanda*-level is a reflexive turning back in which, as it were, ordinary subjectivity shows itself as being a kind of content. Self-awareness for Yoga (and Sāṃkhya) is a *cittavṛtti* (a functioning of ordinary awareness) or *antaḥkaraṇa-vṛtti*, that is, *buddhi, ahaṃkāra* and *manas* functioning together as a single "internal organ". To the extent that *cittavṛtti or antaḥkaraṇavṛtti*, which is a manifestation of primordial materiality (*prakṛti*), is identified with consciousness (*puruṣa*) it is, of course, a mistaken or incorrect awareness. The notion of *asmitā* is the most important "affliction" (*kleśa*) after ignorance (*avidyā*) itself, and separating out or distinguishing

---

*The best examples, in my view, are from the discussions in Sanskrit regarding aesthetic "taste" or *rasa*. It is no accident that the great Abhinavagupta was a highly achieved (Tantric) *yogin* as well as a great aesthetic theoretician. See Gerald J. Larson, "The aesthetic ascetic: Abhinavagupta's perspective on poetry, religion and visual art", in *Marg:A Magazine of the Arts*, Volume 56, No. 2, December 2004, pp. 54-61.

(*viyoga, vivekakhyāti*) *cittasattva* or *buddhisattva* from *puruṣa* is one of the highest goals of Yoga. It is the "*ṛtambharā prajñā*" ("truth-bearing insight"), *dharmameghadhyāna* ("*dharma*-cloud meditation") and "supreme or ultimate reflection" (*prasaṃkhyāna*) referred to earlier (and found in YS I.48 and Vyāsa *Bhāṣya* on YS I.2). This awareness involves the discriminative realization (*vivekakhyāti*) that *cittasattva* or *buddhisattva* may be described (*savikalpa*) as a material process derived from primordial materiality that is to be clearly distinguished, both ontologically and epistemologically, from consciousness (*puruṣa*). This would be the *sāsmitāsamādhi* or *nirasmitāsamāpatti*. The *nirasmitāsamādhi* or *nirasmitāsamāpatti* counterpart would be, of course, the pure being (*sattāmātra*) (Vyāsa *Bhāṣya* on YS II.19) of primordial materiality itself (*mūlaprakṛti*, or the "*aliṅga*") (YS I.45 and YS II.9). Some possible modern examples of these sorts of discussions about the nature of subjective awareness might be in regard to certain areas of science and the philosophy of science. One thinks, for example, of identity theorists (J. J. C. Smart, et al.) in the field of philosophy of mind, or of "eliminativists" (Paul and Patricia Churchland, etc.). Also, research in artifical intelligence (AI) comes to mind. Such modern examples, of course, would only be appropriate for *sāsmitā samāpatti*. To my knowledge, the fields of philosophy of mind, cognitive psychology and experimental work in AI have yet to find ways of characterizing or experimenting in any measurable way the possibility either for *nirasmitā samāpatti* or the notion of a non-intentional consciousness (*puruṣa*).*

---

*Throughout my discussion of the *samāpattis* I am indebted to the brilliant discussion of these matters in Koelman, op. cit. He uses, to be sure, a philosophical idiom (largely Thomistic) which is quite different from mine, but his discussion of the eight levels of "one pointed" *samāpatti* is without doubt, in my view, the best available in the current scholarly literature. See especially pp. 198-224.

In any case, to conclude the discussion, all of these eight levels of awareness (*samādhi* or *samāpatti*) have some sort of content or "seed". Even the highest *nirasmitā samāpatti* of *sattāmātra* (the *aliṅga* or *mūlaprakṛti*) is a "seeded" awareness (YS I.46). Moreover, the highest "seeded" awarenesses, that is, the *nirvikalpa* awarenesses and the truth-bearing insight, are cognitive awarenesses that differ from inferential or verbal *(savikalpa)* awarenesses, inasmuch as they provide a unique or special cognitive apprehension that is direct and/or immediate (YS I.49). When these unique awarenesses come into play they generate predispositions or habits of mind which counteract and restrict ordinary awareness, that is, the afflictions (*kleśa*) of our everyday mistaken self-understanding (YS I.50), and turn awareness toward cessation (*nirodha*). When the *yogin* turns away even from these highest one-pointed awarenesses, that is, when the *yogin* turns away even from the truth-bearing insight, a seedless concentration arises. As mentioned earlier, the *yogin*'s non-intentional perfect *sattva* rests, then, in the presence of pure, content-less consciousness. There arises spiritual liberation or "isolation" (*kaivalya*), that is, the quiescent co-presence of perfect *sattva* and *citiśakti*.

The Yoga of Action (*kriyā-yoga*) and the Limbs of Yoga (*yogāṅga*)

According to Vyāsa and Vācaspatimiśra, Book Two of the YS, entitled "*Sādhana Pāda*" ("Section on Practical Exercises"), deals with the exercises needed to train those who wish to achieve the levels of awareness described in Book One.[82] The first portion of this Book (YS II.1-27) is a sequence of *sūtras* called the "Yoga of Action" (*kriyāyoga*). The sequence is concerned with those practices, namely ascetic exercises, study and recitation and devotion of one's actions to the yogic God (YS II.1-2), that are to be pursued in order to overcome the five afflictions of ignorance, egoity, attachment, aversion and the clinging to conventional life (YS II.3-17). These afflictions have already been discussed above (see the section entitled "The

Materialism of Yoga"). The section on *kriyāyoga* focuses on these afflictions together with a summary account of the theory of Yoga (and Sāṃkhya) (YS II.18-26). The section ends at II.27 which states that a sevenfold insight is the culmination of this Yoga of Action. According to Vyāsa and Vācaspatimiśra the sevenfold insight includes the following: (1) The knowledge of what is to be abandoned has been understood. (2) The factors or causes that give rise to what is to be abandoned have been weakened. (3) The abandonment has been accomplished by means of attaining the concentration that leads to cessation. (4) The means for the achievement of the abandonment, namely the realization of discrimination (of *prakṛti* from *puruṣa*) has been attained. These first four components of the sevenfold insight have to do with the actions that have to be accomplished, and are obviously parallel with the four noble truths of the Buddhist tradition.[83]

The final components of the sevenfold insight have to do with three liberating insights. These are (5) The *buddhi* has fulfilled its purposes and is no longer operative. (6) The three *guṇas* have fulfilled their task. (7) The presence of consciousness (*puruṣa*) has been revealed as being distinct from the *guṇas*. The philosophical and conceptual basis for all of this has been described in some detail in what has gone before and requires no further comment here.

The second part of the second Book contains a sequence of *sūtras* (YS II.28-55) known as "the limbs of Yoga" (*yogāṅga*) (YS II.28), eight in number (YS II.29), the first five of which limbs are set forth in II. 30-55. The remaining three limbs are set forth in the first five *sūtras* of Book Three. The first five limbs include behavioral restraints (*yama*), purificatory ritual observances (*niyama*), correct meditation postures (*āsana*), appropriate breathing exercises (*prāṇāyāma*), and sense-withdrawal exercises (*pratyāhāra*). The final three limbs include spatial fixation on the object of meditation (*dhāraṇā*), temporal flow regarding the object of meditation (*dhyāna*), and cultivation of one-pointed states of awareness (*samādhi*).

The first five limbs are largely practical exercises and have little to do with the philosophical content of Pātañjala Yoga. They are described as "external limbs" (*bahiraṅga*) (YS III.7-8), that is, outer preliminary and/or preparatory meditative exercises. The first limb, behavioral restraint, includes a conventional list of behaviors widely valued in Indian culture, including nonviolence (*ahiṃsā*), speaking the truth (*satya*), not taking what belongs to others (*asteya*), celibacy (*brahmacarya*) and non-covetousness (*aparigraha*). (YS II.30 and 35-40). The second limb, purificatory ritual observances (*niyama*), includes cleansing the body (*śauca*), suppressing desire for the sake of contentment (*santoṣa*), ascetic practice (*tapas*), study and recitation (*svādhyāya*). and meditation on (or deep longing for) the yogic God (*īśvarapraṇidhāna*). Again, both the Vyāsa *Bhāṣya* and Vācaspatimiśra construe "*īśvarapraṇidhāna*" in the sense of dedicating all one's actions to God without getting attached to the fruits of action (YS II.32 and 40-45, and, of course, YS II.1 as well). The third limb, correct meditative posture (*āsana*), means simply any posture of the body that is "comfortably steady" (*sthirasukha*) for the sake of extended meditative practice (YS II.46). These postures enable the practicing *yogin* to remain comfortably in the same position for a long period in a relaxed fashion (YS II.47) and without being troubled by cold or heat, and so forth (II.48).* The fourth limb, appropriate breathing (*prāṇāyāma*), has to do with cutting off or lessening the processes of inhalation and exhalation (YS II.49) so that the practicing *yogin* can increase the periods of

---

*The Vyāsa *Bhāṣya* lists a variety of postures under this limb, including the *padmāsana, vīrāsana, bhadrāsana, svastikāsana* and so forth. These are all *saṃjñā or* "naming" terms, that is, technical terms having to do with conventional postures that *yogins* utilize. Perhaps the best secondary source for a simple and accurate description of the most important postures may be found in Feuerstein 1990. For excellent illustrations of the most important postures, see Burley, pp. 258-271.

the retention of breath (either after inhalation or after exhalation) (YS II.50). Moreover, breath exercise involves focusing the breath on a particular place in the body, measuring the length of time of each inhalation and exhalation, and retention and counting the number of breaths (YS II.50). Eventually a level of breathing arises that transcends the ordinary awareness of inhalation, exhalation and retention (YS II.51) and that enables the practicing *yogin* to move to higher levels of meditation (YS II.52-53). The fifth and final "external" limb, sense-withdrawal exercises (*pratyāhāra*), involves detaching one's attention from the objects of the various sense-organs. When all of these preparatory practices have been properly cultivated under the guidance of an appropriate teacher, the practicing *yogin* is ready to move on to the final three internal (*antar-aṅga*) limbs of the practice of Yoga. These are, as already mentioned, spatial fixation, temporal flow and one-pointed states of awareness.**

Comprehensive Reflection (*saṃyama*) and the Extraordinary Cognitive Capacities (*vibhūti, siddhi*)

According to Vācaspatimiśra, Book One of the YS has to do with the correct understanding of concentration. Book Two of the YS has to do with the meditative practices needed to prepare the *yogin* for the cultivation of concentration. Book Three, says Vācaspatimiśra, has to do with the "extraordinary cognitive capacities" (*vibhūti*) that arise from pursuing the higher levels of yogic awareness, and these are brought about

---

**As was the case in the discussion of *samādhi* and *samāpatti*, the eight limbs of Yoga perhaps bear some sort of relation with the eightfold path of the Buddhists. In fact, however, the two lists have very little in common beyond the number eight and the possible similarity between the final three components of the Buddhist way (effort, mindfulness and concentration) and the internal limbs of the *yogāṅga* (*dhāraṇā, dhyāna,* and *samādhi*).

or effected by the practice of comprehensive reflection (*saṃyama*).* "Comprehensive reflection" refers to the final three "internal" limbs of Yoga (YS III.4). The term "*saṃyama*", as Ram Shankar Bhattacharya has pointed out, is a *saṃjñā*-word, that is, a technical term.[84] It is a word "used in some peculiar sense rather than in its strictly etymological meaning, e.g., as a proper name".[85] Thus, YS III.4 ("*trayam ekatra saṃyamaḥ*") is a *saṃjñāsūtra*, that is, a naming *sūtra* or technical term. Hence, the meaning is something like the following: "The name '*saṃyama*' is given to the three internal limbs taken together". Etymologically the word is derived from the root *yam* plus the adverbial particle *saṃ* meaning "holding together", "restraint", or "control". As a naming term however, it names a threefold exercise of *dhāraṇā*, *dhyāna* and *samādhi* practiced simultaneously that generates the extraordinary cognitive capacities.

The sixth limb of the eightfold "limbs of Yoga" or the first of the "internal" limbs, is "meditative fixation" (*dhāraṇā*) of one's awareness on a specific location in space (YS III.1). The Vyāsa *Bhāṣya* indicates that the content of such fixation may be based on certain parts of the *yogin*'s body. These include the vital center of the navel (*nābhicakra*), the lotus of the heart (*hṛdayapuṇḍarīka*), the light in the head (*mūrdhni jyotis*), the tip of the nose (*nasikāgra*), the tip of the tongue (*jihvāagra*), and so forth. Or, says the Vyāsa *Bhāṣya*, the focus can be on any external object.

---

*In the Sanskrit, this is what Vācaspatimiśra says literally: "*tṛtīyapāde tatpravṛttyanuguṇāḥ śraddhotpādahetavo vibhūtayo vaktavyāḥ*", that is, "in the third Book, extraordinary cognitive capacities are to be discussed, which are the causes for the awakening of faith in keeping with the undertaking of authentic Yoga". The reference to faith (*śraddhā*) undoubtedly refers back to Book One (YS I.20), which begins "*śraddhā*...", referring to the *upāya-pratyaya* of authentic Yoga. See RSB on YS, p. 104, and Woods, p. 203. See also RSB on YS, p. 22.

The seventh limb of the eightfold limbs of Yoga, or the second of the the internal limbs, is meditating or contemplating (*dhyāna*) or attaining an even (temporal) "tone" (*ekatānatā*) of awareness in regard to the object in that particular place attained by fixation (YS III.2). The Vyāsa *Bhāṣya* states that this means a similar flow from moment to moment of the notion of the object that is fixed in the *yogin*'s awareness with no apprehension of any other object.

The eighth and final limb of the eightfold limbs of Yoga, or the third of the internal limbs, is one-pointed concentration (YS III.3), already discussed at some length in the preceding section. The Sanskrit reads as follows: "*tad eva arthamātra-nirbhāsaṃ svarūpaśūnyam iva samādhiḥ*". This may be rendered "That same (*dhyāna*-state) in which only the object shines forth as if devoid of the inherent cognizing presence of the practitioner is one-pointed awareness". This obviously refers back to the description of *nirvitarkā samāpatti* (YS I.43) in which the very same expressions is used, namely "*svarūpa-śūnya iva arthamātranirbhāsā*". The slight difference between the two expressions has to do only with the respective gender inflections (neuter in the case of YS III.3 and feminine in the case of YS I.43). In any case, these three internal limbs, meditative fixation, meditation and concentration, taken together make up comprehensive reflection (*saṃyama*).

When the *yogin* has mastered comprehensive reflection, then the light of insight (*prajñāloka*) shines forth (YS III.5). "*Prajñāloka*" appears to be synonymous with "truth-bearing insight", the "*dharma*-cloud meditation", the "supreme" or "ultimate" reflection (*prasaṃkhyāna*) and "the realizaiton of discrimination (of the difference between *prakṛti* and *puruṣa*)" (*vivekakhyāti*). Or, one might say that all of these terms are "names" (*saṃjñā*-words) for the highest discriminative realization of Yoga. The *yogin* advances to this highest level of discrimination sequentially (YS III.6), but it must be remembered that this highest level of awareness is still one step below the "seedless" awareness (*nirbījasamādhi*). Just as the first five limbs are preparatory or "external" to the three "internal" limbs of fixation, meditation and concentration (YS III.7), so the internal limbs themselves, when the true goal of Yoga is properly understood, become external limbs to the "seedless" (*nirbīja*) awareness (YS III.7-8).

Following the discussion of comprehensive reflection, a sequence of *sūtras* (YS III.8-15) is introduced having to do with the theory of dynamic transformation or change (*pariṇāma*) in Yoga (and Sāṃkhya). Once again it is important to keep in mind the basic materialist conception of ordinary awareness, and the Yoga (and Sāṃkhya) theory of causation known as *satkāryavāda* or the theory that the effect (*kārya*) pre-exists or is latent in the cause (*kāraṇa*). Ordinary awareness is a manifestation of primordial materiality, made up of collocations of the three constituent processes of *sattva, rajas* and *tamas.* Ordinary awareness and/or *prakṛti* changes at each moment. Each change or transformation is an effect that pre-exists or is latent in its original material cause. In terms of personal experience, the changes that result leave predispositions and/or traces that influence future developments. The goal of Yoga is to increase the operational influence of pure awareness *(cittasattva)* and to render *rajas* and *tamas* inoperative. At no point can *rajas* or *tamas* be destroyed or eliminated, but they can be rendered inoperative.

Keeping in mind this general background, it is possible to discuss change or transformation either from the perspective of the practicing *yogin* (YS III.9-12) or from the perspective of the external, phenomenal world (YS III.13-15). Regarding the practicing *yogin,* three types of change or transformation are discussed. The first type of change refers to the transformation that takes place when the *yogin* overcomes his orientation to the external world of the emergent state (*vyutthāna*) and begins to exhibit an orientation to the cessation of the fluctuations of ordinary awareness (YS III.9). This is called the "cessation-transformation" (*nirodhapariṇāma*). The *yogin* begins to form traces that will eventually issue in a peaceful, even flow of awareness (YS III.10). The second type of change refers to the transformation that takes place when the *yogin* turns away from the multiplicity of contents in awareness and focuses increasingly on the one-pointed awareness (YS III.11). This is called the "awareness-transformation" (*samādhipariṇāma*). The third type of change refers to the transformation that takes place when the *yogin*'s awareness regarding a single object becomes the same in each successive moment of meditation (YS III.12). This is called the "one-pointedness transformation" (*ekāgratāpariṇāma*).

In a similar fashion, the changes or transformations characteristic of the external, phenomenal world as apprehended by the sense-organs can be explained (YS III.13). The first type of change is said to be a transformation in external characteristic (*dharma*). The second type of change is said to be a transformation in temporal variation, that is, in terms of the characteristics of past, present and future (*lakṣaṇa*). The third type of change is said to be a transformation in the depth or intensity of awareness of a single content (*avasthā*). The Vyāsa *Bhāṣya* illustrates the three types of transformation or change in the phenomenal world with the example of clay and a jar. Clay being transformed into a jar is an example of change of external (spatial) characteristic (*dharma*). The same clay transformed from a past condition of mud to a present condition of jar and looking to a future condition of broken shards is an example of change in temporal variation (*lakṣaṇa*). Finally, the same jar as it is transformed from being new to becoming old is an example of change in condition (*avasthā*).

All changes or transformations, however, presuppose an underlying material basis or substance (*dharmin, mūlaprakṛti,* or *citta*). In other words, the various changes are simply "characteristics" (*dharma*) of a basic underlying substratum (*dharmin*). Changes, therefore, are simply aspects of *prakṛti* and/or *citta* either in its latent form (derived from the past), its current manifestation (in the present) or what it is yet to be in the future (YS III.14). Such a determinate manifestation of sequence (*kramānyatva*) is, thus, the reason for the sense of change or transformation (YS III.15).*

We come now to the difficult, yet important and intriguing, portion of the YS having to do with the extraordinary cognitive capacities. I have used the terms "extraordinary" and "capacities" to pick up the force of the words "*vibhūti*" and "*siddhi*" in Sanskrit, since these notions clearly call attention to what most people would call unusual and powerful abilities. I also use the word "cognitive", however, since, as is hardly noticed in many interpretations of Book Three of the YS, the terms "*vibhūti*" and "*siddhi*" seldom appear in Book Three. The term "*vibhūti*" is only used in the traditional title of the Book. In the *sūtrapāṭha* itself, the term "*siddhi*" is only directly mentioned in YS III.37, and it is implied in YS III.45. The mention in YS III.37 is highly ambiguous and probably only refers to the preceding *sūtra* (YS III.36). The reference in III.45 is clearly to the traditional eight extraordinary capacities. These include the awareness or sense of becoming small (*aṇiman*), becoming large (*mahiman*), becoming light (*laghiman*), becoming dense (*gariman*), becoming all-pervasive (*prāpti*), attaining all desires (*prakāmya*), gaining power over elemental forces (*īśitva*), and instant gratification (*yatrakāmāvasāyitva*). Various interpretations have been put forth about these traditional extraordinary capacities, which need not detain us. My own view is that these are best understood as the "highs" in awareness that naturally occur among those who engage in serious yogic practice.[86] In any case, they are not at all central to Book Three of the YS.

The term that is regularly used throughout Book Three is the term "*jñāna*", which means knowledge, cognition or

---

*This, of course, is the Yoga (and Sāṃkhya) interpretation of the notion of time, and it bears an interesting comparison with Buddhist discussions, especially the Sarvāstivāda tradition.

cognitive awareness. The term "*jñāna*" is used thirteen times, and the term appears to be consistently used in the sense of the higher cognitive awarenesses that occur as a result of doing comprehensive reflection that is, the simultaneous exercise of meditative fixation, meditation and concentration. The thirteen specific higher cognitive capacities or cognitions that arise include the following:

(1) The ("extraordinary") or higher cognitive capacity to understand the nature of the past and future, that is, "...*atīta-anāgatajñāna*" (YS III.16). For Yoga (and Sāṃkhya), of course, this means *guṇapariṇāma*, and specifically the "*pariṇāmatraya*" explained just before in YS III.9-15. In other words, this is the cognitive capacity to understand the essence of time.

(2) The cognitive capacity to understand intelligible "sounds" (*ruta*) of all sentient creatures, or in other words the manner in which sentient creatures communicate in terms of the relations between "sounds' or "words" (*śabda*), "objects" (*artha*) and "meanings" (*pratyaya*), that is, "...*sarvabhūtaruta-jñāna*" (YS III.17). For Yoga (and the older Sāṃkhya) this means a certain theory of language or communication together with a theory of meaning.* Neither the YS itself nor the Vyāsa *Bhāṣya* use the technical term "*sphoṭa*", but, according to Vācaspatimiśra, this is precisely what is being discussed in YS III.17. The word "*sphoṭa*" means something like the "burst of meaning" that occurs in the *citta* and of *buddhi/manas* when language is properly understood. Does meaning arise from the individual letters (*varṇa*), the words (*pada*) made up of letters, or the sentences (*vākya*) made up of words? This question had been asked all the way back to the time of Patañjali the

---

*I use the expression "older Sāṃkhya", since the later Sāṃkhya of the *Sāṃkhyasūtras* rejects the theory of *sphoṭa*. There is a misunderstanding here, however. The later Sāṃkhya rejects the notion of *sphoṭa* of Bhartṛhari and the notion of *śabdabrahman*. This is most likely not the theory of *sphoṭa* set forth in the YS.

grammarian and possibly earlier. The Yoga answer to the question is not completely clear, but Vācaspatimiśra seems to indicate that the individual word is the primary meaning-bearer. Just after the collocations of sounds that make up a conventional word have been heard or grasped, the *sphoṭa* or burst of meaning from the *citta/buddhi* occurs. Ram Shankar Bhattacharya points out that this is not the *sphoṭa*-theory of Bhartṛhari or of the grammarians generally, including the grammarian Patañjali. Yoga has its own theory of *sphoṭa*, says Bhattacharya.[87]

(3) The cognitive capacity of becoming aware of preceding rebirths, that is, "...*pūrvajātijñāna*" (YS III.18). Such awareness arises through the *yogin*'s growing familiarity with the fundamental predispositions that influence the process of becoming (*saṃsāra, bhava*). In this regard it is important to remember the cosmology of Yoga (see above, section entitled "The Theism of Yoga") that is beginningless and continually influenced by the traces, subconscious impressions and karmic residues operating in all living creatures.

(4) The cognitive capacity of intuiting the meaning of what another mind or mind-stuff may be thinking, that is, "...*para-cittajñāna*" (YS III.19-20). Ordinary awareness or mind-stuff, though all-pervasive and beginningless, is always individuated (*nirmāṇacitta*) because of the afflictions (especially *avidyā* and *asmitā*) (YS IV.4). When the afflictions become diminished, the boundaries that ordinarily inhibit inter-subjective communication may be weakened, and it may well become possible to intuit what others may be thinking or feeling.

(5) The cognitive capacity of intuiting the approach of one's own death, that is, "...*aparāntajñāna*" (YS III.22). The practice of comprehensive reflection provides increasing sensitivity to one's own karmic tendencies. This would include, perhaps obviously, the possibility of an awareness that one's death may be near.

(6) The cognitive capacity of intuiting the nature of objects that are subtle, hidden or distant, that is, "...*sūkṣmavyavahita-*

viprakṛṣṭajñāna" (YS III.25). Deep and intensely focused reflection over time on a given object or problem often provides an intuitive awareness of what initially appeared to be impossible to grasp.

(7) The cognitive capacity of intuiting the (correspondence between the macrocosmic and microcosmic) universe by way of meditating on the sun-gate or entrance (*sūryadvāra*) in the body, that is, "*bhuvanajñāna*" (YS III.26). Ram Shankar Bhattacharya has argued that the term "*sūrya*" is a "technical term" (*paribhāṣika*) for the expression "*sūryadvāra*", that is, the solar entrance or "suṣumnādvāra" in the *yogin*'s body.[88] In other words, the *sūtra* has little to do with astronomy. It refers, rather, to the *yogin*'s body and the manner in which the *yogin* looks for correspondences between the body and the cosmos, utilizing traditional cosmological notions (see section above entitled "The Theism of Yoga").

(8) The cognitive capacity of intuiting the lunar mansions (*tārāvyūha*) (and their correspondence with the *yogin*'s body) by way of meditating on the moon-gate or entrance (*dvārā*), that is, "...*tārāvyūhajñāna*" (YS III.27).[89] If the solar-entrance has to do with the linkage between Yoga and traditional cosmology, possibly the lunar-entrance links up with traditional astrological speculations.

(9) The cognitive capacity of intuiting the "movement of the stars" (*tadgati* = *tārāgati*) (and their correspondence with the *yogin*'s body) by way of meditating on the polar-star (*dhruva*), that is, "...*tadgatijñāna*" (YS III.28).[90] Here again there is a possible linkage with astrology and the lunar mansions. More than that, Ram Shankar Bhattacharya refers to a reference in "various *yoga* works", viz. "*dhruve nāṣāgram ucyate*", that is, "The name 'pole-star' is said to refer to the tip of the nose."[91]

(10) The cognitive capacity of intuiting the orderly arrangement (*vyūha*) of the structure of the body (*kāya*) by way of meditating on the "vital center" (*cakra*) of the navel (*nābhi*), that is, "...*kāyavyūhajñāna*" (YS III.29). If one combines the reference here to the "vital center of the navel" with the

preceding three *sūtras* (YS III.26, 27 and 28), that is, the solar entrance, the lunar entrance, and the pole-star, and puts these together with the following *sūtras*, that is, the "region of the throat" (*kaṇṭhakūpa*) (YS III.30), the "tortoise-channel" (*kūrma-nāḍi*) (YS III.31), the "light at the top of the head" (*mūrdha-jyotis*) (YS III.32), and the region of the "heart" (YS III.34), it could well be the case that this very sequence of *sūtras* (YS III.26-34) represents an early, if not the earliest, evidence for what will later come to be known as the system of Haṭha Yoga ("Exertion Yoga"). This is perhaps especially the case if one, then, combines these references to the list of "postures" (*āsanas*) enumerated by the Vyāsa *Bhāṣya* under YS II.46 and the breath exercises of YS II.49-51. The basic components for Haṭha Yoga are all largely in place. There is an implicit "vital center" (*cakra*) theory. The notions of a solar entrance (*suṣumnādvāra*) and a lunar entrance (*candradvāra*) are in place. There appears to be a theory of channels or veins (*nāḍī*). The notion of the "lotus of the heart" (*hṛdayapuṇḍarīka*) and the idea of an illumination at the top of the head or skull (*mūrdhajyotis*) are present. These components, when combined with a focus on a variety of body postures and an intensive concern for breathing exercises, appear to be the basic skeletal structure for later Haṭha Yoga. Whereas in Pātañjala Yoga these components are for the most part tangential or auxiliary to the main parameters of Yoga philosophy and practice, in Haṭha Yoga, of course, they become the primary focus.[92]

(11) The cognitive capacity of intuiting the presence of *puruṣa*, that is, "...*puruṣajñāna*" (YS III.35). This is the "truth-bearing insight", the "*dharma*-cloud meditation", and the "supreme reflection", or, in other words, the discriminative realization of the distinction between *sattva* and *puruṣa*.

(12) The cognitive capacity of intuiting the difference between *sattva* and *puruṣa* through focusing on the "moment" (*kṣaṇa*) and its sequence, that is, "...*vivekajñāna*", (YS III.52). This appears to be clearly cognate with the "triad of transformations" (*pariṇāmatraya*) and the "determinate

sequence" (*kramānyatva*) of YS III.15-16.

(13) There is one additional reference to "realization of discrimination" (*vivekajam jñānam*) or the cognitive intuition of the difference between *sattva* and *puruṣa* (YS III.54) in which the focus is on the non-intentional or content-less nature of the awareness. This cognitive intuition is said to be "liberating" (*tāraka*), encompassing all determinate objects (*sarvaviṣaya*), encompassing all of time (*sarvathāviṣaya*), and direct or immediate (*akrama*). Such a cognitive intuition calls to mind the reference to the intuitive (*pratibhā*) cognitive apprehension of everything in YS III.33 (*pratibhād...sarvam*) as well as the reference to the higher "subtle" or intuitive capacities of hearing, touching, seeing, tasting and smelling of YS III.36. Finally, YS III.49 comes to mind, that is, the awareness of omnipotence (*sarvabhāvādhiṣṭhātṛtva*) and "omniscience" (*sarva-jñātṛtva)* that occurs when the *yogin* has come fully to understand the difference between *sattva* and *puruṣa*.

In addition to these extraordinary cognitive capacities that are described with the word "knowledge" or "cognition" (*jñāna*) in Book Three, an additional ten *sūtras* deal with what are usually thought to be "paranormal" powers. These include the following:

(1) the power to become invisible (YS III.21);

(2) the power to have the strength of elephants and other animals (YS. III.24);

(3) the power to enter the body of another (YS III.38);

(4) the power to rise above the earth (YS III.39);

(5) the power of having burning energy (YS III.40);

(6) the power of flying through the air (YS III.42);

(7) the power of becoming disembodied for periods of time (YS III.43);

(8) the power of attaining perfection of the body (YS III.45-46);

(9) the power of complete control over the sense-organs (YS III.47); and

(10) the power of quickness of mind, the ability to operate

beyond the sense-organs, and power over *prakṛti* (YS III.48).

These powers are most likely imaginative (*kalpita*) fantasies that arise in the process of doing *yoga*, very much on analogy with the traditional extraordinary capacities (*animān* and so forth,) mentioned earlier. Two *sūtras* in Book Three express a degree of skeptical caution about these powers, thereby providing some textual evidence that these experiences were not meant literally. The first caution, set forth in YS III.37, indicates that such powers, while certainly being manifest in ordinary experience, are nevertheless obstacles (*upasargas*) with respect to the attainment of concentration. The second skeptical caution is expressed in YS III.51. The *yogin* should not become attached or prideful about these higher levels of achievement, since such attachment or pride may lead to unwanted consequences. Having said this, it would be a mistake, however, to underestimate the importance of these imaginative fantasies for the practice of *yoga*. They probably had an important role to play as signs or marks of progress on the yogic path.

Book Three under YS III.51 lists a hierarchy of four levels of achievement by way of marking the progress of *yogins*. They are as follows:

Prathamakalpika ("first-level aspirant" in whom the light of understanding is just beginning);

Madhubhūmika ("honey-state" in which the "truth-bearing insight" has occurred);

Prajñājyoti ("the light of insight" in which control has been gained over the elements and sense-organs and in which the *yogin* is deeply committed to ongoing spiritual practice), and

Atikrānta-bhāvanīya ("having gone beyond what is to be accomplished" in which the level of pure *sattva* has been achieved along with the sevenfold *prajñā*).

These are all "naming" terms (*saṃjñā*-words) that identify the various levels of yogic competence. They probably coincide with the two other fourfold hierarchies mentioned in Vācaspatimiśra's *Tattvavaiśāradī*. The first reference is under YS

I.1 in which Vācaspatimiśra explains the expression "all states" (*sarvabhauma*) with the following fourfold hierarchy:

Madhumatī ("honeyed condition");
Madhupratīka ("honey-faced");
Viśokā ('sorrowless condition"); and
Saṃskāraśeṣa ("predisposition-trace").

These again are "naming" terms, and they are discussed respectively at YS III.43, YS III.48, YS I.36 and YS III.9. They appear for the most part to be parallel with the preceding fourfold hierarchy of the Vyāsa *Bhāṣya*. Finally, there is one other fourfold hierarchy introduced by Vācaspatimiśra in his commentary under YS I.15 as follows:

Yatamānasaṃjñā (the "awareness of striving" or the beginning stage of yogic practice);

Vyatirekasaṃjñā (the "awareness of distinguishing" in which the *yogin* is aware of what has been accomplished and what remains to be accomplished);

Ekendriyasaṃjñā (the "awareness of one sense-organ" in which the mind (*manas*) alone functions with only a faint awareness); and

Vaśīkārasaṃjñā (the "awareness of complete mastery" in which the mind has turned away from all contents).

The use of the term "*saṃjñā*" in this final fourfold hierarchy, according to Ram Shankar Bhattacharya, is not as a "naming" term but rather in its general meaning of "awareness".[93]

The precise meaning of these various hierarchies is difficult to determine in the absence of additional evidence in the extant textual tradition. Much of the traditional Yogic practice has been handed down orally from teacher to teacher and was not written down in texts. It may well be the case, however, that the various "*vibhūtis*", "*siddhis*", and "*jñānas*" were all important signs or marks by means of which the teachers of Yoga interpreted the meaning of the unfolding experience of their students. Likewise, the "*vibhūtis*", "*siddhis*" and "*jñānas*" were also important signs or marks by means of which the teachers assessed the progress of their students towards *samādhi*, and eventually , spiritual liberation.*

----

*Regarding the benefits of Yoga practice, my own view is that Yoga provides benefits comparable to the mental skills of highly disciplined researchers in all fields of intellectual inquiry and the physical skills of highly trained athletes. In this regard there is an interesting survey of recent scientific studies of the physiological benefits of Yoga conveniently summarized in Burley, pp. 226-238. Increased lung capacity, smoothness of breathing, stable heart rate, increased cardiovascular efficiency, improved blood flow, muscular dexterity, reduction of stress, greater capacities for relaxation, and sharpened mental awareness, and so forth, are just some of the important benefits that come from prolonged meditation and training in Yoga. These studies are focused primarily on the practice of Haṭha Yoga, but it is probably fair to say that similar benefits accrue from the practice of Pāṭañjala Yoga. These sorts of benefits, in my judgment, are much more relevant for taking seriously the importance of Yoga than the paranormal benefits highlighted in some of the popular literature on Yoga.

Spiritual Liberation (*kaivalya*)

As was noted in the preceding sections, the first five limbs of the eightfold Yoga are referred to as "external limbs" (*bahir-aṅga*), and the final three are referred to as "internal limbs" (*antar-aṅga*) (YS III.7). These final three limbs taken together are called "*saṃyama*" or "comprehensive reflection", and the practice of *saṃyama* brings about the "extraordinary cognitive capacities". All of these cognitions and cognitive capacities, resulting from *saṃyama*, are "seeded" (*sabīja*) awarenesses, or in other words "awarenesses with content" (*samprajñāta-samādhi*). It has also been noted that there are altogether, at least according to Vācaspatimiśra, eight levels of "seeded" concentrations or engrossment, culminating in the highest "seeded" state, namely the *nirasmitā* engrossment or the awareness of "being itself" (*sattāmātra).*

Even these highest levels of comprehensive reflection, however, according to YS III.8, must finally be considered only "external limbs" from the perspective of the "seedless" or content-less awareness. The Vyāsa *Bhāṣya* (under YS I.2), as I have cited before, puts the matter as follows: "On the one hand, therefore, there is pure consciousness (*citiśakti*), which is unchanging and does not mix with anything else, has objects presented to it and is eternal–on the other hand, opposite from that is this realization of discrimination (*vivekakhyāti*) whose essence is the *guṇa sattva* (or *cittasattva*)....when the *citta* or *cittasattva*) has become indifferent to that realization of discrimination, it (*cittasattva*) renounces or turns away even from that discriminative realization. At that point, it tends towards a condition of [abiding only in the residual predispositions (*saṃskāras*)]. That is a state of awareness that is content-less or seedless. Therein nothing at all is known–it is a state of awareness without content (*asaṃprajñāta*)."

At this point the functioning of ordinary awareness has ceased (*cittavṛttinirodha*) and the *yogin* has attained concentration without content.. This, then, is the basis for YS I.3: "Then there is the condition of the seer in its own inherent form (*tadā draṣṭuḥ svarūpe 'vasthānam).*" The Vyāsa *Bhāṣya* glosses: "Then, the power of consciousness (*citiśakti)* is established in its own inherent nature (*svarūpa*), as it were, in isolation (*kaivalya*)."

The notion of isolation in this context refers to the clear distinction that has emerged in awareness that awareness itself (*cittasattva, buddhisattva*) is not consciousness (*puruṣa, citiśakti*). Ordinary awareness, whether subject, object or the cognizing relation between subject and object, has revealed itself as being a transformation of the sequence of moments made up of *sattva*, *rajas* and *tamas.* More than that, however, "isolation" in this context refers to a pure, content-less, non-intentional consciousness which has always been present in awareness and always will be present in awareness, since awareness cannot itself be apprehended in the absence of consciousness. This pure consciousness, however, which is distinct from ordinary awareness, has become mistaken for ordinary awareness, due to the incorrect understandings that have occurred through the beginningless cycles of becoming. These incorrect understandings have left predispositions and traces that continue to influence the nature of ordinary awareness and must be removed if a correct understanding of the distinction between awareness (*citta*) and consciousness (*puruṣa*) is ever to become possible.

Given this background, Book Four of the YS is a useful summary of the overall discussion that has occurred in the preceding Books. In *sūtras* 1-6 it is emphasized that although there is one all-pervasive *citta (prakṛti)* that encompasses all possibilities, nevertheless, *citta* always appears in individuated forms (*nirmāṇacitta*) because of egoity (YS IV.3).[94] These variegated forms take shape because of the influence of the latent predispositions born from preceding rebirths (YS IV.1). Moreover, even though there are many *cittas* (in individual forms), there is only one single *citta* overall (YS IV.5). Finally, there are various ways of attaining the extraordinary capacities, for example, by reason of inborn capacities from the past, herbal and chemical remedies, auditory incantations, ascetic practices, and the correct practice of comprehensive reflection (YS IV.1). Only the authentic way of yogic meditation through *dhyāna* and *samādhi,* that is, the practice of comprehensive reflection, will not leave traces of a negative sort (YS IV.6).

In *sūtras* 7-13 there is a concluding discussion of karma and traces. Karma is said to be fourfold (YS IV.7), black, white and black, white, and neither white nor black. Black karma is characteristic of evil-natured folk. White and black karma pertains to most people whose interacting lives generate a mixture. White karma is for those who engage in ascetic exercises, recitation of sacred texts, and study. Neither black nor white karma pertains to renunciants who are no longer attached either to white or black karma and who have overcome the afflictions. The karmic traces shape the process of rebirth and maintain the continuity through various rebirths (YS IV. 8-9). The process of becoming is beginningless (YS IV.10), but interventions in the process are possible through the practice of *yoga* (YS IV.11). The past and future actually exist as manifest or unmanifest aspects (of the individual *citta*), and they are made up of the *guṇas* (YS IV.13-14).

In *sūtras* 14-23 the reality of a single existing world is affirmed, since there is a uniform intelligible process of transformation (YS IV.14-15). Although there are many individual ordinary awarenesses, there is an underlying substratum (*vastu, dharmin, prakṛti*) that remains (YS IV.16-17). The individuated awarenesses are not self-reflective , since they themselves become reflected in a *puruṣa* which is not subject to continuous transformation (YS IV.18-21). Content-less consciousness takes on the form of the intellect (*buddhi*), and the changing contents of the intellect incorrectly appear as if they were the same as consciousness (YS IV.22). Ordinary awareness becomes possible when this coming together of pure consciousness with awareness has occurred (YS IV.23).

Finally, in *sūtras* 24-34, the presentation of Pātañjala Y oga is brought to conclusion. Ordinary awareness, although variegated by the beginningless trajectories of traces, functions for the sake of consciousness in the sense that it can only appear by reason of the presence of consciousness (YS IV.24). Consciousness because it is content-less can only appear as what it is not, and ordinary awareness can only appear as consciousness by appearing as what it is not. When this distinction is beginning to be understood, ordinary awareness begins to incline more and more towards isolation. In other words, *cittasattva* or *buddhisattva* recognizes that it is not inherently conscious (YS IV.25-26). Through comprehensive reflection, the predispositions leading towards cessation are wearing away the predispositions leading towards worldly involvement (YS IV.27, YS III.9). These predispositions leading to worldly involvement must be worn away just as the afflictions must be worn away (YS IV.28 and YS IV.30). Then, the *yogin* begins to be indifferent even to the supreme reflection of the difference between *puruṣa* and *prakṛti* and begins to abide in the "*dharma*-cloud awareness" (YS IV.29). At this point there is a cessation of karma and the afflictions, and little remains to be known (YS IV.30-31). The *guṇas* of *prakṛti* have completed their tasks in the sense of *cittasattva* having attained perfect excellence and *rajas* and *tamas* having been rendered inoperative (YS IV.32-34). Even perfect *sattva* relinquishes its realization of discrimination (YS IV.34 and Vyāsa *Bhāṣya* on YS I.2). Or, according to YS IV.34, "...spiritual liberation is the standing forth of pure consciousness in its own inherent nature".

The Haṭha Yoga System and Other Satellite/Sectarian Yoga Traditions in India

In addition to Pātañjala Yoga, as noted at the outset of this Introduction, there are all sorts of other traditions that use the term "*yoga*" in a different, nonphilosophical sense. That is, there are a variety of traditions that are clearly influenced by Pātañjala Yoga but diverge considerably from it. These traditions either explicitly disavow an interest in the philosophy of Pātañjala Yoga, or perhaps more to the point, choose to make use of some of the terms and practices of Yoga for purposes that are often quite distinct from Pātañjala Yoga. Moreover, they are all without exception sectarian religious traditions.

I have used the term "satellite" in regard to these sectarian uses of Yoga in the sense that they are to some degree dependent on Pātañjala Yoga but are also thoroughly independent traditions in many respects. On the one hand, they are influenced by many of the terms and concepts that are central to Pātañjala Yoga and clearly look to Pātañjala Yoga for establishing their own cultural legitimacy. On the other hand, however, they all appear to have distinct agendas from Pātañjala Yoga. They are perhaps best characterized as religious or theological traditions, and the notion of yoga employed in most of these traditions has to do with ritual practice of one kind or another.*

One of the early and well-known examples of such a satellite use of the notion of yoga is the widely cited typology found in the *Bhagavadgītā*.[95] The Gītā makes reference to three type of Yoga, the "discipline of knowledge" (*jñāna-yoga*), the "discipline of action" (*karma-yoga*) and the "discipline of devotion" (*bhakti-yoga*), but the focus of the text is really on Kṛṣṇa-*bhakti*. Many Sāṃkhya and Yoga notions find their place in the Gītā, especially in Chapters 2 and 3, but philosophy is hardly a central concern of the Gītā. The same is true for the use of "yoga" in other later Śaiva and Vaiṣṇava *bhakti* traditions. The tendency is to utilize primarily some components of the "limbs of Yoga" (*yogāṅga*) portion of the YS (II.28ff.) with respect to practical meditative exercises but then to move quickly on to one or another type of *bhakti* spirituality.

In the late Upaniṣad texts, it is even more the case that the notion of yoga is being employed in a "satellite" sense. In the late *Yogatattva Upaniṣad* (number 71 of the works summarized in this Volume), again widely cited in primary and secondary sources, various types of Yoga are enumerated. There is little interest in philosophical discussion beyond a rather unsophisticated or semi-popular Vedānta assertion of the oneness of Brahman and Ātman.[96] The *Yogatattva* mentions four types of Yoga, the "discipline of auditory recitation" (*mantrayoga*), the "discipline of dissolution" (*layayoga*), the "discipline of exertion" (*haṭhayoga*) and the "sovereign or principal discipline" (*rājayoga*). Most of these late texts such as

*Perhaps needless to say, "yoga" in this general sense of ritual performance is as old as the liturgies reflected in the hymns and ritual instructions found in the Veda.

the *Yogatattva* assert that Rāja Yoga is the eight-limbed Pātañjala Yoga and that Rāja Yoga is the culmination of Yoga. In almost every instance, however, little more than lip service is given to Rāja Yoga. In the *Yogatattva* itself, for example, almost the entire text is given over to the description of Haṭha Yoga with only a passing mention of Rāja Yoga.

There is also the massive literature of the Tantra in its Śaiva, Vaiṣṇava, Śākta, (not to speak of Buddhist and Jaina formulations.)[97] Tantra, as is becoming clear in recent research, is quite different from ordinary *bhakti*-spirituality. In terms of general definition, David Gordon White cites the excellent characterization of André Padoux as follows: "(Tantrism is)...an attempt to place *kāma*, desire, in every sense of the word, in the service of liberation...not to sacrifice this world for liberation's sake, but to reinstate it, in varying ways, within the perspective of salvation. This use of *kāma* and of all aspects of this word to gain both worldly and supernatural enjoyments (*bhukti*) and capacities, and to obtain liberation in this life (*jīvanmukti*), implies a particular attitude on the part of the Tantric adept toward the cosmos, whereby he feels integrated within an all-embracing system of micro-macrocosmic correlations."[98]

The Tantra traditions, whether Śaiva, Vaiṣṇava, Śākta, Buddhist or Jaina, involve an incredible proliferation of gods and goddesses and an equally incredible array of eroticized ritual practices. These become prominent in India, especially from the eighth and ninth centuries onwards in such regions as Bengal and the Northeast, Kashmir and the Northwest and in some areas of south India as well. To some extent Tantra picks up strands in South Asian folk religiosity that are very old. The Tantra also places a premium on the importance of what might be called femininity, that is, the role of the goddess and the sacred *yoginīs* in ritual practice. The cultural significance of these Tantra traditions is just beginning to be understood, and as yet there is no scholarly consensus regarding the precise meaning of the various strands of Tantra spirituality. Much will depend on tracing possible foreign influences (from China,

Tibet, Mongolia, the Middle East, and so forth) together with much more detailed studies of vernacular or non-Sanskritic texts.[99] In any case, the term "*yoga*" appears again and again in all branches of the Tantra but hardly in the sense of Pātañjala Yoga. In most instances, the references to *yoga* have to do primarily with Haṭha Yoga, and even Haṭha Yoga is only one component in the vast ritual details of Tantra.

In this volume we have included summaries of some of these later satellite Yoga traditions, especially the texts important for the development of Haṭha Yoga. While they may not be especially interesting from the perspective of the philosophy of Pātañjala Yoga, they are certainly interesting from the perspective of understanding some of the later "satellite" traditions of Yoga in the medieval and modern period. Furthermore, various contemporary Yoga groups, both in India and elsewhere, make use of these satellite traditions. They may be briefly summarized as follows.

Haṭha Yoga

As mentioned earlier in our discussion of the "extraordinary cognitive capacities", it may be the case that Haṭha Yoga grows out of the sorts of notions found in YS III.26-34 (the *sūrya-dvāra, candradvāra,* and so forth). When these notions are combined with a more focused emphasis on posture and breath exercise, it is plausible to think that this may have been the framework from which the later Haṭha Yoga developed. In this sense there is some possibility of historically linking Pātañjala Yoga with Haṭha Yoga. Such a connection, however, is tenuous at best, nonexistent at worst.

The later Haṭha Yoga Yoga texts, to be sure, all refer to the eight-limbed Pātañjala Yoga (or, in other words, to what is usually referred to as Rāja Yoga) and give lip service to its superiority. Overall, however, there is a remarkable absence of any serious discussion of Pātañjala Yoga in later Haṭha Yoga environments. The texts generally leave the impression that Haṭha Yoga is really a distinct satellite form of Yoga.

P. V. Kane puts the matter in the following way: "...(t)here are really only two main systems of Yoga, viz., the one expounded in the *Yogasūtra* and its *Bhāṣya* by Vyāsa and the other dealt with in such works as the *Gorakṣaśataka*, the *Haṭhayogapradīpikā* of Svātmarāmayogin with the commentary called *Jyotsnā* by Brahmānanda. Briefly, the difference between the two is that the Yoga of Patañjali concentrates all effort on the discipline of the mind, while Haṭhayoga mainly concerns itself with the body, its health, its purity and freedom from diseases."[100]

The origins of Haṭha Yoga, apart from the possible tenuous links with Pātañjala Yoga, are usualy traced to two famous spiritual figures (*mahāsiddhas*), namely Matsyendranātha and Gorakṣanātha, who lived probably c. 900 CE. Both were Śaiva ascetics. Elaborate legends surround both figures, and some have suggested that both figures may only be legendary.[101] The current scholarly consensus, however, is that both were historical figures.

Matsyendranātha is said to be the founder of Haṭha Yoga and may have been as well the founder of the Nātha sect.[102] He is also said to have been a proponent of (or possibly even the founder of) the Yoginī Kaula tradition, an important Tantra lineage in the region of Kashmir. In Nepal he is considered to be a Buddhist *bodhisattva*, Avalokiteśvara. The important text, *Kaulajñānanirṇaya*, is attributed to him.

Gorakṣanātha was supposedly a student of Matsyendranātha and is said to be the founder of the Kānphaṭa ("split-eared") sect of yogis.[103] The sect gets its name from the special earrings worn, which require ear piercing. Many Haṭha Yoga texts are attributed to Gorakṣanātha, for example, the *Gorakṣaśataka* and so forth. Other important Haṭha Yoga works are the *Haṭhayogapradīpikā* (c. fourteenth century), the *Gheraṇḍa-saṃhitā* (c. seventeenth century), and the *Śivasaṃhitā* (c. seventeenth century).

According to the *Yogatattva Upaniṣad*, Haṭha Yoga has twenty basic subdivisions. [104] The first eight are the same as the "eight-limbed" Yoga of Pātañjala Yoga, enumerated at YS II.29. The additional twelve subdivisions are for the most part the various bonds (*bandha*) and "bodily exercises" (*mudrā*) of Haṭha Yoga practice. These have to do with positions of the body that block off and redirect the various breaths and fluids. The focus overall is on an elaborate network of bodily postures and an elaborate system of breathing exercises for the sake of bodily purification and control. The term "*haṭha*" is from the root *haṭh* meaning "to treat with violence" or "to oppress", and hence, the expression "Haṭha Yoga" means something like "the discipline of (bodily) exertion. [The word "Haṭha" is to be pronounced in English simply as "hut" as in English "grass-hut", followed by the syllable "*ha*"–hence, "hut-ha" and never "hath" as in English "bath".] Some of the *mudrās* of Haṭha Yoga involve peculiar exercises such as sucking the seminal fluids back up the urethra after ejaculation (*vajrolīmudrā*), drinking urine and using the fluid as a nasal douche (*amarolīmudrā*), and so forth.[105] Haṭha Yoga also involves "six actions" of cleansing. These include cleaning the teeth and body (*dhauti*), cleansing the bladder (*vasti*), cleansing the nasal passages (*neti*), exercising the muscles of the abdomen (*naulī*), cleansing the eyes by staring until the eyes water (*trāṭaka*), and removing phlegm (*kapāla-bhāti*).

In terms of the basically Śaiva theology of Haṭha Yoga, the body is made up of an elaborate network of channels or veins (*nāḍīs*), three of which are especially important. There is the *īḍā* channel that functions on the left side of the body, and the *piṅgalā* channel that functions on the right side. In the center is the *suṣumnā* channel. Running up through the body from the base of the spine to the top of the head is a series of vital centers (*cakra*) that control the various functions of the body. Usually six or seven vital centers are discussed, but the numbers vary depending on various textual traditions. The theory of vital centers may possibly derive from medical texts such as the *Carakasaṃhitā* in which the body's vulnerable places (*marman*) are listed, for example, the head, throat, heart, navel, bladder, and rectum.[106] At the base of the spine in the area of the rectum and the genitals is the *mūlādhāracakra*, the vital center in which is located the psycho-spiritual energy of the body symbolized as the *kuṇḍalinīśakti* ("serpent power"). Ordinarily this powerful spiritual energy is blocked or "sleeping". The purpose of Haṭha Yoga is to awaken the serpent power and redirect the energies of the two sides of the body into the *suṣumnā* channel. The *yogin* then raises the *kuṇḍalinīśakti* up through the various vital centers of the body until the spiritual energy reaches the top of the head, known as the "thousand-petalled lotus" (*sahasrāra*), the abode of Śiva. When the spiritual power has reached the top of the head, the *kuṇḍalinī-śakti* "unites" (*yoga*) with Śiva, and spiritual enlightenment or spiritual liberation occurs.

Many Haṭha Yoga texts give a folk etymology of the term "*haṭha*", breaking the word into two syllables, *ha*, signifying the sun, and *ṭha*, signifying the moon. This allows various correlations such as the "union" of the body's breaths, the "union" of male and female, the "union" of sound and silence, and, of course, the "union" of macrocosm (the world) and microcosm (the body of the *yogin*.) Finally, of course, there is the "union" of Śakti (*kuṇḍalinīśakti, kula*) and Śiva (the supreme *akula*).

Pāñcarātras

These satellite Yoga traditions are overwhelmingly Śaivite in their sectarian orientation, but there is also the Vaiṣṇava Pāñcarātra tradition worth mentioning as well. Of some significance is the *Ahirbudhnyasaṃhitā* of the Pāñcarātra, which derives from somewhere between 300 and 800 CE.[107] The text is important because it mentions five major philosophical traditions, namely Trayī (the Vedic tradition), Sāṃkhya, Yoga, Pāśupata and Sāttvata. The *Ahirbudhnya* describes Sāṃkhya in section 12 (verses. 18-30) as a *ṣaṣṭitantra* ("system of sixty topics"), composed by the Vaiṣṇava sage Kapila, and divided into two parts of thirty-two "principal notions" (*prākṛtamaṇḍala*) and twenty-eight "derived notions" (*vaikṛtamaṇḍala*). The texts then describes a Vaiṣṇava "*yogānuśāsana*" ("inquiry into Yoga") (section 12, verses 31-36), also divided into two parts, namely a *nirodhasaṃhitā* and a *karmasaṃhitā*. Yoga is described as derived from Viṣṇu in the form as Hiraṇyagarbha. Ram Shankar Bhattacharya has argued that this Vaiṣṇava redaction of Yoga is probably an important source for the tradition that Hiraṇyagarbha was the founder of Yoga.[108]

Pāśupatas

Also deserving of brief mention is one of the earliest Śaiva ascetic traditions. The tradition's founder was Lakulīśa, whose name means something like "lord of the club" (*lakula*), referring perhaps to one of the characteristic marks of these early ascetics. Lakulīśa lived probably in the second century of the Common Era. The sect's name, Pāśupata, refers to Śiva as the "*paśupati*" or "lord of beasts", and calls to mind both older traditions of animal sacrifice as well as the sacrifice of one's own body and soul to Śiva. Later, in the more sophisticated philosophical contexts of Śaiva Siddhānta and Kashmir Śaivism, the notion of "*paśupati*" comes to refer to the triad of the lord (*pati*), the individual soul (*paśu*) and the fetters (*pāśa*) that bind the soul.

Regarding the early Pāśupata tradition, however, Feuerstein comments as follows about the group: "What was so controversial about the Pāśupatas was their insistence on shocking the public with their eccentric behavior, such as babbling, making snorting sounds...and making sexual gestures in the presence of women...As is evident from the *Pāśupata-sūtra,* ascribed to Lakulīśa, the earlier schools of this tradition were heavily ritualistic, and philosophy played only a secondary role. The ritual Yoga of the Pāśupatas included many ecstatic practices, such as singing, dancing, and laughter".[109]

The tradition of *pāśupatayoga* is described in the fifth

chapter of the *Pāśupatasūtra* and is a highly ritualistic form of Yoga. It is also mentioned in various Purāṇas, but the *pāśupata-yoga* of the Purāṇas is much closer to Pātañjala Yoga.[110]

Kāpālikas

The early history of this Śaivite ascetic sect is not known, but it was likely an outgrowth of the older Pāśupata tradition. The name of the sect means something like "skull-bearer" and refers to the practice of carrying a human skull which evidently functioned as a vessel for food. The followers of the sect also carry a "stick" (*khaṭvāṅga*), smear their bodies with ashes and engage in a variety of unconventional rituals for which they were widely criticized. Feuerstein comments as follows about the group: "The Kāpālikas, like the Pāśupatas and Kālāmukhas, were worshippers of Śiva–but Śiva in his terrifying aspect as Bhairava. The purpose of all the Kāpālika rites was to achieve communion with God, through which the practitioner acquired both extraordinary capacities and liberation. They offered human flesh at their ceremonies and have been accused–probably rightly–of occasionally performing human sacrifice."[111]

The Aghora Panthīs of the fourteenth century are the later successors of the old Kāpālika tradition. The term "*aghora*" means "not terrific" and may refer to one of the forms of Śiva.[112]

Kālāmukhas

The Śaiva Kālāmukha sect became prominent in the region of Karnataka from the eleventh through the thirteenth centuries. It appears also to have been a branch of the Pāśupatas. The name of the sect evidently refers to the practice of wearing a "black mark" on the forehead (hence, "*kālāmukha*" or "*kālamukha*", which means "black-faced"). David N. Lorenzen, who has written the definitive monograph on the Kāpālikas and Kālāmukhas, comments as follows about the tradition: "Judging from the large number of epigraphs recording donations to Kālāmukha temples and *maṭhas*, these ascetics must have wielded considerable influence in the region. Unfortunately few indications of their beliefs and ritual survive apart from the information which can be gleaned from these epigraphs."[113]

Lorenzen has also discussed one interesting aspect of the sect that appears to relate to the Pātañjala YS, namely the notion of the *mahāvrata* or "great vow". The notion of the *mahāvrata* is mentioned in YS II.31. Says Lorenzen, "According to Patañjali's *Yogasūtra* ii.30-31, when the five *yamas*...are practiced without exception being made for status, place, time, or occasion, the observance is known as the Mahāvrata. Its performance is incumbent on *yogins* at all stages. This Mahāvrata, we believe, is the Mahāvrata of the Kālāmukhas... ...(t)he texts of the Pāśupatas, the section most closely related to the Kālāmukhas, lay particular emphasis on the performance of the five *yamas*."[114] If Lorenzen is correct, this would appear to indicate that the "limbs of Yoga" ((*yogāṅga*) section of the YS II.28-III.8) may well be one of the oldest layers of the YS as J. W. Hauer suggested many years ago. There are also interesting associations in this regard with the old Vrātya traditions going back to Vedic times, as has also been suggested by Hauer.[115] In any case, it is clear that these old Śaiva sectarian traditions are important for understanding the rise of what I am calling satellite traditions of Yoga in the later centuries.

Nātha Siddhas, Kānphaṭa Yogis and the Kaula Cult

The Nātha Siddhas, also known as Nāth Yogīs, the Nātha *sampradāya*, Kānphaṭa ("split-eared") Yogīs, Jogis and Gorakhnāthis in modern north India, are all linked in one way or another with the Haṭha Yoga traditions of Matsyendranātha and Gorakṣanātha mentioned earlier as well as with various Tantra groups. The notion of the *siddha* or "perfected one" refers to the tradition of veneration of certain perfected beings collectively known as the "*siddhas*" or "*mahāsiddhas*". Altogether the northern Indian traditions recognize some eighty-four *mahāsiddhas* who enjoy both liberation as well as extraordinary capacities. There are various *siddha*-lists, almost all of which include Matsyendranātha and Gorakṣanātha as well as a variety of other Śaiva, Śākta and Buddhist *siddhas*. David Gordon White, whose work is the most recent update of these traditions since Mircea Eliade, comments as follows: "As a proper noun, Siddha becomes a broad sectarian appellation, applying to devotees of Śiva in the Deccan (Maheśvara Siddhas), alchemists in Tamil Nadu (Sittars), a group of early Buddhist tāntrikas from Bengal (Mahāsiddhas, Siddhācāryas), the alchemists of medieval India (Rasa Siddhas), and most especially, a mainly north Indian group known as the Nāth Siddhas...The medieval Nāth Siddhas and Rasa Siddhas further interacted with a third group. This was the *paścimāmnāya* (Western Transmission), a Śākta sect devoted to the worship of the goddess Kubjikā which, based mainly in Nepal, also incorporated tantric, yogic, and alchemical elements into its doctrine and practice."[116]

This latter Śākta sect is one of the traditions of the Yoginī Kaula lineage mentioned earlier and linked with the name of Matsyendranātha and the text attributed to him, the *Kaulajñānanirṇaya*.

White then concludes with the following summary: "...[w]e may quite safely characterize the emergence of the Nātha Siddhas as a marriage between Nāths (i.e. Śaiva groups–Pāśupatas, Kāpālikas, and Śāktas–for whom Śiva had long been called Nāth, "Lord") and Siddhas (Maheśvara and Rasa Siddhas and Sittars, as well as the Buddhist Siddhācāryas) which took the institutional form of the Nāth *sampradāya*. Starting in this period [ca. twelfth or thirteenth centuries], all manner of preexisting Śaivite and Siddha clans, lineages, or sects would have funneled themselves into the [twelve] Nāth suborders or have been identified as Nāth Siddhas by outside sources. In addition to groups already mentioned, we also find the Vaiṣṇava Avadhūta *sampradāya* (founded by Dattātreya), Dasanāmī Nāgas, Jainas, Sufi Muslims and a group of snake charmers claiming allegiance, in the fourteenth and later centuries, to one or another of the twelve subsects."[117]

Much remains unclear about these later satellite traditions of Yoga especially with respect to the many Tantra lineages. Also unclear is the relation of these satellite traditions to the great systematic philosophies and theologies of the later centuries, not simply to Classical Sāṃkhya and Pātañjala Yoga, but to Advaita Vedānta, Śaiva Siddhānta, Kashmir Śaivism and the various Vaiṣṇava *sampradāyas*.

Contemporary Yoga Movements

While this volume has focused primarily on Pātañjala Yoga and satellite traditions of Yoga in India from the beginning up to the present time, various forms of Yoga have also developed elsewhere in the world, especially in the United States. For the sake of rounding out this introductory overview of Yoga traditions, we include here a summary account of some contemporary Yoga movements. The survey is not exhaustive, but it provides a suitable sampling of contemporary movements.*

---

*For those interested in detailed treatments of the variety of modern Yoga movements both in India and outside of India, two recent works are especially to be recommended. The first is Joseph S. Alter's *Yoga in Modern India: The Body Between Science and Philosophy* (Princeton: Princeton University Press, 2004). The second is Elizabeth De Michelis's *A History of Modern Yoga: Patañjali and Western Esotericism* (London: Cotinuum, 2004). Alter's book looks at a variety of modern popular Yoga movements in India from the perspective of cultural anthropology. De Michelis' book focusses primarily on Neo-Hindu and Neo-Vedānta approaches to contemporary popular Yoga from the perspective of religious studies. Both books focus almost exclusively on what I have called elsewhere the "Indo-Anglian" orientation in modern India. That is, they are oriented around the modern westernized and nationalist re-interpretations of Yoga deriving from the late nineteenth and

Credit for piecing together the following survey goes to Autumn Jacobsen, a current graduate student in Religious Studies at the University of California, Santa Barbara. Her survey begins with a brief summary of N. E. Sjoman's book, *The Yoga Traditions of the Mysore Palace.*[118] Many contemporary Yoga groups use Haṭha Yoga *āsanas* that are not mentioned in traditional Sanskrit texts. Sjoman's work helps to explain the reasons for the proliferation of Haṭha Yoga *āsanas* among contemporary Haṭha Yoga groups. It should be noted that diacritical marks are for the most part not utilized in this section, since the various groups surveyed choose not to use diacritical marks in their popular literature.

Summary by Autumn Jacobsen

The Yoga Tradition of the Mysore Palace

By the twentieth century, Haṭha Yoga systems consisted of hundreds of *āsanas* that have no basis in the HaṭhaYoga textual tradition. The origin of these *āsanas*, previously unknown, is the subject of N. E. Sjoman's book *The Yoga Tradition of the Mysore Palace*. Sjoman identifies the Haṭha Yoga of T. Krishnamacharya as the predominant source of the numerous *āsanas* present in modern Haṭha Yoga systems, and he maintains that the Haṭha Yoga of Krishnamacharya was a continuation of the Haṭha Yoga tradition of the Mysore Palace.*

---

twentieth century reformist movements. In this regard, see the section entitled "the Indo-Anglian (c. 1757-Present)" in Larson 1995a, pp. 119-141.

*Krishnamacharya was guru to B. K. S. Iyengar, Sri K. Pattabhi Jois, Indra Devi and T. K. V. Desikachar, all of whom have shaped many modern Haṭha Yoga systems. Sjoman focuses primarily on the work of B. K. S.Iyengar and Sri K. Pattabhi Jois, and he claims that Iyengar's tradition is the most

The Haṭha Yoga of the Mysore Palace, argues Sjoman, is a synthesis of the Haṭha Yoga, gymnastic, and wrestling traditions of Karnataka and the origins of its *āsanas* can be traced to texts of the three traditions.

Central to Sjoman's argument is the mid-nineteenth century Haṭha Yoga section of the *Śrītattvanidhi*, a Sanskrit text written in the Old Kannada script.* The *Śrītattvanidhi* describes and illustrates one hundred and twenty-two *āsanas*. Although eighteen *āsanas* of the text belong to the Haṭha Yoga textual tradition, most of the *āsanas* of the *Śrītattvanidhi* are borrowed from the gymnastic and wrestling textual traditions. Sjoman relies upon two Kannada texts, the late nineteenth century *Vyāyāma Dīpikā: Elements of Gymnastic Exercises*, a compilation of gymnastc exercises appropriated from the British,** together

---

influential Haṭha Yoga of the twentieth century. Iyengar Yoga is one of the most prominent forms of Haṭha Yoga and is the basis of numerous Yoga styles, but Jois's Ashtanga Yoga is also influential. He maintained Krishnamacharya's *vinyāsa* method, which has since been incorporated in many *āsana* regimens. It must be noted that most *āsanas* of Iyengar Yoga and Ashtanga yoga are taken directly from the Yoga of Krishnamacharya. Thus, Sjoman's claim that the Haṭha Yoga of Krishnamacharya is the source for most Haṭha Yoga systems of the twentieth century appears to be well-founded.

*The *Śrītattvanidhi* is attributed to Mummadi Krishnaraja Wodeyar (1794-1868) of the royal Wodeyar family of Mysore, who wrote the text sometime between 1811-1868.

**The *Vyāyāma Dīpikā* authored by S. Bharadwaj was published in 1896, several decades after the *Śrītattvanidhi*. Sjoman mainly uses the text to demonstrate its influence on the Yoga of Krishnamacharya. It is probable that the *āsanas* of the *Vyāyāma Dīpikā* that appear in the *Śrītattvanidhi* were common to the gymnastic tradition. Sjoman notes that the Wodeyars

with indigenous wrestling exercises, and the *Mallapurāṇa*, a wrestling manual dated to 1640.*

Sjoman identifies *āsanas* specific to the Yoga of Krishnamacharya and traces them to the *Vyāyāma Dīpikā*, the *Mallapurana*, and the *Śritattvanidhi*.** Especially unique to Krishnamacharya's Yoga is the *vinyāsa* method, which uses breath-coordinated movements to transition from one *āsana* to another. Sjoman presents the *Vyāyāma Dīpikā* as the source of Krishnamacharya's *vinyāsa* method. He explains that Chapter Two of the *Vyāyāma Dīpikā* outlines the "*daṇḍa*" exercises, "variations of push-ups" that "appear to be the primary foundation of Krishnamacharya's *vinyāsas*.[119]

Sjoman has shown that the Yoga of Krishnamacharya, like the Yoga of the Mysore Palace upon which it is based, is a

---

"were closely connected with the British" from 1799 through the early twentieth century, and that their gymnastic tradition is the foundation of the gymnastic tradition of Mysore, dated to the early eighteenth century. Sjoman writes, "the exercise system of the Crown Prince, Krishnaraja Wodeyar, is a combination of the indigenous Indian exercise systems and western [British] gymnastic." Sjoman also mentions that Bharadwaj introduces the *Vyāyāma Dīpikā* as a revival of Indian exercises inspired by and incorporating British exercises consisting of "gymnastics, trapeze, parallel bars, and so on."

*The *Mallapurāṇa* may be dated to the twelfth or thirteenth centuries, although no manuscripts exist. Sjoman maintains that the wrestlers migrated from Gujarat and were patronized by the Maharajas.

**Krishnamacharya authored two Kannada texts, *Yogamakaranda* and *Yogasanagalu*. Sjoman only touches on the contents of *Yogamakaranda* and he ignores *Yogasanagalu*, a text that describes the *āsanas* of the primary, secondary and advanced series taught by Jois.

syncretistic tradition. In other words, Krishnamacharya built upon *āsanas* present in the *Śrītattvanidhi* and added to them based on his own knowledge of Yoga philosophy, Āyurveda, and so forth, to create a complex *āsana* system that, in his judgment, maintained continuity with traditional Haṭha Yoga. As Sjoman relates, two of Krishnamacharya's key disciples, B. K. S. Iyengar and Sri K. Pattabhi Jois also contributed to the evolution of the Haṭha Yoga tradition of Mysore by adding their own innovations and methods.[120]

(The following contemporary groups are listed in alphabetical order.)

Anusāra Yoga

Anusāra Yoga was founded in 1997 by John Friend. By 2005, Anusāra Yoga was being practiced in Europe, South America, Australia and South Asia. Described by Friend as "heart-oriented", an Anusāra Yoga class claims to lead a practitioner through a series of *āsanas* designed to open the heart to divine grace. Friend is a retired businessman, devotee of Siddha Yoga (see below), and a certified Iyengar teacher (see below). He claims to have studied Tantra and Yoga philosophies, anatomy, physiology, and numerous forms of Haṭha Yoga. Simply put, he spliced an Iyengar-influenced *āsana* routine with Siddha Yoga theology and used his business expertise to create a carefully crafted system of Haṭha Yoga. Friend also emphasized the history and philosophy of Yoga by employing Religious Studies scholar Douglas Brooks to accompany him on tours and give lectures on Yoga and Tantra. Like Iyengar Yoga, Anusāra Yoga focuses on the physical details of *āsana* practice but it does so in accordance with the three "A"s of Anusāra–attitude, alignment, and adjustment. "Muscular and organic energy", "spirals" and "loops" denote Anusāra concepts concerning the physical body. Anusāra's unique Siddha Yoga-inspired spiritu- ality is reflected in the opening and closing of each class, which recognize the divine by means of "centering" or meditation.[121]

Ashtanga Yoga

Sri K. Pattabhi Jois (1915-) began teaching Ashtanga Yoga at the Mysore Sanskrit College in 1937 and established the Ashtanga Yoga Research Institue of Mysore in 1963, where he continues to teach. Since 1971 Haṭha Yoga students from around the world have journeyed to Mysore to study with Jois. Ashtanga Yoga classes and *śālas*, "schools", can be found in North and South America, Europe, Asia, Africa, Australia and New Zealand. Although it is one of the most physically rigorous styles of Haṭha Yoga, Jois makes use of a simplified Vedānta philosophy with which he supplements the practice. He insists that his system is the "real" *aṣṭāṅga* Yoga of Patañjali, and is designed to cleanse and strengthen the body, mind and spirit, thus enabling the practitioner to "see God everywhere". Jois' system, which he learned from T. Krishnamacharya between 1927-1937, consists of six series of increasingly difficult *āsanas* linked by *vinyāsas* ("breath coordinated movements") and emphasizes classic Haṭha Yoga techniques. A "Mysore-style" class follows Jois' tradition of instruction. That is, students typically do a two-hour "self-practice" six days a week and progress through the series at their own pace under the guidance of an Ashtanga teacher who is authorized or ceritifed by Jois.[122]

Bikram Yoga

Bikram Choudhury (1946-) learned Yoga from Bishna Ghosh (Pramahamsa Yogananda's younger brother), created his Yoga system under the guidance of Ghosh, and began teaching in India in the 1960s. In 1972 Choudhury settled in Los Angeles and in 1973 he founded the first Bikram College of India in Beverly Hills. By the beginning of the twenty-first century, the Bikram College of India has become internationally known with branches in North and South America, Europe, Africa, Asia, Australia and New Zealand. Bikram Yoga promises total physical health through the repeated performance of twenty-six *āsanas* and two breathing exercises in a room heated to one hundred and five degrees Fahrenheit. The twenty-six postures of Bikram Yoga are common to many forms of Haṭha Yoga.[123]

Integral Yoga

Swami Satchidananda (1919-2002) emerged as a popular meditation teacher in the late 1960s when he began teaching his Integral Yoga in the U.S. Integral Yoga spread to South America, Europe, Asia, Australia and New Zealand and in 1986 devotees of Satchidananda established the international headquarters for Integral yoga at the Satchidananda Ashram in Youngsville, Virginia. He became associated with the Sivananda lineage in 1949. In 1966, Satchidananda settled in the U.S., where he taught a simple Vedanta philosophy that "Truth is One, Paths are Many." This simple message resonated with spiritual seekers of the 1960s counter-culture. Satchidananda named his Yoga "Integral Yoga" because it integrates six Yoga disciplines–Haṭha, Rāja, Bhakti, Karma, Jñāna and Japa ('chanting")–into one system. In addition to lecture tours, Satchidananda authored numerous books, including a commentary on the *Yoga Sūtras* of Patanjali. Although *bhakti*, especially toward Satchidananda, prevails at the ashram, a typical Integral Yoga class is a gentle Haṭha Yoga session consisting of simple *āsanas*, *prāṇāyama,* meditation, and auditory incantations.[124]

Iyengar Yoga

B. K. S. Iyengar began teaching Yoga in Pune, India in 1937. Prominent international figures such as violinist Yehudi Menuhin made Iyengar known to the western world. Iyengar has taught Yoga in Pune and abroad since the early 1950s. In 1975, Iyengar opened the Ramamani Iyengar Memorial Institute in Pune and by the beginning of the twenty-first century Iyengar institutes were prevalent in North and South

America, Africa, Europe, Asia, Australia and New Zealand. Iyengar studied under his uncle, T. Krishnamacharya, for just three years (1933-1936) before leaving Mysore to teach Yoga in Pune. Iyengar studied the body from the perspective of Western medical science and then applied his knowledge of anatomy and physiology to Haṭha Yoga. Iyengar devised a Haṭha Yoga technique that required holding an *āsana* for an extended period of time and emphasized precise alignment of the body. In 1966, Iyengar published the detailed physical and mental benefits of one hundred and eighty-six *āsanas*, complete with instructions and photographs. The book, *Light on Yoga*, has been translated into eighteen languages and is still considered an essential text by Haṭha Yoga teachers and students of all styles. Iyengar has had a profound impact on the contemporary practice of Haṭha Yoga.[125]

Jivamukti Yoga

Sharon Gannon and David Life created Jivamukti Yoga in the early 1980s and they established the first Jivamukti Yoga center in New York City in 1984. Jivamukti Yoga teachers can be found in Yoga studios in the U.S., Canada, Germany and England. Gannon and Life teach that the goal of Haṭha Yoga is "jivamukti", that is, "liberation while living" Yoga. Classes in Jivamukti Yoga guide students through flowing sequences of *āsanas* punctuated with teachings concerning scripture, *bhakti, ahiṃsā* ("non-violence"), music and meditation. The eclectic nature of a Jivamukti Yoga class reflects the multiple interests of its founder, Sharon Gannon and David Life. Gannon is a dancer, choreographer and musician. Life is an artist and performer. Both are certified Ashtanga Yoga teachers.

Kundalini Yoga

Yogi Bhajan (1929-2004) began teaching Kundalini Yoga, otherwise known as 3HO, the "Happy, Healthy and Holy Organization", in the U.S. in 1968. By the twenty-first century Kundalini Yoga had become an international organization with institutes in North and South America, Europe, Africa, Asia, Australia and New Zealand. Yogi Bhajan, born Harbhajan Singh Puri, was a Sikh from Pakistan who reportedly accomplished the Hindu art of awakening *kuṇḍalinī* at the age of sixteen. Kundalini Yoga aims to awaken *kuṇḍalinīśakti*, the "serpent power" coiled and asleep at the base of the spine. Described as "tapping the *kuṇḍalinī*", the experience of *kuṇḍalinī* is believed to usher in physical health, a calm mind, and heightened spiritual awareness. Yogi Bhajan developed Kundalini Yoga by putting a new spin on old Haṭha Yoga practices and appropriating some Sikh traditions as well. Yogi Bhajan teaches that by practicing the Haṭha Yoga techniques of *āsana, prāṇāyāma, kriyās* (bodily cleansing routines), and incantations, the practitioner can "tap" into *kuṇḍalinī* and become a healthy, happy and holy human being.[126]

Kripalu Yoga

Amrit Desai (1932-) began teaching Kripalu ("compassionate") Yoga in 1966 and founded the Kripalu Center in Pennsylvania in 1972. The Center relocated to Lenox, Massachusetts in 1981 and was renamed the Kripalu Center for Yoga and Health. It offers ongoing courses and services concerning Haṭha Yoga, Āyurveda (traditional Indian medicine), meditation and so forth. By the beginning of the present century Kripalu yoga was taught at many U. S. Yoga studios. Desai studied a form of *kuṇḍalinī* Yoga taught by Swami Kripalvananda (1913-1981) in India. In 1962, Swami Kripalvananda commanded Desai to go to the U.S. and to teach a style of Haṭha Yoga that would be appropriate for westerners. Over a span of several decades, Desai and his followers blended Indian philosophies and practices with Western psychology, eventually presenting their method of awakening *kuṇḍālinī* as a means for personal growth. Self-discovery and personal transformation are the goals of Kripalu Yoga.[127]

Power Yoga

Power Yoga names a type of Ashtanga-based Haṭha Yoga focused on physical fitness. Although the appellation is credited to both Beryl Bender Birch and Brian Kest, Birch and Kest developed separate styles of Power Yoga. After a few years of practicing Ashtanga Yoga, Birch began teaching Yoga at the New York Road Runner's Club (NYRRC) and at her own newly established Yoga studio, The Hard and Soft Ashtanga Yoga Center, in 1981. Charged with the special task of teaching Haṭha Yoga to athletes at the NYRRC, Birch modified the primary series of Ashtanga Yoga and portrayed her Haṭha Yoga as a strenuous "workout". Her 1995 publication, *Power Yoga*, popularized her method. Like Birch, Kest drew from his Ashtanga background to create rigorous *āsana* routines, but unlike Birch, Kest presented Power Yoga as a means of self-reflection and self-knowledge. He also put a greater focus on the role and importance of the teacher.[128]

Self-Realization Fellowship or Kriya Yoga

Self-Realization Fellowship is an organization focused on the teachings and meditation techniques of Paramahamsa Yogananda (1893-1952), who founded the Fellowship in 1920. Yogananda established the international headquarters of the movement in Los Angeles in 1925. It now has chapters in South America, Asia, Europe, Africa, Australia and New Zealand. Yogananda came to the U.S. in 1920. One of the first yogis to reside in the U.S., Yogananda authenticated the philosophy and practice of Haṭha Yoga by presenting his Kriya Yoga, "Yoga of Action", as a scientific technique applicable to any religion. His first lecture in the U.S. was entitled "The Science of Religion". After two decades of teaching and touring, Yogananda published *Autobiography of a Yogi* in 1946. In addition to enticing his audience with tales of Indian yogis, the book emphasized the common ground between science and religion, Christianity and Yoga. A classic among students of Haṭha Yoga and New Agers, *Autobiography of a Yogi* has sold over one million copies, gone through thirteen English editions, and been translated into eighteen languages. The Self-Realization Fellowship emphasizes meditation techniques as a means toward strengthening the mind, re-energizing the soul, and experiencing God.[129]

Siddha Yoga

Siddha Yoga arose in India in the 1930s and gained international attention in the 1970s. By 2005, the Siddha Yoga Dharma Association (SYDA) had ashrams and centers all over the world, with two major ashrams in the U.S., the Shree Muktananda Ashram in South Fallsburg, New York and the Siddha Yoga Meditation Ashram in Oakland, California. SYDA is a form of *guru-bhakti* Yoga centered on the living guru and the teachings of past gurus of a particular lineage of Siddhas or "perfected ones". Related to the Tantric traditions of Kashmir Śaivism, the lineage supposedly began with Swami Nityananda (d. 1961), continued with Swami Muktananda (1908-1987), and is presently under the guidance of Gurumayi Cidvilasananda (1955-). Gurumayi initiates devotees into the Siddha Yoga lineage by transmitting divine energy (*śakti*) into the initiate through a glance or touch. Called *śaktipat*, "descent of divine energy", the initiations usually take place during two-day meditation retreats known as "intensives" held at SYDA ashrams. The ashrams also offer courses, retreats, and workshops in Sanskrit, chanting, Yoga and Tantra philosophies, Haṭha Yoga, and meditation.[130]

Viniyoga

In 1976, T. K. V. Desikachar (1938-) founded the Krishnamacharya Yoga Mandiram (KYM) in Chennai, India. Over the next several decades he taught Viniyoga to thousands of students, Indian and foreign, at the KYM and abroad. By 2005, Viniyoga was popular in many countries, especially in Europe and the U.S. Desikachar studied *āsana, prāṇāyama,* chanting, Sanskrit, Indian philosophy and Āyurveda under his father, T. Krishnamacharya, from 1960-1989. In the later years of his life, Krishnamacharya met privately with students, evaluated their physical, mental and spiritual health, and designed practice regimens to fit the individual needs of students. Desikachar followed in his father's footsteps. He began meeting with students individually, assigning them *āsana*, *prāṇāyama*, and chanting practices and recommending diet and lifestyle changes. He called his Haṭha Yoga method "Viniyoga", which means "distribution" or "application", because he insisted that practices associated with Haṭha Yoga must be tailored to the individual. Viniyoga teachers commonly spend several years studying with Desikachar and his family in Chennai and they maintain Desikachar's method in their home countries by holding private sessions with students or by teaching courses and workshops on *prāṇāyama*, recitation and philosophy.[131]

Vinyasa Yoga

Vinyasa yoga is a general style of Haṭha Yoga that arose in the U.S. in the 1980s. It has since become one of the most popular types of Yoga in the U.S., being taught in most Yoga studios, and it has spread to other countries, mostly in Europe. A Vinyasa Yoga class "flows" by means of breath-coordinated movements called "*vinyasas*" from one *āsana* to another. T. Krishnamacharya developed the *vinyasa* method in the 1920s and 1920s and Sri K. Pattabhi Jois preserved the method in his Ashtanga Yoga system, which gained popularity in the U.S. in the 1980s. Although many Yoga enthusiasts were attracted to the rigorous "flow" of Ashtanga Yoga, some found the regimented system of Ashtanga Yoga limiting and created their own style of Haṭha Yoga that retained the *vinyasa* method.[132]

White Lotus Yoga

Ganga White and Tracey Rich developed "flow Yoga" in the 1980s, established the White Lotus Foundation in Santa Barbara, California in 1983, and proceeded to train hundreds of teachers in their innovative style. Ganga White studied a variety of Yoga disciplines, beginning with the Haṭha Yoga of Sivananda in the 1960s. He also studied Iyengar and Ashtanga Yoga in the 1970s and 1980s. Tracey Rich, a student of modern dance, studied Kripalu and Ashtanga in the 1970s and 1980s. Together White and Rich fashioned a non-dogmatic approach to *āsana* practice that combined the alignment of Iyengar yoga and the flow of Ashtanga Yoga while departing from the rigidity of both styles.

PART TWO

SUMMARIES OF WORKS
(ARRANGED CHRONOLOGICALLY)

PĀTAÑJALA YOGA TRADITIONS

1.PATAÑJALI, *Pātañjalayogaśāstra* (*Yogasūtras*)

Translation and Summary by Gerald James Larson

The identity of Patañjali has been discussed at length in the Introduction. The compilation of the *Yogasūtra* and the Vyāsa *Bhāṣya* can be dated approximately in the fourth century (350-400 CE) and certainly no later than the fifth century (400-500). In addition to the discussion of Patañjali in the Introduction, see also the discussion in Larson-Bhattacharya 1987, pp. 27-29 and 165-166.

The edition used for this summary is RSB on YS, pp. 1-184. Although the translation here is new, two older English translations are recommended for the general reader: Mukerji 1983, pp. 1-407, and Woods 1966, pp. 3-348. The latter translation is recommended for accuracy, but is awkward to use for non-Sanskritists. The former translation is recommended for readability and, more than that, as a rendering by a practicing *yogin*, even though the rendering may not always exhibit the technical scholarly treatment provided by the Woods translation. The translation referred to by "T" in the summary that follows is the one by Woods.

Since the *sūtras* themselves are already a highly condensed summary of the Yoga system, a reasonable way to proceed by way of a summary is to present a direct translation of the *sūtras* themselves without accompanying commentary. Because the *sūtra*-style is so highly condensed, of course, it is in some instances impossible to render a *sūtra* without having utilized the interpretations of some commentators. Wherever possible in the following, however, every attempt has been made to offer an accurate translation of the *sūtras* themselves. Also included is the Sanskrit for each *sūtra* so that readers with some acquaintance with classical Sanskrit may have a sense of the original terminology.

BOOK ONE: ON ALTERED STATES OF CONCENTRATION (*Samādhipāda*)

Introduction (*yogānuśāsana*) (YS I.1)(E1; T1)

I.1 Herein begins an inquiry into disciplined meditation based upon past tradition (*atha yogānuśāsanam*).

Functioning of Ordinary Awareness (*citta*): (YS I.2-I.16) (E4-19; T6-44)

I.2 (E4-19; T6-44) Disciplined meditation involves the cessation of the functioning of ordinary awareness (*yogaścitta-vṛttinirodhaḥ*).

I.3. Then, (that is, when the functioning of ordinary awareness has ceased) there is the condition of the seer (that is, *puruṣa*) as it is in itself (*svarūpa*) (that is, without any content, or, in other words, pure content-less consciousness (*tadā draṣṭuḥ svarūpe 'vasthānam*).

I.4. Otherwise, there is conformity with the functioning of ordinary awareness (*vṛttisārūpyam itaratra*).

I.5 The functions of ordinary awareness are fivefold and are afflicted or unafflicted (*vṛttayaḥ pañcatayyaḥ kliṣṭākliṣṭāḥ*).

I.6 Correct awareness, error, verbal construction, sleep and memory (are the five functions of ordinary awareness) (*pramāṇaviparyayavikalpanidrāsmṛtayaḥ*).

I.7 Correct awarenesses arise from perception, inference and reliable testimony (*pratyakṣānumānāgamāḥ pramāṇāni*).

I.8 Error is false cognition based on the form of something appearing as what it is not (*viparyayo mithyājñānam atadrūpa-pratiṣṭham*).

I.9 Verbal (or conceptual) construction depends upon cognition arising from language alone without any substantive referent (*śabdajñānānupātī vastuśūnyo vikalpaḥ*).

I.10 Sleep is a function of ordinary awareness based on the notion (or experience) of absence (*abhāvapratyayālambanā vṛttir nidrā*).

I.11 Memory is the retention of previously experienced

cognitions (or contents) (*anubhūtaviṣayāsaṃpramoṣaḥ smṛtiḥ*).

I.12 The cessation (or restriction) of these functions of ordinary awareness is accomplished through practice and dispassion (*abhyāsavairāgyābhyāṃ tannirodhaḥ*).

I.13 In regard to these two means, practice is restraint with respect to attaining cognitive stability (*tatra sthitau yatno 'bhyāsaḥ*).

I.14 Furthermore, it (practice) is a steady state brought about by uninterrupted effort over a long period of time (*sa tu dīrghakālanairantaryasatkārāsevito dṛdhabhūmiḥ*).

I.15 Dispassion is a cognitive realization of complete control of (the Yogin) who has turned away from all perceptible and scriptural objects (*dṛṣṭānuśravikaviṣayavitṛṣṇasya vaśīkāra-saṃjñā vairāgyam*).

I.16 That is supreme dispassion wherein there is a turning away from all the three *guṇas* due to the realization of the presence of *puruṣa* (*tat paraṃ puruṣakhyāter guṇavaitṛṣṇyam*).

Concentration (*samādhi*) (YS I.17-51)(E19-50; T17-112)

I.17 Concentration having content [relevant for disciplined meditation or yoga] is that derived from forms of empirical awareness, rational awareness, aesthetic awareness and self-awareness (*vitarkavicārānandāsmitānugamāt saṃprajñātaḥ*).

I.18 The other (concentration, namely *asaṃprajñata-samādhi* or content-free concentration) is a condition presupposing the practice of the contemplative realization of cessation wherein only predispositions that are outside of ordinary awareness remain operative (*virāma-pratyayābhyāsapūrvaḥ saṃskāraśeṣaḥ 'nyaḥ*).

I.19 The notion of becoming continues to be the case for the disembodied, and for Yogins who attain only dissolution in primordial materiality (*bhavapratyayo videhaprakṛtilayānām*).

I.20 Among others (that is, those Yogins who follow the proper way of Yoga), (their path to concentration) presupposes the practice of faith, energy, mindfulness, the cultivation of concentration, and insight (*śraddhāvīryasmṛtisamādhiprajñāpūrvaka itareṣām*).

I.21 Concentration is close at hand for those *yogins* who practice with the greatest intensity (*tīvrasaṃvegānām āsannaḥ*).

I.22 Even within that group (of *yogins* practicing with the greatest intensity) a distinction can be made between mild, middling and extreme (practice) (*mṛdumadhyādhimātratvāt tato 'pi viśeṣaḥ).*

I.23 Or, content-filled concentration (*saṃprajñātasamādhi*) can also be attained through focusing on God (as the object of meditation) (*īśvarapraṇidhānād vā*).

I.24 God is a particular or unique consciousness (*puruṣa*) among consciousnesses, untouched by the afflictions, karmic tendencies, karmic fruits and long-term karmic predispositions (that are characteristic of all other sentient beings associated with *puruṣas*) (*kleśakarmavipākāśayair aparāmṛṣṭaḥ puruṣaviśeṣaḥ īśvaraḥ*).

I.25 In God the pinnacle of omniscience has been attained (*tatra niratiśayaṃ sarvajñabījam*).

I.26 (God is) the teacher even of all preceding teachers inasmuch as God is not limited by time (*pūrveṣām api guruḥ kālena anavacchedāt*).

I.27 The verbal expression for God is the sacred syllable (*praṇava*) (or, in other words, the syllable *oṃ*) (*tasya vācakaḥ praṇavaḥ*).

I.28 Repetition of it (the sacred syllable) (and) meditation on the object of the expression (namely God) (should be practiced in order to achieve concentration) (*tajjapas tadarthabhāvanam*).

I.29 Then, (when concentration has been properly cultivated) there is a going over into one's own pure consciousness and the disappearance of the obstacles as well (*tatah pratyakcetanādhigamo 'py antarāyābhāvaś ca*).

I.30 The distractions of awareness, namely illness, dullness, doubt, heedlessness, laziness, worldliness, erroneous perception, failure to attain stability and restlessness–these are the (principal) obstacles (*vyadhistyānasamśayapramādālasya-aviratibhrāntidarśanālabdhabhūmikatvānavasthitatvāni citta-vikṣepās te 'ntarāyāḥ*).

I.31 Frustration, depression, trembling of the body and irregular breathing are the accompaniments of these distractions (*duḥkhadaurmanasyāṅgamejayatvaśvāsapraśvāsā vikṣepasahabhuvaḥ*).

I.32 The (meditative) practice (of focusing on) one principle or reality (*ekatattva*) is appropriate for the sake of negating these distractions (and their accompaniments) (*tat-pratiṣedhārtham ekatattvābhyāsaḥ*).

I.33 Peace of mind (or stability of awareness) arises from the practice of friendliness towards those who are happy, compassion towards those who are in pain, joy towards those who are meritorious, and dispassion towards those who are behaving in a nonmeritorious manner (*maitrīkaruṇāmuditā-upekṣānāṃ sukhaduḥkhapuṇyāpuṇyaviṣayānāṃ bhāvanātaś citta-prasādanam*).

I.34 Or, (stability of awareness, that is, the overcoming of the distractions) can be accomplished through retention and exhalation of breath (*pracchardanavidhāraṇābhyāṃ vā*).

I.35 Or. when there is the apprehension of certain kinds of contents, stability of the mind (can become possible) (*viṣayavatī vā pravṛttir utpannā manasaḥ sthitinibandhanī*)

I.36 Or, (stability of the mind can become possible) when the functioning of awareness is free from grief (and) brilliantly clear (*viśoka vā jyotiṣmatī*).

I.37 Or, (stability of the mind can become possible) when the contents of awareness are free from attachment (*vītarāga-viṣayaṃ vā cittam*).

I.38 Or, (stablity of the mind can become possible) through focusing on the contents of knowledge that derive from sleep or dreaming (*svapnanidrājñānālambanaṃ vā*).

I.39 Or, (stability of the mind can become possible) through reflective meditation on any pleasing object (*yathā-abhimatadhyānād vā*).

I.40 The complete control achieved by the *yogin* (who has attained stability of mind) extends from the smallest particle of reality to the largest entity (*paramāṇuparamamahattvānto 'sya vaśīkāraḥ*).

I.41 (When the *citta* [of the Yogin]) has been sufficiently cleansed of the dysfunctional functioning (*kṣīnavṛtti*)(and become) like a transparent jewel, there arises an engrossment with gross and subtle objects, the process of cognizing, and the subject of cognizing. (The *citta*) then shows forth or highlights the true nature of those contents (*kṣīnavṛtter abhijātasya iva maṇer grahītṛgrahaṇagrāhyeṣu tatsthatad-añjanatā samāpattiḥ*).

I.42 The engrossment related to empirical awareness (*vitarka*) is mixed with verbal constructions (*vikalpa*) involving conventional sounds (words), objects (referents) and the resulting cognitions (*tatra śabdārthajñānavikalpaiḥ saṃkīrṇā savitarkā samāpattiḥ*).

I.43 Engrossment with an empirical object becomes purified (*nirvitarkā*) when memory has been purified and only the object itself shines forth–as if even the act of cognizing is absent and there is only the object itself (*smṛtipariśūddhau svarūpaśūnyā iva arthamātranirbhāsā nirvitarkā*).

I.44 In the same way is to be explained the engrossment with subtle (intellectual or ideational) contents (*sūkṣma-viṣaya*), whether relating to specific intellectual notions (*savicārā*) or pure intellectual contemplation (*nirvicārā*) (*etayā eva savicārā nirvicārā ca sūkṣmaviṣayā vyākhyātā*).

I.45 And subtle objectivity encompasses all the nonempirical contents of awareness up through the unmanifest (*aliṅga*) (that is, primordial materiality or *mūlaprakṛti*) (*sūkṣmaviṣayatvaṃ ca aliṅgaparyavasānam*).

I.46 All these engrossments represent content-filled concentration (or, in other words, all these are intentional awarenesses) (*tā eva sabījaḥ samādhiḥ*).

I.47 When the *yogin* has gained skill in cultivating the highest concentration (that is, the *nirvicārasamādhi*), there arises a tranquility pertaining to the presence of the real self (*nirvicāravaiśāradye 'dhyātmaprasādaḥ).*

I.48 Therein (that is, when there is tranquility in regard to the self as a result of skill in attaining the *nirvicārasamādhi*), (the Yogin has attained) "truth- bearing insight" (*ṛtambharā tatra prajñā*).

I.49 This is a particular kind of awareness (direct perception) whose content is different from (the contents of) the cognitions arising from inference and reliable authority (*śrutānumānaprajñābhyām anyaviṣayā viśeṣārthatvāt*).

I.50 The trace (*saṃskāra*) born of that special cognition counteracts all other traces (*tajjaḥ saṃskāro 'nyasaṃskāra-pratibandhī*).

I.51 When there is cessation of even that special cognition, inasmuch as there is the cessation of everything (that is, all contents), there is a concentration without content (that is, a concentration that is "without seed" or content, *nirbīja*) (*tasya api nirodhe sarvanirodhān nirbījaḥ samādhiḥ*)

BOOK TWO: ON PRACTICE (*Sādhanapāda*)

Systematic Practice: Part One (*kriyāyoga*) (YS II.1-27)

II.1 The structured practice of disciplined meditation involves ascetic exercises (for the body), sacred study/recitation (for speech and voice) and focusing on God (as a content of meditation)(for the mind) (*tapaḥsvādhyāyeśvarapraṇidhānāni kriyāyogaḥ*).

II.2 (The structured practice of disciplined meditation or *kriyāyoga*) is for the sake of cultivating the various altered states of awareness and for the sake of decreasing the force of the afflictions (*samādhibhāvanārthaḥ kleśatanūkaraṇārthaś ca*).

II.3 The five afflictions are ignorance, egoity, attachment, hatred and clinging to ordinary life (*avidyāsmitārāgadveṣa-abhinaveśāḥ pañcakleśāḥ*).

II.4 The first of the five, namely ignorance, provides the basic context for the subsequent four (egoity, attachment, hatred and clinging to life)–and these latter four may be quiescent, decreased, interrupted or active (*avidyā kṣetram uttereṣāṃ prasuptatanuvicchinnodārāṇām*).

II.5 Ignorance is the apprehension of what is permanent, pure, pleasant and the self in what is impermanent, ugly, painful and not the self (*anityāśuciduḥkhānātmasu nityaśuci-sukhātmakhyātir avidyā*).

II.6 Egoity is the appearance of the power of consciousness (*dṛś* or *puruṣa*) and of the power of ordinary awareness (*darśana* or *citta*) as if they were the same thing (*dṛgdarśana-śaktyor ekātmatā iva asmitā*).

II.7 Attachment is closely related to what is pleasant (*sukhānuśayī rāgaḥ*).

II.8 Hatred is closely related to what is frustrating or painful (*duḥkhānuśayī dveṣaḥ*).

II.9 Clinging to ordinary life in the sense of going with the flow of one's ordinary impulses is characteristic even of a learned person (*svarasavāhī viduṣo 'pi tathā rūḍho 'bhiniveśaḥ*)

II.10 These subtle (afflictions) are to be overcome by reversing one's ordinary functioning (*te pratiprasavaheyāḥ sūkṣmāḥ*).

II.11 The functioning of these (afflictions) are to be overcome by means of reflective meditation (*dhyānaheyās tad-vṛttayaḥ).*

II.12 The storage place of karma whose base content is the collocation of afflictions will be experienced or reach fruition in the present or a future rebirth (*kleśamūlaḥ karmāśayo dṛṣṭa-adṛṣṭajanmavedanīyaḥ*)

II.13 So long as this base content continues to exist, there is the ripening of that stored karma in terms of the form of life, the length of life and the quality of life (that a sentient being will assume in its next rebirth) (*sati mūle tadvipāko jātyāyur-bhogāḥ*).

II.14 Inasmuch as a person's stored karma has been meritorious or non-meritorious, so those resulting experiences will have fruits that are pleasant or painful (*te hlādaparitāpa-phalāḥ puṇyāpuṇyahetutvāt*).

II.15 By reason of the frustrations brought about by

fundamental change, pain (both mental and physical) and the resulting predispositions, and inasmuch as the three *guṇas* operate in contrary but inextricable ways, everything in ordinary experience is frustrating to the discriminating Yogin (*pariṇāmatāpasaṃskāraduḥkhair guṇavṛttivirodhāc ca duḥkham eva sarvaṃ vivekinaḥ*).

II.16 Future frustration can be avoided (*heyaṃ duḥkham anāgatam*).

II.17 The contact between the seer (*draṣṭṛ*, that is, *puruṣa*) and the seen (*dṛśya*, that is, *citta* or *prakṛti*) is the reason for the frustration that is to be avoided (*draṣṭṛdṛśyayoḥ saṃyogo heyahetuḥ*).

II.18 The manifest world (*dṛśya*, or in other words *citta*) has for its purpose both ordinary experience and spiritual release, and encompasses all objects as well as all subjective apprehensions, and is constituted by the three constituent processes of intelligibility, activity and objectification (*prakāśa-kriyāsthitiśīlaṃ bhūtendriyātmakaṃ bhogāpavargārthaṃ dṛśyam*).

II.19 The components of the three *guṇas* include gross elements (*viśeṣa*), subtle elements (*aviśeṣa*), the internal organ (*liṅga* or *liṅgaśarīra*, made up of intellect, ego, mind, the five sense-organs and the five action-organs) and the unmanifest primordial materiality (*aliṅga* or *mūlaprakṛti*) (*viśeṣāviśeṣaliṅgamātrāliṅgāni guṇaparvāṇi*)

II.20 The seer (*draṣṭṛ* or pure consciousness), which is only sheer seeing, though inherently pure (or content-less), comes to reflect the intellectual creation (or the *pratyayasarga* of *buddhi* or *citta*) (*draṣṭā dṛśimātraḥ śuddho 'pi pratyaya-anupaśyaḥ*).

II.21 The manifest world exists just for the sake of this pure seeing (that is, *tad-artha* = *puruṣa-artha*), [literally: "the nature or essence of the to-be-seen is just for the sake of that"] (*tad-artha eva dṛśyasya ātmā*).

II.22 (The manifest world), though ended in regard to any (*yogin*) whose purpose has been accomplished, is not ended totally inasmuch as the manifest world is common to all others (*kṛtārthaṃ prati naṣṭam apy anaṣṭaṃ tadanyasādhāraṇatvāt*).

II.23 Contact between the power of what is owned and the owner (or, in other words, between the power of *prakṛti* and that of *puruṣa*) is the occasion for the ascertainment of the inherent form of each (and the eventual dissolution of the contact) (*svasvāmiśaktyoḥ svarūpopalabdhihetuḥ saṃyogaḥ*).

II.24 The cause of that contact is ignorance (*tasya hetur avidyā*).

II.25 When ignorance becomes absent, there is absence of contact, which means abandonment or, in other words, the realization of spiritual liberation (*kaivalya*) of the seer from the seen (*tadabhāvāt saṃyogābhāvo hānaṃ taddṛśeḥ kaivalyam*).

II.26 The means to abandonment is unshaking discriminative awareness (*vivekakhyātir aviplavā hānopāyaḥ*).

II.27 The ultimate insight of that (*yogin*) is sevenfold (*tasya saptadhā prāntabhūmiḥ prajñā*).

Systematic Practice: Part Two (*yogāṅga*) (II.28-III.3) (E88-105; T202-252

II.28 When impurities have been destroyed as a result of the systematic practice of the limbs (or levels) of disciplined meditation, knowledge comes to include the full illumination of discriminative awareness (*yogāṅgānuṣṭhānād aśūddhikṣaye jñānadīptir ā vivekakhyāteḥ*).

II.29 Restraint, observance, posture, breath control, withdrawal of sense-organs, fixation, reflective meditation and cultivation of altered states of awareness are the eight limbs (or levels) (of disciplined meditation) (*yamaniyamāsanaprāṇāyāma-pratyāhāradhāraṇādhyānasamādhayaḥ aṣṭau aṅgāni*).

II.30 Restraints include nonviolence, truth-telling, non-theft, celibacy and non-avarice (*ahiṃsāsatyāsteyabrahmacarya-aparigrahā yāmāḥ*).

II.31 (These restraints) which pertain to all conditions, regardless of form of life (species), place, time or specific circumstance, are known as the Great Vow (*mahāvrata*) (*jāti-*

deśakālasamayānavacchinnāḥ sārvabhaumā mahāvratam).

II.32 Observances include purifications, contentments, ascetic exercises, study/recitation and focusing on God (as a content of meditation) (*śaucasantoṣatapaḥsvādhyāyeśvara-praṇidhānāni niyamāḥ*)

II.33 When these (restraints and observances) get turned aside by this or that improper impulse, an appropriate counteracting meditation should be practiced (*vitarkabādhane pratipakṣabhāvanam*).

II.34 Appropriate opposing meditative exercise (should be directed against) improper impulses such as violence and so forth accompanied by greed, anger or delusion, either committed or caused to be committed or acquiesced in, that are mild, medium or intense, and the fruits of which entail unending pain and ignorance (*vitarkā hiṃsādayaḥ kṛtakārita-anumoditā lobhakrodhamohapūrvakā mṛdumadhyādhimātrā duḥkhājñānānantaphalā iti pratipakṣabhāvanam*).

II.35 When nonviolence has been established (by the *yogin*) there is abandonment of hostility (among all creatures) when drawing near to him (*ahiṃsāpratiṣṭhāyāṃ tatsannidhau vairatyāgaḥ*).

II.36 When truth-telling has been established (by the *yogin*), there is a proper foundation for action and its fruits (*satyapratiṣṭhāyāṃ kriyāphalāśrayatvam*).

II.37 When nontheft (generosity) has been established (by the *yogin*), there is the coming forth of all kinds of wealth (*asteyapratiṣṭhāyāṃ sarvaratnopasthānam*).

II.38 When celibacy has been established (by the *yogin*), there is the acquisition of virility (*brahmacaryapratiṣṭhāyāṃ vīryalābhaḥ*).

II.39 When nonavarice has become steady (for the *yogin*) there arises understanding how rebirth occurs (*aparigraha-sthairye janmakathantāsambodhaḥ*).

II.40 As a result of bodily purification, there is disgust with respect to one's own body and avoidance of contact with others (*śaucāt svāṅgajugupsā parair asaṃsargaḥ*).

II.41 (Also, as a result of purification), there is purification of the intelligibility constituent (*sattva*) (of the *buddhi* or *citta*), cheerfulness, one-pointedness, control over the sense-organs and ability with respect to apprehending the self (*sattvaśuddhi saumanasyaikāgryendriyajayātmadarśanayogyatvāni ca)*.

II.42 As a result of contentment, there is the highest acquisition of happiness (*santoṣād anuttamaḥ sukhalābhaḥ*).

II.43 As a result of ascetic exercises, there is the perfection of the body and the sense-organs inasmuch as impurities have been destroyed (*kāyendriyasiddhir aśuddhikṣayāt tapasaḥ*).

II.44 As a result of study/recitation, there is contact with one's own chosen deity (*svādhyāyād iṣṭadevatāsamprayogaḥ*).

II.45 As a result of focusing on God (as a content of meditation) there arises the perfection of concentration (*samādhi-siddhir īśvarapraṇidhānāt*).

II.46 Posture should be comfortably steady (*sthirasukham āsanam*).

II.47 (Posture is perfected) through relaxed effort and engrossment with the infinite (*prayatnaśaithilyānanta-samāpattibhyām*)

II.48 Then, (the *yogin*) is not tormented by dualities (*tato dvandvānabhighātaḥ*).

II.49 When (posture) has been perfected, there arises breath control which involves stopping or control of the process of inhalation and exhalation (*tasmin sati, śvāsapravāsayor gati-vicchedaḥ prāṇāyāmaḥ*).

II.50 (Breath control is) the operation of exhalation, inhalation and suspension, observed with regard to place, time and number, becoming long and subtle (*bāhyābhyantara-stambhavṛttir deśakālasaṃkhyābhiḥ paridṛṣṭo dīrghasūkṣmaḥ*).

II.51 A fourth (level of breath control) pertains to going beyond external and internal operations (*bāhyābhyantara-viṣayākṣepī caturthaḥ*).

II.52 Then the covering over the light (of knowledge) is destroyed (*tataḥ kṣīyate prakāśāvaraṇam*).

II.53 And, the mind is then ready with respect to the

meditative fixations (*dhāraṇeṣu ca yogyatā manasaḥ*).

II.54 The withdrawal of the sense-organs (occurs) when there is non-contact with their own objects–just as the inherent functioning of the mind (ceases when not being engaged) (*svaviṣayāsamprayoge cittasya svarūpānukāra iva indriyāṇāṃ pratyāhāraḥ*).

II.55 Then, there is supreme control of the sense-organs (*tataḥ paramā vaśyatā indriyāṇām*).

BOOK THREE: ON EXTRAORDINARY COGNITIVE CAPACITIES (*vibhūtipāda*)

III.1 Focus on a specific place (or object) is (known as) fixation of ordinary awareness (*deśabandhaś cittasya dhāraṇā*).

III.2 (When fixation has been accomplished, the achievement of) an even flow of thought (in regard to the place or object) is (known as) reflective meditation (*dhyāna*) (*tatra pratyayaikatānatā dhyānam*).

III.3 That reflective state (that is, the *dhyāna* condition) in which only the object itself appears as if devoid of the presence of the meditator is (known as) concentration (*samādhi*) (*tad eva arthamātranirbhāsaṃ svarūpaśūnyam iva samādhiḥ*).

Systematic Practice: Part Three (*saṃyama, vibhūti*) (YS III.4-55) (E106-155; T253-345)

III.4 This triad (that is, *dhāraṇā, dhyāna* and *samādhi*) functioning together as one is (known as) comprehensive reflection (*saṃyama*) (*trayam ekatra saṃyamaḥ*).

III.5 When comprehensive reflection is achieved, there arises authentic insight (*tajjayāt prajñālokā*).

III.6 The application of this comprehensive reflection can be directed at all levels of awareness (*tasya bhūmiṣu viniyogaḥ*).

III.7 Of the eight limbs of disciplined meditation, this final triad (that is, the comprehensive meditation of *dhāraṇā, dhyāna* and *samādhi*) may be considered to be the internal limbs or levels–(while the first five may be considered to be external limbs or levels) (*trayam antaraṅgaṃ pūrvebhyaḥ*).

III.8 But even those internal limbs or levels are only to be considered as external limbs of the ultimate content-less state of awareness (*tad api bahiraṅgam nirbījasya*).

III.9 The coming into prominence of the predisposition towards cessation and the overcoming of the predisposition towards further ordinary awareness is (known as) the fundamental change tending towards cessation which is characterized by (slowly increasing) moments of actual cessation (*vyutthānanirodhasaṃskārayor abhibhava-prādurbhāvau nirodhakṣaṇacittānvayo nirodhapariṇāmaḥ*).

III.10 On account of this trace (namely the tending toward cessation), there arises a tranquil flow within ordinary awareness (*tasya praśāntavāhitā saṃskārāt*).

III.11 When the many contents (in ordinary awareness) begin to subside and when one-pointedness becomes prominent, (this is known as) the fundamental change tending towards concentration (*sarvārthataikāgratāyoḥ kṣayodayau cittasya samādhipariṇāmaḥ*).

III.12 Then, when the notion maintains continuity or remains the same, whether past or present, (this is known as) the fundamental change tending towards one-pointedness (*tataḥ punaḥ śāntoditau tulyapratyayau cittasya ekāgratā-pariṇāmaḥ*).

III.13 These three fundamental changes (tending toward cessation, toward concentration and toward one-pointedness) which relate respectively to change in characteristic (*dharma*), change in temporal mode (*lakṣaṇa*) and change in overall condition (*avasthā*), have been described with respect (to understanding the various changes that occur) in the external, objective world (the *bhūta*-realm) and in internal, subjective awareness (the *indriya*-realm) (*etena bhūtendriyeṣu dharma-lakṣaṇāvasthāpariṇāmā vyākhyātaḥ*).

III.14 There is a substrate (*dharmin*, that is, a basic materiality) underlying these various characteristics of past, present and future (*śāntoditāvyapadeśyadharmānupatī dharmī*).

III.15 Variance in sequence (of characteristics) is the reason with respect to understanding the variance of fundamental changes (*kramānyataṃ pariṇāmānyatve hetuḥ*).

III.16 Comprehensive reflection on these three kinds of fundamental change generates knowledge of the past and the future (*pariṇāmatrayasaṃyamād atītānāgatajñānam*).

III.17 Inasmuch as word (*śabda*), object (*artha*) and notion (*pratyaya*) are mutually superimposed on one another, there is a basic confusion (in understanding how communication occurs among sentient beings). To the extent that these components are distinguished through the practice of comprehensive reflection, knowledge of the various modes of symbolic communication through sound among all sentient creatures becomes possible (*śabdārthapratyayānām itaretarādhyāsāt saṃkaras tatpravibhāgasaṃyamāt sarvabhūtarutajñānam*).

III.18 Inasmuch as traces (come to be) intuitively perceived (by *yogins* through comprehensive reflecton), knowledge of previous births becomes possible (*saṃskārasākṣātkaraṇāt pūrvajātijñānam*).

III.19 Inasmuch as a notion or idea (of someone else comes to be intuitively perceived through comprehensive reflection), knowledge of the cognitive contents of the minds of others becomes possible (*pratyayasya paracittajñānam*).

III.20 But such knowledge does not include knowing actual objects; it refers, rather, to the non-objective cognition involved (*na tu sālambanaṃ tasya aviṣayībhūtatvāt*).

III.21 Inasmuch as the physical form of the body becomes the focus for comprehensive reflection, to the extent that the capacity of grasping that physical form can be stopped through breaking the connection between light, the eye (and the physical body), invisibility becomes possible (*kāyarūpa-saṃyamāt tadgrāhyaśaktistambhe cakṣuḥprakāśāsamprayoge 'ntardhānam*).

III.22 Inasmuch as action, whether undertaken or not undertaken, becomes the focus for comprehensive reflection relating to omens of one kind or another, knowledge of (impending) death becomes possible (*sopakramaṃ nirupakramaṃ ca karma tatsaṃyamād aparāntajñānam ariṣṭebhyo vā*).

III.23 Inasmuch as universal friendliness and so forth (namely *maitrī, karuṇā, muditā* and *upekṣā*, and cf. I.33 above) become the focus for comprehensive reflection, various powers become possible (*maitryādiṣu balāni*).

III.24 Inasmuch as these powers become the focus for comprehensive reflection, the strength of an elephant and other (comparable) extraordinary strengths become possible (*baleṣu hastibalādīni*).

III.25 From practice (i.e. meditation on) seeing the higher functioning (of the mind), knowledge of what is subtle, concealed or distant becomes possible (*pravṛttyālokanyāsāt sūkṣmavyavahitaviprakṛṣṭajñānam*).

III.26 When the sun [*sūryadvāra* or "gate" in the region of the navel or heart] becomes the focus for comprehensive reflection, knowledge of (various) universes becomes possible (*bhuvanajñānaṃ sūrye saṃyamāt*).

III.27 When the moon [*candradvāra*, another "gate" in the body] becomes the focus for comprehensive reflection, knowledge of the orderly arrangement of the stars (or constellations) becomes possible (*candre tārāvyūhajñānam*).

III.28 When the pole star [yet another "gate" or region] becomes the focus for comprehensive reflection, knowledge of the motion of the stars or constellations becomes possible (*dhruve tadgatijñānam*).

III.29 When the circle of the navel becomes the focus for comprehensive reflection, knowledge of the orderly arrangement of the body becomes possible (*nābhicakre kāya-vyūhajñānam*).

III.30 When the base of the throat becomes the focus for comprehensive reflection, cessation of hunger and thirst becomes possible (*kaṇṭhakūpe kṣutpipāsānivṛttiḥ*).

III.31 When the "tortoise-vein" (the *kūrmanāḍī* or bronchial tube) becomes the focus for comprehensive reflection, steadiness becomes possible (*kūrmanāḍyāṃ sthairyam*).

III.32 When the light at the top of the head becomes the focus for comprehensive reflection, a vision of the *siddhas* (the accomplished *yogins* of the past) becomes possible (*mūrdha-jyotiṣi siddhadarśanam*).

III.33 Or, (from comprehensive reflection on) higher intuition, (knowledge of) everything becomes possible (*prātibhād vā sarvam*).

III.34 When the heart region becomes the focus for comprehensive reflection, consciousness of ordinary awareness becomes possible (*hṛdaye cittasaṃvit*).

III.35 The subject-object world (*parārtha*) of ordinary experience (*bhoga*) is a cognitive condition wherein there is no distinction between the intelligibility constituent (*sattva*) and consciousness (*puruṣa*), even though, in fact, the two are always separate; when one's own unique (and separate) consciousness becomes the focus of comprehensive reflection, cognition of the presence of *puruṣa* becomes possible (*sattva-puruṣayor atyantāsaṃkīrṇayoḥ pratyayāviśeṣo bhogaḥ para-arthatvāt svārthasaṃyamāt puruṣajñānam*).

III.36 Then, higher intuition, subtle hearing, subtle feeling, subtle seeing, subtle tasting and subtle smelling become possible (*tataḥ prātibhaśrāvaṇavedanādarśāsvādavartā jāyante*).

III.37 These extraordinary capacities can be hindrances when (the *yogin*) is in concentration, but they can be considered (valuable) psychic capacities in ordinary life (*te samādhau upasargā vyutthāne siddhayaḥ*).

III.38 Inasmuch as the causes of bondage are being loosened and inasmuch as there is a feeling of suppleness in awareness, there arises the sensation of being able to enter the body of another (*bandhakāraṇaśaithilyāt pracārasaṃvedanāc ca cittasya paraśarīrāveśaḥ*).

III.39 Inasmuch as the up-breath (the *udāna* or speech-breath) has been controlled (there arises a sense of) dispassion in regard to earthly things like water, mud, thorns, and so forth, and a sense of moving upwards (*udānajayāj jalapaṅkakaṇṭaka-ādiṣu asaṅga utkrāntiś ca*).

III.40 Inasmuch as the middling breath (*samāna*, that is, the digestive breath) has been controlled, (there arises) burning energy (*samānajayāj jvalanam*).

III.41 When the relation between hearing and space becomes the focus of comprehensive reflection, celestial hearing (the so-called "divine hearing") becomes possible (*śrotra-ākāśayoḥ sambandhasaṃyamād divyaṃ śrotram*).

III.42 When the relation between the body and space becomes the focus for comprehensive reflection, and there is a sense of becoming very light like cotton, the sense of moving about in space or levitation becomes possible (*kāyākāśayoḥ sambandhasaṃyamāl laghutulasamāpatteś ca ākāśagamanam*).

III.43 Ordinary experiencing when it detaches itself from its intentional contents (that is, its outward involvements), becomes completely disembodied; then there is the elimination of the covers over the light (of pure consciousness) (*bahir akalpitā vṛttir mahāvidehā tataḥ prakāśāvaraṇakṣayaḥ*).

III.44 When gross materiality, its inherent form, its subtle materiality, its relations, and its overall purposiveness become the focus for comprehensive reflection, control of the gross objective world becomes possible (*sthūlasvarūpa-sūkṣmānvayārthavattvasaṃyamād bhūtajayaḥ*).

III.45 Then there occurs the manifestation of (the extraordinary cognitive capacities) becoming small like an atom and so forth, as well as perfection of the body and overcoming the noxious effects of gross embodiment (*tato 'ṇimādi-prādurbhāvaḥ kāyasampat taddharmānabhighātaś ca*).

III.46 Perfection of the body involves beauty, gracefulness, strength, virility and muscularity (*rūpalāvaṇyabalavajra-saṃhananatvāni kāyasampat*).

III.47 When cognizing, its inherent form, its egoity, its relations and its overall purposiveness become the focus for comprehensive reflection, control of the subtle subjective realm of cognition becomes possible (*grahaṇasvarūpāsmitānvaya-arthavattvasaṃyamād indriyajayaḥ*).

III.48 Then, there is quickness of mind, the power of acting beyond the sense-organs, and the control of *prakṛti* (*tato manojavitvaṃ vikaraṇabhāvaḥ pradhānajayaś ca*).

III.49 For the (*yogin*) given solely over to the discriminative realization of the difference between *sattva* and *puruṣa* there arises a sense of supremacy over all beings and omniscience (*sattvapuruṣānyatākhyātimātrasya sarvabhāvādhiṣṭhātṛtvaṃ sarva-jñātṛtvaṃ ca*).

III.50 From renunciation even of these attainments, when there has been destruction of the seeds of all faults, (there arises) spiritual liberation (*tadvairāgyād api doṣa-bījakṣaye kaivalyam*).

III.51 Should there occur an invitation from high beings (*sthānins* or gods, and so forth), however, (there should arise in the *yogin*) neither pride nor attachment, since this would entail unwanted consequences (*sthānyupanimantraṇe saṅga-smayākaraṇaṃ punar aniṣṭaprasaṅgāt*).

III.52 When the (notion of) moment and sequence of moments become the focus for comprehensive reflection, discriminative knowledge becomes possible (*kṣaṇatatkramayoḥ saṃyamād vivekajaṃ jñānam*).

III.53 Then, there occurs the ascertainment of two always separate but similar entities (namely *prakṛti* and *puruṣa*, which are both unmanifest and existent ultimates), even though in ordinary awareness they cannot be distinguished in terms of species, temporal character or spatial location (*jātilakṣaṇa-deśair anyatānavacchedāt tulyayos tataḥ pratipattiḥ*).

III.54 Discriminative knowledge is universal (*tāraka*), all-encompassing, all-pervading and immediate (*tārakaṃ sarva-viṣayaṃ sarvathāviṣayam akramaṃ ca iti vivekajaṃ jñānam*).

III.55 When the *sattva* and *puruṣa* have been clearly distinguished,, (there arises) spiritual liberation (*sattva-puruṣayoḥ śuddhisāmye kaivalyam iti*).

BOOK FOUR: ON SPIRITUAL LIBERATION (*Kaivalyapāda*)
Summary Notations on Awareness and Consciousness (YS IV.1-34) (E156-184; T346-407)

IV.1 (The experience of) extraordinary capacities may occur naturally (that is, as a result of inborn capacities at the time of rebirth), or from taking herbal medications (*oṣadhi*, including elixirs and hallucinogens), or from incantations (*mantra*), or from ascetic practices (*tapas*), or finally from concentrations (*samādhi*) (that occur as a result of practicing the comprehensive reflections just describe in the preceding section) (*janmauṣadhimantratapaḥsamādhijāḥ siddhayaḥ*).

IV.2 Dynamic transformation into another form of life (at the time of rebirth) is due to the potency or abundance of primordial materiality (*jātyantarapariṇāmaḥ prakṛtyāpurāt*).

IV.3 (There is) no need for an efficient cause among these potencies of materiality; but there is the assisting task of removing obstructions, like a farmer (who opens a water gate to allow water to flow into a field) (*nimittam aprayojakam prakṛtīnāṃ varaṇabhedas tu tataḥ kṣetrikavat*).

IV.4 Individualized awarenesses (arise) solely from egoity (*nirmāṇacittāny asmitāmātrāt*).

IV.5 With respect to difference in functioning (among the many different awarenesses), there is only one (pre-individualized) awareness providing the impetus for the many (individualized awarenesses) (*pravṛttibhede prayojakaṃ cittam ekam anekeṣām*).

IV.6 Therein the awareness characterized by even-flowing reflective meditation does not become involved in perpetuating latent tendencies (*tatra dhyānajam anāśayam*).

IV.7 The karma of a *yogin* is neither black nor white; for others, it is threefold (that is, black, white or some mixture of black and white) (*karma aśuklākṛṣṇaṃ yoginas trividham itareṣām*).

IV.8 Then (that is, on account of the karmic accumulation), there is the manifestation of subconscious impressions in keeping just with their appropriate karmic propensities (*tatas tadvipākānuguṇānām eva abhivyaktir vāsanānām*).

IV.9 Since memory and traces are uniform, there is a basic continuity (from rebirth to rebirth) even though there may be considerable separation in terms of form of life, location or time (*jātideśakālavyavahitānām apy ānantaryaṃ smṛti-saṃskārayor ekarūpatvāt*).

IV.10 Furthermore, these (latent tendencies) are beginningless, since the wish or desire to be is permanent (*tāsām anāditvaṃ ca āśiṣo nityatvāt*).

IV.11 Since subconscious impressions are triggered by cause, effect, mind-set and object, when these latter are absent, so they (that is, the impressions) also are absent (*hetuphala-āśrayālambanaiḥ saṃgṛhītatvād eṣām abhāve tadabhāvaḥ*).

IV.12 The past and future actually exist, since their characteristic features have distinct existing modes (*atīta-anāgataṃ svarūpato asty adhvabhedād dharmāṇām*).

IV.13 These characteristics (of the existing modes of past, present and future) are either manifest or subtle (that is, manifest in the case of the present, and subtle in the case of the past and future) and have the *guṇas* as their essence (*te vyakta-sūkṣmā guṇātmānaḥ*).

IV.14 There is such a thing as objective reality, since the fundamental changes (of material reality) remain uniform (rational) throughout (*pariṇāmaikatvād vastutattvam*).

IV.15 Since there are separate awarenesses apprehending a uniform world, there must be two distinct dimensions (of realty, that is, subject and object) (*vastusāmye cittabhedāt tayor vibhaktaḥ panthāḥ*).

IV.16 The objective world is not dependent on a single awareness; (if such were the case) when there was non-apprehension of a thing by that single awareness, what (or where) would the thing be? (*na ca ekacittatantraṃ vastu tad-apramāṇakaṃ tadā kiṃ syāt*).

IV.17 An objective thing is known or unknown to the extent that ordinary awareness is influenced by it (*taduparāga-apekṣitvād cittasya vastu jñātājñātam*).

IV.18 The functionings of ordinary awareness are always being cognized, since *puruṣa* as the reflective power over ordinary awareness is not subject to fundamental change (*sadā jñātāś cittavṛttayas tatprabhoḥ puruṣasya apariṇāmatvāt*).

IV.19 It (that is, ordinary awareness) is not self-reflective, since it is an object that can be apprehended (*na tat svābhāsaṃ dṛśyatvāt*).

IV.20 And, again, it is not possible to ascertain both (that is, awareness and its object) at the same time (*ekasamaye ca ubhayānavadhāraṇam*).

IV.21 In the event that one momentary awareness is to be perceived by another momentary awareness, this would entail a vicious infinite regress from intellect to intellect and would also lead to confusion of memories (*cittāntaradṛśye buddhi-buddher atiprasaṅgaḥ smṛtisaṃkaraś ca*).

IV.22 Although consciousness is not subject to change, the experience of one's intellect (*buddhi*) as if it were (itself) consciousness (*sva*) (occurs) when consciousness takes on or reflects the forms of awareness (*citer apratisaṃkramāyās tadākārāpattau svabuddhisaṃvedanam*).

IV.23 Ordinary awareness influenced by the seer (i.e. consciousness) and what is seen (what is not consciousness) is all-encompassing (*draṣṭṛdṛśyoparaktaṃ cittaṃ sarvārtham*).

IV.24 That (ordinary awareness), even though variegated by innumerable subconscious impressions, (nevertheless) works or functions for the sake of another (that is, for the sake of a *puruṣa*)(*tad asaṃkhyeyavāsanābhiś citram api parārthaṃ saṃhatyakāritvāt*).

IV.25 For the one who sees the distinction (between *citta* and *puruṣa*) there is a cessation of having to meditate upon the existence of the self (*viśeṣadarśina ātmabhāvabhāvanā-vinivṛttiḥ*).

IV.26 Then at that time ordinary awareness is inclining towards discrimination and is headed for spiritual liberation (*tadā vivekanimnaṃ kaivalyaprāgbhāraṃ cittam*).

IV.27 In the interstices (or gaps) in this (awareness), there are other notions (leading in different directions) arising from (residual) traces (*tac-chidreṣu pratyayāntarāṇi saṃskārebhyaḥ*).

IV.28 Abandonment of those is said to be like abandonment of the afflictions (*hānam eṣāṃ kleśavad uktam*).

IV.29 Of the (*yogin*) taking no interest even in the highest elevation, the Cloud of Truth (*dharmamegha*) concentration (shows itself) all around on account of the realization of discrimination (*prasaṃkhyāna 'py akusīdasya sarvathā viveka-khyāter dharmameghaḥ samādhiḥ*).

IV.30 Then there is the cessation of afflictions and actions (*tataḥ kleśakarmanivṛttiḥ*).

IV.31 Then at that time, because of the vast extent of knowledge unencumbered by any obstructions or impurities, there is very little more to be known (*tadā sarvāvaraṇamala-apetasya jñānasya ānantyāj jñeyam alpam*).

IV.32 Then, (there is) completion of the sequence of fundamental changes of the *guṇas* whose purposes have now been accomplished (*tataḥ kṛtārthānāṃ pariṇāmakrama-samāptir guṇānāṃ*).

IV.33 (The notion of) sequence, understood as the terminal point of a fundamental change, is a counterpart of (the notion of) moment (*kṣaṇapratiyogī pariṇāmāparāntanirgrāhyaḥ kramaḥ*).

IV.34 The reversal or turning back of the *guṇas*, which now no longer have to function for the sake of consciousness, is spiritual liberation, or, put somewhat differently, there is now the presence of the power of pure consciousness (*citi-śakti*) in its own inherent form (*puruṣārthaśūnyānāṃ guṇānāṃ pratiprasavaḥ kaivalyaṃ svarūpapratiṣṭhā vā citiśaktir iti*).

2.VYĀSA, *Bhāṣya* on Patañjali's *Yogasūtras*

Summary by Ram Shankar Bhattacharya

The date and identity of Veda-vyāsa or Vyāsa have been discussed in the Introduction. Both the *Yogasūtra* and the Vyāsa *Bhāṣya* are roughly contemporary and may be dated approximately in the fourth century (350-400 CE) and certainly no later than the fifth century (400-500 CE).

As with the summary of Patañjali's *Yogasūtras*, the E for this summary is RSB on YS, and the T is Woods.

BOOK ONE

I.1 (E1-3; T3-4) Yoga is provisionally defined as concentration, which is a property of awareness. Awareness has five stages (*bhūmi*), namely distracted (*kṣipta*), sluggish (*mūḍha*), partially distracted (*vikṣipta*), one-pointed (*ekāgra*) and suppressed (*niruddha*). The awareness of the fourth stage (one-pointed), called content-filled (*samprajñāta*), illumines a real thing and is able to destroy the afflictions and to slacken the knots of karma. The fifth stage (the suppressed) is called content-less (*asamprajñāta*); in it all fluctuations of awareness are suppressed.

I.2 (E4-6; T8-9) Because "*yoga*" does not mean suppression of all fluctuations of awareness, content-filled concentration (in which a single thought is kept in awareness) also comes under the denomination of "*yoga*". Though such awareness involves the three *guṇas*, the *sattva guṇa* is predominant in it and it tends toward merit (*dharma*), knowledge (*jñāna*), dispassion (*vairāgya*) and supremacy (*aiśvarya*) or toward their opposites (namely demerit, ignorance, passion, and failure of supremacy) according to the appropriate influence of *rajas* and *tamas*. When the stain of *rajas* is removed, awareness remains in its own nature and tends toward concentration called *dharmamegha* (cf. IV.29). Discriminative discernment (*vivekakhyāti*) is contrary in nature to the immutable consciousness (*citiśakti*), i.e. the *puruṣa* principle. Awareness suppresses even this discernment. The resulting state, in which only traces subsist, is known as seedless (*nirbīja*) concentration.

I.3 (E7; T113) When all fluctuations of awareness are suppressed, the immutable awareness, which is the knower of the cognition in the intellect, remains in its own nature. In the emergent state (*vyutthāna*), however, it does not seem so.

I.4 (E7-8; T14) Since in the emergent state objects are shown to the *puruṣa*, it appears (to ignorant persons) to be identical with the fluctuations of awareness. The correlation between the *puruṣa* and awareness is that of proprietor (*svāmi*) and property (*svam*), and it is said to be beginningless.

I.5 (E9-10; T17) Fluctuations caused by the afflictions give rise to the accumulation of stored-up karma. Fluctuations having discriminative discernment as their basis obstruct the functioning of the *guṇas*. Traces and fluctuations help each other to come into existence. When awareness has finished its task, it abides in its own nature and becomes dissolved (in its own material cause).

I.7 (E10-12; T0-21) Perception, one of the three kinds of correct awareness, is that fluctuation which comes into existence when awareness becomes affected by external things through the channel of the organs. This fluctuation is predominantly cognitive of the particular properties of an object, which is comprised of generic and specific properties. Inference is that fluctuation which is derived from a mark (*liṅga*) existing in things belonging to the same class and not existing in things belonging to a different class. Inference is chiefly concerned with general properties. (Knowledge from) reliable testimony is that fluctuation which arises in the awareness of a person who hears the statements of trustworthy persons (*āpta*) who possess knowledge of things seen or heard. Testimony becomes unreliable (erroneous) if a trustworthy person declares things of which he does not actually have knowledge.

I.8 (E12-13; T24) Error is not correct awareness since it is capable of being sublated (*bādha*) by knowledge. An instrument of knowledge has as its content an existing thing (*bhūtārtha*). For example, seeing that there is really just one moon sublates the double-moon experience. Erroneous cognition is of five kinds, which are the same as the five afflictions, namely ignorance and so forth (see below under YS II.3).

I.9 (E13-14; T26-27) Conceptual construction (*vikalpa*) is neither knowledge nor error. Though it is without a real object it has its own utility for persons acting or thinking in a way based on words. To think that the self (*puruṣa*) has immutable consciousness (*caitanya*) as its property is an example of this kind of fluctuation. Consciousness is not a property of *puruṣa*. It *is puruṣa*! Again, "the arrow comes to a stop" attributes motion where there is none.

I.10 (E14-15; T29) Since there is memory of the sleeping state, that state must be regarded as an experience (*pratyaya*), for memory presupposes the existence of traces which are themselves caused by experiences.

I.11 (E15-16; T31-32) It is not the experience only, nor the content of the experience only, that is remembered, but both the experience and its content are remembered, though the content is what chiefly is remembered. The things to be remembered are either imagined, as in the dreaming state, or not imagined, as in the waking state. Memory arises out of the above-named fluctuations which are characterized by pleasure, pain and delusion. All these fluctuations are to be suppressed in order to attain concentration.

I.12 (E16; T14) The activity of awareness runs either toward good, that is, when it goes onward to liberation and downward to discriminative knowledge, or toward evil, that is, when it goes onward to the mundane existence (*saṃsāra*) and downward to undiscriminating awareness. Dispassion (*vairāgya*) helps one to check the inclination toward content-filled awareness; likewise, the practice of meditation helps to achieve discriminative knowledge.

I.13 (E16-17; T34-35) Stability is the undisturbed flow of non-fluctuating awareness..

I.14 (E17; T35) If practice (of meditation) becomes confirmed it is not suddenly overpowered by traces from the emergent state.

I.15 (E17-18; T36) Cognitive realization of complete control (*vāśīkāra-saṃjñā*), which is the essential nature of dispassion, is devoid of the sense of receiving or rejecting things. It arises in that awareness which perceives fault in an object with the help of discriminative discernment.

I.16 (E18-19; T37-38) A person whose intellect has become satisfied by the persevering presence of self-vision becomes extremely detached from the *guṇas* whether manifest or non-manifest. This extreme dispassion is nothing but the undisturbed calm of knowledge. Liberation is inseparably connected with it.

I.17 (E19-20; T40) The four kinds of content-filled concentration can be attained with the help of supporting objects *(ālambana)*. Each succeeding meditation is bereft of the preceding one's supporting object.

I.18 (E20; T42) In content-free concentration there remains no functioning of awareness, but only traces. Supreme dispassion is the only means to it. Awareness, while cultivating this concentration, which is devoid of supporting objects, becomes as if it were nonexistent. This is seedless concentration.

I.19 (E21; T43) A variety of seedless concentration is called inclination toward becoming (*bhavapratyaya*); it is found in the disembodied *(videha)* gods who live in a state which their traces have brought about but who experience a liberation-like state. This concentration is also found in those dissolved in *prakṛti (prakṛtilaya)*, who experience a liberation-like state. The awareness of both these two types of *yogins* is liable to rebirth, since it has not fulfilled its tasks.

I.20 (E22-23; T46-47) The concentration of proper *yogins* is called *upāyapratyaya* (it is also a variety of seedless concentration). It has the five varieties mentioned in the *sūtra*.

I.21 (E23; T47) The practices followed by *yogins* are of three kinds–gentle, moderate, and vehement. Each of these may be associated with mild, middling, and intense eagerness.

I.23 (E23; T48) God becomes inclined to a *yogin* for his devotion and favors him. Owing to divine grace he then attains concentration.

I.24 (E24-27; T49-50) That particular *puruṣa* who is uncontaminated by experience, that is, untouched by the traces resulting in the fruition of karma stemming from the afflictions, is called God. He is never involved with the three kinds of bondage, and consequently he is eternally liberated and is always possessed of supremacy. Scripture (*śāstra*) is the proof of the existence of eternal excellence (*utkarṣa*) in God. Both the scripture and supremacy are eternally present in him in whom the *sattvaguṇa* exists in its highest developed form.

I.25 (E27-29; T55-56) The cognitive capacity found in the individual selves it to be known as the seed of omniscience. This seed must reach its utmost excellence in some being, since it admits of degrees. The highest degree of excellence is God's. The special qualities of God are to be known from scripture. Although he has no feeling of self-gratification the motive of his action (i.e. the imparting of divine knowledge) is to be found in his compassion. A similar example is to be found in the first enlightened sage Kapila who, assuming a created mind, declared the doctrine (*tantra*) to the inquiring Āsuri.

I.26 (E29; T39) God with his perfection is present in all past creations.

I.27 (E29-30; T50) The relation of the syllable *oṃ* with God is fixed. Conventional usage (*saṃketa*)reveals this relation, as for example the pre-established relation of father and son is revealed by some verbal statement. Such conventional usage was practiced in previous creations also. Sages hold that the relation between words and their meaning is eternal (*nitya*, i.e. it is always present in some form or other).

I.28 (E30; T61-62) A verse is quoted which says that recitation (i.e. the repetition of sacred syllables) and the practice of yoga help each other. Through a constant practice of these two the supreme self is revealed.

I.30 (E31-32; T63-64) Illness is the (result of the) disorder of bodily constituents, secretions, and organs. Dullness is lack of mental activity. Doubt is knowledge of two contrary properties in one and the same object. Heedlessness is a failure to reflect on the means of achieving concentration. Laziness is disinclination caused by heaviness in body and mind. Worldliness is addiction to sense-objects. Erroneous perception is error. Failure to obtain stability (in a state of concentration) is self-explanatory. Restlessness is the incapability of remaining in an acquired yogic state.

I.31 (E32; T65-66) Frustration, depression, etc. do not appear in concentration.

I.32 (E32-35; T66-70) It is wrong to hold that awareness is momentary and limited to one content only, for had awareness been of this nature it would have been wholly one-pointed and consequently there could arise no distraction. Awareness, however, does become one-pointed if it is withdrawn from its (ordinary)objects and set on a chosen content. One-pointedness cannot be said to be a property of the flow of ideas, since there could be no possibility of any sort of flow if awareness was only momentary. Again, it cannot be held that awareness is made up of different ideas accidentally related, for this view would repudiate the feeling of identity found in one's cognition of oneself. The direct perception of the self-same egoity cannot be denied. Therefore, it is reasonable to conclude that awareness is a single thing, stable (i.e. not momentary), and that it has many intended objects.

I.33 (E35; T71) Cultivation of friendliness, compassion and joy (the *bhāvanās* or sentiments) is termed "purification" (*parikarman*). This brings about pure merit (*śukla dharma)* and makes the *citta* undisturbed and one-pointed.

I.34 (E35; T72) Exhalation must be practiced with a special

effort.

I.35 (E36; T72-77) There are five sense-activities (*pravṛtti*) connected with supernormal (*divya*) smell, taste, color, touch and sound. These activities, by dispelling doubt, make awareness stable. Secondary sense-activities also arise with the sun, the moon, etc. as their objects. Though the true nature of things can be known through scripture, inference, and the instruction of teachers, yet so long as nothing is experienced correctly and directly, knowledge of transcendental things remains indirect and such knowledge is not helpful in producing a firm idea about subtle things. This is why some particular property must be recognized in order to dispel doubt regarding the instructions received from teachers

I.36 (E37; T74) The supernormal power called undistressedness (*viśokā*) is two-fold, namely pertaining to objects and pertaining to ego; both are called "luminous" (*jyotiṣmatī*). In the former the intellect is perceived as resembling objects like the sun, the moon, etc. In the latter, the mind (that is, awareness) becomes engrossed in egoity. Here the realization of the subtle self takes place in the form of "I am".

I.39 (E38; T77) If awareness can achieve stability regarding objects it can become stable elsewhere also.

I.40 (E38-39; T77) The awareness of a *yogin* reaches stability which extends to the state of smallest magnitude and of greatest magnitude. In this highest form of mastery a *yogin* has no need for purification by practice (of meditation).

I.41 (E39-40; T78-79) Things that are to be grasped include the subtle elements, the gross elements (*sthūla*, i.e. the five *(mahābhūtas*), and the gross things made up of the *bhūtas*. The knower includes the *puruṣa*-endowed-with-*buddhi* as well as the liberated selves. Knowing includes the process of sensing or cognizing. When awareness rests on knower, known, and knowing, and becomes tinged by them, it appears to have assumed the forms of knower, known, and knowing, and this state is called engrossment.

I.42 (E40; T80-82) The properties of words, their intended contents, and the ideas associated with them are different. But in empirical (*savitarka*) engrossment objects appear to be permeated or intermixed through the constructing of identity of words, their meanings, and ideas.

I.43 (E41-42; T82-83) In engrossment purified of empirical awareness (*nirvitarka*) an object is known only in its true nature, and this insight is construction-free. The knowledge derived from empirical engrossment does not arise from verbal or inferential knowledge, nor can it be influenced by any other means of knowing, In this engrossment it is the object only which is cognized as a formation of a single mental act. The existence of such an object is proved by its manifest effect. All intercourse is concerned with this whole *(avayavin)* which is to be understood as single, great or small, tangible, and transitory. The view that there are no wholes is untenable, for on that view everything would be reduced to erroneous cognition. There could arise no correct knowledge, owing to the absence of intended objects (all such objects being nothing but wholes having parts). Thus it is reasonable to accept the existence of a whole having properties like size and so forth. It is the whole that is the content of the *nirvitarka* engrossment.

I.44 (E44-45; T89) The contents of *savicāra* engrossment are the subtle elements, which are conditioned by space, time, and causation. In this engrossment the content is cognized as a single unit of a subtle element with manifest properties. The object of the *nirvicāra* engrossment is such as is not characterized by past, present, and future properties. It corresponds or refers to all properties, and it is also the substratum of all properties. The awareness derived from this engrossment is as if free from (knowledge of) its own nature *(svarūpaśūnya iva)*. The intended object of *savitarka* and *savicāra* engrossments involves predication, while that of *nirvitarka* and *nivicāra* engrossments is without predication.

I.45 (E45; T91) The subtle element smell is the intended object corresponding to the earth particle (or atom, *aṇu*).

Similarly, the subtle element of taste corresponds to the watery particle, etc. Again, the subtle contents of these subtle elements are the ego, which as the principle of the "I-sense" and in its subtlety reaches its utmost degree. *Puruṣa*, not being a material cause, has no connection with this subtlety.

I.46 (E45-46; T92) A concentration is termed "seeded" because its supporting object is an actual external thing.

I.47 (E46; T93) When there arises a clear and steady flow of quiescence of the illuminating intellect in *nirvicāra* engrossment, the *yogin* achieves undisturbed peace in the instruments of perception or in the intellect. This peace is nothing but the clear light of knowledge whose content is really existent and which acts without any sequence of time.

I.48 (E46; T94) The insight named "truth-bearing" , which arises in *nirvicāra* engrossment, is bereft of all misconceptions. Insight is acquired with the help of scripture, inference, and constant meditation.

I.49 (E47-48; T94-96) The content of verbal knowledge is general (*sāmānya*), since words are unable to connote particularity. Similarly, inference proves the existence of a thing in general. Though particularity (*viśeṣatva*) residing in subtle elements or in the *puruṣas* cannot be known through verbal knowledge, inference or ordinary perception, it cannot be said that particularity does not exist, for it is known through the insight born of meditation.

I.50 (E48; T96-97) The traces arising from the insight born of meditation inhibit the traces of the emergent state. Meditation comes into existence if ideas are suppressed. From meditation comes insight which gives rise to traces. These traces do not provide awareness with any further task as they destroy the afflictions. The movement of awareness culminates as soon as discernment arises.

I.51 (E49-50; T98) Seedless meditation is antagonistic to both the insight born of meditation and the traces created by that insight. The existence of the traces in a suppressed awareness may be inferred from the duration of time during which the awareness was suppressed. In seedless meditation, awareness merges in its material cause, *prakṛti*, along with all kinds of traces. When awareness ceases to function, the self abides in itself and is called "liberated".

BOOK TWO

II.1 (E51-52; T103) Ascetic exercises are capable of reducing impurity caused by the afflictions and karma. They should, however, be practiced in a moderate manner. Recitation is the reciting of sacred syllables such as *om*. Focusing on God is either the offering of all actions to him or the renunciation of the results of action.

II.2 (E52; T103) The *yoga* of action not only attenuates the afflictions but also makes them powerless like roasted seeds. As a result of this attenuation discriminative discernment becomes dissolved in its cause after finishing its tasks.

II.3 (E52-53; T106) The five afflictions, namely ignorance and so forth, strengthen the activity of the *guṇas*, determine their mixture and bring about the ripening of karma.

II.4 (E53-55; T106-108) The nature of the four stages of the four afflictions named egoity, attachment, hatred and the will to live is as follows. The quiescent state is that in which the afflictions remain in a potential state and are capable of rising again. (There is actually a fifth state, in which the afflictions totally lose their power to rise again, just as a parched seed does not germinate. This state is to be found in those *yogins* who possess perfect knowledge and who are said to be in their final body.) The declining) state is that in which the afflictions are overpowered by cultivation of their opposites. The interrupted state is that in which the afflictions intercept each other frequently, that is, in this state one affliction is interrupted by another for a considerable period. The active state is that in which an affliction has direct relation with its object. All these afflictions are manifested by karmic causes and are countered by the cultivation of contradictory karmic meditations (*pratipakṣabhāvanā*). All of these afflictions are but varieties of ignorance as they rise and decay upon the rise and decay of ignorance.

II.5 (E55-57; T110-112) An example of the apprehension of permanence in what is impermanent is the idea that the earth, etc. are permanent. Similarly, an example of taking there to be purity where there is impurity is the notion of purity in the highly repulsive body. This recognition includes the notion of merit in demerit and the notion of usefulness in uselessness. The taking of pleasure where there is pain is described in YS II.15. The taking of self where there is not self is to be found in external things, in the living organism and in the mind. Ignorance, which is the root of stored-up karma and its fruit, is to be considered as a really existing thing. It is not the absence of knowledge but the opposite of knowledge.

II.6 (E57; T115) The affliction called egoity is the feeling that the *puruṣa* and the *buddhi* (though they are different in nature) are one. So long as this wrong identification exists there arises experience. If these two entities are distinguished liberation takes place.

II.7 (E58; T116) The affliction of attachment is the desire of a person for pleasure or the means to pleasure.

II.8 (E58; T117) The affliction of hatred is anger, wrath or repulsion of a person toward frustration or the means to frustration.

II.9 (E58-59; T117-118) On account of the instinct of self-preservation in the form of "may I not cease to live and may I live (on)" as found in all sentient beings, the existence of previous births is proved. The fear of extinction is the affliction called the will to live, which is spontaneously felt by the stupid as well as the wise who have understanding of the prior limits of lives.

II.10 (E59; T119) These five afflictions must be overcome. They become inactive like burnt seed and then disappear with the disappearance of awareness that has fulfilled its functions.

II.11 (E60; T120) The gross fluctuations of the afflictions, being attenuated through the practice of the *yoga* of action, become capable of being eschewed with the help of the ultimate reflection (*prasaṃkhyāna*), an awareness nearly the same as discriminative discernment.

II.12 (E60-61; T121) Stored-up karma possessing merit or demerit has its source in greed, delusion, or anger. The meritorious type bears fruit quickly if actions are performed with intense auditory recitation, austerity, concentration and so forth directed toward God and the gods. The demeritorious kind bears fruit early if vicious actions are performed repeatedly against frightened, diseased or pitiable persons or to those who are noble-minded and the like.

II.13 (E61-65; T122-126) So long as there are afflictions, the stored-up karma will produce its results. One act cannot reasonably be held to be the cause of one birth, for in that case there would be uncertainty or irregularity of the succession of results of innumerable actions. Likewise one act cannot be the cause of many births, for in that case there would be no time for the fruition of the remaining karma. Many acts cannot be the cause of many births, for they do not happen simultaneously. Therefore it is reasonable to conclude that many acts (i.e. a diverse accumulation of stored-up karma) remaining variously in predominant and subordinate states become manifested at the time of death and thereby cause a single birth. Stored-up karma (having birth, length of life and quality of experience as its three kinds of results) is mainly accumulated in one birth only. The stored-up karma which is operative in a given life brings about either the kinds of things experienced or both experience and length of life. Those traces that cause memory only are called subconscious impressions. Stored-up karma sometimes does not produce all its results, i.e. is of uncertain maturation. The sort of stored-up karma whose maturation is uncertain and is not to be seen in the present life has three kinds of outcome: (1) it may be destroyed through proper means; (2) it may be mixed up with a dominant stored-up karma; or (3) it may remain in a dormant state for a long time, being overshadowed by some dominant stored-up karma.

As the time, place, and cause of the manifestation of the results of karma are indeterminate, the course of karma is not easily discernible.

II.14 (E66; T131) *Yogins* experience frustration even when they are experiencing pleasurable objects.

II.15 (E66-70; T132-135) The frustration of change (*pariṇāma*) is that which is experienced as a result of the functioning of stored-up karma caused by attachment, aversion, etc. Pleasure, which arises when the senses become satisfied owing to the gratification of thirst for objects, is also a source of frustration, for enjoyment increases attachment. The frustration of suffering is the result of that stored-up karma which is chiefly associated with aversion. Being incited by aversion one behaves with others in a favorable or unfavorable way. The frustrations of traces are the traces' arising respectively from pleasurable and frustrating experiences. The beginningless flow of frustration causes distress to *yogins*. Observing the eternal flow of misery a *yogin* takes refuge in knowledge. Since change is the nature of all modifications of the *guṇas*, awareness changes every moment. It has various forms and fluctuations which are constantly reacting on one another. This is the reason for the frustrating character of ordinary life. Ignorance is the source of all frustration, and knowledge is the cause of the disappearance of ignorance. This science (of Yoga) has four divisions dealing with mundane existence, the cause of this existence, release, and the means to release.

II.16 (E70; T139) It is only future frustration that hinders *yogins*. Present and past frustrations cannot be forsaken after they have been experienced.

II.17 (E71-72; T140-141) The seen, which is defined here as the properties deposited on the *buddhisattva* (i.e. on awareness), is the property of the *puruṣa*, which is the seer. As the seen serves the purpose of another entity (the self) it is not independent. The beginningless correlation between the seer and the seen, which is effected for a purpose (either experience or liberation), is the cause of frustration which can be escaped if the cause of this correlation is avoided.

II.18 (E72-75; T144-145) The seen (as defined under II.17) has the nature of the three *guṇas*, namely *sattva, rajas* and *tamas.* These *guṇas* have the nature of influencing one another and though they are mutually dependent their properties are not mixed up. They produce effects according to their relative predominance. They act by proximity to the self as a magnet draws iron. The activity of the seen is not without an impelling force (*prayojana*). It exists for the sake of experience (i.e. the result of identifying the knower with the knowable) and for the sake of liberation (*apavarga*), the ascertainment of the nature of the immutable enjoyer. Agency lies in the three *guṇas* while the self is the witness of their activity. Both experience and liberation, bondage and release, lie in the intellect (that is, in awareness, but they are wrongly attributed to the self. Likewise the functions of the intellect, namely the processes of cognizing, attending, and so forth, are erroneously assumed to exist in the *puruṣa*-principle.

II.19 (E75-78; T148-150) The five gross objects, the five sense-organs, the five organs of action and the internal organ fall under the category of gross elements (*viśeṣa*). The five *tanmātras* and the ego-principle are called subtle elements (*aviśeṣa)*. They are the sources of the gross elements. The subtle elements are the modifications of the intellect and eventually become dissolved in their material cause, the unmanifest *prakṛti*. This unmanifest state is uncaused, which is why it is called "eternal". All the other three gross elements have the aims of life (*puruṣārtha*, namely experience and liberation) as their (efficient) cause. The *guṇas* neither disappear altogether nor are they born. All effects, after remaining in their respective material causes, become differentiated and consequently assume manifested form. The gross elements are not transformed into any emergent principles, but they have mutations in the form of characteristic form (*dharma*), temporal variation (*lakṣaṇa*), and condition (*avasthā*) (cf. YS III.13).

II.20 (E78-80; T154-155) The seer, the reflector of the intellect, is nothing but the power of seeing untouched by any qualifications. He is not similar to the intellect, since the latter is mutative, composed of the three *gunaṣ*, and acts in cooperation with its parts for others. *Puruṣa*, the seer, on the other hand is immutable, is the witness of the activities of the *guṇas*, and exists for its own sake. *Puruṣa* is however not entirely similar to the intellect, since it oversees the ideas formed in the intellect and consequently (falsely) appears to be identical with those ideas.

II.21 (E80; T157) Since the seen is nothing but an entity that is enjoyable by the *puruṣa*, it is said to exist for the benefit of the self. When the seen achieves experience and liberation fully, it is no longer seen by the self and consequently it attains cessation though it is not destroyed utterly (i.e., it exists in an unmanifested form.

II.22 (E80; T159) The correlation of seer (*puruṣa*) and the power of seeing (*darśanaśakti*, i.e. awareness or intellect) is beginningless and consequently the connection of *puruṣa* with the *mahat*-principle and the other evolutes has no beginning.

II.23 (E81-84; T160-162) Contact between the self, the proprietor, and the seen, the property, is the cause of both experience and liberation. It is knowledge which is the cause of their disunion (*viyoga*). Similarly, non-discrimination (*adarśana*) is the cause of the contact. Absence of bondage (i.e. release) comes as the result of the disappearance of non-discrimination.

II.24 (E84-86; T166) It is subconscious impressions of ignorance which are the cause of the said contact. So long as the intellect remains colored by erroneous thinking it becomes unable to achieve knowledge of the self. When the intellect achieves this knowledge and its functions become fulfilled it does not appear again as there remains no cause of bondage. The cessation of intellect is called liberation (*mokṣa*). Non-discrimination is removed by correct knowledge, i.e. discriminative discernment.

II.25 (E86; T168) Once liberation is achieved there arises no contact with the *guṇas* in the future. In the state of escape (*hāna,* i.e. liberation) the self remains grounded in its own self.

II.26 (E86; T169) Discriminative discernment consists in realizing the difference between *sattva* (*citta*) and *puruṣa*. When erroneous cognition ceases to be productive this discernment becomes clear, as a result of which, erroneous thinking being powerless, fails to act. This is the way to liberation.

II.27 (E87-88; T170-171) A *yogin* possessing discriminative discernment acquires insight which has seven phases. The first four phases, those to be achieved through effort or practice, are respectively concerned with the avoidable (*heya*), the causes of the avoidable (*heyahetu*), escape (*hāna*)through concentration based on the cessation of fluctuations, and the means to that escape (*hānopāya*). The last three are known as *cittavimukti*. In the fifth phase it is realized that the intellect (i.e. awareness) has fulfilled its task. In the sixth the conviction arises that the *guṇas*, getting merged into their cause, will not rise again. In the seventh the real nature of *puruṣa* is revealed. These seven phases of insight can be experienced even in this lifetime by a *yogin* who is proficient (*kuśala*, i.e. a *jīvanmukta*).

II.28 (E88-90; T172-174) The impurity to be eradicated by the practice of the aids to meditation (*yogāṅga*) is ignorance, etc. that is, the afflictions. The following up of the aids is the cause of separation from impurity.

II.30 (E91-92; T178-179) Nonviolence is absolute abstinence from malice. Truth-telling (i.e. abstinence from lying) is the correspondence of speech and thought to fact. A true sentence must not delude others or create a wrong notion in others or appear meaningless to its hearer. Non-theft means abstention from taking things illegally that belong to others. Celibacy is the control of the organ of generation by a person who is the master of his senses. Non-avarice is to desist from taking things with the observation that their acquisition, etc. breeds frustration.

II.32 (E93; T181-182) Purification is either external (by

using external things) or internal (i.e. removal of the impurities of awareness). Contentment is the absence of desire for more than immediate necessities. Ascetic exercise is the ability to bear extremes. Vow is included in it. Study/recitation is either the reading of authoritative texts on liberation or the repeating of *oṃ*. Focusing on God is offering up all actions to him.

II.33 (E94; T183) Counteracting meditation comes about by practice of these five.

II.38 (E96; T187) A *yogin* grounded in celibacy becomes able to transfer his thoughts to his disciples.

II.40 (E96-97; T188) One who practices cleanliness becomes able to perceive faults in the body.

II.41 (E97; T188) The purification of *sattva* and so forth, mentioned in the *sūtra*, are ordered as cause and effect–the preceding item being the cause of the following quality.

II.43 (E97; T190) Extraordinary capacity of the body is explained as the supernormal powers of atomization (*aṇiman*) and so forth (cf. YS III.45), and extraordinary capacity of the senses means powers like clairvoyance, clairaudience, etc.

II.44 (E97; T190) *Iṣṭadevatās* include deities, sages, and perfected beings (*siddhas*).

II.45 (E98; T190) Attainment of concentration is said to bring about knowledge of things that happen even in another life, place or time.

II.46-48 (E98-99; T191-192) The author mentioned some of the most important postures. Relaxation of effort is said to be the cause of the non-shaking of the limbs. Heat and cold is an example of a pair of opposites; it is subdued by the practice of postures.

II.49-50 (E99-100; T193-194) Inhalation is defined as the drawing of external air, exhalation as the expelling of the abdominal air. The external and internal operations of breath control are defined respectively as suspension of movement (holding) after exhalation and after inhalation. The suppressed operation is effected by one effort without paying any notice to the previously-mentioned two operations. Breath-control observed according to number constitutes what is called "stroke" (*udghāta*), which is either mild, moderate, or acute.

II.51-53 (E100-102; T195-197) The fourth breath-control consists in a suspension of movement that arises gradually as a result of acquiring mastery of stage after stage in succession by observing the objects of the first two operations of breath-control. It should be noted that in the third aspect of breath-control (of suppressed operation) which is also a kind of suspension of movement there is no regard to these objects.

II.54-55 (E102-105; T197-199) Since suppression of the organs necessarily follows suppression of awareness, there is no need for applying other means to suppress the organs. Some definitions of "withdrawal" offered by the ancient teachers have been quoted here.

BOOK THREE

III.1 (E104-105; T203) The *Bhāṣya* mentions some of the bodily places (the navel, the heart, etc.) on which awareness is to be focused, and remarks that awareness is bound to external objects through its fluctuations alone.

III.2 (E105; T204) The even flow of ideas is explained as the flow that is similar to previous thought and not interrupted by another idea.

III.3 (E105; T204-205) Reflective meditation appears as if it were devoid of its own form owing to its having been colored by the nature of the supporting object of that meditation.

III.4 (E106; T205) The author says that "*saṃyama*" (comprehensive reflection) is a technical term of yogic tradition.

III.5 (E106; T206) As comprehensive reflection gets established so does insight born of concentration become developed.

III.6 (E106-107; T206) It is not possible to master the higher stages of comprehensive reflection without possessing mastery over the lower stages. If, owing to divine grace, one attains higher stages, one has no need to practice comprehensive reflection on lower stages. It is through *yoga* that one becomes aware of the superiority and inferiority of the stages.

III.7-8 (E107; T207-209) Seedless concentration arises when there is absence of the last three aids.

III.9 (E108; T208-209) Since the traces of the emergent state are attributes of awareness, and since they are not experienced, they cannot be suppressed by suppressing ideas. The momentary change of traces in one and the same awareness is to be understood as *nirodhapariṇāma*, that is, awareness when it is becoming suppressed.

III.10 (E109; T210-211) "Traces" in this *sūtra* means the traces of the suppressed state. These traces of suppression may be overcome by the traces of the emergent state.

III.11 (E109; T211) Awareness possesses two attributes called "all-pointedness" (*sarvārthatā*) and "one-pointedness" (*ekāgratā*). When these attributes (which are not different from the awareness itself) possess the character of decaying and arising respectively, then the awareness becomes concentration.

III.12 (E199; T211-212) The evolving of the one-pointed sort remains until concentration is disturbed.

III.13 (E110-116; T212-217) An example of change in characteristic is the becoming invisible of emergence and the becoming visible of suppression in a substance, or vice-versa. Examples of change in temporal mode are the states of past, present, and future of suppression or of emergence. Examples of change in overall condition are the firmness and infirmity of traces. A substance changes through its properties, which mutate through temporal modes and these in turn mutate through states. No substance can exist being bereft of these three kinds of transformations or changes even for a moment. The ever-changing nature of the *guṇas* is the cause of their activity. In reality, the change in properties is the major change, and the other two are connected with it. While properties change, the property-possessor remains unchanged. The relation between properties and their possessor is not one of absolute identity nor one of absolute difference. Yoga holds the relation to be "the non-acceptance of either of these two (alternatives)". In fact this whole universe loses its manifested state but remains in a subtle one (in its material cause). On account of this subtlety the universe is not perceived. A present thing is not untouched by its past and future states. The same reasoning is to be applied with respect to a past or a future thing. It cannot be urged that if a thing is extant in the three times there would arise the fault of confusion of times (*adhva-saṃkara)*, for each time-variation does not appear simultaneously, but gradually. A property-possessor is changed through its properties, which again are changed through temporal variation. The properties are either noticed (they are manifested) or unnoticed (they are in the past or future state). An earthen thing may be new or old but while undergoing change of state the thing does not lost its earthen character. It is wrong to say that a thing will be absolutely permanent if the view of the evolving of temporal variation is accepted, for though the *guṇa*-possessor persists yet the *guṇa*s change constantly. A cause is more permanent with reference to its effect; for example, the *tanmātras* are indestructible with reference to their effects, the elements; the essential core *(liṅga)*, which is indestructible with reference to its effects, is destructible with reference to its causes, the *guṇas*. In essence all the three kinds of change are nothing but change of state. These changes do not transcend the property-possessor (*dharma-dharmin*) relation. Change is the rise of a property after the cessation of (another) property in a (relatively) permanent substance.

III.14 (E116-118; T224-226) A property of a property-possessor is its "power" (*śakti*) as characterized by its capability (*yogyatā*). The existence of properties is proved by the difference in the production of effects. The present (i.e. manifested, uprisen) property is different from past and future properties on account of its peculiar function. A property is either peaceful, having gone away after performing its function, uprisen or functioning, or indeterminate (*avyapadeśya*) because it is incapable of being described or determined through belonging to a future time. A present property is immediate or next in succession to a coming property. Though everything may be regarded as identical with everything (i.e. every thing may produce everything) owing to the non-destructible character of universal properties (*jāti*), there is no possibility of simultaneous manifestation. Each entity requires a particular place, time, form, and cause for its origination. That which constantly follows the manifested and the unmanifested properties is a property-possessor, which is in reality an assemblage of generic and specific properties. Those who hold that there are only properties but no persisting element cannot explain the phenomenon of experience and of recollection. Moreover the existence of a persisting substance is proved by the recognition of objects. Thus it is wrong to hold that the thing is an attribute only without a persisting substance.

III.15 (E118-120; T229-230) The rise of properties in succession is called a sequence (*krama*). (In the *Bhāṣya* the property itself is called "*krama*" figuratively.) A sequence exists among the three changes (as stated in III.13). It is the present and the future that have sequence but there is no such sequence with relation to the past, for immediacy presupposes the relation of antecedent and consequent which is wanting in the past. The sequence in change of properties and temporal change is clear. Regarding the sequence in the changes of state it should be noted that oldness as found in a jar is the result of the sequence of changes that take place momentarily. Sequences are perceived if there is a distinction between the substance and its properties. When this distinction ceases from the transcendental standpoint then the substance goes by the names of its properties. An awareness has two kinds of property: perceptible (the fluctuations that are known) and imperceptible (those capable of being inferred). The latter attributes are seven in number, namely the suppressed state, merit, traces, change, life, movement and power.

III.17 (E121-127; T233-236) The organ of speech utters syllables only; the ear can hear only those syllables which are caused by resonance *(dhvani)*. A word is grasped by the intellect, which follows the syllables and gather them by retaining the memory of the syllables. The syllables (in a word) are not uttered in one and the same moment and they are non-interdependent in nature. They, without presenting a word, appear and disappear and as such they cannot be regarded as forming a word. A syllable having the essence of word is said to be filled with the power to furnish expressions for everything. It, coming into juxtaposition with other syllables, assumes a particular form. Thus a group of syllables with a particular order becomes able to convey a meaning, being regulated or limited by a convention. For example, the three syllables (represented by the the English letters) "c", "o" and "w", being arranged in that order, convey the idea of a cow. One intellectual presentation of the grasped order of sounds, which are regulated in some sense, is a denotative word. The word which is the content of a single mental process is brought up by one effort (of the mind). It is devoid of sequence and parts. It is brought into its function by means of the idea of the final syllable. If a man wants to convey information to another he must use those words which according to the sanction of usage or common understanding are thought to be something real. In accordance with conventional usage a word, though partless, can be analyzed. For example, the summation of the syllables (represented by) "c","o" and "w" is a word which has some object to signify. Convention *(saṃketa)* is essentially handed down by memory and in essence it is the erroneous identification of the word with the thing signified by it. Thus the word, the thing signified, and the idea become confused on account of the erroneous identification of each with the other. A person who knows the distinction of these three knows all the meanings of words uttered by all creatures. Every word has the power to express a sentence. Even the single word "tree" must be taken as meaning "a tree is", since existence cannot be detached from any entity. Similarly, there can be no action without the means (the *kārakas* or cases, namely the agent (*kartṛ*), *karman*, and so forth). This is why the word "*pacati*" (meaning the present action of cooking by somebody) must presuppose the existence of all relevant *kārakas*. Sometimes one single word is used to signify the sense of a whole sentence, as for example the single word "*śrotriya*" means a person who studies the Vedas. Since a word may signify the sense of a sentence it is necessary to analyze words into the stem and suffixes. Otherwise there may arise confusion regarding the intended meaning of words. It is to be noticed that the meaning (*artha*) of a word has its own status. It is not invariably united either with the word or with the idea, for a change in one does not necessarily lead to a change in the other two. Thus it follows that a word, its meaning, and the idea it produces are different in nature. A *yogin* practicing comprehensive reflection on the distinction of these three acquires knowledge of the manner in which creatures communicate.

III.18 (E127-128; T247-248) Traces are either the causes of memory and afflictions as subconscious impressions, or are the causes of the three changes or transformations at the time of rebirth in terms of birth, length of life and experience due to merit or demerit. These traces are the unseen properties of awareness, but their presence can be intuited by a highly competent *yogin*. One's own previous births and the previous births of others are known in this way.

III.21 (E128; T250) Likewise the sounds and other properties belonging to the *yogin*'s body may become invisible.

III.22 (E129-130; T251) Karma (whose result is the length of life) of the *sopakrama* type is that which bears fruit quickly, and of the *nirupakrama* type is that which bears fruit only after a long time.

III.23 (E130; T252) The *sūtra* is explained in the light of YS I.33, and it is remarked that since detachment (*upekṣā*) from evil persons does not fall under the sentiments (*bhāvanā*), it being positive in character, power or strength (*ala*) cannot be acquired through comprehensive reflection on detachment.

III.25 (E151; T253) The light of activity (*pravṛttyāloka*) is the same as the "brilliantly clear" mentioned in YS I.36.

III.26 (E131-134; T254-257) The universe consists of seven regions (*loka*). The physical world (*bhūr loka*) extends from the lowest hell (*avīci*) to the summit of (Mount) Meru; the astral world (*antarikṣa*) extends from the top of Meru to the Pole Star; the heavenly world (*svarga loka*) is the region of Mahendra; the *mahar loka* is the region of Prajāpati; the *jana, tapas,* and *satya lokas* are the regions of Brahmā. The physical world comprises the six hells (*naraka*), and the seven underworlds (*pātālas*) as well as the earth, which is divided into seven islands (*dvīpa*), namely Jambū and so forth, surrounded by seven oceans. In the center of the earth is situated Mt. Meru, which is surrounded in the four directions by the countries named Bhadrāśva and so forth. It is the pleasure-ground of the gods. This whole structure has an egg-like form and is to be regarded as a minute fragment of *prakṛti*. The earth is inhabited by Asuras, Gandharvas, and others. In the astral world the planets and so forth are tied to the Pole Star. Six kinds of divinities (*deva*) reside in the third region, called "Mahendra". In the fourth region, called "Mahat", there are five kinds of divinities. In the last three mentioned regions there reside particular kinds of divinities possessing supernormal powers in varying degrees. The Videhas and Prakṛtilayas do not reside in any region but in the *mokṣapada*, a state nearly the same as liberation.

III.30-31 (E135; T260-261) The "*kaṇṭhakūpa*" is located below the throat, and the tortoise-vein is in the chest.

III.32 (E135; T261) *Siddhas* are those who frequent the space between the earth and the sky.

III.33 (E136; T261) Intuition is said to be the deliverer (*tāraka*) knowledge, a preliminary form of discriminative discernment.

III.34 (E136; T262) The seat of consciousness is said to be of the form of a tiny lotus in the *brahmapura* or "city of

Brahman".

III.35 (E137-138; T265) These powers (mentioned in the *sūtra*) arise even without any desire to acquire them as a result of comprehensive reflection on an object which exists for its own sake.

III.36 (E136-137; T262-263) Awareness dominated by *sattva* realizes the distinction between the intellect and *puruṣa* when it becomes able to subdue *rajas* and *tamas*. *Puruṣa*, who is nothing but immutable awareness, is absolutely different from the intellect. Experience is the awareness of these two principles as non-distinct; it is ascribed to *puruṣa* though it belongs to the intellect. As it is seen, so it must be regarded as existing for the sake of another. It is wrong to suppose that the intellect actually perceives *puruṣa*; on the contrary, it is *puruṣa* who sees the intellect, which depends on the image of the self as entered into it.

III.37 (E138; T265-266) It is argued that since intuition and so forth (III.36) stand in the way of realizing *puruṣa* they are to be known as obstacles to concentration.

III.39 (E139; T267) Life (*jīvana*) (more precisely, the effort of maintaining life) consists in the functioning of the whole complex of organs and is characterized by the five breaths (*prāṇa*). The function of breath extends as far as the heart; of the middling breath (*samāna*) as far as the navel; of eliminating (*apāna*) as far as the foot; of the arising (*udāna*) as far as the head; of breathing generally (*vyāna*) to the whole body.

III.40 (E139; T268) The radiance in the body is said to be caused by the pulsation of *tejas*.

III.41 OE140-141; T268-269) *Ākāśa* is the basis of ears and sounds. The quality of being the locus of sound and of unveiling (*anāvaraṇa*) are characteristic marks of *ākāśa*, which is said to be all-pervading (*vibhu*) on account of its being not limited in extent.

III.42 (E141; T271) Because *ākāśa* pervades the space occupied by a body, the body is invariably associated with *ākāśa*. A *yogin* performing comprehensive reflection on this relation and acquiring engrossment with the atoms can render his body light and thereby becomes able to walk on water and so forth.

III.43 (E141-142; T272) The meditative fixation called disembodied (*videha*) is a fluctuation of awareness held outside the body. This is called constructed (*kalpita*) if the *manas* abides in the body; it is called unconstructed if the fluctuation remains independent of the body. The former is the means to the latter (also called *mahāvideha*) through which *yogins* have the experience of entering other bodies. The afflictions and karma, with their threefold result, are said to be the covering of brightness of the intellect's *sattva*, whose essence is nothing but illumination.

III.44 (E142-145; T273-274) The gross aspects of the elements are the particular types of sound, touch, color, taste and smell residing in earth, water, fire, air, and *ākāśa* characterized by various forms and other properties. The essential aspects of the elements are the five generic forms (*svasāmānya*), namely hardness of earth, liquidity of water, heat of fire, mobility or air, and going everywhere of *ākāśa*. Sound and so forth are said to be the particularities (*viśeṣa*) of a generic form (*sāmānya*). A substance (*dravya*) is an aggregate (*samudaya*) of general and particular properties. A collection of aggregates (*samūha*) either consists of the component parts, the differentiation between which has disappeared, or it consists of parts whose separateness is indicated by words. An aggregated entity may be intentionally considered either as identical or as different from its component parts. Again, an aggregate is said to possess its parts either separately (*yutasiddha*) or inseparably. According to Patañjali the latter is called a substance. The subtle forms of the elements are the *tanmātras* whose modification is the atom and which consists of general and particular properties. The positive concomitant form of the elements is the state of the *guṇas* following the nature of the effects. The purposeful form of the elements is their possessing the *guṇas* as the means of experiencing and gaining liberation.

By practicing comprehensive reflection on these five forms of the elements a *yogin* masters the elements.

III.45 (E145-146; T278-279) Atomization (*aṇiman*) is that power by which the body can be reduced to the minutest form. Lightness of weight (*laghiman*) is that power through which one becomes weightless. Magnification (*mahiman*) is that power by which one becomes magnified. Acquisition (*prāpti)*) is the power of extending the body or its limbs to a distant thing. Irresistibility (*prākāmya*) is the power that makes the will irresistible. Control (*vaśītva*)is the power that enables one to put the elements and their products under one's control. Lordship (*īśitva*) is the power by which one gains sovereignty over the origination and so forth of the elements. *Yatrakāmāvasāyatva* is the power of wish fulfilment.

III.47 (E146-147; T280-281) The activity of the sense-organs toward a perceivable object is called sense-cognition (*grahaṇa*) As the senses receive both the general and particular properties, the mind can determine both these properties. The essential aspect of the senses is a kind of substance, which is a particular aspect of the illuminating intellect's *sattva*. The ego aspect of the senses is the *ahaṃkāra*. The fourth aspect of the organs consists in possessing the *guṇas* in their receptive (*vyavasāyātmaka*) form. The fifth aspect of the organs is containing the *guṇas* which act for the *puruṣa*.

III.48 (E147; T282) The three capacities mentioned in the *sūtra* are called *madhupratīka*.

III.50 (E148-149; T284-285) When a *yogin* realizes that discriminative discernment is an attribute of the intellect's *sattva* and as such forsakable, and that *puruṣa* is immutable, pure, and different from the intellect, then the seeds of the afflictions become unproductive and finally disappear with the disappearance of the mind. Thus *puruṣa* ceases to experience the three kinds of anxiety. The absolute dispassion of *puruṣa* from the intellect takes place when afflictions, actions, and the results of actions have fulfilled their purpose. In liberation the immutable consciousness, that is, *puruṣa*, remains grounded in itself.

51 (E149-150; T285-286) *Yogins* are of four kinds. A *prathamakalpika* is that *yogin* in whom insight has just dawned. A *madhubhūmika* is that *yogin* who has achieved the insight named "truth-bearing" (*ṛtambharā*). A *prajñājyoti* is that *yogin* who has mastery over the elements and the senses. An *atikrāntabhāvanīya* is that *yogin* who has only the task of dissolving his awareness into its cause and is possessed of sevenfold insight (cf. II.27). A *yogin* who has achieved the second stage above (i.e. *madhubhūmika*) is invited by the gods to enjoy various kinds of pleasurable tings, namely nymphs and the like. A *yogin* is advised not to attach himself to these things but to ponder the frustrating nature of mundane existence and to take resort to *yoga*. He is also advised not to take pride so that he may not be deluded by heedlessness.

III.52 (E150-151; T287-288) As an atom is a substance possessing minimal limit, so a moment (*kṣaṇa*) is the minimal limit of time. The continuous flow of moments is called sequence (*krama*). As there is no real summation of moments and their sequences, so the periods (day, night, and so on) are to be regarded as mental summation (*buddhisamāhāra*). That is, they have no gross, objective reality. To an ordinary person time appears as if it were a substance, though in reality it is a construction based on verbal awareness (*śabdajñānānupatti*). A moment is a real thing and it rests upon sequences. Sequence, consisting in the uninterrupted succession of moments, is, according to the *yogin*, the essential nature of time. Present time is a single moment and in that single moment the whole universe passes through a change.

III.53 (E152-153; T290-291) The space correlated to one moment is different from the space correlated with another moment. Two exactly similar things placed in the same place in two successive moments can be known distinctly with the help of discrimination, for these two things have experienced different momentary changes with reference to the same place. Since properties like shape etc. are enough to distinguish one thing from another, there is no need to accept individuators as the Vaiśeṣika does. The change in each moment is capable of being known by *yogins* only.

III.54 (E154; T294) Discriminative knowledge is called the "deliverer" (*tāraka*). It comes from one's inborn faculty without any instruction from others. It is without any sequence. Yoga with-an-intended-object (here called *yogapradīpa*) is a part of this knowledge and it extends from the *madhubhūmika* stage to the sevenfold insight (cf. II.27).

III.55 (E154-155; T295-296) The purity of (a) *puruṣa* is the absence of experience which is wrongly ascribed to him. When the intellect realizes discriminative knowledge and becomes devoid of afflictions, then it gains purity. In this state a person, whether he achieves supernormal powers or not, attains liberation. As a matter of fact, correct knowledge is the cause of the absence of the afflictions, as a result of which there arises no karmic fruition. In this state the *guṇas* fulfill their tasks and consequently they cease to exist as seen. This is what is known as the state of liberation (lit., of "isolation") (*kaivalya*).

BOOK FOUR

IV.1 (E156; T299) An extraordinary capacity produced from birth is that which arises at the time of rebirth. Extraordinary capacity through herbs and alchemy is found in the abode of the Asuras. Flying in the sky is an example of extraordinary capacity through spells. And through ascetic practices one acquires fulfillment of his wishes (*saṃkalpasiddhi*). Extraordinary capacities deriving from concentration have already been described in the preceding section.

IV.2 (E157; T300) The evolving of a body or an organ into a different species is due to the impenetration (*anupraveśa*) of the new constituent parts. Through this process the material causes (*prakṛti*) of the body and the organs assume their own modifications depending upon efficient causes like merit, etc.

IV.3 (E157-158; T301-302) Efficient causes such as merit and so forth do not account for the material causes of the body and the organs. Merit simply destroys the obstructing factor, namely demerit. The obstruction being destroyed, the material causes fill up their own modifications. Merit is the cause of the cessation of demerit and vice-versa; it does not give rise to the activities of the material causes of the body and organs.

IV.6 (E159; T304) Awareness perfected through concentration is untouched by virtue and vice owing to the decay of the afflictions.

IV.7 (E159-160; T305) Karma is of four kinds: (1) black, the works of the wicked; (2) black-white, that performed through external means and that hurt or benefit others; (3) white, those mental works that do not hurt others, that are free from external means and are performed by persons cultivating austerities and performing recitations; (4) neither white nor black, performed by *sannyāsins* who have reduced their afflictions and are not going to be born again. This last kind of karma is called neither black nor white owing to its being characterized by renunciation of results and dispassion as well,

IV.9 (E161; T307-308) The fruition of karma being manifested by some appropriate cause of manifestation takes place in spite of the interval of birth, distance and time (between the original action and its fruition) on account of the affinity between (the) memory (of the initial agent's action) and (the) traces (in the later agent's mind). Moreover, it is (for example) a (previous) cat's karma that is the cause of rebirth as a cat, for instance, and the traces caused by the (first) cat's experiences correspond to the (later cat's) subconscious impressions. Memories arise from traces and traces again produce memories. The traces conveyed by memory are brought into play (in the later cat) by stored-up karma. Since there is no break in the relation between cause (here, stored-up karma) and effect (here, the traces), there is similarity in the members of the causal stream even though they may be separated by birth, distance and time.

IV.10 (E161-164; T307-310) The desire to live is natural, for the fear of death which is caused by the memory of pain is found in all creatures at birth. Awareness is commingled with eternal subconscious impressions and it exists for the experience of the seer. Some are of the opinion that awareness is shaped by the dimension of the body in which it resides and it has a contracting and expanding nature. Yoga holds to the contrary that awareness is all-pervading and that its fluctuations are contractive and expansive in nature.

IV.11 (E164-165; T314) Subconscious impressions are held together by the following four factors: (1) cause, exhibited by the six-spoked wheel of mundane existence originating from ignorance--the wheel shows the origination of attachment to and aversion from pleasure and pain respectively, and the origination of pleasure and pain from merit and demerit; (2) result is that object with reference to which merit and so forth becomes operative; (3) locus is the awareness' possessing the power of functioning; (4) supporting object is the stimulus by which subconscious impressions become manifested. In the absence of these four factors, impressions cease, since they are invariably associated with these four factors.

IV.12 (E165-166; T315-316) A future entity is one which will appear later. A past entity is that whose manifestation has been experienced. A present entity is that which exists with its own functions. Since there is knowledge of past and future things and since knowledge has invariably its own objects, past and future things must be accepted as present in their own forms (i.e. they exist in subtle forms in their respective material causes). An object has many properties, which exist in different periods of time. At the time of appearance of one aspect of a substance the other two (past and future) remain in a dormant state.

IV.13 (E166; T317) The properties of a substance belong to the three phases of time. The present state is that which is manifested. In the past and future states properties remain in the form of non-particulars. All things are but special collocations of the three *guṇas* and their essence is nothing but the *guṇas*.

IV.14 (E167-168; T318-319) The three *guṇas*, whose natures are respectively illumination (*prakāśa*), change (*kriyā*) and stability (*sthiti*), have a modification of the nature of grasping (*grahaṇa*), namely the capacity of the organ, for example, the hearing of the ear. Likewise, they have another modification of the nature of the object cognized (what is grasped, *grāhya*), for example, sound. These subtle sounds, touch and so forth give rise to the elements which in turn produce gross substances, namely earth, water, cow, tree, and so forth. Some do not accept the reality of objects on the ground that no object can be conceived without its cognition, while cognition can exist without having any corresponding object, as we find in a dream state. Such a view is untenable as the objects appear to us by virtue of their existence.

IV.15 (E169-170; T323-324) Each thing is to be regarded as existing in general, since it is the supporting object of many awarenesses. It is not constructed by either one or many awarenesses. It is grounded in itself. According to the influence of merit, demerit, ignorance and knowledge, one and the same object causes different feelings, namely pleasure, pain, stupor and detachment. A content is of the nature of what is known while its cognition is of the nature of knowing. According to Sāṃkhya, an object is nothing but a particular collection of the three *guṇas*, which possess the nature of perpetual change.

IV.16 (E170-171; T325) According to some, a thing, being a content of experience, is dependent on its perception, existing at the present time only. This view is untenable, for if a thing were to depend for its existence on being known it would not exist when awareness becomes inattentive or suppressed. There would then be no reason for the reappearance of that thing later. Moreover, if a thing is said to come into being with its perception the thing will have no unknown parts. Therefore, it is reasonable to hold that a thing is grounded in itself. It is common to all, and it is cognized when it becomes connected with awareness.

IV.17 (E171; T327) As a magnet attracts iron, so objects attract or affect awareness. An object becomes known when it is connected with awareness. The evolving nature of awareness is proved on account of the knowability and unknowability of things.

IV.18 (E172; T328) Had the lord of awareness (*puruṣa*) suffered change, the fluctuations of awareness would have been known and unknown (as objects are sometimes known and sometimes not known). Since awareness is constantly known, it is established that the lord of awareness is unchanging.

IV.19 (E172-173; T328-329) It cannot be held that awareness is self-illuminating (*svabhāsa*). As it is an organ it must be regarded as a seen thing. Had it been self-illuminating it would not have been known. It is a fact that a person experiences his feelings, a fact which could not have happened had awareness not been known.

IV.20 (E173-174; T330) According to upholders of the doctrine of universal momentariness, the result, the action, and the agent are identical.

IV.21 (E174; T331) As a result of the confusion of memories (that follows from that doctrine's acceptance) there would be non-ascertainment of any single act of memory. The Vaināśikas have confused everything by not accepting the existence of a *puruṣa* that reflects *buddhi*. The Sāṃkhya-Yoga school speaks of the existence of *puruṣa*, the lord, as the experiencer of awarenesses.

IV.23 (E176; T334) Awareness (here, *manas*) becomes colored by the thing thought of and is also connected with *puruṣa*, the subject (*viṣayin*). Though insentient, awareness seems to be sentient and it looks like both the subject and the object. This is why the inanimate awareness (*citta*) is regarded as sentient by undiscerning persons. Some hold that all is nothing but awareness (*cittamātra*). This is untenable, for a cognizable entity exists as reflected in the insight born of concentration. If that cognizable entity were awareness itself, the insight could not have ascertained it, the insight being itself the reflection. It is *puruṣa* by which the reflected entity is enabled to appear. Those who can understand the distinct character of knower, knowing and known are to be recognized as possessing perfect knowledge, for they are able to realize the *puruṣa*-principle.

IV.24 (E177; T336) Awareness acts for the sake of others and not for itself. It is an organic whole, that is, a thing that acts in conjunction with its parts, and it does not work to serve its own interest. The entity for which awareness acts is the *puruṣa*, which is not a whole that acts with its parts.

IV.25 (E178; T337-338) Every person naturally possesses the desire to know about the existence and states of one's own being. This desire ceases 'if the person becomes able to comprehend the difference between the intellect and *puruṣa*. Since in the absence of ignorance *puruṣa* cannot be associated with pleasure or pain, it is reasonable to conclude that the aforesaid desire ceases in a person who possesses discriminative knowledge.

IV.27 (E170; T339) Even in an awareness that constitutes discriminative discernment there sometimes arise ideas concerning me or mine on account of those traces whose germs are in the process of decaying.

IV.28 (E179; T340) Traces of knowledge will continue to exist till the end of the functioning of awareness, and afterwards they will naturally disappear with the quiescence of awareness.

IV.29 (E179-180; T340-341) Owing to decay of the seeds of traces there remains no possibility for the rise of any fluctuation or distraction.

IV.30 (E180; T341) On the cessation of the afflictions and karma an enlightened aspirant becomes liberated in his lifetime for the simple reason that such a person is not born again.

IV.31 (E180-181: T341) When *tamas* and *rajas* have become inoperative, eternal *sattva*-knowledge becomes manifest.

IV.32 (E181; T343) The *guṇas* cannot operate even for a moment if they have fulfilled their two functions, namely experience and liberation.

3.VĀCASPATIMIŚRA, *Tattvavaiśāradī* on Patañjali's *Yogasūtras*

Summary by Karl H. Potter

According to tradition, this famous interpreter of Indian philosophy was a Maithila Brāhmaṇa from the region of Bihar. He lived either in the middle of the ninth century (ca. 841 CE) or toward the latter half of the tenth century (ca. 976 CE). The matter is yet to be decided, but the consensus appears to be growing in favor of the later date. For a discussion of the life and works of Vācaspatimiśra, see Larson-Bhattacharya 1987.

The edition and translation used for this summary are the same as for the previous two works.

BOOK ONE

I.1 (E1-4; T3-8) The commentary begins with a discussion of what is presupposed in one who embarks on the study of *yoga* and in what sense the *Yogasūtras* are authoritative.

The definition of *yoga* as something which is a property of awareness is intended in distinction to the (Vaiśeṣika) philosophers who think of the fluctuations of awareness as inhering in the self. "*Citta*" indicates the internal organ (*antaḥkaraṇa*) or intellect (*buddhi*). The pure, unchanging consciousness-power (*citiśakti*) cannot have the fluctuations of awareness as properties, but the intellect can.

Objection: If *yoga* characterizes all stages of awareness, it must apply to the distracted, depressed and partially distracted ones as well!

Answer: The five states are as follows: (1) the distracted stage is very unstable, being directed toward this or that object by *rajas*; (2) The depressed stage, dominated by *tamas*, is the fluctuation of sleep; (3) the partially distracted differs from the distracted in that though it is generally unstable it sometimes remains stable, and the general instability is either natural or produced by conditions such as disease or sloth; (4) the one-pointed state is focused on one thing; (5) the suppressed occurs when all fluctuations are suppressed so that only traces are left. Now the first two are so far from being in any way causes of liberation that (Vyāsa) does not bother to deny that they are properly termed "*yoga*". But the third, since it sometimes is stable, might be supposed to qualify as *yoga*, but since it is influenced by restlessness it cannot be so. So it is only the last two (one-pointed and suppressed) which properly qualify as "*yoga*".

What is *yoga*, then? The fourth, one-pointed stage qualifies; it illuminates a real thing, not superimposed ones. But sleep also has a real object as its supporting object, namely *tamas*, which is why he says that the fourth state illuminates a distinct thing as well, but one in which *sattva* predominates.

Now both inference and verbal testimony illuminate, but they do not destroy the ignorance which is direct experience. For example, those two do not remove such errors as the double-moon illusion or spatial disorientation. That is why he indicates that the fourth stage "fully" illuminates its object–he means immediately illuminates, that is, perceives.

As for the fifth stage, when he says "all fluctuations...are suppressed," he means that even the *sattva*-predominated ones are suppressed.

I.4 (E7-8; T14-17) The meaning is this: when the difference between the *buddhi* and the *puruṣa* is not grasped because of their proximity, then the deluded person superimposes the fluctuations of the intellect on the *puruṣa* and comes to think "I am peaceful", "I am frustrated", "I am deluded". It is as in the case of the confusion of a rose and a crystal, or like thinking one's face is dirty when it is seen in a dirty mirror. This is also taught in Sāṃkhya; the *Bhāṣya* quotes Pañcaśikha, indeed.

The "proximity" between awareness and *puruṣa* spoken of here is not to be thought of as spatial or temporal, but rather as a kind of fitness (*yogyatā*). The functioning of ignorance in the form of proprietor and property related is beginningless since the conditions of ignorance are beginningless; the stream consisting of ignorance and subconscious impressions is like that of the seed and the sprout.

I.5 (E8-10; T17-19) The fluctuations which are afflicted and/or unafflicted–correct awareness and the others–operate by first deciding on the putative nature of their objects and then become attached or averse to them, thus accumulating stored-up karma.

Objection: All beings are subject to desires, so there are only afflicting fluctuations. And even if there could be non-afflicting fluctuations, since they are born in beings subject to desires, they could not produce their effects. Thus suppression of the afflictions by non-afflicting fluctuations is merely a fancy.

Answer: Practice and dispassion are bred by steady attention to verbal communications and inferences and to one's teachers. These are non-afflicting even though they occur in the midst of afflictions. As the non-afflicting traces mature they suppress the afflictions.

I.7 (E10-12; G21-24) Knowledge (*pramā*) is the awareness of the nature of a thing not previously presented which is caused by the ordinary experience (*vyavahāra*) of human beings. A *pramāṇa* is an instrument of knowledge.

A "trustworthy person" is one in whom are found properties of thought, compassion and skillful use of the sense-organs. Some examples of erroneous verbal knowledge are offered.

I.8 (E12-13; T24-27) The difference between error and conceptual construction is that the sublating notion is evident in common people in the case of error, while in constructions only the learned recognize what sublates them.

The five kinds of error under their alternative names are explained. *Tamas* is the recognition of the self in eight forms which are not the self–that is, as unmanifest (*avyakta*) *prakṛti*, *mahat*, ego (*ahaṃkāra*) and the five *tanmātras*. Delusion (*moha*) is the supposition of prosperity (*śreyas*) where it does not exist, for example, in atomization and the other forms of supremacy of *yogins*. It is worse than *tamas* and is equivalent to egoism. Having obtained supremacy and being perfected, if one resolves to enjoy the objects of the world this is "great delusion" (*mahāmoha*) or attachment. Then if he is frustrated because his powers fail him he gets *tāmisra* or hatred. Finally, if he is successful in his powers but fears that all will come to an end, this is *andhatāmisra* or the will to live.

I.9 (E13-14; T27-29) Conceptual construction is not an instrument of knowledge since it is without an actual object, and it is not error, since it "arises from awareness involving words". That is to say, a man may attribute difference to identical things, or find identity where there is difference. Now since identity and difference are not perceptible objects, their cognition here is not valid, but since what is said does not deviate from ordinary understanding, it is not a case of error either. The examples offered in the *Bhāṣya* show this, and several of them are offered in order to answer schools that deny such a category as conceptual construction.

I.11 (E15-16; T32-34) The "not letting go" (*asampramoṣa*) characterizing memory alludes to the fact that all the other fluctuations grasp a previously unpresented thing, while memory alone grasps nothing that goes beyond previous experience.

Objection: Even memory may go beyond previous experience, as when in a dream the dead are remembered as present at a time and place other than that in which they actually flourished.

Answer: This case is not actually an instance of memory, but rather error, though it is commonly called "memory" because it resembles memory proper.

I.15 (E17-18; T36-37) Objects involve the three kinds of liberation, which constitute their fault. Direct awareness through meditation is called the supreme or ultimate reflection (*prasaṃkhyāna*). There are four kinds of cognitive realization (*saṃjñā*)– (1) awareness of effort, in which one is aware of trying to bring about maturation of desires and other faults in awareness which turn the senses toward those objects so that they will no longer operate thus; (2) awareness of discrimination, coming next after some faults have matured and others are about to, and one is aware which are which; (3) awareness of the single sense, i.e. the internal sense-organ (*manas)*, in which the faults persist faintly even after they have left the other organs; and (4) awareness of mastery, when even this faint desire is destroyed.

I.19 (E21-22; T43-45) Vācaspati construes "*bhavapratyaya*" to mean "worldly" means to concentration (*samādhi*) as contrasted with "spiritual" (*upāya*) ones. "*Bhava*" is equated to ignorance. It has to do with sense-organs and substances. The Videha gods and Prakṛtilayas are described as having internal organs which contain nothing but traces, and who have shed the gross body as well as the sense-organs. The state they achieve is "liberation-like" since there are no fluctuations in it, but since there are still traces, it is not liberation.

I.20 (E22; T46-47) Faith is distinguished from other mental states in that it has as content something known through verbal authority or inference but which provides extreme delight and incites one to great effort.

Smṛti is construed not as memory but rather as meditation–it is here glossed as reflective meditation (*dhyāna*). And insight is glossed as exceptional discrimination, which is the occasion for liberation.

I.21 (E22-23; T47-48) This section is intended to explain why some *yogins* get different results than others and take longer or shorter getting there. The answer is that they try harder or less hard according to the force of traces, and so forth.

I.24 (E23-27; T50-55) Objection: Since there are in the universe only conscious and unconscious beings, God must be one or the other. But if He is unconscious He is *prakṛti* and is therefore unable to "become inclined" toward any as *sūtra* 23 says He can be. On the other hand, if he is conscious, since the consciousness-power (*citiśakti*) is indifferent (*audāsīnya*), it cannot be "inclined".

Answer: This *sūtra* (24) answers the foregoing objection. God is a self (*puruṣa*), but is so endowed that He does not become involved with an intellect as other selves do. Nevertheless, because of His excellence He resolves to inspire the rest of the selves so as to liberate them, and to do this He assumes a *sāttvika* character. This is only an appearance, as He is quite unrelated to anything, even *sattva*, which as to do with ignorance; He is like an actor, unaffected by the role He plays.

Objection: His desire to inspire other selves is only possible on the assumption of His possessing *sattva*, but you say that his possessing *sattva* comes after His desire to inquire–so there is mutual dependence (*anyonyāśraya*).

Answer: That might be so if this were the very first creation. But creation, maintenance and destruction of the world goes on beginninglessly. Now, as God is destroying the world in *pralaya*, He thinks "I must assume a perfect *sattva*-quality", and thus there is set up a subconscious impression which is activated at the time of the next creation (when that *pralaya* ends). It is analogous to the way Caitra thinks "tomorrow I must get up at dawn" just before going to sleep, and the subconscious impression produced thereby wakes him up at dawn.

The "scriptures" which prove God's existence are *śruti, smṛti,* epics (*itihāsa*) and *purāṇas*. But what proves their validity? The fact that God has perfect *sattva*, and this in turn is evidenced by noting that incantations and medical texts (*āyurveda*) are composed by God, and that their authority is shown by their effectiveness in accomplishing their respective purposes. So scripture provides an authority which is not based in turn on *pramāṇas* such as inference or even perception.

I.25 (E27-29; T56-59) The inference set forth in this *sūtra* depends on the general rule that whatever admits of degrees of excellence is capable of reaching the extreme limit of excellence. The example given by Vyāsa is "as in the case of any ascending scale". Likewise thinking admits of degrees of excellence, and thus there must be some thinking thing which reaches the upper limit, namely omniscience.

Objection: The Buddha and other beings are authors of sacred books–are all of them then omniscient? And if not, which ones are?

Answer: Those so-called sacred books written by the Buddha and others are not really scripture for they are contradicted by other instruments of knowledge. Only those scriptures that celebrate God under the descriptions we give are authoritative.

Objection: If God is eternally free and has no desires for Himself, and if He is compassionate, He should create a world in which there is no suffering. Since this world is full of suffering it cannot have been created by a God such as you describe.

Answer: He creates a world containing both pleasures and pains in order to encourage men to learn to discriminate and thus achieve liberation. In doing this He is not without compassion.

I.27 (E29-30; T60-61) Words are by nature capable of referring to things of all sorts. The conventions instituted by God both manifest this natural expressive power in words and also delimit the specific application of a given word to a certain kind of object. God makes his conventions conform to those he issued prior to *pralaya*.

I.32 (E32-35; T67-70) This argument is identified as directed toward Vaināśīkas, that is, Buddhists, and it is explained at some length. In closing, Vācaspati directs us to his *Nyāyakāṇika* and *Brahmatattvasamīkṣā* for more arguments on this point.

I.33 (E35; T71-72) Specifically, cultivation of friendliness to happy folk eliminates envy, of compassion towards those who suffer eliminates any desire to injure others, of gladness toward those of merit eliminates jealousy, of detachment toward the non-meritorious eliminates anger.

I.34 (E35-37; T72) The word "or" ("*vā*") in the *sutra* does not mean that breath-control is an alternative to cultivation of the sentiments mentioned in the previous *sūtra*, but begins a series of alternatives set forth in the five succeeding *sūtras*.

I.36 (E37; T75-76) Vācaspati Miśra here reviews the physiology lying behind the attainment of stability. Here "lotus of the heart" is conceived of as situated between the chest and the stomach, and it contains planes (*maṇḍala*) corresponding to waking, dream, deep sleep and the fourth (*turīya*) state as well as channels (*nāḍī*) connecting these planes. Of these the channel at the center of the body passes through various planes, and this passage is the locus of awareness, so that by concentrating on it one becomes aware of awareness in the two ways described in the *Bhāṣya*.

I.42 (E40; T81) Properties of words are, for example, their pitch–high, low, and so forth. Properties of intended contents include such as inertness and materiality. Properties of ideas include such as being illuminating and freedom from shape, etc.

I.43 (E41-44; T83-88) Inference and language involve conventional usage and arise from conceptual construction. By practice one learns to concentrate on the intended object alone, and to set aside the memory of the conventional usage, which in turn suppresses conceptual construction; the object remains unclothed by constructs, and that is *nirvicāra* engrossment. This is the "higher" perception.

Objection: How can *yogins* teach the truth about objects without using inference and language which, you say, involve conceptual construction?

Answer: The *yogins* have a knowledge which is the seed of inference and language–those two arise from this kind of knowledge. And they then use conventional usage to express themselves through a medium involving words.

By saying that in this engrossment the object is cognized as a formation of a single mental act, the author of the *Bhāṣya* means to suggest that what is known is not many but single. Atoms are not its objects; since they are subtle and many, they are not fit to be the object(s) of a single idea of something of large dimension.

Objection: Supposing atoms exist, then the grossness is an apparent property which is confined (*saṃvṛta*), that is, which is a subjective appearance.

Answer: But that is what constitutes the intended object. It is a special kind of conglomeration that is undergoing change different from other changes. Such an object is in some respects the same as its atoms, in other respects different. Since such an object has manifest results and serves everyday purposes it is to be proved by inference to the opponent. But the form in which we know it does not persist. A pot eventually get smashed into pieces.

Objection: This might be so if it did not involve contradiction, but it does. For a whole both occurs at a place and does not occur in that place, is covered and not covered, is red and not red, moves and does not move.

Answer: But we do have the idea of a whole, and that idea must be based on something.

Objection: The atoms of color, taste, smell and touch provide the basis, for they form a continuous series and we fail to perceive their subtleness.

Answer: Since they are intermingled, these series are not continuous. So our idea of a single object is a construction, false. But it is self-defeating to say that we come to know subtle, imperceptible atoms as gross objects through their association with other subtle, imperceptible atoms, if we cannot know a gross object in some way that does not involve construction and so is false.

I.44 (E44-45; T89-91) In explaining how the subtle elements are "conditioned by causation", Vācaspati explains that an earth-atom is produced from five *tanmātras* in which smell predominates. An atom of water is produced from four *tanmātras* in which taste predomoinates. A fire-atom is produced from three *tanmātras* (color, touch and sound) in which color predominates. An air-atom is produced from two *tanmātras* (smell and touch) in which touch predominates. Finally, *ākāśa* arises from the sound *tanmātra* alone. Now when subtle elements are spatially and temporally and causally identified they are capable of being known in the *savicāra* way, analogously to the way in which *savitarka* engrossment works. But atoms are not spatially or temporally identifiable, nor are they really single, being conglomerations of *tanmātras* as we have just seen. So the knowledge of them as spatially, temporally and causally conditioned comes by way of conceptual construction, and it is ultimately confused, just like the *savitarka* engrossment. Whereas the objects of *nirvicāra* engrossment are not related to specific properties of these sorts–they indeterminately correspond to any, all or none of them.

I.49 (E47-48; T95-96) Why are not words able to denote particularity? Because a word is infinite in its possible application, and it may be applied to any given instance. Convention does not connect a word with any particular instance, but only with the general property connoted. Nor can the meaning of a sentence be a particular; notably, sentences expressing inferences refer generally to pervader and pervaded and not to particulars.

Objection: But why cannot we grasp particulars by ordinary perception–surely this "higher perception" or insight is not necessary to grasp an individual thing? Perception does not involve knowledge of word-meanings.

Answer: But it does involve the sense-organs, and there is no special fitness-relation (*yogyatā*) connecting the senses with particular objects. Rather, we perceive things as qualified by their sensible qualities.

Objection: Then there are not particular things, since there is no *pramāṇa* left to grasp them.

Answer: Just because the *pramāṇa* which knows x ceases to operate it does not follow that x ceases to exist. So it is the *samādhi*-born insight which cognized individuals in themselves.

I.50 (iE48-49; T97-98) Since it is the nature of our thinking to prefer ideas which portray things as they actually are, the traces arising from insight into the true nature of things naturally inhibit those traces arising from the emergent state.

BOOK TWO

II.1 (E51-52; T103-104) The second Book is intended for those for whom practice and dispassion do not come easily. It is for those whose *citta* is emergent and who must purify their *sattva*, and it provides the means to accomplish such purification.

II.3 (E52-53; T106) Ignorance is just error. The others have ignorance as their material cause (*upādāna*) and so they too are just error. So when ignorance is destroyed all are destroyed.

II.4 (E53-55; T105-110) "Cultivation of their opposites"–this can mean either that the afflictions become overpowered by their opposites, viz., the *yoga* of action, or else that ignorance is overpowered by its opposite, namely right awareness (*saṃyagjñāna*). Each of the other afflictions has its specific opposite–discrimination is the opposite of egoism, detachment is the opposite of attachment and aversion, and the cessation of the idea of continuing is the opposite of the will to live.

II.5 (E55-57; T112-115) Objection: There are other kinds of ignorance besides the four listed in this *sūtra*–e.g., loss of one's sense of direction, or seeing a circle of fire in the whirling torch, and so forth.

Answer: Of course there are other kinds, but only these four constitute the seeds of *saṃsāra*.

Objection: "*Avidyā*" ("ignorance") can be construed in different ways. (1) One way of understanding it is to take the negative prefix "-*a*-" as the chief member of the compound, which would be to construe it as the *prasajyapratiṣedha* kind of negation, that is, a negative description of a positive state, but in this sense *avidyā* could not be the cause of the afflictions. (2)

Another way would be to construe it as having "*-vidyā*" as its chief member: then it would mean "knowledge" (*vidyā*) of the absence of something", and then *avidyā* would not cause the afflictions but rather (since it is negative) destroy them! Or (3) if something else altogether is the chief member, "*avidyā*" would have to be construed as referring to an intellect in which *vidyā* is absent. But that cannot be the cause of the afflictions *per se*, since we would have to then admit that such a state even when preceded by discriminative insight causes afflictions, since it is equally the absence of knowledge. So *avidyā* is not the cause of the afflictions.

Answer: *Avidyā* is none of your alternatives (1)-(3), but a fourth thing, namely an erroneous cognition contradictory to *vidyā*. That is, the negative prefix contradicts the chief, final member of the compound and so suppresses the thing that member describes, and this is sometimes found in common usage, as for example "*amitra*", a "non-friend", which is used to mean an enemy.

II.9 (E58-59; T118-119) The fear of death or extinction is not acquired through perception or inference or language in this life; thus it must be inferred that death has been experienced in a previous life, since even children tremble at danger to their lives. So, this fear arises from everything painful or frustrating, and proves that the will to live reproduces itself over and over in successive lives through the operation of subconscious impressions. Even worms behave thus.

II.10 (E39; T119) "...to the original state", i.e. to the state of their cause.

II.11 (E60; T120-121) "Perfect knowledge" (*prasaṃkhyāna*) is explained by Vācaspati as a process involving effort by which the attenuated afflictions, returned to the causal state by reversal (*pratiprasava*), are then rendered inoperative.

I.12 (E60-61; T121-127) Delusion produces nothing but demerit, but wrath sometimes breeds merit as in the case of Dhruva whose anger at his father spurred him to meritorious deeds. Usually it breeds demerit only.

II.13 (E61-65; T126-131) The *Bhāṣya* discusses four cases. The first is the supposition that each birth is caused by a single and distinct act. In that case, however, in a given lifetime, even though one makes many karmas dwindle, since there will be innumerably many more karmas still active, even the subtraction of those which have dwindled will leave so many still active that men will become discouraged. Even the wisest won't be able to show that meritorious actions have beneficial results.

The second case is the supposition that each karma causes more than one birth, which merely makes the situation described above worse.

The third case is where many karmas cause many births. But since these births must occur successively, the case is still no better than before.

Thus by elimination it follows that the fourth case–that many karmas cause one birth–is the only reasonable theory.

The stored-up karma brings about the form, length and quality of life. The distinction is that between the case of Nandīśvara and of Nahuṣa. In Nandīśvara's case both his length of life–a brief eight years–and the kind of experiences he had during that time resulted from a specific kind of meritorious karma produced by vehement activity. Now in the case of Nahuṣa his length of life resulted from his high status, but his specific experiences in that life resulted from the demerit he earned when he touched Agastya with his heel.[133]

II.14 (E66-68; T132-137) Stored-up karma sometimes does not produce all its results in one birth (though Vācaspati seems to imply that usually it does). Three instances are discussed. Case 1 is the case where some stored-up karma is destroyed in some subsequent birth in the same way that we see karma destroyed in this life, that is, by being removed through another action of great merit, for example, involving non-injury and so forth, all by itself. Case 2 occurs in the case of the *jyotiṣṭoma* and other rites. An animal is killed, which should breed bad results, but since it is done in the course of virtuous activity it remains intermixed with the fruits of the dominant (good) karma and can be removed by penance and so forth, along with the dominant karma's results. Or if penance is not due and the combined karma lingers on, still its effects will involve so little displeasure that it is negligible. Case 3 is not a case of an accessory to a rite. Rather, it is a case of involvement in a dominating action, which breeds such powerful karma that there is no appropriate opportunity for its maturation, and so the karma continues in the form of a seed. It will later ripen when an appropriate opportunity arises.

II.15 (E69-70; T138-139) Some think that the destruction of the one who escaped is liberation; it is like the blowing-out (*nirvāṇa*) of a lamp. Others teach that liberation consists in the purification of knowledge (*vijñāna*) produced by the destruction of the afflictions. But no reasonable person ever tries to destroy himself.

Objection: There are those intent on suicide.

Answer: True, there are some, but they are not ordinary transmigrators, and even so, they desire liberation. Self-destruction is not one of the aims of man (*purusāṛtha*), so should not be accepted as constituting liberation.

Objection: Then let it be that the one who escapes is in his very nature what is to be accepted (*upādeya*).

Answer: Then he is impermanent, being an effect, and he might backslide from (apparent) liberation. But (real) liberation is deathlessness.

Objection: Then the purified endless series is liberation.

Answer: No, for the series is not anything over and beyond its members, and so does not end really, since the members of the series are not eternal. So we want a theory which holds immortality (*śāśvatavāda*), so that liberation can be the aim of man.

II.17 (E71-73; T141-143) Objection: The relation between the seer and the seen must be either natural or accidental. If it is natural, the two terms of the relation being permanent the relation must be permanent, and so rebirths will be without end. If the two terms are accidental, there is mutual dependence (*parasparāśraya*) between the afflictions, karma and subconscious impressions, on the one hand, and the internal organ on the other. And it is impossible that creation is beginningless, since then *saṃsāra* would never have arisen. It has been said: "Even for those who say that the self is non-agent, how can the *guṇas* have brought about the first action? For karma did not yet exist, nor false awareness nor passions nor aversions, all these fluctuations of the internal organ, which has not yet come to be."

Answer: "The beginningless correlation between seer and seen...is affected for a purpose (either experience or liberation)...". That is, the relation is not natural but accidental, but it is nevertheless beginningless, being the result of a condition (*nimitta*) which is beginningless, namely ignorance.

18 (E73-75; T145-148) Objection: Let us grant that the *guṇas*, even though intermingled and mutually dependent, are not mixed up. But then the *guṇas* cannot be supposed to work in harmony, for we know that things whose powers are quite different from each other do not work in harmony together. For example, threads do not cooperate with pieces of earth and dry grass to produce a jar.

Answer: "They produce effects according to their relative predominance", that is, in the example offered, since it is a jar which is to be produced, the threads and grass do not work together, for they are not the appropriate material. Likewise, when it is a divine body to be produced, *sattva* dominates and *rajas* and *tamas* are subordinate, whereas when a human body is to be produced *rajas* dominates, and for an animal body *tamas* is dominant. In each case the dominant item becomes intensified.

Objection: Which instrument of knowledge tells us that at such a time the "subordinate" items are even there at all?

Answer: As in magnetism, they act by mere proximity. When any one of the three *guṇas* act, the others cooperate without any other cause.

II.19 (E75-78; T150-153) The sense-organs are particular things having egoity and dominated by *sattva*. The motor organs are dominantly *rajas*, and the internal organ (*manas*) is essentially dominated by both *guṇas* (*rajas* and *tamas*) equally. And here the five *tanmātras* have the intellect (*mahat*) as their cause, since they are non-particular like egoity.

This intellect exists, that is, is capable of actions serving a purpose; anything capable of serving a purpose is included in *mahat*. Vyāsa denies that it is completely imaginary (*tuccha*), and thus shows that the evolutes of *prakṛti* are real and not merely apparent (*vivarta*). By contrast, non-existence (*asat*) is imaginariness, that is, uselessness as regards human purposes. "What is neither real nor unreal", that is, neither exists nor does not exist, characterizes the non-resolvable *prakṛti*. As long as the *guṇas* are in equilibrium *prakṛti* is of no use for human purposes, but it is not for that reason worthless, since it is capable of changing into something useful.

II.22 (E80-81; T159-160) An object of awareness ("the seen") does not cease when one self has accomplished its purposes, since it also seen by other selves. Though colors cannot be seen by the blind it does not follow that they do not exist, since those not blind can see them. The self is not single like *prakṛti*. The apparent teaching of scripture that the self is single must be only figurative, since only if we assume plurality of selves can we explain the order of birth and death, pleasures and pains, etc. Anyway, scripture (for example, *Śvetāśvatāra Upaniṣad.* 4.5) clearly implies that selves are many.

II.23 (E81-84; T162-165) The eight views on the nature of non-discrimination are explained: (1) Construing the "non-" in the *paryudāsa* way (as forming a compound which denotes a positive thing contradictory to its final element), "non-discrimination" might be taken to denote the ability of the *guṇas* to produce the connection of a self and its intellect . (2) Or construing the "non-" in the *prasajyapratiṣedha* manner (as indicating a denial of something which it is possible to affirm) "non-discrimination" is the non-production by awareness, which is able to entertain objects, of (a connection to) either sounds, etc. or of discrimination–both being possible contents of awareness. (3) Or, construing the "non-" in the *paryudāsa* way (again), "non-discrimination" might be the *guṇas*' possessing objects (in potency). (4) Again in *paryudāsa* manner "non-discrimination" is just ignorance, which at the time of the involution of creation back into *prakṛti* is suppressed, so that a subconscious impression of this ignorance is precisely the non-discrimination referred to. (5) Again as *paryudāsa*: "non-discrimination" is the going out of equilibrium on the part of the *guṇas* because of the traces of *prakṛti* when the stable traces generated by the equilibrium have been burned off. (6) (Again *paryudāsa*) "Non-discrimination" is the power of sight belonging to *prakṛti*. (7) The "non-discrimination"is the power of sight belonging to both *prakṛti* and *puruṣa*, that is, the properties of the *buddhi* appear as if they were properties of consciousness (*caitanya*), since there is assumed to be no difference between intellect and consciousness. (8) "Non-discrimination" is just perception of sounds and so forth–it denotes all perception except the discrimination of the self from the intellect.

Of these he favors the fourth alternative, because all the others would result in there being no differences among the experiences of the several selves, since non-discrimination on all the other views is common to all selves.

II.28 (E88-90; T174-177) Examples of each of the nine kinds of causes: (1) the internal organ is the cause of the origin of awareness; (2) the fact that the self has purposes is the cause of the sustenance of the internal organ; (3) illumination of colors is a cause of the manifestation of objects; (4) the cause of the modification of one object is another object, for example, when fire cooks rice; (5) an existing object is the cause of our idea of it; (6) the cause of acquisition is the nature of a thing, for example, it is the *sattva*-nature, which naturally breeds effects, which causes discrimination; sometimes this natural causative action is blocked and needs to be helped by other means, in the present case by practice of the eight aids (*yogāṅga*); (7) that which causes discrimination also causes disjunction from effects lower than that; (8) the cause of transformation of gold into bracelets, and so forth, is the goldsmith; fire's cooking rice is not a cause of transformation but of modification (see 4 above), since in the case of gold the difference between cause and effect is emphasized whereas in the case of rice it is not–examples of internal causes of transformation are also given: infatuation with a woman causes a man to become dejected when she takes up with another; (9) the cause of support is that without which the effect would not be maintained–e.g., the body's cause of support is the sense-organs and other parts of the body, and the relation is mutual (the body supports the parts), for each body depends on the ingestion of other bodies for its support.

BOOK THREE

III.1 (E104; T203-204) Auspicious external objects to which awarenesses are bound include Hiraṇyagarbha, Vasava, Prajāpati and so forth. Purāṇas are quoted to illustrate.

III.4 (E106; T205-206) "*Saṃyama*" ("comprehensive reflection") is a technical term standing for attention, contemplation and concentration collectively.

III.13 (E110-116; T217-224) Examples of things which evolve in these various ways: a cow or a jar are changes of property of earth and so forth. Such things are young and become older; evolvings of temporal variation, these temporal slices have had changes of state–newness or oldness. Again, sense-organs have changes of property such as seeing blue, etc. which in turn have temporal variations–seeing a jewel, and so forth–which aspects of temporal variation have states such as clearness or opacity, etc.

III.17 (E120-127; T236-247) Vyāsa says "a word is grasped by an intellect which follows the syllables and gathers them by retaining the memory of the syllables".

Objection: The syllables themselves have each a meaning,

so a word cannot be grasped in the way you state, since the syllables are many and the word is one.

Answer: Either each syllable arouses an idea which corresponds to a word, as each peg on which a net is hung supports the net, or else the syllables only collectively arouse the idea, like stones which in combination support a pot. Now the first alternative is impossible here, since the idea (of the word's meaning) does not arise from the first syllable, and if it did the rest of them would be unnecessary. So the second alternative remains. But the syllables, unlike the stones, are not all there at the same time: they appear and disappear without being all there at once to convey (the word's) meaning. So that alternative will not do either. However, if each syllable itself has expressive power–"g" having the power to express an indefinite number of meanings associated with the words in which it occurs–the problem vanishes. Each syllable's power is conditioned by those of the syllables near it, so that as the syllables are pronounced traces are laid down which limit the expressive power of those which follow. These traces are not the kind which produce heaven from sacrificing and so forth (*apūrva*); rather, they are memory-traces. In this way the collection of syllables constitutes a word with a single meaning because of its specific meaning (*sphoṭa*). This is why the syllable "g" does not produce an idea of a cow until the syllable "o" follows: then the *sphoṭa* is manifested. It is also why the same syllables pronounced in a different order do not produce the same idea. And so a word is a single, partless thing, and only appears to be composite.

Objection: If a word is partless, is not constituted of syllables, why do we think that it is so constituted? When a thing–for example, a piece of glass–is covered with red paint, and then the paint is removed, it is still transparent.

Answer: It is not an apt analogy. Words are not known except as associated with syllables, and so it is natural for men to treat them as if they were constituted of syllables.

Now, just as each syllable has the power in itself to convey any word-meaning, so each word has the power in itself to convey any sentence-meaning, although no meaning will be conveyed unless the word appears in the context of other words.

III.44 (E242-243; T274-275) Lists are offered of the qualities of the gross substances. Earthy qualities include shape, weight, roughness, resistance and stability. Watery qualities are liquidity, subtlety, brilliance, whiteness, sinuosity, weight, coolness, protectiveness, purification, cohesion. Fiery qualities are tending-upwards, purification, burning, cooking, weightlessness, brightness, destructiveness. Airy qualities include horizontal motion, purification, felling, impulsion, power, changeability, being without shadow, aridity. The qualities of *ākāśa* include pervasiveness, interpenetration, unobstructiveness.

III.52 (E150-151; T288-290) Vācaspati introduces this section as an explanation of the omniscience which has been equated with discriminative knowledge. It is not that everything whatsoever is known–past, present and future–for at any moment past and future are conceptual constructions.

BOOK FOUR

IV.10 (E161-164; T310-314) The discussion on the size and shape of awareness is developed.

Objection: ("Some are of the opinion..." that) awareness only functions within the body. Now, awareness cannot be of the smallest dimension (*aṇu*) since then it could not affect simultaneous experience of the data belonging to more than one sense. And it cannot exist outside the body, for its effects do not occur outside the body. So it must have the same size as the body. Otherwise it could not reside in an appropriate locus so that it could enter the blood and semen of the parents of the new body it enters. *Saṃsāra* would be impossible.

Answer: No, it is only the fluctuations of awareness which expand and contract; awareness itself is all-pervading. For if it must have an "appropriate locus", namely a subtle body, in order to enter the new gross body, then it must likewise have an "appropriate locus" to get into the subtle body in the first place–and what could that be? An infinite regress will result. So there must be a subtle body continuously throughout all *saṃsāra*–from creation to *pralaya*. Thus awareness does not itself transmigrate–nowhere in scripture does it say so.

IV.14 (E167-169; T319-321) The objector ("Some do not accept...") is identified as a "destructionist", that is, a Vijñānavādin, who holds that from the highest standpoint objects are nothing but ideas. From the two facts (1) that all objects of which we have evidence are known (*vedya*) and (2) that every knowing of an object is accompanied by knowing of the idea of that object (*sahopalambha*), the Vijñānavādin deduces that objects are nothing but ideas, since they always occur together in experience. The apparent difference between idea and object is a conceptual construction, like the illusion of two moons.

Answer: Objects have characteristics of their own which are not possible qualifications of ideas–for example, grossness and externality–and the objects which appear to have these properties actually do have them, so there is no conceptual construction involved.

Objection: First the coarseness and so forth is grasped in a construction-free (*avikalpaka*) awareness; then a construction-filled (*savikalpaka*) awareness ensues which is conditioned by and limited to the form of the first awareness' object.

Answer: If it were so the "coarse and external object" would be quite unreal (*alīka*), but since according to you the idea is identical with its object it too must be quite unreal, which is unacceptable to you. Anyway, the mere fact of regular accompaniment (*sahopalambhatva*) does not prove identity. Nor does the fact of being known (*vedyatva*). Two things may in fact accompany each other because of their natures or because of some obstruction in our thinking of them. And "being known" does not necessarily imply "being identical". So the Vijñānavādin's thinking, based on fallacious reasons, is itself a case of conceptual construction. (Vācaspati directs us to his *Nyāyakāṇika* for more details.)

IV.33 (E181-183; T345-347) The point of the latter part of the discussion is explained as follows. The person asking the question about whether *saṃsāra* will end is inclined to infer that eventually there will be liberation for all and *saṃsāra* will come to a final end. But this inference conflicts with scripture, since *śruti, smṛti,* Purāṇas and tradition all attest that *saṃsāra* is without beginning or end. So there must be countless (transmigrating) beings.

4.ŚAṂKARĀCĀRYA (?), *Vivaraṇa* on Patañjali's *Yogasūtras* (*Pātañjalayogaśāstravivaraṇa*)

The identification of the author of this work with Śaṃkara the Advaitin, author of the *Brahmasūtrabhāṣya*, has been a controversy that has plagued the scholarly world for many years. T. S. Rukmani has dealt with this question in detail in the Introduction to her two volume work, *Yogaśāstrabhāṣyavivaraṇa of Śaṃkara.*[134] She argues that the work is not an authentic work of Śaṃkara, the Advaitin. The text appears to be dependent on Vācaspatimiśra's *Tattvavaiśāradī*, thereby suggesting that the work is considerably later than the 8th-9th century, the presumed date of Śaṃkara the Advaitin.[135] Gopinath Kaviraj has argued that the *Vivaraṇa* is a fourteenth century work by a certain Śaṃkarārya who is also the author of the commentary *Jayamaṅgalā* on the *Sāṃkhyakārikās.*[136] Tuvia Gelblum has also argued for a later date of the *Vivaraṇa*, as has Usharbudh Arya.[137] On the other hand, Paul Hacker, Hajime Nakamura, Sengaku Mayeda and, of course, Trevor Leggett have argued that the *Vivaraṇa* is an authentic work of Śaṃkara. Their argument is based largely upon certain key terms that are characteristic of genuine works by Śaṃkara, for example, *adhyāsa, adhyāropa, parivijṛmbhita* and so forth. Overall, the arguments of Rukmani, Gelblum et al. appear to be stronger, and so we are placing the *Vivaraṇa* chronologically after Vācaspatimiśra, somewhere between the eleventh and fourteenth centuries. We recognize, however, that the issue of authenticity has not yet been completely settled.

In this summary, following the convention of T. S. Rukmani, the author of the *Vivaraṇa* will be identified as "the VKS" (=Vivaraṇakāra Śaṃkara). The work has a loose style overall. There is also a strong Nyāya methodology used by the VKS in advancing his arguments which again further suggests a post-Udayana period in Indian philosophy (or, in other words, post-1000 CE). Very often the VKS just repeats whole passages from the Vyāsa *Bhāṣya* in his *Vivaraṇa* without adding much to the contents. In spite of these minor defects, the *Vivaraṇa* is an important work in the field of Yoga.

Rukmani has used her two volume annotated English translation (Rukmani 2001), as the basis for the following summary. The page numbers refer to both the Sanskrit text and the attached English translation.

Summary by T. S. Rukmani

BOOK ONE

I.1 (ET I.1-16) The VKS starts with a lengthy discussion of the wording of YS I.1.

Objection: If cessation of pain is the end and its means is insight, the *sūtra* should be worded "*atha vivekakhyāty-anuśāsanam*".

Answer: The means to *yoga*, which is *vivekakhyāti* (i.e. insight) will in any case be discussed because the end is the result of the means followed. Moreover, *yoga* itself is the eight-fold means to insight as mentioned in YS II.28. Therefore, there is nothing amiss in the wording of YS I.1 as "*atha yoga-anuśāsanam*".

Vyāsa's definition of *yoga* as concentration and its belonging to all parts of the mind next come up for discussion. The VKS justifies this usage, since it makes clear that the jurisdiction of concentration is over things like the mind and not over things like the self, the body or the sense-organs. There is an interesting reference to the Vaiśeṣika definition of *yoga*.

One point of departure from commentators like Vācaspatimiśra et al. is the following remark: As content-filled (*samprajñāta)* concentration is the initial stage its definition should normally be mentioned first; but since the commentator deems it proper to mention in this context the definition of content-free (*asamprajñāta)* concentration he says that he will speak of content-filled *yoga* later. The definition of *asamprajñāta* concentration is given at this point in order to indicate that content-free concentration can be achieved through superior dispassion without dependence on content-filled concentration.

I.2 (ET 16-23) The VKS first gives the reason why "all" is not included in the definition of *yoga* and also concludes that though content-filled concentration can be understood as the meaning of the definition, he believes that this *sūtra* is in fact a definition of content-free concentration itself. Significantly he does not recognize the word "twofold" accepted by other commentators on Vyāsa under YS I.2. He emphatically states that YS I.2 is for the sake of defining content-free concentration only.

I.3-4 (ET 23-31) At the time of content-free concentration there is only the intellect without any known content; in other words, *puruṣa* alone is both the knower and knowledge in this stage. At other times, *puruṣa* identifies itself with the modifications of the mind. A lengthy discussion follows as to how one need not assume anything other than knowledge for the phenomenon of knowledge to arise. It appears that the VKS is using the Vijñānavādin's argument here as an objection (*pūrvapakṣa*). He also raises another objector's argument for the self's being an inherent cause in the knowledge episode. The VKS's predilection for Nyāya is clearly seen here. Another objection, recalling the Buddhist theories of *skandhas*, dependent origination and not-self is also brought in. He clinches the discussion by comparing the mind to a magnet possessing *puruṣa*, its master.

YS I.5-7 (ET 31-60) The nature of the fluctuations of the mind and the kinds of fluctuations are discussed in these three *sūtras*. Though fluctuations are endless they can be classified in terms of five kinds as the text does, and also as afflicted and non-afflicted. The afflicted are caused by afflictions to perpetuate the cycle of karma and rebirth, while the non-afflicted will lead to insight. There can be non-afflicted fluctuations in the stream of the afflicted and vice-versa.

A lengthy discussion ensues on the means to knowledge, which are three, direct perception, inference and authoritative language. Perception is what comprehends the special characteristic of an object. The VKS then engages in a polemic against the Buddhist Vijñānavāda theory that denies the existence of an external object. He also discusses the question of the validity of knowledge. As opposed to the Buddhist and Nyāya schools the VKS maintains that the validity of knowledge is "knowledge of the fluctuations of the mind as belonging to *puruṣa*".

Objection: But that the fluctuations are knowable is not proved. It is not possible for an instrument to become the object also, any more than a knife's cutting itself.

Answer: (1) Action by its very being is the cause for a result and one speaks of it as an instrument only figuratively. So a fluctuation by its existence is the cause of the result. (2) A fluctuation can be known since it has the power to manifest itself just as a lamp can manifest an object even while being knowable itself. Such is the case with mental fluctuations.

Further discussion of (2): (a) In the case of the senses like the eye, as the light in the eye and the light outside arise simultaneously there is confusion about perceiving itself. It is like the lighting up of many lamps simultaneously which creates the confusion of distinguishing which light belongs to which lamp. (b) Moreover, the mental fluctuation is not distinguishable from and not distanced from *puruṣa*. *Puruṣa*, being inseparable from the mind and its fluctuations, owns the fluctuation in that the content of awareness belongs to it. Thus *puruṣa* has the result, knowledge (*pramā*), belonging to it.

The VKS next discusses inference. The discussion follows the Nyāya pattern. The well-known instances of Caitra and the Vindhya mountains are given as examples of concomitance and exclusion in an inference of something possessing a distinguishing mark.

The subsequent section deals with language (*śabda, āgama*, scripture) and brings comparison (*upamāna*) under inference.

I.8-11 (ET 61-75) These *sūtras* deal with the other fluctuations like error, conceptual construction, sleep and memory. Under the discussion of error the VKS exhibits his predilection to steer away from the main topic by questioning the grammatical adequacy of terms.

I.12-16 (ET 75-82) Constant practice of dispassion helps the mind to work towards liberation. The distinction between complete control (*vaśīkara*) and dispassion (*vairāgya*) is discussed in I.15. While dispassion is common to all four stages of yogic progress, complete control is a prelude to the highest dispassion, which is a dispassion from the *guṇas* themselves. And the highest dispassion that results in liberation is the subject of discussion in I.16.

I.17-18 (ET 82-88) In *sūtra* 17 there is mention of the four kinds of content-filled concentration. The question as to how self-awareness (*asmitā*), which is an affliction, can be connected with concentration is raised and answered: (1) In the state of self-awareness there is appearance of the form of egoity's higher cause (that is, being itself, *sattāmātra* or *prakṛti*). (2) There is the disappearance of all other objects. (3) There is the feeling of selfhood–so there is no harm in accepting it as a form of concentration. Moreover, a *yogin's* mind is not afflicted by ordinary egoity, since it is no more qualified by ignorance and, thus, generates no further karma. The VKS does not enter into further divisions of the four content-filled concentrations as do Vācaspatimiśra and Vijñānabhikṣu.

The state of content-free concentration is described as the other concentration, which has only subliminal impressions without any sense of subject or object.

I.19-20 (ET 88-91) The state of content-free concentration is of two kinds: The first is attained by means of the practice of *yoga.(upāyapratyaya)*. The second has to do with the process of natural rebirth (*bhavapratyaya*).

I.21-22 (ET 91-93) There is a classification of *yogins* into nine types depending on the intensity of their practice of the means.

I.23-29 (ET 93-142) These *sūtras* introduce God (*īśvara*) as a principle different from *puruṣa* and *prakṛti*, who can be used for attaining concentration.

The VKS spends quite some time on the arguments for the existence of God in I.24-25. Since Sāṃkhya does not know of God, there is need for proof of the existence of God. There must be mention of God's special nature. The answer to this is I.24 where God is defined as untouched by afflictions at all times. And in answer as to how God is eternal excellence, the VKS seems to suggest that tradition (*śāstra*) is the cause for knowing God, since traditional knowledge is the effect of the pure *sattva*. Unlike commentators such as Vācaspatimiśra and Vijñānabhikṣu, the VKS does not use, in this place, the efficacy of the incantations of the Vedas and the proven utility of Āyurveda as proof for the authority of the *śāstras* on the existence of God. Scriptural knowledge leads to the inference of the *sattva* mind, which in turn leads to the knowledge of God.

I.25 is the longest section in the entire *Vivaraṇa*. The VKS brings in a lot of unnecessary quibbling under this *sūtra* which states that in God there is unexcelled omniscience. Knowledge growing in excellence reaches a limit in omniscience, and in God knowledge reaches its limit. Such a one has unexcelled omnipotence, says the *Vivaraṇa*. But the discussion, then, in the mouth of an objector, proceeds without a focus.

Objections: (1) The word "*īśvara*" ("God") cannot denote one who is omniscient, since it is only a word, like "pot" and so forth. And (2) the unique arrangement of the universe capable of being experienced is a natural phenomenon, similar to the natural rising and setting of the moon, sun, stars and so forth.

Answer: (1) There is no evidence for earth and so forth coming into being naturally, and it is not proved. (2) It is proper to understand the creation of the earth for the sake of experiencing the results of one's own karma.

The VKS draws attention to the opponent's use of the word "*īśvara*" without its denoted meaning. (1) The denial of omniscience in God implies the acceptance of omniscience but only its denial in God. It is like the statement "a rabbit has no horn", where there is denial of a rabbit having a horn but not the denial of the existence of a horn or of a rabbit. (2) It can also mean that someone other than God can have omniscience. It is only denied in God. After many permutations and combinations of arguing in the same vein, the VKS concludes that the pure *sattva* of God is as follows: (1) God's *sattva* has the characteristics of eternal strength, knowledge and power that are unexcelled. (2) God's *sattva* is all-pervasive. (3) God's *sattva* illumines all objects. (4) God's *sattva* is not associated with merit or demerit. (5) Finally, even though without a body or sense-orgnas, God's *sattva* is nevertheless omniscient.

God, not being conditioned by time, is the *guru* of all other *gurus* like Brahmā and so on. The word denoting God is "*oṃ*", and there is some discussion (in I.27) of the derivation of the word "*praṇava*", which is unique in a commentarial work. The VKS indulges in some discussion of the fixed relationship that exists between *oṃ* and *īśvara*.

In I.28 there is advocacy of repeating "*oṃ*" either mentally or in a low voice, which will result in one-pointedness of the mind. The added effect of overcoming obstacles by devotion to God is the subject of I.29.

I.32 (ET 147-159) In order to remove distractions, the *yogin* must practice concentration of mind on a single entity.

This leads to a refutation of the Buddhist theory of momentariness, and the VKS presents some argumetns against the theory of the storehouse consciousness (*ālayavijñāna*) of the Vijñānavādins.

I.33 (ET 159-160) The mind can attain clarity (steadiness) by also practicing virtues such as friendliness, compassion, joy and dispassion towards those who are happy, miserable, virtuous and evil-minded. The VKS asks why dispassion towards the evil-minded is mentioned, since it cannot be the cause for giving rise to *dharma*. The reply given is that in the absence of dispassion, the mind would get engaged in the thought of evil deeds and that will obstruct the mind from meditating on friendliness and so forth.

I.34-39 (ET161-169) These six *sūtras* prescribe alternate means for gaining stability of the mind. They are exhalation and retention of breath, experiencing directly the object of meditation when there is luminous sense-activity, meditating on an attachment-free mind, meditating on a dream object or state of deep sleep, or finally, by choosing any object for meditation which helps to gain stability.

I.41 (ET 170-176) This *sūtra* introduces the word "*samāpatti*", "engrossment", and there is some discussion on that. The balanced state of mind of engrossment is becoming one with the object, be it an outside object, the sense-organs, or self-awareness. The VKS makes an important point of distinguishing *samāpatti,* engrossment, from *saṃyama,* comprehensive reflection.

Objection: This *sūtra* does not serve a purpose, since in the third Book the object of engrossment will be understood as the effect of comprehensive reflection.

Answer: (1) This *sūtra* shows the result of the practice of complete control. The state of content-filled concentration has been mentioned as accompanied by empirical awareness (*vitarka*) and so forth. If engrossment is not mentioned then it is not possible to indicate the nature of empirical awareness and so forth, since empirical awareness, etc. are the characteristics of engrossment.

There are also comments on the cosmic *mahat* and cosmic *ahaṃkāra* and how ordinary experience will be absent on those levels.

Objection: *Puruṣas* can know each other mutually.

Answer: This is not so. Since the *puruṣas* are identical in nature there cannot be a relation of subject and object between them. They are like two lamps indistinguishable as subject and object.

Objection: How can one accept the existence of a *puruṣa* other than oneself?

Answer: Just as one sees another face through another mirror, similarly one *puruṣa,* seeing the transformation of its own mind into the form of another mind which is like the second mirror, comes to know another *puruṣa*. The experience "This is his self", "This is my self", however, comes about inferentially through the special mark (*liṅga*) belonging to a mind different from one's own.

I.42-48 (ET 176-197) These seven *sūtras* describe different kinds of engrossments culminating in the highest, purely intellectual contemplation described as "tranquility in the presence of the self" (*adhyātmaprasāda*).

I.42 describes *savitarka* engrossent, in which there is mixture regarding word, its meaning, and the idea or object conveyed. The VKS accounts for this first stage by saying that "being qualified by latent impressions of the knowledge of the conventional relation between word and meaning in many births, the first engrossment of the *yogin* is the same as the idea that one finds in the ordinary world". In other words, it is a highly focused empirical awareness.

I.43 describes the next stage of purified engrossment (*nirvitarka samāpatti*) that is free from this mixture or confusion, that is, free from predication. While *savitarka* engrossment is common to all, this *nirvitarka* kind only belongs to a highly disciplined *yogin*. This is a state in which memory is purified of all error of verbal convention, scriptural knowledge and inference. There is a lengthy discussion of the merits of *satkāryavāda* (of Sāṃkhya and Yoga) as opposed to the *asatkāryavāda* of the Nyāya school. The VKS also criticizes the Buddhist school of Vijñānavāda.

In I.44 the VKS in turn describes *savicāra* and *nirvicāra* engrossments. In the first there is engrossment with reference to a subtle object conditioned by place, time, and experience. In the latter, these factors are absent.

In I.45 the VKS discusses the range of subtle objects from *tanmātras* up through (unmanifest) *prakṛti*.

I.47-48. The VKS indicates that these *sūtras* describe how insight (*prajñā*) comes into being. The process by which the "truth-bearing insight" unfolds is threefold: First, one listens and follows the *śāstra* as taught by the teacher or *guru*. Second, one follows the reasoning as taught in the *śāstra*. Finally, one meditates continuously. In I.47 there is a description of the state in which there is great clarity (*vaiśāradya*) of the super-reflective (*nirvicāra*) engrossment. In I.48 that stage is called "the truth-bearing insight".

I.49 (ET 197-199) The content of "truth-bearing insight" is different from that which arises from scripture and inference. It is direct perception having a particular content.

Objection: No ordinary perception can perceive the particulars (*viśeṣa*) pertaining to subtle elements or to *puruṣa*. Nor is there a means of proof, other than the three instruments of knowledge (perception, inference, testimony), to know those particulars.

Answer: Anything that exists can be known through an instrument of knowledge. Therefore, this insight can be grasped by the wisdom that is concentration (*samādhiprajñā*), which is a special kind of perception.

I.50-51 (ET 199-204) These two *sūtras* describe the process of the rise of content-free concentration. Traces born of insight obstruct other traces and also obstruct the traces of activity. Then insight and the traces of insight take over.

Question: Why is awareness not connected with subliminal impressions or the traces of activity at this stage?

Answer: Activity traces have afflictions such as ignorance as their causes. But since the traces born of insight oppose activity traces, the mind is not inclined towards activity. It is like a person in whom thirst has disappeared and who, therefore, has no desire to drink anything.

In I.51 even the curtailment of the traces born of insight is advocated for the sake of attaining content-free concentration. Then, when the mind has lost its power to bind, it is absorbed into *prakṛti*. Release, finally, is the cessation of the modifications of the mind (*cittavṛttinivṛttir eva muktiḥ iti*).

BOOK TWO

II.1-2 (ET 205-211) The first Book was addressed to the one who has a steady mind. The second is begun for anyone who desires to attain *yoga*. And the means for such a one is *kriyāyoga*, which comprises ascetic practices, study of sacred texts and devotion to God. The VKS states that the first Book is called *Samādhi Pāda* because concentration (*samādhi*) is explained therein, whereas this second Book is called *Sādhana Pāda* because the contents determine the heading of the section, namely practice.

Objection: How can ascetic practice, which causes pain to the body, achieve *yoga* through steadying the mind?

Answer: One who looks upon the body and so forth as the self, as very delicate, etc. and is engaged in averting pain to the body, sense-organs and mind, cannot achieve *yoga*. Thus ascetic practices is included, and *kriyāyoga* is important, since it helps in minimizing the afflictions and bringing about concentration.

II.3 (ET 211-214) Ignorance, egoity, attachment, hatred and clinging to ordinary life are the five afflictions and by mutual cooperation they bring about karma and its fruit. And each of them is a misapprehension.

II.4 (ET 214-223) The last four afflictions, namely egoity, attachment, hatred and clinging to life, are of four types:

quiescent, decreased, interrupted and active. Ignorance is the breeding ground and cause of all the others. When the afflictions are burnt, it signifies that the *yogin* has continuous true insight and that is known as the burnt-seed stage. After describing the nature of quiescent and decreased afflictions, there is a discussion of what interrupted afflictions are.

Objection: There is no characteristic like being interrupted in addition to being quiescent, decreased, or fully active.

Answer: If the interrupted affliction is not accepted because it is not seen (to exist), then when attachment exists in one place its nonexistence in another place can be its total absence. And that is not feasible, since it comes into being again.

Question: What is the distinction between that which is quiesccent and that which is interrupted, since in both cases they are not seen?

Answer: The VKS finally admits two kinds of interrupted state. The first kind is that in which there is disappearance altogether of the continuity of the affliction due to the overpowering influence of some obstacle. There is another kind that is manifest with reference to a particular object but is not manifest with reference to another, even when the cause of manifestation is there. Caitra's attachment to his wife and his non-attachment to other women at the same time is given as an example.

II.5 (ET223-231) This *sūtra* defines ignorance as the idea of permanence in impermanence, of purity in impurity, of pleasure in pain, and of self in not-self. There is an elaborate discussion based on grammar regarding the word "*avidyā*". The conclusion reached is that "*avidyā*" is a type of *tatpuruṣa* compound (a *nañtatpuruṣa* like "*agospada*" or "*amitra*") meaning a different awareness which is the opposite of true awareness.

II.6 (ET231-234) Egoity (*asmitā*) is defined as the identity between the power of seeing and the power by which one sees. While *avidyā* is ignorance of the true nature of *puruṣa*, the cause of egoity is the coloring of the mind by the seer and the seen.

II.7-9 (ET 234-237) These *sūtras* define the nature of attachment, aversion and the desire to live (long or forever).

Question: What does one learn from this craving for living?

Answer: Through this craving for the continuity of the self the previous experience of death is inferred, since there has been no experience of death in this life either directly or indirectly. And since death cannot take place without birth, the experience of a previous life is also inferred. And also the continuity of birth and death is inferred.

II.10-11 (ET 238-239) These two *sūtras* deal with the methodology of weakening the modifications of the afflictions by *kriyāyoga* and then through meditation (the ultimate reflection, *prasaṃkhyāna*) how they are reduced to the subtle and burnt-seed stage.

II.12 (ET 240-245) This *sūtra* describes elaborately how the stored karma *(karmāśaya)* has the afflictions as its basis and how it is experienced either in a present or future life.

II.13 (ET 245-261) The results of the presence of afflictions are birth, length of life and type of experience. A discussion ensues as to the relationship between stored karma and the number of lives. Many permutations and combinations such as one karma leading to one life or many lives, or many karmas leading to one life or many lives, are discussed. The conclusion is stated by the VKS as follows: Just as the contact of seed, soil and potential to sprout is the cause for the manifestation of a sprout, similarly death also is the cause for the manifestation of compatible seeds. The karmas come together and become unified and then give rise to one birth. But not all karmas are experienced in that birth. As for the karmas to be experienced in future lives, other than the ordinary ones described above, as well as the karmas from beginningless time, some will be destroyed by expiatory deeds. Some will be absorbed in a stronger karma that has to happen quickly. Some will be dormant until a similar, compatible karma becomes the manifesting cause.

Objection: But if the karmas in one life come together and give rise to the next rebirth, how can there be other karmas destroyed, absorbed or overpowered by other karmas?

Answer: The stored karma causing one birth is difficult to understand. It can be understood as starting a life whose fruition of karma is not quite determined. It can also be interpreted as an exception overpowering the general rule, that is, that the karmas from one life come together and determine the next life. In other words, there is some ambiguity in accounting for the fruition of karma.

II.14-15 (ET 263-264) In II.14 the results of karma are given as pleasure and pain and in II.15 it is said that the result, whether pain or pleasure, is always pain to the discriminating wise *yogins*. The distinction between the *yogin* and an ordinary person is brought out through the analogy of the eye being hurt even by a fine thread of wool, which does not hurt when falling on other parts of the body. The *yogins* are like the eye whereas ordinary humans are like the other parts of the body. The science of *yoga* like the science of medicine has four divisions as follows. The world is filled with pain, which is to be got rid of. This pain has a cause which is contact between *puruṣa* and *prakṛti*. There is an end to this pain of *saṃsāra* and there is a means to it (that is, proper awareness).

There is a lengthy discussion of the nature of the self (*puruṣa, ātman*) under II.15. The *puruṣa* is not fit to be destroyed like the world of pain, which can be destroyed. The VKS concludes that the *puruṣa* is eternal.

II.16-17 (ET 284-292) II.16 describes how pain, which is yet to come, is to be avoided and II.17 deals with the cause of pain, which is the association between the seer and the seen. An interesting discussion is found here of the nature of the relation between what is possessed (that is, the object, *citta*) and the possessor (that is, the true self or *puruṣa*).

Question: How can something which is independent be a possessor? Similarly, anything that functions on its own does not need to function for another. The answer is the traditional one of necessity.

Answer: Since it serves the purpose of another through accomplishing the twin purposes of the *puruṣa*, namely experience (*bhoga*) and release (*apavarga*), *prakṛti* or *citta* is a possession of the *puruṣa*.

Towards the end the VKS asks a question: If *puruṣa* is thus not pained and *prakṛti* operates for the sake of the *puruṣa*, is it not illogical to say that *puruṣa* assumes the form of the modifications of awareness?

Answer: Because there is absence of activity in the changeless *puruṣa*, when there is proximity of an object of perception, there is the assuming of the form of that object. This is like a crystal taking on the form of red color in the proximity of red shellac.

II.19 (ET 300-310) The nature of the *guṇas* are the particularized gross (*viśeṣa*), the unparticularized subtle (*aviśeṣa*), that which is its cause (*liṅga*), and that which is without any indicator (*aliṅga*). Gross elements, subtle elements, the internal organ and *prakṛti* are all discussed.

II.20 (ET 310-317) The nature of the seer is consciousness alone. Though pure he witnesses the transformations of awareness. *Puruṣa*, the seer, is not similar to the intellect's creation, nor is he dissimilar to the intellect's creation.

Objection: There is change in *puruṣa* as well, due to known and unknown objects, similar to the changes in the intellect's creation.

Answer: The intellect itself, taking on the form of the object, is the object of *puruṣa* and not the object of its own self. Since the intellect's creation is at all times known, there is no change in *puruṣa*.

Objection: Then it is the object determined by the intellect that *puruṣa* perceives.

Answer: The meaning of the "object determined by the *puruṣa*" only means that *puruṣa* perceives the form taken by the intellect.

Objection: But only the intellect's creation constitutes

knowledge and not what is created.

Answer: It cannot be so, for then the body and so forth, which are the intellect's creation, will have knowledge!

II.21-22 (ET 317-320) The seen object exists only for the sake of the *puruṣa*, says II.21, and II.22 further adds that for a liberated *puruṣa* objects cease to be effective; but they are very much present for the *puruṣas* not yet liberated.

II.23 (ET 320-329) Association (*saṃyoga*) between the seen-intellect (here, the owned, *sva*) and the seer (here, the owner, *svāmin*) is the means to know the true nature of the powers of both. And ignorance is the cause of that association. Once there is insight into the true nature of the seer and the seen, there is liberation, which is permanent. A long discussion of the nature of ignorance (non-seeing, *adarśana*) ensues. Eight types of ignorance are discussed. A preference is expressed for the view that ignorance is positively incorrect awareness.

II.24 (ET 329-333) The cause of the special relationship of each *puruṣa* to its own intellect is ignorance.

Objection: It has been said that the mind (intellect) does not cease after the rise of insight.

Answer: Ignorance ceases to exist after the rise of insight.

II.25-26 (ET 333-336) Liberation as defined in *sūtra* II.25, and II. 26 deals with insight, which is the means for liberation. There is an interesting observation on the problematic nature of liberation, since it is not a substance. The answer is that cessation of ignorance is liberation and that it is accomplished by effort. When insight is present, ignorance is absent. Therefore, even if ignorance is not a substance, it can be realized.

II.27 (ET 336-340) Insight (*prajñā*) is said to be of seven types. The VKS like Vācaspatimiśra takes the seven kinds to refer to the insight of a *yogin*.

II.28-35 (ET 340-378) Here and following are twenty-eight *sūtras* dealing with thte first five limbs of the eightfold limbs of *yoga* (*yogāṅga*). II.28 introduces the sequence. There is mention, generally, of the nine causes understood in the tradition. They are origin, sustenance, manifestation, change, knowledge, attainment, separation, otherness and support. In this context the cause (which is the practice of *yoga*) is only twofold, that is, the cause for destruction of impurity and the cause for the rise of insight. Then, from *sūtra* II.30-55 the five external limbs are discussed.

BOOK THREE

III.1-4 (ET 1-4) The first three *sūtras* define the internal limbs meditative fixation, meditative reflection and concentration respectively. The VKS makes it clear that one is talking about fixing of the mind on the region of the navel, and so forth.

Question: What is the difference between concentration as means and concentration as end in III.3.

Answer: The description of *yoga* as concentration is to indicate a special state of the mind which is the end, whereas concentration as means is the series of thoughts taking on the nature of the object of meditation. The fourth *sūtra* defines *saṃyama* ("comprehensive reflection") as the technical term in Yoga which denotes the application of the three internal limbs collectively to the object to be mastered.

III.5-6 (ET 4-7) Mastery of comprehensive reflection leads to insight. III.6 mentions the application of comprehensive reflection in ascending order. While in general comprehensive reflection can only proceed gradually from gross to subtle and more subtle until insight is achieved, exceptions, due to devotion to God enabling the aspirant to reach the highest stage without going through the lower stages, are allowed by all commentators, including the VKS. But the VKS disagrees with someone* that gaining comprehensive reflection on the higher

---

*(Summarizer's note) Somebody whom I identify with Vācaspatimiśṛa in keeping with my view that the *Vivaraṇa* is

stage enables one to gain it on objects of the lower stage.

III.7-12 (ET 7-15) In these *sūtras* the superiority of the internal means is proclaimed and the process of change from activity to content-free *samādhi* is laid out.

III.13-14 (ET 15-39) These two *sūtras* elaborate on the threefold changes in terms of characteristic, temporal mode, and change in overall condition as the theory of dynamic transformation (*pariṇāma*) in Sāṃkhya and Yoga. It is made clear, in keeping with the *satkāryavāda* of Yoga (and Sāṃkhya), that the substance (*dharmin*) undergoes these changes and there is no coming into being of something new. The VKS shows his familiarity with Nyāya at many places in the discussion. There is a lengthy discussion of the permanence or non-permanence of the substance mind (or internal organ) and its threefold aspects. In the course of his different arguments the VKS touches upon the Nyāya theory of *asatkāryavāda* and refutes the criticism that the denial of change of the object, along with the denial of its permanence, is a case of contradictory middle term. The VKS states that the single qualified substance has both a manifest form and a perennial form. In the manifest form it is non-eternal and in the potential form it is eternal.

YS III.16-34 (ET 44-122) This set of nineteen *sūtras* dwells on the powers that come to the *yogin* by the practice of comprehensive reflection on different objects. In III.17 the VKS speaks at length (pp. 45-69 in ET) about the practice of comprehensive reflection separately on a word, its meaning or object, and the idea conveyed, which will enable the *yogin* to gain knowledge of the sounds of all living beings. Discussion of the nature of words leads to consideration of many views regarding the nature of understanding meaning from words and sentences, and there is also a tacit assumption of the *sphoṭa*-theory. The VKS states his view in accordance with Yoga that

---

post-Vācaspatimiśra.

the word is one. Word is directly experienced by all. By the mature understanding of the intellect caused by the traces brought together by the rise of the sequence of the letters or syllables, the meaning of a word emerges just after the last syllable is uttered, accompanied by the remembered sequential functioning of the earlier syllables. The VKS introduces a set of verses from Kumārilabhaṭṭa's *Ślokavārttika* which does not support *sphoṭa*, but he then rephrases them to suit his theory which supports *sphoṭa*. He thus says that the mind-substance or intellect is illumined by the ripening of a series of impressions brought about by each preceding syllable. At the moment of the birth of the final syllable, there arises an illumination of intelligence capable of being grasped by a single idea without parts. The VKS is even more specific regarding *sphoṭa* when he asserts that sometimes when the uttered letters are destroyed and not in existence, there is the understanding of meaning apart from syllables, and that is *sphoṭa*.*

III.55 (ET 123-125) This last *sūtra* of the Book defines liberation in two ways: as the purity of the *sattva* intellect and as the purity of the self (*puruṣa*), since there are no more "presented" objects in that state of awareness. The VKS emphatically states that the purpose of the *yogaśāstra* is to accomplish insight and not to bring about extraordinary capacities.

BOOK FOUR

IV.1 (ET 127-128) The VKS introduces this Book as necessary in order to indicate the accomplishment of liberation by way of counteracting bad karma. The VKS repeats the statement of the *Yogasūtras* that extraordinary capacities arise from birth, herbs, incantations, *tapas* and concentration.

---

*Summarizer's note: The VKS's strong support of the *sphoṭa*-theory, of course, is an important argument against his identity with Śaṃkara, the Advaitin.

IV.2-3 (ET 128-131) Rebirth occurs through the inherent and beginningless power of *prakṛti*.

IV.4 (ET 131-132) *Citta*, though all-pervasive, always appears in individuated forms.

IV.6-9 (ET 133-144) Here the VKS gives a summary discussion of karma, indicating the various types, namely black, white and black, white, and neither black nor white.

IV.14-21 (ET 160-184) The VKS presents a series of *sūtras* giving the standard critique of the Buddhist Vijñānavāda position of momentariness and of the Buddhist denial of a real world of mind (*citta, prakṛti*) and consciousness (*puruṣa*).

IV.22-23 (ET 184-190) These two *sūtras* come back to the Yoga theory of knowledge being a mistaken oneness of *puruṣa* with the mind through reflection (IV.22). The mind colored by the object is like a magnet, which attracts *puruṣa* to the transformations of the mind into the object.

IV.24 (ET 190-194) The mind serves the purpose of *puruṣa* by working in combination with sense-organs, objects, and so forth. The VKS concludes the discussion in this *sūtra*, which again has some polemics against the Buddhists, by asserting that there is an experience of that which serves the purpose of another and for which contact (of *puruṣa* and *sattva*-intellect) is the cause. When there is separation from the contact, liberation (*kaivalya*) results.

IV.25-26 (ET 194-197) The nature of a true *yogin* forms the subject-matter of these two *sūtras*. The true *yogin* is enthralled by hearing about the path leading to liberation. The VKS also mentions that this can come about through accumulated good karma over many lives, or, interestingly, due to the capacity of the virtue of non-acceptance of gifts in this life itself. In that state, the mind inclines towards insight, and is tilted heavily towards liberation.

IV.27-28 (ET197-198) The mind tilted towards liberation can still have episodes of other thoughts, which are due to the earlier traces. But these traces will reach the burnt-out state through the traces of insight and will not give rise to any further emergent-state activity. The traces of insight will stay in the mind without binding it.

IV.30-31 (ET 200-202) The *dharma*-cloud realization leads to cessation of afflictions and karma. But it does not lead to liberation directly. We have to understand, therefore, that the VKS means that it is very close to liberation and not that it leads to liberation.

IV.32 (ET 202-203) At this state the *yogin* has the capacity to know everything. The VKS raises an interesting question in this context.

Question: How can knowledge, which has discarded the taint of *rajas*, have the capacity to know?

Answer: The *sattva*-mind is set in motion by *rajas* and is like the impact of the wind on a huge collection of clouds. *Sattva guṇa* by its own nature does not act. Only the *guṇa rajas* has that capacity. The VKS seems to hint at the threefold *guṇa* composition even at this stage. The task of *rajas* is not so much impelling to activity but removing the obstructions to knowing everything.

IV.32 (ET 202-203) The *guṇas* are no longer active once the *dharma*-cloud realization has come into existence.

IV.33 (ET 203-208) The concept of sequence is given as something which is grasped at the conclusion of a mutation. The example of an old cloth is used to indicate that the mark of change from newness to oldness is "sequence".

Objection: It will be illogical to speak of the end of the sequence of mutation in the case of the imperishable *guṇas*.

Answer: In the case of the *guṇas*, their essence in the form of illumination, activity and inertia is not destroyed. Therefore, they are eternal, though inoperative.

IV.34 (ET 208-211) This last *sūtra* of Book Four defines the nature of liberation (*kaivalya*). The VKS mentions different views pertaining to liberation before defining *kaivalya* in Yoga. For some, liberation is absolute cessation of the flow of consciousness (that is, the Buddhist Vijñānavādins). For others it is the cessation of new qualities in the self, such as knowledge, pleasure, pain and so forth, and the state of existence without awareness (that is, the Nyāya-Vaiśeṣika). For still others it is attaining oneness with God (perhaps reference to the many *bhakti* schools). And again, for others, it is the state similar to God because of omniscience.

Kaivalya in this last *sūtra* is defined in two ways. (1) First, it is the gaining of their natural state by the *guṇas*. (2) It is the state of the *puruṣa* abiding in its own self, that is, in "isolation" *(kaivalya)*. The VKS mentions "*oṃ*" and gives a set of seven verses as a conclusion to the *Vivaraṇa*. From these verses it appears that VKS was a Viṣṇu *bhakta*. The first verse praises Kṛṣṇa while the second verse refers to the ten *avatāras* of Viṣṇu. He alludes to Śeṣa-nāga on which Viṣṇu rests in the same verse. The belief that Patañjali is an incarnation of Śeṣa is mentioned in the third verse. The traditional identification of the grammarian Patañjali with the author of the *Yogasūtras* as well as with the author of a medical treatise is referred to in the fourth verse. The author of the VKS also seems to be a committed *yogin*, since he devoutly refers to Patañjali as the one who proclaims *dharmameghasamādhi*, which gets rid of the threefold pain. He again refers to *dharmamegha* in the next verse as well. The last verse says "I bow down to that unequalled Śaṃkara Bhagavatpāda, the powerful guru who has the full moon on his face, who is not holding a serpent (and) who does not have ashes as his decoration".*

---

*Summarizer's comment: This last seventh verse clearly indicates that the VKS is not the same as Śaṃkara Bhagavatpāḍa. Our author draws a distinction between Śiva and Śaṃkara Bhagavatpāḍa who is considered to be an incarnation of Śiva in the tradition.

5.AL-BĪRŪNĪ, "*Book of Patañjali*"

Summary by Tuvia Gelblum

A hitherto unidentified, fairly elaborate commentary on Patañjali's *Yogasūtras*, independent from extant commentaries, has become available in its Arabic translation done by Abū-Rajiḥān Muhammad ibn Ahmad al-Bīrūnī (CE 973 - ca. 1050). The Arabic version has the force of a dialogue of questions and answers between "the ascetic roaming in the deserts and the forests" and Patañjali, respectively. Incorporated in this expository dialogue are most of the *sūtras* themselves, occurring generally in their original sequence, though interwoven with the commentary material used by the Arabic translator.

The Arabic text has survived in a single and poor manuscript (Koprulu 1589, fols. 417a-424), discovered in Istanbul by L. Massignon in 1922.[138] The text is written on the margins surrounding another unrelated text, and hence the delay in its identification. A critical edition of the Arabic text was published by H. Ritter in 1956,[139] and an English rendering has since been published by the present writer in collaboration with Shlomo Pines.[140]

In his well-known *India*, al-Bīrūnī not only refers to the fact of his having translated the work in question,[141] but also quotes from it copiously.[142] These quotations furnish useful parallels for the reconstruction of the Arabic version from the unique manuscript. In the past, however, on account of being studied in isolation, these quotations frequently misled scholars attempting to identify their source. Thus E. Sachau categorically declared, "Alberuni's Patañjali is totally different from 'The Yoga Aphorisms of Patañjali'".[143] Similarly, S. N. Dasgupta concluded that the author of the underlying original text was a third distinct Patañjali, different from both Patañjali the grammarian and Patañjali the author of the *Yogasūtras*.[144] It was R. Garbe who first related the quotations in *India* to the text of the *Yogasūtras*.[145] Yet, his identification of the commentary material contained in those quotations–at first as that of Vyāsa's *Yogabhāṣya*,[146] and later as that of Bhojarāja's *Rājamārtaṇḍa*,[147] –on the basis of similarity of some ideas, cannot be borne out. For such similarities as found by him can readily be accounted for as independent free borrowings from a common tradition. It is precisely from the fact of being independent of extant commentaries that the underlying Sanskrit commentary derives its significance. Apart from its intrinsic value, it would appear to point to a possible lost richness of commentary traditions related to the *Yogasūtra*. Furthermore, there is some evidence to suggest that the Sanskrit commentary translated by al-Bīrūnī is not much younger than Vyāsa's *Bhāṣya*. For, as S. N. Dasgupta cogently argues, the commentary under consideration contains cosmographical descriptions which run counter to the descriptions as given in the *Bhāṣya* (under 3.26), and from this we can infer that it was probably written at a time when the *Bhāṣya* had not yet attained any great sanctity or authority.[148]

The head-title of al-Bīrūnī's version may be rendered in English as "the book of the Indian Patañjali on liberation from the afflictions (lit. 'burdens', i.e. *kleśas*)".[149] Other descriptions of the work by al-Bīrūnī may be rendered as "the translation of Patañjali's book on the liberation from the entanglement",[150] "a book on the liberation of the soul from the fetters of the body", "(the book of) Patañjali on seeking liberation and union of the soul with its intellectum (i.e. object of meditation)".[151] Al-Bīrūnī's Arabic version characteristically speaks of the goal as "liberation and union with God".[152] This major distinctive characteristic of al-Bīrūnī's version, it may be noted, is a far cry from the goal of *yoga* as defined by the *Yogasūtra* (IV.34): "the energy of thought being grounded in itself" (*svarūpa-pratiṣṭhā...citiśaktir iti*). According to S. N. Dasgupta, we can fairly assume that the description of the goal in al-Bīrūnī's version faithfully reflects an authentic modification of the *yoga* doctrine in its development.[153] It is however also conceivable that the emphasis in the Arabic text on union with God as the ultimate goal is due to the translator's own interpretation as a

Muslim addressing readers of his own persuasion.[154]

The Arabic text opens with a preface by the translator providing the personal background of his undertaking. This is followed by an introduction giving particulars about (a) the "state of these people" and (b) "the state of the book". Under (a) we find a general characterization of the Hindu community as preoccupied with concepts such as *saṃsāra* and *mokṣa*. Under (b) the translator offers an apology to the reader for abridging the original "over-lengthy commentary", omitting mainly those parts which are concerned with grammar and language.

The text proper, namely "the book of Patañjali, text interwoven with commentary", then opens with a *maṅgala* (benedictory statement), which is given here in full. It may be a key for identifying the original Sanskrit source. "I prostrate (myself) before Him above whom there is nothing, and I glorify Him who is the beginning of things and to whom they shall return, Him who knows all beings. In the second place I exalt, with a human soul and a pure intention, the angels (=*devas*) and other spiritual beings who are below Him, and I call upon them to help me in my exposition–which I wish to keep short–according to the method of Hiraṇyagarbha."[155]

There follows an introductory discussion in which the author of the commentary itself attempts to justify his undertaking by claiming it "will have for the reader a status of sense-perception productive of conviction". This is preceded by a traditional reference to the *puruṣārthas* (goals of life) and epistemological reflections on the relevance of the *pramāṇas* (instruments of knowledge) to the supreme goal of life, "liberation of the entangled soul". "As long as ambiguities beset the soul, the latter is given over to perplexity and cannot give heed to that which (procures) its liberation from this entanglement and its deliverance from toil and bondage, and (gives) it an eternal sojourn, in which there is neither death nor birth."[156]

Some impression of the character and style of al-Bīrūnī's version may be conveyed through the following excerpt from its

English translation.

"Question 1. Is it possible for you to show me by arguments and demonstrations what is sought for in order that by grasping it I should be assisted against doubts and misgivings?"

"Answer: Patañjali said: This is possible...Listen then, since you have asked. That which you seek is *praxis*, which has (in the first place) causes and thereupon results and consequences and an agent (bringing) this (about). Accordingly you ought to have a true knowledge of each (factor) and criticize the various opinions concerning it, rejecting the erroneous views. A part of *praxis* is, as it were, activity, and another part is, as it were, desisting from activity. If you grasp this matter you will find that it includes knowledge. For (it consists in) compression of that which spreads out from you towards external (things), so that you are not concerned with anything but yourself. (It also consists in) the quelling of the faculties of the soul, so that they should not cling to that which is not you.* (It consists finally in) every (faculty) engaging in the work which is assigned to it by you. This activity comprises both knowledge and *praxis*."[157] Subsequently two methods of the yogic process are expounded: (1) that which is "of a practical nature, namely habituation", and (2) that which is intellectual, namely mental asceticism, which consists of contemplating the consequences with the eye of the heart, and considering the evil of existents, which come into being and pass away..."**

---

*Cf. *Yogasūṭra* Ī.2: *Yogaś cittavṛttinirodhaḥ* "Yoga is the suppression of the modes of functioning of the mind".

**Ritter pp. 171-172. Cf. Pines/Gelblum 1966, pp. 316-317. For a corresponding statement in al-Bīṛūṇī's *India* cf. Hyd pp. 58-60. Sachau 1964 at I.76 wrongly identifies method (1) with *kriyāyoga*. He also translates the description of method (2) as "renunciation (the *via omissionis*): (loc. cit., p. 79); but the Arabic text here should evidently be amended: for *yhafḷī*

(1) manifestly corresponds to *abhyāsa* (practice) as defined in *Yogasūtra* I.13: "of these, repeated practice is the effort to remain in the state (of suppressed *vṛttis*)" (*tatra sthitau yatno 'bhyāsaḥ*). (2) corresponds to *vairāgya* (dispassion) as defined in *sūtra* I.15: "Dispassion is the consciousness of (self-) control on the part of the one who is no longer thirsting for objects that are perceivable or promised by scriptures" (*dṛṣṭānuśravika-viṣaya-vitṛṣṇasya vaśīkara-saṃjñā vairāgyam*). A third method is expounded in the second section of the text for the less advanced aspirant, which serves as a preliminary to (1) and (2). It is referred to as "worship" and corresponds to the *kriyā-yogaḥ* of *sūtra* II.1: *tapaḥsvādhyāyeśvarapraṇidhānāni kriyā-yogaḥ*", "Yoga of ritual acts consists in asceticism, recitation (of formulae) and the directing of one's mind to the *īśvara*". Unlike all other translators, al-Bīrūnī seems to have correctly understood *kriyā* in this context to stand for "ritual act"and not "activity, practice" in general.[158]

Reference has already been made above to the divergence between the elaborate cosmographical account in the Arabic version (under *sūtra* YS III.26, commenting on *bhuvanajñānam*, ("knowledge of the universes") and the one occurring in the extant commentaries. Similarly some material concerned with astronomy and medical doctrine is retained in the Arabic version without being paralleled in the extant commentaries (under *sūtras* III.28 and III.29 respectively). An otherwise unknown tradition modifying the Sāṃkhya theory of the three *guṇas* by reducing the latter to a dual scheme may be reflected in al-Bīrūnī's characterization of *rajas* as being a mixture of the other two *guṇas*, i.e. *tamas* and *sattva*.[159]

In evaluating the text under consideration, it may finally be noted that apart from its significance for the history of the text of the *sūtras* themselves and the information which it contains

---

("neglecting") read "'*aqli*" ("intellectual") which, except for some diacritical dots are indistinguishable in the Arabic script.

concerning an otherwise unknown text, al-Bīrūni's translation *as such* is distinctly of value for the understanding of the tradition of classical Yoga. Its limitations, failures and misunderstandings, not less than its insights, are illuminating for students of comparative thought.

6.BHOJA, *Rājamārtaṇḍavṛtti* on Patañjali's *Yogasūtras*

Summary by Ram Shankar Bhattacharya

Bhoja, Bhojarāja or Bhojadeva was from the clan of the Paramāras who were originally feudatories of the Rāṣṭrakūṭas in Gujarat. The Paramāras claimed Rajput status for themselves and asserted independent rule in the region of Malwa (Madhya Pradesh) in the mid-tenth century. They made the city of Dhar their capital. Bhoja came to the throne of Dhar somewhere ca. 1010 and ruled, according to tradition, for some fifty years. In addition to his political skills, he was also a scholar and worked in such areas as philosophy, poetics, veterinary medicine, phonetics, archery, yoga and medicine.[160] His commentary, *Rājamārtaṇḍavṛtti* ("commentary of the sun-king") on the *Yogasūtras*, thus can be dated in the middle of the eleventh century, roughly contemporary, in other words, with Al Bīrūnī. As was mentioned in the Introduction to this volume, in verse 5 of the opening of his commentary, the identity of the two Patañjalis, namely the Patañjali of the *Mahābhāṣya* and the Patañjali of the *Yogasūtras*, is asserted.

The Sanskrit edition (E) used for this summary is Dundhiraja Sastri 1982. There is no complete translation of the text.

BOOK ONE

I.1-4 (E1-8) Bhoja thinks that *sambandha* (connection), *abhidheya* (subject-matter) and *prayojana* (purpose) are tacitly stated in this *sūtra*. The connection is either the relation of *pratipādyapratipādaka* (a thing to be known and that which tells of it) between *yoga* and this treatise, or the relation of *sādhyasādhana* (a thing to be realized and its means of realization) between *yoga* and its result, liberation. Yoga with its means (*sādhana*) and results (*phala*) is the subject-matter . The purpose (also called *phala*) of the work is either the expounding of *yoga* or the state of isolation to be achieved through *yoga* as expounded in this treatise. The word "*anuśāsana*" in the expression "*yogānuśāsana*" (in I.1) is explained as the exposition in which the nature, kinds, means and results (of the entity defined) are described.

The suppression of the fluctuations of awareness which is a modification of *sattva* (bereft of blemishes) is their dissolution (*laya*) in their material cause. While dealing with the *bhūmis* (the states in which awareness exists habitually), Bhoja mentions those beings who are in possession of these states: e.g., the Daityas and the Dānavas are said to possess the distracted(*kṣipta*) state. The one-pointed state is defined as the cessation of the external fluctuations of awareness and the suppressed state as the dissolution of the fluctuations and traces.

3. It is remarked that in the state in which the seer abides in itself, the intellect becomes devoid of all mutations and the notion of agency (*kartṛtvābhimāna*) ceases.

I.5-11 (E 8-16) 5. A fluctuation (*vṛtti*) is defined as a modification of awareness which is of the nature of a whole (*avayavin*).

7. Correct awareness (*pramāṇa*), one of the five fluctuations, is defined as a cognition which corresponds with its object (*avisaṃvādijñānam*).

8. It is remarked that doubt (*saṃśaya*) comes under error (*viparyaya*) since it is not based on the actual form of the object.

9. Conceptual construction (*vikalpa*), a fluctuation of awareness, is explained as an ascertainment (*adhyavasāya*) without having any reference to the real nature of an actual

entity (*vastu*).

11. *Asampramoṣa* is explained as the rising up (*āroha*)of the objects experienced previously through traces in the intellect (*buddhi*). It is remarked that the object of dreamless sleep (*nidrā*) is not capable of being experienced.

I.12-16 (E16-20) 12. "Suppression" (*nirodha*) is defined here again as the existence of fluctuations assuming the nature of potential energy in their material cause, *citta*.

13. Stability (*sthiti*) is said to be a fluctuation of awareness which is devoid of (other) fluctuations. This fluctuation is to be known as being fixed in itself (*svarūpaniṣṭhā*).

15. The word "*vaśīkārasaṃjñā*" ("complete control") is explained as a kind of reflection that the objects are under my control and that I am not to be affected by them.

16. It is remarked that extreme dispassion (*paravairāgya*) is highly conducive to the cessation (i.e. seedless) concentration.

I.17-22 (E 21-28) 17. Bhoja understands *samprajñāta* ("content-filled") concentration as a practice (*bhāvanā*) that is explained as "the repeatedly taking in, in the mind, of the obejcts to be meditated on by eradicating other objects." The objects to be meditated on (*bhāvya*) are divided into two groups, *jaḍa* (the twenty-four *tattvas*) and *ajaḍa* (i.e. God (*īśvara*). Bhoja shows the character of objects of the four kinds of content-filled concentration by associating them with the three kinds of engrossment as shown in I.41. Thus the *savitarka* and the *savicāra* come under the engrossment with the objects cognized (*grāhya*), the *sānanda* and the *sāsmitā* content-filled concentrations fall under the engrossment with the instruments of cognition and on the cognizer (the *grahaṇa* and the *grahītṛ* engrossments respectively). It is remarked that the Videha (disembodied) are said to come under the group of *yogins* who are perfect in the *grahaṇa* engrossment.

18. *Virāma* is explained as the leaving off thoughts of the form of *vitarka*, etc. (as mentioned in I.17). "Content-free" (*asamprajñāta*) concentration is explained as having no object

to be experienced and having no seed.

19 The "notion of becoming" concentration is taken as pseudo-*yoga* since the *videhas* and the *prakṛtilayas* fail to realize the ultimate principle.

21. "Practice" (*saṃvega*) is explained as a firm impression which gives rise to action.

I.24-29 (E 28-36) 24. Bhoja remarks that it is the will of God which is the cause of the conjunction of *prakṛti* with *puruṣa* and of the disjunction of *puruṣa* from *prakṛti.**

28. According to Bhoja, *praṇava* (i.e. *oṃ*) has three *mātrās* and a half (each of the letters a, u, and m has one *mātrā,* and the half belongs to the nasal sound).

I.30-32 (E36-39) 30. It is remarked that the disorder of the bodily constituents is the cause of diseases, viz., fever, etc.**

32. The word "*ekatattva*" is explained as any desired principle (*abhimāna tattva*).

I.33-40 (E39-47) 33. Bhoja remarks that the purifications (*parikarman*) (cultivation of friendliness, etc.) are external actions and they are to be understood as factors helping one to

---

*Summarizer's remark: This view, however, is untenable, for a will (whether it is divine or otherwise) being itself a product of *saṃyoga* cannot be the cause of a *yoga* that is found in all sentient beings. Moreover, it is held that the conjunction of *prakṛti* and *puruṣa* is beginningless (*vide* the statement of Pañcaśikḥa quoted in *Vyāsabhāṣya* II.22.

**Summarizer's remark: It appears to me that Bhoja deliberately offered his explanation of disease with a view to dispelling a doubt that arises from the definition of *vyādhi* as given in the *Bhāṣya*. The *Bhāṣya* seems to hold that it is the disorder (of humors, etc.) which is the same as disease, while Bhoja takes the disorder as the cause of diseases. Here the wording of the *Bhāṣya* is not to be taken literally since the teachers of Āyurveda take disorder as the cause of diseases. Such inappropriate expressions are frequently met with in ancient works.

concentration. The words "*sukha*", etc. are taken in the sense of "endowed with *sukha*", etc.

35. Bhoja does not seem to read "*manasaḥ*" in the *sūtra* as is read by others.

36. Dreaming (*svapna*) is defined as the state in which there arises experience (*bhoktṛtva*) through *manas* only, whose functions through the external organs have dwindled away.

I.41-51 (E47-58) 41. *Tatstha* signifies one-pointedness and *tadañjanatā* the quality of being engrossed. It is remarked that the order of "*grahītṛ, grahaṇa,* and *grāhya*" is to be changed into "*grāhya, grahaṇa,* and *grahītṛ*" so as to make the order consonant with the order of the *bhūmikas*. "*Grahītṛ*" is to be taken in the sense of *asmitā*.

45. The fluctuations of the *guṇas* have four subdivisions, viz. *viśiṣṭaliṅga* (the gross objects and the sense-organs), *aviśiṣṭaliṅga* (the *tanmātras* and the *antaḥkaraṇa*), the *liṅgamātra* (i.e. the *buddhi*) and the *aliṅga* (*prakṛti*. here *pradhāna*). This division is based on II.19.

51. It is remarked that in the seedless concentration *puruṣa* abides in itself.

BOOK TWO

II.1-2 (E60-62) 1. Focusing on God is explained as the surrender of all actions to him, the highest *guru*. This surrender must be associated with the idea of abandoning hankering after the fruits of actions.

II.3-11 (E62-71) 3. Ignorance, etc. are called afflictions as they give rise to suffering. These afflictions are said to strengthen traces, the products of the three *guṇas*.

4. It is argued that since egoity, attachment, aversion and clinging to conventional life appear and disappear according as the existence and nonexistence of ignorance, it is reasonable to hold ignorance to be the source (*mūla*) of egoity, etc. Ignorance is also said to be the material as well as the efficient cause of egoity, etc. Each of these afflictions is able to distract the *citta*.

5. Ignorance is defined as the apparent presentation of the

attributes of one thing in another.

9. Clinging to conventional life (*abhiniveśa*)is said to be the same as fear (*bhaya*), whose essential nature is self-protection (of the form of "let the objects and the body not be taken away or detached from me").

II.12-14 (E71-75) 12. "*Karma*" in the word "*karmāśaya*" is explained as the subconscious impressions (*vāsanā*). It is remarked that all the three fruits of *karmāśaya* felt in the present birth are not experienced by all. Some experience birth only, while others experience birth as well as length of life.

II.15-17 (E75-79) 15. Owing to excessive greed and lust, pleasure and pain become inevitable and they give rise to suffering afterwards. Such sufferings are to be taken as examples of pain caused by dynamic mutations (*pariṇāmaduḥkha*). That pain is to be taken as the result of anxiety (*tāpa*) which has its basis in hatred. Such pain can arise even at the time of experiencing pleasure. *Saṃskāra duḥkhas* are those pains that are caused by traces. It is remarked that on account of the non-destructibility of afflictions, traces and fruition, every thing is to be understood as pain (i.e. the source of pain).

17. "Contact" (*saṃyoga*) is explained as the proximity which consists in being of the nature of experiencer (*bhoktṛ*)* and *bhogya* (what is to be experienced, the object of the action of experiencing).

II.18-22 (E 79-85) 18. The word "*ātman*" in the expression "*bhūtendriyātmaka*" is explained as change (*pariṇāma*) not altogether different from the *dṛśya* itself.

20. Bhoja employs the word "*cetanā*" as a synonym of "*dṛśi*",

---

*Summarizer's note: The nature of *bhoktṛ* (an appellation of *puruṣa* or *draṣṭṛ*) is to be understood properly. Though grammatically it means the agent of the act of experiencing, yet in Sāṃkhya-Yoga it means the immutable illuminator of the cognitive faculty (*pravṛtti*) in *antaḥkaraṇa*.

and remarks that the relation of *dharma* and *dharmin* is not to be applied in *draṣṭṛ*. The reason for calling the seer *(draṣṭṛ)* "reflecting" (*anupaśya*) is his nature of perceiving *pratyayas* (i.e. the cognitions colored by the objects) directly without undergoing any transformation.

22. A corollary is drawn from what is stated in this *sūtra* that there is no possibility of liberation of all beings when one being is liberated.

II.23-27 (E85-90) 23. Bhoja observes that this *sūtra* points out the results of contact, which is taken as the mark (*lakṣaṇa*) of contact. It is the contact between them by which one (i.e. *prakṛti*) becomes capable of being experienced and the other (i.e. *puruṣa*) one who experiences.*

25. Bhoja aptly remarks that it is improper to think that there can be no such contact since contact requires a corporal body limited in extent. Rather, the contact (between *puruṣa* and *prakṛti*), being caused by non-discrimination, ceases when discriminative discernment comes into existence.

26. The essence of discriminative discernment is said to be the entering of the shadow of consciousness (*cicchāyāsaṃkrānti*) into *buddhi* which is not subjugated by the blemishes of *rajas* and *tamas*. After a constant flow of discriminative discernment the role of the seen (*dṛśya*) ceases and consequently liberation *(kaivalya)* is realized.

II.28-34 (E90–98) 28. "Systematic practice of the limbs" (*anuṣṭhāna*) is explained as their practice after due consideration (*jñānapūrvaka abhyāsa*).

29. Bhoja observes that reflective fixation (*dhāraṇa*) and meditation (*dhyāna*) give rise to concentration *(samādhi)* directly, while restraint (*yama*), etc. bring about concentration

---

*Summarizer's note: We have already stated that in this system *puruṣa* is called "experiencer" in the sense of "immutable illuminator of experience". Experience, a product of the *guṇas*, really exists in the *guṇas*.

in an indirect way uprooting the improper impulses (II.34), viz., violence and the like.

30. Nonviolence is mentioned in the first place in the *sūtra* because violence to other beings is to be abandoned at all times.

34. Bhoja observes that the order in which the causes "directed against the improper impulses", viz., greed, anger and delusion, are enumerated should be changed into "delusion, greed and anger" since it is delusion which is the root cause of all the afflictions.

39. Non-avarice (*aparigraha*) may be practiced even with reference to one's own body. The assuming of the body, which is the instrument of experience, is to be conceived as a kind of avarice. So long as there exists attachment to the body, knowledge of reality will not come into existence.

41. "Control over the sense-organs" (*indriyajaya*) is explained as the residing of the organs in the self. "Ability with respect to apprehending the self" (*ātmadarśana*) is the same as discriminative discernment (*vivekakhyāti*).

II.46-48 (E104-106) 47. "Engrossment with the infinite" (*anantasamāpatti)* is explained as the engrossment of mind in the infinitude existing in the sky and the like.

II.49-53 (E106-111) 50. Bhoja understands *bāhyavṛtti* as the same as *śvāsa*, also called *recaka* (exhalation); similarly, he takes *abhyantaravṛtti* (Bhoja reads *antarvṛtti*) as the same as *praśvāsa*, also called *pūraka* (inhalation).* The significance of

---

*Summarizer's note: This is not in consonance with the Vyāṣa *Bhāṣya*, which takes "*śvāsa*" as the drawing in of the external air and "*prāśvāsa*" as the exhalation of the internal air. This shows that according to the *Bhāṣya śvāsa* is *pūraka* and *praśvāṣa* is *recaka*. One is tempted to read "*praśvāsa*" in place of "*śvāsa*" so that there would arise no contradiction. This amended reading might be taken as original since Bhoja explains *śvāsa* and *praśvāsa* strictly in according with the

the word "*kumbha*" (a jar) in the word "*kumbhaka*" (another name of the *stambhavṛtti*) is shown by pointing out the similarity of stillness (*niścalatā*) existing in the water in a jar and in the breaths in the body (of a *yogin* practicing *stambhavṛtti*). "*Udghāta*" is defined as the impulse felt either for inhaling or exhaling after stopping breathing for a considerable period.*

II.54-55 (E112-114) 54. The word "*pratyāhāra*" is analyzed as "*pratīpam āhriyante asmin*", i.e. a practice in which the organs are drawn back from the objects.

BOOK THREE

III.1-8 (E 114-121) 1. Meditative fixation is said to be related to the field of the content-filled concentration alone.

5. Curiously enough, Bhoja explains the word "*āloka*" (in *prajñāloka*) as *prasava* (generation). Since no *Dhātupāṭha* reads the root *lok* in the sense of generation or creation and the like, it appears that the printed reading is corrupt.

8. The seedless concentration is spoken of as possessing no supporting object (*ālambana*, a support or object to be meditated upon). It is remarked that *śūnyabhāvanā* (contemplation of void) is another name of this concentration.

III.9-15 (E121-130) 9. It is remarked that suppression (*nirodha*) is that change of awareness in which there is the predominance of *sattva* which is designated as *prakṛṣṭa*, i.e. devoid of the blemishes of *rajas* and *tamas*. It is also held that awareness can never remain unchanging. The change called suppression is to be understood as of the nature of stability only (i.e. it is not to be taken as a state involving no change).

11. The fundamental change tending toward concentration

Bhāṣya (II.49) in commenting on *sūtra* I.31.

*Summarizer's note: This seems to be the clearest of all the definitions given by other commentators.

(*samādhipariṇāma*) is said to arise in an awareness which possesses *sattva* in abundance.

12. Those notions are said to be "the same" whose supports are of one form.

14. Bhoja remarks that that power is called a "substrate" (*dharmin*) which is conditioned or characterized by the capacity that consists in the invariable connection of the effect and the cause.

III.16-28 (E130-141) 16. Since an awareness is nothing but a pure illuminating factor, the power to comprehend all objects lies inherently in it. This power, however, is obstructed by the afflictions like ignorance, etc.

17."Word" *(śabda)* in this *sūtra* is taken either in the sense of sound which possesses sequence (*krama*) and which is perceived by the ear, or in the sense of *sphoṭa*, which does not possess any sequence and which is perceived by the intellect. An "object" (*artha*) is either a universal (*jāti*), a quality (*guṇa*), or an action (*kriyā*).

18. Traces (*saṃskāra*) are either subconscious impressions (*vāsanā*) which give rise to memory only, or the causes of karmic ripening (*vipāka*), viz., birth, length of life and type of experience.

19. A notion (*pratyaya*)(a modification of the intellect in the form of an object) of a person is perceived by a *yogin* with the help of some sign or mark, e.g., the complexion of a face and the like.

20. Bhoja remarks that the foreknowledge of death through portents can be acquired by non-*yogins* also. Such a knowledge becomes characterized by general features only and as such it may give rise to doubt. On the contrary, the foreknowledge of a *yogin* becomes bereft of error and doubt as if it were a perception, since the *yogin* is able to know the exact time and place of death.

23. In the "etc." following friendliness Bhoja 's enumeration follows what is found in *sūtra* I.33. The inclusion of dispassion (*upekṣā*) here is not in consonance with the Vyāsa *Bhāṣya*, for

it expressly states that since *upekṣa* is not a practice (*bhāvanā*) it cannot be the object of comprehensive reflection.

26. The word "*sūrya*" in this *sūtra* is explained as the lustrous sun, and it is remarked that this luster is *bhautika*, belonging to the field of the gross elements.

III.29-37 (E 142-150) 32. *Mūrdhan* is the same as the *brahmarandhra*, an aperture in the head. Since it contains luster, "*jyotis*" is used with it. The *sāttvika* radiance emitted from the heart assumes the form of a lump in this region.

34. "Consciousness of ordinary awareness" (*cittasaṃvid*) is explained as the knowledge of the subconscious impressions existing in the awareness of a person practicing comprehensive reflection and also as the knowledge of attachment, etc. existing in the awarenesses of other persons.

35. "One's own unique" (*svārtha*) consciousness is that notion whose supporting object is nothing but the *puruṣa*-principle only. In other words, *svārtha* is the same as the entering of the shadow of consciousness (*cicchāyāsaṃkrānti*) in the *sattva* (i.e. the *buddhi*) that has given up egoism.

36. Bhoja takes words like "*pratibhā*", "*śravaṇa*", etc. in the sense of particular cognitions (*jñāna*) and remarks that through these cognitions a *yogin* perceives subtle (*divya*) sound, touch, etc. (The Vyāsa *Bhāṣya* seems to take these words as the names of supernormal powers (and not as the forms of cognitions) through which a *yogin* can acquire six kinds of *divya* knowledge.)

III.38-48 (E150-162) 38. Bhoja notes that there is a channel (*nāḍī*) through which flow the fluctuations of awareness and remarks that this channel is different from those channels through which flows lymph, etc.

39. Life (*jīvana*) is defined as a fluctuation of all the organs, all of which give rise to it simultaneously. This simultaneous rise is like the simultaneous blazing of husks.

41. The essential characteristic of celestial hearing consists in its capacity to perceive subtle, obstructed or remote sounds.

44. Bhoja, while dealing with the inherent aspect of gross

materiality, remarks that in this aspect smell is to be taken as the feature of earth. (The Vyāsa *Bhāṣya*, however, mentions solidity or hardness as the feature of earth in its inherent aspect.)

45. Bhoja enumerates the extraordinary capacities (also called *mahāsiddhis*) as atomization, lightness of weight, magnification, *gariman*, irresistibility, control, lordship and wish fulfilment. The Vyāsa *Bhāṣya*, however, mentions acquisition (*prāpti)* and does not mention *gariman*. Bhoja thinks that the touching of the moon by fingertips is an example of *gariman*, while the *Bhāṣya* takes it as an example of acquisition. The definitions of, and the order of listing of, control and lordship as given by Bhoja are different from those given in the *Bhāṣya*.

III.49-55 (E162-171) 49. Bhoja remarks that the discriminative discernment that arises from comprehensive reflection practiced toward the *sāttvika* mutation of the intellect consists in the slackening (*sthitibhāva*) of the notion of agency that lies in the *guṇas*.*

55. Bhoja understands the purification (*śuddhi*) of the intellect as its entering its material cause. This state comes into existence after the cessation of the notion of agency in *sattva* (i.e. the *buddhi*). The Vyāsa *Bhāṣya*, however, understands *śuddhi* as the state in which *buddhi* is occupied with discriminative discernment and also as the state in which the seeds of affliction have become burnt.

---

*Summarizer's remark: This is, however, not in consonance with the original Sāṃkhya doctrine that the *kārtṛtva* really lies in the *guṇas;* cp. *Sāṃkhyakārikā* 20 ("*guṇakartṛtve ca tathā*" and also the statement by Pañcaśīkhā ("*ayam thu khala triṣu guṇeṣu kartṛsu*") quoted in the *Bhāṣya* on *Yogasūtra* II. 18. *Vivekakhyāti*, however, consists in the knowledge of difference between *buddhi* and *puruṣa*.

BOOK FOUR

IV.1-5 (E171-177) 1. Bhoja remarks that the psychic capacity that occurs naturally (i.e. through birth) (*janma-siddhi*) includes those extraordinary capacities also which come into existence even after birth. Such capacities, known as *sāṃsiddhika,* may be found in Kapila and other *maharṣis*. It is concentration practiced in a previous birth which is the actual cause of all the four kinds of extraordinary capacities, and birth, drugs, etc. are to be taken as the sources of their manifestation only.

IV.6-11 (E177-185) 7. Bhoja takes sacrifice (yāga*),* said to be constituted by *dravya, devatā* and *tyāga*, as an example of white karma conducive to beneficial results. These white karmas are said to be performed by those who are endowed with *dāna* (charity, gift), *tapas* (penance), sacred study and recitation (*svādhyāya*) and the like. It should be noted in this connection that if animal killing is involved in a sacrifice (*paśūyāga*) then the sacrifice cannot be regarded as a white karma from the yogic point of view.

9. Bhoja refers here to the view held by some ancient teacher that memory and traces are different in nature. Bhoja contends that in this view there will be no cause-effect relation between memory and traces owing to the absence of simultaneity.

10. "Wish or desire to be" (*āśis*) is explained as the spontaneous longing for the means to pleasure and is considered to be the same as great delusion (*mahāmoha*). Awareness (*citta*) is defined here as colored with experiences and traces and as having expansion and contraction as its properties. It takes various forms according as it is affected by stimuli.

11. The nature of the absence of subconscious impressions is shown as similar to the state of burnt seeds.

IV.12-16 (E185-192) 12. Since there can be no absence of the existent and no genesis of the nonexistent it is justified to accept that there exists a property-possessor with its own form and which constantly changes through its modifications. It is the properties which are either past, future, or present. An awareness is of the nature of a property-possessor which exists until liberation (*apavarga*) of the absolute knower is achieved.

13. The three *guṇas* viz., *sattva, rajas* and *tamas*, are identical (respectively) with pleasure, pain and stupor and all the internal or external entities exhibit these three essential characteristics, a fact which shows that all entities are nothing but the modifications of the three *guṇas*.

14. A dynamic transformation (*pariṇāma*) of the *guṇas* consists in the predominance of one *guṇa* and the subordination of the other two. The word "*vastutattva*" is explained as the unity (*ekatva*) of an entity (*vastu*).

15. Here Bhoja shows the futility of the notion of the creation of an actual entity by many awarenesses simultaneously. He concedes that there can be no relation of cause and effect between the entity and the awareness and as such an actual entity is to be regarded as essentially different from its cognition.

17. "*Uparāga*" (influence) is defined as *ākārasamarpaṇa*, i.e. when an awareness being affected by a stimulus assumes the form of an object, then it becomes aware of that object.

IV.17-23 (E192-202) 21. "Memory trace" (*smṛtisaṃskāra*) is defined as the capability of understanding the particular object whose memory occurs in an awareness.

22. The characteristic of change of qualities (*guṇa-pariṇāma*) is a change in which one of the three *guṇas* becomes predominant and the other two become subordinate.

23. An awareness is said to be "influenced" (*uparakta*) by the seer when it appears as if it assumed the form of *puruṣa* owing to proximity. Bhoja appears to hold the view that the awareness does not really assume the form of the *puruṣa*. The awareness, however, really does become affected by the object seen (*dṛśya*) and it assumes the form of a thing which has become its object.

Bhoja states that in this philosophy two kinds of fluctuation of awareness are accepted. The first is *nityodita*: it is the same as the *sattva (buddhi)* which becomes manifested owing to the proximity of *puruṣa*. Consciousness (*caitanya*) becomes manifested in this fluctuation. The (second kind is the) *abhivyaṅgya* fluctuation of awareness, which assumes the capability of being experienced (*bhogyatā*) of *puruṣa* and is closely connected with it. It is the state of being the experiencer of pleasure and pain. The appellation "*śāntabrahmavādin*" is given to the Sāṃkhyas. According to the doctrine of *śānta-brahman* the ultimate state is that in which *brahman* or the immutable *puruṣa* abides in itself after the complete cessation of all modifications of awareness.

A statement of Vindhyavāsin on the nature of experience (*bhoga*) is quoted here. It is the *cittasattva* which is really affected by experience though it is attributed to *puruṣa*.

A view of some ancient teacher on the nature of *pratisaṃkrānti* is shown here. It is compared with a reflected image (*pratibimba*). The possibility of experience has also been discussed here. The character of two kinds of change, namely *anuloma* and *pratiloma* has been shown precisely. The former is from the *mahat* to the *mahābhūtas* and is called *bahirmukha* (proceeding from the subtle to the gross form), and the latter is from the *mahābhūtas* to self-awareness (*asmitā*) (i.e. from the gross to the subtle form) which happens when the effects enter their material cause. The *buddhisattva* which contains both traces caused by objects and the shadow of consciousness leads its whole life by acquiring knowledge of objects.

IV.24-34 (E202-216) 25. Meditation on the existence of the self is explained as the wrong self-awareness (*abhimāna*) that awareness is the real actor, cognizer and experiencer.*

---

*This may show that according to Bhoja it is *puruṣa* who is to be taken to be the doer, knower and experiencer, or it may simply mean that the *puruṣa* is the witness presence that allows the doer, knower and experiencer to function. According to the

28. From the statement that discriminative discernment gives rise to the *dharma*-cloud realization, Bhoja infers that the efficient cause of *jñāna* must be held to be the exalted (*prakṛṣṭa*) *sattva*.

34. Here Bhoja holds a lengthy discussion on the nature of liberation accepted by different schools like the school of Śaṃkara, the Naiyāyikas, the Mīmāṃsakas, the Jainas, the Śaivas, and the like. After refuting the views of these schools Bhoja concludes that the only logical view about the nature of liberation is that in the liberated state of the self who is nothing but consciousness, the self abides in itself. Here again, the Sāṃkhyas are referred to as *śāntabrahmavādins.*

In the course of refuting the views of the various schools Bhoja stresses the following points: (1)Liberation (*mokṣa*) cannot reasonably said to be *ānandamaya* (full of bliss, or bliss in essence). (2) The theory of ignorance as propounded by Advaitins cannot be accepted as reasonable. (3) The view that the self becomes intelligent when associated with intelligence (*cetanā*) is untenable. (4) It is wrong to hold that the self is perceptible with the help of the I-notion (*ahampratyaya*). (5) The immutable self cannot be said to have a magnitude equal

---

traditional view *kartṛtva* really lies in the *citta* (and not in the *puruṣa*). The knowerhood and experiencer-ness which are correctly attributed to *puruṣa* are not to be understood as the two forms of agency as is commonly held by some schools of philosophy. In Sāṃkhya-Yoga *jñātṛtva* and *bhoktṛtva* signify the quality of being the immutable illuminator of the cognitive and conative faculties. Thus it is clear that *jñātṛtva* and *bhoktṛtva* have no connection with mutation. That *puruṣa* is bereft of all qualities and actions is one of the principal tenets of Sāṃkhya-Yoga.

to that of the body in which it lies.

7.SĀYANA MĀDHAVA, *Sarvadarśanasaṃgraha*

Summary by Gerald James Larson

Mādhavācārya was a follower of the Advaita Vedānta tradition and has usually been dated in the fourteenth century. He is said to have been a minister in the court of King Bukka I (1356-1377) of Vijayanagara.[161] His work, *Sarvadarśana-saṃgraha*, provides a summary treatment of the various philosophical and religious systems prevalent in his period.[162] Altogether he treats some sixteen systems in what appears to be a hierarchical manner. His treatment begins with the Cārvāka-darśana and culminates in the following sequence: Pratyabhijñādarśana (Kashmir Śaivism), Raseśvaradarśana (Alchemy), Vaiśeṣikadarśana, Naiyāyikadarśana, Jaiminidarśana (Mīmāṃsā), Pāṇinidarśana, Sāṃkhyadarśana, Yogadarśana, and, finally, Śaṃkaradarśana. Regarding his treatment of Pātañjala Yoga, two observations are pertinent. First, he refers to Yoga as "*śeṣvara-sāṃkhya*", that is, "theistic Sāṃkhya", which also has another name, "*sāṃkhyapravacana*", that is, "an explanation of Sāṃkhya". Second, it is interesting to note that he places Yogadarśana even higher in his hierarchy of systems than the Sāṃkhya. Pātañjala Yoga is just one system below Śaṃkaradarśana. His treatment of Yoga overall follows the *Yogasūtras* closely and calls for no further summary here.

8.RĀMĀNANDA SARASVATĪ, *Maṇiprabhāvṛtti* on Patañjali's *Yogasūtras*

Rāmānanda Sarasvatī was a student of Ācārya Govindānanda, who can be dated in the late sixteenth century, which suggests that Rāmānanda Sarasvatī himself lived in the early seventeenth century. A follower of the Advaita Vedānta of Śaṃkara, he wrote *Brahmāmṛtavarṣinī*, a sub-commentary on the *Brahmasūtras*. His commentary, *Maṇiprabhāvṛtti* ("Jewel-

Luster Sub-commentary"), on the *Yogasūtras* for the most part follows earlier commentaries.

The Sanskrit edition, indicated as E below, used for this summary is Bhattacharya, n.d.

Summary by Anima Sen Gupta

BOOK ONE

I.1 (E 2) Awareness has two forms–content-filled and content-free. The fluctuations the states of awareness (*citta*)* and so the cessation of these fluctuations, which is called "*yoga*", is also a state of awareness. Awareness possesses five levels: distracted, sluggish, partially distracted, one-pointed and ceased. The first three do not pertain to *yoga* proper, but the fourth and fifth levels do relate to *yoga* in the proper sense. The fourth or one-pointed has to do with content-filled concentration where awareness is fixed on a single object. The fifth has to do with content-free concentration in which there is no content at all.

I.2 (E 2) "Yoga" means cessation of the fluctuations produced by the effective functioning of *rajas* and *tamas*. This definition, therefore, is applicable to content-filled concentration, when the mind remains occupied with the fluctuation of the *sattva*. A single awareness is supposed to possess many levels in the forms of distracted and so on because it is constituted of the three *guṇas*.

I. 3 (E 5) When all the functionings of awareness, which are of the forms of calmness, turbulence and delusion, are

---

*Professor Sen Gupta uses the term "mind-stuff" to translate "*citta*". For consistency's sake, and to eliminate possible confusion due to the connotations of the term "stuff", the General Editor has replaced "mind-stuff" throughout with the briefer term "awareness" which is taken as a standard translation of "*citta*" in this Volume.

stopped, the *puruṣa* remains in its own natural form. The *puruṣa* is mere consciousness: it never assumes the form of a fluctuation.

I.4 (E 5) In the emergent state awareness undergoes various fluctuations which are calm, turbulent, etc. The intellect (*buddhi*), possessing fluctuations , is not differentiated from the *puruṣa* and as a result of non-discrimination the *puruṣa* falsely appears as identical with the intellect and consequently, through mistake, it is supposed to be the calm, miserable and delusive ego of worldly experiences. In reality, the *puruṣa* never loses its own nature. When awareness stops functioning there is liberation, while bondage occurs in the emergent state during which awareness undergoes fluctuations.

I.5 (E6-7) The author quotes Bhoja's commentary, which says that in order to explain the cessation of the fluctuations of awareness the author of the *Yogasūtras* has defined awareness as that with the cessation of which there is liberation and with the awakening of which there is bondage. The fluctuations have been divided into harmful and beneficial with a view to indicating their unwholesome and wholesome natures. The harmful fluctuations are the causes of the afflictions like attachment, aversion, etc, and these are the producers of the state of bondage. All living beings (after experiencing objects through the instruments of knowledge) develop passions, etc. under the spell of which they perform actions. These actions, by producing pleasures, etc. keep living beings entangled in worldly life. The beneficial fluctuations, which lead to the realization of the difference between intellect and *puruṣa* through practice and dispassion, take their rise in the midst of the harmful fluctuations and, being increased by repeated practice, destroy the harmful ones. Then through the practice of the supreme dispassion these beneficial fluctuations too are stopped. There is then the dissolution of awareness. This is the state of liberation.

I.7 (E7-8) Instruments of knowledge are three in number The common characteristic of these instruments is that each one of them produces knowledge. Knowledge relates to that awareness of an object which was not known before. An awareness is a reflection (of the *puruṣa*) in a fluctuation. The fluctuations of the intellect in the form of the object is the instrumental cause of it. The reflection of the *puruṣa* in the objectified fluctuation of the intellect also assumes the form of the object through the functioning of the fluctuation and becomes the result (i.e. knowledge). When through the knowledge of the pervasion between the mark (*liṅga*) and the thing to be proved (*sādhya*), and also through the knowledge of the presence of the mark in the subject (*pakṣa*) of the inference, there arises the fluctuation yielding knowledge of the things to be proved in a general way. This is called inference. The fluctuation, yielding knowledge of the object which is gained through the utterances of a trustworthy person who has known it either through perception or through inference, is said to be produced by verbal testimony. The Vedas are composed by God, who is trustworthy.

I.8 (E8-9) The awareness that does not remain steady in regard to the content it embraces and is also finally removed by another awareness is to be regarded as error. A false awareness, being false, does not cover vague cognition, which remains outside of its scope. The incorrectness of misunderstanding is admitted by all, and error is sublated. This type of removal is not possible in the case of conceptual constructions.

I.9 (E9) When one hears of such words as "man's horns" he has a vague awareness in his mind having no specific object corresponding to it. This vague awareness is called conceptual construction. As this type of awareness and the use of words for it cannot be avoided in practical life in spite of the fact that it admits of correction, it is different from ordinary error.

I.10 (E10) Sleep is the fluctuation of awareness which arises when there is absence of the modes of waking or of the dream state, and which is supported by inertia born of the "materiality constituent". The word "fluctuation" is used in connection with sleep with a view to refuting the contention that the sleeping state is one in which awareness is absent. A person getting up from sleep remembers "I was sleeping peacefully".

I.11 (E10-11) Memory is the reproduction of a previous experience only. It does not reproduce anything which was not previously experienced.

I.12 (E 11) The river-like minds of all living beings flow naturally towards the worldly-life, which is a life of experience. When a man becomes disinterested in the experiencing of object he can put a stop to the flow of his mind toward the world. By practicing discrimination between the intellect and the *puruṣa* he can direct his mind inward. Practice and dispassion make the mind free from the fluctuations having *rajas* and *tamas* as their practically effective inherent force. The fluctuations, having that "thought-constituent" as their practically effective inherent force, then arise in the mind and stability prevails. "Practice" refers to careful performance of restraint, observance, etc. which serve as the means for the attainment of *yoga*. If practice can be made steady and deep-rooted by continuing it for a long time with self-control, learning and reverence, then it cannot be disturbed by empirical affairs. Dispassion developed towards all sorts of objects, either of this world or of the next, is the supreme form of dispassion.

I.16 (E17) Cessation is the disappearance of all fluctuations of awareness. Such cessation is brought about by the supreme type of dispassion. When only the subliminal impressions remain, the content-free concentration takes place. The highest form of dispassion overpowers the traces of the content-free form of concentration. It is seedless because it has no support; it is also devoid of the seeds of action.

I.20-21 (E18-20) Faith, energy, etc. leading to knowledge may be included in the means. Owing to the force of subliminal impressions from the previous births, faith etc. may be either gentle or moderate or intense. *Yogins* also are classified into three categories: (1) those possessing subliminal impressions in a small quantity; (2) those possessing a quantity which is neither large nor small; (3) those possessing a quantity which is very large. Again, the forcefulness of the subliminal impressions may be less, moderate or great.

I.23 (E20-21) If a *yogin* can have whole-hearted devotion to God, if his body, mind and words are dedicated to God, then he can attain concentration quickly. The word "or" in the *sūtra* is used here to show that devotion to God is an alternative path to the one mentioned before.

I.27-28 (E24-25) God is indicated by the mystic syllable "*oṃ*". The *yogin* understands the relation that exists between the mystic syllable and God; so he repeats "*oṃ*", meditates upon its meaning and thereby makes his mind steady and one-pointed.

I.37 (E32) The *yogin* can make his mind stable by meditating on the dispassionate minds of the great sages like Vyāsa, Śuka, and others.

I.47 (E 39) When the impurities of *rajas* and *tamas* are removed, then awareness, being devoid of afflictions and impurities, manifests its illuminating (*sattva*) nature: it, then, assumes the form of a transparent and motionless flow of pure brilliance

I.48 (E40) Owing to the attainment of such proficiency, knowledge (full of truth) arises in the pure and engrossed mind. This knowledge is called "truth-bearing insight".

I.50 (E41-44) By the repeated arousal of the traces of concentration, the afflictions are destroyed. Awareness is completely detached in relation to worldly enjoyment. Such a mind is then drawn towards the *puruṣa* principle. After attaining discriminative insight and thereby serving the supreme end of the self, awareness gets merged in the *guṇas*. The final end of all efforts of awareness is the realization of the distinction between the *puruṣa* and itself.

I.51 (E34) When the traces of seedless concentration are accumulated, awareness, in the absence of a cause for its existence, gets merged by nature. When awareness is dissolved, the *puruṣa* remains in its own pure form; it is dissociated from awareness and this state of aloofness of *puruṣa* is its liberation.

BOOK TWO

II.1-2 (E44) These two *sūtras* indicate that yogic knowledge can be attained by the "*yoga* of action" (*kriyāyoga*), which consists of ascetic exercises, study, and devotion to God. "Ascetic exercises" (*tapas*) implies: (i) practicing sex control, serving the teacher, truth-telling, and observing silence completely, discharging duties relative to one's stage of life, etc. and also (ii) the power to put up with difficulties caused by heat, cold, hunger, thirst, etc. "Study" requires that the aspirant should utter the syllable "*oṃ*" etc. He should study those scriptures which speak of liberation. Devotion to God requires that the aspirant should dedicate all fruits of his actions to the most respected teacher (i.e. God). If the afflictions remain forceful then concentration cannot take place. As a result of the yoga of action these afflictions are attenuated. This brings about concentration.

II.5 (E47) Ignorance prompts a man to regard the non-eternal as eternal, the impure as pure, the finally sorrowful as the pleasurable, and the non-self as the self. These forms of ignorance lie at the root of bondage or worldly life.

II.6 (E48) The false identity of the seer (*puruṣa*) with the seen (the intellect) is expressed iṇ the form "I am". The two radically distinct entities like the experiencer and the experienced falsely appear united through ignorance. The followers of Vedānta call this egoity "the knot of the heart".

II.7 (E48) The thirst for worldly enjoyment, which arises on account of the arousal of the traces of the same type of enjoyment, is the manifestation of a state of mind which is called "attachment" (*rāga*).

II.8 (E48) "Aversion" refers to the feeling of anger towards misery and its causes arising out of remembrance of previously experienced pain.

II.9 (E48-49) Inborn fear of death, which exists in the minds of both wise and unwise due to subliminal impressions arising out of the painful experiences of previous deaths, is called the will to live (*abhiniveśa*).

II.10 (E50) When discriminative knowledge arises awareness disappears in the ego-sense which is its cause. Then the subtle afflictions, that is afflictions which have become like burnt seeds, are destroyed.

II.15-16 (E56) Just as medical science is to be learnt in four parts, namely disease, its cause, cure of the disease, and the cause of cure, in the same manner this science (of Yoga) is to be learnt in four parts: (1) what is to be removed, (2) the cause of that which is to be removed, (3) removal of that cause, and (4) the means that lead to that removal. Pain which is yet to come is to be removed.

II.18 (E37) The three *guṇas* go by the name of their primary cause (*prakṛti*). These are called the "seen" (*dṛśya*). They exist in the form of elements and also in the form of sense-organs. The elements are both gross and subtle. The organs are divided into five organs of cognition and five organs of action plus the intellect, the ego-sense and the mind (the three internal organs). The "seen" serves the purposes of enjoyment and liberation of the *puruṣa*. It is because of this characteristic that all elements and organs are treated as the "seen".

II.19 (E58) The diversified modifications are sixteen in number, namely five gross elements in the forms of space, air, fire, water and earth, ten organs of cognition and action, and the mind. These are not capable of producing further categories of a different order. The six non-diversified modifications are the five subtle physical elements and the dynamic ego. According to Sāṃkhya, the five subtle physical elements originate from the dynamic ego whereas the Yoga regards the five subtle physical elements as the effects of the intellect, appearing after the origination of the dynamic ego. The intellect is (also) called the "*liṅgamātra*". The word "*mātra*" implies difference from both the diversified and the non-diversified. The primary cause which is the original state of the three constituents is to be regarded as *aliṅga* (that which does not merge into anything else). The *guṇas* serve the purposes of the *puruṣa*.

II.20-23 (E59-61) Although the *puruṣa* is unchangeable and pure, still exhibiting the changes of the intellect and falsely appearing as similar to those changes, revealed by it, the *puruṣa* appears as identical with the knowing faculty of the intellect. The essence of the object of sight then disappears in regard to the liberated *yogin*, it still continues to operate in regard to all other worldly-minded people Both experience and liberation are due to contact between the seer and the object of sight. Awareness of the knowable in diversified forms of sound, etc. is experience, and realization of the true nature of the seer is liberation.

II.26 (E63) Knowledge of the distinction between the seer and the seen is what is called discriminative knowledge. In the initial stage, from the study of the scripture, discriminative knowledge arises in a general way; being indirect it cannot destroy beginningless ignorance. Then the *yogin* contemplates rationally and by becoming disinterested in all worldly objects he allows his mind to flow towards the *puruṣa* all the time. The discriminative knowledge that results from content-filled concentration eliminates error and being unimpaired becomes the means to liberation.

II.28 (E65) If the accessories to *yoga* are practiced regularly, then the five forms of afflictions are destroyed completely. The purity that arises from the performance of the eight-fold limbs of *yoga* serves to awaken the highest knowledge.

II.30-31 (E66-67) Restraint, observances, posture, breath-control, withdrawal of sense-organs, fixation, meditation and concentration are the eight limbs (of disciplined meditation). These should be practiced universally by all *yogins* without making any distinction of class, place, time and so forth.

BOOK THREE

III.1 (E83) With a view to attaining content-filled concentration the *yogin* fixes his mind either on the navel region or on the heart or on the tip of the nose, and thereby makes his mind steady. This is called "meditative fixation" (*dhāraṇā*).

III.2 (E84) The mind is withdrawn from all other objects and is fixed steadily on the object of attention. The thought process relating to the object flows continuously without break. This is called reflective meditation (*dhyāna*).

III.3 (E85) When meditation in the form of a continuous and transparent flow of "thought-process" deepens so much that the object only shines forth in the mind, the meditation assumes the form of concentration. Meditation is the flow of the "thought-process" of the three forms of awareness, namely awareness of the object of meditation, of the act of meditating, and also of the meditator in an unbroken fashion. The awareness of the object alone bursts forth in the mind in the state of concentration. In the content-free concentration there is not even the awareness of this object of meditation.

III.11 (E89) By practice, the distractions of the mind are gradually eliminated and one-pointedness is consequently increased.

III.55 (E124) When through discriminative knowledge subliminal impressions of inhibition only remain in the intellect and the intellect also becomes free from all impurities of *rajas* and *tamas*, resulting in the cessation of objective fluctuations, then this state of the intellect is regarded as the state of purity. The ever-free self too ceases to be falsely associated with imaginary enjoyments and so it is also in its state of purity. This likeness in purity of the intellect and the *puruṣa* results in liberation.

BOOK FOUR

IV.17-18 (E140-141) Awareness is no doubt all-embracing and it possesses, by nature, the capacity of revealing objects. When an awareness is influenced by an object through the operation of the sense-organs, it assumes the form of the object, which is manifested by the reflected consciousness residing in the awareness. By means of its own image formed in the intellect, the object makes itself an object of apprehension by the *puruṣa*. Thus the awareness, depending on its fluctuations in the form of the objects related to it, knows an object at one time and at another time (when the awareness is not so related) the object remains unknown. On account of the knowability and unknowability of objects, awareness is subject to change.

All the fluctuations of awareness which are capable of being revealed by the *puruṣa* are always so revealed to the master (i.e. *puruṣa*). Thus *puruṣa* is unchangeable.

IV.19 (E142-144) Since an awareness is knowable in the form "my mind is peaceful", it is not self-luminous. It is not self-reflective as is the *puruṣa*. Since awareness falls under the category of an object of sight (*dṛśya*) it is revealed by a seer other than itself. Owing to recollection in the form of "I am that", it is not momentary.

IV.20-21 (E142-144) The doctrine of universal momentariness cannot be supported because of the fact that illumination of awareness and consciousness at the same moment is not possible. Given momentariness, an awareness cannot be both subject and object at the same time. If the object is a product of an awareness then the awareness cannot exist at the moment when the object is produced. If the object is not produced by the awareness, then also in spite of being contemporaneous it cannot be cognized by the awareness because of the absence of causal connection and essential identity. Nor can one awareness be supposed to be illumined by another awareness. If the awareness in the form of blue is illumined by another awareness, then that will be illumined by yet another and so on. This will result in infinite regress. if there are many minds, there will be many traces and many memories; so it will be difficult to have clear recollection of a particular experience. In the absence of a cognizer and also in the absence of clear apprehension of a particular memory, there is bound to the mixing together of different memories.

IV.23 (E145-146) An awareness is affected on the one hand by consciousness and, on the other, by an object. Since the awareness is an object to be enjoyed, a distinct principle as the enjoyer is to be admitted. The enjoyer is eternally manifested and is regarded as the *puruṣa*.

IV.24 (E146) Although awareness assumes diverse forms of pleasures and pains, being affected by innumerable impressions, still it serves the purposes of enjoyment and liberation of the *puruṣa*. The awareness is not the enjoyer because it performs the activities of enjoyment, etc. being associated with the body, organs, etc.

IV.29-30 (E150-151) When the *yogin* realizes the distinction between *prakṛti* and *puruṣa*, he becomes indifferent to this special knowledge also; he comes to possess all-around discriminative knowledge and attains the stage of concentration called *dharma*-cloud realization. On the attainment of this stage, the five-fold afflictions and all traces of actions are eradicated.

When infinite knowledge and supreme dispassion result from the concentration called *dharma*-cloud realization, the modification of the three *guṇas* (from the *mahat* to objects like a jar) appearing gradually (prior to enjoyment and liberation) disappear in the reverse order.

IV.34 (E155-160) The intellect, etc. which are the effects of the *guṇas*, disappear in the reverse order (in which they appeared after *pralaya*) in relation to the successful *yogin* whose purposes of enjoyment and liberation have been fulfilled. All forms of traces are resolved into the mind. The mind disappears in the ego-sense. The ego-sense disappears in the great principle (*mahat*), which in its turn disappears in the *guṇas*. As a result of such accomplishment, the primary cause is not provided with any purposes for creation in relation to that successful self. The self or the *puruṣa* remains in its own excellence by its own nature: the state of the "self-in-itself" is said to be attained when there is absolute dissociation (*viyoga*) of the *puruṣa* from the intellect, ego-sense, etc. From the pont of view of the eternal, pure, non-attached, and illuminating *puruṣa* this "isolation" is supreme liberation.

9.RĀGHAVĀNANDA SARASVATĪ, *Pātañjalarahasya* on Vyāsa's Yogasūtrabhāṣya and Vācaspatimiśra's *Tattvavaiśāradī*

Summary by Ram Shankar Bhattacharya

Rāghavānanda says that his purpose in composing this commentary is to supplement gaps and omissions in Vācaspati Miśra's commentary. According to the author, the benedictory verse "*yas tyaktvā rūpam ādyam...*" belongs to the Vyāsa *Bhāṣya*. This verse has been commented on by Vijñānabhikṣu, but not by Vācaspatimiśra. Most traditional scholars in India consider the verse to be a later interpolation.

The author Rāghavānanda (also known as Rāghavendra Sarasvatī) was the disciple of Advayabhagavatpāda, the disciple of Vāsudeva Bhagavatpāda (see colophon). Some of his works are: (1) *Tattvārṇava*, a commentary on the *Tattvakaumudī* by Vācaspati, (2) a commentary on the *Manusmṛti*, (3) a commentary on the *Saṃkṣepaśārīraka*, and (4) a commentary on the *Mīmāṃsāsūtras*. According to Gopinath Kaviraj, he may be placed some time in the sixteenth century.[163]

There are no new philosophical insights in the commentary beyond what is found in Vyāsa and Vācaspatimiśra and therefore there is no need for a full summary.

10. VIJÑĀNABHIKṢU, *Yogavārttika* on Patañjali's *Yogasūtras*

Summary by T. S. Rukmani

It is generally accepted that Vijñānabhikṣu (hereafter, Bhikṣu) lived in the sixteenth century CE. He thus lived at a time when all the three schools of Vedānta, i.e. Advaita, Viśiṣṭādvaita and Dvaita had been established and also after the *bhakti* movement had reached new heights during the time of Caitanya. Being at heart a theist, for which there is ample evidence both in his *Sāṃkhyapravacanabhāṣya* and his *Yogavārttika*, Bhikṣu was vehemently opposed to Śaṃkara's Advaita Vedānta.

The picture of Bhikṣu that emerges from the *Yogavārttika* is that of an uncompromising ascetic, steadfast in his adherence to the principles of Yoga. He thus differs from Śaṃkara in his interpretation of the *Vedāntasūtras* of Bādarāyaṇa. He also differs from Vācaspatimiśra (hereafter Miśra) and others in his interpretation of the Sāṃkhya system and dismisses the atheistic stand of Sāṃkhya as an academic exercise in trying to show that even if there is no belief in God it is possible to attain *mokṣa* through right knowledge.

Bhikṣu's famous dual reflection theory for the acquisition of knowledge is unique. Neither Miśra nor any other commentator has thought on those lines. One is tempted to draw parallels between the dual incarnation theory of Kṛṣṇa in Caitanya's thought and Bhikṣu's dual reflection theory. Unlike commentators such as Miśra who are able to explain and comment on different systems without their own biases showing through, Bhikṣu's preference is transparent in his commentaries. He is first and foremost a *yogin* and one finds this intense commitment to *yoga* tailored into his interpretation of systems like Vedānta and Sāṃkhya as well. This is perhaps why there are no commentaries available on systems of Pūrvamīmāṃsā and Nyāya-Vaiśeṣika by Bhikṣu. Bhikṣu also differs from Miśra, the other important commentator on the

Vyāsa *Bhaṣya*, at various places. Many such differences will be pointed out in the course of the following summary.

"ET" in what follows refers to Rukmani 1 = Volume I, 1981; 2 = Volume II, 1983; 3 = Volume III, 1987; and 4 = Volume IV, 1989 .

BOOK ONE

In introductory verses Bhikṣu establishes that Yoga is the philosophy *par excellence* for those seeking liberation. He claims that the essence of the meaning of all the Vedas is mentioned here (in the *Bhāṣya*) by Veda Vyāsa under the pretext of a commentary on the *Yogasūtras* (YS). Therefore this is the only path for those desiring liberation. Just as all rivers such as the Gaṅgā are present in the parts of the ocean, so also schools of philosophy such as the Sāṃkhya are present totally as parts of this (Yoga) philosophy.

I.1-2 (ET 1.19-43) The traditional definition of "*yoga*' by Vyāsa that "it is concentration and it is a quality of the mind* in all its fields" is examined. When awareness is active on the objects alone through the quality of *rajas*, it is distracted; it is sluggish when, through *tamas* it is engaged in sleep; the partially distracted is better than the distracted; that lamp-like awareness which has its flame-tip in one object alone is one-pointed. Even though there is some one-pointedness in the three (states of) distracted, etc. the definition of "*yoga*" does not cover those. "Suppressed" is the state where all activities of awareness are restricted and only traces are left. Amongst the five states of awareness mentioned above only the last two (one-pointed and suppressed) qualify as "*yoga*". It is not just

*Rukmani translates "*citta*" as "mind". As is our policy (see previously), from here on we replace her "mind" in this sense with "awareness", since "mind" also is used to translate, e.g., "*manas*" and other terms that also appear regularly in Yoga texts.

one-pointed (awareness) which qualifies as *yoga* but also the destruction of the afflictions.

Yoga also has a lower and higher stage called content-filled and content-free respectively. While in the former the content of concentration is revealed in its true form along with removal of the five afflictions, in the latter even this state is transcended through superior dispassion (*paravairāgya*). An awareness at this stage has only a series of traces of content-free concentration and has no more power to continue the cycle of birth and death. It then merges into its primal cause.

In the commentary on *sūtra* I.2 Bhikṣu states his definition of "*yoga*" clearly as "the restriction of the fluctuations of awareness, accompanied by the destruction of the afflictions and of karma.

The Vedāntin says that in content-free concentration also, pure awareness of the self is present in the form of a fluctuation of awareness into its true self. This is to be rejected because it is without authority. Pure awareness of the self is present at the time of content-filled concentration itself and thus it is lower than content-free concentration.

I.3 (ET 1.41-43) Question: In content-free concentration does the *puruṣa* (a) exist as consciousness itself, or (b) does the *puruṣa* cease to exist like a lamp on the destruction of the wick?

Answer: At the time of content-free concentration the *puruṣa* stays in itself as consciousness alone like the clear crystal in the absence of the red rose in its proximity.

I.4 (ET 1.43-55) Question: Since *puruṣa* as consciousness is changeless, in what form does it exist during activity?

Answer: Like an image and its reflection, in activity there is identification of the fluctuations of the intellect and the "modification of *puruṣa*". "Modification of *puruṣa*" refers to its reflection in the intellect. The simile of an image and its reflection is to indicate the identification of the two.

Objection: How can there be modification of the changeless *puruṣa*?

Answer: Because of being informed about the object by the

intellect. And informing is placing the object, which is present in oneself in consciousness, in reflection. Thus there is no real change in *puruṣa*, but like the crystal there is an apparent change, and this is what constitutes the *puruṣa*'s "knowledge".

Unlike Miśra and other commentators, Bhikṣu believes in the double reflection theory. Just as there is reflection of the intellect in consciousness, so there is reflection of consciousness in the intellect also; otherwise the knowledge of *puruṣa* could not be explained owing to the contradiction of the subject and the object being the same thing. According to Bhikṣu, when there is reflection of *puruṣa* in the intellect it is only the content of the intellect which is the content of awareness and the second reflection of *buddhi* in *puruṣa* makes *puruṣa* the subject of that awareness. One should understand all this happening simultaneously and not as various steps in a process or series. There is a beginningless relationship of "owned" and "owner" between a (particular) intellect and a (particular) *puruṣa*. This special relationship of owned and owner takes care that at no time is there identity of one *puruṣa* with a fluctuation of the intellect of another *puruṣa*.

I.5-11 (ET 1.55-91) The fluctuations of awareness, though broadly divided into afflicted and non-afflicted, are only of five types. While the afflicted are those which result in pain and perpetuate the cycle of karma, non-afflicted are those which oppose ignorance and are connected with discriminating between what is true and what is untrue, and can result in discriminative discernment.

Correct awareness is awareness of something not cognized before; the means are perception, inference and the utterances of trustworthy persons. Points made in the course of the discussion are as follows: (1) A fluctuation of awareness is a substance like light; (2) Since in dreams, meditation, etc. it is seen that there is experience of a pot, etc. it is proved that ideas can give rise to outside shapes as well; (3) Thus we agree with the Buddhists (the Vijñānavādins) partially but also disagree with them because we accept external objects. (Bhikṣu differs with Miśra as to the location of awareness and it is in the commentary under *sūtra* I.6 that he develops fully the dual reflection theory.)

Objection: Some (e.g., Miśra) say that awareness takes place in the intellect and that consciousness, by being reflected in the mirror of the intellect, obtains the fruit (of knowledge) through identification with both the fluctuation and the object of the fluctuation of the intellect; and this reflection of *puruṣa* is known as *cicchāyā* and is a quality of the intellect.

Answer: This is not so. Reflection is only a change into an image of the intellect through a particular limitation of it; Moreover, mutual reflection is established in the scriptures and the *smṛtis*; therefore, it is proper that *puruṣa*, conditioned by the reflection of the intellect alone, is associated with awareness. The reflection in *puruṣa* of the intellect is desired for the awareness by the *puruṣa* in the form of agent (i.e. of the subject, "I") as, without superimposition of the intellect (on the *puruṣa*) there will be the contradiction that the subject and the object in a knowledge are the same thing.

Error is misapprehension or false awareness (*mithyājñāna*), under which is included the five-fold ignorance in the system of Yoga. Doubt is also included under error. In the system of Yoga, error is in the form of positive mistaking one thing for another (*anyathākhyāti*). It is not just nondiscrimination as in the Sāṃkhya system. It is also different from the Vaiśeṣika *anyathākhyāti* type of misapprehension, as (in Vaiśeṣika) there is no superimposition of the silver outside (on to the shell). Thus imagining any (or all) of the following eight–i.e. *avyaktaprakṛti, mahat, ahamkāra,* and the five *tanmātras*–which are not self to be the self is also error.

Conceptual construction is that awareness which is followed by words and the knowledge of the meaning of words. Conceptual construction is different from correct awareness since its content is not a real thing, and it is not error, since it is followed by knowledge of the meaning of words.*

Sleep is a fluctuation and its content is *tāmasa* awareness. The Vedānta theory of the absence of (fluctuations of) awareness in deep sleep is incorrect. If it were so, then during waking and dreaming also the fluctuations could arise due to ignorance as in deep sleep, and there would be no need of awareness at all. Therefore, as in waking and dreaming, so also in deep sleep there are fluctuations of awareness.

Memory is the non-loss of fluctuations and the contents of fluctuations, and it comes into being only through traces.

I.12-16 (ET 1.91-104) It is through dispassion and continued practice of different means of cessation that the various fluctuations are restrained. The different means of cessation are faith, effort, concentration, meditation, one-(pointed)ness, concentration and insight. Dispassion has to be understood at two levels. The first, called "complete control" (*vaśīkāra*), has three stages before maturing into dispassion. The first (called *yatamāna*) is the effort to break attachment. The second (*vyatireka*) is the thought that non-attachment toward certain objects has been achieved and it is to be achieved toward other objects. When the spent-out attachment stays only in the mind it is *ekendriya* and when even that is destroyed it is known as complete control. Detachment even from complete control is superior.

Objection: While Patañjali mentions non-attachment to the *guṇas*, how can Vyāsa classify it as a form of knowledge?

Answer: There is no problem. Absence, in our opinion, is not a special category, but absence of attachment to the *guṇas* only implies a special state of knowledge. Thus the non-attachment from the *guṇas* can be the cause, and mere peacefulness of knowledge (*jñānaprasādamātra*) the effect. This

*Summarizer's note: Bhikṣu differs from Miśra and other commentators in giving this meaning to "*vikalpa*", which resembles the grammarians' theory of *vikalpa* and that of Buddhist Vijñānavāda.

kind of knowledge ensures content-free concentration and liberation.

I.17 (ET 1.111) The four kinds of content-filled concentration are those accompanied by deliberation (*vitarka*), by reflection (*vicāra),* by bliss (*ānanda*) and by egoity (*asmitā*). Each succeeding stage is superior to the earlier one. And both Miśra and Bhikṣu agree that the first two are divided into a further division as *savitarka* and *nirvitarka* and *savicāra* and *nirvicāra*. But when it comes to the third and the fourth stages Miśra divides them into *sānanda, nirānanda, sāsmitā* and *nirasmitā*. However, Bhikṣu disagrees with these further divisions of content-filled *samādhi;* according to Bhikṣu there are only six.

I.18-20 (ET 1.111-120) Content-free concentration comes after content-filled concentration and it is of two types called respectively "inclination toward becoming" (*bhavapratyaya*) and "inclination toward the correct means" (*upāyapratyaya*). Those with inclination toward becoming are also of two kinds, (1) the disembodied (*videha*), who have experience without reference to bodies, i.e. they are without gross bodies like the gods; and (2) those dissolved in *prakṛti (prakṛtilaya)* along with their subtle bodies.

(Miśra and Bhikṣu differ in their understanding of "inclination toward becoming". According to Miśra "*bhava*" means "*avidyā*", so "*bhavapratyaya*" means that which is caused by ignorance. But Bhikṣu takes "*bhava*" to mean birth: therefore "*bhavapratyaya*" means that which is caused by birth. Also Miśra believes that both *videhas* and *prakṛtilayas* come back to earth after their traces have fructified, while Bhikṣu states that they attain liberation.)

Content-free concentration is achieved by *yogins* who practice the various means like faith, etc. and they are those inclined toward correct means. In *sūtra* 20 the means are given as faith, energy, memory, concentration and insight. Each one of them is connected to the limbs of *yoga* by Bhikṣu. Since faith (*śraddhā*) connotes great desire for *yoga* it can denote all the five limbs up to withdrawal of the sense-organs (*pratyāhāra*). From faith comes energy (*vīrya*), which means meditative fixation (*dhāraṇā*), and from energy comes memory which is reflective meditation (*dhyāna*), and from that comes concentration (*samādhi*) and insight (*prajñā*). Those who practice these means constantly and with speed attain concentration fastest. Subdividing the *yogins* depending on the abundance of their practice there are nine kinds of *yogins*, and the ninth kind can be further sub-divided into little, middling and abundant practice, thus giving rise to twelve kinds of *yogins* in all.

I.23 (ET 1.123-126) Concentration and liberation can also be obtained fastest by deep meditation on God, which is a special kind of practice.

Objection: What is the logic in saying that insight with reference to God achieves content-free concentration even without abundant, quick practice?

Answer: God, due to the devotee's devotion, desires his liberation to be fast even when he follows the means slackly.

I.24 (ET 1.127-147) Who is this God and where does he fit into the Yoga system? God is not a liberated self *(jīva)* since then he would have had connection with afflictions at some time. While Hiraṇyagarbha and other liberated selves are freed only after breaking the bonds, God is free at all times from bondage. God is eternally connected with pure *sattva*, is omniscient, and has no afflictions or temporal limitations. It is due to God's desire that the dissimilarity in *prakṛti* is caused at the time of creation.

Is there any proof for the existence of God? It is perceived that through the sacred books there is establishment of God, and through God's direct perception as pure *sattva* the authority of those same sacred books is established. Thus there is what is known as the defect of mutual dependency.

Answer: This is not so. The authority (effectiveness) of the Vedic incantations and the medical treatises (*āyurveda*) proves the authority of the scriptures as well as the *sattva*-mind of God.

God is unequalled. The reasons for that are: (1) Only that which is unequalled (which has reached the limit of supremacy) is supreme. (2) In the presence of another there can be no free desire. Since God has unobstructed desire he is supreme.

I.25 (ET 1.147-154) It is seen that knowledge has degrees of excellence; it has to reach the limit somewhere because of this nature: this is so in the case of any ascending scale. The purest limit of knowledge is omniscience.

Objection: The above inference only generally establishes an omniscient being–but how does one know his particular name?

Answer: This and other details like his possession of complete bliss, extreme compassion, true selfhood, being the support of the world, etc. is to be learned from the scriptures.

Objection: Since God is eternally liberated his action does not stand to reason as there is no goal to be achieved.

Answer: This is not so. (1) Action is eternal in God, so there is no need for a cause of it. (2) Though God has no goal there is the purpose of blessing and uplifting the devotee and removing his pain.

Objection: God only blesses His devotees and causes pain to others. Thus He is partial.

Answer: Partiality comes only through attachment and hatred, and not by action alone. Though God has the desire to remove the pain of all beings He is restricted by the influence of His devotees and is delayed in His work.

I.26 (ET 1.154-156) By the argument of His being the omniscient supreme being God is proved to be so at all times. He is the father of all other selves including Brahmā, Viṣṇu, and Śiva.

I.27 (ET 1.157-159) The name of that God is *oṃ*. There is an eternal relationship between the two. Similarly the relationship between words and their meanings is eternal, a word only reveals a meaning already present.

I.28-31 (ET I.160-179) Connecting "*oṃ*" with devotion and

meditation on God (*īśvarapraṇidhāna*), Bhikṣu mentions here that "*praṇidhāna*" is meditating on Brahman (*īśvara*) along with repeating the word "*oṃ*" and it should be done knowing the eternal relationship between the two. Through this devotion there arises one-pointedness and then through superior dispassion there arises content-free concentration.

Moreover, devotion has the added result of the removal of obstacles to liberation. There are nine obstacles: they are sickness, idleness, doubt, negligence, sloth, lack of dispassion, misapprehension, failure to attain any state (of concentration), and inability to stay (in the stage of concentration attained). These are distractions of the mind and are enemies of Yoga. They also give rise to pain, unsteadiness, trembling of the limbs, inhaling and exhaling great quantities of air.

I.32 (ET 1.179-188) The above obstacles can be removed through dispassion and practice (of reflection and concentration) on a single entity. While Miśra understands God by the word "*ekatattva*" Bhikṣu understands that word as denoting any entity. In this context refutation of the arguments of the Buddhists who believe in the momentariness of awarenesses is given, since the basis for concentration is an enduring awareness.

I.33 (ET 1.189-191) Along with faith, etc. mentioned in I.20, practice of friendliness towards those who are happy, compassion towards those who are unhappy, joy towards those having merit, detachment towards those having demerit help in stabilizing the mind. (There are minor differences of interpretation of *sūtras* 33-39 by Miśra and Bhikṣu.)

I.34 (ET 1.191-193) Various alternative or supplementary means for stabilizing the mind are discussed. They are: (1) exhaling and retaining breath. Breath-control will be mentioned in the second Book as one of the eight limbs of yoga for a beginner, whereas here, this breath-control is the best, therefore there is no repetition. (2) Superior sensory activity directed towards the objects smell, etc. results in the direct perception of (divine) smell, etc. (3) Two types of luminous sensory activity which are without sorrow, one directed towards the intellect and the other directed toward egoity. In this context Bhikṣu describes in detail the yogic concept of the eight-petalled heart-lotus with its connections with *oṃ*, the four stages of waking, dreaming, deep sleep and the fourth (*turīya*) state, the different nerve centers, and so on. (4) Fixing one's awareness on other minds which are devoid of attachment, like that of Sanaka, etc. (5) Having dreaming as a support of the mind helps it to realize the dreamlike nature of the waking world. Thus it helps in steadying the mind. (6) Meditating on the image of one's desired deity.

I.41-42 (ET 1.206-215) The word "*samāpatti*" is dẹfined as the fruit of content-filled concentration. In concentration, the last of the eight limbs of yoga, the mind loses the nature of thought and becoming one with the object appears to have lost its awareness aspect. But engrossment (*samāpatti*) is the result of content-filled concentration and is the same as insight (*prajñā*). The various kinds of content-filled concentration, from the point of view of engrossment, are analyzed from *sūtra* 42 onwards and have to be read along with *sūtra* I.17.

I.43-44 (ET 1.216-234) While all awarenesses based on scriptures and reasoning generally involve superimposition of word and meaning, in the *nirvitarka* and *nirvicāra* engrossments pure knowledge with reference to meaning and idea arises without any other superimposition.

Since error is natural in judgments generally, *savitarka* engrossment also involves that same error. But when awareness transcends that stage, paying attention only to meaning, there arises *nirvitarka* engrossment where there is knowledge in the form of the essence of meaning alone. While in *savitarka* and *nirvitarka* engrossment the support is a gross object, in *savicāra* and *nirvicāra* engrossment the support is a subtle object. And all these are seeded concentrations. In this context (as in I.17) Bhikṣu again elaborates his difference from Miśra about the divisions of content-filled concentration and reiterates his previous statement that content-filled concentrations are only six and not eight as maintained by Miśra.

I.47-49 (ET 1.243-251) It is in *nirvicāra* engrossment that one attains great clarity. It is a one-pointed flow of *sattva*-awareness of the nature of brightness from which all dirt has been removed. In this state there is an immediate grasp of the true nature of the object without any reference to the order (like past, present, etc.) and this is the state of truth-bearing insight. Thus it is only that insight which arises in *nirvicāra* engrossment that can be called "truth-bearing", that which bears the truth and only the truth.

I.50 (ET 1.251-257) The traces of insight obstruct the traces of activity.

Objection: When it is possible to obstruct the traces of activity by a trace which arises through one individual insight and its continuance, what is the purpose of practicing content-filled concentration again?

Answer: Attaining insight once does not obstruct the traces of activity. This is known from *śruti* and *smṛti* texts which advise practice of content-filled concentration again and again. It is only through the stronger traces born of a series of insights that there is overpowering of the weaker traces of the emergent state (*vyutthānasaṃskāra*).

Moreover, once the traces of the emergent state are burnt immediate liberation results by the two *yogas* (content-filled and content-free) overcoming even stored-up (*prārabdha*) karma.

Objection: How can stored-up karma, whose time span has been fixed, be destroyed by the traces of insight?

Answer: The fixed time-span is only for such deeds which destroy and are fit to be destroyed. One even finds mention in the scriptures of expiatory deeds and deeds of appeasement which destroy evil (the result of demerit) whose time-span has not been reached.

Objection: But even traces of insight can give rise to rebirth.

Answer: It is only when the mind has afflictions like

ignorance, etc. that it has power to bind the *puruṣa* and give rise to rebirth. But since insight is the cause of the destruction of afflictions, there are no more actions which bind and therefore no rebirth.

I.51 (ET 1.257-264) The traces of insight on reaching excellence give rise to content-free concentration through superior dispassion (cf. I.18). A complete absorption of the traces of insight is the result of the stronger series of those traces born of content-free concentrations. Since the mind is absorbed back into *prakṛti*, its cause, *puruṣa* is liberated.

BOOK TWO

II.1-2 (ET 2.1-9) While the first Book was directed towards those superior aspirants of *yoga* for whom practice and dispassion are easy, this Book is directed toward all other who have minds facing outwards.

Ascetic practice, self-study and devotion to God are together called "*kriyāyoga*". Even though restraint (*yama*), etc. are also "*kriyāyoga*" , and "observances" (*niyama*) include these three (ascetic practice, etc.) as part of itself, still the three are mentioned separately because they are superior to the others; thus even by practicing these three intensely *yoga* is achieved.

Īśvarapraṇidhāna in this context is also different from that mentioned in the first Chapter (cf. I.23). Here it is devotion, an offering of all worldly and sacrificial deeds to God. *Kriyāyoga* weakens the afflictions and prepares the aspirant for liberation.

Objection: It is only through destruction of the afflictions that rebirth can be stopped, so what is use of weakening them?

Answer: *Kriyāyoga* will make the afflictions similar to burnt seed and give rise to the fire of supreme reflection (*prasaṃkhyāna*, i.e. insight) and from insight results liberation.

II.3 (ET 2.9-11) The five afflictions are errors. By mutual association with each other the continuity of the results of karma (*karmavipāka*) is accomplished.

II.4 (ET 2.11-18) Ignorance is the basis of the other afflictions. Each of the others are divided into four further types as being quiescent, decreased, interrupted and active. Thus there are sixteen divisions of the afflictions of which the basis is ignorance, i.e. lack of awareness of reality. According to Bhikṣu the practice of *kriyāyoga* weakens the afflictions. But Miśra elaborates it further, since knowledge opposes ignorance, insight into difference opposes the ego-sense, neutrality opposes attachment and aversion, and cessation of the thought of remaining alive opposes clinging to life.

II.5 (ET 2.19-26) Ignorance is the ascription of permanence to impermanent things, of purity to impure things, of pleasure where everything is actually painful, of self to that which is not a self.

Objection: Etymologically the word "*avidyā*" can mean "other than knowledge" or "absence of knowledge" or "most excellent knowledge" and not necessarily the wrong awareness of taking one thing for another.

Answer: This is like the words "*amitra*" and "*agospada*" which mean respectively an enemy and a big place. Thus "*avidyā*" can mean false awareness or absence of awareness. Thus the philosophy of *anyathākhyāti* is established.

II.6 (ET 2.26-30) The absolute identity, as it were, between the seer and the instrument (*karaṇa, buddhi*) is the error called egoity (*asmitā*). Though there is no marked difference between ignorance and egoity, ignorance can be described as the cause and egoity the effect.

II.9 (ET 2.31-36) The will to live is the desire to go on living without dying; it is due to the fear of death experienced in a previous existence, since it could not have been experienced in this life. According to Bhikṣu the trace of the fear of death is stronger than other traces and is destroyed only by the mind and not by truth-bearing insight. Thus, this is the difference of the destruction of these traces from that of the traces of ignorance.

II.10-11 (ET 2.36-39) Through *kriyāyoga* the afflictions are weakened, and through the insight born of concentration or reflection, which arises by continued practice of *kriyāyoga*, the weakened afflictions are reduced to the burnt-seed state. And then through content-free concentration these burnt-up afflictions are absorbed into *prakṛti* along with the mind.

II.12 (ET 2.39-42) The afflictions have to be destroyed as they are the source of the deposit of good and bad deeds. These deposits in turn have to be experienced either in this life or in future lives.

II.13 (ET 2.42-59) The results of the traces of birth, life-span and kind of experience together are called "ripening" (*vipāka*). A lengthy discussion ensues in this context as to whether one deed gives rise to one birth or to many births or whether many deeds give rise to many births or one birth. The first three options are rejected and the fourth is accepted and called "*ekabhāvika*", "giving rise to one existence". Thus many deeds cause one birth. Just as traces are experienced either in this life or future lives, the fruition of traces or ripening also is divided as that whose fruition takes place in a limited time and that whose fruition takes place in an unlimited time. The latter is correct, because (a) the traces can be restricted or restrained without giving their results, (b) a trace can be absorbed into another important deed and yield its results along with it; (c) it can be overpowered by an important deed which is to yield its fruit and stay without giving fruit for a long time.

There is a difference between Miśra and Bhikṣu while discussing the connection between a trace and its rule for fruition in this life or future lives. One can understand "trace" (i.e. a karmic residue) in any one of the following ways: (A) A karmic residue which exhausts itself in this life cannot have a result in another life. (B) A trace which is to be felt in future lives and has a time limit for fruition has to bear its fruit in one life only. (C) A trace which is to be experienced in future lives has no time limit for its fruition. It appears that Miśra understands that there is the fruition of a karmic residue fixed in the present life itself. Thus he is inclined toward (A). But Bhikṣu accepts both (A) and (B). As a corollary to this logic Bhikṣu also says that it is not all one's deeds which come together and result in one birth after causing death as already mentioned, but only the trace which has a fixed time for its experience, i.e. which is to be experienced in the life following death.

Objection: But in this way the theory of (a trace's) giving rise to one existence is destroyed.

Answer: Though there are exceptions, we accept the general theory of one existence as the effect.

II.14 (ET 2.59-61) The fruit of traces (their ripening) has pleasures and pains as results in a worldly sense, but in the yogic sense has only pain.

II.15 (ET 2.61-79) Pain is further elaborated and classified in this *sūtra* along with the statement that to one who discriminates everything is pain.

The cause of rebirth is contact between the seer (*puruṣa*) and the seen (through the intellect). The total removal of the said contact is liberation and the means for that removal is insight into the truth. Now (1) Does destruction of contact, i.e. liberation, mean the destruction of the self with which there is contact? (2) Or does the destruction of contact give rise to a new self? As for (1), destruction or removal is possible only when there are two entities, i.e. the remover and the thing to be removed. But here there is only one entity and the removal is only of a false relation. Therefore this theory falls apart. As for (2) a new self emerging will mean change in self and the unchangeability of a self will fall apart. Thus the doctrine of the permanence of the self is established by reduction.

II.16-17 (ET 2.79-90) All pain yet to come is to be removed. And the cause for pain (as already stated) is contact between seer and seen.

Objection: But if contact is accepted, the neutrality of *puruṣa* will be lost.

Answer: In the case of *puruṣa,* as that of (water on) a lotus leaf, even when there is contact there is neutrality. This is so, since only that contact which is the cause of change of its support causes attachment; and that kind of contact is not there in *puruṣa*. These two *sūtras* should be read along with *sūtras* II.23-24, where the nature of contact and its cause are discussed in detail.

II.18 (ET 2.90-106) All seen objects are of the nature of illuminating brightness, activity and stability; they are from the three *guṇas* having those natures. Only an insentient cause having the three *guṇas* can have insentient effects having the three *guṇas*. And the purpose of their existence is to effect experience and liberation for a *puruṣa*.

Objection: But how can you say that the destruction of pain for *puruṣa* is the goal of the *guṇas*, since only the destruction of one's own pain can be his goal and not that of another?

Answer: Even wise men accept content-free *yoga* as that which destroys pain. Because *puruṣa* is informed of the object by the *sattva* intelligence, when *sattva* is hurt *puruṣa*, becoming similar to it as its reflection (*pratibimba*), appears to be hurt. Thus, since even the wise have to get rid of this pain due to the reflection known as experience, one cannot say that *puruṣa* is goalless. This defect, on the other hand, applies to the present-day Vedāntins (*advaita*) alone.

Liberation can be viewed in two ways: (a) it is a state where all the *guṇas* have stopped their modifications and are absorbed in *prakṛti*, and (b) it is a condition where *puruṣa* has regained its natural state. Thus liberation is for both *puruṣa* as well as the *guṇas*.

II.19 (ET 2.106-134) *Guṇas* based on different states are (1) those which are causes for further changes (the unparticularized (*aviśeṣa*) and (2) those which are effects alone (the particularized (*viśeṣa*)); (3) that which indicates its cause (*mahat*), and (4) that which has no indicator of its cause (*prakṛti*).

Miśra and Bhikṣu differ as to the meaning of the word "*liṅga*". While Miśra interprets it as "that which gets absorbed", Bhikṣu explains the word "*liṅga*" (mark) literally as (1) that which serves as a mark to infer its cause, or (2) that which being the first effect indicates all the other effects.

Prakṛti is also "existent always" because even in liberation there is no total removal of this equilibrium of the *guṇas*. Otherwise the further creation of evolutes, which in the system is a continuous refilling by *prakṛti,* will not be possible if it had exhausted itself.

II.20-22 (ET 2.135-152) *Puruṣa*, for whom the *guṇas* strive, has a dual nature: it is similar and dissimilar to the intellect. It is similar because it along with the intellect cognizes its content, and it is dissimilar because it does not change, etc.

Puruṣas are many and *prakṛti* is one, common to them all. Therefore when liberation is achieved for one *puruṣa* the *guṇas* are no more effective for that *puruṣa*; but they are not lost with reference to the other *puruṣas* who are not liberated.

II.23-26 (ET 2.152-172) While contact between intellect and *puruṣa* is the cause of pain, knowledge up to the stage of insight is also born out of this connection, which results in the separation of the contact and the attainment of the true nature of the seer. The cause for the connection is ignorance, and ignorance opposes insight. Thus ignorance is the cause for connection and insight is the cause for separation.

A lengthy discussion on the meaning of "*avidyā*", considering eight alternatives dependent on whether the negation in the term is connected with the verbal stem or the nominal form, ensues. The accepted yogic view of "*adarśana*" is stated as "the traces of ignorance", since that is the reason for the contact between *prakṛti* and *puruṣa*. Because of the power of the traces of ignorance the intellect does not achieve the limit of its own duty which is insight, and so again get connected with *puruṣa*. When the intellect reaches the end of its duty by giving rise to superior dispassion and insight it has its duty accomplished. Then there is cessation of ignorance, and in the absence of the cause–ignorance–there is no more contact with *puruṣa*.

II.27 (ET 2.172-178) This *sūtra* is interpreted differently by Miśra and Bhikṣu. While insight itself is considered by Bhikṣu to have seven divisions, Miśra takes it to be the seven kinds of insight of a *yogin*. In the first type there is complete knowledge of that which is to be destroyed. The second type is when all the afflictions have been weakened. The third is the direct perception at the end of meditation of the liberation which is to come in the form of cessation of all pain. The fourth deals with the perfected state of insight through which the final result is achieved. The next three divisions automatically make their appearance after the first four, as follows: (5) when the intellect has accomplished its dual task of experience and liberation; (6) when the *guṇas* of pleasure, pain, etc. of the mind, along with the mind, are absorbed into *prakṛti*, (7) when *puruṣa* is free from the relationship with the intellect and is of the nature of pure consciousness; this is the *jīvanmukti* stage similar to that of liberation but still embodied.

II.29 (ET 2.187-188) Just as practice and dispassion are the means for a superior aspirant and *kriyāyoga* is for an average aspirant, the eight limbs of *yoga* are to be practiced by a beginning aspirant. From this *sūtra* onwards there is a detailed description of the eight limbs of *yoga*.

II.49-53 (ET 2.220-234) These *sūtras* deal with breath control. Bhikṣu describes it in great detail and with great insight, giving the impression that he was a practicing *yogin*.

In comparison to the other six limbs restraints and observances are considered external.

Breath control is the suspension of the natural movement of breath and it is followed by *recaka, pūraka* and *kumbhaka,* described differently as "holding of the breath easily". "*Recaka*" is suspension after exhalation; it is not just exhalation or expulsion of air. *Pūraka* is suspension after inhalation. And when there is absence of both *recaka* and *pūraka* without any continuous practice and with just one single effort, that is *kumbhakaprāṇāyāma*. This threefold control of breathing is regulated by space, time, and number which are given in detail by Bhikṣu. "*Kevala kumbhaka*" can theoretically be described as transcending the stages of *pūraka* and *recaka* and can only be attained by constant effort. The third kind of breath-control, *kumbhaka*, on the other hand, exists only between inhalation and exhalation.

Control of breathing, along with practice and dispassion, has been mentioned as a means to liberation for a superior aspirant in Book One itself. Thus breath control is the best means for weakening the covering of awareness.

Bhikṣu assigns a high place to breath control in the achievement of *yoga*. Miśra, on the other hand, warns that controlled breathing cannot weaken bad (*pāpa*) behavior and only austerity can accomplish that.

II.55 (ET 2.237-240) Withdrawal of sense-organs (*pratyāhāra*) is the state when the sense-organs imitate the restrained mind by having no contact with their objects even when they are present. Various definitions of withdrawal are mentioned in *sūtra* II.55. According to some it is sensory activity which is entirely within one's control, and according to others it is sensory activity where pleasure and pain are absent. But all these only partially satisfy the definition of withdrawal given by Patañjali.

BOOK THREE

III.1-3 (ET 3.1-7) Definitions of the next three means is given. Meditative fixation (*dhāraṇā*) can be on any place (both external and internal). There are special spots for it like the navel, the lotus on the top of the head, etc. While one can fix one's mind on an object for varying durations of time it is only when concentration lasts as long as it takes to complete twelve (sessions of) breath-control that it can be called "fixation".

Fixation is fixing the mind only through the fluctuations of awareness, whereas reflective meditation (*dhyāna*) is a succession or flow of fluctuations of awareness with reference to the spot or the end of continuous fixation. It is really reflective meditation when it is qualified by the time taken to complete twelve fixations. While in reflective meditation there is present the awareness of the knower, the known, and the knowing process, in concentration (*samādhi*), involving oneness with the object of meditation, this awareness is absent. Here the special distinction of concentration is the period of time, which is a multiple of twelve meditations.

III.4 (ET 3.7) In the system of *yoga* "comprehensive reflection" (*saṃyama*) is a technical term for fixation, meditation and concentration taken together.

III.5 (ET 3.7-8) By attaining proficiency in comprehensive reflection there arises the effulgence (*āloka*) of insight. In this state there is direct perception of subtle objects.

III.13-15 (ET 3.21-72) A lengthy discussion and a repetition of ideas broached already in II.19 in the context of changes in the state of the mind and in the elements and sense-organs is found here.

Every substance has the three changes of characteristics, temporal quality, and change of state. If the mind is taken as an example of a substance, then the disappearance of activity (*vyutthāna*) and the appearance of restraint (*nirodha*) is the change of characteristics in the mind. When the existence characteristic gives up its not-yet-manifest quality and takes on the quality of the present, that is a change of temporal quality. In keeping with the doctrine of *satkāryavāda* the present state is mentioned as only a manifestation of the present when the not-as-yet-manifest state disappears and the past is only an appearance when the present state disappears. In the same mind change of temporal quality is the increase (strength) and decrease (weakness) of the traces (of cessation and emergence respectively). This is like the "newness" and "oldness" of a pot.

Although one can look at a substance in various ways, due to the non-difference between the characterized and the characteristics, one understands that the underlying substratum (*prakṛti*) alone pervades all changes. But this permanence is different from the permanence of non-change of *puruṣa*.

From this *sūtra* onwards till the end of this Book the powers that come to a *yogin* by the practice of comprehensive reflection on various objects are described; by one who desires liberation only, reflection on the distinction between the *sattva*-

intellect and *puruṣa* should be practiced.

III.17 (ET 3.74-94) This *sutra* is significant as it clearly assumes the *sphoṭa*-theory, and it is clear that he assumes it as well in I.42. In the world, when a word is uttered there is superimposition of the word, its meaning, and the thought on each other, and there is produced one unified impression. If comprehensive reflection is practiced on each of them separately, the knowledge of the sounds of all living beings is acquired. Thus a word has a sound value, a meaning value and a "knowledge" value and it is possible to practice comprehensive reflection on each separately.

In this connection Bhikṣu first points out how "*śabda*" is used indiscriminately for a letter, a sound, and a word. Sounds which are kinds of changes in the air one breathes, come in contact with the organ of speech; these sounds reach the ear of the listener; they are different sounds. But because awareness of something denoted arises when words like "*gauḥ*" ("cow") are uttered one accepts the sounds "*g*", "*au*", "*ḥ*", etc. as one word and when the last letter ("*ḥ*") is uttered the intelligence through traces binds them together and brings about a unity as "*gauḥ*" meaning "cow" as one word: this is a partless (*akhaṇḍa*) (whole), it arises all at once and is called a "*sphoṭa*". It is called "*sphoṭa*" because it reveals the meaning.

III.19 (E 3.100) The word "*pratyayasya*" (in the *sūtra*) is interpreted differently by Miśra and Bhikṣu and so the meaning of the *sūtra* is different for each. Miśra takes it to mean the idea of other minds (*parapratyayasya*) in order to justify the power of knowing other people's minds. Thus only when comprehensive reflection is practiced on another's mind can it be known in totality, according to Miśra. But Bhikṣu interprets "*pratyayasya*" as "one's own fluctuation of the mind". Thus by practicing comprehensive reflection on one's own mental awareness there is direct perception of the qualities of everything, i.e. as the support of thoughts, and from that he gets to know the minds of others as well.

III.20 (ET 3.100-102) Bhikṣu differs from Miśra and others

by taking this *sūtra* to be a continuation of the commentary of Vyāsa on III.19. In the knowing of the mind of another the question arises as to whether idea in the other mind is known along with its supporting object. Bhikṣu's reasoning is that since one's own mind is the supporting object for comprehensive reflection here, it cannot have another mind's content as its support. In other words, only the thoughts in other minds are perceived and not the objects of those thoughts as well. This *sūtra* has to be read along with III.54.

III.33-36 (ET 3.128-144) *Pratibhājñāna* arises out of intuition,which arises spontaneously (*anaupadeśika*). It is the means for crossing the round of births and deaths and so it is called "*tāraka*", "deliverer". While Bhikṣu favors the idea that an intuition is a spontaneous flash which arises without instruction or deliberation, Miśra uses the word "*ūha*" ("reasoning") to describe intuition.

Intuitive knowledge is the stage when the *yogin* knows all. This is a state prior to the dawn of insight into the difference between the intellect and *puruṣa*, i.e. prior to insight as interpreted in *sūtra* III.33. But in *sūtra* III.36 it appears that intuition is a state after insight into the difference between *puruṣa* and the *sattva*-intellect, i.e. immediately after insight. Since truth-bearing insight or supreme reflection is the direct link to liberation, intuitive knowledge cannot be superior to it. It is a state co-existent or arising with the first flash of insight. Thus intuitive knowledge is (1) a state when the *yogin* knows everything; (2) it is born immediately after discriminative knowledge or is an immediate by-product of discrimination which is co-existent with it; (3) it is a state when the *yogin* knows all things at all times and in this state knowing has no sequence. The extraordinary capacity which arises due to practice of comprehensive reflection on various objects can be of the nature of knowledge (direct perception) as knowledge of the past, present and the future, knowledge of the difference between *puruṣa* and the intellect, and so on.

BOOK FOUR

IV.2-3 (ET 4.2-10) The method by which different changes (like a body, sense-organs, fire, pot, etc.) come into being is through the independent filling-in process of *prakṛti* and not just by the desire of the *yogin* or God.

IV.7 (ET 4.17-21) Action (*karman*) is fourfold: dark, which results in pain; bright and dark, which yields both pleasure and pain, bright, which yields pleasure; and neither bright nor dark, which is devoid of any result in the form of pleasure and pain. The actions of a *yogin* are neither bright nor dark as the sense of doer is absent in him.

IV.8-9 (ET 4.22-26) From deeds follow their results and the manifestation of only those traces which are in conformity with that result. If there is birth as a cat after the life as a human being then the traces of a cat's life at some previous birth will now be manifested; it also means that the traces (here, *adṛṣṭa*) of that particular birth, i.e. a cat's, are ready to give fruit. Even if the present cat's life is separated from the earlier cat's life by many other kinds of lives in many preceding births it will be considered as having continuity. This is so because memory and traces are of the same nature. And traces are beginningless.

Sāṃkhya objection: The beginninglessness of traces is possible only if its support of the mind is permanent and if it is not different in each body. Then if the mind is all-pervasive, its coming into being after dissolution and its residence in another body after death cannot be explained. If it is atomic then the experience simultaneously of more than one sense-datum, as in the case of eating where the sense of smell, taste, sight, and touch are evident, cannot be explained. Therefore the mind must change size according to the size of the body it occupies.

Answer: The mind is all-pervading. And the fluctuation of awareness, which is a substance, is what expands and contracts depending on merit and demerit as efficient causes. Thus the beginningless traces having a support has been satisfactorily explained.

IV.11 (ET 4.36-40) The six-spoked (wheel) of *saṃsāra*, like the Buddhist wheel, is graphically drawn by Bhikṣu. The six spokes are merit, demerit, pleasure, pain, attachment and aversion–the rotator of this wheel is ignorance. Thus ignorance is the cause of traces (as already discussed in Book Two).

IV.14-16 (ET 4.51-69) The Buddhist Vijñānavādin says that objects are just ideas in the mind and they have no external existence as they always occur in experience. They are just like dream objects. Bhikṣu states that this argument is not correct. It is mere prattle (*apālāpa*) and incorrect because (1) the waking state object-experience is not sublated as a dream-object is; (2) objects are known through interaction with the sense-organs and are not imagined; (3) both schools accept that in dreams there is awareness without an outside object, but an object lacking the capacity for being a content is not accepted even by others; (4) some absurd results will result from interpreting objects as subjective. Thus when the stomach (the front side of the body) is experienced the back of the body not being seen will, according to the Buddhist, cease to exist. This contradicts everyday experience.

IV.17-19 (ET 4.69-83) The mind knows an object sometimes and does not know it at other times, where the self is always known (through reflection). Can the mind also be known?

There is an interesting comparison to construction-free (*nirvikalpaka*) and construction-filled (*savikalpaka*) awareness in connection with the dual reflection theory of Bhikṣu (cf. *sūtra* 19). In every awareness there is the cognizer and the cognized, so even in self-illumination there is this two-fold nature.

The process of cognizing is as follows: Initially in anger, etc. there is a bare, construction-free awareness (*nirvikalpakabodha*) associated with *puruṣa* (this is the first reflection). When in the second instant there is the reflection of the mind (second reflection), in *puruṣa* there is the possession of awareness as belonging to the ego-sense.

IV.22-23 (ET 4.93-107) Self-realization or knowledge born

of insight is also due to the reflection of the *puruṣa* in the fluctuation as *puruṣa*: thus, like the mind's assuming the form of an object in any object experience, in self-awareness it takes on the form of the self (*ātman*). Thus the knowing of the mind itself is the knowing of objects and the knowing of oneself. Just as a single crystal by reflecting a red rose and a sapphire situated on either side of it assumes as it were, together with its own form, three forms, so also the mind by reflection of both the object and the self (*puruṣa*) has the three forms of knower, known and the process of knowing. Therefore it is known as "having all as objects" (*sarvārtha*).

IV.25 (ET 4.111-115) There is a difference of interpretation of this *sūtra* between Bhikṣu and Miśra. Bhikṣu interprets "*viśeṣadarśanaḥ*" as the first stage (a special insight) of liberation; but Miśra takes it to stand for an awareness of the distinction between one who is fit for liberation and one who is not.

IV.28-34 (ET 4.118-143) The burning up and absorption of the traces along with the mind into *prakṛti* is achieved as follows: When contentful insight is there at all times it is called the *dharma*-cloud stage. This is the stage when all traces have been burnt, i.e. it rains *dharma*, which uproots afflictions and deeds. The direct experience of insight is the supreme reflection, whereas its continuous presence is the *dharma*-cloud. This is the first liberation. The second liberation is the burning up of all afflictions except the will to live and karma. This is the liberation-while-living stage. The third is *kaivalya*, liberation from embodiment.

11.VIJÑĀNABHIKṢU, *Yogasārasaṃgraha*

Summary by Ram Shankar Bhattacharya

This short summary of the larger *Yogavārttika* was written by Vijñānabhikṣu after having written his *Sāṃkhyasāra*,

Brahmādarśa, and *Sāṃkhyabhāṣya,* since all of these works are mentioned in the *Yogasārasaṃgraha.*

The edition (E) used for this summary is V. Sarman 1933. The revised edition of a translation by Ganganatha Jha (Jha 1933), which he first published in 1892, is identified as the same Volume (#10) of the series in which E is found, though it is separately printed. This is our T.

BOOK ONE

(E1; T1-2)In the first two benedictory verses the author pays obeisance to God, to Patañjali, and to the teachers of *yoga*. In the third benedictory verse he informs us that the present work was composed after the composition of the *Yogavārttika*.

(E1-4; T2-9) Yoga, which is the means by which the *puruṣa* permanently abides in its own form, is defined as the inhibition of the fluctuations of awareness.* This inhibition exists in both forms of *yoga*, namely content-filled and content-free concentration. The realization of the self's abiding in its own form is nothing but the cessation of its artificial, contingent (*aupādhika*) form which is caused by limiting adjuncts (*upādhi*).

While the content-filled form of *yoga*, which eradicates afflictions, etc. leads to liberation through the direct realization of the principles of reality (*tattva*), the content-free form, which transcends the actions that have already begun to produce effects (*prārabdhakarman*), leads to liberation through its power of destroying traces. The word "*yoga*" is also used in the sense of yogic means, namely knowledge, devotion, karma and the like. Mental fluctuations that are capable of being inhibited are of five kinds, namely correct cognition, etc. Desire (*icchā*)and other fluctuations are restricted as a result of

*As above, we replace other translations of "*citta*" with our "awareness".

restricting these five. As soon as a fluctuation is affected by an object it assumes the form of the object. A fluctuation is not a quality of the intellect but a substance (*dravya*) as it possesses action. The reflection of the object in the *puruṣa* is called knowledge (*pramā*), i.e. the result of correct cognition. It is experienced as belonging to the *puruṣa* (*pauruṣeyabodha*), for the functions of the organs serve nothing but the purposes of *puruṣa*. The author has defined here the five kinds of fluctuations in accordance with the *(Yoga)Bhāṣya*.

Restriction of these fluctuations is not characterized as either destruction or negation, for the system of Yoga does not regard an absence (*abhāva*) as an entity. A restriction is positive in character, it creates traces. Both activity (*pravṛtti*) and inactivity (*nivṛtti*) are to be regarded as positive in nature. One is not the negation of the other.

(E4-5; T9-12) Yoga (the cessation of the fluctuations) is either one-pointed, content-filled concentration or content-free concentration. In the former all fluctuations except the one being experienced are restricted. This form of *yoga* is the cause of realizing the object of meditation. It also checks the mind from running towards undesired objects by suppressing the subconscious impressions concerning the objects. Awareness is all-pervasive and is capable of apprehending all objects. It can perceive objects of meditation without any external help when its *tāmasa* covering is reduced as a result of restricting the subconscious impressions.

Content-less concentration is the complete cessation of all mental fluctuations. In this state there remain traces only. There is no object to be known in this state. Even the trace of the knowledge of reality ceases.

(E 5-8; T8-18) The perceptible (*dṛṣṭa*) results of one-pointed awareness are the cessation of pain arising from mental fluctuations. The (imperceptible or non-worldly) subtle (*adṛṣṭa*) results are the direct perceptions of the essence of objects to be meditated upon. The subjugation of the elements and of the organs is also the result of this concentration. The subtle result of the unconscious concentration is an immediate release from both the karma that has already commenced to produce their effects (*prārabdhakarman*) and their traces. Yoga successfully eradicates these actions.

Content-less awareness is essential even after the attainment of knowledge. A liberated being is not born again on account of the cessation of ignorance. While the one-pointed awareness is capable of destroying vicious traces that obstruct knowledge, content-less awareness is capable of eradicating all kinds of karma. The destruction of karma means to render acts incapable of producing effects by uprooting their auxiliary causes. This uprooting is also known as "burning" (of karma).

The auxiliary causes just referred to are no other than the subconscious impressions causing experience of objects. The impressions of the emergent state are uprooted by the more powerful impressions of restriction. The non-experienced portion of the *prārabdhakarman* of a person attaining content-less concentration is destroyed with the destruction of his mind, which loses its identity as soon as the purposes of that *puruṣa,* which is the cause of sustaining the mind, come to an end.

(E8-14; T18-30) One-pointed awareness has four stages as accompanied by four factors: *vitarka, vicāra, ānanda* and *asmitā*. Each stage is progressively more subtle than the former. The order of the arising of these four factors is natural and one cannot attain to a following stage without mastering the preceding one. It is only through the grace of God that a practitioner can reach a higher stage without attaining a lower stage.

One is required to accept one and the same supporting object for practicing the aforesaid stages of conscious concentration *(bhāvanā)*. A supporting object is that on which concentration is fixed. It may be a deity or even an inanimate thing.

Direct perception *(sākṣātkāra)* through fixation, meditation, and concentration on the peculiar qualities existing in gross entities which exist in the three phases of time, or which are concealed or remote, is called "*vitarka*". Yogic perception of a thing is different from ordinary perception.

The *vicāra* form of awareness consists in the realization of the subtle aspect of the same object as was meditated on by the *yogin* in the *vitarka* stage. The word "subtle" means *tanmātras*, *ahaṃkāra*, *mahat* *(buddhi)* and *(avyakta)* *prakṛti*. As a gross thing is nothing but an effect of subtle things (an effect being essentially identical with its material cause), it is quite logical to hold that a thing may be perceived in a subtle way. The subtle form of a thing is perceived through the power of *yoga*.

Ānanda (the third factor) is joyful perception. It arises when fixation, meditation, and concentration are fixed on pleasure or joy existing in the twenty-four (types of) things (comprising the (Sāṃkhya-)Yoga categories of *prakṛti*). Though *prakṛti* (the ultimate material cause) contains pain and stupor or delusion, there is a specific purpose in mentioning *ānanda* alone in the *sūtra* on conscious concentration. One finding fault in joy would take it as pain and would consequently cultivate disinterest toward all objects.

The fourth state (*asmitā*) is the perception of the unchanging and all-pervading self as different from the previously mentioned entities with the help of the aforesaid supporting objects. It is in the form of "I am different from the body", etc. This is the ultimate stage, and it culminates in the concentration called "*dharma*-cloud realization". Such a perception arises when one becomes able to find fault in the preceding three factors. The *asmitā* form of awareness has two objects to be meditated on, namely (1) the self in general as different from the twenty-four things, and (2) the supreme self different from the twenty-five principles. As the supreme self is more subtle than the individual self, the latter is recognized first.

The self is the object of discernment into the difference between *sattva* (i.e. the mind predominated by the *sattva guṇa*) and *puruṣa*. Devotion to God (cf. YS I.23) is called "*paramātmayoga*".

(ET 14-16; T30-33) The aforesaid four stages of awareness, consisting in the direct perception of gross entities, subtle entities, joy and the self, are technically called "engrossments" (*samāpatti*). The author has described the four kinds of engrossment, namely *savitarka, nirvitarka, savicāra* and *nirvicāra*, with necessary details. The notion that words, their meanings and verbal cognitions are identical is what is known as conceptual construction (*vikalpa*). The *savitarka* perception is also known as construction-filled (*savikalpa*)). Similarly the *nirvitarka* perception is also known as construction-free (*nirvikalpa*). The assertion of modern logicians that *nirvikalpa* consists in directly perceiving the self and other entities without any connection with their qualities (*viśeṣaṇa*) has no basis (*apramāṇika*).

The *savitarka* form of engrossment may be regarded as a "lower perception" (*aparapratyakṣa*) as it is associated with ignorance (conceptual construction being a form of ignorance). The *nirvitarka* form of engrossment may be regarded as the highest perception (*parapratyakṣa*) because it is not subject to superimposition of any kind. Since these four stages of conscious concentration are qualified by contents of meditation, they are called *sabīja* ("seeded") or *sālambana* (having a (supporting) object). In all of these stages there exist fluctuations and their traces.

(E 16-19; T33-37) There are four classes of *yogins* who practice conscious concentration. (1) *Prathamakalpikas* are those who possess the *savitarka* form of engrossment. (2) *Madhubhūmikas* are those who possess the *nirvitarka* form of engrossment. These *yogins* are endowed with the insight called "truth-bearing". (3) *Prajñājyotis* are those who have conquered objects up to unmanifest *prakṛti*. (4) *Atikrāntibhāvanīyas* are those who have acquired the fourth state of conscious concentration which culminates in the *dharmamegha* (*YS* I. 29) The person possessing this concentration is called *jīvanmukta* (liberated though living).

It should be understood that the two forms of liberation,

namely liberation while living (*jīvanmukti*) and liberation after death *(videhamukti)* may be acquired without possessing supernormal powers. The Sāṃkhya view, that these two kinds of liberation come into existence whenever attachment, aversion, etc. which are the auxiliary causes of the transmigratory existence, are annihilated even in the absence of supernormal powers, is in consonance with the Yoga view. Content-less awareness leads one to liberation immediately by destroying the subconscious impressions and by transcending the actions that have already begun to bear fruit.

(E 18-20; T37-41) Content-less awareness is of two kinds, namely *upāyapratyaya* and *bhavapratyaya*. *Upāyapratyaya* is that type which is caused by faith, energy, memory, concentration and insight. Both of the two forms may also be acquired through devotion to God.

God is that particular *puruṣa* who is never affected by the afflictions, by actions, by merit and demerit, and their results. He is the same as the *brahman* of the *Vedāntasūtras*. His lordliness and omniscience are not excelled by other deities. He is the teacher of all former teachers and is signified by the sound *oṃ*. Devotion to god enables one to get rid of all obstacles, namely disease, etc., and brings about its results in less time.

The second form of content-less awareness is called "*bhavapratyaya*" since it causes birth (*bhava*). This concentration is to be found in the disembodied (*videha*) gods who have no gross body but only a subtle body, and the *prakṛtilīnas*, those who having crossed the universe and having surpassed all the minor coverings, have reached the veil or covering called *prakṛti* and have become similar to God on account of acute practice of knowledge and dispassion.

(E 20-21; T41-45) Though content-less awareness is of the nature of cessation, it produces traces. As these traces are developed so the fluctuations and their traces, including the awareness of reality (*tattvajñāna*), are attenuated. When all kinds of traces get burnt, past actions already bearing fruit (*prārabdha*) become incapable of producing their effects. As soon as the purpose of the mind becomes fully served, it gets dissolved into its material cause along with all actions and traces thereof. This is the great sleep (*mahānidrā*) of awareness (*citta*), which is commonly known as the isolation of the *puruṣa*. In this state there arises absolute disjunction from all forms of *dṛśya* (the essence of which is nothing but pain).

BOOK TWO

(E 22-24; T46-50) Three kinds of persons are qualified to practice *yoga*, namely (1) *ārurukṣu*, those wishing to attain *yoga*, who belong to the lowest stage, (2) *yuñjana*, those who are striving for concentration, who belong to the middle states, and (3) *yogārūḍha*, those who have attained concentration, who belong to the highest stage.

"Renunciation (*tyāga)* concerning those who have attained concentration" must be taken to mean the renouncing of external actions which are obstacles to *yoga*. Different from these are the internal actions designated as internal sacrifice (*antartyāga*).

(E 24-26; T50-54) Practice (*abhyāsa*) is exertion to bring about the flow of undisturbed one-pointedness. By means of practice one can check the mind from running toward undesired objects.

Dispassion (*vairāgya*) is not the absence of passion (*rāga*) but conviction that all objects are useless. It has two aspects, namely ordinary and extreme. Ordinary dispassion consists in the absence of longing for all kinds of object on account of perceiving fault in the acquisition, preservation, etc. of objects. It has four phases. The first phase (called *yatamāna*) consists in perceiving faults only. The second phase (called *vyatireka*) consists in ascertaining the number of organs controlled or yet to be controlled. The third phase (called *ekendriya*) consists in uprooting attachment, hatred, etc. from the mind. The fourth state (called *vaśīkāra*) consists in the organs remaining unperturbed in spite of their proximity to the objects. While the first three forms are to be practiced by the *yogins* called *yuñjanas*, the last form is to be practiced by those who are established in yoga practices (*yogarūḍhas*).

Supreme dispassion (*paravairāgya*) consists in the realization that all kinds of knowable things are useless due to their being inherently faulty. It is caused by the knowledge of the distinction of the self from the non-self and also by the cessation of ignorance. As liberation is its immediate result, it is called supreme. As the mental flow towards an object is obstructed by dispassion, the flow of the mental fluctuations become steady, assuming the form of the object to be meditated on. The cessation of the fluctuations depends upon both these means.

(E26-30; T54-61) There are six internal means called "purifications" (*parikarman*) which are helpful in bringing about steadiness, i.e. a peaceful mind. The fourth, fifth and sixth purifications are not obligatory. Purifications are the means to practice. Both practice and dispassion are the means to conscious concentration. Dispassion is the direct means to the cessation of mental fluctuations, while practice is the indirect means as it acts through concentration. Practice based on some supporting object becomes the means to non-conscious concentration through the realization of discriminative knowledge.

(E30-32; T61-64) *Kriyāyoga,* austerities, study and devotion, are said to be the chief means to be adopted by those possessing middling qualifications (known as *yuñjanas*). Practice and other means are also to be taken up according to one's own ability.

Austerity consists in enduring the opposites, such as heat and cold. Study is the reading of treatises on emancipation or the repetition of sacred syllables. Devotion consists in surrendering all actions to God, the supreme teacher, or in renouncing the results of actions. To think that the supreme God is the enjoyer of the results of actions is what is known as the offering of the results of actions. God's experiencing the results of actions means His causing the embodied selves to enjoy the results of their actions. Here experience is to be taken in a secondary sense. God cannot be supposed to enjoy directly the results (e.g., heaven or hell) of actions performed by individual selves.

The word "*yoga*" in the expression "*kriyāyoga*" signifies a means. The result of *kriyāyoga* is both the attenuation of the afflictions and the cultivation of concentration.

The five afflictions are described. Each preceding affliction is the cause of the following. Thus ignorance is the source of all the four afflictions that follow, which disappear on the disappearance of ignorance.

(E32-34; T65-68) The afflictions are at first attenuated by *kriyāyoga* and afterwards are rendered powerless by discriminative knowledge. This is the state of liberation while still alive (*jīvanmukti*). These afflictions disappear when the mind gets dissolved. This is the state of highest liberation and in this state *puruṣa* does not experience pain. Afflictions, actions, etc. become unable to produce their results as they are rendered completely impotent. Though merit (*dharma*) is the cause of heavenly pleasure, in reality this pleasure has frustration as its invariable consequence. Afflictions give rise to *dharma* and *adharma*; these in turn produce birth, the span of life, and experience. Pleasure and pain arise from these three. Bondage (*bandha*) is what is known as the experience of pleasure and pain.

(E34-36; T68-73) The cessation of ignorance which is the result of the realization of the distinction between the self and the non-self, leads to the cessation of the rest of the afflictions (namely egoity, etc.) Actions that have not begun to produce their results as yet fail to produce their results on account of the destruction of the afflictions, which are the cooperating causes of actions. Those actions that have already begun to fructify are destroyed by the fruition of knowledge. This is why there is no rebirth for him who has left his body after enjoying the fruits of *prārabdhakarman.* This is what is known as the stage of emancipation, which is nothing but the termination of pain.

(ET36-39; T73-78) An account of the paths leading to discriminative discernment that are helpful to persons wishing to attain *yoga* are given here. These are eight in number–restraint (*yama*)and so forth.

Violence sanctioned or enjoined by scripture (*vaidhahiṃsā*) is regarded as non-violence. It falls under the purview of either the duty of a householder or inevitable violence. Even the renunciation of such violence constitutes what is called a great vow (*mahāvrata*). The term "great vow" is applied to the restraints only, for leading to cessation they are capable of being practiced without any limitation. This cannot be said of the observances (*niyama*), which are of the nature of an activity (*pravṛtti*) and as such are invariably controlled by space, time, etc.

(E39-44; E78-86) The number of yogic postures are said to be equal to the number of the postures found in all kinds of creatures. Only three postures, namely *svāstika, padma* and *ardha* are said to be the best. It is remarked that an elaborate account of yogic postures and purification of the nerves, etc. is to be found in the treatises on Haṭhayoga and Rājayoga.

Breath control is said to be of three varieties, namely inhalation, exhalation, and stopping of breath. A fourth variety called *kevalakumbhaka* is also mentioned in some treatises.

Withdrawal of the senses consists in subjugating the sense-organs after withdrawing them from their respective objects. The subjugation of organs means to put them under control so that they may be used in accordance with one's own will.

The purpose of the first five auxiliaries to yoga is to subjugate the body, vital air and the organs, while the purpose of meditative fixation, reflective meditation and concentration is to subjugate the mind.

(E44-47; E86-90) Meditative fixation is the fixation of the mind on certain regions of the body, namely the heart, navel, head, etc. Reflective meditation is the flow of undisturbed fluctuations assuming the form of the object of meditation, namely Viṣṇu and other deities. Again, the place of meditation is the heart, the fluctuations of awareness, etc. When meditation assumes just the form of the object and the distinctions of the act of meditating, the object of meditation, and the state of the meditator cease on account of the fusion or absorption into the object, then it is called concentration. It is incapable of being disturbed, unless contact of organs with stimulating objects occurs.

Though the mind is naturally capable of perceiving all intended objects, it fails to perceive them on account of its being affected by non-intended objects. This is why the restriction of fluctuations directed toward non-intended objects is regarded as the direct cause of perceiving intended objects. Concentration is a subordinate helping factor in this perception. Restriction of fluctuations is, however, the principal factor, and concentration is the last auxiliary to *yoga* called conscious.

(E47-51; T90-99) The joint application of fixation, meditation and concentration to any supporting object is called comprehensive reflection (*saṃyama*), which may be directed gradually to all stages beginning with the gross objects and ending with the supreme self.

(E51-52; T99-100) The last three auxiliaries to yoga are regarded as internal in comparison to the first five, which are regarded as external. While the chief purpose of the former group is to purify the mind, that of the latter group is to purify the body, vital air, and the organs. A person may achieve yoga in the present life even by following the last three auxiliaries in his previous life. Yoga can never be attained without practicing the last three auxiliaries.

BOOK THREE

(E53-54; T101-103) The purpose of enumerating the extraordinary capacities is either (1) to pacify the craving for powers which are an obstacle to knowledge, etc. or (2) to ascertain the power of comprehensive reflection. The purpose of presenting these powers to persons who are desiring to attain liberation is to show the undesirable character of these powers. One aspiring for liberation is required to shun desires for omniscience and the like.

These powers are in fact innumerable and only a few are mentioned in the *Yogasūtras* and the *Bhāṣya* thereon. An extraordinary capacity is the realization of the contents of comprehensive reflection.

(E54-56; T103-109) The author has first given an account of those reflections that are helpful to realize the self. It is also remarked that the reflection mentioned in III.35 enables one to realize that the *puruṣa* is absolutely different from the fluctuations, and it concludes that there is no other way besides this reflection for directly realizing the self. True *yogins* are said to look upon the extraordinary capacities with detachment.

(E56-64; T109-125) The powers which result from comprehensive reflection on the cognizer, instrument of cognition, and the object cognized are stated here.

BOOK FOUR

(E64-67; T126-131) Stating that liberation is the chief result of knowledge and yoga, the author has quoted and explained *Yogasūtra* IV.34 and remarked that the three *guṇas* are incapable of being destroyed. This *sūtra* offers two definitions of isolation (i.e. liberation). According to the first defintion isolation is an attribute of *prakṛti,* while according to the second it is *puruṣa*'s abiding in his own form. Both of these two definitions show that the absolute cessation of the experience of pain is the end or goal (*puruṣārtha*).

(E68-71; T133-139) The word "sound" (*śabda*) has three significations. (1) It is the object of the organ called speech (i.e., it is produced in the palate, etc.) (2) It is that entity which, being produced by sound, exists in the ear and is apprehended by the ear. (3) It means the words like "jar", etc. which are apprehended by the intellect. A "*sphoṭa*" is different from the uttered sound and is caused by a single effort. The author finds no reason to reject even the view that a whole sentence constitutes a *sphoṭa*.

(E71-73; T139-145) Each *puruṣa* has an eternal internal organ which must be all-pervasive as *yogins* perceive all objects through it. The veil (*āvaraṇa*) dominated by *tamas* existing in the internal organ is destroyed by the power of yoga, as a result of which the internal organ becomes able to know all simultaneously.

Motion in the all-pervasive internal organ is to be ascribed to its limiting adjuncts (*upādhi*), namely the vital force, organs, etc. Though all-pervasive it is an effect (i.e. a product of the three *guṇas*) as is declared in the authoritative texts.

(E73-75; T145-148) Time (*kāla*) is nothing but the moment. Brief arguments have ben advanced here to prove that the scriptural statements about the eternity of time simply show its eternal changing-ness (*pravāhanityatā*). A moment is not altogether different from *prakṛti* or *puruṣa*; it is a particular kind of extremely transitory fluctuation of *prakṛti*. The usage of "*muhūrta*" (a period of 48 minutes), "day", "night", etc. is dependent on the sequence of moments.

12.BHĀVĀGAṆEŚA DĪKṢITA, *Pradīpikā* on Patañjali's *Yogasūtras*

Bhāvāgaṇeśa Dīkṣita was a direct disciple of Vijñānabhikṣu and can be dated, therefore, along with Vijñānabhikṣu in the latter half of the sixteenth century. His *Ṭīkā* on the *Tattvasamāsasūtra*, entitled *Tattvayātharthyadīpana* ("Illuminating the Complete Meaning of the Truth") is the oldest commentary on the *Tattvasamāsa* after the *Kramadīpikā*. He also composed a brief commentary on the *Pātañjalayogasūtra* called *Pradīpikā*. In most respects it is a summary paraphrase of his teacher Vijñānabhikṣu's *Yogavārttika*. For the Sanskrit text, see Dundhiraja Sastri 1982.

13.NĀRĀYAṆATĪRTHA, *Yogasiddhāntacandrikā*

Summary by Anima Sen Gupta

Nārāyaṇa Tīrtha was well versed not only in Sāṃkhya and Yoga philosophy but also in the philosophical systems of the Nyāya-Vaiśeṣika school and the Vedānta. He was a Telugu *brāhmaṇa* from Kaza in Guntur district. In later life he traveled and lived in various places, including Varanasi, Prayag, Mathura, Puri and so forth. He was a devotee of Kṛṣṇa. He wrote three works on Yoga, the *Yogasiddhāntacandrikā*, the *Sūtrārthabodhinī* and the *Pātañjalasūtralaghuvṛtti*. Only the first two texts are available. Japanese scholar Ko Endo has studied the life and works of Nārāyaṇa Tīrtha extensively and has concluded that he is best dated 1600-1690 C.E.[164]

The heavy emphasis on devotional *bhakti* should be noted. Also, the inclusion of Haṭha Yoga and aspects of Tantra practice is worth noting. "E" here refers to Bhatta 1910. Page numbers have not been provided in the summary, but the individual *sūtras* are easily accessible in the edition.

BOOK ONE

Introduction (E1-2) The author indicates that yoga has been earlier explained by Brahmā, sages, and scholars, but he tries to explain its deeper points in a simpler fashion.

For the highest aim of self-realization, the Upaniṣads have laid down the necessity of meditation (*nididhyāsana*) for unhindered communion with the self. Concentration is attained through unfaltering commitment to Rājayoga. As aids to it sixteen forms of yoga are mentioned based on practice, knowledge, actions and devotion, etc. such as *kriyāyoga, jñānayoga, karmayoga, premabhaktiyoga*, etc.

I.1 (E3) Yoga means concentration. By "*anuśāsana*" is meant a beginning of the scripture on yoga detailing definition, result, and means. The result is liberation (isolation, *kaivalya*) and the person deserving it is one desirous of it. The relation between this scripture and its consequence is that of an inducer to the object of inducement, and between the work and its subject is that of the expositor and the subject matter.

I.2-3 (E3-9)Fluctuations are external and internal changes of state of the internal organ of threefold nature as awareness, mind and the ego-sense, like that of a candle, its wick and flame. Its suppression is merger lapsing in its source (*prakṛti*), like fuel-less fire. At the time of the suppression (of fluctuations) the subject (seer) stays in his own nature as pure consciousness. Thus the content-free fluctuation is the suppression of other fluctuations through unswerving concentration on the self.

Abhāvayoga is attained when all other fluctuations are suppressed to concentrate the mind on the self. *Mahāyoga* is when the content of concentration is God.

Or, suppression means stopping of the fluctuations so that the mind is free from them. The pure knower (*kṣetrajña*) becomes one with the highest self and attains liberation. According to the *Yogavāsiṣṭha* there are two ways of destroying awareness–yoga, which is suppression of fluctuations, and knowledge (*jñāna*), which is appropriate grasp (of things).

Yogins are of two types, those disciplined (*yukta*) and those undisciplined. The first is of tranquilized mind. He wants only liberation. The second is not of peaceful mind, and seeks yogic powers, etc. Whereas undisciplined *yogins* can be of various types according to circumstances, what about those who are disciplined? Staying in its own nature of the *puruṣa* is the attainment of self-luminousness, free from fluctuations as existence-consciousness (*saccidrūpa*), which is liberation while living (*jīvanmukti*).

I.4 (E9) In the emergent state (i.e. out of concentration) *puruṣa* appears as fluctuations of three types, viz., peaceful, cruel and deluded. But the self does not depart from its true nature even when it appears in fluctuations, just as a crystal does not turn red due to reflection of that color. This is because an unreal change does not alter a thing.

I.5 (E9-10) Fluctuations are of five kinds, and are afflicting and non-afflicting according as they are harmful or beneficial. The afflicting fluctuations are based on various desires toward objects and are of the nature of *rajas* and *tamas*, and hence productive of suffering leading to merit or demerit according as they are of the nature of kindness or cruelty towards others.

Non-afflicting fluctuations are opposed to the above types, and are based on discriminative knowledge of the *sāttvika* nature related to the means of attainment (*sādhanā*). Thus with the help of instruments of knowledge, when the self is realized, sorrow ends. Under the category of error, when the *śālagrāma* stone is taken as Viṣṇu it generates religious merit. According to Advaita Vedānta the great saying "that thou art" (*tat tvam asi),* of the nature of wrong conceptual construction, leads to liberation by indicating non-difference. Sleep gives happiness. And perceiving blue clouds, if one remembers Śrī Kṛṣṇa, generates good (unseen, *adṛṣṭa*) results. Hence these good fluctuations, conducive to liberation, are not to be suppressed indiscriminately with the fluctuations of the afflicting type, but are to be given up only at the final state, since they are not directly of the nature of liberation (*nirvāṇa*).

I.6 (E10) Instruments of knowledge (*pramāṇa*) are different in category from purposes and consequences, and, as such, are not fluctuations to be directly suppressed.

(Inference by) agreement and difference is classified under illusion by Vedāntins, as they are (occasionally, or according to that system, generally) grounds for erroneous awareness. Yet that is not logical. We (in the Yoga system) do not admit beginningless, inexpressible *avidyā*, but do admit the illusoriness of the instruments of knowledge as fluctuations of awareness. The cases of shell-silver also are fluctuations of the internal organ, of the nature of sublated as non-sublated, and hence of the form real-and-unreal. This is the basis of *sadasadkhyāti,* to be clarified later.

I.7 (E10-11) Comparison (*upamāna*) is to be classified under perception. Presumption (*arthāpatti*), possibility (*sambhava*), and gesture (*ceṣṭā*) are to be placed under inference. Non-perception (*anupalabdhi*) is to be placed under perception, and tradition (*aitihya*) under testimony (*śabda*).

Inference (*anumāna*) is that knowledge of a thing to be proved (*sādhya*), based on generality, that is gained through pervasion (*vyāpti*) together with the presence of the *hetu* in the *pakṣa*.

I.8 (E12) Error (*viparyaya*) is false awareness intended to establish something as different from what it is. What is sublated by a contrary perception is not established; for instance, the perception of silver is sublated on the realization that the object is a shell.

I.9 (E12) Conceptual constructions (*vikalpa*) are fluctuations produced by such words or awarenesses to which no objects correspond, for instance, in a quarrel it might be said of a man that he has horns. It is not an instrument of knowledge, being without an (actual) object, and it is not error, because it is not sublated. It is a verbal concept produced without contact with the senses, and different from ordinary errors, as in the case of metaphor. Naiyāyikas also admit that even if words present certain meanings, for want of fitness (*yogyatā*) there is no verbal knowledge.

I.10 (E13-17) With reference to the *Chāndogya Upaniṣad* the author opines that scripture will also bear out that in sleep awareness merges (in the self), because of which there is semblance of the bliss of Brahman. Sleep is a fluctuation of ignorance, in spite of the merging of awareness. In sleep the awareness does not reside in its cause, the self, but only has an absence (for the time being) of its external propensity. Else it would not rise again. Sleep being a state of the mind, the attendant bliss is due to *sattva* and not to the self.

According to scripture deep sleep is a state of joy, and hence it cannot be just absence of all awareness. If it were such a want, the feeling of bliss on awakening would be an inference, and deep sleep would be an absence of awareness and suffering as in a liberated self; and the attribute of bliss would be only due to absence of suffering. But if deep sleep be not known, there would be no locus for the inference, nor can there be an inference that sleep's temporality (while asleep) was empty, since there is no temporal universal in *sāmānyalakṣaṇa* perception. Nor can it be an inference that out of eight parts of day and night, six being wakeful, the remaining two must be of sleep, because that would be common to all men, and not a matter of individual experience. In our view, deep sleep being a transformation of the mind, there is no difficulty about remembering it.

I.11 (E17-19) A memory is an idea corresponding to an object experienced without adding or changing it. In memory both the object and its awareness are remembered together, just as the two go together in experience. No second act of awareness (after-cognition, *anuvyavasāya*) is needed to experience it. This is the view of Vedāntins also. Such a second act would lead to infinite regress.

I.12 (E19-20) Corresponding to afflicting and non-afflicting fluctuations already considered (cf. I.5), there is a distinction of functions of fluctuations, such as those having external objects and those internal ones like sleep, etc. Just as water tending to flood villages, etc. is controlled with a dam, etc. and for irrigation directed into channels, so the above two types of fluctuations are to be controlled by dispassion and practice respectively.

I.13 (E20-21) By effort one attains stability (concentration) on God or conscious reality through enthusiasm, courage, patience, spiritual knowledge, service of noble persons, restraints, rules, and discipline. These constitute practice.

I.15 (E21-22) The controlled state of awareness due to lack of desire for objects, whereby objects are indifferent (*upekṣā*) to one, is dispassion (*vairāgya*). It has four stages: first, while with a strong desire to discard objects one is unable to do so; second, when one discards the rest except the dearer ones; third, without attachment one keeps using things externally; finally, one discards them altogether. Or, the first is discrimination of the essential and the nonessential, second is the remnant of objective attachments, third, only mental interest in them, and fourth, ignoring them.

I.16 (E22-23) The reference to knowledge of *puruṣa* is a pointer to the laziness of those content (with slight effort). Discriminative wisdom lies in faith in *prakṛti* as the doer of all things, or, having seen the defects of the worldly objects, in reliance on the knowledge of the self, which is free from attachment, calm and enlightened.

I.17 (E23)is based on the *Tattvavaiśāradī*.

I.18 (E23-24)The first part mentions the method, and the second part the result. The former, by stating the discipline for bringing about the cessation of fluctuations, excludes the *prakṛtilayas*, and the latter excludes the state of being liberated while living, who are endowed with only enlightened wisdom as stated in the Upaniṣads. Due to extreme resignation there arises content-less concentration having only subliminal impressions.

I.19 (E24) is based on the *Tattvavaiśāradī* and Bhoja's *Rājamārtaṇḍa*.

I.20 (E24-25) When seedless concentration is attained with the self of the nature of reality and consciousness resting like a non-flickering wick of a lamp as stated in *smṛti*, that is Rājayoga. In the previous *sūtra* the origin of gods, etc. has been mentioned. They do not rely on content-less concentration because their thoughts and senses implies that their awarenesses are content-filled. They have become enlightened *yogins* by worship of God or *prakṛti* in special bodies. They get liberated after their attainments end.

I.21 (E25)Renunciation (*saṃvega*) means dispassion (*vairāgya*).

I.23-26 (E26-40) By constant meditation, love and devotion to God concentration becomes easy. By His grace a good teacher comes to the aid of the seeker, God being the supreme teacher and all other teachers being His incarnations.

Some hold that Brahmā, Viṣṇu and Śiva (as supreme) mean

just a quality-less great self (*guṇātīta paramātman*), because Brahman has not even a body of *māyā*. But when referred to as residing in their abodes with form, they are (especially powerful) individual selves (*jīva*). That is why they are referred to as teaching each other occasionally. This view is not correct, because for the sake of grace to the devotees the supreme principle assumes other sportive forms (*līlāvigraha*) also and rules over everything, and Brahmā, Viṣṇu, and Rudra also create. They are of two types, as described in scripture and the *Purāṇas*. In the first type they are the incarnations of pure God; in the second they are particular individuals of the world with its activities and results. But due to non-difference between a power and its owner, they are also called great God, though actually it is not so. The main powers are the three mentioned above, and similar are also incarnations like Rāma.

As omniscient, God is the teacher (*guru*). When Brahmā, etc. receive instructions, God in His manifold capacity appears as more or less enlightened for the benefit of the devotees.

God is manifest in two ways, as inner-dweller in sentient creatures and as outer-dweller in the world as its regulator. He appears in form for the worshipers, and as pure consciousness for others. He is again two-fold in terms of permanent power and sportive power. The first has been mentioned above: the second again is two-fold as (the incarnations) Vyūha and Avatāras. If among the highest trio of Brahmā, etc. there are conflicting accounts of who created whom, these refer to different cosmic periods without meaning any kind of pervasion or inclusion between them.

I.27 (E40-44) For adjunctless God, "undifferentiated *oṃkāra*" is a non-derivative name. In this sense God is unseen and unheard, realizable only by feeling and devotion. "*Oṃ*" is a word for God. The relation of a word and its corresponding object is identity (*svarūpa*) with difference (*vibhāgarūpa*). Word and meaning are one. In this manner of mutual non-difference "*oṃkāra*" indicates Brahman as stated in scripture.

There are other specific incantations for different gods.

Why the pre-eminence of "*oṃ*"? The reason is that by reciting "*oṃ*" all incantations are covered. The *praṇava* (i.e. *oṃ*) is the bow and the Upaniṣads are the arrows. "*Praṇava*" is used instead of "*oṃ*" because the latter is to be kept secret due to its mystic nature. "*Praṇava*" means bowing (*praṇāmayati, namayati)* to the Vedas, etc.

I.28 (E45-46) *Praṇava* is to be recited with proper pronunciation. As its meaning one should reflect on God with unthinkable powers, and also try to discriminate between *puruṣa* and *prakṛti*. Or the meaning of "*praṇava*" is non-difference between God in his perfection and the individual self (*jīva*), "*a*" being self, "*ṃ*" being Brahman, and "*u*" being a resolution of their difference. Its recitation is auditory recitation (*mantrayoga*), attaining of discriminative knowledge by reflection on its meaning is *jñānayoga*, and mediating on the non-difference is *advaitayoga*.

I.29 (E46-48) By the above three forms of meditation and devotion arises knowledge of the limitations of individual selves and knowledge of God as a consciousness-of-consciousness (*cetanaścetana*), as stated in scripture. In this knowledge one realizes "I am not, naught is mine", by firm direct encounter, which becomes the cause of isolation.

I.31 (E49-51) The first paragraph is as in the *Bhāṣya*. The external attempts to overcome distractions require a great deal of effort. But recitation of God's name easily produces great results, like a spark of fire that sets a haystack ablaze. Such concentration and devotion to God is of four types. The first is love like the *gopīs*', the second is constant meditation on God, the third is devotional fasts, etc. and the fourth is resignation of the fruits of actions and consecration of them to God as the supreme teacher. Corresponding references to the twelfth chapter of the *Bhagavadgītā* are given.

I.34 (E53) Breath is gradually inhaled, for some time the wind is kept out, and then gradually exhaled. This is an early form of breath control. In breath control breathing and awareness are conquered, all sins are destroyed, and the awareness becomes single-pointed in concentration. Breath control is known as *haṭhayoga* or the seed of yoga (*yogabīja*). "*Ha*" stands for the sun, and "*ṭha*" for the moon. In "*haṭha*" they come together.

I.35 (E54) By concentration on the front part of the nose wonderful smell is felt. These and similar experiences strengthen faith in the efficacy of yoga. Hence it is called *lakṣyayoga*.

I.36 (E54-55) The process of *brahmayoga* is this: First the eight-petalled lotus turned downwards is to be turned upwards in exhalation. In it there is a solar *maṇḍala* of twelve *kalās*, representing the waking state of the form "*a*". Above that is the *maṇḍala* of the moon of sixteen *kalās* representing the dream-state of the form of "*u*". Above that is the circle of fire of ten *kalās* of the nature of deep sleep, and "*m*". Further above it is *nāda*, the fourth (*turīya*) state of Brahman. Where that mind merges is the supreme state of God (Viṣṇu).

This state is bright, effulgent, and free from sorrow as the mind gets concentrated on the delight of consciousness in *nāda*. Or it is free from sorrow because of the quieting of the mind or concentration of sight in the middle of the brows on the effulgent inner self (*pratyagātman*). This is *śivayoga*, free from the hardships of *haṭhayoga*. This is called *śāmbhavī mudrā*. Thereby *kāmacarī, bhūcarī, khecarī* and *nirvāṇa mudrās* also become possible.

I.37 (E55-56) *Vāsanāyoga* is practiced by negating other desires by good desires of the *sāttvika* type.

I.38 (E56) "*Jñāna*" here stands for the object known (*jñeya*). It is a type of *vāsanāyoga*. In dream, if God is seen in the form that is dear and an object of worship, it consists in making the mind dwell on that form.

I.39 (E57-63) By concentration on anything liked, such as Hari, the sun, etc. the mental fluctuations can be restrained, whereby the capacity for fixing the attention on God develops. Attention can also by made single-pointed by fixing it on sacred places (*tīrtha*) inside the body like Ayodhyā, at the thousand-petalled center at the head, or at Kāśī at *ājñā cakra*, etc. at the tip of the nose, or where *īḍā* (Ganges) and *piṅgalā* (Yamunā) flow, or where Prayāga is located. Similarly, other channels are the Narmadā and other sacred rivers for visiting *tīrthas* in the course of the yogic pilgrimage from the basal center (*mūlādhāra*). In this process the three regions of the body, below the waist, from the waist to the throat, and above that, are to be covered; also fourteen forests in hairy parts of the body and barren tracts in hairless regions. Then follows a section reflecting on different aspects of personality as gods: *puruṣa* of the nature of self-luminous consciousness as Śiva, *prakṛti* with *guṇas* as Śakti, awareness as *Vāsudeva, buddhi* as Brahmā, the *ahaṃkāra* as Śiva, etc.

Next follows reflection on different parts of the body as different cosmic regions, from the nether world in the soles of the feet to the region of truth (*satyaloka*) in the head. Further there is an account of reflection on colors, after which comes a description of different vital centers in the body, as elsewhere.

In the middle of the body, in the place of *anāhata nāda*, there is a drooping young lotus. It has to be reflected as raised. Here, impelled by breath and according to past deeds, the *jīva* of the nature of knowledge and spirit roams day and night.The *yogin* focuses breaths on each petal of the lotus, meditating on *ākāśa*, air, fire, water and earth. In this way he covers one petal in nine hundred breaths, and of eight petals in 7,200 breaths. This process is repeated thrice within a day and a night. In this way the number of breaths is counted for life. Hence by control of breath longevity is gained.

Breathing in different petals, different mental attitudes arise, as stated in the *Haṃsopaniṣad* and already summarized in connection with the *Dhyānabindu Upaniṣad*. When the self leaves a petal and is in *ākāśa*, he momentarily enjoys the bliss of Brahman as he is in the fourth (*turīya*) state, but returns to the next petal like a hawk on a string. But if a *yogin* can hold his breath fixed in this interval, he continues in such bliss. In this state of breath, if he considers himself in the state of Indra, he attains that state.

The breath flows in the channels *īḍā* and *piṅgalā*. In the former the breath is in the left nostril and is called "moon", and is of the nature of *śakti* and cool. *Piṅgalā* is to the right, of the sun, of the nature of Śiva and hot. If a *yogin* manages so that the breath flows in the left nostril during the daytime heat, and the right nostril during the cool of night, he gets a conqueror's death. The above method is called *dhyānayoga*.

I.40 (E63-64) It is *siddhayoga* when by non-fluctuating awareness the greatest magnitude becomes accessible, unhindered by any of the obstacles like hunger, thirst, etc.

I.41 (E64-65) Joy or bliss (*ānanda*) has not been separately mentioned because it belongs to the ego-sense. In this way the content-filled concentration of four types, assuming forms either of empirical awareness or of rational awareness or joy or the sense of egoity, are produced. Of these the first three pertain to the content of awareness (*grāhya*) while the last is the cognizer (*grahītṛ*).

I.46 (E66) "Content-filled " means that a part (aspect) of one's being is placed before his awareness for (eventual) concentration.

I.47 (E66)"Tranquility pertaining to the presence of the real self" means that the self, together with the intellect, becomes capable of experiencing bliss due to *sattva*.

I.49 (E67-68) A particular (*viśeṣa*) awareness means one that is construction-free (*nirvikalpa*). Words and inferences produce awarenesses limited by the pervasiveness limited by an object (in plain language, general concepts). But a particular awareness is unable to deal with such general concepts, and therefore it is of the object alone, unqualified by predicates.

BOOK TWO

II.1 (E70-71) "*Tapas*" means drying of the body through fasting and austere vows. This together with study and devotion is called "*kriyāyoga*" because it involves use of speech, body, etc. Although these have already been mentioned earlier, together with purity and contentment, as part of the rules for yoga, they are separately mentioned here because of their special efficacy in the control of body, sense, and mind.

II.2 (E71) *Tanūkaraṇa* means making subtle or less dense.

II.4 (E71-72) The four afflictions (other than ignorance) are dormant in the case of those merged in *prakṛti*, attenuated in the case of *kriyāyogins*, and sustained or intercepted in the case of humans attached to objects.

II.5 (E72-77) The (Advaita) Vedāntic view of *sadasad-anirvacanīyakhyāti* and the notion of *avidyā* as the cause of the world are both untenable. If ignorance were the cause of the world, as soon as someone knew something the dispelling of ignorance should have brought the world to an end. Hence ignorance is a series of illusions and a function of the internal organ. It is of the nature of real-unreal, which is established by the method of agreement and difference. When due to distance, etc. the ropeness of a rope not seen, it is taken as a snake, but on perceiving its ropeness the illusion ceases. For this, ignorance without support is not the cause; but attachment, etc. that produce incapacity to perceive properly is the cause. The illusory object is unreal as it is sublated, but it is real because it appears. Hence it is both real and unreal (*sadasat*).

II.9 (E78-79) The five afflictions–ignorance, etc.–are also called (respectively) *tamas, moha, mahāmoha, tāmisra* and *andhatāmisra*.

II.10 (E79-80) It cannot be maintained that the afflictions are the cause of the world, and that hence they should be destroyed for liberation, and not awareness itself. (So long as awareness remains) the residues of afflictions, like burnt seeds, might happen only to be displaced, but might lead to fresh sprouts.

II.11 (E80) The elimination of gross afflictions is the first step. But the merger of awareness (into *prakṛti*) being the real goal, the inverse process has been mentioned.

II.13 (E81-85) The afflictions cooperate with karmas for their fruitions in three forms of birth, span of life and its experiences, Only when the self is wet with the water of afflictions does the sprout of fruition (of karma) arise, not otherwise. A causal condition does not have the efficiency to produce an effect without the (required) support of other conditions making up the collection (*sāmagrī*) constituting a sufficient condition. When by knowledge, etc. afflictions are overcome, so also are the fruits of actions.

II.15 (E86) "*Guṇavṛttinirodha*" might be taken in two ways: (i) The suppression of the *guṇas* and their (respective) awarenesses, pleasure, pain, and delusion, by subordinating one another; (ii) The suppression of the awarenesses of the *guṇas*, i.e. of pleasure, pain and delusion, as each arises by subordinating the others.

II.20 (E87-88) The percipient seer is only an observer as pure consciousness, not as having awarenesses, etc. It perceives presented ideas as reflected in the fluctuations of the intellect by synthesis (union) of discrimination with fluctuations. The seer is here indicated as an instrument of knowledge, as without him the world cannot be cognized.

II.22 (E88-89) For the realized *puruṣa, prakṛti* does not act. It acts for the *puruṣa* that has not attained (the goal). Only for him do *mahat*, etc. develop.

II.24 (E89-90) The reason for the union of the seer and the seen is ignorance of the nature of taking the flow (of experience) as the self, their relation being like seed and sprout. "I am" in this form of the illusion of the non-difference of seer and seen merges in *prakṛti* at dissolution, to arise again at the next creation from traces laid down before for *puruṣa*'s enjoyment and liberation.

II.26 (E90-91) Discrimination (*viveka*) is that the seer and the seen are different, and the resulting knowledge (*khyāti*) is that the *guṇas* are different from the *puruṣa*. This is *aviplava* in the sense that it is free from the successive rise of subconscious impressions that generate false awarenesses. This is the method for removal of suffering. The serial steps for it are thus: First by knowledge goes ignorance. Thereby goes the hold of *prakṛti*, and awareness merges. Hence its union with *puruṣa* goes and thereby ends suffering. The other means of yoga are not irrelevant, but it is knowledge that gives liberation.

II.28(E92-98) By repeated practice of yoga and its parts, by removal of impurities like fickleness, afflictions and sins, comes growth of knowledge leading to proper discrimination. This is either by the discipline of Sāṃkhya-Yoga or by ancillaries of yoga like six acts and exercises *(mudrā)*. *Dhautī**, etc. are acts for bodily purification, while *mahāmudrā, mahābandha*, etc. are the bodily postures. These belong more to bodily practice of Haṭhayoga than to Rājayoga.

II.30 (E98-100) As violence (*hiṃsā*), causing suffering to creatures, is the root of every evil, it is to be avoided in thought, speech and actions. Nonviolence is stated to be the first restraint (*yama*). Truth lies in use and practice according to what is actually seen, etc. Truth is behavior calculated to make things understood as they are; with that intention it can be verbal and behavioral. *Steya* is misappropriation of another's things like property. *Brahmacarya* is restraint of senses in all ways, abstaining from all aspects of sexual intercourse. *Aparigraha* is non-acceptance of enjoyments beyond what is necessary for maintenance of the body.

II.31 (E100) These are of the nature of abstinence and renunciation, and as such parts of yoga.

II.32 (E100-102) Devotion to God stands for such activity which pleases God and thereby leads to release from the world. Already stated once under *kriyāyoga* (II.2) it is again stated as part of the great vow. The devotee of the highest self (*paramātman*) rests in supreme joy, self-luminous and self-witnessing its own self, due to identification with Brahman.

---

*Monier-Williams 1899, p. 520, column 3 informs us that "*dhautī*" is "a kind of penance consisting in washing a strip of white cloth, swallowing it and then drawing it out of the mouth".

II.36 (E104) The results rest on words uttered. When truth is observed, the words become pure and incantations become complete. Thereby words uttered produce desired results due to unfailing utterance. Great is the consequence of truth, bad is the consequence of falsehood. By truth all is attained; in truth everything resides; by truth all infirmities are shed and the self attained.

II.38 (E105)By restraint of semen the conscious power is not dissipated in externality, but thereby body, senses, and mind develop great capacity. In those whose semen flows upwards great energy (luster, *tejas*) is observable. According to the *Chāndogya Upaniṣad* they can move unobstructed at will.

II.43 (E106-107) The extraordinary capacities of attaining atomicity or great dimension mentioned in I.40 are included here also, but not mentioned separately as part of Haṭhayoga. These can be attained through other means like medicine, etc.

II.46 (E107-114) The *padma, siddha* and other postures (*āsana,* sitting) are so-called as they are primarily sitting postures of eighty-four types.

II.47 (E114) By meditation on the endless (*ananta)*, when the concentration becomes firm, and by working off karma, when endless favor is won, posture becomes firm.

II.50 (E115-116) *Prāṇa* is wind in the body and, therefore, the lengthening of breath is *prāṇāyāma* having the three aspects-- *recaka, pūraka, kumbhaka*, that is, exhaling, inhaling and holding.

The place for practice of yoga should be a lone hill or fort or sacred place or attractive hermitage, free from noise and excessive heat or cold. The man who practices should be adolescent or a youth. He should take moderate and non-irritating mild food. He should also be free from sorrow, worry, etc.

If the above rules are not followed various defects and afflictions arises like disease, inertness, amnesia, speechlessness, and stupidity, and desires that bring about total failure assail him.

BOOK THREE

III.1(E133-134) *Dhāraṇā* is fixed attention (of awareness) on one spot, to the exclusion of others, either on some part of the body or on an external object. The aim is to fix the mind steadily on God.

III.2 (E134-136) Reflective meditation (*dhyāna*) is continuous fixation of attention on one fluctuation, undisturbed by another. It may be with qualities (*saguṇa*) or without them (*nirguṇa*). In the first category would be contemplation on the trinity of Brahmā, Viṣṇu, and Maheśa constituting *oṃkāra*. For the second the supreme principle, as changeless ground of all things, with eyes and limbs everywhere, would be fit.

III.3 (E136) For content-filled concentration, according to the *Garuḍa Purāṇa*, the mind should be held steadily on Brahman for a period of twelve controlled breaths (*prāṇāyāma*).

III.5 (E136) Through concentration direct (immediate) insight about the object of meditation arises.

III.9 (E138-139) Becoming invisible (*abhibhāva*) is reduction of the heart (i.e. of the pains) of such states as distraction, etc. due to content-filled concentration. Becoming visible is to be manifest at present.

III.11 (E139) Changes of awareness, in terms of the ascendance and subsidence of diverse and unitary meditations, are simultaneous developments during yoga.

III.13 (E140-141) The three forms of change in form (*dharma*), temporal variation (*lakṣaṇa*) and condition (*avasthā*) are applicable to subtle and gross elements, internal organ, senses, knowledge, and actions. When the substance alters its prior property to assume another property it is called a change in form. Change in temporal variation means reverting to a past state. The two together are called changes of condition. These changes are inevitable as pertaining to the *guṇas*.

III.14 (E141-142) The repository of properties (*dharmin*) has a property that has appeared, or lapsed, or that is inexpressible as either. Thus under *satkāryavāda*, if the effect is already present in the cause, how can there be its fresh production? But if it is not present, that runs counter to the causal theory. It will not do to say that the effect, though present, was not revealed, but now becomes revealed, for then "revelation" would go counter to causal theory. To meet this difficulty, our author tells us that in *sattva guṇa* capacity to reveal is always present, but obscured due to *tamas*, so that only the latter has to be removed for "revelation".

The question arises whether a thing has one change or many. Though the former might be simpler, actually, due to diversity of accessory factors, there must be many changes of qualities.

III.15 (e142-143) Due to different actions (on it) the same thing undergoes different states. All things are continually changing. Even if changes of form do not occur every moment, changes of state do. Due to this, the world has been taken as a dream, as in the *Māṇḍūkya Upaniṣad*. But this position is not correct, because dream objects lack self-consistency, stability, and practical efficiency.

III.16 (E143) Comprehensive reflection brings about the predominance of *sattva* by removing the restrictions due to ignorance. Thereby all things are known. Similarly reflection removes obstacles in other fields also.

III.17 (E143-144) A word like "cow" conveys a unitary meaning by reason of the *sphoṭa*-theory. The syllables cannot be uttered simultaneously, but the last syllable uttered, together with the traces of the earlier ones, come together and trigger *sphoṭa*.

The three–the word, the corresponding object, and its idea–in a person's knowledge of an individual thing are ordinarily confused due to superimposition between them. When, by reflection on their differences, each of the three become directly perceptible.

III.19-20 (E145) By reflection on one's own awarenesses and attachments, etc. the contents of another's mind become known.

III.21 (E145) By reflection on one's own words one also becomes inaudible to others.

III.22 (E145-150) Having known the appropriate portents in advance, *yogins* without fear or perturbation can regulate their last days, so as to have proper consequences after death.

III.29 (E159) In the middle of the body is the vital center of the navel, like the root of a banyan tree, from which the rest of the body, above and below, are like branches. By meditation on it, the state of fluids, wastes, nerves, life, etc. and their process become known.

III.31 (E159) The heart's lotus is the abode of Brahman. Hence, on entering it, awareness gains special joy, and does not stray elsewhere.

III.32 (E159-160) On meditation on the self-luminous light in the Brahman-orifice, perfected beings (*siddha*), residing between earth and heaven, become visible.

III.34 (E160) By concentration on the heart's lotus one sees one's own and others awarenesses, together with their desires.

III.35 (E160) Enjoyment (*bhoga*) is (a state) of the intellect with a predominance of *sattva*. It arises because of a particular change in the internal organ in a *yogin* who has not yet realized his goal. It is based on egoism due to failure to attain insight into the self as pure witness. This confusion (of self with the intellect)has to be ended by concentration on the self as witness.

III.37 (E161-162) According to the *Yogavāsiṣṭha*, for realized souls extraordinary yogic powers hold no attraction.

III.45 (E164-165) Here *gariman* is mentioned among the powers.

III.50 (E166) This is realization due to termination of traces. Non-attachment is part of the discipline for one who seeks liberation.

III.52 (E167) The cause-effect relationship is one of identity in this system, the uncaused cause being *prakṛti*. Everything passes into its next state at every moment. By meditation on a moment all things in this process can be known, which is discrimination.

III.53 (E167) In *puruṣa* who is free from all fluctuations, *sattva* also goes. Such a *puruṣa* is devoid of any enjoyments, and is liberated. In this state, there is no scope for extraordinary capacities.

BOOK FOUR

IV.1 (E169-170) For the five types of extraordinary capacities (*siddhi*), Those of different sages like Viśvāmitra, Yājñavalkya, etc. are given as examples. These accomplishments arise due to good deeds of past lives that end sins.

How do transformations into atomicity or largeness, or different bodies, occur due to accomplishments? It cannot be merely by resolve, because one thing is not capable of changing into another (without transformation in *prakṛti*). Concentration, etc. are only efficient causes.

IV.2 (E170) According to merits, etc. these transformations occur, being filled in by *prakṛti*. These changes can occur by resolve of *yogins* or God, or not. In the first case the independence of *prakṛti* vanishes, and in the latter case the scriptures are contradicted. Actually, the case of not being filled in by *prakṛti* does not arise.

IV.3 (E170-171) Efficient factors like merit, demerit or resolve do not become causes without being filled in by *prakṛti*. Independence of *prakṛti* is an admitted fact, because atoms are in activity in empty space, even without merits or resolves.

(The text the summarizer was using breaks off at this point. Our E provides the remaining portion, which we do not attempt to summarize here.)

14.NĀRĀYAṆATĪRTHA, *(Sūtra)Arthabodhinī* on Patañjali's *Yogasūtras*

Summary by Ram Shankar Bhattacharya

This is a brief summary on the *Yogasūtras*. Its chief purpose is to afford easy explanations of the *sūtras*. It is based on *Tattvavaiśāradī* and also on the *Rājamārtaṇḍa* commentaries.

The edition used for this summary is Bhatta. Since the summary is little more than scattered notations, page numbers are not included here, the numbering indicating *sūtras*.

BOOK ONE

I.1 The word "*atha*" is said to made an auspicious term by being pronounced.

I.2 Suppression (*nirodha*) is the restriction of the mental fluctuations caused by inverse mutation (*pratiloma pariṇāma*).

I.3 The essential nature of *puruṣa* is nothing but immutable consciousness (*caitanya*).

I.4 Liberation comes into existence when the restricted state arises, and bondage when the emergent state occurs.

I.5 Bondage is said to be caused by afflicted fluctuations and liberation is caused by unafflicted fluctuations.

I.11 Dream consciousness comes under error.

I.12 The purpose of persevering practice (*abhyāsa*) is to check sleep, which may occur when the flow of the fluctuations is restricted by dispassion.

I.16 "Knowledge of the nature of the *puruṣa*" (*puruṣakhyāti*) means the direct perception of *puruṣa* as distinct from *prakṛti*.

I.18 A concentration is called "seedless" when it is devoid of the seed of karma.

I.19 Ignorance is said to be at the root of the concentration called *bhavapratyaya*, as in this state the not-self is regarded as the self.

I.24 The word "*viśeṣa*" in the expression "*puruṣaviśeṣa*" indicates that God is different from the embodied self.

I.29 The inner self (*pratyagātman*) is an ignorant self and is different from God.

I.34 Awareness becomes tranquil as a result of practicing breath-control, as the practice destroys sin and enables one to control the mind.

I.45 *Prakṛti* (here, *pradhāna*) is called "*aliṅga*" as it does not get dissolved into anything.

BOOK TWO

II.2 Concentration gives rise to discriminative discernment (*vivekajñāna*) which in turn destroys false awareness with subconscious impressions.

II.6 The word "*darśana*" in this *sūtra* means *prakṛti*.

II.15 The words "*pariṇāma*", "*tāpa*", and "*saṃskāra*" in this *sūtra* refer to future, present, and past miseries respectively.

II.19 The three, *sattva*, etc. are called "*guṇas*" as they serve the purpose of the intelligent self.

II.20 The seer is nothing but immutable consciousness. Knowledge is not to be regarded as its attribute. The seer perceives sounds, etc. when he identifies himself with the intellect and becomes indistinguishable from its modifications.

II.23 The association of the seer with the object of sight (i.e. the intellect, etc.) is to be inferred from its effects.

II.26 The discriminative discernment which arises from the authoritative sentences is indirect and as such it is unable to uproot ignorance.

II.30 The restraints are enumerated before all other aids to yoga, since they are independent of the others.

II.38 Celibacy consists in restraining semen from falling.

BOOK THREE

III.1-3 Meditative fixation is bereft of dissimilar ideas; in reflective meditation there is no stoppage of the flow of fixity. The object of meditation, being dissociated from all connection with others, is perceived in concentration. In content-free awareness, consideration of even the awareness of an object ceases.

III.17 A word is, in fact, not formed by letters but is manifested by them; similarly a sentence is manifested by words. The object signified (*artha*) may be either denoted (*vācya*) or implied (*lakṣya*).

III.26 Since the rays of the sun suppress the light of the stars, comprehensive reflection on the sun does not bring about knowledge of the stars.

III.38 In the supernormal power of penetrating into another's body, the *yogin* takes the other's body as his own.

III.54 Isolation (*kaivalya*), which is the absence of future miseries, is manifested after the cessation of ignorance as a result of the direct perception of *puruṣa*.

BOOK FOUR

IV.1 Usually people practice yoga through faith. If supernormal powers do not arise in the present birth in spite of yoga-practice, one should expect their appearance in the coming birth.

IV.3 In Sāṃkhya, the future aim of man (*puruṣārtha*) is the instigator of *prakṛti*'s evolving, and God plays no role.

IV.11 Causes (*hetu*) and other factors mentioned in this *sūtra* are beginningless in the sense that they are always either in a manifested or unmanifested state.

15-16.NĀGEŚA (or NĀGOJĪ) BHAṬṬA, *Vṛttis* on Patañjali's *Yogasūtras*

Nāgeśa lived in the first part of the eighteenth century, according to Keith and others, and worked in the areas of philosophy of language, grammar, Nyāya, Vedānta, Yoga and Sāṃkhya.[165] He composed two commentaries on the *Yogasūtras*, a shorter one, entitled *Laghvī*, and a longer one, entitled *Bṛhatī*. Both commentaries, while full of thoughtful comments about the grammar and language of the *Yogasūtra*, closely follow the views of Vijñānabhikṣu and hence need not be summarized in this volume.[166]

17.SADĀŚIVENDRA SARASVATĪ, *Yogasudhākara* on Patañjali's *Yogasūtras*

Summary by Ram Shankar Bhattacharya

It is a brief commentary on the *Yogasūtras* which in many places is similar to the *Maṇiprabhā*. The author Sadāśivendra Sarasvatī was born in the Chola country near the town Karur in south India. He seems to belong to the eighteenth century. He was a householder who was initiated into *sannyāsa* by Paramaśivendra Sarasvatī. He was a follower of the Advaita tradition. Besides this work he composed a number of other works mainly on Advaita Vedānta and the Upaniṣads.

The edition used for this summary is Dundhiraja Sastri 1982. Only the important points stated in the commentary are noted in this summary.

BOOK ONE

I.4 Awareness (*citta*) is said to be that which is being restricted. Consciousness (*citiśakti*, that is, the *puruṣa* principle) abides in itself, and in the emergent state seems as if not established in its own nature.

I.7 Knowledge (*pramā*) is said to be the reflection (*pratibimba*) of the *puruṣa* principle in the mental fluctuations. Knowledge is that whose object has not been cognized before.

I.10 The non-apprehension (*abhāvapratyaya*) of a thing is explained as caused by the *guṇa tamas*.

I.17 The four forms of the content-filled concentration are precisely described.

I.19 Inclination toward becoming and towards correct means are said to be the two forms of the content-free concentration.

I.32 "*Ekatattva*" here refers to God.

I.34 Inhalation, though not stated, is implied in the process discussed this *sūtra*.

I.47 *Adhyātmaprasāda* is explained as the apprehension (*khyāti*) of *citiśakti*, the *puruṣa* principle.

BOOK TWO

II.1 The word "*kriyāyoga*" is explained as referring to those actions which are the means to yoga.

II.9 It is remarked that clinging to conventional life (*abhiniveśa*), which is characterized by fear, arises without any instrumental (*nimitta*) cause.

II.11 "*Dhyāna*" is taken to be meditation on the *puruṣa* principle.

II.13 It is remarked that *bhoga*, i.e. the experiencing of pleasure and pain, is the chief of the three effects of karmic residues (*karmāśaya*).

II.15 The three kinds of pain mentioned in the *sūtra* are said to be respectively connected with the past experience of pleasure, present experience of pleasure, and the future destruction of pleasure.

II.17 *Saṃyoga* here is explained as the state of being possessor and possessed (*svasvāmibhāva*) which is caused by ignorance.

II.20 *Puruṣa* is devoid of awareness (*jñāna*) and other attributes.

II.23 *Saṃyoga* is a conjunction of *puruṣa* and the intellect and it is inferred only through its effects.

II.27 The seven stages of insight are said to be associated with the cessation of the desire to know (*jijñāsā*), the desire to forsake (*jihāsā*), the desire of obtaining (*prekṣā*) the desire of doing (*cikīrṣā*), lamentation (*śoka*), fear (*bhaya*) and uncertainty (*vikalpa*) respectively.

II.30 The restraints are said to be of the nature of prohibition.

II.32 The observances are said to be of the nature of injunction.

II.51 It is remarked that the fourth form of breath-control is to be practiced by those who can subjugate sleep.

II.52 *Prakāśāvaraṇa* is that *tamas* which causes sleep and laziness.

BOOK THREE

III.3 It is remarked that the cause of the content-filled concentration is the lower dispassion (*aparavairāgya*) and that of content-free concentration is the highest form of dispassion (*paravairāgya*). It is further remarked that the essential difference between reflective meditation (*dhyāna*) and concentration (*samādhi*) consists in the respective presence and absence of the traces of agency and instrumentality.

III.5 The authenticity (lit. "shining", *āloka*) of authentic insight (*prajñāloka*) is said to be the quality of being truth-bearing (*ṛtambharā*).

III.16 Awareness is said to be able to know all without the help of the instruments of knowledge if the hindering stain of *rajas* and *tamas* is diminished.

III.26 Knowledge of the three universes (*bhuvana*) is the extraordinary capacity called *madhumatī*

III.27 Since the stars become invisible while the sun shines, comprehensive reflection on the sun cannot give rise to knowledge of the stars' arrangements.

III.29 The supernormal powers enumerated from *sūtras* 16 to 28 are said to be external, while from III.29 on they are to be known as *adhyātmika*, pertaining to the fields of the mind and body.

III.45 The supernormal power heaviness (*gariman*) is included in the *aṇimādi* group.

III.50 The attainment of isolation (i.e. the abiding of *puruṣa* in its own form) is to be known as the extraordinary capacity named *saṃskāraśeṣa*, the state in which only traces persist.

III.52 A moment (*kṣaṇa*) is said to be indivisible.

BOOK FOUR

IV.3 It is remarked that while the atheistic Sāṃkhya takes human purpose as the instigator of the activity of *prakṛti*, the theistic Yoga takes God as the cause.

IV.9 A trace (*saṃskāra*) is defined as the potential state of acting, cognizing, and so forth.

IV.20 It is the *puruṣa* which illuminates both the mind and its objects; the mind itself cannot illuminate objects.`

18.ANANTADEVA, *Yogacandrikā* on Patañjali's *Yogasūtras*

Summary by Ram Shankar Bhattacarya

The *Yogacandrikā* (called *Sūtrārthacandrikā* and *Padacandrikā* in the benedictory verses at the beginning and the end respectively) appears to have been written in the eighteenth century. It is very brief and it never discusses any question elaborately, although here and there it tries to criticize others' views. It resembles the *Arthabodhinī* by Nārāyaṇa Tīrtha in terms of content. Nothing is known about the author.

The edition used is again Dhundhiraja Sastri 1982. Like the *Yogasudhākara*, the commentary is brief, and only a few important comments will be noticed in the summary.

BOOK ONE

I.2 Inhibition of the fluctuations of awareness means their dissolution in their material cause on account of the stopping of their moving towards objects.

I.7 The Vedas, which are revealed by God, constitute verbal authority, one of the instruments of knowledge.

I.8 Doubt is included in error, since it is not established on what is the true form of an object.

I.15 It is the feeling of tastelessness which gives rise to dispassion.

I.18 One is required to follow the way indicated in the

Upaniṣadic passage *neti neti* ("not this, not this", *Bṛhadāraṇyaka Upaniṣad* II.3.6) in order to restrict the fluctuations that arise in the state which consists only of traces.

I.32 The word "*ekatattva*" is explained as any intended principle of reality.

I.38 In the dream state the self experiences through the mind.

I.47 *Adhyātmaprasāda* is said to be the same as firmness in tranquility (*sthiti*).

I.49 Not only subtle objects but also concealed and distant objects are perceived in the insight called "truth-bearing".

BOOK TWO

II.17 *Saṃyoga* is defined as proximity in the form of *puruṣa* being experiencer (*bhoktṛ*) and *prakṛti* being capable of being experienced (*bhogya*).

II.20 *Puruṣa* is said to be a witness (*anupaśya*) since it illumines influences (*uparāga*) that arise in the intellect.

II.23 Contact between seer (*puruṣa*) and seen (the intellect) is to be regarded as a self-linking connector (*svarūpasambandha*), that is, a relation which is essentially identical with the things concerned, or a relationship in which all things concerned appear the same.

BOOK THREE

III.29 The *nābhicakra* (situated in the navel region) is said to possess sixteen spokes, a view frequently found in the works of Tantra.

III.34 The word "*citta*" is taken as refering to the awareness of the *yogin* and also of other persons.

III.35 *Bhoga* is taken in the sense of the experience of pleasure only.

III.44 Smell is said to be an attribute of the *svarūpa*-aspect of the element earth.

III.45 Heaviness (*gariman*) is included in the group of supernormal powers known as *aṇimādi*.

BOOK FOUR

IV.10 *Āśis* is said to be the same as *mahāmoha*, which is characterized by the resolute desire "let me possess all means of pleasure and let me not be devoid of any such means".

IV.12 Awareness remains a substance until liberation is realized.

19.ŚAṂKARĀCĀRYA, *Rājayogabhaṣya*

Summary by Ram Shankar Bhattacharya

The editor, C. T. Kenghe, of the present printed text (Kenghe 1967) of the *Rājayogabhāṣya*, ascribed to Śaṃkarācārya, offers the following observations about the work in an introductory editorial note in Sanskrit. (1) This text was first published in 1896 with English translation prepared by Ananta Kṛṣṇa Śāstrin. (2) The present printed text (based on several manuscripts) is also known as *Vijṛmbhitayogasūtra-bhāṣya*, a name which suggests that the work speaks of secret doctrines which are not usually expressed in the Yoga philosophy. (3) In some of the manuscripts the text has been divided into three or four chapters instead of just two. (4) Though it does not appear to be a regular commentary on any work, it seems to be connected with the *Triśikhibrāhmaṇopaniṣad*.

It is obvious that this text was not written by the great Śaṃkarācārya. It is, rather, a modern Haṭha Yoga text, and its philosophical basis is a simplified version of Vedānta. The text contains some interesting comments about Rāja Yoga, Tāraka Yoga and Amanaska Yoga, all of which are themes and variations on Haṭha Yoga. Rāja Yoga in this text is clearly not Pātañjala Yoga.

The edition (E) used for this summary is Kenghe 1967. In that edition the text begins on p. 11.

CHAPTER ONE

(E11-12) The text is in the form of a dialogue between a certain spiritual teacher and his disciple (the word "*prākṛta*", "ignorant", has been used to denote a disciple, a person capable of being taught). The benedictory verse contains a eulogy of Īśāna, who is dscribed as *puruṣa* in the form of a shadow (*chāyāpuruṣa*). The word "Rājayoga" is explained in two ways, namely (1) yoga deserving to be practiced by kings, and (2) the king (i.e. the best) of the *yogas*. This yoga with its eight auxiliaries is said to lead one easily to emancipation.

The power to control heat and cold, tranquility, etc. are the restraints. Devotion to the spiritual teacher, etc. are the observances. Yogic posture consists in sitting comfortably in a desired position. The breath becomes motionless as a result of practicing the three operations (namely inhalation, exhalation, and stoppage of breath) of breath-control effortlessly with the idea that the world is illusory. This is said to be the view of Sāṃkhya and Yoga. Withdrawal of the senses consists in drawing the mind inward so that consciousness (*caitanya*) gets dissolved into the supreme self. Reflective meditation consists in thinking the individual to be similar to the supreme self by cultivating the idea expressed in the expression "*so'ham*" ("I am he"). Meditative fixation is the act of observing the internal as well as the external principles (*tattva*). In the state of concentration mental fluctuations become devoid of all conceptual constructions, and the mind attains perfect steadiness.

(E12-13) Traditions other than Rājayoga are incapable of expressing the nature of *brahman* directly. Knowledge of reality (*tattvajñāna*), according to Rājayoga, is as follows: From *ātman* proceeds *ākāśa* which produces the ear, sound, etc. From *ākāśa* proceeds air (*vāyu*) which gives rise to the mind, the *vyāna* breath, touch, etc. Air is the cause of fire, which produces the intellect, the *udāna* breath, the eye, color, etc. From fire comes water, which produces awareness (*citta*), the *prāṇa* breath, the organ of taste, etc. Water creates earth which produced the ego-sense, the *apāna* breath, the olfactory organ, smell and the excretory organ.

The ten external organs and the five internal organs (namely awareness, mind, intellect, the thinking organ, and the ego-sense) are to be known as *ādhyātmika* (concerning the self). The fifteen objects, namely sound, etc. are to be known as *ādhibhautika* caused by supernatural influences). The fifteen deities, namely *dik*, etc. are known as *ādhidaivika.* The transcendental *brahman* is realized by a person who knows all the aforesaid entities.

(E13-14) A person at first becomes aware of the difference between the individual self and *brahman*. Gradually he comes to know of his identity with *brahman* and of his difference from the sixteen modifications (the ten organs, the mind, and the five objects, namely sound, etc.). According to some the subtle body (*liṅga*) consists of the vital air, the sense-organs, the mind, and the intellect.

(E14) The following are enumerated: eight *prakṛtis*, namely Brahmā, etc.; three basic powers (*śakti*), namely desire, etc.; three kinds of individual selves, namely *viśva*, etc.; three subdivisions of time, namely morning, etc.; three kinds of bodies, namely gross, etc.; three kinds of states (*avasthā*), namely waking, etc.; three fires, namely *Gārhapatya*, etc.; three regions, namely heaven, etc.; three kinds of blemishes (*mala*), namely *kārmika* (pertaining to karma), etc.; threefold miseries, namely *ādhyātmika*, etc.; threefold desires, namely desire for wife, etc.; three *guṇas*, namely *sattva*, etc. An aspirant is required to know that all of these are the illusory creations of *māyā* and that the self is different from these.

The process of how a gross evolute (e.g., a gross element) dissolves into its subtle cause is given here. The supreme self is said to be the ultimate cause of all. The self is either not associated with anything or endowed with the organs. The defining attributes of the one supreme self are *sat, cit* and *ānanda* (existence, knowledge, and bliss).

CHAPTER TWO

(E15-16) The view of one particular school of Sāṃkhya is given here. The means of subduing the five blemishes, namely passion (*kāma*), anger, breathing, fear and sleep, and the gradual process of attaining the supreme goal (*paramapada*) by an embodied self are described here. Knowledge (*jñāna*) is said to be the only means to liberation. A detailed description of Tārakayoga ("liberation yoga") is given here with a discussion on the meaning of the word "*tāraka*".

(E16-17) *Suṣumṇā*, the *brahma* channel, is said to be situated from the *mūlādhāra cakra* at the base of the spine to the *brāhmarandhra* in the region of the head. A person piercing *kuṇḍalinī* residing in the *suṣumṇā* becomes liberated. One is required to hear the secret sounds and to perceive the flame in the heart, etc. in order to gain liberation. This process is known as internal gazing (*antarlakṣya*)). To perceive various kinds of luster in the tip of the nose or in the other regions of the body is called external gazing (*bahirlakṣya*). *Madhyalakṣya* (gazing at the central point) consists in perceiving luster in the sky through a particular process of yoga. An account of various kinds of *ākāśa* (namely *parākāśa, mahākāśa*, etc.) is given here and it is remarked that the way called Tāraka leads to the mindless (*amanaska*) state.

(E17-18) *Amanaska*, also called Rājayoga, is the second half of Tāraka. Introspection (*antardṛṣṭi*) is the chief means for acquiring Tāraka yoga, which has two aspects, namely *mūrtitāraka* (up to the field of the organs) and *amūrtitāraka* (that which transcends the two eyebrows). *Brahman* is perceived through the introspection of a tranquil mind. The colors or forms of *brahman* as described in scripture are to be known as the creations of *māyā*.

(E19-20) The *amūrta tāraka* (a form of Tāraka yoga) is the same as the mindless state *(amanaska)* known as Rājayoga. The mind-priest should offer the oblation of vital air and organs in the fire (*jyotiḥkuṇḍa*) of yoga in order to attain the state called *unmani* (the state transcending the mind) which enables one to unite with *brahman*. One is required to practice the *śāmbhavī* and other bodily exercises in order to get rid of transitory existence. An aspirant is required to visualize a flame (the deity Śiva, the *puruṣa* of the size of a thumb, and the like) in the *sahasrāra* (the thousand-petalled lotus in the head, i.e., the brain). A *jīva* (i.e. an embodied self) is said to be the twenty-fifth entity. For liberation the self should leave *prakṛti*, consisting of twenty-four principles, and should become identified with the supreme self, the twenty-sixth entity. This state of the person is regarded as liberation while still alive.

(E20-21) A few secret yoga practices are described here which are not clearly intelligible. It is remarked that the *śāmbhavī* exercise (*mudrā,* the "seal" pertaining to Śiva) is the same as the *khecarī* exercise. The control of air depends upon the control of the mind. Rājayoga, but not Haṭhayoga, can bring about perfect control of the mind and air.

(E22-24) The yogic process of the dissolution of the mind is given here with necessary details. It is remarked that a Rājayogin remains unattached to his actions, and he experiences identity with *brahman*. Such a *yogin* has no need for external worship. A vivid description of mental worship is given here. In the highest state the distinction of *dhyeya* (the object to be meditated on), *dhyātṛ* (the meditator) and *dhyāna* (the act of meditating) ceases. A person remaining in the highest state of yoga is not overcome by the states like waking, etc. Transmigratory existence comes to an end for a person in the state of concentration. Volition or wish (*saṃkalpa*) is co-existent with bondage. A person, who is free from all kinds of distractions is to be known as liberated while living.

(E24-26) A detailed description of the yogic process of attaining the fifth or highest state called "the state beyond *turīya*" (*turīyātīta*) is given here (the other four being waking, dream, sleep and the *turīya* state). The experience that "I am identical with the absolute non-dual *brahman* is regarded as the highest of all experiences. Dattātreya and others are said to be persons possessing this experience. It is remarked that oneness with pure non-duality (*śuddhādvaitasāmarasya*) is the teaching of Yogaśāstra and that Rājayoga is called by such names as *unmani, sahaj, amanaska,* etc.

(E26-27) The characteristics of *amanaska*, together with the means (e.g., practice of the *śāmbhavī* exercise, the seal of Śiva) of acquiring it and the external as well as the internal signs (e.g., remaining like a dry log of wood) of a person established in this state, are described here. It is remarked that the experience of identity with the supreme self immediately follows the state of *amanaska*. The relationship of a spiritual teacher with his disciple who has acquired the highest state is shown here.

(E27-30) Here is given a long account of the precepts of a a spiritual teacher to his disciple who has realized the bliss of *brahman*. Haṭhayogins like Nārada and others got rid of pain and other undesired factors (an account of these factors is given here with the necessary details). At the end an account of the path of *brahman* for attaining liberation is given in which there is mention of the awakening of *kuṇḍalinī, suṣumṇā*, and piercing of the knots, namely Brahmā, Viṣṇu and Rudra, and of the six vital centers .

20.BALARĀMA UDĀSĪNA, *Bhāṣya* on Vācaspatimiśra's *Tattvavaiṣāradī*

Balarāma Udāsīna, born in 1855, was a follower of the Udāsīna sect and studied Vedānta with Rāmamiśra Śāstrin. He studied Nyāya in Bengal for some time, but spent the last part of his life in Varanasi. He composed a short Sanskrit commentary on the *(Vyāsabhāṣya) Tattvavaiśāradī*, which simply summarizes the larger commentary of Vācaspatimiśra. Hence, there is no need to include a summary in this Volume. He also composed a Hindi commentary on the *Yogasūtras* and a few works on religious matters. He is also the author of a sub-commentary on Vācaspatimiśra's *Tattvakaumudī* entitled *Vidvattoṣiṇī*, which was summarized in Larson/Bhattacharya

1987, pp. 509-520.

21.HARIPRASĀDA SVĀMIN, *Vaidikavṛtti* on Patañjali's *Yogasūtras*

The author of this commentary, who was a disciple of Ātmārāma, a *sannyāsin* of the Udāsīna sect, lived in the first quarter of the twentieth century, and this commentary was published during his lifetime (in *saṃvat* 1961 = 1904 CE.). He seems to be a follower of the school of Dayānanda, the founder of the Ārya Samāj. Besides this text, he composed a commentary on the *Sāṃkhyasūtras* entitled *Vaidikavṛtti* and on the *Tattvakaumudī* entitled *Cittaprasādinī.* In most places the commentary follows the Vyāsa *Bhāṣya* closely.

22.HARIHARĀNANDA ĀRAṆYA, *Śivoktayogayukti*

Summary by Ram Shankar Bhattacharya

Swāmī Hariharānanda Āraṇya, a Bengali *sannyāsin,* lived from 1869 to 1947. He is the founder of the Kapila Maṭha, located in Bihar, a monastic community claiming to maintain the tradition of Sāṃkhya and Yoga in modern India. Hariharānanda was a disciple of Swāmī Trilokī Āraṇya, but nothing is known of this teacher.

Hariharānanda wrote a number of works on Sāṃkhyayoga in Bengali and Sanskrit. His best known work in Bengali is the *Kapilāśramīyapātañjalyogadarśana,* which has been partly rendered into English by P. N. Mukerji under the title *The Yoga Philosophy of Patañjali* (Calcuta: Universityof Calcutta, 1963).

The present work, *Śivoktayogayukti*, is edited from West Bengal:Kapilāśrama, Hooghly, 1914. This is our E. To our knowledge there is no translation into a Western language

(E1-8) (The text is in the form of a dialogue between Śiva

and Devī). In the initial stages the practice of yoga seems to be painful, but at the end it affords bliss. The self (*ātman*), which is the dearest of all things, is realized through yoga. This is why one should practice yoga disregarding all other activities.

(E9-14) The experience that "I am existent" is self-evident. The existence of "I" can in no way be negated. What is regarded as belonging to the "I" cannot be taken as identical with the "I", who is the knower, the subject. The subject, which is self-luminous (*svaprakāśa*) and is called consciousness (*caitanya*, absolute awareness), is absolutely different from an object (i.e. that which is capable of being cognized). The subject which is indivisible, eternal, pure, and devoid of parts is the efficient cause of creation.

(E15-22) Entities are either subjects or objects. They are respectively known as the seer and the object of seeing. The former transcends space and time while the latter is ever-changing. The cause of all manifested things must be an assemblage or whole made of *puruṣa* and *prakṛti*, which are both to be regarded as absolute. The self becomes devoid of lordly powers on account of (its association with) ignorance, which can be annihilated through yoga. By uprooting ignorance a person attains limitless knowledge and power. Yoga can eradicate all kinds of miseries.

(E23-34) As all mutable things are perishable, pleasure, depending on them, must come to an end. This phenomenon is known as "pain based on anxiety" (*tāpaduḥkha*). All acts create traces which in turn become the operative cause of birth. This is known as pain based on traces. Since yoga enables one to get rid of pain and to attain eternal bliss, one should practice yoga.

(E35-43) Truthfulness, charity, compassion, nonviolence, etc. can be successfully practiced by a person who is a practitioner of yoga. It is a *yogin* who cultivates virtue to the highest degree. A *yogin* knows that he is not identical with his body on which depend all immoral and vicious acts. By cultivating absolute nonviolence, etc. a *yogin* endeavors to realize the self.

(E44-57) Attachment to the body and mind (i.e. taking both body and mind as really belonging to "I") is the cause of misery or bondage. One can uproot the proprietary feeling (*mamatva*) of the object of the senses with the help of meditation, which paves the way for concentration. Concentration is the source of insight which is the direct means to release. Having gained this insight one becomes able to forsake actions and to transcend his attachment to the body. A person having no egoism is called a liberated person.

(E58-64) Persons who are desirous of practicing yoga are of three kinds, namely mild, moderate and intense. In this Kāli age there is hardly a person who is to be known as belonging to the "intense" group, that is, whose vital energy naturally flows towards the *suṣumṇā* nerve. Since these persons practiced the external accessories of yoga in their previous birth, they are able to follow up the internal accessories of yoga in their present life. An ordinary person should follow up all of the accessories of yoga. Those persons whose intellect is tainted by the strain of *rajas* and *tamas* fall down if they try to follow up the internal aids of yoga only.

23.HARIHARĀNANDA ĀRAṆYA, *Paribhaktisūtra* and *Lalitā* thereon

Summary by Ram Shankar Bhattacharya

The edition ("E") used is issued by the Kapilamaṭham, Madhupur, Bihar, 1925. The text is a *sūtra*-work on devotion in accordance with the doctrines of Sāṃkhya and Yoga with the autocommentary *Lalitā*.

CHAPTER ONE

(E1-3) The path of devotion is followed by all schools of philosophy in some way or other. Devotion, in this *sūtra*, is defined as a desired state (of the mind) which has a glorified person (*mahāpuruṣa*) as its object (i.e. in devotion the mind becomes grounded in, or abides in, the desired *puruṣa*). Devotion cannot be regarded as of the nature of passion or attachment since it refers to an entity which transcends speech and mind.

A glorified person is either (1) attributeless and referred to by the notion of the ego (*asmatpratyayalakṣya*) or (2) God or any great being or ordinary respected man, who is referred to by the notion of non-ego (*yuṣmatpratyayalakṣya*). When the mind becomes grounded in any one of these, the state is called devotion. There would arise the fault of under-pervasion (*avyāpti*) if devotion is taken as a kind of passion or attachment. To hold that "grounding in God only" is devotion is equally wrong, as devotion is cultivated by the atheist Buddhists also. The practice of devotion brings about appropriate results according to its particular character. Both heaven and liberation are attained as a result of practicing different kinds of devotion.

(E4-5) Devotion directed to such glorious persons as Rāma, Kṛṣṇa, Buddha and others is to be known as lower (*aparā*). This devotion is characterized by attachment (or passion, *rāga*). If devotion is directed to the immutable awareness (i.e. one's own pure self, called *pratyagātman*, the interior self) is known as supreme (*parā*). It is devoid of passion, etc. and in this state one becomes grounded in immutable consciousness.

CHAPTER TWO

(6-7) In the state of supreme devotion which is beyond the field of thought and speech, the self becomes firmly grounded in its own form. The word "*ātmarati*" ("one delighting in the self") used in the *Upaniṣads* means "a person abiding in the self" who is absolutely free from all attachment to not-selves. Devotion is neither *jñāna* only nor absolutely different from *jñāna;* it is the flow of knowledge characterized by some sentiment. It is not momentary knowledge.

(E8-9) The lower devotion is characterized by pleasure.

The pleasurable feeling is called *bhaktirasa,* "flavor of devotion". The supreme devotion is characterized by *śānti* (cessation of the activities of the mind and organs.

CHAPTER THREE

(E10-12) Supreme devotion is attained with the help of lower devotion when the mind is restricted by supreme dispassion. Devotion is developed as a result of practicing some favorable means, namely fortitude (*dhṛti*), forbearance (*kṣama*), restraint of external organs (*dama*), austerity, breath-control, etc. These, if practiced with a tranquil mind, enable the practitioner to direct his mind towards God.

(E13-14) Devotion should be practiced through certain sentiments, namely peace, etc. in accordance with the practitioner's liking or taste. Among all the sentiments, tranquility (*praśāntabhāva*) in which the element of cessation is predominant is the highest, for it leads to liberation which is declared by the scripture to be the ultimate goal. This tranquility is of two kinds, namely *paramapreyas bhāvanā*, the feeling that the self is the dearest of all, and *paramapūjyabhāvanā*, the feeling that the deity possessing divine qualities is the dearest and most adorable of all. The followers of the latter type of sentiment also realize their own self. Supreme devotion gets accomplished through these two forms of tranquility.

(E15-16) External worship of a deity is prescribed for those who possess a distracted mind. This form of worship consists in offering flowers, chanting incantations or singing songs, and, behaving like a servant (*paricaryā*). This worship gives rise to firm attachment or love (*rati*).

(E17-20) Internal worship is the chief means of devotion that has been prescribed for those who possess firm love for the adorable deity. There often arise joyful tears, a feeling of uncanniness, loss of sensitivity in the body (*kāyajāḍya*), forgetfulness of external objects in a person practicing internal worship. The last stage of this worship consists in the awareness of the deity only .

CHAPTER FOUR

(E21-22) In the highest state of devotion the mind, organs, and the vital breaths of the devotee become tranquil, for the mind rests on the adorable deity only. The restriction of the mind, etc. is essential for the attainment of this state. The chief result of lower devotion is knowledge of the essential nature orf the adorable *puruṣa*. It has other results also, namely attainment of the same region with the deity (*sālokya*), etc. The devotee becomes able to realize Godhead and his inner self.

(E23-26) When the principles (*tattva*) (as stated in Sāṃkhya) along with the essential nature of the adorable deity are understood, then the absolute self is perceived. Direct perception is essentially different from indirect realization. The self can be realized directly through meditation or through devotion to God. The supreme form of devotion is found in those who are absolutely dispassionate and are capable of abiding in the self. The distractions of the mind can be checked by highest detachment (*paravairāgya*) which is based on knowledge of the principles. The result of highest passionlessness is eternal peace.

24.HARIHARĀNANA ĀRAṆYA, *Yogakārikā* on Patañjali's *Yogasūtras*

Summary by Anima Sen Gupta

Our E is the third, 1966 edition of the work published by Kapilamaṭha from Madhupur, Bihar. There is no date for the first edition. The *Yogakārikā* is a versified commentary (with a short Sanskrit commentary) on the *Yogasūtras* of Patañjali.

BOOK ONE

I.2 (E5-6) Every state of knowing is called a fluctuation of awareness. Awareness possesses three dispositions: (1) disposition toward rational reflection (*prakhyā*), (2) disposition towards sense-activity (*pravṛtti*), and (3) disposition towards stability (*sthiti*). When all the fluctuations of awareness are restricted the stage of content-free concentration is reached: when all other fluctuations except the desired one are stopped, the stage of content-filled concentration is attained by an aspirant. These two forms of the cessation of the fluctuations of awareness which result in the destruction of the threefold misery of life are termed "Yoga".

I.3 (E12-13) When all the fluctuations of awareness are stopped, the consciousness-principle shines in its own light. "Shining in its own light" and "not shining in its own light" are only descriptions from outside and are so described only from the empirical point of view when our intellect is not clear and our vision is clouded on that account.

In empirical life the fluctuations of awareness are not stopped. Though the *puruṣa* or seer is by nature pure and unreal, being colored by the fluctuations, it falsely appears to be identical with the fluctuations of awareness. This is why the fluctuations are manifested by the *puruṣa* and the latter, being the revealer of the fluctuations, appears to be indistinguishable from them.

I.5-6 (E14) The fluctuations of awareness are classified into two groups with a view to facilitating spiritual practice. Of the non-discriminative fluctuations, those which have ignorance at their root are called "afflicted" and these produce pain. Those which are the results of knowledge (that is opposed to ignorance) are called "non-afflicted") and these lead to mental peace. These afflicted and non-afflicted fluctuations again are of the five kinds indicated below.

I.7 (E15) The source that produces knowledge (*pramā*) is an instrumental cause of knowledge (*pramāṇa*).

I.8 (E18) When we perceive an object in a form which it

does not possess, then it is called error or "wrong awareness". It is not the negation of awareness.

I.9 (E19) There are words which have no corresponding real objects. When we hear such words, vague cognition arises in our minds. That is called a fluctuation due to conceptual construction.

I.13 (E24) "Practice" refers to repeated and determinate efforts of an aspirant to make the mind steady by stopping mental modes. Efforts should, however, be voluntary.

I.14-16 (E25-31) Dispassion is to be cultivated with a view to withdrawing of the mind from the disturbing influence of external objects. It is to be acquired gradually. The highest form of dispassion makes a mind wholly disinterested toward all objects of this world and also of the next.

Content-filled concentration is gained in the highest stage of concentration. When this fluctuation of awareness is also stopped, then that is the state of aloofness which is called content-free or seedless concentration.

I.41 (E61) The awareness in which all fluctuations except one have disappeared, if rested on an object, appears to be absorbed in it in such a manner as to take on its nature. This sort of absorption is called "engrossment" (*samāpatti*).

I.42 (E63) Such engrossment is of different forms. The word, the gross object suggested by it, and the knowledge of that object are different. In the initial state, the *yogin* follows the process of meditation by mixing up the word, the object, and the knowledge of the object. Here, because the three distinct things are treated as one, the process is only an early level of engrossment.

I.50 (E74) The *yogins* who have reached the highest level have attained the state of complete cessation of awareness, and this seedless concentration is called content-free (*asamprajñāta*). This state is the state of permanent peace.

BOOK TWO

II.1-2 (E78-79) The *sūtras* indicate that an ordinary person who cannot give up external actions totally can attain yogic knowledge by the Yoga of Action (*kriyāyoga*).

"Ascetic practice" (*tapas*) stands for control of thought, emotion and will. The aim should, however, be the attainment
232 of knowledge and the purification of the mind. To go through physical suffering without making any attempt to enrich the mind with knowledge, pure thoughts and emotions, is futile. "Study" means that the aspirant should utter the syllable "*oṃ*" or any other incantation that can produce an idea of God. He should study those scriptures which speak of liberation. "Devotion to God" means that the aspirant should dedicate all fruits of his actions to God. As a result of such surrender of all actions to God, the aspirant has the feeling that he is doing actions, being moved by the Lord who is his indwelling principle. The actions belong to God and so he should perform actions in a disinterested manner, fixing his mind on God.

II.3 (E83-84) In the case of a *yogin* who has acquired discriminative knowledge, the afflictions reach the state of burnt up seeds. "Dormancy" here means that the afflictions are incapable of sprouting like burnt seeds. When an affliction remains inoperative for some time either due to excessive enjoyment or due to absence of any support, then the affliction is said to be in a state of interruption.

II.5 (E83) Ignorance prompts a man to regard as permanent what is impermanent. Under the spell of ignorance one also regards the impure as the pure, the sorrowful as the pleasurable, and the non-self as the self. Ignorance is, thus, a sort of contrary cognition and is erroneous.

II.6 (E87) The false identity of the seer with the intellect (i.e. the inner organ) is expressed in the form "I am the seer".

II.7 (E87) The desire for objects of pleasure, which arises because of the arousal of traces of pleasure enjoyed in the past, is the manifestation of a state of mind which is called a state of attachment.

II.8 (E89) "Aversion" refers to the feeling of resistance,

anger, etc. towards objects producing misery arising out of remembrance of previously experienced pain.

II.9 (E89) Inborn fear of extinction which exists in the mind due to subliminal impressions arising out of the experience of the pain of death is the affliction called the will to live.

II.15 (E95-96) All these afflictions can be removed by studying the science of liberation (*mokṣaśāstra*) in four parts: (i) what is to be removed, (ii) the cause of that which is to be removed, (iii) removal of the cause, and (iv) the means that lead to that removal.

II.18 (E99) The "seen" is that which serves the purposes of enjoyment and liberation of the *puruṣa*. All objects and organs possess this characteristic and are treated as the "seen".

II.19 (E102) Five subtle elements and the principle of self-consciousness (*asmitā*) are the six non-specific evolutes. The five subtle elements have five gross elements as their specific products. The specific products of the principle of self-consciousness is expressed in the form "I exist". That which is uncaused, unstable, eternal, of the form of three *guṇas*, and unconscious is called the "unmanifest" (*avyakta*). That which originates to serve the purposes of *puruṣa* (i.e. the purposes of the *puruṣa* cause it to originate) and is also revealed by the *puruṣa* is called the "manifest" (*vyakta*).

II.20 (E109) The seer is the awareness that is reflected in self-consciousness in the form "I am the knower". This awareness is self-revealing. That which is not revealed by any other thing and is also wholly opposite to the seen in nature is called the *puruṣa*. *Puruṣa* is the seer. The fluctuations of awareness are revealed by the seer through reflection.

II.22 (E109) Though the seen disappears in relation to the liberated *yogin*, still it continues to operate in relation to all other worldly-minded people.

II.23 (E111) Contact (i.e. apprehension of the *puruṣa* and the intellect as one, which is wrong) is inseparable from the cognition of objects, because the fluctuations of awareness in the form of objects result from such contact. Both experience and liberation, being states of awareness, are due to contact between seer and the seen.

II.24 (E113) It is discriminative knowledge that brings about separation between the *puruṣa* and the intellect. Therefore, ignorance, which is opposed to discriminative knowledge, is the cause of the contact (between *puruṣa* and intellect).

II.26 (E115) The highest stage of dispassion known as "complete control" *(vaśīkāra)* removes all desires for enjoyment of objects here and hereafter. Discriminative knowledge reduces ignorance to a state of burnt-seed. This is the way to gain freedom from misery.

II.29 (E120) When the accessories to yoga are practiced regularly, then the impurities of awareness are destroyed completely. Knowledge goes on becoming clearer and more perfect until discriminative awareness is attained. It is the highest form of knowledge and it is also the last limit of knowledge.

BOOK THREE

III.1 (E147) When the sense-organs are under proper control, the *yogin* fixes his mind on a particular part of the body. In the case of an inner part of the body, the mind is fixed directly through feeling; but in the case of an external object, the mind is fixed through sensory modification of that form. Thus that fixation of the mind in which there is awareness of the desired object only and the external sense-organs, being withdrawn, no longer seek other objects, is called (meditative) fixation (*dhāraṇā*).

III.2 (E148) In the case of (meditative) fixation, the thought process relating to the object of meditation flows in succession. When through repeated practice the thought flows continuously in an unbroken fashion, this is called "reflective meditation" (*dhyāna*). In the case of fixation, the thought of the *yogin* flows in succession like drops of water, but in the case of reflective meditation, the flow of knowledge is continuous like the flow of oil.

III.3 (E149) When meditation on the desired object is so deep that the object only shines in the mind, the *yogin* loses, as it were, consciousness of himself, and then the meditation assumes the form of concentration (*samādhi*). Knowledge of everything else is lost in the nature of the object of concentration.

BOOK FOUR

IV.4 (E217) Self-awareness is the cause of the "mind", i.e. (further) mental awarenesses. Self-awareness remains like a burnt seed when discriminative knowledge is attained. By this self-awareness, the *yogin* (who has full control over the body, mind and organs) can create new "minds" voluntarily for giving moral and spiritual instructions. These created "minds" can be stopped at any time by the will of the *yogin* and so these minds do not preserve impressions of ignorant actions and, thus, do not produce bondage.

IV.19 (E237) The mind,. being knowable, is not self-luminous. Fluctuations of awareness expressed in the form of anger, resentment, etc. are revealed and known as objects. The mind is therefore not the seer but the seen. The seen is always to be revealed by some other principle and is not self-revealing. So, the mind is basically unconscious and is different from the *puruṣa* or the seer.

IV.26 (E245) At the time of acquiring discriminative knowledge, the mind of the *yogin* flows in the channel of discrimination with the ideal of isolation (*kaivalya*) shining in front. Just as a river, flowing downwards, terminates at the bottom of a hill, in the same way, the river-like mind, flowing downwards along the channel of discrimination, disappears on reaching the highest state of liberation.

25.HARIHARĀNANDA ĀRAṆYA, *Bhāsvatī* on Patañjali's *Yogasūtras*

Summary by Anima Sen Gupta

The text used ("E") is the fifth edition of the work, published from Calcutta by the University of Calcutta in 1967. The work was originally published in 1934. There is at least one more recent edition (University of Calcutta, 2000), but the pagination here represents the 1967 version.

BOOK ONE

I.1 (E322-323) In the Introduction, the author expresses his own view according to which Hiraṇyagarbha, the propounder of the Yoga philosophy, is identified with Kapila, who was the promulgator of both Sāṃkhya and Yoga. Patañjali edited and presented Yoga philosophy in a condensed aphoristic form (i.e. in the form of *sūtras*) at a time when the common people were experiencing difficulty in following Yoga because of the variety of interpretations given to it by different commentators.

I.2 (E324-326) The definition of Yoga as the state of the cessation of fluctuations of awareness is free from the defects of being either too wide or too narrow. Since an awareness exhibits the characteristics of the three *guṇas* it is to be regarded as the composite of the those three. The highest form of intellectual cognition is discriminative knowledge, which is the limit of excellence attainable by the intellect or *cittasattva*. The intellect differs from the *puruṣa* because the *puruṣa* is immutable, devoid of all sorts of fluctuations, untransmissible illuminator of all intellectual modes leading to manifestation of things presented, pure and infinite in the sense that finitude cannot be ascribed to it. The intellect is illuminating in the sense that it can reflect consciousness, but it is not self-illuminating. Discriminative awareness, being intellectual, is changeable in nature and falls under the category of an object of sight ("seen", *dṛśya*). As such, it is also different from a *puruṣa* and is to be stopped. Supreme dispassion stops this discriminative discernment. In the arrested state, fluctuations possess only traces and no thought. The mind gets dissolved in the state of isolation. When, after the attainment of knowledge, that too is stopped, awareness becomes completely devoid of fluctuations (i.e., the mind reaches the stage of total restriction). The concentration at this stage is called "seedless" since it is devoid of any supporting object.

I.3 (E325) The *puruṣa* is the knower of the intellect. The intellect also disappears when all fluctuations of awareness are restricted. The *puruṣa* remains in its own real nature, being free from the falsely ascribed fluctuations of the state of emergence.

I.4 (E326-327) In the emergent state, owing to the illumination of the modifications of the intellect by the light of the *puruṣa*, the latter appears to be non-different from the modifications illuminated by it. The word "*sannidhāna*", "proximity" is not to be understood in the sense of nearness in space. It really means that the *puruṣa*, who is the seer, and the intellect appear in a non-distinguishable manner in a single cognition. The awareness that the intellect is "mine" is the proof of this relation happening through non-discrimination. Since the *puruṣa* and *prakṛti* are eternal, the contact (between them) is also beginingless like the beginninglessness of the seed and the seedling. That contact is not a separate positive entity. It has a cause and when that cause is destroyed, the contact also disappears. So the contact, though beginningless, is not eternal.

I.5 (E328-329) The fluctuations are five-fold, and classified into harmful and beneficial. The harmful ones produce pain and worldly suffering. They become the loci of the traces of actions (*karmāśaya*) while the good fluctuations are related to discriminative knowledge. When the fluctuations become imperceptible, they assume the form of unseen traces. When these traces are revived in the expressed form of fluctuations, we get what is called memory. Thus, the fluctuations produce traces and the impressions in their turn lead to the arousal of fluctuations. All fluctuations are generated by traces.

I.7 (E329-332) A fluctuation reveals both the universal and the specific characteristics of an object, but in the case of perceptual cognition the awareness of the specific characteristic becomes more important. Of course, there is no concrete external entity in the form of a universal (*sāmānya*). In fact, the mental awareness of a property as belonging to many individuals of the same class is the apprehension of a universal property. "Particularity" refers to the real, unique characteristic of every individual by means of which each is differentiated from the others. A universal is fit for apprehension only through words.

I.9 (E332-333) A conceptual construction is aroused by the use of such a word as is expressive of a non-entity in the sense that there is no real object corresponding to it. Even then, such words are potent to cause vague awareness. So long as our practical life remains confined to the use of words, conceptual constructions cannot be done away with. It is only when intellectual (*nirvicāra*) meditation, meditation without the use of language, is achieved that the aspirant makes himself free from the use of words.

I.11 (E335-337) Here the word "*buddhi*" is used in the sense of an instrument of knowledge of an object which was not known before. In this case, the function of knowing plays the dominant role, whereas in recollection the already known object plays the predominant part. In cognition of the form "I am knowing the jar" the cognitive process is the predominating one, but in the cognition "It is a jar" the modification in the form of the jar is the important factor and this is a memory of the jar. All fluctuations of awareness are saturated through and through with pleasure, pain and delusion. Delusion, again, is of three kinds: (i) delusion relating to deliberation (*vicāramoha*); (ii) delusion relation to physical and mental activity (*ceṣṭāmoha*), and (iii) delusion relating to feeling in which pleasure cannot be distinguished from pain (*vedanāmoha*).

I.12 (E337) All modes of awareness can be stopped by

practice and dispassion. Dispassion prevents the thought process from flowing toward an object of enjoyment and the practice of discrimination strengthens the flow of discriminative awareness. Thus, the cessation of mental activity depends on practice and dispassion. Discrimination is the primary means of arresting the fluctuations of awareness. The constant pursuit of other means for acquiring discrimination also falls under "practice".

I.13 (E337) That effort which aims solely at mental stability is known as practice. The steadiness that the mind attains after the cessation of all mental modes is to be regarded as the primary steadiness.

I.16 (E339-340) The higher dispassion culminates in discriminative awareness which is the highest form of intellectual cognition. This is the state in which the impurities of *rajas* are completely removed and the *yogin* remains in this state with calmness and discriminative insight.

I.17 (E340) Content-filled concentration is immediate awareness of the principles through deliberative concentration, etc. The five gross physical elements, the five organs of cognition, the five organs of action, mind, and the five vital airs are directly experienced in awareness through the form of content-filled concentration and known as deliberative concentration (*vitarka*). The *tanmātras*, the ego, and the gross elements become the objects of realization in the second form of content-filled concentration known as *savicāra*. When the external and internal organs become steady, the predominant *sattva guṇa* produces bliss, which becomes the content of the third form of content-filled concentration..

When the mental fluctuation in the form of "I am" becomes the supporting object and when the *yogin* feels "I am the knower of bliss", that is the final form of content-filled concentration, called egoity (*asmitā*). Supreme dispassion (*virāmapratyaya*) is the cause of the cessation of all mental fluctuations. Since the traces remain embedded in awareness, they possess the potency of producing fluctuations even in the arrested state. When all fluctuations are arrested and awarenesses are devoid of any content, that is the state suitable for the attainment of content-free concentration. Supreme dispassion serves as the means for its attainment (because it inspires the aspirant to stop even the remaining fluctuation of egoity). The absence of overt activity in awareness gives it an appearance of a nonexistent entity although it is not so. Awareness cannot be destroyed because that which is existent can never be made nonexistent. In the completely arrested state, the concentration called content-free takes place. This is a state in which the intellect is also restricted. As in this state there is no cognition either of the knower or of the process of knowing or of an object known, it is said to be "content-free".

I.19 (E343-346) Inclination towards becoming (*bhavapratyaya*) is a kind of seedless meditation which is attained by those who have not attained discrimination. The expression refers to traces which produce birth (*bhava*). Those (*videhas*) who realize the defects inherent in natural objects but do not possess knowledge of the *puruṣa* become dissociated from the gross and subtle bodies. When the force of the traces of dispassion gets exhausted, the concentration of these aspirants comes to an end. Again, those who have not been able to attain discriminative knowledge but have discovered fully the three-fold suffering associated with mundane life (the *prakṛtilayas*) remain dissolved in *prakṛti* so long as the force of the traces of dispassion persists. The awareness of these *yogins* possesses a tendency to arise again. When these *yogins* assume new bodies they come to possess supernormal powers of a high order. These *yogins* are different from (i) the presiding deities and (ii) the gods meditating on the elements (*bhūta*). The *yogins* who are the seekers of liberation attain content-free concentraton by means of faith, energy, remembering, concentration, wisdom, etc. "Faith" (*śraddhā*) here means interest in those objects which are fit for awakening discrimination. It leads to sincere efforts which in turn produce constant energy; this latter leads to concentration which produces wisdom. Wisdom reveals all the principles in their true forms. By repeated practice of discrimination, all traces of the empirical life are annihilated and the supreme dispassion causes content-free concentration. Those *yogins* who are forcefully inclined to attain liberation by constant spiritual discipline can attain their goal very quickly.

I.23 (E345-346) Liberation can be attained through devotion to God as well. One has to meditate on God constantly after dedicating all his actions to him. "*Praṇidhāna*", however, is not simply the dedication of all actions to God: it means devotion. The devotee feels in his mind the presence of God through constant meditation and then surrenders himself completely to the loving divinity with adoration and intense attachment.

I.24 (E341-352) The twenty-five principles constitute both the material and the efficient cause of the world. *Prakṛti* is the root material cause and the *puruṣa* is the efficient cause. This is the view of the Sāṃkhya-Yoga school. God is neither *prakṛti* nor an ordinary *puruṣa*. He is a special kind of liberated *puruṣa*, endowed with power, purity, and knowledge (i.e. He is an assemblage (*samāhāra*) of *puruṣa* and *prakṛti*. His mind always remains under His control. He can make the mind manifest and non-manifest at His own sweet will. God is not a creator. He is indifferent to both creation and dissolution of the world, as He is ever free. It is illogical and also against scriptural testimony to hold that the world is created by an ever-free self. The creation and maintenance of the world are the functions of Hiraṇyagarbha, who attained the highest form of content-filled concentration in his previous birth. Creation proceeds from the divine impressions of his purely and highly enriched mind.

I.32 (E355-358) While practicing meditation on God, the mind of the aspirant at first reflects on different divine characteristics. By means of practice, these different attributes are blended to form a single object of thought. The mind is, then, fixed on that single object. In the case of meditation on God, the aspirant should feel that he is residing in God, and that he is like God. Of all practices, the practice of keeping awareness fixed on a single object is the best.

I.41 (E363-364) Concentration attained in the one-pointed mind is called engrossment (*samāpatti*). The cognizer, the instrument of cognition and the content of cognition become the support of engrossment. That state of awareness which remains fixed on the desired object and gets tinged with the nature of the object is called engrossment.

I.43 (E368) The position of the Buddhists, who admit all objects as mere aggregates of factors (*dharma, skandha*), is not justifiable, since their position reduces all knowledge to error.

Truth is also of two kinds: (i) practical, relating to events and objects of the practical life, and (ii) metaphysical truth relating to liberation. These two kinds are further divided into relative and absolute. If an awareness that arises is relative to a particular situation, then that awareness is dependent on that situation and the words which express that awareness are true only relatively. Awareness that relates to the metaphysical principle is finally true. In the state of concentration the instruments of knowledge become completely steady and wholly pure; so knowledge that arises from the concentration that takes place in the one-pointed level of the mind is the supreme knowledge. Truths which cover the principles (*tattva*), are regarded as metaphysical although relative, because these truths assist the aspirant to achieve the highest and the best. That metaphysical truth which embodies the immutable *puruṣa* is the truth of the final goal. So knowledge of this truth is absolute. The absolute truth may have either a changeable eternal principle as its object or an immutable eternal *puruṣa*.

I.49 (E373) Specific knowledge of an object is many-sided and so all these diversities cannot be expressed through words. The knowledge conveyed through words is always of a general character. Hence both inference and verbal testimony are productive of general knowledge. Specific knowledge of the principles is immediately gained through concentration.

I.50-51 (E374-375) Discriminative knowledge is the highest

achievement of the *yogin* through content-filled concentration. When this knowledge bursts forth, all activities of the mind stop immediately. By stopping even this discriminative knowledge through supreme dispassion the *yogin* attains the completely arrested state of awareness and enters into seedless, content-free concentration. This concentration results in the cessation of all forms of mental activities and their traces.

BOOK TWO

II.1 (E377-378) The involved mind of an ordinary person is incapable of practicing meditation and detachment continuously. Even then an ordinary person can become successful by performing some actions conducive to concentration. These actions are: (i) self-purificatory conduct involving mental, moral and physical discipline (*tapas*), (ii) meditation on the syllable "*oṃ*" and study of the scriptures relating to liberation (*svādhyāya*), and (iii) surrender of all actions and fruits of actions to God (*īśvarapraṇidhāna*). By practicing these the aspirant can withdraw himself from external activities; being endowed with suitable qualities, he can practice concentration.

II.3 (E378-379) Those erroneous fluctuations which are painful and are opposed to the supreme goal are called afflictions (*kleśa*). These are of five kinds. These afflictions, by increasing themselves in the forms of ideas and traces, strengthen the effect-producing power of the three *guṇas* and thus cause the appearance of the fluctuations of the *guṇas* in the forms of the great principle, etc.

II.4 (E379) The afflictions remain latent in two forms: (i) in the form of power which will produce activities in the future; (ii) in the form of burnt seeds which have completely lost the creative-power. The afflictions of the first type become operative as soon as they are confronted with suitable objects, but not those of the second type.

II.5 (E381) Ignorance is not negative. It is not merely the absence of knowledge, nor is it an entity of a different kind. It is the erroneous belief in one thing as another. All false cognitions are errors (*viparyaya*). Only that erroneous cognition which causes rebirth is called "*avidyā*". *Avidyā* is not indescribable, for it can be described as believing one thing to be another (i.e. knowing a thing in a form which it does not possess).

II.10-11 (E384) That dissolution which is opposed to evolution in the sense that it does not lead to a further process of emergence is called reversing "one's ordinary functioning" (*pratiprasava*). The affliction which has been attenuated and which, for that reason, remains simply as an ingredient of a discriminating awareness, is removed by such reversing. Discriminative discernment stops finally the functioning of awareness. Owing to the cessation of all mental activity the afflictions, too, become ineffective. Then by practicing supreme dispassion discriminative awareness too is stopped. Owing to the absolute cessation of all fluctuations of awareness the afflictions, too, are destroyed totally and finally. It is because the subtle afflictions can be removed only when awareness gets dissolved that this type of affliction is regarded as the most powerful enemy of the aspirant. Awareness cannot be dissolved without practicing supreme detachment and this also is the outcome of the cognition of the true nature of the *puruṣa* which is devoid of the three *guṇas*. This supreme knowledge is very rare.

II.12 (E386) Action is nothing but the functioning of awareness, organs and vital airs. The traces of actions which again get manifested in the forms of appropriate desires, efforts, etc. and cause the origination of the body and organs, are called karmic residues (*karmāśaya*). These traces also produce pleasures and pains (which are the fruits of actions).

II.15 (E392-395) Attachment, aversion, and delusion give rise to mental and bodily karmic residues. Those which originate from attachment, etc. in their purely mental forms are mental, but the karmic residues that originate from the combined actions of the body and the mind are physical.

Suffering is not merely conditional (i.e. suffering does not arise merely from the contact between awareness and object), but suffering also originates from the inherent nature of awareness and all its objects. The *guṇas* undergo constant changes owing to their essentially changeable character.

II.23 (E415) Discriminative discernment does not immediately culminate in liberation because liberation in the true sense is obtained when this discrimination, too, is stopped. It is, nevertheless, a secondary cause as it is a preceding condition for liberation.

II.24 (E417) "Ignorance" (*avidyā*) means traces of erroneous awareness which are effective in producing a disposition towards incorrect appreciation of the facts of life: These traces, being the root cause of error, produce corresponding errors as a result of which the contact between the intellect and the *puruṣa* persists. Awareness completely ceases to function when the true nature of the *puruṣa* is realized and the practice of supreme detachment is adhered to.

II.26 (E418) When the *yogin* comprehends correctly the nature of the intellect and also appreciates its difference from the *puruṣa*, he attains what is called undisturbed discriminative discernment. The *puruṣa* is also realized as the witnessing principle lying behind the intellect.

II.27 (E420-421) In the highest or last state of knowledge beyond which there cannot be anything more to be known, awareness comes to realize that the *puruṣa* is free from relationship with the *guṇas* etc. In this condition the *yogin* is regarded as liberated while living (*jīvanmukta*) and proficient. Although he is a living person (of the world) still he is called a liberated self. One who is not affected by misery is to be regarded as liberated. When awareness is merged finally, the *yogin* is called a *muktakuśala*, that is, the *yogin* attains incorporeal emancipation by transcending the sphere of the *guṇas*.

II.29 (E421) A collection of parts (*aṅga*) is called a whole (*aṅgin*). There is no whole apart from the parts. It is because restraints, observances, etc. are productive of the steadiness of "yoga", that these are called "limbs" of *yoga (yogāṅga)*, which is the suppression of the fluctuations of awareness. These limbs of Yoga are classified into external and internal. Just as the first part of the five-fold vital air (or breath, *prāṇa*) is called by the same name (viz., *prāṇa*), in the same manner the last limb of Yoga (viz., *samādhi*) goes under the name of *samādhi*.

II.52 (E431-432) Through breath-control the vital airs become quiet and this condition of breathing produces steadiness of the body. This again leads to cessation of actions which in turn destroys or weakens traces, thereby making awareness (knowledge) brighter and more illuminating.

BOOK THREE

III.1 (E434) Intense concentration is the highest state of the steadiness of awareness. The common characteristic of concentration is that in this state awareness remains fixed on a particular object only and all other thoughts and ideas about other things are completely stopped. By attaining the steadiness of mind designated as "concentration" the *yogin* attains complete knowledge of the subject, the object and the sense-organs. This is called content-filled concentration. When this content-filled concentrtation too is stopped, the *yogin* attains the content-free state of concentration in which all fluctuations are stopped.

III.9 (E436) When all fluctuations are stopped awareness seems to assume the form of a void and nothing is explicitly noticed in this state. Even in that state awareness does possess the potency for undergoing changes. Both confused and one-pointed states are states of fluctuations. Fluctuations possess two characteristics: awareness and traces. The traces of fluctuations are not of the nature of cognition and so when awarenesses are stopped those traces are not destroyed. In the state of arrest awareness possesses only traces owing to the disappearance of awareness, and only these traces undergo changes in this state.

III.11 (E437) The eagerness to receive everything is a characteristic of awareness. Awareness can also be one-pointed. The weakening of the tendency of awareness to receive everything and the strengthening of the tendency toward one-pointedness is what is called change of mind in the direction of concentration.

III.13 (E329-443) "*Dharma*" means the characteristic qualities by which an object becomes known, and "*dharmin*" refers to the substratum (the object) having such qualities. The qualities of the cause become the substratum of the effect. So, the quality or *dharma* is of the nature of the substratum or *dharmin*. Qualities like jarness, etc. are of the same nature as the lump of clay, the substratum. The lump of clay, which is the *dharmin*, is nothing but the collection of qualities like jarness etc. *Dharma* simply manifests the changes which are gradually taking place in the *dharmin* by the annihilation of one form of transformation on the appearance of another. The qualities which are present in the *dharmin* undergo changes and these changes are specified as past, present and future characteristics.

III.14 (E445-446) Qualities are the powers the possession of which enables the substances to become known at all times. The differences in the production of appropriate objects exhibited by these powers serve as the basis for inferring their existence in all times. One and the same substance may possess many qualities. An object is known by its quality and so the qualities are the things to be known through different instruments of knowledge. These characteristics are originally of three kinds: (i) of the form of illumination, (ii) of the form of motion, (iii) of the form of inertia. Each one of them is again divisible into real, imaginary, or merely semantic. From the point of view of temporal difference, all of them are divided into quiescent or past, emergent or present, and unmanifested or future. Only some of the characteristics are emergent whereas the quiescent and unmanifested characteristics may be innumerable.

III.15 (E448) The oldness of the jar is not to be identified with its worn-out state because the latter is the indicator of changes relating to characteristics. When differentiation is made from the point of view of the time of origination of a jar, during the prevalence of the same characteristic, expressions like "it is old","it is new", etc. are used. Change of location is also a change of state.

III.34 (E459) One awareness cannot be directly apprehended by another awareness. It is the illuminating flow of the recollected actions of receiving involved in the feeling of ego which is called internal fluctuations of awareness.

III.52 (E470) "Assemblage of objects" (*vastusamāhāra*) means that objects like jars, etc. when put together, seem to exist side by side, but an "assemblage" of movements does not imply such a type of togetherness because the past and the future moments are not present. Hence the concept of an assemblage of moments referred to by "day" or "night", etc. is nothing but a creation of the intellect. Such intellectual concepts relating to assemblages of moments are thought of in practical life as real and are admitted as such. A moment is the substratum of an object but it itself is not an object. It is also the substratum of a non-object imagined as an object. Moments cannot be really collected or "assembled" because moments which are past and future are connected with changes and are conceptual constructs. So, only one moment is existent and that is called the present. The past, present, and future characteristics of all objects are supported by that single moment because all past and future characteristics are existent in subtle forms.

III.53 (E472) According to one view, there are some ultimate differentiating characteristics which give rise to an awareness of distinction between two things. The upholders of this view also maintain that spatial difference, difference in characteristics, and difference in shape or species are the final differentiating factors. Such differentiation is possible only in the cases of the great principle (*mahat*), etc. The primary cause which is the original source of all does not admit of any such differentiation. Hence Vārṣagaṇya has said "In the primary cause, the question of such differences in position, in shape, and in species does not arise as there is no differentiation in that stage".

BOOK FOUR

IV.4-5 (E477) The *yogin* voluntarily creates one or many minds out of the pure and (for that reason) barren "I-feeling" which has become unproductive like a burnt seed owing to the arrival of discriminative knowledge. These created minds enable the *yogin* to impart spiritual instruction to those who are steeped in ignorance. The basic mind is the efficient mind which can control all subordinate minds at one and the same time.

IV.6 (E477) Here, the created mind is to be understood in the sense of the mind that has become successful through yogic concentration. Such a successful mind is devoid of traces. The concentration that leads to liberation is not the result of any traces in his lifetime and is not born again.

IV.10 (E479) That which is natural does not arise owing to the operation of any cause. That which always is, or that which arises with the object at the same time and remains with it, is called "natural". Here the view of another school, the Jaina school, has been discussed. According to this view, the mind is like a lamp placed in a pot or kept in a palace. Just as the light of the lamp assumes the form either of the pot (in which the lamp is placed) or of the palace (in which it is kept), in the same manner the mind also assumes the form of the body which it inhabits. This view is not correct. Awareness is not a spatial object. It exists in time and is of the form of activity. As the non-concrete awareness cannot be measured, its largeness and smallness are inconceivable. Since awareness does not consist of spatial parts it is all-pervading. In other words, it is related to all contents of awareness. Its all-pervasiveness is not to be understood in the sense of pervading the entire space because it is of the nature of a receiving instrument. According to Yoga, its mode alone is capable of expansion and contraction. Awareness when it becomes discriminative knowledge becomes omniscient, and when impure or non-illumined it is limited.

IV.11 (E481-482) Subconscious impressions are collected in the mind by causes like merit, demerit, etc. Memory arises from an existent object because nothing can arise from nonexistence. Impressions, too, are collected from memory. Objects are the support of impressions which get manifested being directed towards objects like sound, etc. If the causes and effects which help the accumulation of impressions are removed, then these too disappear.

IV.12 (E482) Awarenesses can never be content-less. All cognitions refer to objects. Awarenesses of the past as well as of the future are related to their special objects. Ordinary human beings refer to these objects, which are imperceptible to the sense-organs, by taking into consideration the variations in time.

IV.14-15 (E483-485) Vijñānavādins do not accept the existence of external objects. According to them, an exteral object has no metaphysical reality. This very denial of the reality of an external object by the Vijñānavādin establishes the existence of an external object, because like all schools of philosophy they also agree in holding that the highest and the best can be achieved only by being disinterested in external objects. Now, if an external object does not exist, then how can one cultivate a dispassionate attitude towards it? If the object is cognized in a form different from what it actually possesses, then also the existence of an object which has been so cognized will have to be admitted. Dream-objects are not the products of pure imagination. Objects like color, etc. cognized previously are remembered or reconstructed in dreams through imagination. Sound, color, etc. are experienced through the sense-organs which receive impressions from external objects. A man who is born blind can never perceive any color in his dreams. So, cognition of objects is not controlled merely by awareness: it arises in awareness because of the influence of external objects. The Vijñānavādin who asserts that the object is merely a creation of consciousness (*vijñāna*) may be asked to point out that particular consciousness which is creating those objects. He can answer only by saying "it is not any particular consciousness", since, in fact, different persons know differently one and the same object; this proves that the object and the cognition of the object are different. According to Sāṃkhya the naturally mutative constituents undergo modifications independently without being moved by anybody's imagination. Objects which have been formed in accordance with merit and demerit become related to the relevant awarenesses.

IV.16 (E485) If it is held that an object of awareness arises along with the awareness and that it does not exist prior to the awareness or posterior to the awareness, then this contention, too, is not logical. If the existence of an object depends on a particular consciousness, then what will happen to the object when that particular consciousness ceases to think of it? An external object is not the creation of a particular consciousness and is not dependent for its existence only on that consciousness. The object of cognition is common to all awarenesses and awarenesses are different. From the relation between the mind and the object comes the experience of the seer who considers it either as beneficial or as harmful.

IV.18 (E487) It is through the contact with the *puruṣa* that all fluctuations (of awareness) become known. Had a present fluctuation been absent (even though contact with the *puruṣa* is there) then the *puruṣa* would have been regarded sometimes as a knower and sometimes as a non-knower. Thus *puruṣa* would be become subject to change.

IV.19-20 (E487-488) There is no self-revealing object in the realm of the seen, because to be seen is to be revealed by some other object. Fire cannot serve as an instance of a self-revealing principle. A self-illuminating object is that which is not illuminated by any other principle. If consciousness is to be treated as self-illuminating, then it should illumine itself as well as the object. Had it been so, then the nature of consciousness and also of the object would have been ascertained at the same moment. This, however, does not happen. The mental function which ascertains the nature of consciousness is not identical with the mental function which determines the nature of the object. The awareness of a sound and the awareness that I am cognizing a sound cannot take place simultaneously. So awareness reveals the object only. It is not self-revealing. The upholders of the theory of momentariness assert that knower, known and knowledge originate at one and the same moment and are also revealed together. This view is implausible and not in agreement with human experience.

IV.21 (E490) Future awareness cannot justifiably be held to know present awareness. If one awareness is to be known by another awareness, then we shall be forced to admit the existence of innumerable knowing awarenesses. If one awareness is to be known by another awareness, then this process will lead to infinite regress. This will also cause confusion of memory. (According to this view) the preceding awareness becomes the cause of the succeeding awareness. If the awareness of the present moment is the knower of previous awarenesses, then it will also be the knower of the memories of all these awarenesses at the same moment. Such a state is sure to produce confusion of memory.

IV.23 (E492) According to Vijñānavādins only consciousness, which is the root of illusory cognition and which is also capable of assuming different forms and odors, is an existent entity. They have faith in concentration; but in concentration the object which becomes the support of the concentrating awareness is not a creation of awareness. Had this object been non-different from concentration, then awareness would not cognize itself as awareness. Hence, some self-revealing object has got to be admitted. That self-revealing object is the *purusa*.

IV.25 (E494) An aspirant can attain discriminative knowledge spontaneously if the seed of discrimination is present from previous births. When the ordinary awarenesses of the self are gone, the *puruṣa* shines in its own true form.

IV.29 (E495) The intellect of the *yogin* who has acquired discriminative knowledge remains absorbed in that knowledge alone and as such he is always the possessor of pure and true knowledge.

IV.34 (E500) The *puruṣa* or *citiśakti* always remains in its true form; but owing to its contact with the intellect it appears as being other than what it is. When the intellect is fully dissolved, spiritual liberation or, on other words, the "isolation" (*kaivalya*) of the *puruṣa* is established.

26.BALADEVA MIŚRA, *Yogapradīpikā* on Patañjali's *Yogasūtras*

Summary by Ram Shankar Bhattacharya

In the introductory verses the author gives an account of his genealogy. Besides this commentary he composed *Sandhyāprakāśa*, *Gṛhasthācāradarpaṇa* and some other religious works. The present commentary is said to have been composed by following Vācaspatimiśra's *Tattvavaiśāradī*. In the Sanskrit introduction it is stated by the editor that the commentary was published in *saṃvat* 1987 (=1930 CE) when the author was still alive. It is published in Dhundhiraja Sastri 1931.

BOOK ONE

I.1 The word "*anuśāsana*" shows that the author has dealt with Yoga's defining characteristic (*lakṣaṇa*) as "that which is the instrumental cause of joining something" (*yujyate anena*). This is why yoga is explained in the *Bhāṣya* as concentration, which consists in the union of the mind with the self. The word "*samādhi*" is used in two different senses. It means either (1) the eighth member of yoga in accordance with the derivative sense "that by which the mind is rendered one-pointed", or (2) the state in which all fluctuations of awareness are inhibited.

I.2 The word "*citta*" ("awareness")in the *sūtra* refers to the intellect. "Cessation of the fluctuations of awareness" is to be interpreted as the inhibition of those fluctuations in which there is predominance of *rajas* and *tamas*. In the content-filled form of yoga there appear fluctuations in which *sattva* is predominant. These fluctuations are also inhibited in the content-free form of yoga. This inhibition must be associated with the eradication of afflictions and karmic residues. A detailed exposition of the five states, distracted and so forth, has been given here.

I.4 On account of the *puruṣa*'s proximity to the intellect, *puruṣa* superimposes the fluctuations of the intellect on itself and consequently considers itself as afflicted by pain.

I.8 Though the fluctuation called conceptual construction does not reflect the true form of the object it cannot be regarded as error, for it is not sublated by an instrument of knowledge as error is.

I.10 A person in dreamless sleep has internal insight (*antaḥprajñā*). Though there is similarity between sleep and one-pointedness, yet the former is dominated by *tamas* and is opposed to concentration.

I.11 Memory has been defined in two ways. (1) It is that fluctuation which consists in the appearance of the experienced object in the intellect through traces. (2) It is a particular kind of fluctuation whose content is the object experienced previously and in which there is no surreptitious addition.

I.17 As the *vitarkānugata* variety of content-filled concentration has two subdivisions, namely with (*savitarka*) and without (*nirvitarka)* empirical awareness, and as the *vicārānugata* variety has two subdivisions, namely with (*savicāra*) and without (*nirvicāra*) rational content, so too the *ānandānugata* and the *asmitānugata* varieties of content-filled concentration have two subdivisions each. (The commentator is closely following Vācaspatimiśra in this regard.)

I.18 In content-free concentration the mind, being devoid

of fluctuations, assumes the form of *brahman*. It is remarked that the traces created by suppression destroy not only the traces caused by one-pointedness but also themselves.

I.19 Inclination towards becoming (*bhavapratyaya*) has been explained in two ways: (1) it is that concentration which is caused by the superimposition of *prakṛti* and other not-selves on the self, and (2) it is that concentration whose result is to be born again and again on account of ignorance. It is remarked that content-free concentration (in which all fluctuations are suppressed) is of two kinds. (1) It is that which is caused by the dissolution of *prakṛti, mahat*, etc. and that which, due to association with ignorance, is the cause of return to transmigratory existence. (2) It is that which is caused by faith, etc. and which leads to emancipation. The latter is said to be the chief form of content-free concentration.

I.24 The perfected mind of God is a modification of the *guṇas*. It is beginningless, consists of pure *sattva*, and it possesses the power of unexcelled knowledge and activity.

I.29 The commentator reads the *sūtra* with the word "*pratyakcetana*" as well as "*pratyakcetanā*" and explains it accordingly. While the former means *puruṣa* possessing ignorance, i.e. the *jīva* or embodied self, the latter means the seer.

I.32 "*Ekatattva*" is explained as meaning *īśvara* or qualified (*saguṇa*) *brahman*.

I.38 "*Nidrālambana*" is explained as sleep dominated by *sattva* in which the mind becomes one-pointed. The pleasure in this state can be taken to be a supporting object (*ālambana*) and thus the awareness can attain the state of steadiness.

I.46 Engrossments are eight in nmber. Two have the gross aspects of objects (*grāhya*) as their content, two focus on the subtle aspects, two focus on the organs (*grahaṇa*) (based on the presence and absence of conceptual constructions), and two concern the subject (*grahitṛ*) (based on the presence and absence of constructions).

I.50 An awareness has two functions: experiencing sounds,

etc. and discriminative discernment. The former function is associated with afflictions and karma. Discriminative discernment arises in an awareness whose afflictions and karma have been uprooted by the traces created by insight and which is also devoid of any role (*adhikāra,* defined by Vācaspati in I.51 as that karma which is caused by destiny and which is the cause of the creation of the body).

BOOK TWO

II.1 it is remarked that devotion to God in this *sūtra* is not construed as *bhakti* but as surrender.

II.4 It is remarked that the opposite of ignorance is knowledge of reality. Egoity is the opposite of the knowledge of the difference (between the *puruṣa* and the organs). Passion and hatred is the opposite of detachment. Egoity and other afflictions become active in connection with some object when the object is known through ignorance.

II.12 It is an established fact that karmic residues are characterized as merit and demerit, both of which are caused by desire, etc. For example, one incited by desire performs those actions which are capable of fulfilling some particular purpose (*kāmyakarman*), and through this one acquires merit which is the means to heaven and other goals.

II.17 Since only the intellect is seen by *puruṣa*, a question may arise regarding the validity of the view that "sound, etc. are objects seen by the *puruṣa*". The intellect becomes modified by the forms of sound, etc. when those are received by the intellect through the channels of organs. That is why the seer (i.e. *puruṣa*) is called possessor (*svāmin*, the intellect being the *sva*, the thing possessed). The relation between the seer and the *buddhi* is not natural; it has a cause, though it is beginningless.

II.20 Since *puruṣa* is reflected in the intellect it is called the perceiver of the intellect. Though *puruṣa* is immutable, to the ignorant it seems to assume the same forms fashioned by the fluctuations of the intellect, and this act is known as *puruṣa*'s perceiving those fluctuations.

II.22 The unmanifest (*avyakta*) *prakṛti*,whose existence has been accepted in the Vedas and the *smṛtis*, is said to be one without parts, all-pervading, and eternal. Though unmanifest *prakṛti* is one, *puruṣas* are many.

II.28 The eight accessories of yoga give rise to discriminative discernment by directly removing obstacles. Those who practiced the accessories to yoga in their previous births are not required to practice them again in the present birth, since impurities existing in those previous lives have already been eradicated.

II.45 It is remarked that since the restraints are not dependent on any other accessories they are mentioned in the first place, and each of the following seven accessories of yoga mentioned in this *sūtra* is dependent on the preceding accessory. Purification of the mind is capable of giving rise to devotion to God, and the first seven accessories of yoga are the means for acquiring purification of the mind. This is achieved through the intermediary operation of unseen (*adṛṣṭa*) merit.

II.47 It is remarked that there are two kinds of efforts. One is the sustainer of the body; it is not antagonistic to the practice of yogic postures. The other is natural and antagonistic to the practice of yogic postures. This second effort has been referred to in this *sūtra*.

BOOK THREE

III.3 Since concentration is stated to be a particular variety of meditation (*dhyāna*) it must be regarded as not conditioned by space though it is conditioned by time. This view is shown to be upheld by the Purāṇas.

III.8 It is remarked that the content-free form of concentration comes into existence when comprehensive reflection is dissolved by the force of supreme dispassion, characterized by tranquility produced by wisdom.

III.13 It is not to be held that increase and decrease pertain to a substance and not to qualities, for we have the experience that qualities like color, etc. have increase and decrease. A color with a developed shade is regarded as the same color. This fact is proved by recognition (*pratyabhijñā*). It is remarked that cognition, desire, etc. exist for two moments only and that the change of intensity (*avasthā pariṇāma*) of these occurs in the second moment.

III.14 It is remarked that the attributes remain in a substance so long as that substance exists. An attribute (*dharma*) is a power (*śakti*) and there is no real distinction between a power and the substance possessing the power (*śaktimat*).

III.18 As to why the Sāṃkhya and Yoga philosophers are eager to establish the immutability of *puruṣa*, the commentary states that if *jñāna*, etc. are regarded as special attributes (*viśeṣa guṇa*) of *puruṣa*, all or some of these attributes would be destroyed in the state of liberation. On account of their destruction *puruṣa* also would be destroyed, like the earth which gets destroyed as a result of the destruction of its attribute smell. Awareness, which is the object of *puruṣa*, assumes the forms of objects like sound, etc. This assuming of forms exists in the reflection of *puruṣa* existing in the awareness. Desire, pleasure and the like are its fluctuations. According to Yoga, the self (*puruṣa*) is devoid of dimension. But since *puruṣa* is realized as existing in the heart, he is falsely regarded as limited by the size of the heart. For the purpose of worship the self is sometimes described as possessing the size of a thumb.

III.43 Though the *Bhāṣya* does not mention *gariman* (the power of becoming heavy) in the list of eight supernormal powers, it is to be accepted because *laghiman* (the power of levitation), the opposite to *gariman*, has been mentioned in this list. In some lexicons *gariman* is found to have been read in the group of the eight supernormal powers. The name of the eighth power is said to be *kāmāvaśāyitva* and not *yatrakāmāvaśāyitva* as read by the *Bhāṣya*.

BOOK FOUR

IV.2 The commentary takes both *mahat* and *ahaṃkāra* as *asmitā*, the material cause of the organs.

IV.3 It is remarked that according to the atheistic Sāṃkhya it is a future human purpose (i.e. experience and liberation) which is the impeller or inciter of *prakṛti* (i.e. of the body and the organs), while according to theistic Yoga God is the inciter. In fact, a future aim is to be accepted as the cause of permanence or sustenance (*sthiti*). This does not, however, prove that merit and demerit cease to be the efficient causes (of experience and liberation) for their agency is accepted in removing obstacles.

IV.4 The word "*citta*" in this *sūtra* must mean *manas* (mind), for egoity is said to be the cause of *manas*. Like the created (*nirmāna*) *citta* (a highly perfected mind created by a *yogin*), there are also *nirmāṇa* intellects and *nirmāṇa* egoities. It is to be noted that each created mind has a body of its own.

IV.13 It is remarked that although the fluctuations of *prakṛti* are changing in each moment, *prakṛti* is eternal and fundamentally real (*paramārtha*).

IV.14-16) The commentary has elaborately explained the refutation of the doctrine of consciousness(-only) (*vijñānavāda*) as given in the *Bhāṣya*.

IV.29 The word "*dharma*" in "*dharmamegha*" means "that action which is known as not-white-not-black". It may also mean the direct realization of one's innermost self. In this state there arises no idea characterized by ignorance.

IV.30 It is remarked that if anything other than the twenty-five principles of Sāṃkhya exists, that also is known to an awareness in which the *sattva guṇa* is predominant.

IV.33 According to *sūtra* IV.32 the sequence of changes must have an end. This view is applied only to the field of modifications (*vikāra*). Unmanifest *prakrti* is eternal, or more precisely, permanent though changing (*pariṇāmanitya*), thus there can be no end to its mutations. The flow of creation is not only beginningless; it is also endless. Consequently the theory of "the liberation of all beings" becomes untenable. This view cannot be proved through inference, and it is not maintained in any statement of scripture. Scriptural texts are in favor of the view that transmigratory existence (*saṃsāra*) has neither beginning nor end. That is why there can be no annihilation of *saṃsāra* as a result of the liberation of all beings.

IV.34 Liberation (*mokṣa*), that is, isolation (*kaivalya*) is ascribed to both *prakṛti* and *puruṣa*. In respect to *prakṛti*, isolation means non-association of *prakṛti* with that *puruṣa* with which it has been wrongly associated. In regard to *puruṣa*, isolation means *puruṣa*'s abiding in itself owing to non-association with the intellect. According to the commentary, bliss is realized in this state.

27.KṚṢṆAVALLABHĀCĀRYA, *Kiraṇā* on Patañjali's *Yogasūtras* and Bhoja's *Rājamārtaṇḍa*

Summary by Ram Shankar Bhattacharya

Kṛṣṇavallabhācārya was a teacher of the Swāmi Nārāyaṇa sect. As well as the present text, he wrote a commentary entitled *Kiraṇāvalī* on Vācaspatimiśra's *Tattvakaumudī*. Our E is Sastri and Sastri 1939. The subcommentary of Kṛṣṇavallabhācārya largely repeats older commentaries and only a few summary notations will be included in this summary.

BOOK ONE

I.1 Isolation is said to be attained by the certain and final termination of the three kinds of pain, or by taking refuge in the supreme God associated with the complete and eternal cessation of all pains.

I.6 Knowledge (*pramā,* the result of *pramāṇa*) is the apprehension of *puruṣa* (reflected in the cognitive principle, the intellect) which is not doubted, contradicted, or previously known.

I.8 The reason for the classification of doubt under error is given here by showing their partial similarity. While erroneous awareness (a mental state not based on the form of the object) is associated with cognition, in doubt it is associated with the object.

I.9 A person knows the falsity of his erroneous cognition, though he may fail to understand the non-validity of a conceptual construction. This is because conception is based on words, which may be misleading.

I.16 The dispassion called "complete control" is caused by discriminative cognition. It is superior to concentration.

I.17 While the commentary (by Bhoja) takes *puruṣa* as the only example of a conscious being, the subcommentary of Kṛṣṇavallabhācārya mentions both the individual self and the supreme self as conscious entities.

It is remarked that, in the *savitarka* form of content-filled concentration, contemplation (*bhāvanā*) follows the relation of substance and attribute, contemplation in the *nirvitarka* form of concentration is devoid of this relation. In the *nirvicāra* concentration the contemplation is related to the substance only (*dharmimātra*); it follows the spatial and temporal relation, etc. in the *savicāra* form of concentration.

I.19 Hiraṇyagarbha and others are regarded as the *videhas*, who have only subtle bodies. The *prakṛtilayas*, those merged in *prakṛti*, are those who have transcended the cosmos and have dissolved themselves into the eight *prakṛtis*.

I.24 The word "*viśeṣa*" in the expression "*puruṣaviśeṣa*" indicates that there is the highest development of omniscience, omnipotence, etc. in God.

I.23 The definitions of the *kalpapralaya* and *mahāpralaya*, along with ar. account of four kinds of dissolution, namely *nitya, naimittika, prākṛta* and *ātyantika*, are given here.

I.34 The *mātra*-measure (in connection with the practice of breath control) is discussed.

I.42 The nature of *sphoṭa* as accepted by Grammarians is shown.

BOOK TWO

II.13 The word "*bhoga*" ("experience") is said to have three senses, namely (1) the thing to be enjoyed, (2) pleasure and pain, the results of experience, and (3) the organs, i.e. the instruments of the act of experiencing. (It is an established principle that the intended meaning is to be ascertained through context, etc.)

II.15 Explanation of the words "*anaikāntikī*" and "*ātyantikī*" (adjectives to *duḥkhanivṛtti*) is given.

II.24 The author gives a justification of Bhoja's view that association (*saṃyoga*) is the same as discriminative discernment. It is further remarked that the reading of the expression "*vivekakhyātirūpa*" embodying the aforesaid view is corrupt and it should be corrected to "*avivekakhyātirūpa*".

II.26 The doctrine of the self's reflecting in the intellect is elucidated. The nature of isolation is said to be either (1) absolute negation of the three kinds of pain, or (2) taking refuge in the supreme God.

II.47 Though Bhoja reads "*ānantyasamāpatti*" in the *sūtra*, Kṛṣṇavallabhācārya takes the word as "*anantasamāpatti*" and explains *ananta* as the "great snake" (*śeṣanāga*). He evidently follows *Tattvavaiśāradī*.

BOOK THREE

III.7-8 Reasons for regarding meditative fixation, reflective meditation and concentration as internal means and as external means to the seedless concentration are stated here clearly.

III.17 Some of the epithets of sound (i.e. word) and *sphoṭa* (the word-principle) are explained. It is held that *sphoṭa* is manifested by letters (*varṇa*).

III.31 The tortoise-nerve (*kūrmanāḍī*) is said to be the same as the *nāḍīcakra* in the heart.

III.35 It is remarked that the image of *puruṣa* is called "shadow" (*chāyā*) and that "*puruṣajñāna*" means knowledge of the image of the self.

III.38 The epithet "all-pervasive" (*vyāpaka*) shows that both the self and awareness possess great magnitude.

BOOK FOUR

IV.1 The word "*oṣadhisiddhi*" is explained to mean the development of both health and passion.

IV.12-15 The *prima facie* views are ascribed to the Buddhists.

IV.16 It is remarked that the sentence "*nacaikacittatantram...*" is read as a *sūtra* by Vijñānabhikṣu and not by Vācaspati and others, who take it to be a *Bhāṣya*-passage.

IV.21 When the reflection of the sentient self (*cit*) in the cognitive principle becomes affected by the fluctuations, the self is said to have entered the *buddhi*. When the mind receives the reflection of the self, it is illuminated by the self.

IV.22 The supreme self is also called "*śāntabrahman*". It is remarked that according to the atheistic Sāṃkhya there is no God (*parameśvara*) different from the pure self.

IV.32 The term "*kṣaṇapratiyogin*" is explained as that which has the sequence of moments as its locus.

IV.33-34 Isolation or liberation is said to be either the absolute negation of three kinds of pain, the self's abiding in its own form, taking refuge in the supreme self, or realizing eternal bliss in the state of absolute surrender to the supreme self.

28.SWĀMĪ JÑĀNĀNANDA, *Bhāṣya* on Vyāsa's *Yogasūtrabhāṣya*

Swāmī Jñānānaṇanda (1845-1950) is the well-known founder of Bhārata Dharma Mahāmaṇḍala, a religio-cultural organization of Varanasi. His work is an elaboration of the Vyāsa *Bhāṣya* on the *Yogasūtras*.

In the summary provided below we have replaced Dr. Bhatt's translations of technical terms by those in use in the present Volume.

Summary by Govardhan Bhatt

BOOK ONE

I.1 The first *sūtra* enjoins the practice of yoga, for which a person with a *sāttvikī* intellect alone is fit. As defined in the *(Bhagavad)Gītā,* a *sāttvikī* intellect is that which knows what ought to be done and what ought not to be done, i.e. one with a highly developed moral sense. Those whose intellect is *rājasī* or *tāmasī* are not entitled to the practice of yoga. A *rājasī* intellect has an underdeveloped moral sense and needs proper moral education through the study of scripture and instruction by a religious teacher. A *tāmasī* intellect is still more unfit for the practice of yoga, as it has a perverted moral sense. A person having this type of intellect is a potential sinner and so deserves to be dealt with rather severely by the state and the society.

I.2 But what is yoga? It is the suppression of the fluctuations of awareness or mind. By "suppression" (*nirodha*) is meant the merger of the fluctuations in their cause, viz. the mind, and it results in the attainment of two supernormal fluctuations known as content-filled concentration and content-free concentration. The former is characterized by a triple consciousness of the cognizer, the cognition and the cognized object, while in the latter this also drops completely.

Normally there are five states (*bhūmi*) of yoga, of which three are ordinarily experienced by all and two are specifically experienced by aspirants advanced in yoga practice and so are called "extraordinary".

The first state is called "sluggish" *(mūḍhā)*, in which the mind being under the influence of *tamas guṇa* lacks the sense of good and evil, is overcome by sloth and forgetfulness and, like an unbridled horse, runs about restlessly. The second state is called "distracted" (*kṣipta*) and is due to the excess of *rajas guṇa*. In this state the mind, like a bridled horse, engages in some work after some intellectual planning and some purpose in view. The third state is called "partially distracted" (*vikṣipta*).

It is caused by an excess of *sattva guṇa* and is experienced for a very short duration. In it the mind is devoid of pleasure, pain, thought, sloth, etc. The fourth and fifth states, viz. "one-pointed" (*ekāgra*) and "suppressed" (*niruddha*), are more important for the aspirant. In the one-pointed state there is no manifestation of anything other than the meditator, meditation and the object meditated upon. This is accomplished by practice and leads finally to the suppressed state, which is the cherished goal of the aspirant. In it awareness becomes absolutely fixed and totally free from all kinds of fluctuations, and in the course of further practice it gives rise first to content-filled concentration and then to content-free concentration.

I.3-4 When the fluctuations of awareness are completely suppressed, the seer (self) stands in its real form as pure consciousness. In the ordinary empirical state the seer identifies itself with the fluctuations of awareness and assumes the alien roles of a doer and an enjoyer. Awareness or the internal organ has three parts, viz., mind (*manas*), intellect (*buddhi*) and ego(maker) (*ahaṃkāra*) which, as a matter of fact, are three different functions of awareness. Mind wanders from object to object. Intellect is more stable and judges things in terms of goodness and badness. The ego(maker) makes one think of oneself as an independent entity. It is responsible for the bondage of the self (*puruṣa*) which really is pure consciousness. As we know, the self in the bound condition identifies itself with the mind which, like a mirror, assumes the form of whatever object comes into contact with it. When like the wavy surface of a pond the mind is agitated and constantly modified into various objective shapes, it cannot reflect the self in its true character. But when all the fluctuations have ceased it becomes calm and is able to reflect the true image of *puruṣa*. This is the very purpose of the practice of yoga.

I.5-11 Now, the fluctuations of awareness are broadly of two types, viz. afflicted (*kliṣṭa*) and unafflicted. The preponderance of *sattva guṇa* in the mind generates unafflicted modes, while that of *tamas* gives rise to afflicted ones, which in their turn produce merit and demerit respectively. The aspirant is advised to suppress the afflicted modes with the help of the unafflicted ones, and all including the unafflicted fluctuations should ultimately be destroyed by supreme detachment (*paravairāgya*).

From another point of view, the fluctuations of awareness are of five kinds, viz., correct awareness, error, conceptual construction, sleep and memory.

Correct awarenesses (*pramāṇa*) are of three kinds only, viz., perception, inference, and testimony. They, however, give rise only to extrinsic knowledge, not that of the intrinsic nature of the self, and so they should be suppressed. Error (*viparyaya*), which is erroneous or doubtful cognition, should obviously be suppressed still more. Conceptual construction (*vikalpa*) is accepting a thing simply on the basis of hearsay without any rational consideration of its truth value, e.g. "the sun rises in the east". Sleep (*nidrā*) too is a fluctuation arising when the mind is overpowered by *tamas guṇa*. It is caused by ignorance and so is opposed to the state of meditation based on a discriminative knowledge of *puruṣa* and *prakṛti*. All these fluctuations including the last one, memory (*smṛti*), being the causes of pleasure, pain and delusion, are to be suppressed by the one who desires to establish his self in its true form.

I.12-16) Practice (*abhyāsa*) and dispassion (*vairāgya*) are the two means of suppressing the fluctuations of awareness. Dispassion checks the outward flow of the mind toward worldly enjoyment and practice makes it flow inward more vigorously. Practice is a steadfast effort to attain one's true form. When awareness becomes absolutely calm by uninterrupted practice it is enabled to reflect the highest truth. This gradual and steadfast practice which strengthens and encourages the aspirant for the attainment of a godly state is called spiritual practice (*sādhanā*). This practice should be continued without a break for a long time with faith in the scriptures, in the teacher and in continence. Then it becomes firmly rooted and is converted into habit and succeeds in giving the desired spiritual insight.

Dispassion is getting rid of the desire for worldly and heavenly enjoyments by the consideration of their momentary character and their origination from ignorance. It has four stages. In the first one (*yatamānasaṃjñā*) the aspirant endeavors to think out what is of permanent value and what is merely transient in ths world. In the second stage (*vyatirekasaṃjñā*) he tries to assess how much progress he has already made and how much still remains. The third state (*ekendriyasaṃjñā*) is attained when the senses have ceased to be attracted by the objects of enjoyment but the thirst for them still lurks in the mind. The last stage (*vaśīkārasaṃjñā*)is reached when even this hidden thirst is completely destroyed and the aspirant becomes conscious that he is the master and not a slave of sensuous phenomena. This is known as supreme dispassion (*paravairāgya*) characterized by a complete loss of interest in the objects of the world.

I.17 By practice and dispassion the fluctuations of awareness are arrested and thereafter the aspirant achieves the state of concentration (*samādhi*) which, as stated before, is of two kinds. The content-filled concentration is of four kinds according as it is accompanied by empirical awareness (*vitarka*), rational awareness (*vicāra*), bliss (*ānanda*) and self-awareness (*asmitā*).

In the empirical concentration the mind concentrates on the problem of creation and is fixed on the idea of God as different from creation. In this state it engages in the search for causes and proceeds from gross objects to subtle ones. In the rational concentration the ideas of gross or external objects leave the mind and only the subtle thought of the cogniser (self), cognition, and the cognized (God) remains. In the next state only bliss is experienced, and in the fourth state there remains only the consciousness of self-existence. In addition, all the four states of content-filled concentration are characterized by a triple consciousness of the cognizer, cognition, and the cognized, which becomes latent in the fourth state.

I.18 In the content-free concentration this triple consciousness is totally destroyed and as a result of practice and supreme dispassion pure consciousness characterized by perfect knowledge arises. This is also called "seedless" (*nirbīja*) "construction-free" *(nirvikalpa)* concentration and is the state of perfection attainable equally well by the methods of yoga, *vedānta*, and devotion (*bhakti*). This state produces two types of great men, biz., *brahmakoṭi* and *īśakoṭi*. Men of the former type totally dissociated themselves from the world. They appear to be intoxicated, insensible, and inactive. Men of the second type become spiritual leaders of society like the ancient *ṛṣis* and engage themselves in action with altruistic motives alone.

I.19 The progress, however, to this highest state of concentration is not easy and smooth. An obstacle which is likely to arrest progress appears when there is deficiency in the intensity of practice and dispassion. In such a case the aspirant, though he might have outgrown the ordinary man's identification of the self with the physical body, identifies his self with *mahat* or the other primary evolutes of *prakṛti* of having merged himself in the causal *prakṛti* itself falls into the error of taking the reflection of consciousness in his internal organ as the real self and thus complacently stops further effort. Ths obstacle is named "*bhavapratyaya*" as it causes regression to the ordinary worldly consciousness.

The aspirant can avoid the risk of getting thus stranded at a lower stage by the cultivation of faith, energy, memory, concentration and wisdom. Faith (*śraddhā*) is firm belief in and fondness for one's objective. Energy (*vīrya*) is intense enthusiasm for attaining the objective. Memory (*smṛti*) is remembering the joy which goes on increasing gradually as the aspirant advances towards the goal. Concentration (*samādhi*) (in a special sense here) is the joyfulness of mind when memory becomes steady. And wisdom (*prajñā*) is the light that appears in the mind in this joyful state.

The attainment of the goal becomes speedier when the eagerness (*saṃvega*) of the aspirant increases in intensity.

Obviously this motivation is an important additional factor and is especially helpful in getting over the obstacles. Motivation is primarily of three types according to its mild, medium and intense degrees, and each type has three sub-types, when the intensity of faith, etc. also is taken into consideration.

I.23-29 There are other means as well leading to content-free concentration and ultimately to liberation, and some of them are certainly easier than the eightfold yoga. Devotion to God is one of these. This consists in leaving everything to the will of God, surrendering all one's actions to Him and then, having turned one's back to the whole world, thinking all the time of God alone with a heart overflowing with His love. As a matter of fact, the root cause of bondage is egoity, which makes man believe in his own powers and gets him involved in this mesh of suffering. Devotion to God is a powerful means of getting rid of this egoity and loosening the bonds of karma.

God is a spiritual being like the other *puruṣas* or selves in kind but different in that while the ordinary empirical selves have assumed doership and enjoyership due to ignorance and thus have gotten entangled in this transmigratory world, He, being absolutely and eternally free from ignorance, is untouched by the taint of afflictions, actions, their fruits and traces. He has perfect knowledge and infinite power, and is eternally free from the bondage of nature to which empirical individuals are subject. He can be directly known through intuition by *yogins*.

God is omniscient. Knowledge in the case of empirical selves is sometimes less and sometimes more, since the mind, being subject to the limitations imposed by space and time and ignorance, has a variable degree of unsteadiness. God, on the other hand, being the master of *prakṛti*, is eternally free from all limitations and has infinite knowledge which cannot be excelled by anyone.

God is the original teacher, the teacher of even the most ancient teachers, because He is beginningless. All the great sages who have appeared on the earth to give enlightenment to mankind from time to time are buy special forms of divine manifestation (*vibhūti*).

God is expressed by *praṇava* or the mystic syllable *oṃ*. Whenever some action takes place it gives rise to vibrations which in turn produce a sound. The divine act of creation and maintenance of the world too must give rise to vibrations. Such vibrations produce the sound of *oṃ*. That is why *oṃ* has become the sacred name of God and it is as good an object of devotion as God Himself.

The aspirant following the method of devotion should repeat the mystic name of God and concentrate on its meaning. By this means his mind becomes calm and steady. Then the aspirant attains the knowledge of his inner nature and getting over all the obstacles of his path he succeeds in achieving content-free concentration and ultimately freedom from bondage.

The progress of the aspirant, however, is not smooth and uniform. It is likely to be impeded by a number of obstacles. There are nine primary obstacles which distract the mind, and five secondary ones which assist the primary ones or accompany them.

As has been already indicated, these obstacles can be checked by the repetition of the divine name, which is a theistic method. But one can also adopt a non-theistic method in the form of the practice of one-pointedness of the mind, which consists in turning it away from sensuous objects and making it flow inwards, i.e. stopping its inborn multiform extroverted movement and making it acquire a uniform introvertedness.

There are seven ways of attaining this uniform introvertedness of mind. First, the aspirant should cultivate the feeling of joy towards happy people, of compassion towards the miserable, of friendliness towards the virtuous and of indifference towards the vicious. This practice makes his mind calm and serene. Secondly, since mind and vital breath are identical in substance the control of breath becomes a reasonable means of acquiring steadiness of mind. Thirdly, the aspirant should draw the mind away from gross objects and fix it on one of the subtler elements. Fourthly, he may also concentrate his mind on the blissful point of light which is actually pure *sattva guṇa* of *prakṛti* and appears first occasionally in the course of practice but is constantly seen in advanced stages. Fifthly, the aspirant may concentrate on the minds of the great men who have already achieved the perfect state of desirelessness, or he may himself try to make his mind absolutely free from passion through the practice of detachment. Sixthly, fixing the mind on the dream state or on that of dreamless sleep may also lead to the desired result. And lastly, the aspirant may fix his mind on any object in which he feels interested provided it is free from associations of a sensual nature. All these alternative ways lead to the attainment of a uniform introverted state of mind which gives the aspirant the power to overcome the obstacles to yoga and to concentrate his mind on any subtle or gross object at will without any difficulty.

A superior result of the constant practice of the one-pointed introverted state of mind appears in the form of engrossment (*samāpatti*), which is a new name of the conscious concentration already discussed. When the fluctuations of awareness disappear completely the mind becomes perfectly steady and transparent like a crystal. In this state it acquires the capacity of getting transformed into or assuming the shape of whatever object is happens to contemplate. The attainment of this state is gradual and is completed in several stages.

The lowest stage is called "with discernment" (*savitarka*). In it the fluctuation of awareness of a content is mixed with its verbal symbol, the meaning of the symbol and its cognition. The next stage is called "without discernment" (*nirvitarka*) and in it the identification of the mind with the object is more complete as its verbal and cognitive associations and inferential elements are dropped by the mind. Both these stages are inferior, for the aspirant is not yet able to transcend nature. The object whether gross or subtle still belongs to the sphere of nature.

In still more advanced stages, called "with" or "without

rational awareness" (*savicāra, nirvicāra*), the object is spiritual. In the *savicāra* stage the aspirant is able to have a bare indirect experience of the self with the aid of subtle elements while he remains subject to space, time, and causality. But in the *nirvicāra* stage he is able to get rid of his relation with subtle elements and other natural conditions and has a direct experience of the self with an exclusive reliance on God. When the *nirvicāra* stage is reached the mind is purged of all impurities. It then becomes free from all miseries, and experiences a blissful state which resembles the spiritual bliss of the highest order (*brahmānanda*). This state is known as *adhyātmaprasāda*. As a result of the complete disappearance of *rajas* and *tamas* from the mind the intellect acquires the ability of knowing everything in its real character and there remains no likelihood of illusion. This sort of intellect is termed *ṛtambharā* (truth-bearing). Knowledge thus acquired is different from ordinary knowledge based on perception, authority and inference, since unlike the latter it is perfect and free fromspatial and temporal limitations and the inherent faults of the sense-organs. On the appearance of this truth-bearing insight dispositions of ordinary empirical life are completely destroyed and as a result the aspirant attains knowledge of his true nature. This occurs in the content-less concentration which is the culminating stage of yoga known as *nirbīja samādhi* as distinguished from the four stages of *savikalpa samādhi* known as *sabīja samādhi*. It is seedless (*nirbīja*) because in this state there is a total destruction of all the traces including even those of *nirvicāra samādhi* and thus the aspirant is liberated forever.

BOOK TWO

The main theme of the first Book was the nature of yoga. Now the author of the *sūtras* undertakes a discussion of the various means of attaining the goal.

II.9 Penance, study, and devotion to God are recommended as the means for a second-grade aspirant, i.e. a person not so well equipped mentally as the first-grade person or the wise and gifted; the second-grade aspirant has not yet got rid of his mental impurities though he has a keen desire for liberation. These three means are named *kriyāyoga* or the yoga of action (as distinguished from the means recommended in the first Book which lay emphasis on mental discipline rather than action).

Now penance (*tapas*) is the discipline of the body, mind, and speech which subdues their instinctive and impulsive demands and dissociates the aspirant from object of sensuous pleasure. It resut in increasing one's power to even supernormal degrees and making the mind absolutely pure.

Study (*svādhyāya*) includes reading scriptures and repeating the mystic syllable or the name of the Lord for the attainment of liberation. It raises the intellectual level of the aspirant.

By "devotion to God" (*īśvarapraṇidhāna*) is here meant what is called *gauṇi bhakti* or devotion through such rituals as hearing the name of God and stories promoting the love of God, reciting His name, etc. It includes the well-known nine types of acts described in the devotional texts and leads to supreme devotion (*parabhakti*) which loosens the roots of the afflictions.

But what are afflictions (*kleśa*)? They are the fluctuations of awareness obstructing or antagonistic to merit-giving fluctuations and are five in number. Among them ignorance is the chief one, rather the root cause of the remaining four, attachment, aversion, egoity and the will to live. And all these exist in four states, viz., dormant, attenuated, intercepted, and fully manifest. They are dormant when there is no external stimulus to arouse them and so they are not felt. They are attenuated when they lose strength due to the dominance of opposite fluctuations. Interceptedness is a temporary non-experience, e.g., an emotion, when some other fluctuation comes in the focus of consciousness. The fully manifest state appears when a fluctuations becomes fully operative.

Ignorance is false awareness showing an object in a form

contrary to its real nature. It is one of the two forms of the cosmic power (*mahāmāyā*) deluding the empirical self into believing that what is sinful is virtuous, what is not to be done is what ought to be done.

II.10-11 These afflictions bind the self to the ever-continuing cycle of births and deaths and so they are to be destroyed first by the aspirant. They have two forms, subtle and gross. It is easier to get rid of the gross afflictions. The subtle ones are not really fluctuations of awareness but their causes and so their destruction is effected by a different method, viz., dissolving the mind itself in which they reside in seed-form by meditation. The gross afflictions which are gross fluctuations disappear automatically when the mind is brought under control and made steady by the practice of meditation.

II.12-14 Afflictions serve as the basic motives for action. Activated by them the individual persons develop good and bad actions which give rise to merit and demerit. These latter are stored in the mind in the form of subconscious impressions (*vāsanā*) and remain there until they become mature for fruition in the form of enjoyment and suffering. The subconscious impressions of actions are of two types, viz., those which fructify in the present birth (*dṛṣṭajanmavedanīya*) and those which fructify in a future birth (*adṛṣṭajanmavedanīya*). The former are extra-powerful ones which cannot wait and so intercept current fruition and produce their own fruits immediately. This is different from the classifications of types of karma (accepted in other systems) into those of past births which are stored up and waiting for fruition in future births (*sañcita),* those of present birth which are being stored up (*kriyamāna*), and those of past births whose fruition has commenced in this birth (*prārabdha*).

As long as the roots of subconscious impressions in the form of afflictions are not destroyed they continue to produce birth, length of life and experiences as their threefold results. Subconscious impressions are like seeds which give rise to the tree of life. Birth is the appropriate species, kind or caste in which one is born. Length of life is the period from birth to death. And experience is bodily and sensory pleasure and pain.

(II.15) To the wise and discriminating person, however, all is pain and suffering. All pleasure is accompanied by pain as its consequence. The anticipation of its loss is painful. When the capacity for enjoyment is lost with advancing age, the very memory of youthful pleasures causes nostalgic pain. Pleasure gives rise to fear, anxiety, jealousy, hatred, etc. which are all painful. To the wise sensuous pleasure and pain both serve as a chain binding the self to the empirical world. Both are caused by ignorance and so are to be avoided equally by a prudent person. They give rise to an unending cycle of births and deaths. This transmigratory world is like a disease and its removal is to be planned in a scientific way.

II.16 It is the future pain that is to be avoided. There is no point in exerting to avoid the pain one has already experienced or is currently experiencing. But it is quite sensible to get prepared and devise means of avoiding the pain which is in store and waiting to be experienced. Incidentally, pain is of three kinds, viz., that which is self-caused (*ādhyātmika*), that which is caused by nature and supernatural agencies (*ādhidaivika*), and that which is caused by animals and other human beings (*ādhibhautika*).

II.17 But what is the origin of pain? It is certainly, as has already been said, the false identification, under the influence of beginningless ignorance, of the seer, i.e., the subject or conscious *puruṣa* in the form of *antaḥkaraṇa*. The self is ever pure, intelligent, and free by nature and so beyond pain which is a mere fluctuation of awareness. But due to this false identification it imagines the alien qualities of pain, etc. as its own. Here starts the whole trouble and if the self is to get free from this mesh it has to undo this identification.

II.18-19 The whole of this objective world is the product of the evolution of *prakṛti* which is non-intelligent and consists of the three *guṇas*. When these three are in a state of disequilibrium the process of creation starts, in which twenty-three *tattvas* appear at various stages of evolution as conceived in the Sāṃkhya system. The purpose at the root of this evolution is twofold, viz. experience (*bhoga*) and liberation (*apavarga*) of the selves who have somehow identified themselves with objective nature due to the influence of ignorance. Ignorance is *prakṛti* itself together with its twenty-three evolutes causing bondage to the *puruṣa.* It is knowledge (*vidyā*) when *prakṛti* returns to its original state of equilibrium in which it consists of pure *sattva* and liberates the *puruṣa*. This is what *prakṛti* exists for. It is a sort of unconscious teleology inherent in nature.

The total number of *tattvas* is twenty-four including *prakṛti* itself. They make their appearance in the course of evolution in which four stages are clearly marked. In the first stage the three *guṇas* of *prakṛti* are in perfect equilibrium and there is no evolution. That is the unmanifest stage (*aliṅga*). When the equilibrium is disturbed the evolutionary process starts and *mahat* makes its appearance. This is a barely manifest state (*liṅgamātra*) of *prakṛti*. Then a real differentiation of the primordial matter takes place and five subtle elements and *ahaṃkāra* are evolved. This is a slightly particularized state (*aviśeṣa*). In the last stage *prakṛti* is fully differentiated and particularized (*viśeṣa*) into the five gross elements, five organs of sense, five organs of action, and *manas*.

II.20-24 Now what is the nature of the seer (*puruṣa*)? It is pure consciousness. The latter is not its attribute but its very nature. As a matter of fact, it has no attributes at all. Its purity consists in its being free from all sorts of fluctuations and attributes. It is not even a seer. Seership is its phenomenal character. Just as a transparent crystal appears to be colored due to the proximity of a colored object, so the pure *puruṣa* appears to be a seer due to its intimate association with the objects of nature. It is the reflection of *puruṣa* in *buddhi* which creates the false notion of seership in *puruṣa* and this is the state of bondage. Freedom from this state is to be effected and the earlier it is, the better.

All this objective world is relative to the needs of *puruṣa*. It has a meaningful existence only in this context. The very purpose of *prakṛti* is to give *puruṣa* experience in the state of bondage and then when discriminative knowledge has arisen it withdraws itself from view. *Prakṛti* has no purpose of its own. After one *puruṣa* has achieved liberation *prakṛti* ceases to exist for him. But for other *puruṣas* who are still in bondage the phenomenal world continues to exist as usual. *Prakṛti* is infinite and beginningless and so are *puruṣas*, and there will be no time when no bound *puruṣa* remains. Binding the self by creating the relation of subject and object is a natural function of *prakṛti*. The stream of creation will ever continue to flow, since an infinite number of selves *(jīva)* or psycho-physical complexes will ever continue to be created by it as ignorance. And as knowledge giving freedom to the selves by removing the bonds of subject and object it is also an equally natural function of *prakṛti*. It is *mahāmāyā*, the divine cosmic mechanism creating bondage by *rajas* and *tamas* and effecting liberation by *sattva*.

II.25-28 *Hāna* consists in destroying the contact *(saṃyoga)* of *puruṣa* with the internal organ by removing ignorance. The moment we acquire perfect knowledge of the real nature of self and not-self the illusion that they are related is at once shattered and liberation is achieved. Thus discriminative knowledge is the means we are seeking. When this knowledge becomes firm and free from all traces or seeds of ignorance and there remain absolutely no chances of relapsing to the older stage, all suffering is gone forever.

Attainment of this sort of knowledge is not sudden but a gradual seven-stage process. And before the light of this knowledge appears the aspirant has to wash off his impurities by a vigorous pursuit of the path of yoga consisting of eight parts of steps.

II.29 The *aṣṭāṅga yoga* recommended here is a graduated system of moral, physical and psychological training in which perfection at each stage is to be achieved before the aspirant can pass on to the next higher stage. The eight well-known parts, steps, or stages of the whole course of ethico-psychological practices are divided into two broad parts. The first five steps constitute the external discipline (*bahiraṅga sādhanā*) which aims at achieving purity of mind, and the last three steps constitute the internal (*antaraṅga*) discipline which aims at achieving the one-pointed state of mind, this latter being the direct means to liberation.

II.30-32 The first two steps in the practice of yoga are *yama* which means restraint or abstinence from certain immoral types of conduct, and *niyama* or observance.

II.33-34 At these initial stages of moral training the aspirant should be on his guard against a very frequent source of trouble, viz., *vitarka*. *Vitarkas* are ideas of sinful acts such as violence, intemperance, etc. causing a setback to his progress. They are born of greed, anger, and false belief and have a varying degree of intensity. The aspirant is advised to fight them out by cultivating ideas of opposite virtues. Whenever he is disturbed by an undesirable idea he should think of good things and throw the idea out of his mind. He may also counteract them by remembering the instructions of his teacher and the infinite suffering in hell, etc. that he may have to undergo as a result.

II.35-43 A successful practice of the first two states of yoga is rewarded by the acquisition of certain supernormal powers. when the aspirant has perfected his practice of nonviolence even the natural enemies and killers like tigers forget their hostilities in his presence. This is made possible through the cosmic awareness. The individual awarenesses (*cittakośa*) join together to form a collective mind (*cidākāśa*) which is the mind of God. This collective mind serves as a medium for transmitting the superior energy of the aspirant's mind which subdues the inferior mind of the killer. The transmission of kindness, sympathy, love, etc. also is explained on the same principle.

By the perfection of truthfulness the aspirant acquires *vāksiddhi* and his words become infallible, i.e. whatever he utters turns out to be true. By the perfection of non-stealing even rare things become easily available to him. Perfection of sensual restraint leads to unusual physical and mental energy. When the practice of non-possession is perfected the aspirant acquires the ability of remembering all his past lives.

Perfection of observances also results in extraordinary acquisitions, e.g. purity and serenity of mind, one-pointedness, physical powers of making the body minute like an atom, mental powers of extrasensory perception, the vision of deities and so on.

II.45-48 In the third stage the aspirant has to practice a bodily posture or *āsana* which is a position in which the body is comfortable, the mind is steady, and the spirit is cheerful. As many as eighty-four postures have been described in Haṭhayoga texts and only four are recommended in Layayoga texts. The practice of a posture is brought to perfection when it becomes easy and natural to the aspirant, i.e. he has no feeling of fatigue and all his muscles are completely relaxed. On the attainment of this state the aspirant develops a wonderful capacity for endurance, his body becomes immune to the bad effects of heat and cold, his mind remains unperturbed under all extreme conditions and is able to get completely absorbed in the thoughts of the infinite.

II.49-53 The fourth state is that of breath-control (*prāṇāyāma*). One with an unsteady or restless mind is not qualified for the practice of this stage. A restless mind goes with a restless body . So only one who has perfected postures is fit for breath-control which consists of the three phases of inspiration (*pūraka*), expiration (*recaka*), and retention (*kumbhaka*). But the main thing is retention of breath. There is a fourth phase also in which the mind having attained complete stability is wholly devoid of the idea of internal or external objects. Breath-control should be practiced under the guidance of an expert. Perfection of breath-control results in the dwindling away of the veil of impurities covering the light of knowledge and then the aspirant acquires a free access to the internal world of the mind.

II.54-55 The fifth stage is withdrawal (*pratyāhāra*) of the senses from external objects. Its practice also involves a complex technique like breath-control and so requires the expert guidance of a competent teacher. The senses have a natural tendency to seek external objects. But the practice of withdrawal makes them turn inwards to the world of the mind, and when it is perfected the aspirant ceases to be a slave to the senses and becomes their master instead.

BOOK THREE

III.1 The sixth stage in yogic training is fixing (*dhāraṇā*), which consists in the practice of focusing the mind on a particular thing of the internal world, i.e. not on any actual thing but on an idea or image only. It is of two kinds, viz., gross or subtle according as the thing represented is a gross part of the body, e.g. navel, or is one of the five subtle elements. Again, fixing may be extra-organic (*bāhya*) or intra-organic (*abhyāntara*) according as the object of attention lies outside the body of the aspirant or is a part of it.

The seventh stage is meditation (*dhyāna*). It consists in first fixing the mind on an object and then keeping the consciousness steady for a long time. In this state the awareness assumes the shape of the object and remains as such continuously for a long time depending presumably on the strength and length of the practice the aspirant has already put in. Meditation is of four kind, *sthūla, jyotiḥ, bindu* or *brahma* according as the object is a gross image of one's desired deity, a flame, a point of light, or *saccidānanda.*

The eighth stage of yoga is just an advanced state of meditation which comes to be known as concentration (*samādhi*) when there remains the consciousness of the object alone without the consciousness of the meditative act. What is called "meditation" (*dhyāna*) involves the awareness of the cognizer, cognition, and object as separate entities. And the same is called "concentration" (*samādhi*) when the independent existence of the three is lost. There are three sub-stages here. The first is *sādhāraṇa samādhi* or common concentration in which there is no awareness of the cognitive act and the object becomes one with the cognizer himself. Then comes the second sub-stage called content-filled (*samprajñāta*) concentration in which the aspirant acquires the ability of knowing super-sensible objects despite the presence of the three factors. The third and last sub-stage is content-free (*asamprajñāta*) or construction-free (*nirvikalpaka*) concentration in which isolation from *prakṛti* is achieved.

III.4-6 The practice of fixation, meditation and concentration, all three together with regard to the same object, is technically named comprehensive reflection (*saṃyama*). It is the co-application of the three processes to the same object. Out of the three sub-stages of concentration it is the common one which is included under comprehensive reflection, because a sense of duality is implied by the attaiments (*siddha*) resulting from the practice of comprehensive reflection to be dealt with in the sequel, while in the third sub-stage the sense of duality completely vanishes. A successful completion of the practice of comprehensive reflection brings about the light of knowledge which is free from error and productive of perfections. By the application of comprehensive reflection higher planes or advanced levels of yoga are attained gradually.

III.7-8 Out of the eight stages of yoga the first five are the external means as they are not directly related to concentration and only the last three, called comprehensive reflection, are the internal means as they are directly related to conscious meditation. But to the seedless meditation even they are not internal, since that results in the supreme attainment in the form of liberation to which the attainments resulting from conscious concentration are obstructive rather than conducive.

III.9-10 What is an internal part of or a direct means to seedless meditation is called *nirodhapariṇāma* or the suppressive modification of mind. It is a state of awareness appearing when the usual extroverted stated called "emergent" (*vyutthāna*)appears, in which awareness moves from object to object, disappears and the introverted state called suppression born of the practice of one-pointedness appears. It is an intermediate state in which all the fluctuations have been suppressed but their seeds or traces have not yet been destroyed. When this happens the aspirant enjoys a unique spiritual state. He is liberated while having a body. The store of his subconscious karmic residues is burnt up by the fire of knowledge and the fresh accumulation of karma is stopped. In this state awareness becomes absolutely calm and serene. The highest spiritual knowledge is then born and its appearance destroys the elements of *rajas* and *tamas* and as a result the aspirant attains the state of highest bliss and absolute peacefulness.

III.11-12 As distinguished from this state the change of mind which is inferior in quality and accompanies the attainment of conscious meditation is called *samādhipariṇāma* or change of concentration. It comes when the usual multi-objective or many-pointed state of mind disappears and one-pointedness appears by the practice of comprehensive reflection. It results in seeded concentration and is the basic cause of the numerous divine powers attained in construction-filled meditation.

Just after this change of mind and preceding the actual attainment of divine powers there appears as the cause of the latter another change called *ekāgratāpariṇāma* or change into one-pointedness. When this change occurs the mind of the aspirant desirous of attaining a supernatural power becomes entirely free from multi-pointedness and hence calm like the surface of a ripple-less pond. This state is called *śāntapratyaya*. Simultaneously there also appears another state called *uditapratyaya* in which the mind assumes a pro-attitude towards the supernatural power expected by the aspirant to be produced by the force of his craving for it.

III.13-15 Not the mind alone but all the substances undergo modification which is of three kinds, viz. *dharmapariṇāma, lakṣaṇapariṇāma,* and *avasthāpariṇāma.* The first is modification through change of quality. For example, when earth is shaped into a pot it leaves the quality of lumpiness and takes on that of potness. The second is a modification through change of mark. It is of three kinds, viz. *bhūtalakṣana, vartamānalakṣaṇa,* and *anāgatalakṣaṇa* depending respectively on the pastness, presentness, and futureness of the change. *Avasthāpariṇāma* is modification through change of state and is seen in the newness of things and their becoming old.

Amidst all these changes, however, the substance always remains the same. Qualities alone change from time to time. One quality is past and gives place to the present one which also in its turn will be replaced by a future one. But despite this appearance and disappearance the substance continues as the same. First there is powder which is turned into a lump and then into a pot by the potter. But it is the same clay in all these different forms. And this diversity of change is quite compatible with the unity of the substance, because the changes appear one after the other in a sequence rather than simultaneously.

III.16 Comprehensive reflection on modification through change of quality gives the aspirant the power to know the past; reflection on modification through change of mark gives the power to know the present; and reflection on modification through change of state gives him the power of knowing the future. Thus he becomes omniscient and this power he can profitably use for knowing the obstacles to yoga beforehand and avoiding them.

III.17 Concentration on the differences of the sound produced by the different animals gives the power of knowing their inner feelings and emotions from their natural sounds and or knowing future events from their unnatural sounds.

III.18 Concentration on the subconscious deposits of good and bad actions done in previous births gives a "photographic" knowledge (*yathātathā parijñāna*) of previous births. Comprehensive reflection practiced successfully converts the mind into a photographic camera as it were.

III.19-20 Concentration on cognition gives knowledge of other persons' minds. This knowledge, however, is not comprehensive and fully detailed but vague and general. For a knowledge full of specific details of other minds further concentration on their specific contents is needed.

III.22 *Yogins* concentrate mainly on the karma which has started fruition and secondarily on that which is just being stored up for the ascertainment of length of life. Concentration on portents also gives a foreknowledge of death. Portents are *ādhyātmika, ādhidaivika* and *ādhibhautika*. The first kind involves some inner sense-deficiency. The second kind is due to supernatural agencies, e.g. appearance of ghosts, spirits of forefathers, etc. The third kind involves morbid physical changes, e.g. sudden change of a fat body into a very thin one. Portents occur when death is to come rather suddenly and very shortly.

III.23 Concentration on the four attitudes of friendliness, etc. which the aspirant was asked to cultivate under I.33, gives spiritual strength.

III.25 By concentration the *yogin* can fix at will the point of light named *jyotiṣmatī* referred to under I.36 on anything, e.g., the minute channels and nerve centers and the six mystic channels inside the body or things remotely distant, or hidden under water or ground. He can thus have a direct knowledge of such things.

III.26 Concentration on the sun generates knowledge of all the gross and subtle worlds. The gross world consists of our earth and the stars, planets, and satellites all around and the subtle worlds are the seven celestial worlds and seven nether worlds. The sun has three forms. The basic cause of *jyotiṣmati pravṛtti* is the spiritual sun. The presiding deity residing inside the solar disc is the sun god. And the gross visible sun is the physical sun.

III.33 In the course of practice the *yogin* sees a star-shaped light during meditation. This is named *prātibha*, which is a forerunner of the steadiness of intellect. By concentration on this the *yogin* attains universal knowledge. Through this power the sacred texts were known by the ancient Vedic seers to whom everything was visible like a fruit placed on the palm.

III.34 The fourth vital center is placed at the level of the heart. By concentration on this the *yogin* attains a full knowledge of his own awareness which is the receptacle of all the old and new karmic traces.

III.38 The power to enter other bodies at will is acquired by the *yogin* when the bonds linking his subtle body to his gross body are gradually loosened on the attainment of concentration. By concentration he acquires knowledge of the channels through which he enters a gross body and goes out of it. This power comes at the stage of content-free concentration (*vide* I.17).

III.45 Conquest of the elements is followed by the attainment of the eight well-known powers, e.g., *aṇiman, laghiman,* etc. In this list the name of *yatrakāmāvasayitva* enumerated by Vyāsa is missing and *gariman* not mentioned by Vyāsa is included. The former implies that whatever the *yogin* wills comes out to be true. The latter is the power of making the body as heavy as one wishes. The power named *prāpti* is explained differently as the ability to go at will from one world to another. According to Vyāsa it is the ability to touch even such distant objects as the moon with one's fingertip.

III.49-50 When the *yogin*'s mind becomes transparent he clearly perceives the distinction between the objective intellect and the subjective *puruṣa*. Then he becomes the master of all and the knower of everything. This is the supreme perfection (*parasiddhi*) and this state of the *yogin* is known as *viśokā* or the sorrowless state. All the other supernatural powers are inferior attainments. As a result of this *viśoka* state the *yogin* becomes absolutely detached and steering clear of the wayside temptations he attains the ultimate goal of absolute isolation (*kaivalya*).

There are three classes of aspirants: the best, the middle, and the mean. The mean one is he who uses his supernatural powers for worldly gains. The middle one is he who does not use his attainments for worldly prosperity and enjoyment. And the best is he who has no desire at all for such powers, and he alone is fit for liberation.

BOOK FOUR

IV.1 In the previous Book it was stated that supernatural powers are attained by a *yogin* in the course of his practice aiming at liberation at the stage of conscious concentration on various objects. But such powers can also be congenital or acquired by other means such as drugs, *mantras* and penance. Śukadeva and Kapila possessed such powers from their very birth. Drugs can make one ever youthful and blessed with a long life. Incantations give the power of traveling in space, killing the enemy, etc. Through penance Viśvāmitra attained Brahmanhood and Nandīkeśvara became a god while still a man. However, powers derived from means other than concentration are inferior in nature and concentration is found to be at least an auxiliary cause in each case. The attainment that seems spontaneous and congenital is always preceded by *sādhanā* in previous births and in other cases apparent causes, e.g., penance, etc. really make body and mind as fit as by concentration.

IV.2 A miraculous change such as took place in the case of Nandīkeśvara who became a god from a man in the same birth is possible by virtue of an unusual mental force which can effect appropriate atomic transformation of the body.

IV.3 What is the role of merit and demerit in such transformation of nature? They are not as a matter of fact directly causative. Demerit is a sort of barrier obstructing an appropriate change in nature while merit has the function of removing this obstruction or breaking the barrier only. Nature is self-causative, able to bring about changes by itself. Merit counteracts demerit and this helps nature in an indirect way only.

IV.4-5 Sometimes a *yogin* wishes to exhaust his karma by experiencing the fruits of actions simultaneously. For this purpose he by the power of his yoga converts his accumulated (*saṃcita*) karma into *prārabdha* and assumes numerous bodies in a single birth for which he creates equally numerous minds by dividing his share of *ahaṃkāra* just as numerous sparks are produced out of a single spark of fire. And the bodies and minds created thus by the *yogin* through his supernatural power do not act independently but are controlled by the *yogin*'s own mind.

IV.6-7 A *yogin* not interested in the inferior powers derived from concentration attains the state of higher concentration which should be considered as the supreme attainment. In this state his mind becomes free from all stains and transcends merit and demerit, pleasure and pain, action and inaction. This is *jīvanmukti* or the attainment of liberation while in an embodied state. In this state the inferior powers are sometimes manifested spontaneously by the will of God.

The actions of such a *yogin* are also of a unique type. They are neither white nor black while the actions of ordinary human beings are white, black, or of a mixed type. The *yogin* being free from egoity, there is no accumulation of the traces of actions done by him. A desire for the well-being of all is the only motive behind his actions which are like burnt seeds devoid of the power of producing sprouts. Because of an absence of personal motives they are unable to bind him and so are non-white and non-black.

IV.8 Actions are ordinarily of three kinds, viz., natural (*sahaja*), giving rise to plant life, animal kingdoms, and the whole creation, divine (*aiṣa*), and those (*jaiva*) done by empirical selves. The *jaiva* ones are further divisible into *saṃcita, kriyamāna* and *prārabdha* ('already discussed) and each one of these is again subdivided into white, black and mixed. All these actions produce traces. The traces thus produced give rise to cravings which again produce traces. This cycle of actions producing traces and traces producing actions goes on forever like seeds producing sprouts and sprouts again producing seeds, and thus the empirical selves ever remain bound to this transmigratory world unless they make special efforts to get out of this endless course and attain liberation.

IV.9 Actions done leave permanent traces which are accumulated and remain waiting indefinitely for an appropriate time to manifest their fruits. Traces differ in strength. The more powerful ones have early fruitions and the weaker ones have delayed fruition.

IV.10-12 The empirical selves are tossed about by the waves produced in this ocean of karma by experienced actions, their unconscious deposits, and instinctive cravings giving rise to one another from beginningless time. This process is beginningless. The universality of the will to live and never to die cannot be explained without this assumption. The instinctive wish for eternal life and one's own good is seen even in small ants, new-born babies, and an old man on his deathbed. This is a natural phenomenon not depending on learning through experience. It has, therefore, no first cause and so is beginningless.

However, it is not endless for that reason, as it can be terminated by the practice of yoga and attainment of concentration. A thing may be beginningless, but its continued existence depends on a constant source of nourishment. If the supply is cut it will die of starvation. So is the case with subconscious impressions. Their existence depends on such factors as experience, attachment, body, mind and objects, the most basic factor being ignorance. By self-knowledge ignorance is destroyed and everything else including subconscious impressions coming in its train. A *vāsanā* is a fluctuation of awareness and when by the practice of concentration such modification is stopped the mind ceases to undergo qualitative changes and hence temporal changes also. In this state the flow of time stops and the mind becomes as good as nonexistent.

IV.13-14 Now what is a property (*dharma*)? It is that on whose cessation a thing ceases to exist, since it is only through its qualities that the existence of a substance is known. Conversely, that which destroys the existence of a thing is a non-property (*adharma*). When a quality remains in a seed-state it is said to be latent and when it assumes a plant-state it is manifest. And qualities are modifications of *sattva, rajas* and *tamas* which acting in a cooperative manner give unity to a thing in spite of their multiplicity, because when they combine one of them becomes the principal and the rest become its subordinates.

IV.21 The assumption of self cannot be replaced by the theory of one mind cognized by another mind, because in that case one will have to assume an infinite number of minds unnecessarily and there will result a confusion of memory, which is repugnant to our logical sense.

IV.22 How, then, is knowing possible? *Puruṣa* is of the nature of consciousness and absolutely unchangeable. It is reflected in awareness to which its light of consciousness is thus transferred. And when awareness is modified into the forms of objects by contact with them the sham-consciousness of mind derived from the reflection of *puruṣa* converts the unconscious mental modes into knowledge.

IV.23 Mind becomes the revealer of all including subject, object, and cognition by virtue of its connection with the subject on the one hand and the objects on the other. Like a crystal it catches the reflection of whatever is placed in its proximity. This is because of its peculiar constitution in which the element of *sattva* predominates. When by the practice of yoga mind is made pure after a complete elimination of the *rajas* and *tamas* elements it acquires the capacity of even revealing God.

IV.24 Mind has no ends of its own. Whatever it does is for the sake of *puruṣa* who is the master. Mind is a mere servant, a mere instrument for accomplishing the ends of its master, the self. It is an unconscious product of *prakṛti* and like a bed, etc. it serves with the help of other unconscious things the purpose of giving experience and enjoyment to the self.

IV.25-26 The *yogins* who are already blessed with the

supreme attainment see the world differently. They know the distinctness of *prakṛti* and *puruṣa* and have a perfect knowledge of truth. As a result they know the answers to the usual philosophical questions about the self and thus they are no longer curious. They can very well be recognized by their complete detachment and keen interest in religious and spiritual activities. Their minds turn away from the objective world and towards the supreme goal of *kaivalya*.

IV.34 The ultimate goal which is consciously and deliberately pursued by the aspirant through a planned and systematic course is *kaivalya* or absolute independence of the self. It is the fully mature state of superconscious concentration which is the culminating point of yogic *sādhanā*. It can be described in two ways. Objectively, it is the return of the *guṇas* to the original state of equilibrium of *prakṛti* by a process of involution or gradual merger of the later stages of development into the earlier ones after they have fulfilled the transcendental purpose for which the whole creation takes place. And subjectively, it is realization by the self of its essential nature or its remaining in its essential form of seership. It is a state of freedom from bondage to the *guṇas* and freedom from ignorance which causes the self to separate it from the non-dual, universal reality called *brahman* and limit it within one small individualized center. Independence is the braking of the boundaries of this center and the consequent loss of the sense of individuality. This is what has been variously described by other systems as a nondual state (*advaitabhāva*), absolute cessation of pain, *brahman*-consciousness, becoming one with or absorption in the supreme spirit (*brahmasadbhāva*).

THE HAṬHA YOGA SYSTEM AND OTHER SATELLITE TRADITIONS OF YOGA

We come now to what we have identified as "Haṭha Yoga and Other Satellite Traditions of Yoga". What is most striking about the texts from this point on to the end of the Volume is the paucity of discussion of any of the important philosophical aspects of Pātañjala Yoga. To be sure, Pātañjala Yoga is referred to by name, usually but not always under the designation "Rāja Yoga". For the most part, however, as indicated in the Introduction, this is little more than lip service whose purpose appears to be largely a matter of seeking cultural legitimacy. Clearly the texts of Haṭha Yoga exhibit little if any interest in philosophical issues. What little philosophy there is amounts to, first, what can be characterized as a simplified, monistic Vedānta as found, for example, in many of the so-called "Yoga Upaniṣads". Second, there is an equally simplified version of Śaiva and/or Śākta theology that focuses on bringing about the union of Śākti (*kuṇḍalinīśakti, kula*) and Śiva (*akula*) in an erotic-cum-metaphysical embrace that appears to analogize the experience of orgasm with the experience of spiritual liberation.* Moreover, the ritual manipulations also are designed to bring about the coalescence of the awareness of the practitioner's body (microcosm) with the universe (*bhuvana*) as a whole (macrocosm).

The interest is focused, in other words, on the ritualistic manipulation of the body's postures, the body's fluids and the body's breathing mechanisms for the sake of attaining enhanced physical strength, greater mental clarity and altered states of awareness of various kinds. Sectarian considerations play an increasingly important role, largely Śaiva and Śākta (but also

---

*I prefer the term "analogue" to the term "homologue" since the relation is one of similarity, hence, analogous, without a common origin, in contrast to the "homologue" which suggests a common origin.

Vaiṣṇava, Bauddha and Jaina as well). Also, the massive material of the Tantra comes into play. This material has yet to be properly researched. There appears to be more than a little foreign influence, as P. C. Bagchi has noted. Also, much additional work in vernacular, non-Sanskritic sources has to be done before one can properly understand the significance of the Tantra.

29.MATSYENDRANĀTHA, *Kaulajñānanirṇaya*

Summary by Gerald James Larson

As indicated in the Introduction, Matsyendranātha is one of the important figures in regard to the origins of Haṭha Yoga, the Nātha sect, and the Yoginī Kaula tradition of Tantra. He is one of the eighty-four *mahāsiddhas* ("great accomplished ones") and was a teacher of Gorakṣanātha, the founder of the Kānphaṭa tradition of Haṭha Yoga. There are many legends and myths about the life of Matsyendranātha, and his precise date and place of origin remain obscure. Some have claimed that he is only a mythical figure, but in more recent studies it appears that he was an historical figure.

According to P. C. Bagchi, Matsyendranātha most likely lived in the early part of the tenth century (900-950) in the region of Bengal and Assam. He is said to be the author of one of the earliest texts on Haṭha Yoga, the *Kaulajñānanirṇaya* ("Discussion of the Knowledge Pertaining to the Kaula Tradition"). The text has been edited by P. C. Bagchi and translated by Michael Magee.[167] This is the ET for our summary. Bagchi has also written an extensive introduction to the text, describing the many legends about Matsyendranātha and providing a useful abstract of the text.[168]

The text is replete with elaborate eroticized ritual prescriptions and performances. The precise meanings of these are probably only to be known to initiates. David Gordon White

(White 2003) provides some interesting speculations about the significance of some of this symbolism.

The text makes no reference to Pātañjala Yoga and represents primarily a tradition of Haṭha Yoga and early Tantra. The text contains twenty-four "*paṭalas*" or sections in the form of a verse-dialogue between Bhairava (Śiva) and Devī. The summary below is divided into those twenty-four sections.

1 (ET1) The text of the first section is missing, but there are two verses remaining from it suggesting that the section had to do with a description about creation.

2 (ET2-3) Devī inquires about the process of destruction or dissolution of the world. Bhairava responds with a description of dissolution that appears to refer to the world (macrocosm) but also, and perhaps primarily, to processes of dissolution in the *yogin*'s body and to the dissolution of Śakti into Śiva.

3 (ET4-8) Devī inquires about the characteristics of the Kula (that is, *śakti* and by implication *kuṇḍalinīśakti*), the self and awareness. Bhairava responds with an elaborate summary regarding vital centers, incantations, channels, and the eternally erect *vajra liṅga*.

4 (ET9-12) Devī inquires about the results that occur from intense practice. Bhairava again responds with elaborate ritual references to Śakti, *nādabindu*, channels, incantations and the supreme *liṅga*.

5 (ET13-18) Devī asks Bhairava to speak freely about the conquering of death. Bhairava responds by describing the use of alchemy (*rasāyana*), various incantations and meditation on the moon and some eleven vital centers in the body.

6 (ET19-23) Devī asks about the characteristics of the self and of the results and greatness of ascetic exercise (*tapas*). Bhairava responds by describing various ritual procedures involving bodily fluids (*rasa* and *amṛta*).

7 (ET24-29) Devī asks about the knowledge of the three *tattvas* and the knowledge relating to old age and decay, and the destroyer of fever and death. Various ritual performances

are described, and it is said that only a Kaulika may do these things. The text comments (28), "Without knowing (Kaula) Śāstra, (Kaula) *guru*, (Kaula) incantations and (Kaula) Śiva and unless one is a Nātha of the Kaula Āgama, one is a beast (*paśu*)".

8 (ET30-39) Devī asks about the Kula Siddha and the type and order of *sādhana*. Bhairava responds with long lists of incantations and seed-syllables for ritual performance.

9 (ET40-43) Bhairava describes the various *yoginīs* and *siddhas* of the Kaulācāra.

10 (ET44-49) Bhairava describes the various vital centers in the body

11 (ET50-56) Devī inquires about non-duality and food. Bhairava describes various rituals involving the use of wine, flesh and sexual intercourse.

12 (ET57-59) Devī asks about the "simple way of acting as a Kaula, and of the nature of vessels". Bhairava describes worship of the *guru*.

13 (ET61-63) Bhairava describes knowledge giving liberation in terms of ritually projecting seed-syllables on different parts of the body.

14 (ET63-79) In one of the longest sections in the text, Devī asks about becoming free from time, free from the vital centers, the nature of the extraordinary capacities, the nature of the body and leaving the body. Bhairava describes vital centers, incantations, bodily exercises, the Kaulika path, the various centers in the body, the secret place in the skull, the various *yoginīs*, and the creation of the supreme body.

15 (ET80-84) Devī asks about the results of birth and the method of producing divinity. Bhairava describes rituals related to the vital centers.

16 (ET83-94) In another of the long sections in the text Devī asks Bhairava to speak to her about the three sacred lands and the mountain temples. Bhairava describes the basic myth by means of which he acquired the sacred knowledge. Verse 37 comments, "Though being a Brāhmiṇ...I acted as a fisherman.

As Brahma rescued the knowledge from the stomach of a fish by killing it, he is known as *matsyaghna*. Because the Lord of the Brāhmaṇas acted like a fisherman, he became *kaivarta* (fisherman)."

17 (ET95-101) Devī inquires about the characteristics of the self. Bhairava speaks about the regions of the body, the coming together of Śiva and Śakti and various ritual performances involving incantations.

18 (ET101-103) Devī asks about the Kula island of *siddhas*, the *kāma* of the Kaula *siddhas* and the significance of the "anointing" (*abhiṣeka*).

19 (ET106) Devī asks about the placing of the lotuses in the body of the *siddhas*.

20 (ET107-110) Bhairava describes liberation in this world through the interaction of the *vīra* and his *śakti*--Śiva and Śakti, and male and female in sexual interaction.

21 (ET111-112) Devī inquires as to the various schools of the Kula, and Bhairava provides a list.

22 (ET113-114) Devī asks about the *kaulāmṛta*, the nectar of the Kaula. Bhairava describes the hidden *liṅga* and the worship of the *guru*.

23 (ET115-117) Devī asks how the Kaula *yoginīs* move about the earth.

24 (ET118-120) Devī asks Bhairava to speak of *siddhapūjā* in the body one last time.

30.GORAKṢANĀTHA, *Siddhasiddhāntapaddhati*

Summary by Dolgobinda Shastri

Siddhasiddhāntapaddhati is regarded as the most authoritative scripture on the philosophy of the Nātha Yoga cult of India. All the schools of this cult follow this scripture as the guideline of their *sādhanā* including practice and theory.

Gorakṣanātha has used in this book hundreds of technical

terms which are largely unknown to the general reader. Only a few of the most essential terms will be summarized here. Among such terms used, *samarasa* is of special importance and its connotation aims at the highest ideal goal of the *siddha yogins* of the Nātha cult. The highest goal of all other schools of Indian philosophy, including the Yoga of Patañjali, is liberation (*mokṣa, nirvāṇa, samādhi*). *Samarasakaraṇa* is a superior stage to *samādhi*, according to this tradition. *Mokṣa* or *nirvāṇa* is a negative approach. According to Gorakṣanātha, *samarasa* is a state of divine enjoyment of the individual soul after union with the supreme self. The *yogin* sees and enjoys himself in all and all in himself along with the supreme self in himself and himself with the supreme self.

Mallik 1954, the first printed edition of this work, contains a long introduction by the editor, Dr. Kalyani Mallik.

Gorakṣanātha and his purported *guru* Matsyendranātha, the two stalwarts of the Nātha Yoga cult, are famous throughout India and Nepal. For centuries both of them have been worshipped as the incarnations of Lord Śiva and Viṣṇu respectively. Gorakṣanātha is regarded as the Lord of the State (*rāṣṭradevatā*) of Nepal. The Nepalis are called "*Gorkhās*", i.e. protected by Gorakṣa or Gorakha. The coins and currency notes of Nepal bear the name of Gorakṣanātha.

More than fifteen books are ascribed to Gorakṣanātha of which *Siddhasiddhāntapaddhati* is probably the most important for understanding Haṭha Yoga. Gorakṣanātha is often said to be the founder of Haṭha Yoga, but probably there were Haṭha Yoga traditions that are considerably older than both Gorakṣanātha and Matsyendranātha.

Regarding the date of Gorakṣanātha scholars differ considerably. Since P. C. Bagchi has placed Matsyendranātha in the first half of the ten century, it is reasonable to place his purported student, Gorakṣanātha, in the later tenth century, or possibly in the first part of the eleventh century. This is somewhat problematic, since the Nātha cult with which Gorakṣanātha is associated did not become prevalent until a bit later, that is, in the twelfth or thirteenth century. This suggests that there may have been intervening teachers between Matsyendranātha and Gorakṣanātha or that the linkage between Matsyendranātha and Gorakṣanātha is only a later notion in the tradition. In any case, the only reasonable conclusion is to allow a wide variance with respect to Gorakṣanātha's date, ranging from the late tenth or early eleventh century to the thirteenth century. Regarding his place of origin, a similar reservation must be maintained. Gorakṣanātha is associated with Assam, Bengal and Orissa but also with the Punjab region and Kashmir as well.

The main theme discussed in the *Siddhasiddhāntapaddhati* is the truth or theory (*tattva*) of the coalescence of the individual body (*piṇḍa*, microcosm) and the cosmos (*brahmāṇḍa*, macrocosm). The book contains six chapters or "instructions" (*upadeśa*).

CHAPTER ONE

I.1 The author, Gorakṣanātha, bows to the primordial Lord (Ādinātha––that is, Śiva)) who is united with his supreme power (*śaktiyuta*) and who is the teacher of the universe.

I.2-14 Before beginning to discuss the theory of the evolution of bodies, it is admitted by the author that fundamentally there is really no origination of the cosmic order. He explains the origin, etc. as conceived by the School of the Enlightened Yogis or seers (*sat sampradāyataḥ*) for the sake of satisfying the natural curiosity of people in general. From the viewpoint of the highest concentration there is neither origination nor destruction. The Absolute Reality unveils itself into our consciousness in its super-sensuous, supramental, super-intellectual, transcendental state in which the subject-object relation vanishes and consciousness realizes itself as perfect identified with the Absolute Reality. In this state, time and space and all existence in time and space are merged in perfect unity and shines as Ultimate Reality.

On the other hand, we experience the phenomenal world

order in our cognition, and this experience cannot be denied. Its origin must be traced to the Absolute Reality. Therefore Gorakṣanātha makes an attempt in this book to link together the transcendental experience of an enlightened *yogin (siddha)* and the intellectual demand of a common man. The purpose is to refine and elevate the consciousness of truth-seekers (*sādhaka*) of all orders and to discipline their thought-process in the proper direction.

According to Gorakṣanātha the Supreme Reality is termed "nameless" (*anāma*) before any sort of creation whether spiritual or material world-order. His divine will evolves as his supreme energy (*nijāśakti*) for creation. This energy manifests itself with its five evolutes as *nija, parā, aparā, sūkṣma*, and *kuṇḍalinī* (serpent power). These five energy-aspects have five qualities, altogether making twenty-five, the sum total of which is terms *parapiṇḍa* or supreme organism.

I.15-35 The supreme organism is expressed in five primordial causal attributes termed *aparampara* (fully unmanifest chief constituent factor), *paramapada* (subtlest unfolded spirit), *śūnya* (void but rich with infinite potentialities), *nirāñjana* (the Absolute Spirit experiencing Himself as pure) and *paramātman* (universal self). After the manifestation of the above five attributes, the *parapiṇḍa* is next designated *anādyapiṇḍa*.

The next manifestation is called *ādyapiṇḍa* when the above five attributes multiply each by being expressed in five qualities and thus making twenty-five in all.

From the *ādyapiṇḍa* comes the *mahāsākārapiṇḍa* or the five great formal elements, i.e. the great *ākāśa*, the great air, the great fire, the great water, and the great earth, each one evolving from the previous one. Again each of these five great elements possesses five attributes making twenty-five in all.

I.36-42 The same Śiva as *mahāsākārapiṇḍa* is manifested in eight divine personalities in gradual order: Śiva-Bhairava, Śrīkaṇṭha, Sadāśiva, Īśvara, Rudra, Viṣṇu, Brahmā. From Brahmā evolves the material body which is termed *prakṛtipiṇḍa*, which inherits five qualities of each of the five great elements, making twenty-five in all.

I.43-66 The material body (*prakṛti-* or *bhūta-piṇḍa*) constitutes a mental body with five attributes (*antaḥkaraṇa pañcaka*) such as mind, intellect, ego, awareness and pure consciousness, each of which possesses five qualities.

The next manifestation of the mental body is termed *kulapañcaka*, In the present context, *kula* is explained as the sum total of five qualities influencing the psycho-phyiscal phenomena of a person. These are *sattva, rajas, tamas, kāla* and *jīva*, each of which again have five attributes. *Sattva* manifests as kindness (*dayā*), righteousness (*dharma*), pious deeds (*kriyā*), devotion (*bhakti*) and faith (*śraddhā*). *Rajas* manifests in charity (*dāna*), enjoyment (*bhoga*), love for luxury (*śṛṅgāra*), appropriation of property (*vastu grahaṇa*) and acquisition for selfish desire (*svārthasaṃgraha*). *Tamas* manifests in controversy (*vivāda*), quarrelsomeness (*kalaha*), melancholia (*śoka*), killing (*vadha*) and deception (*vañcana*). *Kāla* manifests as calculation (*kālana*), creative aptitude (*kalpanā*), confusion (*bhrānti*), temporary insanity (*pramāda*) and accidental misfortune (*anartha*). *Jīva* manifests as waking state, dream state, deep sleep, perfect concentration on the self (*turīya*), and concentration on the state of absolute union of the individual self with the Supreme Self (*turīyātīta*).

The next topic dealt with is *vyaktipāñcaka* or five modes of self-expression. "*Vyakti*" here means expression. It is classified as desire (*icchā*), action (*kriyā*), pretension (*māyā*), temperament (*prakṛti*) and speech (*vāc*). Each of these five are again expressed on five forms of which speech needs enumeration. According to Gorakṣanātha, speech has five states: *parā, paśyantī, madhyamā, vaikharī,* and *mātṛkā*.

The first expression of speech is *parāvāk*, which is called *śabdabrahman* or the ultimate reality in the form of sound. The Vedic and Upaniṣadic name of *parāvāk* is *praṇava* or *oṃ*, which is also accepted by Gorakṣaṇātha.

The second stage is *paśyantī*. It is an inner perception. In the third state (*madhyamā*) *vāc* comes down as a vibration in the physiological system. *Madhyamā vāc* stands midway between the ideal form and articulate form of speech. In the stage of *vaikharī, vāc* is expressed through vocal organs. In the last state it is called *mātṛkā* or ultimate phonetic constituents of alphabets, that is, words, sentences and so forth.

Then come five perceptible organs (*pratyakṣakaraṇa-pañcaka*): activity (*karman*), sexual instinct (*kāma*), physical effects of the moon (*candra*), sun (*sūrya*) and fire (*agni*). Each of the first two are again manifested in five forms. *Candra, sūrya* and *agni* work as agents for digesting food, preserving health, and developing the physical form.

Gorakṣaṇāṭha describes *candra* as having seventeen, *sūrya* as having thirteen, and *agni* as having eleven attributes (*kalā*), which are actually diverse kinds of forces.

I.67-73 Among the ten principal channels in a body, *suṣumnā* or *brahmanāḍī* starts from the spot between the navel and the generating organ (*mūlādhāra*), passes through the spinal column, and meets the cerebrum or brain (*sahasrāra cakra*). *Suṣumnā* is of vital importance to all the aspirants of yogic culture. The *yogin* makes the *kuṇḍalinī* pass through the *suṣumnā*, which finally attains *sahasrāra cakra* (the brain, "a wheel of a thousand spokes").

The next two important channels are *iḍā* and *piṅgalā* or, in other words, *candra nāḍī* and *sūrya nāḍī* running through the left and right nostrils respectively. *Sarasvatī nāḍī* connects the mouth or speech organ. *Gandhārī* and *hastijihvā* are two channels connecting the two ears. *Kuhū* is connected with the anus for excreting refuse materials from the body. *Śaṃāhinī* is connected with the generating organ.

The next topic taken up by Gorakṣanātha is the location of the main airs (*vāyu saṃsthāna*). The airs are ten in number: *prāṇa, apāna, samāna, udāna, vyāna, nāga, kūrma, kṛkara* or *kṛkala, devadatta* and *dhanañjaya*. The first five are most important so far as the yogic practice of breath-control is concerned.

A brief account is given of the gradual day-to-day growth of the human body in the mother's womb from the first day of its conception until its birth in the ninth month. The root causes for various types of children are discussed--male, female, eunuch, twin, deformed, blind, dwarf, etc.–and the amount of flesh, blood, numbers of bones, etc. in the human body.

CHAPTER TWO

II.1-9 In this second *upadeśa* a still deeper reflection (*vicāra*) on the inner structure of the human body as perceived by the enlightened *yogin* is discussed.

The inner body contains nine vital centers, sixteen containers (*ādhāra*), three objects of concentration (*lakṣya*), and five voids or skies (*vyoman*). A *yogin* must be acquainted with the above constituents without which he is a *yogin* in name only, not real.

Nine vital centers: The serpent power (*kuṇḍalinī*) starts from the generating organ through the spinal cord and reaches the brain (*sahasrāra*) passing some vital centers conceived as in the central channel (*suṣumnānāḍī* or *brahmamārga*), i.e. the spinal cord. These vital centers represent particular planes of spiritual experience in the course of yogic practice or *sādhanā*. Spiritual progress is achieved after piercing or passing the nine vital centers one after the other until the *yogin* attains *samādhi* or the state of perfect union of the individual self with the supreme self.

The first vital center is *brahmacakra* in *mūlādhāra* or *kāmarūpa pīṭha*. This spot is conceived as being between the anus and the generating organ. This is the starting point of the serpent power, *kuṇḍalinī*, which is ordinarily asleep. The *yogin* arouses this power and makes her ascend upward passing through the vital centers until it reaches the brain, where it is united with Śiva.

The next is *svādhiṣṭhāna cakra* which is located at a center close to the generating organ. This station is also named *uḍḍīyāna pīṭha*. Here the *yogin* worships a very beautiful bright-red-colored Śiva in meditation.

The third is *nābhi cakra* located at the navel. The fourth is the heart (*hṛdaya) cakra* (or *anāhata cakra)*. The fifth is *kaṇṭha* or *viśuddha cakra* located near the throat. *Tālu cakra* is located at the root of the palate. The *yogin* tastes nectar (*amṛta*) which flows from the brain. The seventh is *bhrū cakra*, located at a nerve center in between the two eyebrows. The *yogin* perceives here a bright burning lamp. His vision attains perfection. Whatever he speaks turns out to be true.

The eighth is *nirvāṇa cakra* and this spot is called *jālandhra pīṭha. Jāla* means net. The individual self is caught by this network of phenomenal suffering of birth and death. When the spiritual aspirant reaches this stage, he perceives the supreme net-holder and attains liberation. The last is the *sahasrāra cakra* or *pūrṇagiri pīṭha*, i.e. the seat of the highest mountain of eternal absolute experience.

II.10-25 Sixteen *ādhāras* are discussed here. "*Ādhāra*" means that which contains or holds. These are the principal seats of vital psychic functions utilized by the *yogin* for spiritual progress. These sixteen spots cover the entire human body beginning from the toe to the utmost portion of the head.

II.26-38 Three kinds of *lakṣyas* or objects of concentration during meditation are discussed here. A *yogin* must practice the habit of concentration on a particular object in order to attain concentration easily and speedily. The three kinds are termed "inner" (*antar*), "outer" (*bahir*) and "in between" (*madhyama*).

"Inner concentration" (*antarlakṣya*) means that one should choose for concentration any of the objects within one's own body. Gorakṣanātha advises the *yogin* to concentrate upon the *kuṇḍalinī* as *mūlādhāra*, or a point on the forehead at the front part of the brain. One may also concentrate on the hind part of the brain which is called *bhramaraguhā*. This is the central store of the vital fluid (*bindu*). During sexual excitement this fluid is dislodged and flows downwards. By concentration on *bhramaraguhā* a *yogin* can attain control over the sexual instinct and can draw the vital fluid upwards. Preservation of vital energy is essential for a *yogin*. Another point of concentration is the *dhum dhum* sound heard within the brain while closing firmly both ones' ears by the forefingers. While doing this, no external sound distracts one's attention. This particular *dhum dhum* sound gradually enables the *yogin* to hear "*oṃ*" or *praṇava.*

"Outer concentration" (*bahirlakṣya*). The trainee may concentrate on any object of white, red, yellow, or blue color, or a flame according to his choice while in meditation.

The next topic is the five *vyomans* or parts of the sky. The sky or *vyoman* is one. The five *vyomans* are five different names for the same sky in different ethereal layers. They are *ākāśa, parākāśa, mahākāśa, tattvākāśa* and *śūnyākāśa*. The *vyoman* is conceived as the subtle form of the united Śiva and Śakti and the *yogin* should meditate on the theory of *vyomans* in order to attain pure and universal consciousness.

The last subject of discussion is the eight states of yoga (*aṣṭāṅgayoga*). Simple definitions of all the eight states have been given here with slight variations from those in the *Yogasūtra* of Patañjali.

CHAPTER THREE

The third chapter reveals the inner perception of the individual body. The individual body contains the universal body, i.e. everything in the cosmos.

III.1-5 The word "*piṇḍasaṃvitti*" has another meaning. It also means "a *yogin* who experiences the whole cosmic system in the individual body is the true realiser (*saṃvitti*) of the body (*piṇḍa*)". A *yogin* is designated as "*piṇḍasaṃvitti*" when he sees the whole universe within himself.

Seven lower worlds (*saptapātāla*). *Kūrma* or the divine tortoise-incarnate is perceived in the yogic conception at the bottom and he is the supported of the cosmic body. *Pāṭāla, talātala, mahātala, rasātala, sutala, vitala* and *atala* are the seven lower worlds constituting the lower parts of the individual body from the toes to the thighs. Anger in the body is perceived as *kālāgni* Rudra.

The three worlds, namely *bhu, bhuva,* and *sva,* are located in the anus (*guhyasthāna*), generating organ (*liṅgasthāna*), and the navel (*nābhisthāna*).

The four higher worlds, namely *mahā, jana, tapas,* and *satya*, are perceived in the higher and deeper regions of the spinal cord.

Then the locations of twenty-one regions with a deity in each of them are described to be in the upper portion of the individual body. The various deities are listed.

III.6-12 The four castes (*varṇa*) are perceived to be located in the nature of the individual, i.e. Brāhmaṇa in righteous conduct (*sadācāra*), Kṣatriya in valor and courage (*śaurya*), Vaiśya in business (*vyavasāya*) and Śudra in service (*sevā*). A *yogin* experiences all men and women of all races and castes within himself. Therefore he has no hatred for anybody. He has love for every being.

The location of seven islands (*sapta dvīpa*), seven oceans (*sapta samudra*) are also perceived in this body. The solid parts like bones, flesh, etc. are the sites of seven islands and liquid fluids like urine, blood, semen, etc. are said to be seven oceans. The nine regions such as *Bhārata khaṇḍa, Kaśmīra khaṇḍa*, etc. are experienced in this individual body. The nine channels are the nine great rivers such as Gaṅgā, Yamunā, Sarasvatī, etc. The other small rivers and streams on the earth are the seventy-two thousand small channels.

III.13-14 Twenty-seven stars (*nakṣatra*), twelve signs of the zodiac (*rāśi*), nine planets (*graha*), fifteen lunar days (*tithi*), thirty-three crores of gods (*devatā*), all demons (*dānava*), aboriginal races like *yakṣas* and *piśācas*, evil spirits (*bhūta)* and ghosts (*preta),* heavenly musician races like *gandharvas*, *kinnaras*, *apsarās*, all trees, all heavenly bodies, creepers, bushes and grasses, clouds, insects–every object in the universe is perceived to be within this body by an enlightened *yogin*.

A *yogin* also experiences heaven in his happiness, hell in his misery, bondage, liberation, etc. in his own body.

At the end of this chapter the concluding verse says: Thus in the entire individual body the cosmic body (*viśvarūpa*), the supreme lord (*parameśvara*), the supreme soul (*paramātman*) with his undivided nature resides in every individual body, in essential consciousness (*citsvarūpin*) as like the sky (or void, *vyomavat*).

CHAPTER FOUR

IV.1-12 All the bodies, whether cosmic or individual, are contained in and sustained by the supreme power (*nija śakti*) of the absolute supreme reality. This power is all-pervading and all-regulating energy. She is the desire (*icchā*) of the supreme spirit, embodiment of transcendental knowledge. Though the absolute reality does not create, the power represents him as the creator. Actually, *Śakti* manifests herself as the creation of the spiritual and material world-order. So she is said to be the *ādhāra* or container of phenomenal creation. She is Śiva in unmanifest state (*nirutthānadaśā*).

The unmanifest supreme reality is termed *akula* and its manifested state as *kula,* expressed in five forms: *parā, sattā, ahantā, sphuratā,* and *kāla*. *Akula* is that state when the supreme being is one without a second, having no name, no form and no duality. In this state the absolute reality merges within himself. His power is not manifested then. During such a state the supreme reality is termed "(all-)powerful" (*śaktimān*). The states of *kula* and *akula* are explained by giving the simile of bubbles on the surface of the water. The bubbles are "*kula*" and called "*akula*" when the bubbles merge in the water. *Akula* is the non-dual state of the all-powerful.

Therefore, the infinitely-powerful Śiva manifests himself with the help of his supreme energy (*śakti*) in so many forms of the creation whether animate or inanimate. This is his divine sport.

IV.13-15 The all-powerful spirit can do nothing without the help of his *śakti*. It is with the help of *śakti* only that Śiva can manifest everything.

The other name of *śakti* is *kuṇḍalinī* in yogic terminology. This *kuṇḍalinī* has two states: awakened (*prabuddha*) and sleeping (*aprabuddha*). The individual self becomes engaged in all worldly affairs other than aspiring for spiritual progess when the *kuṇḍalinī* is in a sleeping state. But when the same *kuṇḍalinī* inspires the individual self to refrain from all worldly affairs and makes him pursue a spiritual path, it is said to be in the awakened state and marching upward through the *brahmanāḍī* to meet *sahasrāra*. *Kuṇḍālinī* and *śakti* are the same, identical.

Kuṇḍalinī is said to be in the lower stage when it sleeps and the individual self experiences the affairs of the external sense-organs in the physical and intellectual planes. It is said to be in the middle state when it awakens and the individual self experiences the urge for spiritual enlightenment and is engaged in *sādhanā* under the guidance of an enlightened divine master. The consciousness of phenomenal existence and experience does not vanish altogether during this state. *Kuṇḍalinī* is said to be in the upper state when the self transcends phenomenal existence and experiences perfect union with the supreme spirit. The consciousness of duality vanishes in this state.

The aspirant experiences Śiva and Śakti in transcendental oneness. Śiva is immanent in Śakti and Śakti is immanent in Śiva. No difference is seen within Śiva and Śakti, as the relation between the moon and the moonlight. The moonlight has no existence apart from and independently of the moon.

In the last stage *kuṇḍalinī* is named "pure consciousness" (*parasaṃvit*). In all orders of substance it is the same consciousness that reigns as the unifier of all parts and attributed. This all-glorious *saṃvit* reveals itself in all orders of phenomenal existence, manifests itself in all finite changing and diversified objective forms. Thus this power unfolds the eternal consciousness, manifests reality in perfect bliss, and stands as the basic container of the individual and cosmic body.

CHAPTER FIVE

V.1-12 Supreme reality is termed *paramapada* in the language of Gorakṣanātha. *Samarasa* or union of the individual with the supreme self cannot be achieved by any kind of empirical awareness excepting the mercy of the divine master (*guru*). It is to be realized in one's own self (*svasaṃvedya*). No other aid, whether material or intellectual or yogic, can reveal the supreme self. Intellectual discourse fails to reveal him. Devotional service and the mercy of an enlightened teacher can reveal the supreme self. The divine master of this yogic path can help the individual self to be united with the supreme self who is the embodiment of perfect existence-consciousness-bliss (*saccidānanda*). The spiritual aspirant through the divine mercy of the divine master sees and enjoys his own self in the supreme self. This sort of union is *samarasa*.

V.13-33 An aspirant of this spiritual path of yoga aiming at *samarasa* or final union with the supreme self must follow some outward disciplinary methods. He should wear a conch (*śaṃkha*) and round earrings prescribed by the *siddha yogins* of the Nātha cult. He must stay in a secluded place and observe the rules for daily worship and day to day behavior. But he should not attach too much importance to the external wear or other outward observances. Union with *paramapada* cannot be achieved by wearing some particular garments or observing mechanically some rules or regulations. A particular garment or outward observances are only signs for the inspiration of others. Ordinary people may be attracted and inspired to follow this spiritual path by seeing the dress and behavior of the aspirant.

Union with *paramapada* in the state of *samarasa* can be achieved through the four gradual stages of *sahaja, saṃyama, sopāya* and *advaita*. The word "*sahaja*" has a special connotation. This word previously was misused by a section of the followers of Tantra and Buddhism. The Buddhists and Tantric Sahajīyas gave a misleading interpretation of the word "*sahaja*". They allured the pseudo-aspirants to their path by advising them to supply enough food to the sense-organs to the point of saturation. Satiation of subconscious impressions is termed "*sahaja sādhanā*". Gorakṣanātha was conscious of this deviation and gave a correct interpretation of *sahaja sādhanā*. According to him "*sahaja*" means "effortless", "easy", "spontaneous" and "natural". The divine touch becomes as easy, etc. as breathing itself. This *sahaja* state cannot be achieved without the mercy of the *guru* or divine master.

V.34-53 The spiritual aspirant achieves the final goal in twelve years of continual *sādhanā*. In the first year he becomes free from diseases and is liked by all. In the second year, the aspirant gains the knowledge of all human languages. In the third year, his body becomes divine and ferocious creatures like snakes and tigers do not cause any harm to him. In the fourth year he has no feeling of hunger, thirst, heat, or cold and can hear sounds from far-off distances. In the fifth year he attains the power to enter into other bodies. No weapon or thunder can hurt him in the sixth year. In the seventh year he can travel without touching the ground and see objects which are out of sight to others. In the eight year he gains eight kinds of extraordinary capacities. In the ninth year he can swim in the sky to all locations. In the tenth year he gains the power to go wherever he likes. He becomes omniscient in the eleventh year. In the twelfth year he becomes equal with Śiva himself. Only through the mercy of a divine master can the aspirant achieve all the above powers.

The disciples of a Nātha *guru* are divided into five categories:

1. Disciples who have received special mercy and can transmit the same to others;

2. Those who live in monasteries, temples and preach the doctrine;

3. Those who can show occult powers in order to attract the public to pursue the yogic path;

4. Those who have attained the Nātha *svarūpa* or highest goal and lead others who are specially worthy for the same;

5. Those who have achieved all *siddhis* and guide others

according to their receptivity.

V.54-81 Various religious sects of Indian culture and philosophy have enjoined and sanctioned various rules and regulations, strict disciplinary methods to be observed physically and mentally. But all these superficial, ritualistic methods will not enable a spiritual aspirant to achieve the final goal. Only the mercy of the divine master and sincere and truthful endeavor, both united, will enable him to be united with *paramapada*. The divine master leads a sincere and true disciple to *paramapada* by his words, merciful look even for a moment, by transmitting divine power into his body and by giving his personal services (*sevā*). This kind of divine master is to be served, worshipped, and followed with all sincerity, honesty and devotion.

Union of the individual self and the supreme self, i.e. *samarasa*, is revealed in those who serve the *guru* with all love and devotion. Such devoted selves can see and enjoy the most beautiful and blissful unity or the divine sport (*cidvilāsa*) of Śakti after the union of both the selves in the transcendental plane of pure consciousness.

CHAPTER SIX

VI.1-20 A *yogin* who has realized the perfect ideal of *samarasa* as explained in the previous Chapter, who has shaken off all desires and attachments, all cares and fears, all senses of difference and plurality, is called an *avadhūtayogin*. Such a *yogin* is the real *nātha* or master of his senses and circumstances. This *avadhūtanātha* is truly worthy of being a *sadguru*.

An *avadhūtayogin* has some external signs such as smearing the body with ashes, putting on a piece of loin cloth, shaving the head, wearing big round earrings, holding a stick, etc. All these external signs stand as symbols. These are the symbols of some particular inner qualities or spiritual attainments. It matters little whether the *avadhūta* takes such outward signs or not, but he must be endowed with the inner qualities behind those signs.

An *avadhūta* is said to have shaved his head when he shakes off the bondage of pains and pleasures. He is smeared with ashes when he is saturated with the memory of the divine.

An *avadhūta* cannot be recognized by his external behavior only. At times he pretends to be very much engrossed with worldly pleasure. At another moment he is away from all those worldly affairs. Now he behaves like a king. The next moment he is a beggar in the street. His ways are unforeseen.

VI.21-75 The author observed the diversified branches of the Indian spiritual path with sectarian rules and regulations, outward ritualistic behavior, each condemning the other. He keenly observed the diversity among those philosophical branches and explored the unity in all such diversities. Therefore he says that an *avadhūta yogin* of the Nātha cult combines in himself all the attainments of the adepts of all other sects. Gorakṣanātha gives the real definitions of *Śākta*, Vaiṣṇava, Śaiva, Vaidika, Naiyāyika, Vaiśeṣika, Mīmāṃsaka, Brāhmaṇa, Kṣatriya, Vaiśya, Śudra, *brahmacārī*, *gṛhastha*, *sannyāsī*, and the *avadhūta* of the Nātha cult combines in himself all of them. He is the unifying embodiment of all sects, all religions, all spiritual thoughts ever revealed in the culture of India. This *avadhūta* is the *sadguru* of the highest order and he is to be worshipped and followed sincerely.

VI.76-94 Thus the author explores the grand synthesis of all spiritual cults in their pure perspective. Next he refutes the sectarian attitudes, modes or worship or *sādhanā* of dogmatic sects who boast of their external signs, and special characteristics which distinguish each from the other. This sort of narrowness and antagonistic attitude never helps an aspirant in his spiritual progress. He despises such attitudes of Vedāntins, Vaiśeṣikas, Vaiṣṇavas, Tāpasas, Yogins, Cārvākas and all other sects who engage themselves in quarreling and finding fault with one another. Even the *yogins* who follow the methods of yoga strictly, but are devoid of a sublime attitude, are discarded. All their pains and austerities are futile without the experience of the unity with *paramapada*.

VI.95-117) A *yogin* of the Nātha cult utters the words "*ādeśa ādeśa*" whenever he meets another of his own cult, whether a junior or senior *sādhaka*, a householder or a *sannyāsī*. The word "*ādeśa*" has a special meaning. Ordinarily it means order or command. In the language of Gorakṣanātha, however, *ādeśa* means the united form of a trinity. There is (i) the self (*ātman*), that is, Nātha the formless; (ii) *paramātman*, that is, Nātha the divine form or divine will for creation, and (iii) the individual self (*jīvātman*) or Nātha the qualified (*saguṇa*), that is, the effect of creation. A *yogin* while uttering the word "*ādeśa*" is in constant remembrance of the basic identity expressed as unity in trinity. Thus the *yogin* attains *paramapada* shaking off all diversities by contemplating the word "*ādeśa*".

The instruction given in this book must be kept secret and it should not be imparted to a disciple of any other person. It should not be given out of friendship, affection, or by pressure or for any other cause. It is to be imparted only to a devoted, pure, truthful, kind and righteous disciple initiated into the Nātha cult by a *sadguru*. It should not be taught to a disciple who is impure, hypocritical, atheistic, cruel, quarrelsome, or turned away from the righteous conduct of a *yogin*. A disciple should be tested very strictly before he receives this lesson. It is to be given only for the spiritual progress of a true and sincere aspirant or for the continuity of this spiritual order.

Thus *Siddhasiddhāntapaddhati* ends with a benedictory verse invoked by Gorakṣanātha where he praises the mercy of Śiva-Śakti and Gaṇeśa to shower blessings on the readers and followers so that they may enjoy eternal bliss.

31.GORAKṢANĀNĀTHA, *Gorakṣaśataka*

What is known about the date and life of Gorakṣanātha has already been mentioned in the preceding entry. Regarding the text known as *Gorakṣaśataka*, there appear to be several texts or several collections of verses all claiming to be the original text. One well-known version of *Gorakṣaśataka* is Briggs 1982, pp. 284-304. This version contains 101 verses. The critical edition has been published in Nowotny 1976, and includes 207 verses! In any case, nearly all of the verses have been published in one or another text attributed to Gorakṣanātha, and the verses contain very little that has not been summarized in the preceding summary of the *Siddhasiddhāntapaddhati*. Many of the same verses also appear in the later *Haṭhayogapradīpikā*. A reasonable conclusion is that there were some original verses of Gorakṣanātha that circulated widely in Nātha circles and came to be incorporated in a variety of HaṭhaYoga texts.

32.GORAKṢANĀTHA, *Gorakṣapaddhati*

Summary by Dolgobinda Shastri

The theory and basic principles of the Nātha school have been presented in the summary of the *Siddhasiddhāntapaddhati*. Here in *Gorakṣapaddhati* (also known as *Gorakṣasaṃhitā*) Gorakṣanātha narrates the most important practical aspects of Haṭha Yoga–what to practice and how to practice. Hence these two texts taken together give a reasonably clear picture of the Nātha tradition. The edition used for this summary is Mahidhara Sharma 1967.

The text is divided into two parts, each named "*Śataka*", consisting of approximately one hundred main verses (*ślokas*), but some numbers include many other inserted verses. The first *Śataka* consists of one hundred and ninety-nine verses dealing with postures, exercises and bonds. The second Śataka deals with the sixfold acts (*ṣaṭkarma*) from postures through concentration. The whole book contains three hundred and twenty-six verses in all.

The numbering used below refers to the verses in sequence from 1-326 without regard to the separate numbering used for the inserted verses in the Sharma edition.

PART ONE

1-27 Gorakṣanātha, after salutations to the divine master with humble devotion, describes yoga, which is the means to perfect bliss. A *yogin* can attain *paramapada* or the highest goal and can make himself free from the threefold miseries. Generally yoga is treated as having eight limbs, but in this work only six have been dealt with, beginning with postures *(āsana)* and excluding restraints *(yama)* and observances (*niyama*). These two are preliminary to all spiritual paths. Posture is the sitting posture of an aspirant (*sādhaka*) while practicing yoga. Postures are eighty-four in number, of which *siddhāsana* and *padmāsana* are the most important and essential for Haṭhayoga.

If a *yogin* is not acquainted with the six vital centers, sixteen *ādhāras*, two *lakṣyas* and five *vyomans* in his individual body he cannot attain perfection. The individual body is like a vertical abode having nine doors: a mouth, two eyes, two ears, two nostrils, anus, and genitalia. There are also the five residing deities of the five constituent elements, Brahmā in earth, Viṣṇu in water, Rudra in fire, Īśvara in air, and Sadāśiva in the sky. None can attain perfection in the practice of yoga without knowledge of the above.

Lotuses and vital centers. The lotus at *mūlādhāra cakra* has four petals, at *svādhiṣṭhāna* has six petals, while *maṇipūra cakra* at the navel contains ten petals. The fourth, *anāhata cakra* in the heart, has twelve petals. It is also known as *pūrṇagiri pīṭha*. The fifth is *viśuddha cakra* in the throat having sixteen petals. The sixth is *ājñā cakra* between the eyebrows. The lotus here is of two petals. The last, *sahasrāra cakra*, has one thousand petals. This is the seat of *paramaśiva* or the supreme reality.

28-60 Seventy-two thousand channels rise from the central point in between the navel and the root of the genitalia and cover the whole body. This sport of origination of the channels is oval shaped. Out of the seventy-two thousand channels only seventy-two are important and of them only ten are essential for the purpose of yoga. These are: *iḍā* in the left, *piṅgalā* in the right, *suṣumnā* in the middle (spinal cord), *gāndhārī* in the left eye, *hastajihvā* in the right eye, *pūsā* in the right ear, *yaśasvinī* in the left ear, *ālambuṣā* in the mouth, *kuhū* in the genitals, and *samkhinī* in the anus.

Out of the ten airs (*vāyu*) inhaling (*prāṇa)* lies in the heart, exhaling *(apāna)* in the anus, *samāna* in the navel, *udāna* helps the twinkling in the eyes, *kṛkāra* for sneezing, *devadatta* for yawning: *dhanañjaya* remains in the whole body even up to four hours after death.

Inhaling and exhaling work out the influence of ignorance (*avidyā, māyā*) over the conditioned self. The considered self confined in the physical body moves up and down by the influence of inhaling and exhaling as a ball jumps up and down when kicked by a player or like a bird tied to a long rope.

Inhaling at the *ājñā cakra* and exhaling at the *mūlādhāra cakra* attract each other. Yoga means union of these two airs. An aspirant unites the two airs by breath-control. This is called "Haṭha Yoga". The word "*haṭha*" has two letters–"*ha*", which means exhaling, and "*ṭha*", which means inhaling. Thus by due attention during control of breathing the practitioner spontaneously mutters the word "*haṃsa*" while breathing. From sunrise to sunset a man mutters the word "*haṃsa*" 21,600 times automatically. A seeker is only to perform a solemn vow (*saṃkalpa*) in due process after rising from his bed. Only this much is needed, then the reciting (*japa)* (of "*haṃsa*") goes on automatically in breathing. This is the best kind of spiritual practice in the Nātha school.

Kuṇḍalinī sleeps with the mouth downwards obstructing the entrance door of *suṣumnā*. Awakening of *kuṇḍalinī* is successfully accomplished by a special posture for the awakening and upward movement of the *kuṇḍalinī* power.

61-78 Here and following a variety of bodily exercises (*mudrā*) are described.

79-118 *Khecarī mudrā*–Turn the tongue upward and move in towards the inside of the throat so as to reach the pharynx, fix the eyes on the center of the eyebrows. The tongue is to be lengthened for this purpose by the following process of cutting (*chedana*). The joining channel under the tongue is to be cut to the extent of a hair's breadth. By this the obstructing channel is removed and the tongue can be drawn outside to the length of reaching the center of the eyebrows outside and the pharynx inside by the following process of movement (*cālana*) and milking (*dohana*): Open the mouth and bring out the tongue, then go on milking holding it with the thumb and the forefingers of both the hands just as we do while milking a cow holding her teats.

A *yogin* being steady in *khecarī mudrā* for one hour only withstands the poisons of snakes and scorpions, diseases and old age. By practicing for fifteen days he conquers death. This exercise keeps the semen (*bindu*) steady in its abode in *vyoma cakra* even at the time of intercourse with a woman. It is never dislodged as the body is never excited or irritated. The semen, being steady and calm, keeps the body away from decay. *Khecarī mudrā* is the best of all the bodily exercises.

152-175 *Vajrolī mudrā*. This exercise is meant for the married couple only. It is related to intercourse with a woman. *Brahmacārins* and *sannyāsīs* are forbidden to practice this, since they must maintain celibacy. A devoted and faithful wife and milk are essential for this exercise. At the moment of orgasm during intercourse, when the semen is about to come out, the aspirant is to draw the semen upward by the process of contraction of the penis. Even if the fluid is already dropped and mixed with female *rajas*, it is to be drawn up into the male body through the penis by the same process of contraction. Warm milk must be taken after intercourse.

The aspirant has to adopt some preliminary procedure prior to the practice of *vajrolī mudrā*. In the first stage, the *yogin* should practice drawing up water through a silver tube inserted into the penis. When this practice is successfully done, he should practice drawing up semen by the contraction process. Thus *vajrolī mudrā* is mastered. Success in this exercise makes the aspirant conquer decay and death.

Life depends on semen, semen depends on mind; when mind is unsteady, semen becomes unsteady. By practicing *vajrolī mudrā* both mind and semen become steady and unperturbed.

Sahajolī mudrā. After intercourse in *vajrolī mudrā*, both male and female should sit and smear the body with ashes of cow-dung mixed in water which is to be kept ready beforehand.

Amarolī mudrā. While passing urine, leave the first and last flow, preserving the middle flow of urine in a glass. This is to be drunk and used for nasal cleaning after *vajrolī mudrā*.

A female also can practice *vajrolī* during intercourse and draw up both the male and female sexual fluids in the contraction process.

Male and female, after becoming adept in *vajrolī*, attain supernatural powers of knowing the past and the future and can move in the air.

176-199 Reciting *oṃ (praṇava japa)*. *Praṇava* or *oṃ* is regarded as the highest Vedic *mantra* according to the Nātha yoga cult. Hence the opinion of some scholars that the Nāthas are non-Vedic is absolutely unfounded. Gorakṣanātha regards *praṇava* as the united form of the trinity, i.e. *bhuḥ, bhuvaḥ, svaḥ; candra, sūrya, agni; brahmā, viṣṇu, maheśvara.* It is the embodiment of the three times (present, past and future), three Vedas (Ṛk, Sāma, Yajuḥ), three parts of the universe (*loka*), viz., heaven, earth, and underworld, three *svaras* (*udātta, anudātta, svarita*) and three powers (*śakti*), viz., *icchā, kriyā* and *jñāna*. *Praṇava* is the word-form of *parabrahman* or supreme reality. It is to be recited always in the lotus-posture (*padmāsana*) with body, throat and head in a straight line and eyes constantly on the tip of one's nose. It can also be remembered at all places, all stages, and at all hours without discrimination of time and place.

Praṇava may be performed with breath-control. The breathing of air comes out to the length of eighteen inches. All the veins are cleansed by breath-control. Cleansing of the veins is essential for yogic exercises.

Sitting in the lotus position in a secluded place, the *yogin* should start *pūraka* slowly during which span *oṃ* will be recited twelve times. This practice, continued for three months, enables the aspirant to accomplish the cleansing of the channels. The sweat coming out during control of breathing is to be rubbed on the limbs. Milk and *ghee* is the convenient diet during the preliminary stage; no restriction of diet is necessary in the matured stage.

PART TWO

200-214 *Ṣaṭkarma*. It is accepted that breath-control is essential for all the bodily exercises or any procedure of Haṭha Yoga. But there are persons who are unfit for controlling the breath–for example, overweight or sickly persons. Hence, for them, *ṣaṭkarma* or the following six acts are prescribed as stages preliminary to breath-control. These are *dhautī, basti, neti, trāṭaka, nauli* and *kapālabhāti*.

Dhautī. A piece of cloth two inches wide and twenty-four feet long is to be swallowed bit by bit in fifteen days, as advised by the guide. The last end of the cloth must be held fixed by the teeth. The portion swallowed each day must be drawn out slowly bit by bit. This process cleanses the intestine. This exercise, perfectly done, cures diseases like cough, asthma, spleen, leprosy and poisoning, etc.

Basti. Sitting in navel deep water, a bamboo tube, three inches long with one hole, is to be gradually inserted inside the anus and water should be drawn into the stomach by the process of contraction. When the stomach is washed the water should be pushed out. This is the action called "*basti*". No diet, solid or liquid, is to be taken before *dhautī* or *basti*, but must be taken immediately after.

Basti calms seven bodily constituents (serum, blood, flesh, fat, bones, marrow and semen), five sense-organs, and five action-organs (speech, hands, feet, anus, and genitalia). It removes restlessness of mind and body, increases grace and glamor and the digestive capacity.

Neti. This kind of action is done by putting a thread or thin rubber tube into the nostril and bringing one end through the mouth and then moving it back and forth. This removes the impurities stored in the nose and forehead. It enables the aspirant to see very minute objects which common people cannot see. Many kinds of diseases relating to the throat are prevented or cured by this.

Trāṭaka. This consists in looking at a small object constantly without blinking until tears are produced. This process cures or prevents all diseases of the eyes, and it removes dullness, idleness, and anger.

Nauli. Bend the shoulders forward and begin moving the stomach right and left, up and down in a circular motion. This increases the digestive power of the stomach, cures diseases like rheumatism, gout, etc. It is essential for all the other actions.

Kapālabhāti. An aspirant is to practice inhaling and exhaling like the bellows of a blacksmith. This is also known as *bhastrikā prāṇāyāma*. This practice cures twenty kinds of disease involving cough and cold.

215-229. The next topic dealt with is controlling the breath in detail. Breath-control is performed in three stages. The first stage is inhaling. The second stage is holding one's breath (*kumbhaka*), and the third is exhaling. Reciting *oṃ* during these three states is the essential part of breath-control.

Withdrawal of sense-organs (*pratyāhāra*) brings twelve times the result of breath-control. Meditative fixation (*dhāraṇā*) produces 144 times that result, and reflective meditation (*dhyāna)* 20,736 times the results of controlling breathing. In the stage of concentration (*samādhi*) the seeker becomes *siddha* or an adept as he perceives all the presiding deities of all the vital centers from the penis up to the brain, and at last he becomes free from rebirth, karma, and attains liberation *(kaivalya)*.

230-243. The procedure of concentration is narrated briefly.

275-283. An aspirant, firm in posture, adept in control of breathing, and master in withdrawing his senses, should proceed to meditative fixation. This is conceiving the five elements (*bhūta*) separately installed with respective deities in different vital centers in the individual body, after gaining control over the mind and breathing.

284-303 Reflective meditation is constant memory of the self. The mind is to remain fixed on the self. This meditation is of two kinds–qualified (*sakala*) and absolute (*niṣkala*).

Posture for reflective meditation is the lotus position or the *svastikāsana*. Meditation is to be performed with eyes fixed on the tip of the nose, mind along with *kuṇḍalinī* must be fixed gradually on the vital centers such as described previously. Meditation on these centers bestows eightfold attainments (*siddhi*), immortality, liberation, and divine bliss. This is declared by Gorakṣanātha with great emphasis. This meditation is far superior to all the sacrifices prescribed by the Vedas.

304-326 Before beginning to discuss concentration, Gorakṣanātha brings two words "*upādhi*" ("adjunct") and "*tattva*" ("principle") forward for discussion. The former means color or letter (*varṇa*), and the latter means the self (*ātman*). An adjunct is knowledge of the cosmos and the principle is the cosmos or supreme entity. In concentration the *yogin* is freed from all adjuncts. His separate entity vanishes. He becomes one with the self. The state of complete unification of aspirant, practice and attainment is concentration. Duality of self and highest self ceases in concentration.

A *yogin* in concentration rises above time and space. He is impenetrable by any weapon. No animal, no sorcery can do any harm to him. He is above and beyond the reach of any thing material or super-material. He is unattached to any action or its results. He enjoys supreme bliss and oneness (*samarasa*) with the supreme reality.

Gorakṣanātha reveals this most secret knowledge of yoga, which bestows emancipation. This knowledge has been received by him from Ādinātha (Śiva) himself. This is the fruit of bathing in all holy streams, performing all sacrifices, worshiping all deities, and of all offerings to Brahmins and ancestors.

33.GORAKṢANĀTHA, *Yogabīja*

Summary by Ram Shankar Bhattacharya

This is another work attributed to Gorakṣanātha. It is a dialogue between Devī and Śiva. The edition used is Naraharinatha 1959. The numbering refers to verses.

1-11 Being asked by Devī as to how beings who suffer from pleasure and pain, being deluded by *māyā*, could attain liberation with the help of a specific path, Śiva replied: It is the *nāthamārga,* the way accepted in the Nātha system of yoga, which is the destroyer of birth, death, etc. and also the giver of supernormal powers. Isolation can only be attained through that path. Persons even though learned are found to have been deluded by *māyā*. The indefinable (*anirvācya*) luster of the self is incapable of being described. This immutable, taintless, and transcendental entity (i.e. the self) has become embodied (a *jīva*) being associated with the fruits accruing from the virtuous and vicious deeds.

12-19 Being asked by Devī as to how the transcendental *paramātman* assumed selfhood, the Lord (*īśvara*)(i.e. Śiva) said the following: There arises a throbbing (*sphurita*) in the taintless *jñāna* (i.e. the *paramātman*)which gives rise to the sense of ego. From that comes into existence a lump (*piṇḍa*, that is, the body) made up of the five kinds of gross objects (*bhūta*). It is built or bound by the *dhātus* (the main constituents of the body, i.e. the tissues), and is a form of the *guṇas*, associated with pleasure and pain. It is filled with or characterized by the life-principle (*jīvabhāvanā*), and is in essence nothing but the supreme self (*paramātman*). If an individual self becomes bereft of decay, death, lamentation, sleep, hunger, thirst, etc. he is known to be Śiva himself. A means is prescribed here to eradicate the faults just listed. This means is a combination of knowledge and yoga. Neither is able to lead a person to liberation without the help of the other.

20-23 Being asked as to what was the use of yoga, since *saṃsāra* and release were respectively the result of ignorance and knowledge, Śiva replied that one cannot get rid of the blemishes like lust, wrath, etc. through knowledge only.

24-32 Being asked by Devī whether a person who comes to know his original nature as complete (*pūrṇa*) and all-embracing can be supposed to have any touch with injunctions and prohibitions since a man possessing discrimination (*viveka*) is regarded as remaining always in the liberated state, Śiva said the following: The self falls into the delusion of transmigratory existence (*saṃsāra*) because of *kalpanāsphūrti*, that is, the flashing or vibrations of confused cognition. There is no difference between an ignorant person, overpowered by pleasure, pain, and delusion, and a man of learning (that is, a person who has not acquired self-knowledge) who is under the sway of subconscious impressions, for these impressions are equally possessed by both of them. A person though devoted to knowledge and free from passion is unable to attain liberation if he does not practice yoga.

33-47 Being asked by Devī as to how the wise, who are dispassionate and devoted to the self, can attain liberation, Śiva said the following: An embodied being is either fully developed or not fully developed in the practice of yoga. The former's body is bereft of inertia while that of the latter is inert, of the nature of the earth, a source of pain and liable to be affected by heat, cold, etc. The latter is easily misguided by his sense-organs. An individual attains a particular kind of body, which was thought by him at the time of death in his previous birth. An ordinary being, however, is unable to know of his future birth. Without a perfected body no person can practice meditation successfully, for he becomes compelled to leave his imperfect body on account of troubles or pains arising there. If however the dynamic ego is uprooted, then the body is also destroyed; consequently the embodied being gets rid of all diseases. When the ego is destroyed there arises restraint (*śama*) of the outgoing mental propensities, etc. If the ego-sense is destroyed, the body gets rid of all pain.

48-53 Being asked as to how a *yogin* should behave with others and how others should behave with him, Śiva said: Since the *yogins* have full control over their bodies, organs, mind, intellect, passions, wrath, etc. they cannot be subjugated by others. A living organism made up of seven constituents is made perfect by the fire of yoga. A body purified by yogic practices becomes powerful and becomes incapable of being cut, fettered or tied. Such a body is bereft of all impurities and is capable of assuming gross or subtle forms.

54-60 A highly powerful *yogin*, who is not subjected to decay and death, remains independent and acts without any purpose or desire. He can create various bodies and dissolve them in his body according to his will. He never dies as he is already dead. He lives where all die and dies where all live. Neither has he any duty nor has he any attachment to the deeds done by him. He abides in his own self and is said to be liberated during his lifetime. Those who have acquired the indirect knowledge of the self are subjugated by bodily activities. Such persons are incapable of being compared with the *yogins*.

61-66 Being asked about the different paths of the wise attainable after death, Śiva said: A wise man attains the result according to the virtuous and vicious deeds performed by him. As a result of virtuous deeds one comes in contact with a perfected *yogin* and by his grace one attains perfection. The great *yogins* do not fall or come down even in the period when Viṣṇu and other deities are dissolved. Transcendental reality can be realized neither by hearing scripture nor by cultivating acts such as meditation, but by the grace of the teacher, who is similar to the philosopher's stone (*cintāmaṇi*, which is supposed to yield all desires).

67-72 Being asked about the reason for claiming yoga to be the giver of liberation in view of the fact that the wise hold knowledge to be the only means to liberation, Śiva said: Neither knowledge nor yoga alone is capable of leading one to liberation or of bringing about perfection without the help of the other. Yoga can be acquired through the path of knowledge if it is practiced in a goodly number of births; knowledge, however, can be acquired in one birth with the help of yoga. This is why yoga is held to be the highest means to liberation.

73-78 Having acquired indirect awareness of the self one may consider oneself to be liberated, though as a matter of fact one cannot be liberated through thinking (*manana*)alone. By practicing yoga in many births one transcends the cycle of birth and death. Having united the sun and the moon (i.e. the *iḍā* and *piṅgalā* channels) by performing union of exhalation and inhalation a person can strengthen by purification through yoga the body made up of seven constituents. Such a person gets rid of diseases, etc. and remains in the form of the highest *ākāśa*. He never dies, though his body seems to be a burnt piece of cloth (i.e. he exists in his body without taking it as his own and casts it off without any attachment).

79-87 As the mind of an individual self is tied by breath it can be subjugated by air only. Breathing cannot be controlled by studying scripture, etc. One should take up the practice of yoga after learning the ways of breath-control. Otherwise one may suffer. It is disastrous to practice yoga without controlling one's breathing. Self-knowledge appears in the purified mind of that person whose breaths are dissolved, whose mind has become free from all blemishes and whose body is not liable to fall. As yoga can give rise to knowledge in a single birth, an aspirant should practice yoga constantly and should try to subjugate breathing. There is no means that is higher than yoga.

88-98 Being asked by Devī about the nature of yoga and yoga-practice and about the results of yoga, Śiva said: Yoga may be defined as the union of inhaling and exhaling, or of menstrual excretion (*rajas*) and semen (*retas*), or of the sun (the *piṅgalā* channel) and the moon (the *iḍā* channel), or of the individual self and the supreme self. Even the union of opposites is called yoga. One is required to serve one's *guru* who has controlled his breathing and to take his advice as to how to do it.

99-136 Breath is delicate and white. A long section then follows describing the process of moving the *kuṇḍalinī* power through the various vital centers by using the techniques of breath-control.

137-144 Through the grace of the *guru* one should try to control his breathing and then his mind. The dissolution of breath and of the mind are interdependent. By breath-control as well as by the practice of the postures the mind gets dissolved and the semen is checked from falling. When, after the practice of inhalation and exhalation air is restrained, many secret sounds (*nāda*) are heard, and hunger and thirst become suspended. All blemishes are eradicated. As a result of all these, the aspirant becomes established in his own nature, which is nothing but existence-knowledge-bliss (*saccidānanda*). This is the path of *mahāyoga* which has four phases (*bhūmikā*), namely *mantra, haṭha, laya* and *rāja*.

145-152 Being asked about the characteristics of the four phases, a doctrine of the Siddha school, Śiva said: Inhalation and exhalation are performed with the sounds of *ha* and *sa* respectively. All individual selves mutter the incantation *haṃsa* (composed of these two sounds) which can also be uttered in the reverse way in the form of *so'ham* (*saḥ* and *aham*). This is the practice of Incantation Yoga (*mantrayoga*). The sun and the moon (i.e. the *piṅgalā* and the *iḍā* channels) are respectively called *ha* and *ṭha*. The union of these two is called Haṭha Yoga. When as a result of the union of the knower of the *kṣetra* (the living organism, i.e. the *jīva*) and the supreme self, the mind gets dissolved and air becomes tranquil, then the process is called Layayoga. It leads to the state which is identical with the bliss of the self. The union of the two vital airs, namely *prāṇa* and *apāna*, is the essence of Rājayoga.

153-161 Being asked about the ways known as *kāka* (crow) and *markaṭa* (monkey), which are essentially the same but externally different, Īśvara said: Though the great path, declared by Ādinātha, appears to be twofold, yet it is one (i.e. both the paths lead to the same goal). If perfection is achieved in one and the same birth as a result of practicing yoga for a long time, then the process is called the way of the monkey. If with a view to attaining perfection through the western gate (*paścima dvāra*) as early as possible a series of bodies is taken one after another, then the process is called the way of the crow. There is no higher practice than this.

161-170 Perfection in yoga cannot be acquired without performing actions; this is why one should take proper means to achieve the goal. Without the help of the western path no means can lead one to the path of liberation. The eradication of diseases and bodily inactivity, constant flow of the moon, manifestation of the secret sounds, softness in the body, walking in the sky, omniscience, etc. are the results of yoga practice. A *yogin* being all-knowing and all-powerful becomes liberated in this lifetime and wanders all over the world.

171-178 Being asked about the usefulness of the *siddhis*, Śiva said: *Siddhis* are of two kinds, constructed or imagined (*kalpita*) and not constructed (*akalpita*). Constructed are those powers that arise from secretion (*rasa*), medicinal herbs (*oṣadhi*), and *kriyā* (which seems to mean the rites causing such powers as time and the repetition of sacred syllables, etc.). These afford insignificant powers (*alpavīrya*). Sometimes these (constructed powers) arise without any effort (*svatas*, spontaneously). The not-constructed powers are those that are long-lasting (*nitya*) and highly powerful; they are of the nature of desire (*icchārūpa*). They are caused by yoga (i.e. concentration, *samādhi*) in a person who is devoid of subconscious impressions. These lead to the state of *paramātman*. Constant luster (in the body) is the sign of a person perfected through yoga.

179-190 The *siddhis* are the signs of success and they appear naturally. Whether a person is *siddha* or *jīvanmukta* is indicated by these powers. A person possessing no *siddhis* must be deemed as remaining in bondage. The body of one liberated in life is to be known as bereft of decay and death. When the body itself attains *brahman*-hood (this seems to suggest the most perfected state of the body) and the self knows nothing but itself then the self is liberated. When one's body and mind become *cinmaya* (mere consciousness, divine) and undergoes no change, then one is called liberated. Yoga expounded here is to be kept a secret. It must not be imparted to the cruel, cunning, fraudulent, or mischievous, but to those who are devotees of Śiva and are devoted to the path of the Nāthas.

Devī, having heard the science of yoga, bowed down to Śiva.

34.AUTHOR UNKNOWN, *Gorakṣasiddhāntasaṃgraha*

Summary by Dolgobinda Shastri

This is a text from perhaps some time in the thirteenth or fourteenth century in which the author attempts to show that the philosophy of Gorakṣanātha stands unique and superior to all other branches of Indian philosophy. The text was first edited by Gopinath Kaviraj in 1925 in the Sarasvati Bhavan Series, Vidya Vilas Press, Varanasi. Our E is the second edition (Pandeya 1973); sections are identified by the page-numbering in E. The text is in Sanskrit prose with many important quotations from older texts. It contains some sixty-eight pages and appears to be incomplete.

1-3 There is at the outset a definition of "*avadhūtaguru*". The author bows down to Nātha, the supreme absolute entity. He shines as the light in the middle with Śambhu on the left and Viṣṇu on the right, the unqualified principle on the left and the energy on the right. He is the abode of all creative phenomena, all forms of emancipation, etc.

An *avadhūta* is to be accepted as the only *guru* or divine master, none else. An *avadhūta* is he who has shaken off all differences and is above caste or stage of life. No *brahmacārin* or *sannyāsin* can be a *guru* so long as they belong to a caste or stage of life which is within the field of the three *guṇas*. A *guru* must be in the upper state beyond that field. An *avadhūta guru* is beyond even that.

4-7 Yoga is the best of all paths for spiritual enlightenment.

8-12 The outward signs of a *yogin* are described. These signs are: *mudra, nāda, vibhūti* and *ādeśa*.

Literally, "*mudrā*" means two round earrings made out of conch, wood, or marble. These earrings are the symbols for the feeling of ecstacy of the union of the individual self with the supreme self.

Nāda is the sign or symbol of the *anāhata* sound or the sound which comes out without the use of the vocal cords. This is "*haṃsa*" or "*oṃ*", the sound arising from exhaling and inhaling.

Vibhūti is the ashes of burnt cow-dung with which *yogins* smear their body. It is the symbol of fire, which burns all sins.

Ādeśa literally means "command". A Nātha *yogin,* whenever he meets another of his order, whether junior or senior, utters the words "*ādeśa, ādeśa*" as was made customary by Gorakṣanātha. The word "*ādeśa*" symbolizes the unity of the trinity, i.e. the self (*ātman*), the conditional self (*jīvātman*), and the supreme self (*paramātman*). *Yogins* should remind themselves of the above principle whenever they meet.

The next topic discussed is the final goal of attainment or emancipation. According to the views of the Nātha *yogins*, liberation rests with "Nātha-hood" (*nāthasvarūpena avasthāna*). The Nātha *svarūpa* is conceived as above the *advaita* or non-dual. It is the supreme divine bliss. It is neither thinkable nor non-thinkable, but it is both.

Freedom from bondage is liberation.

The inferiority of the philosophy of other religious schools such as Sāṃkhya, Vedānta, Buddhist, Jaina, Vīraśaiva, etc. is shown with logical arguments and verses from the *Siddhasiddhāntapaddhati.*

Yoga and bhoga (enjoyment) are the two most important objects of human life. Only the *siddhas* are engaged in yoga while all other human beings are engrossed in experiencing. The result or fruit of yoga is liberation, and the result of experiencing is bondage and suffering. The path of yoga is difficult at the beginning, but it is blissful in the end. The initial hardship can be easily overcome by the mercy of the *guru* or divine master.

The philosophy of the Mīmāṃsakas is refuted. The Mīmāṃsaka argues that ritualistic performances (*karmakāṇḍa*) according to the Vedic injunctions are the only way to salvation. In the opinion of the author, action (*karman*) cannot be the cause of the cessation of karma, as karma is within the fold of the three *guṇas* and is not independent.

13-20 Advaita or the non-dualistic theory of Śaṃkara is refuted. In the opinion of that school duality is not real but apparent, and is created by the deluding potency of *māyā*. But according to the *siddha* (Nātha) school, supreme reality is free from duality or non-duality. In the course of the argument the life of Śaṃkara is narrated during which it is claimed that in the end that Śaṃkara attained success (*siddhi*) by learning yoga from Tāranātha, a *siddhācārya* of the Nātha school in northern India.

21-27 The *Vedas* are found in various branches. The *Upaniṣads* are more than fifty in number. Śaṃkara, Rāmānuja, and all other *ācāryas* have explained the *Vedas* and *Upaniṣads* according to their respective different interpretations supporting the theory which they have established. But the author says that their views cannot be said to be the real intent of the *Vedas*, etc. The *yogins* of the Nātha school do not require the verses of the *Vedas*. To them the essence of the *Vedas* is *oṃ* and the *brahmagāyatrī.*

Bhuḥ comes from the *Ṛgveda. Bhuva* comes from the

Yajurveda, and *svaḥ from the Sāmaveda*. From these three come out respectively the three letters of *oṃ*, that is, *a*, *u* and *m*. Again from these three letters spring the constituents of creation in order from the subtlest to the grossest form.

Oṃ (praṇava) is the essence of all knowledge. One who meditates on *praṇava* knows everything. He has no fear from any quarter. He is saturated by the divine bliss of *praṇava*. The worshiper of *praṇava* acquires all knowledge.

28-33 The text provides a folk-etymology of the term "*avadhūta*".

The supreme transcendental absolute entity Śiva is all-pervading like the sky. The individual self is neither conditioned nor free, neither born nor dead, neither the enjoyer nor the doer. It is also beyond all mundane speculations. It is neither a form nor formless. The self is ever pure, unattached and transcends all attributes and all descriptions whatever has been said about the self in the scriptures.

Perfection in yoga is achieved neither by performing the rituals sanctioned by the scriptures nor by the study of those scriptures. A *yogin* must abstain from the company of women, fire, wandering too much, or any kind of physical austerity which causes torture to the body and mind. Breath-control, repeating "*oṃ*", practice of *khecarīmudrā*, these three are essential for perfection in yoga.

34-43 The three letters constituting "*oṃ*", viz., *a*, *u*, and *m*, are the unified form of trinity–the three deities, three times,, three worlds, three *Vedas*, three energies, etc.

The three deities are Brahmā, Viṣṇu and Śiva. The three times are present, past and future. The three worlds are earth, space and heaven. The three *Vedas* are *Ṛg, Sāman,* and *Yajus.* The three energies are desire, action and awareness.

A *yogin* is considered a real *guru* or master when he attains spontaneous steadiness of vision, breath, and mind without any effort. In this sense these nine Nāthas are to be accepted as real *gurus*: Ādinātha, Matsyendranātha, Udayanātha, Daṇḍanātha, Satyanātha, Santoṣanātha, Kūrmanātha, Bhavanarjī, and

Gorakṣanātha.

44-51 The philosophy of the Nātha Yoga school accepts the duality of the supreme reality, but his duality or non-duality is beyond empirical conception. The Nāthas wear the sacred thread as the symbol of purity, long life, etc. during the primary state of *sādhanā*. But in the higher stages a *yogin* is to give up the outward sacred thread along with the *śikhā* (the top-knot) and *daṇḍa* (the staff of a mendicant).

Karma activated for the present life (*prārabdhakarman*) is destroyed by either action or knowledge, but only yoga can root out the effects of the deeds of previous lives.

An *avadhūta guru* is endowed with thirty-six qualities, and a qualified disciple must possess thirty-two qualities.

62-55 The two terms "*ācāra*" and "*vicāra*" are discussed. *Brāhmaṇas* put much importance on rituals (*ācāra*) as enjoined by the scriptures, whereas the Nātha *yogin* pays more respect to *vicāra* or right thinking. One need not be guided by some mechanical and formal rules of daily life. No amount of mechanical performance of rituals can lead to liberation. Every thing should be observed with due consideration of its real effect and utility.

The absolute reality transcends the concepts of existence and nonexistence. It has neither origination nor destruction, and it is beyond all empirical or philosophical imagination and speculation.

The extreme Vedānta view of Advaita is not accepted by the Nātha Yoga school. Absolute transcendence does not imply negation or opposition to the relative phenomenal world-order. On the contrary, it indicates perfect assimilation, unification and identification of all relative phenomenal realities within itself. This is the distinct feature of difference between the Nātha Yoga conception and the Vedānta view of the Advaita school.

The behavior of an *avadhūta*, an adept of the Nātha school, is somewhat different from the adepts of other orders. The *avadhūta* is neither the enjoyer nor the renouncer of the necessary objects of life. Hence, he is called *atyāśramī* or one who has transcended caste and the four stages of life.

56-58 The word "*bhāgavat*" needs to be defined. "*Bhaga*" means excellence which is sixfold, namely (1) the divine attributes of power (*aiśvarya*), (2) righteousness (*dharma*), (3) glory (*yaśas*), (4) beauty (*śrī*), wisdom (*jñāna*) and (6) non-attachment (*vairāgya*). A *bhāgavat* is one who possesses all these divine qualities. According to the Nātha school only Śiva or the supreme entity is endowed with all these six divine attributes of perfection.

Nātha is neither the individual self nor the supreme self. Nātha the supreme bestows liberation. The process and function of creation gradually evolves thus: Creation originates from two sources—*nāda* and *bindu*. The nine Nāthas come from *nāda* and *Sadāśiva Bhairava* comes from *bindu*. From the nine Nāthas descend the twelve and eighty-four *siddhas* and the twelve *panthas*.

59-61 Nātha is without origin, whereas all other divine incarnations such as Rāma, Kṛṣṇa, etc. are described as having parents and origins. Other divine incarnations are stated to be the creator, sustainer, and destroyer, etc. Hence they are active, whereas Nātha is inactive.

62-68 Yoga is established as the best form of spiritual realization because yoga has been taught by those who have already attained liberation.

All the spiritual paths other than yoga have prescribed some activites to be followed as part of spiritual practice . But yoga systems never prescribed any activity other than yoga as a part of the *sādhanā* for spiritual progress. Yoga itself is the means for spiritual perfection, because yoga is the union of the individual self with the supreme self.

It is already established that yoga is the subtlest form of the Vedas. The *yogins* are the highest order of Brāhmaṇas as they realize *brahman*. Brahmanism cannot be hereditary as a son of a Brāhmaṇa may not be fit to realize *brahman*. The *yogins* are the Brāhmaṇas in the true sense of the term, as none can be a *yogin* unless he realizes *brahman*.

(The text breaks off at this point.)

35.NITYANĀTHA, *Siddhasiddhāṇtapaddhati*

The text, edited by Pt. Janardanashastrin Pandeya, has been published in Sarasvatī Suṣamā (XIX.1), the research journal of Sanskrit University, Varanasi. The author Nityanātha, also known as Nityanāthapārvatīputra in the colophon, is a well-known teacher in the Nātha tradition of yoga. He has been mentioned as one of the *mahāsiddhas* by Svātmārāma (*Haṭhayogapradīpikā* I.7).

There is another work of the same name by Gorakṣanātha, already discussed and summarized above. The present text in three chapters is almost identical with the first three chapters of the work by Gorakṣanātha.

In the benedictory verses the author pays obeisance to the Eternal Luster, to Mahādeva, and to Ādinātha.

Since the contents of both this work and #29 are mostly identical there is no need for a separate summary. There are a few differences that might be mentioned. One of the most important differences is the placing of *dhyāna* before *dhāraṇā* in the present work. Gorakṣanātha, however, placed it after *dhāraṇā*. In addition, there are different names given for some postures, channels, vital centers, and worlds. There are no important philosophical differences between the two texts, however.

36.AUTHOR UNKNOWN, *Yogayājñavalkya*

Summary by Ram Shankar Bhattacharya

The text is attributed to the Yājñavalkya of the *Yājñavalkyasmṛti*, but it is clearly a Haṭha Yoga text from about the thirteenth or fourteenth century. The summary here is based on the edition of K. S. Sastri in Trivandrum Sanskrit Series, No. 134.

The text is in the form of a dialogue between Yājñavalkya and his wife, Gārgī.

CHAPTER ONE

I.1-9 Yājñavalkya, the *yogin*, was once requested by Gārgī to disclose the nature of yoga.

I.10-19 Yājñavalkya replies that he will describe yoga, which was originally proclaimed to him by Brahmā when he earnestly asked Brahmā to tell him about the nature of knowledge *(jñāna)* and karma.

I.26 There are two ways of attaining knowledge. One is called *pravṛttikarman*, through acts done through mental resolve (*saṃkalpa*) caused by desire. It is the cause of birth. The other is called *nivṛttikarman*, through acts that are accompanied by knowledge and performed without any mental resolve. Persons afraid of the cycle of birth and death should perform acts properly without being motivated by desire.

I.27-40 Persons belonging to the *varṇas* are required to pay off the debts owed to the sages, men, and gods by practicing celibacy, by procreating offspring, and by performing sacrifices. They are to remain in the *āśramas* as prescribed differently for the four *varṇas*. The duty of a Brāhmaṇa consists in studying the Vedas, performing sacrifice, etc. and uniting himself with the self while remaining in the *sannyāsa āśrama*. A Kṣatriya should perform the duties of a *sannyāsa*, a hermit (*vānaprastha*), and a householder. A Vaiśya should perform the duties of a hermit and a householder. A Śūdra should perform the duties of a householder and always engage himself in serving the other three *varṇas*. Some prescribe *brahmacarya* even to Śūdras. Persons belonging to the four *āśramas* are required to perform duties as enjoined in scripture without being motivated by desire.

I.41-42 Since karma associated with knowledge becomes the means to liberation Yājñavalkya describes knowledge as follows.

I.43-48 The essence of knowledge is yoga which has eight accessories (*aṅga*). Yoga is union of the individual self (*jīvātman*) and the supreme self (*paramātman*). The eight limbs are given and explained in the usual order.

I.49-69 The ten restraints are explained: (1) Nonviolence is not creating any trouble to any creature at any time; however, violence sanctioned by scripture is to be known as non-violence. (2) Truthfulness is language that is conducive to the well-being of others.(3) Non-stealing is the absence of desire to possess things that belong to others. (4) Celibacy is abstinence from all kinds of sexual activities. Persons of different *āśramas* have appropriate forms of celibacy. Even to serve respected persons comes under celibacy. (4) Kindness is the will for gratification or benefit of all creatures. (6) Straightforwardness (*ārjava*) is to remain without being disturbed by *pravṛtti* and *nivṛtti*. (7) Forgiveness (*kṣamā*) is the equal assessment toward desired and non-desired things. (8) Fortitude is the tranquility of awareness even if there arises loss or acquisition of wealth or friends. (9) Moderation of diet (*mitāhāra*) is to take the quantity of food as prescribed differently for persons of different *āśramas*. (10) Cleanliness (*śauca*) is either external (done with the help of external things like water, etc.) and internal (i.e. the purification of the mind either by cultivating spiritual knowledge (*adhyātmavidyā*) or by following the precepts of spiritual teachers.

CHAPTER TWO

II.1-19 There are ten observances, as follows. (1) Austerity (*tapas*) is the drying up of the body by practicing vows. (2) Contentment is the undisturbed state of mind on obtaining what comes spontaneously. (3) A believing nature (*āstikya*) is to keep faith in the existence of merit and demerit. (4) Giving is to give away with reverence a thing that has been earned in a right way. (5) Worship of God is to worship Viṣṇu or Rudra with a tranquil mind. The purification of heart, speech, ad body also comes under the worship of God. (6) Listening to the doctrines (*siddhāntaśravaṇa*) is to listen to the Veda in accordance with the rules as prescribed for persons belonging to different *āśramas*. (7) Shyness (*hrī*) is the reluctance to do an act which is declared to be blameable in the authoritative texts like the Vedas. (8) Faith (*mati*) is to hold in high esteem the duties enjoined in the *śāstras*. (9) Recitation (*japa*) is the proper uttering of incantations that are Vedic. Constant reading of the Vedas, etc. is also called *japa*. It is twofold: (a) *vācaka*, performed through utterance, which is either low or high, and b) *mānasa*, performed through mental activity or thinking. The *mānasa* form is higher. Recitation becomes effective if performed by knowing the names of the sages, metres, or incantations. (10) A vow is accepting a particular means (*upāya*) in order to achieve *dharma, artha, kāma* and *mokṣa*.

CHAPTER THREE

III.1-2 The eight principle postures are described, namely *svāstika, gomukha, padma, vīra, siṃha, bhadra, mukta, and mayūra.*

CHAPTER FOUR

IV.1-6 Gārgī asked Yājñavalkya about the nature of the purification of the channels, about the origination and flow of the channels, and about the places and functions of the vital airs.

IV.6-13 Yājñavalkya said: The length of the body of a person is equal to 96 fingers (*aṅgula*, i.e. the breadth of a finger, most probably of the thumb) of his own hand. The measurement of a breath (*prāṇa*) is 12 *aṅgulas* (according to some, fourteen more than the length of the body. That person deserves praise who can make the vital air equal to or lower than the bodily fire. It is desired that one should control the vital air by applying the bodily fire through yoga. The bodily fire of golden color exists in the middle part of the body. This place is triangular in human beings, quadrangular in quadrupeds, and circular in birds. The subtle flame existing in this place is known as the bodily fire.

IV.13-20) The exact place of this fire is the middle part of the body, which exists two *aṅgulas* above the anus and two *aṅgulas* beneath the organ of generation. The middle part of the heart and the navel is to be known as the middle part of quadrupeds and birds respectively.

The place known as *kanda* (bulb) exists nine *aṅgulas* above the middle part which is in the form of an egg having the length and thickness of four *aṅgulas*. There is a center (*nābhi*) in this bulb in which is situated a vital center (or "wheel", *cakra*) of twelve spokes. This vital center is the seat of the individual self (*jīva*). Breath (*prāṇa,* the vital air) flows in the lower part of this center. All individual selves remain alive so long as they are associated with breath.

IV.21-25 In the upper part of this vital center exists *kuṇḍalinī* assuming the form of an eightfold circle. Having encircled the aforesaid bulb, *kuṇḍalinī* exists and she shuts the mouth of *brāhmarandhra* with her own face. *Kuṇḍalī* possessing a serpent form shines forth in the heart and she is awakened by the flow of the *apāna* at the time of practicing yoga. At this time the vital air aided by fire flows towards the *suṣumṇā* nerve which is situated in the middle of the bulb. All the channels are connected with this bulb or with the vital center in the bulb.

IV.26-31 There are fourteen principal channels. Among them, three (*īḍā, piṅgalā* and *suṣumṇā*) are regarded as the chief channels. *Suṣumṇā* is the best of all as it is sustains the body and is regarded as the path or means to liberation. *Suṣumṇā* is situated in the middle part of the bulb and it extends up to the head through the backbone. *Suṣumṇā*, whose deity is Viṣṇu, is called *brāhmarandhra* as it is connected with the means to liberation.

IV.31-35 *Īḍā* (connected with the moon) and *piṅgalā* (connected with the sun) are situated in the left and right side of the *suṣumṇā*. The sun and the moon are respectively full of poison and nectar and are connected with *rajas* and *tamas*.

Suṣumṇā is the eater of time (i.e. it helps one to transcend time).

IV.35-46 The position and place of the channels are given here. A large number of channels are said to come out from these and pervade the whole body.

IV.47-49 In these channels flow the ten vital airs or breaths (given as *prāṇa, apāna, samāna, udāna, vyāna, nāga, kūrma, kṛkara, devadatta,* and *dhanañjaya*). The first five are to be known as principal. Among these five the first two are the most powerful and inhalation is more powerful than exhalation.

IV.50-56 The specific places of the first five airs are stated here.

IV.56-57 A general statement on the places of the second five airs are given here.

IV.57-65 The joint function of inhalation and exhalation (especially their influence on food taken in) has been stated here. It is remarked that there are nine holes from which excreta come out.

IV.66-71 The specific functions of the ten breaths are stated here. The act of purifying the channels is said to depend upon knowledge of the arrangement of the channels as well as knowledge of the places and functions of the airs.

CHAPTER FIVE

V.1-2 Being asked by Gārgī about the means for purifying the channels, Yājñavalkya replies:

V.3-10 A person who performs his duties properly and is free from desires, who practices restraints and observances and follows the customs appropriate to his *āśrama*, should resort to a suitable forest and constructing there a hut (*maṭha*) should practice yoga. Some however hold that any place which is free from (too much) wind and sunshine is suitable for yoga.

V.10-15 A person smearing himself with ashes, uttering appropriate incantations with a view to purifying various limbs of the body, placing *kuśa* grass or a deer-skin on the ground, holding body, head and neck firmly erect, bowing down to his *guru*, facing either the east or the north, should observe the nectar coming out from the eyes.

V.15-21 One should practice breath-control with meditation (as shown here) for a period of three to four years or for a period of three to four months, six times a day, in a solitary place. In this way a person can achieve purification of the channels. Signs like lightness in the body, etc. are to be found in a person who has purified his channels.

CHAPTER SIX

VI.1-10 The essential nature of breath control is the union of *prāṇa* and *apāna*. It has three operations: inhalation, exhalation and the stoppage of breath, which are connected with *a, u* and *m* respectively. A complete description of breath-control with the process of repeating *oṃ* and of the method of meditation is given in verses 4-10. It is prescribed that at first inhalation should be performed with the left nostril and then with the right nostril.

VI.11-19A Different views regarding the number of the incantations and the character–Vedic or secular–of the incantations (to be uttered in breath-control) as well as the process of uttering different incantations by members of each of the four *varṇas* and by women (including prohibitions, e.g., women should not utter *oṃ*) are stated here precisely.

VI.19-23 A Brahmin is required to practice breath-control three times a day. This enables him to eradicate his sins and to attain liberation.

VI.23-34 Proper practice of inhalation, exhalation and stoppage (as defined in VI.23-24) gives rise to sweat in the body (it is called the lowest stage of breath-control), quivering of the body (the middle stage), and the rising up of the body from the ground (the highest state). The third stage yields much pleasure. Inhalation and exhalation are completely absent in this state, which is called *sahita*. There is also another state of breath-control called *kevala kumbhaka*. It has no reference to inhalation or exhalation. The aforesaid *sahita kumbhaka* is a means to this stage. It gives rise to the power called *manojavitva* (possessing the speed of the mind). It is the path of liberation and the source of knowledge.

VI.35-48 Control of breathing is the way to subjugate the vital air. Different results can be achieved by restraining air in different parts of the body or by taking in air in different ways as is precisely stated here. Certain diseases can be eradicated if air is restrained in different parts of the body.

VI.49-57 A particular way of conquering the vital air is to make the vital air reach the *brāhmarandhra* through the *suṣumṇā* channel by restraining air through a particular yogic process (shown in VI.51-53). At this stage a sound similar to that of a lute is heard. Before hearing this sound one may hear the sounds of a conch, wind, etc. When air enters the *brāhmarandhra* the mind abides in the self. Air is now subjugated completely and consequently the individual self enjoys perpetual bliss.

VI.57-64 Some *yogins* say that a person should sit in the *siddha* posture holding his body, head, and neck erect and should utter *oṃ* and practice breath-control. This can be practiced by the members of all the four *varṇas* and by women as well–by uttering sacred syllables concerning deities like Śiva, etc. They should keep a lamp in their hands. Through this process breath reaches the place of fire. The practice is to be followed until the fire is subjugated.

VI.64-73 The body of the practitioner becomes light when air is restrained in the place of *śakti* (or fire, *vahini*, in the Bengali edition). Then the practitioner should try to restrain air in the navel until it is absorbed in the sun residing in the navel. Through this process air reaches the region of *kuṇḍalī*, as a result of which *kuṇḍalinī* is awakened. The ultimate result of all these practices as stated here is the realization of the ever-shining *ātman*.

VI.74-81 If anybody wants to leave his body through yoga he should contemplate *brahman* and should let the vital air pass through the *brāhmarandhra*. He should then unite his own self with the blissful *ākāśa* (i.e. *brahman*) as a result of which he becomes identical with *brahman* and does not assume a body again. It is desired that a person should perform his duties in accordance with the rules and should practice breath-control as taught in the yogic tradition, for a person, being purified through breath-control, attains the highest goal.

CHAPTER SEVEN

VII.1-4 The forcible drawing in of the organs, which naturally run towards or move among their respective objects, is called withdrawal of sense-organs (*pratyāhāra*). To see everything as existing in the self (i.e. in the intellect in the form of the self) is also called *pratyāhāra*. The mental performance of the obligatory duties also falls under *pratyāhāra*.

VII.5-16 To draw air from one vital part (*marman*) and to retain it in another part is also called *pratyāhāra*. Air should be retained in these places with the help of mental force. If anybody is able to draw air from one vital part and to retain it in another vital part, he becomes perfect in yoga and gets rid of all diseases.

VII.17-25 Another way of withdrawal is to restrain air with the help of breath-control in the different places (i.e. the aforesaid *marmans*) of the body with reflection.

VII.25-30 Air inhaled through the two nostrils can be restrained in the two sides of *kuṇḍalinī* simultaneously. Likewise air can be restrained in the heart. This practice is helpful to attain the state of the highest self. Another process to attain the highest goal is given in verse 28. It is desired that one should draw the vital air through the *suṣumṇā* channel and restrain it in the place between the two eyebrows until the mind is dissolved.*

---

*The Bengali edition has been used as there is a hiatus in this passage.

CHAPTER EIGHT

VIII.1-3 Meditative fixation is the steady fixation of the mind on the self. It is also the mental holding of the external *ākāśa* in the cavity of the heart situated in the city of *brahman* (i.e. the living body).

VIII.4-10 There are five attentions to be fixed on the five deities residing in the five elements and which are situated in five different regions of the body. One should practice fixed attention to these five deities by uttering five mystical letters or syllables (*bījamantra*), namely *laṃ, vaṃ, raṃ, yaṃ* and *haṃ.* One should unite oneself with *parameśvara* by turning one's breath and mind toward Sadāśiva, who is the cause of all.

VIII.11-15 In this respect some *yogins* say that a person, after dissolving the effects into their respective causes, should perceive the *brahman-puruṣa,* who is dark brown in color, with the help of *oṃ*. Gārgī is asked to realize the highest self in her mind purified by the practice of mystic sound (*nāda*).

VIII.16-23 According to the *yogins* who are also physicians, the body is made up of five elements and is characterized by three *doṣas* (wind, bile, and phlegm). The nature of a body is to be ascertained according to the nature of those three *doṣas*. Diseases caused by the mind, etc. can be uprooted with the help of various kinds of mental fixation. The aforesaid three *doṣas* can be destroyed by the practice of breath-control. It is required that a practitioner of the restraints and observances should perform duties and practice fixity of mind.

CHAPTER NINE

IX.1-3 Reflective meditation is the direct feeling (*vedanā*) of one's own self through the mind. It is either qualified (*saguṇa)* or non-qualified (*nirguṇa*). There are five higher forms of qualified meditation among which three are the best. Non-qualified meditation is of one kind only.

IX.4-11 The non-qualified kind of meditation is to be practiced by a person who is aware of the nature and functions of the *marmans,* channels and vital airs. It consists in feeling "I am *brahman* who is all-embracing, all-perceiving, all-pervading, pure, and full of bliss". There is also another form of non-qualified meditation on the self who is the embodiment of bliss, who is dark brown and perceived in the city of *brahman* (i.e. the heart) situated in the body.

IX.12-29 A qualified kind of meditation also consists in thinking of the identity of the lotus-heart having eight petals with the highest self who is known as Vāsudeva, Nārāyāṇa or Puruṣottama. The best form of qualified contemplation consists in thinking of the one's identity with the imperishable highest self. The state of *vaiśvānara* is attained through this meditation which leads to liberation. There is also a variation of this meditation. It is the perceiving in the mind of the solar disc which is identical with the golden *puruṣa* with four faces.

IX.30-31 To perceive the lustrous and motionless inner self as existing in the region between the middle part of the body and the head and to think of one's identity with it is said to be a higher form of contemplation.

IX.32-41 Another variation of this (qualified) meditation is the contemplation of the lustrous higher self by a person whose eyes are fixed on the tip of his nose and who has relaxed his body and who has also performed the posture called *paryaṅka*. Afterwards the practitioner is to think of his identity with *paramātman*. Another variation of this meditation is to think of the identity with the imperishable *paramātman* who is the enjoyer, pure, emitting nectar in the lotus-heart having eight petals. By practicing this meditation for a period of six months one can conquer death and by practicing it for a period of one year one becomes liberated in one's lifetime.

IX.42-44 It is desired that one should practice meditation and should abandon desire for the results of actions. Though there are many kinds of meditation, the aforesaid ones are to be preferred. Sages, knowing the self as both qualified and non-qualified, practice meditation.

CHAPTER TEN

X.1-5 Concentration (*samādhi*) is the state of equality of both the individual self and the highest self. It may also be defined as the abiding of the interior self in *brahman*. As one meditates so one attains concentration. One attains concentration on an object to which one is excessively attached. In concentration the individual self and the supreme self become one.

X.6-19 One should endeavor to attach oneself to the supreme self by performing one's own duties without any desire for result and also by following the instructions of one's own spiritual teacher. When one becomes aware of the fact that death is approaching, one should impart one's learning to one's son and should reside in some sacred place. There one, sitting in the *paryaṅka* posture and facing the east or the north, should sit on a seat made of *kuśa* grass or on a seat on which a deer-skin has been placed. One should practice breath-control by restraining the gates of the body, fixing one's mind on the supreme self. One should leave one's body by uttering *oṃ* and should always contemplate the nature of the self. It is declared by *yogins* that whatever one is remembering at the time of death, that is reached by him.

X.20-23 Gārgī was asked to leave her body by meditating on the self in the mind. One attains liberation with the help of knowledge if one performs one's duties without any attachment toward the results. This is the essence of *karmayoga* taught by Brahmā. Gārgī was advised to practice the eight-membered yoga and to forsake mundane existence by attaining *nirvāṇa*.

CHAPTER ELEVEN

XI.1-3 Gārgī asked Yājñavalkya how one should perform one's duties and how one could get expiation if one fails to perform one's duties.

XI.4-10 Yājñāvalkya replied: There is no question of expiation for a person who, with a purified mind, practices breath-control and leaves all actions. It is wrong to leave one's duties at the time of practicing yoga regarding them as painful. As all actions cannot be relinquished by an embodied being they are to be performed till death. After performing the duties one should leave one's body by uniting oneself with the supreme self.

XI.10-22 Gārgī requested Yājñavalkya to expound yoga with its limbs which is the means to liberation.

CHAPTER TWELVE

XII.1-4 A person, after performing the *siddha* posture should behold the flame of fire. *Prāṇa*, being restricted by yogic posture, reaches the fire which gradually shines forth. This practice should be continued for ten days, three times a day.

XII.5-9 Some signs, e.g. lightness in the body, or manifestation of the secret or divine sound (*nāda*), appear in a person who has put the vital air under control. The aforesaid fire is to be restricted in the navel. One should constantly meditate on *kuṇḍalinī* situated in the navel region and should restrain air.

XII.10-14 The self-luminous *kuṇḍalinī*, assuming the form of a serpent, is situated in the navel. He deserves praise, who can meditate on *kuṇḍalinī* and can hear her. She, being heated, is awakened and runs through the whole body. It is also required to draw the air above the navel by conquering the region of *kuṇḍalinī*.

XII.15-22 All diseases are cured when air, being mixed with fire, pervades the whole body by surpassing the navel. At this time air flows towards the *brahmarandhra*. When the vital air with fire is restricted in the heart, then air enters the thousand-petalled lotus (i.e. the *sahasrāra cakra*) and makes its mouth turn upwards. In the citadel of *brahman* (i.e. the heart) the vital air exists and the fire situated in the *suṣumṇā,* which extends up to the space between the two eyebrows, shines. When both air and fire enter the heart then light, etc. are perceived and internal as well as external signs appear. One should behold through the mind's eye the fire-like moon in the forehead and meditate on the inner self in the mind. In the citadel of *brahman* there resides the individual self who is nothing but *brahman* deluded.

XII.23-31 The invisible subtle body (*liṅgaśarīra*) shines either in the middle part of the body or in the heart or in the forehead. A knower of *brahman* perceives the lustrous *śakti* through one-pointed vision. When the mind existing in the space between the two eyebrows becomes dissolved (i.e. becomes devoid of all activities and distractions) then the self is perceived. At this time the crown of the head quivers. Such a practitioner becomes able to perceive the self in the mind and also the sages, *siddhas* and others. So long as the mind is not dissolved in the space between the two eyebrows one should think of absolute bliss or the full moon in the cavity of the mouth. When the mind exists in the *viṣṇupada* (that is, *ākāśa*) it gets dissolved. This is the state which is near to liberation. At this stage bliss is experienced. One is required to make oneself capable of attaining liberation through the practice of yoga.

XII.32-36 *Brahman* is that from which the origin, subsistence, and dissolution of all proceed, and which according to the scriptures shines in the heart. It is subtler than the subtle and greater than the great and is perceived with the purified intellect. One drawing out the vital air should retain it in the head and should mutter sacred syllables. One should leave the body by drawing the vital air upwards and by letting it go through the head.

XII.37-47 After declaring the science of yoga, Yājñavalkya went away to a lonely place to practice concentration and Gārgī, forsaking the world, took refuge in a lonely forest-hermitage and began to practice yoga.

37. SVĀTMĀRĀMA, *Haṭhayogapradīpikā*

Summary by Ram Shankar Bhattacharya

Svātmārāma Yogin lived some time in the fourteenth

century, and his text, *Haṭhayogapradīpikā*, is one of the most well-known texts on Haṭha Yoga.

The text has been edited and translated twice, once in P. Sinha 1914-15, and again in Iyangar 1933, which is our T. There is also a translation (but no text) by Hans-Ulrich Rieker (translated by Elsy Becherer), in *The Yoga of Light. Hatha Yoga Pradipika. India's Classical Handbook* (Herder and Herder: New York, 1971). The edition used here is Kṣemarāj Śri Kṛṣṇadāsa, *saṃvat* 1968 (=1911 CE), Bombay–and the verses in I, III and IV are different in this edition from that used by RSB and by both Sinha and Iyengar.

The text is filled with the technical terms and practices of Haṭha Yoga. In many instances, the technical names are cited without explanation or interpretation. It should be noted that the expression "Rāja Yoga", which supposedly according to many sources refers to Pātañjala Yoga, in fact bears very little relation to Pātañjala Yoga.

CHAPTER ONE

I.1-3 (E2-4; T1-2) In three introductory verses the author pays homage to Ādinātha (Śiva), to his teacher Gurunātha, and indicates that he has composed the work for the sake of the attainment of Rāja Yoga.

I.4-9 (E7-11; T4) Haṭha Yoga was known to Matsyendra and Gorakṣa and was passed on to Svātmārāma. A list of the names of the "great accomplished ones" (*mahāsiddha*) is given, and they are said to have conquered death.

I.10-11 (E11; T4-5) Haṭha Yoga is able to uproot all miseries and it should be circulated in secret by *yogins*.

I.12-14 (E13-16; T5-7) A practitioner of Haṭha Yoga should reside in a small cottage (*maṭha*) in a pious country. It should be built in accordance with the instructions laid down in verse 13.

I.15-16 (E17; T8) There are six impediments to yoga, namely (i) excessive food, (ii) effort causing fatigue, (iii) talkativeness, (iv) cultivation of harmful habits, (v) mixing with people, and (vi) covetousness or fickleness. Similarly, there are six factors that promote yoga, namely (i) enthusiasm, (ii) courage, (iii) fortitude, (iv) knowledge of the principles, (v) determination, and (vi) leaving the association of people.

I.17 (E18; T8-12) Ten restraints and ten observances are listed.

I.18 (E19; T13-14) Posture is regarded as the first limb (*aṅga*) or aid in Haṭha Yoga. It is conducive to firmness, etc. Sages like Vasiṣṭha and *yogins* such as Matsyendra have developed the various postures.

I.19-32 (E20-26; T14-17) The technique of performing the following postures is given in these verses: *svastika* (19), *vīra* (21), *kūrma* (22) *kukkuṭa* (230, *utthānakūrma* (24), *dhanus (25), matsyendra* (26-27) *paścimottāna* (28-29), *mayūra* (30-31) and *śava* (32).

I.33-43 (E26-31; T17-19) The postures *siddha, padma, siṃha,* and *bhadra* are said to be the best among the eighty-four postures and even among these four *siddha* is the highest. *Siddha* is described with its different names (in 35-37) and praised (in 38-43).

I.44-57 (E32-38; T19–22) The postures *padma, siṃha* and *bhadra* are elaborately described and praised (variations in names are also given). It is advised that an aspirant should practice breath-control and bodily exercises along with the postures. The practice of hearing the *anāhata* sound (*nādānusandhāna*) is to be taken up after practicing postures, control of breath, and exercises. A practitioner of yoga observing celibacy, etc. and leaving all contact with objects achieves perfection.

I.58-63 (E39-43; T22-25) Moderation in eating (*mitāhāra*) consists in taking food that is soft and agreeable. One-fourth part of the stomach should remain empty. A list of forbidden food (*apathya*) is given in verse 59. The nature of unwholesome food is uttered in verse 60. It is ordained that one should avoid fire, the company of women, much traveling, etc. A list of edibles is given in verse 62 and the nature of such food is stated in verse 63.

CHAPTER TWO

II.1-5 (E46-47; T26) Breath-control is to be practiced according to the instructions of a teacher. As air has great influence over the activity of the mind and life, it is essential to stop the movements of air, i.e. breath (in the body). It is also necessary to purify the channels in order to possess mastery of the vital air.

II.6-11 (E48-50; T27-28) Inhalation and exhalation are to be practiced through different nostrils (both right, *piṅgalā*, and left, *īḍā*) in a particular way (as shown here) in order to purify the *suṣumṇā* channel. The channels become purified through proper practice of breath-control for a period of about three months. One should practice eighty *prāṇāyāmas* in four sittings (in the morning, midday, evening and midnight).

II.12-18 (E51-56; T28-30) In the initial stage of breath-control sweat comes out from the body of the practitioner, and it should be rubbed into the body. In the middling state of breath-control trembling arises, and in the highest state the air (breath) reaches steadiness. Milk and clarified butter should be taken at the time of beginning the practice of breath-control, which should be performed gradually and without using any force. Though breath-control is able to eradicate diseases, yet it becomes the source of disease if practiced in a wrong way.

II.19-20 (E57; T30) When the channels become purified there arises leanness, and luster in the body and internal sound (*nāda*) becomes manifested.

II.21-35 (E57-66; T30-33) If there is excessive fat or phlegm in the body, one should practice the six purificatory exercises, namely *dhautī, basti, neti, trāṭaka, nauli* and *kapālabhāti* (explained earlier on p. 141). The process of practicing these exercises is given here in detail.

II.36-43 (E66-70; T33-34) A practice of these six exercises enables one to practice breath-control easily, which is regarded by some as the only practice of *yogins*. The stoppage of air makes the mind calm and one-pointed. Breath-control helps the vital air to enter the mouth of the channel *suṣumṇā*; consequently the *yogin* attains the state called *manonmanī* (steadiness of mind). (The practice of *gajakaraṇī*, a type of vomiting, has been incidentally described in verse 38.)

II.44-47 (E70-72; T35-36) Stoppage of breath (*kumbhaka*) is of eight kinds, namely *sūryabheda*, etc. While practicing breath-control one should practice the three *bandhas*, namely *jālandhara* (contracting the throat), *uḍḍiyāna* (drawing back the abdomen) and *mūla* (contracting the anus) so that the vital air can reach the *brahmanāḍī* (that is, *suṣumṇā*).

II.48-70 (E73-88; T36-42) The process of practicing the following eight kinds of breath control with their results has been given in detail: (1) *sūryabheda* (48-50), (2) *ujjāyī* (51-53), (3) *sītkārī* (54-56), (4) *sītalī* (57-58), (5) *bhastrikā* (59-67), (6) *bhāmarī* (68), (7) *mūrchā* (69), and (8) *plāvinī* (70).

II.71-75) (E90-91; T43) Breath-control consists of three operations, exhalation, inhalation, and stopping these two. The latter is either *sahita* or *kevala*. The former (*sahita*) should be practiced as a means to the latter and air is to be retained with ease without performing inhalation or exhalation. The latter (*kevala*) is highly powerful and it enables one to realize the secret power known as *kuṇḍalī* (the same as *kuṇḍalinī*).

II.76-78 (E92-93; T44) One should practice the ways prescribed in Haṭha Yoga and Rāja Yoga until one achieves the extraordinary capacities of Rāja Yoga. One cannot be effectively practiced without the other. By stopping breathing one should render the mind content-free so that one can attain the stage of Rāja Yoga. Signs like leanness of body, calmness in one's face, brightness in the eyes, etc. become manifested in a person who practices breath-control.

CHAPTER THREE

III.1-5 (E94-95; T45) The *kuṇḍalī* or the *ādhāraśakti* (power of sustaining) is said to be the seat of the means of yoga (i.e. all yoga practices are based on *kuṇḍalī*). As soon as *kuṇḍalī* awakens all the lotuses (i.e. the vital centers) become fully opened and the knots get untied. At this time the vital air begins to flow through the *śūnyapadavī* (lit., the way to the void, that is, the *suṣumṇā* channel) and one's awarenesses become untouched by supporting objects. *Suṣumṇā* is called by various names. One should practice the bodily exercises in order to awaken the divine *kuṇḍalinī* residing in the entrance to the *brahmadvāra* (i.e. *suṣumṇā*, i.e. the open door to *brahman*).

III.6-9 (E96-97; T45-46) The ten bodily exercises, namely the *mahāmudrā*, etc. are capable of destroying decay and death and of affording the eight supernormal powers. These are to be practiced secretly.

III.10-18 (E97-101; T46-47) Technique of the *mahāmudrā*. It is to be practiced with the *jālandharabandha* and the *mūlabandha*. This exercise helps *kuṇḍalinī* to awaken. In it respiration is to be practiced slowly. At first it is to be practiced on the left side and then on the right side. It even destroys the effect of poison and removes diseases like consumption, leprosy, and the like.

III.19-25 (E102-104; T47-48) Technique of the *mahābandha*. It is to be practiced along with the *jālandharabandha* and the *mūlabandha*, and to be practiced at first with the left side and then with the right side. Some do not prescribe the contraction of the throat (*kaṇṭhabandha)* in the *jālandharabandha* and say that the tongue-lock (pressing the upper surface of the tongue against the palate) is highly beneficial. This exercise helps the mind to attain to *kedāra*, the place of Śiva (in the middle of the eyebrow). Both the *mahāmudrā* and the *mahābandha* are to be practiced with the *mahāvedha*.

III.26-29 (E105-106; T48-49) It is to be practiced with the *kaṇṭhamudrā* (i.e. *jālandharabandha*). It destroys wrinkles, greyness of hair, etc.

III.30-31 (E107; T49) Praise of the aforesaid three *bandhas*. These are to be practiced gradually, eight times a day, according to the traditional teaching.

III.32-54 (E108-119; T49-56) Technique of the *khecarīmudrā*; why it is so called; it is also called *vyomacakra*. The tongue is to be so thrust as to touch the gullet in the cavity of the skull (*kapālakuhara*) and the eyesight is to be kept in the middle of the eyebrows. The tongue should be put out, rubbed, and elongated in the manner shown in 33-36. The practitioner remains unaffected by poison, etc. The secret name of the tongue's entering into the eyebrow is "the eating of the cow" (*gomāṃsabhakṣaṇa*). The fluid coming out from the middle of the eyebrow is called "the liquor of gods" (*amāravāruṇī*). This exercise enables one to realize one's own self. It is established in the vacuum, which is the source of knowledge and is associated with the five streams (viz., *iḍā*, etc.).

III.55-60 (E120-122; T57-58) Technique of the *uḍḍiyānabandha*; why it is called so; it is also called *udyāna* in III.6. Its practice consists in pressing the belly above the navel backwards. It should be learnt from a competent teacher. One can conquer death by practicing it for six months. It helps one to attain liberation in a natural way.

III.61-69 (E123-126; T58-60) Technique of the *mūlabandha*. The perineum (*yoni*) is to be pressed by the heel and the anus is to be contracted. This practice make exhalation go upwards and this unites inhalation with exhalation, *nāda* with *bindu*. The fire becomes developed being struck by the air (breath) as a result of which *kuṇḍalinī* awakens and she enters the *brahmanāḍī*.

III.70-75 (E127-129; T60-61) Technique of the *jālandharabandha*. It consists in the contraction of the throat and in the pressing of the chin against the chest. It destroys pain in the throat, closes sixteen vital parts (*ādhāra*), and checks the falling of the nectar. This should be united with the *uḍḍiyānabandha* so that the vital air should flow towards the western or posterior direction (that is, to *suṣumṇā*). The aforesaid three *bandhas* are the means to Haṭha Yoga.

III.77-82 (E130-132; T61-63) Technique of the

viparītakaraṇī mudrā. The head is to be placed on the ground and the legs are to be raised. The sun residing at the navel eats up the nectar of the moon situated on the palate. This consumption of the nectar can be checked by this exercise. If practiced for six months it increases appetite and destroys wrinkles, etc.

III.83-89 (E133-137; T63) The technique of *vajrolī mudrā*. Milk and a woman are required for a successful practice of this exercise. It consists in drawing back the semen discharged during sexual intercourse. A *yogin* overcomes death by drawing back semen in the aforesaid way. Sweat smell comes out from the body of a *yogin* who is able to preserve semen. It is required that both the mind and the semen are to be preserved properly.

III.90-103 (E137-143; T63) *Sahajolī* and *amarolī* are variations of *vajrolī*. After practicing *vajrolī* the male and the female *yogins* should smear ashes of cow-dung on their bodies. This is *sahajolī*. Drinking of one's urine in mid-flow is called *amarolī*. It is a favorite practice of the Kāpālikas. *Vajrolī* is to be practiced by women also so that they can preserve their *rajas* (menstrual excretion).

III.104-123 (E144-152; T63-66) Technique of the *śakticālana mudrā*. With the help of *kuṇḍalinī* (called by various names) a *yogin* opens the door of liberation which is covered by her. One attains liberation if one can forcibly move the *kuṇḍalinī* power. If she is awakened as result of catching hold of her tail (the process is to be learnt from a teacher) and of practicing breath-control in a particular way (as stated in verses 114-117) she goes upwards. The seat of *kuṇḍalinī* is above the bulb which is nine inches above the *mūla* (i.e. the *mūlādhāra*). One sitting in the *vajra* posture should awaken *kuṇḍalinī* by practicing the *bhastrikā* form of breath-control and should contract the navel for two *muhūrtas* (ninety-six minutes). By this practice *kuṇḍalinī* leaves the entrance of the *suṣumṇā* and the vital air enters it. One practicing the said way gets perfection within forty days. There are 72,000 channels in the body which are purified by the said practice.

III.124-127 (E153-154; T67) *Suṣumṇā* becomes straight by the practice of yogic posture, etc. Those who have conquered sleep and whose mind has become calm can acquire perfection by the practice of the *rudrāṇī* (*śāmbhavī*) *mudrā*. It is useless to practice breath-control, etc. without following Rāja Yoga. Control of breathing, etc. are to be practiced with a concentrated mind.

III.128-130 (E155-156; T67-68) Every one of these ten exercises is capable of bestowing perfection. A *guru* is a person who can instruct strictly in accordance with the traditional way.

CHAPTER FOUR

IV.1-7 (E157-160; T69-70) Let there be praise of Śiva whose essential nature consists in *nāda, bindu* and *kalā*. Concentration (*samādhi*), the chief topic of this Chapter, is called by by various names, such as *rājayoga, unmanī, manomanī, amanaska* and so forth. Altogether some sixteen synonyms are listed. Concentration is the equality or oneness of the self with the mind. It is also defined as the state of being in complete absorption (*samarasa*), which comes into existence when both the mind and the vital air become dissolved (or motionless). It is also the oneness of the individual self with the supreme self.

IV.8-9 (E160-161; T70-71) In practicing Rāja Yoga one should follow the instructions of a *guru* without whose grace it is extremely difficult to realize the *tattva* or to acquire the state of spontaneous concentrations (*sahaja avasthā*).

IV.10-13 (E161-163; T71-72) When by the practice of posture, etc. *kuṇḍalinī* is awakened and *prāṇa* reaches *śūnya* (i.e. the *brāhmarandhra*), a person naturally attains *sahaja avasthā* (defined as the state of liberation while alive or "the fourth" (*turīya*) if he realizes *kuṇḍalinī* and leaves off all actions. When *prāṇa* flows through the *suṣumṇā* channel and the mind enters *śūnya* (i.e. *brahman* not limited by space and time), then a *yogin* becomes free from all actions (i.e. not affected by their results) and transcends time.

IV.14-17 (E163-177; T72-74) Perfection in the *amarolī-*, *vajrolī-*, and *sahajolī-mudrās* can be acquired if the mind becomes calm and the vital air enters *madhyama* (i.e. the *suṣumṇā* channel). So long as breath, the organs and the mind are alive (i.e. active) knowledge cannot be acquired. He whose breath and mind are dissolved can attain liberation. Having known the process of piercing (*bheda*, i.e. passing) the *suṣumṇā* channel and having made the air run through it, one becomes able to restrain breath in the *brāhmarandhra*. Time (here it means the period of day and night) is regulated by the sun and the moon; it is eaten or destroyed by *suṣumṇā*.

IV.18-19 (E178; T74) In a cage-like body there are 72,000 openings of the channels. The (central) channel *suṣumṇā* is known to be related to Śiva (*śāmbhavīśakti*).

IV.20-25 (E179-181; T74-75) The state of *manomani* (mind not directed to any object) arises when breath flows through *suṣumṇā*. Mind can be restricted if air (i.e. breathing) is put under control and vice versa. Subconscious impressions and air (i.e. breathing) are the causes of mental activity. The destruction of one leads to the destruction of the other. Both the mind and breathing are to be restricted to one and the same point. Both of these are intermingled. The activity and non-activity of the one depend upon those of the other. When both of them are destroyed liberation is attained.

IV.26-29 (E182-183; T75-77) Both mercury (*rasa*) and the mind (*manas*) are constantly restless. As mercury prepared in different ways cures disease, enlivens the dead, and enables one to travel in the sky, so the practice of breath control cures disease, prolongs longevity, and enables one to remain above the ground.

The stability of the mind leads to the stability of breathing, which in turn helps one to preserve semen (*bindu*) as a result of which stability of the body is acquired. Breathing is a matter of the mind, whose dissolution depends upon the secret sound (*nāda*).

IV.30-34 (E184-185; T77-78) According to this school the

dissolution of the mind is liberation. Bliss manifests itself when both the *manas* and *prāṇa* are dissolved. This dissolution is to be regarded as the ultimate goal. It is experienced in one's own self. Both ignorance (in which all effects exist) and *vidyā* (the *śakti* existing in the individual selves) become unnoticed when the mind becomes dissolved in *brahman*. Dissolution is the absence of memory of objects on account of the non-rise of subconscious impressions.

IV.35-38 (E186-188; T78-79) The practice of the *śāmbhavī mudrā* (to be practiced secretly) consists in directing one's vision to the vital bodily centers and at the same time keeping the eyes without blinking. In this state the *yogins* mind and breathing become motionless, and the *yogin* perceives everything with detachment This exercise enables one to realize the *tattva*, which is neither void nor non-void. The *śāmbhavī* and the *khecarī mudrās* enable one to realize bliss as they cause the mind's dissolution in the self, which is nothing but awareness and bliss (*citsukharūpa*).

IV.39-42 (E188-191; T79-81) Technique of the *unmanī mudrā,* not known even by the followers of the *āgama*, etc. The practice of this exercise consists in fixing the gaze on the tip of the nose and raising the eyebrows a little, and in keeping the mind steady. In this exercise the organic function of the *yogin* comes to a stop; the *yogin* realizes the ever shining light which is the cause of all.

IV.43-53 (E191-195; T81-83) The *khecarī mudrā* is accomplished when breathing flows through neither the right (*piṅgalā*) nor the left (*īḍā*) channel but in the middle (i.e. the *suṣumṇā*) channel. The vacuum existing between the said two nerves absorbs air. While practicing *khecarī* which is associated with the *vyoma* channel (i.e. the space between the two eyebrows) the practitioner abides in the space (*antara*) which has no supporting object. *Khecarī* practiced properly leads to the *unmanī* state. The mind dissolves in the space between the eybrows, called the seat of Śiva. *Khecarī* is to be practiced until the yogic sleep (*yoganidrā*, that is, the cessation of all fluctuations) is acquired. In it one must keep one's awareness without any supporting object. Both breathing and awareness become tranquil in this exercise and cease to function. Consequently the *yogin* acquires great strength and a highly developed body.

IV.54-64 (E196-201; T83-86) By associating the mind with *śakti* (i.e. *kuṇḍalinī*) one should attain the highest goal. One should think of oneself as identical with *brahman* and leave all thought. One should relinquish all wishes in order to achieve tranquility or peace, as wishing (*saṃkalpa*) is the root cause of all activities. The mind assumes the form of the *tattva* (that is, truth or the self) if it remains constantly united with it. Knowledge and knowable entities are nothing but the mind itself (owing to their being the creations of mind). On the destruction (or disappearance) of these three nothing exists. Everything is capable of being perceived by the mind. If the mind becomes dissolved (*unmanī*, i.e. if it becomes absolutely bereft of all fluctuations of thoughts) then duality is no longer perceived, consequently isolation is manifested. Various means for attaining concentration have been prescribed by the ancient teachers.

IV.65-68 (E201-203; T86-87) Gorakṣanātha taught the process of meditation on sound (*nāda*, i.e. the process of taking the unstruck (*anāhata*) sound as the chief means). It is the best of all means. A person, sitting in the *siddha* posture and performing the *śāmbhavī mudrā* should hear the secret sound in the right ear with a concentrated mind. Another way to sound-meditation is to close the ear with the fingers and try to hear the secret sound in the purified path of *suṣumṇā*.

IV.69-79 (E204-208; T87-90) The secret sound has four stages. In the first (*ārambha*) stage the *Brahmagranthī* gets untied and bliss comes out from *śūnya* (i.e. the cavity in the heart). The body of the practitioner becomes divine and his heart becomes full of vitality. In the second (*ghaṭa*) state the breath reaches the throat, the *Viṣṇugranthī* gets untied and the sound of a drum is heard in the cavity of the throat. In the third state (*paricaya*) the sound of a drum (*mardala*) is heard in the cavity of the space between the two eyebrows and the *Rudragranthī* is untied. Consequently, the air reaches the space between the eyebrows. The sound of a flute is heard. In the fourth (*niṣpatti*) stage, which is the state of Rāja Yoga in which both the object (*viṣaya*) and the cognizer (*viṣayin*) become unified and the *yogin* becomes similar to *īśvara*. The effort of a person practicing Haṭha Yoga without knowing Rāja Yoga is fruitless.

IV.80-89 (E208-212; T90-92) To meditate on the space between the eyebrows is the means to attain the state called *unmanī*. The dissolution of the mind is the immediate result of the secret sound. By hearing *nāda* one attains bliss. One should keep the mind ready to hear the *anāhata*-sound which conceals all external sounds, as a result of which the practitioner gets rid of all distractions. As the practice of *nāda* get developed subtle and more subtle *nāda*s are heard. The sounds, similar to those of the clouds, ocean, etc. are heard at first, which are afterwards followed by the sounds of a bamboo, lute, etc. One should try to situate the mind to hear the subtle component parts of the loud sounds. Any sound may be taken as a means for concentrating the mind.

IV.90-102 (E213-219 T92) The mind associated with *nāda* gradually gets dissolved and becomes bereft of all desire. An experiencing mind can be restricted by the practice of the *anāhata* sound. This is why an attentive mind should always try to hear *nāda*, which destroys the unsteadiness and distractions of mind and enables it to attain *brahman*. By hearing the secret sounds the mind gradually becomes absorbed. The subjugation of the fluctuations becomes easier if air enters the *brāhmarandhra* through the path of *susumṇā*. The knowable awareness (*jyotiṣ*) is to be perceived in the *anāhata*-sound. It is the highest region (*pada*) of Viṣṇu. So long as there is sound there is *ākāśa*. *Brahman* transcending sound and mind is called the supreme self. All forms of *nāda* are nothing but *śakti*. It is the formless supreme self in whom all *tattva*s get dissolved.

IV.103-109 (E219-222; T95-97) All the means to Haṭha and Laya processes are prescribed to achieve Rāja Yoga, which enables a *yogin* to transcend time. The state of *unmanī* is manifested in the mind that has cultivated the Haṭha-practices characterized by passionlessness. When all sins are destroyed the mind and the vital air are dissolved in the attributeless *brahman*. In the state called *unmanī* the body of a *yogin* becomes absolutely effortless. A *yogin* looks like a dead person. He is not afraid of death nor is he attached to actions. The mind, being functionless, becomes devoid of all knowledge of external objects.

IV.110-114 (E222-225; T97-98) He, whose mind neither sleeps nor wakes nor remembers nor even appears or disappears, is liberated. Such a *yogin* does not experience the pain of opposites. In the waking state he appears like a sleeping person. A *yogin* who has attained *samādhi* cannot be controlled by others, and he cannot be overcome by incantations or *yantras* (magical diagrams). So long as a person is unable to control the breath in the middle channel (*suṣumṇā*), to preserve semen and to practice contemplation easily, his views on wisdom (that is, on the doctrines of this *śāstra*) are to be taken as unreliable and invalid.

38.AUTHOR UNKNOWN, *Gheraṇḍasaṃhitā*

Summary by Ram Shankar Bhattacharya

The work is in dialogue form between Gheraṇḍa, the teacher, and Caṇḍakāpāli, the disciple. The work is named after the name of the teacher, and its authorship is unknown. It is probably a product of the late seventeenth century, roughly contemporaneous with the *Śivasaṃhitā*, another Haṭha Yoga classic text. A large number of verses of this text are more or less similar (not only in meaning but also in form) to verses of the *Haṭhayogapradīpikā*.

The *Gheraṇḍasaṃhitā* has a considerable number of editions with commentaries, some with translations into vernacular language as well as into English.

The text is largely a Haṭha Yoga manual of practice and contains almost nothing of any philosophical significance. As was the case with the *Haṭhayogapradīpikā*, Rāja Yoga (as interpreted here) has very little if anything to do with Pātañjala Yoga.

The text and a translation was long ago (1914) published in Vasu 1914, which is our ET.

CHAPTER ONE

I.1-12 (ET 1-3) In the benedictory verse, Ādīśvara is said to be the first teacher of the science of Haṭhayoga. Caṇḍakāpāli wants to know the yoga concerning the physical body. Yoga is said to be the means for realizing reality (*tattvajñāna*). An embodied being passes through life and death on account of the deeds performed by him. He is required to purify his living organism. The purification involves cleansing, firmness, steadiness, calmness or fortitude, lightness, perception of the self, and isolation (*nirlipta*, non-defilement) by means of the six purificatory acts, yogic postures, exercises, withdrawal of the senses, breath control, reflective meditation and concentration respectively. The six purificatory acts are listed in standard order.

I.13-44 (ET 3-8) The technique of *dhautī* of four kinds is given, namely internal washing, cleansing the teeth, cleansing the heart, and cleansing the rectum.

I.45-60 (ET 8-11)Techniques for performing the last five purificatory acts is given.

CHAPTER TWO

II.1-45 (ET 12-19) Thirty-two yogic postures are said to be highly useful. Their techniques are described.

CHAPTER THREE

III.1-100 (ET 20-35) A list of twenty-five bodily exercises is given and explained.

CHAPTER FOUR

IV.1-5 (ET 36) Withdrawal of the senses consists in withdrawing attention from those objects to which it tends to turn and in bringing the mind under control.

CHAPTER FIVE

V.1-15 (ET 37-39) Success in practicing breath-control depends on four factors: (i) suitable place (the capital of a country, etc. are not suitable); (ii) suitable time (autumn and spring are said to be the only suitable seasons; (iii) taking moderate food, and (iv) the purification of the channels. An account of the months comprising a season (six seasons in all)is given in verses 10-14. A practitioner is advised to construct a suitable hut in a country which is governed properly and in which food is easily available.

V.16-32 (ET 39-41)Discussion on moderation of food: a list of good foods (namely rice, barley, etc.) to be taken by a *yogin*; food (namely bitter, acid, salt) to be discarded; certain acts (namely early bathing, fasting, etc.) to be avoided.

V.33-45 (ET 41-43) The process of purifying the channels by means of breath-control which is either with or without the recitation of sacred syllables. A detailed process of breath-control is given in verses 39-45.

V.46-96 (ET 43-51) A detailed description of eight kinds of breath control. An account of ten vital airs (with their seats in the body, and their functions). The verses on the eight forms of breath control speak of the following: the results of breath control, *bandhas* to be practiced, secret sounds heard at the time of practicing breath control, deities to be meditated on, the *ajapāgāyatrī,* reciting of *haṃsa,* the number of respirations in one day and night, the length of a body, length of the air flowing from the nostrils in different acts, viz., singing, eating, etc.

CHAPTER SIX

VI.1 (ET 52) Reflective meditation is of three kinds:(i) gross (*sthūla*), i.e. the meditation on figures or forms; (ii) luster (*jyotis*, also called *tejas* in the following verses), i.e. the meditation on *brahman* as a mass of light; (iii) subtle (*sūkṣma*), i.e. meditation on *brahman* as *bindu* (without any visible form) who is the same as the supreme deity *kuṇḍalī*.

VI.2-14 (ET 52-53) A detailed description of the gross forms of meditation which consists in meditating in the heart on a deity with its ornaments, vehicles, etc. An alternative process of the gross form of meditation is given in verses 9-11, which is to be practiced on the pericarp of the thousand-petalled lotus (*sahasrāra*).

VI.15-17 (ET 54) The process of meditation called *jyotis* on the *mūlādhāra*. It consists in contemplating the embodied self and taking it as identical with the lustrous *brahman*. An alternative process is given in verse 17. It consists in contemplating on *oṃ* as in the middle of the eyebrows.

VI.18-22 (ET 54-55) The process of the subtle form of meditation. It depends on the awakening of *kuṇḍalinī* as a result of practicing the *śāmbhavī mudrā*.

CHAPTER SEVEN

VII.1-4 (ET 56) In the state of concentration, which is acquired through the grace of a spiritual teacher, the mind becomes separated from the body and gets united with the supreme self. In this state a person feels his identity with the eternally liberated *brahman* which is existence, intelligence and bliss (*saccidānanda*).

VII.5-23 (ET 56-59) Rājayoga has six forms, namely meditation (*dhyāna*), secret sounds (*nāda*), great joy (*rasānanda*), dissolution in or identity with *brahman* (*layasiddhi*), devotion (*bhaktiyoga*) and union of the mind with the supreme self (*manomūrchā*). These are to be accomplished by the six means, namely meditation etc. respectively. The process of each means has been described in detail in verses 7-16. Rāja Yoga. *Samādhi*, *unmanī* and *sahajāvasthā* are said to be the names of one and the same state.

39.AUTHOR UNKNOWN, *Śivasaṃhiṭā*

Summary by Ram Shankar Bhattacharya

This is another late seventeenth century Haṭha Yoga manual. It is edited and translated in Vasu 1914. However, the edition that RSB used is Venkateshvara Steam Press, Bombay, *saṃvat* 2008 (=1951 CE), and the verses in it differ from Vasu 1914.

The philosophical orientation of this text, as clearly indicated in its first Chapter, is an elementary or simplified monistic Vedānta. Again, the so-called Rāja Yoga appears to have very little relation to Pātañjala Yoga.

CHAPTER ONE

I.1-16 After asserting that it is the eternal consciousness (*jñāna*) which is real, the author says that he is going to compose a work on yoga which will enable a person realize self-knowledge by disregarding a large number of erroneous doctrines which are taught by teachers who have the intention to delude others.

I.17-27 A careful study of the scriptures reveals that the *yogaśāstra* is the highest of all. Yoga deserves to be taught to proper devotees. The Vedas have two subdivisions. One deals with actions and the other deals with knowledge. Actions–both prohibited and prescribed–yield appropriate results and are the cause of birth.

I.28-44 It is an established fact that everything is painful. Bondage is full of acts in the form of merit and demerit. All acts characterized by merit and demerit are bondage. This is why one, desirous of yoga, should eschew all activities. One is required to act according to the Vedic view that it is the self which is to be heard of and reflected on. A *yogin* should always think "I am identical with that self from which everything proceeds and gets dissolved". There is a constant unity of the self; its apparent manifoldness is the result of illusion. The duality of the selves is absolutely false. As the notion of a snake in a rope is false, so too the perception of the world in the self is false. The world-illusion comes to an end when the self is perceived. The self is realized as soon as ignorance is annihilated.

I.45-67 In reality the self is never transformed into the world. This transmigratory existence (*saṃsāra*) goes instantly to decay. All this is a projection (*vivarta*, an apparent modification or illusion) in the supreme self caused by ignorance. Since consciousness (*caitanya*) is the source of all, one should resort to (i.e. instantly contemplate) it. The self (i.e. consciousness) pervades all, as does *ākāśa*. It remains unaffected by the things it pervades. The self is one, without a second, self-luminous *saccidānanda*, and devoid of all duality. Its essence is nothing but consciousness. it is eternal and is not limited by time and space. It is not the elements, as they are of the nature of effects. A *yogin* perceives the self in his own intellect with the help of concentration.

I.68-73 It is *māyā* which produces everything. As the body is a product of *māyā* it, in fact, cannot be the object of love (*prītiviṣaya*). All worldly behavior is based on friendliness, enmity, or detachment, and all objects are both pleasure-giving (*priya*) and pain-giving (*apriya*). Knowing that the whole world is a projection of *māyā yogins* become dissolved in *brahman* with the help of the processes known as *adhyāropa* (the act of falsely imagining one thing as another) and *apavāda* (removal of superimposition). When the partless self becomes devoid of all limiting adjuncts (*upādhi*) it becomes taintless.

I.74-85 All creations of ignorance are false. From *brahman* comes *ākāśa*; it produces air, which gives rise to fire; from fire comes water, from water earth. Each of the aforesaid elements is produced by the element that precedes it; for example, the earth is a product of all the other elements. The special attribute of each of the five elements above is respectively sound, touch, color, taste and smell. In each subsequent element the special attributes of the preceding elements also reside. Thus the earth possesses all the five attributes. These five elements are perceived respectively by the ear, skin, eye, tongue, and nose (the nature of the organs is to be understood according to the viewpoint of this school). The earth becomes dissolved in water, water in fire, fire in air, air in *ākāśa*, which gets dissolved in the supreme reality.

I.86-96 *Mahāmāyā*, consisting of *sattva, rajas* and *tamas guṇas*, is inanimate (*jaḍa*) and possesses two functions, namely distracting (*vikṣepa*) and concealing (*āvaraṇa*). According to the predominance of *sattva, rajas* and *tamas, māyā* is known as the goddess Lakṣmī, Sarasvatī, and Durgā respectively. All divinities are perceived in the supreme self. There are two things to be known, namely reality (*tattva*) and nonreality (*atattva*). All objects are capable of being known. An illuminating entity remains even if there is nothing to be illuminated. One becomes liberated when one comes to realize the entity which is one, bliss, all-pervasive and absolute.

I. 97-104 According to previous karma a new body is formed from the physical body of the father. A body is made of the five elements (*bhūta*) in their compound (*pañcīkṛta*) state. It is the sate of experience and is liable to be affected by pain. It comes into existence on account of the fusion of *bindu* (a form of Śiva, that is, semen) and *rajas* (a form of Śakti, that is, female fluid and/or ovum). An embodied self is dissolved in the supreme self when all fruits of his actions come to an end.

CHAPTER TWO

II.1-12 In a body there are islands, rivers, mountains, shrines, the sun, the moon, etc. It also contains the five elements. All activities depend upon the spinal column. The moon with eight digits (*kalā*) is situated on the peak of the *merudaṇḍa* or vertebral column. It sprinkles nectar which flows through the *iḍā* channel, situated on the left side. The sun with twelve digits is situated on the roof of the *merudaṇḍa* and it moves through the *piṅgalā* channel situated on the right side. The sun, who performs creation and dissolution, absorbs the nectar.

II.13-28 There are 3 and 1/2 lacs (=350,000) of channels in the body, of which fourteen are principal. The *iḍā, piṅgalā* and *suṣumṇā* channels are regarded as the chief of these fourteen channels, and *suṣumṇā* is regarded as the supreme channel as all other channels are dependent on it. *Īḍā*, *piṅgalā* and *suṣumṇā* flow downward; they are of the nature of the moon, sun, and fire respectively; they are as thin as the lotus-fiber and attached to the vertebral column. The *citrā* channel is situated in the middle of these three. It is of five colors and is said to be the divine path.

The *ādhāra*-lotus (i.e. the *mūlādhāra*) is situated about three-quarters of an inch above the rectum (*guda*) and below the penis (*meḍhra*). There is a triangular field in the pericarp of this lotus. Here lies the lustrous *kuṇḍalī* making 3 and 1/2 coils. The *īḍā* channel is situated on the left side. The *piṅgalā* channel is situated on the right side. Both *īḍā* and *piṅgalā* are extended to the right and left nostrils respectively through *suṣumṇā*, which is situated in the middle of these two channels. *Suṣumṇā* possesses six powers in six regions and in six lotuses (i.e. plexuses, which will be mentioned by name later).

II.29-38 A large number of channels come out from the *mūlādhāra* and reach the tongue, penis, eyes, (the big toes of the leg), ear, abdomen, armpit, anus, genital organ, etc. These channels are further divided into branches and sub-branches and become 350,000 in number. Air flows through these channels. The *bastī deśa* (bladder below the navel) is the place where fire exists in the middle of the sun with twelve digits. The act of digesting (*pāka*) depends upon it. This fire, called *vaiśvānara,* nourishes, strengthens, and maintains the body.

II.39-49 The embodied self being bound by actions and subconscious impressions resides in the body enjoying the fruits of actions. All mental fluctuations arise according to acts previously done. Virtuous and vicious deeds are the respective causes of pleasure and pain. Time has also its bearing on pleasure and pain. On account of faults one superimposes the world on *brahman*. False awareness continues to exist so long as there are subconscious impressions in an embodied self. Knowledge is regarded as the means to liberation as it eradicates error.

II.50-57 Error ceases on account of the realization of difference. The awareness of manifoldness continues until there arises direct knowledge of the taintless *brahman*. (The act of maintaining the body is regarded as successful if the embodied self endeavors to attain liberation). One desirous of transcending the world should perform one's own duties in accordance with one's *varṇa* and *āśrama* without yearning for the fruits of actions. If one perceives the self in the intellect one can get rid of actions. Reality becomes manifested when desires, etc. are destroyed.

CHAPTER THREE

III.1-9 In the heart there is a lotus adorned with twelve letters–*ka, kha*, etc. It is the seat of the vital energy (*prāṇa*) associated with subconscious impressions, actions, and ego. The vital energy has ten varieties, namely *prāṇa* (situated in the heart), *apāna* (in the anus), *samāna* (in the navel), *udāna* (in the throat), *vyāna* (in the whole body), *nāga* (causing vomiting), *kūrma* (causing the opening of the eyes), *kṛkala* (causing hunger and thirst), *devadatta* (causing yawning), and *dhanañjaya* (causing hiccups). Among these ten, the first five are principal, and *prāṇa* and *apāna* are regarded as the chief of these five.

III.10-20 One should learn yoga from a teacher who should be held in high esteem by his disciple and should be pleased before taking instructions from him. There are six signs of perfection in yoga, namely (1) the conviction that yoga invariably produces its result, (2) faith, (3) worship of the *guru*, (4) even-mindedness, (5) subjugation of the organs, and (6) moderation in diet.

III.21-34 A person should practice yoga in a well-constructed hut. He should sit in the *padma* posture, making his body erect, and he should gradually inhale and exhale with either of the two nostrils and perform twenty *kumbhaka*s (stoppages of breath) in the morning, midday, afternoon and midnight (i.e. eighty in all in four times). The channels become purified after a regular practice of two months. There are many signs indicating the purified state of the channels, namely fragrance in the body, etc. There are four stages of yoga, namely *ārambha, ghaṭa, paricaya* and *niṣpatti*. Acquiring the *ārambha* state a *yogin* becomes extremely beautiful and becomes endowed with enthusiasm and strength.

III.35-45 A *yogin* should avoid food which is sour, dry, pungent, salty, bitter, and should also avoid excessive traveling, morning bathing, stealing, violence, fasting, sensuality, talkativeness, too much eating, etc. He should eat clarified butter, milk, camphor, etc. and should engage himself in listening to the scriptures and in loud singing of devotional songs (*kīrtana*). He should also practice passionlessness, fortitude, forbearance, austerity, cleanliness etc. and should observe some well-established traditional rules for eating as stated in verses 43-45.

III.46-55 In practicing *kumbhaka* air should be checked according to one's own strength. in the first stage sweat oozing from the body should be rubbed on the body; in the second stage there arises quivering in the body; in the third the body stays in the sky leaving the ground. There are many signs indicating perfection, namely little sleep, scantiness of feces, health, absence of sweat and saliva, boldness, and the attainment of the power of entering the earth (*bhūcarī siddhi*).

III.56-64 A person should practice yoga disregarding all

impediments. He should utter the prolonged sound of *oṃ* and practice breath-control in order to destroy sin and to achieve the eight powers, namely *aṇiman*, etc. He can attain the following powers by practicing breath-control: unfailingness of speech, ability to wander everywhere at will, telesthesia, subtle vision, entering another's body, making oneself invisible, moving in space, and the like, among others.

III.65-70 The stage called *ghaṭa* is described here. In this state there occurs union in *prāṇa* and *apāna*, in *nāda* and *bindu*, and in the individual self and the supreme self. By practicing withdrawal of the senses, in this state one becomes able to subjugate the senses.

III.71-78 The stage called *paricaya* is described here. In this state the vital centers are pierced and all actions are destroyed. The practitioner becomes able to perform *kāyavyūha* (a new body constructed with the help of concentration), to conquer the five elements by practicing fixity on the five regions, namely the rectum, the seat of the genital organ, the navel, the heart and the space between the two eyebrows.

III.79-82 The stage called *niṣpatti* is described here. In this state the seeds of actions are destroyed and the *yogin* becomes liberated while living as a result of conquering or crossing all the vital centers.

III.83-99 A *yogin* is advised to take in air through the mouth having made it resemble the beak of a crow, and to practice the *khecarī mudrā*. The practitioner becomes incapable of being overcome by hunger, thirst, sleep, etc.

III.100-118 The technique of the four principal postures, namely *siddha, padma, ugra* (also called *paścimottāna*, the posterior stretching pose), and *svastika* (also called *sukhāsana*) is described here. In practicing these postures the body should be held erect, the tip of the nose should be gazed on, the chin should be placed on the throat as stated here.

CHAPTER FOUR

IV.1-25 Technique of *yonimudrā*. It consists in contracting the perineum (*yoni*) in a particular way with a particular kind of meditation. Extraordinary capacities like infallibility of words (*vāksiddhi*) and others may be achieved by the practice of this exercise. By practicing bodily exercises one becomes able to awaken the coiled energy (*kuṇḍalī*) lying dormant in the mouth of the *brāhmarandhra*. The following ten exercises are of great importance, namely *mahāmudrā, mahābandha, mahāvedha, khecarī, jālandhara, mūlabandha, viparītakṛti* (i.e. *viparītakaraṇī*), *uḍḍāna* (i.e. *uḍḍīyāna*), *vajrolī* and *śakticālana*.

IV.26-36 Technique of the *mahāmudrā*. It is to be practiced with the left and the right sides separately with breath-control. This exercise helps to arouse *kuṇḍalī*.

IV.37-42 Technique of *mahābandha*. It consists in pressing the perineum and in mixing the air *samāna* with *prāṇa* and *apāna*.

IV.43-50 Technique of *mahāvedha*. It consists in commingling the *apāna* with *prāṇa*. It enables one to cut the knot called *brahman*.

IV.60-63 Technique of the *jālandhara bandha*. It consists in placing the chin on the chest in order to check the nectar exuding out of the thousand-petalled vital center from being grasped by the fire residing in the navel.

IV.64-68 Technique of *mūlabandha*. It consists in contracting the anus and in uniting *prāṇa* to *apāna*.

IV.69-71 Technique of *viparītakaraṇī mudrā*. It consists in placing the head below and the navel above.

IV.72-77 Technique of *uḍḍīyānabandha*. It consists in pulling backwards the parts above and below the navel, i.e. the abdomen including the navel.

IV.78-104 The technique of the *vajrolī mudrā*. It consists in drawing out the *rajas* (it is not the same as the l blood but a different kind of secretion) and in associating the same with semen. There are two varieties of this exercise, namely *sahajolī* and *amarolī*, both having essentially the same nature. By following the method of discharging urine as stated in verses 101-102 one becomes able to control the ejaculation of semen.

CHAPTER FIVE

V.1-13 Enjoying objects is the chief obstacle to the path of yoga. The hypocritical performance of religious acts is also a powerful obstacle. The idea that the acts of external purity and verbal knowledge of transcendental entities are the real means to liberation is also an obstacle in realizing the self.

V.14-27 Yoga is fourfold, namely Mantrayoga, Haṭhayoga, Layayoga and Rājayoga. The practitioners of these yogas are regarded as mild, middling, intense, and possessing superlative intensity respectively. The characteristics of these four types have been stated in detail in verses 16-27.

V.28-39 The worship of *pratīkas* (here it seems to mean reflected images, though ordinarily it means symbols) bestows desired results. One perceives the divine light of the self by retaining air in the manner shown in verses 35-36, and one gradually becomes one with the self.

V.40-57 Secret sounds resembling those of a bee, flute, lute, etc. are heard by a *yogin*. Concentrating the mind on these sounds one gets dissolved in the supreme reality. A general description of yoga practice is given in verses 46-57.

V.58-68 As a result of comprehensive reflection upon the trachae (*kaṇṭhakūpa*) there arises cessation of hunger and thirst; upon the bronchial tube (*kūrmanāḍī*) it brings tranquility of mind; on a particular aperture in the cranium (*śiraḥkapālarudrākṣavivara)* it provides sight of the *siddhas* (the beings who rove in the space between the sky and the earth); and on the void, it gives one the power to pass through the air (*ākāśa*). With the help of meditation practiced on the back part of the head a *yogin* conquers death.

V.69-82 From the food taken in, three kinds of *rasa* (essence of food assuming the form of lymph or chyle) are formed. The first kind of food nourishes the subtle body; the second kind nourishes blood made up of seven tissues (*dhātu*, the main constituents of the body); the third kind is transformed into excreta (urine and feces). All the functions of the body are performed by the fourteen channels.

V.83-149 A detailed description of the six vital centers, namely (1) *ādhāra* or *mūlādhāra* (at the bottom of the backbone adjoining the anus), (2) *svādhiṣṭhāna* (at the root of the genital organ), (3) *maṇipūra* (at the navel region), (4) *anāhata* (in the heart), (5) *viśuddha* (in the throat), and (7) *ājñā* (between the two eyebrows), with an account of the petals of each lotus (plexus), the letters connected with the petals, the superintending gods and goddesses residing on them, the results to be achieved through meditation on these vital centers, and some special yogic practices connected with them is given here.

V.150-202 Description of the *sahasrāra cakra*. It is said to be situated above the uvular region of the palate (*tālumūla*) flowing downward to the *mūlādhāra*. In the center of this vital center there is an orifice called *brahmarandhra*. Meditation practiced on the *citrā* nerve existing in the middle of the *suṣumṇā* channel enables one to realize knowledge of *brahman*. The vital air enters *suṣumṇā* if it is checked in the way shown here. There is an orifice called the second *brāhamarandhra* in the perineum (*mūlādhāra*). By practicing meditation on the meeting places of the three channels (namely *iḍā, piṅgala* and *suṣumṇā*) one attains the highest goal. Meditation on the aperture in the skull brings about some supernormal powers. Obstacles are removed by this meditation. The thousand-petalled lotus (*cakra*) is also called *kailāśa*. A *yogin*, by drinking the nectar coming out from this lotus, becomes immortal. This is the place where *kuṇḍalinī* gets dissolved; consequently the partless and taintless knowledge (i.e. *brahman*) becomes manifested. By meditating on the great void outside the cosmic egg one attains various supernormal powers.

V.203-212 In the foregoing verses Rāja Yoga has been described. Next the Rājādhirājayoga (the supreme form of Rājayoga) is described. In practicing this yoga a person should keep his mind without any supporting object or should make the mind steady. He should absolutely subjugate the I-sense and should contemplate the partless *brahman* with the help of the process of superimpositions (*adhyāropa*) and de-superimposition (*apavāda*). In the state described here there is no need for the instructions of a teacher. A householder can also attain perfection. Some general instructions for practicing yoga and the process of reciting in connection with the vital centers with necessary details are given in the last part of the text.

40.PŪRṆĀNANDA, *Ṣaṭcakranirūpaṇa*

Summary by Ram Shankar Bhattacharya

The present work dealing with the system of the vital centers originally was a portion of a larger work of Pūrṇānanda's entitled *Śrītattvacintāmaṇi*. It is a portion of the sixth chapter (*paṭala*)of that work and contains fifty-five verses. Little is known about Pūrṇānanda. Arthur Avalon (Sir John Woodroffe) in Avalon 1964 gives a few background comments (see pp. xiii-xiv, Preface) about Pūrṇānanda, indicating that he was a follower of the Tantra from Bengal and lived some time in the sixteenth (or possibly seventeenth) century. His precise date is not known. Avalon 1964 provides the text (on pp. 1-96) and an English translation (on pp. 317-478). While summarizing the text we have followed the explanations given in the commentary, whose author is unknown, published in Sarman 1899.

1-3 In the left and the right side of the spinal cord (*meru*) there are two channels (called *iḍā* and *piṅgalā* respectively) possessing the nature of the moon and the sun. In the middle is situated the channel called *suṣumṇā* possessing the nature of the moon, sun and fire. It rises from the *mūlādhāra cakra*, and reaches to the head. In the middle of *suṣumṇā* is situated the channel called *vajra* in which there exists the most subtle channel named *citriṇī*. In this nerve there is the *brahmanāḍī* which is a hollow path running from the orifice of the *svayambhū liṅga* (in the *mūlādhāra*) to the center of the thousand-petalled lotus. In the mouth of this *brahmanāḍī* is the *brahmadvāra* which is said by *yogins* to be the mouth of the *suṣumṇā* channel. The *mūlādhāra cakra* is the meeting place of the *kanda* (most probably it is the pelvic floor) and *suṣumṇā*.

4-13 The *mūlādhara cakra* is described here. it is situated in the mouth of *suṣumṇā*, that is, below the penis and above the rectum. This vital center has four petals of red color containing the four syllables *va, śa, ṣa,* and *sa* situated in a clockwise position (*dakṣiṇāvarta yoga*). In the center of the vital center there is a quadrangular vital center containing the syllable *la* (the printed reading *na* is corrupt) which is the secret incantation *(bīja)* of the earth. Brahmā (Indra, according to some) with his vehicle elephant, holding four Vedas in his four faces, resides in the *bīja* incantation. He is to be meditated upon here. The goddess Ḍākiṇī having four hands also resides here.

There is a triangular field called Traipura (i.e. the seat of the goddess Tripurasundarī) in the mouth of the *vajra* nerve. Here flows the *kandarpa* air which sustains and controls the embodied self. In this triangular field resides the *svayambhū liṅga* which is circular in form, golden in color (red, according to some) and is said to be an inhabitant of Kāśī. It can be realized only by means of meditation and knowledge.

Above this *liṅga* exists *kulakuṇḍalinī* in a sleeping state covering the mouth of the *brahmadvāra* (i.e. in the orifice of the *svayambhū liṅga*). It is said that *kuṇḍalinī* has the form of a snake and exists assuming a coiled form of 3 and 1/2 turns. The embodied self remains alive on account of her activities. The supreme deity (*parameśvara*) who is full of bliss and possesses eternal knowledge and luster resides in *kulakuṇḍalinī*. She is all-powerful, is called *kalā*, and is identical with *nādaśākti*.

One acquires various supernormal powers by meditating on *kuṇḍalinī*. The process of meditation is given in detail in the commentary. The commentary quotes verses to show that unmanifested sound (*avyaktātmā rava*) comes from *parabindu*, the sound meaning the coiled form which resides in the central part of the body. The four aspects of speech, namely *parā* (originated in the *mūlādhāra cakra*), *paśyantī* (in the *svādhiṣṭhāna cakra*), *madhyama* (in the *anāhata cakra*), and *vaikharī* (in the *viśuddha cakra*) have been described in the commentary.

14-18 The *svādhiṣṭhāna cakra* is described here. It is situated at the base of the genital organ. It is red in color and has six petals containing six syllables, namely *ba, bha, ma, ya, ra,* and *la*. It is the seat of water. Its presiding deity is Varuṇa and the secret incantation is *vam*. The incantation is white in color, is of crescent form and has the crocodile (*makara*) as its vehicle.

In the secret incantation *vam* resides the blue-colored Viṣṇu holding *śrīvatsa* (a particular mark or curl of hair on the breast of Viṣṇu) and *kaustubha* (a celebrated jewel). He is to be meditated on as sitting on Garuḍa. Here resides the blue-colored goddess Rākiṇī having three eyes and four hands. The person who meditates on this vital center becomes able to subjugate lust, wrath, etc. and to compose charming poems.

19-21 The vital center called *maṇipūra* is described here. (According to some it is the solar plexus.) It is situated on the *svādhiṣṭhāna cakra*, i.e. on the root of the navel (more precisely, on the pelvic region). It is as blue as the sky and it possesses ten petals having ten syllables, namely *ḍa, ḍha, ṇa, ta, tha, da, dha, na, pa* and *pha*. Here lies the triangular seat of fire, whose secret incantation is *ram*. The *ram* is its vehicle. Here one should meditate on the three-eyed, red-colored Śiva who has a bull as a vehicle.

The goddess Lākinī of golden color (*śyāmā, vide* the commentary) having three faces and four hands, resides in the triangular field. One acquires supernormal powers of destroying and protecting the world by meditating on this vital center.

22-27 The *anāhata cakra* is described here. It is called *anāhata* as *śabdabrahman* is realized here. It is situated above the navel, precisely in the heart. It is red in color; it possesses twelve syllables, namely: *ka, kha, ga, gha, ṅa, ca, cha, ja, jha, ña, ṭa* and *ṭha*. Its pericarp is the seat of air. There is a six-angled field in the lotus, in which the secret incantation *yam* exists. The secret incantation is of smoky color and has an antelope (*kṛṣṇamṛga*) as a vehicle. The white-colored and three-eyed Śiva named Īśa is to be meditated on here.

The yellow-colored goddess Kākinī having three eyes and four hands resides here. In the pericarp of the vital center there is a triangular *śakti*, with face downwards, gold in color. Here exists Śiva, called Bāṇa, under which resides the embodied self in the form of a flame. Here Śiva is to be worshiped mentally. One meditating on this vital center becomes equal to the god of learning (i.e. Bṛhaspati) and becomes able to subjugate senses and to enter others' bodies.

28-31 The *viśuddha cakra* is described here. (Most of the modern scholars take it to be the same as the carotid plexus.) Since its meditation purifies the mediator it is called *viśuddha* (from the root *śudh*, to become pure or to be auspicious). It is situated in the throat. It is red or purple in color, possessing sixteen petals containing the sixteen vowels (*a, ā, i, ī, u, ū, ṛ, ṝ, ḷ, ḹ, e, ai, o, au, ṃ* and *ḥ*). In its center there is a triangular field in which exists the orb of the moon, which is the seat of *ham*, the secret incantation of *ākāśa*. It is the seat of the three-eyed, five-faced Śiva, named Sadāśiva, sitting on his vehicle the elephant.

Here resides the four-handed goddess Śākinī, who may be meditated on in two different ways. It is the gate of liberation. Meditation on this vital center with the stoppage of breath (*kumbhaka*) brings about supernormal powers, such as the power to move the three worlds, to know everything without the help of any instruction of a teacher, etc.

32-39 The *ājñā cakra* is described here. It is white in color and is situated in the place between the two eyebrows. In its two petals there are two syllables, namely *ha* and *kṣa*. Here resides the six-handed (four-handed according to some) goddess Hākinī. It is the seat of the mind. In the center of this vital center there is a triangular field which is the seat of Śiva, named Itara, who is to be worshiped by uttering *oṃ*. It is remarked in the commentary that the mind, *oṃ,* Śiva and the goddess Hākinī are situated one below the other, i.e. the mind is situated above all. One meditating on this vital center acquires supernormal powers, such as omniscience, entering others' bodies, etc.

The flame-like inner self (*antarātman*) resides in the inner part of this vital center. *Oṃ*, the crescent moon (*ardhacandra*), the letter *ma* in the form of *bindu*, and *nāda* are situated one above the other (i.e. *nāda* exists above all). The mind gets dissolved here. One perceives Bhagavat in this vital center, which is the seat of Śiva. One enters the transcendental *puruṣa* if one places one's energy on this vital center. (A vivid description of the death of a *yogin* is given in the commentary on verse 38.) Above this vital center there is the seat of Śiva named *mahānāda*. (There is a discussion on the nature of *nāda* and *bindu* in the commentary on verse 39.)

40-49 The *sahasrāra cakra* (*sahasra*=thousand; *ara*, meaning spoke, is used in the sense of a petal) is white in color and is situated above the *ājñā cakra*, precisely on the top of the *śaṅkhinī* channel. The place is known as a void. It contains all the fifty letters. (In the commentary there is a discussion on the nature of *nāda, bindu, bīja, śakti,* and the state called *unmanī*.) In the center of the vital center there is the moon, in the internal part of which there is a triangular field. A void is to be meditated on in its center. It is the seat of Paramaśiva who gives self-knowledge and destroys ignorance.

This vital center is the place of the deity who is called by such names as Śiva, Paramapuruṣa, Harihara, etc. by different sects. The knower of this seat attains supernormal powers and is not born again.

In this vital center exists the sixteenth digit of the moon, which is red in color. Nectar comes out from this digit. A digit called *nirvāṇa* containing the power of bestowing eternal peace exists within this digit. This power is the source of the knowledge of reality and is the path of liberation. One should meditate on the eternal Śiva in this *nirvāṇaśakti.*

50-55 The process of transcending the six vital centers is to be known from a teacher. *Kuṇḍalinī* should be brought to the thousand-petalled lotus with the help of the sound *hum.* *Kuṇḍalinī* reaches the thousand-petalled *cakra* if one can transcend *svayambhūliṅga* (in the *mūlādhāra*), *bāṇaliṅga* (in the heart), *itaraliṅga* (in the place between the eyebrows) and the six vital centers situated in the *brahmanāḍī*. Having brought *kuṇḍalinī* to the thousand-petalled lotus one should meditate on the supreme deity whose essence is nothing but consciousness. *Kuṇḍalinī* comes down to the *mūlādhāra* through the path of the six vital centers after uniting herself with the supreme Śiva. A person well-versed in the science of the six vital centers transcends transitory existence. It is only this science which leads to liberation.

41.AUTHOR UNKNOWN, *Vasiṣṭhasaṃhitā*

Vasiṣṭha, of course, is one of the eight great sages, the family priest and descendant of Raghu, the great-grandfather of Veda-Vyāsa, and so forth. This text, however, is simply a late Haṭha Yoga text deriving from the late sixteenth century of later. It was published in Digambara Svami 1969. The Yogakāṇḍa portion of the text has eight brief chapters in which various aspects of Haṭha Yoga are described.

42.CIDGHANĀNANDANĀTHA, *Ṣaṭkarmasaṃgraha*

This is another late Haṭha Yoga text. The author, Cidghanānandanātha, indicates that he was a disciple of Gaganānandanātha of the Nātha sect. His precise date, however, is not known. His text takes up the subject of the "six (cleansing) actions" (*ṣaṭkarmāṇi*) of Haṭha Yoga as set forth in the works of Gorakṣanātha, and already described in previous summaries. The text contains some 149 verses and develops various subclasses of the six actions. It is published in Horshe n.d.

43.ŚRĪNIVĀSA BHAṬṬA, *Haṭharatnāvalī*

Summarized by Ram Shankar Bhattacharya

The present summary has been prepared on the basis of Reddy 1982, the ET.

From the second introductory verse it appears that the author was a versatile scholar. He was the son of Timmaya and Somambā. He composed works on Nyāya and Vedānta also. He was an inhabitant of Tirabhukti. This Tirabhukti is in the Andhra state.

The work was composed some time in the seventeenth century.

Though the present work is based on the *Haṭhayogapradīpikā* and the like, it contains a few unique views. It enumerates two kinds of *niyamas*, mental and bodily, which is not found in any well-known work on yoga. In the place of the six purificatory acts (*karman*) usually prescribed in Haṭhayoga works, it prescribes two more, namely *cakri* and *gajakaraṇī*.

BOOK ONE

I.1-4 (ET 1-2) After saluting Ādinātha, the author says that Haṭhayoga, which is a means to Rājayoga, was known to Matsyendra, Gorakṣa and others.

I.5-8 (ET 2-3) Several definitions of yoga are given and *mahāyoga* is defined as the inhibition of the fluctuations of awareness with the remark that *mahāyoga* has four stages–Mantrayoga, Layayoga, Rājayoga and Haṭhayoga.

I.9-24 (ET 3-8)Descriptions of the above-mentioned four yogas is given here; views of other teachers are also quoted in a few places.

I.25-55 (ET 8-18) The eight purificatory acts, namely (i) *cakri* (process of cleaning the anus), (ii) *nauli* (rotating the abdomen), (iii) *dhautī* (swallowing a piece of cloth), (iv) *neti* (a means for cleansing the nose), (v) *bastī* (a means for cleaning the abdomen), (vi) *gajakaraṇī* (a process of vomiting), (vii) *troṭana* or *trāṭaka* (a practice for strengthening the eye), and (viii) *mastakabhāti* (also called *kapālabhāti*) (a kind of breathing exercise) are described and the view of the *Haṭhayogapradīpikā* about the number of purificatory acts is criticized. Alternative processes and subdivisions of some of these acts have also been shown.

I.55-66 (ET 18-20) The effects of all these acts, especially the purification of the vital centers by these processes, are stated.

I.67-79 (ET 21-24) The proper residing places of a follower of Haṭha Yoga, the food to be taken or avoided, the process of eating, factors that are helpful (e.g., steadiness, perseverance) and harmful (e.g., overeating, over-exertion) to yoga practice are stated here.

I.80-87 (ET 20-27) A list of the teachers of Haṭha Yoga is given here and it is remarked that some teachers are not in favor of prescribing means other than breath-control for the eradication of impurities.

BOOK TWO

II.1-32 (ET 28-36) A detailed description of the process of practicing eight (or nine according to some) kinds of yogic breathing, namely *bhastrikā, bhrāmarī, sūryabheda, ujjayi* , *sītalī, mūrchā, sitkara, kevala* and *bhujaṅgakaraṇī* (the ninth) has been given here mentioning the general as well as the specific results of each with the process of inhaling, exhaling, and retaining air.

II.33-148 (ET 37-66) A detailed description is given of the process of practicing the ten bodily exercises. The view of *Haṭhayogapradīpikā* about the practice of *vajrolī mudrā* has been refuted. A few authoritative texts and the views of some teachers have been quoted. The author propounds his own view about the technique of the *khecarī mudrā* (II.126) at the time of dealing with the *śakticālana mudrā*.

BOOK THREE

III.1-3 (ET 67) The chapter deals with the eight auxiliaries to yoga. An enumeration of mental vows, namely serenity of mind, contentment, silence, etc. and of bodily observances, namely bathing, cleanliness, etc. is given here.

III.4-40 (ET 68-76) Yogic postures, which bring about steadiness and lightness, and which are adopted by Vasiṣṭha, Matysendra, and others, are said to be the first accessory to Haṭha Yoga. Out of eighty-four postures (described by Śiva), ten are important; the most important of theses are four, namely *siddha, padma, siṃha* and *bhadra* (described here) and among these *siddha* is regarded as the best.

III.41-77 (ET 76-87) The process of practicing twenty-six postures (namely *mayūra*, etc.) is given here in detail.

III.78-99 (87-93) At first the general results of yogic breathing have been stated. The purification of the channels and the manifestation of the secret sound (*nāda*) are the chief results of breath-control. The process of inhaling and exhaling, and the number and duration, etc. connected with the practice of breath-control are stated here.

BOOK FOUR

IV.1-3 (ET 94-95) Concentration (*samādhi*) has been defined as the union of the self and the mind or the equilibrium of the embodied self and the supreme self.

IV.4-16 (ET 95-98) Unstruck secret sound (*anāhata nāda*) and its absorption are said to be observed by *yogins*. *Yogins* having attained concentration through devotion to *nāda* experience indescribable pleasure. *Nāda* brings about the state called *unmanī* (the state of transcending the act of thinking). *Nāda*, which is heard inside the body, is of various kinds. The mind gets absorbed in *nāda*. The dissolution of mind is the result of practicing Rājayoga.

IV.17-30 (ET 98-102) The four stages of yoga, namely *ārambha, ghaṭa, paricaya and niṣpatti* are described here. In the first stage the *anāhata* sound is heard inside the body; in the second the vital air runs through the middle path (i.e. the *suṣumṇā* channel); in the third particular kinds of *anāhata* sound reach the place called *mahāśūnya* (the space between the eyebrows); in the fourth state the knot called *rudra* gets pierced and a particular kind of *anāhata* sound is heard. The characteristics of a *yogin* in the fourth state is elaborately described in verses 25-30.

IV.31-43 (ET 103-106) Yogic description of a body (*piṇḍa*) is given here. A body is said to be of ninety-eight fingers (of one's own) in length; there are thirty-two bones on both sides of the spine and 72,000 channels in the whole body. From the vital center of the channels (*nāḍīcakra*) situated in the *mūlādhāra* channel (perineum) proceed the other channels, among which fourteen are principal. The chief of these are *iḍā, piṅgalā,* and *suṣumṇā*. It is remarked that the description of microcosm (*piṇḍa*) and macrocosm (*aṇḍa* = *brahmāṇḍa*, the cosmic egg) is to be known from the Vedas, the Āgamas and the Purāṇas.

IV.44-51 (ET 106-109) The yogic process of transcending thought and of getting rid of *māyā* (cosmic illusion) is described here.

IV.52-63 (ET 109-111) Various schools of philosophy are found to propound different views. It is remarked that the various schools--Śaiva and so forth–uphold baseless doctrines and that they do not know the realities. That is why one should approach a wise spiritual teacher.

44.SUNDARADEVA, *Haṭhasaṃkeṭacandrikā*

Summarized by Ram Shankar Bhattacharya

This is an unpublished text on Haṭhayoga. The Varanasi Sanskrit University Library (Sarasvati Bhavana Library) possesses a manuscript of this text (No. 29948). The Deputy Librarian has given permission to prepare its summary.

The name of the author if this text is Sundaradeva (a physician, *vaidya*), son of Govindadeva and grandson of Viśvanāthadeva. He belonged to the Kāśyapa *gotra* and was an inhabitant of the Deccan. He was taught yoga by Viśvarūpatīrtha. The work was composed at Kāśī (Vāraṇāsī). The manuscript was copied in 1854. The author's precise date is unknown. He likely lived in the eighteenth or early nineteenth century.

Some of the views of the author deserve special notice. He says that the practice of devotion (*bhaktiyoga*) is the principal auxiliary to Rājayoga. The text quotes a great variety of traditional works.

Since this is a manuscript, only an outline of the contents will be given.

CHAPTER ONE

In the benedictory verses the author eulogizes certain deities and introduces the content of the text. The topics dealt with in this chapter are: the glory of yoga; the preliminaries to yoga; the characteristics of a disciple and a *guru*; the general method of practicing yoga; general instructions for yoga practitioners; the proper place and time for yoga practice; procedure for constructing a hermitage; mental blemishes to be eradicated; purity of food; things fit to be eaten and to be avoided; moderations of diet; drinks to be taken; recreation; bodily developments which show perfection in the practice of breath-control; yogic practices to be engaged in daily; the technique of *gajakaraṇī* (a process for vomiting food lying in the stomach through the throat); signs of those who practice internal yoga exercises; kinds of yoga practitioners; the restraints and observances; yogic postures, including a description of *matsyendra, mayūra, śava, siṃha, yogasiṃha, bhadra, kūrma, uttānakūrma, valgulī* and *vṛścika* postures; the locks (*bandha*) *mūla, gomukha, pārśvopadhāna, padma, siddha, paścimottāna* and *svāstika*; observances (*caryā*) to be performed at the beginning of yoga practice; description of the six acts, namely *āntaranauli, cakrīkarman, bastikarman, gajakaraṇikarman, śaṅkhakarman* and *śaṅkhaprakṣālana-karman*; the means of controlling vital air which can become a source of pain if not properly controlled. It is remarked that the bodily exercises are helpful for the practice of Haṭhayoga; a description of the *mudrās jālandhara, uḍḍīyāna, mūla, vedha* and *śakticāla* is given. (Though there is no mention in the manuscript that the first chapter ends here, from the style of the composition it appears that the chapter has ended.)

CHAPTER TWO

The second chapter features a discussion of bodily exercises (*mudrā*) (processes of controlling the organs with the help of muscular and mental techniques). Various bodily exercises are presented, including the association of the *viparītakaraṇimudrā* with *khecarīmudrā, mūlabandha* (anal contraction), *jālandharabandha* (chin lock), *uḍḍīyānabandha, mahāmudrā, mahābandha, mahāvedana, vajrolī, sahajolī,* food to be taken at the time of practicing an exercise.

CHAPTER THREE

Chapter Three details several means to purify the channels; exercises to be taken up at the beginning of yoga, namely *merucālana, cakrībandha, tānābhyāsa*, etc.; the *kumbhakaprāṇāyāma*; aids to breath-control; kinds of breath-control; the second stage of the purification of the channels; results of the purification of the channels; types of breath-control which are highly capable of purifying the channels; the *mātrākumbhaka,* the *sagarbha* form of breath-control.

CHAPTER FOUR

Chapter Four is a general discussion of the postures that are helpful to the practice of breath control; the definition of "stroke" (*udghaṭa*) in connection with the three operations of breath-control; varieties of stoppage of breath; *āntarabhastrikā,* a variety of *bhastrikā* breath-control; varieties of exhalation, inhalation and holding of breath; four purificatory poses capable of purifying the channels, namely *haṃsakarman, nirañjanakarman, śayanāsanakarman* and *nāsāgrakarman.*

CHAPTER FIVE

This chapter treats the means of controlling the vital energies; the results of conquering each of these vital airs; perfections of some yoga practices. *Siddhāsana* is said to be the factor that brings the most success in practicing breath-control and the *mūlabandha*. A description of piercing of the *svādhiṣṭhāna cakra* is given; *yoginīmudrā; kuṇḍalīśakti; udghaṭa;* the seven states of knowledge; the definition of a person who has attained concentration (*ārūḍhayogin*).

CHAPTER SIX

Chapter Six discusses the *mūlādhāra* channel; ten kinds of fire; discourse on the origination of and manifestation of secret sound; control of semen; the highest form of breath-control; the places of luster; result of the meditation on the six vital centers; the residing place of the embodied self; the gastric fire; the functions of the *īḍā, piṅgalā* and *suṣumṇā* channels; heating the *kuṇḍalī*; ten vital forces (*vāyu*); the nature of *suṣumṇā*; the first stage of yoga practice concerning the *mūlādhāra* channel; reciting the syllable *oṃ*. (The style of the author indicates that here ends the sixth chapter.)

CHAPTER SEVEN

This Chapter gives an elaborate description of the *khecarī mudrā*, with the remark that the *tripurabhairavīvidyā* is to be practiced by those who are unable to practice this exercise; it describes the nature of *kuṇḍalī, suṣumṇā, turīyāvasthā* (the fourth state), and the dissolution of the mind and vital energy; *auṣadhakalpa* (medicinal herbs and their effects) with special mention of *muṇḍīkalpa, vārāhīkandakalpa*, and *dhātrīmahā-kalpa*; the process of drinking *śivāmbhu* (a medicinal preparation); the process of practicing breath-cotrol connected with the *aṣṭāṅgayoga;* the nature of Rājayoga; the process of piercing the six vital centers; a description of *madhyakanda* (most probably it is the central part of the pelvic floor); the definition of *chāyāpuruṣa*.

CHAPTER EIGHT

A discussion of withdrawal of the senses and the process of practicing it with breath-control; the extraordinary capacities as the results of withdrawal the description of the stage called *paricaya*; discussion on *kāyavyūha* (organization of the body); the description of two yogic states, namely *(ārambha)* the initial state) and *ghaṭa* (the concentrated state); *utkarṣaprāṇāyāma* (a developed form of breath-control; the process of *jihvācālana* (moving of the tongue) and *śakticālana*; piercing the knots (*granthibheda*); the state *unmanī* (absence of mind); a note on the order of the practice of the bodily exercises; the practice of *kevalakumbhaka*; the piercing of the three knots known as Brahman, Viṣṇu and Rudra.

CHAPTER NINE

Includes a description of Rāja Yoga and Laya Yoga; the process of piercing the vital centers beginning with the *maṇipūra cakra* and also of the knots beginning with the *brahmagranthi;* the method of practicing the *apakarṣa* breath-control; means of transcending time; a description of concentration and *śūnyaka* breathing, with the remark that the latter is to be practiced by one who has acquired the *dharmamegha* concentration (see *Yogasūtra* IV.29).

CHAPTER TEN

Includes a brief account of dissolution (*laya*); a description of the *gorakṣa mudrā*, the embryonic state of *nādānusandhāna* (contemplation on secret sound); a particular way of controlling breathing known as *sanmukhikaraṇa*; *nādopāsana* (focusing consciousness on the secret sound); *dakṣyayoga* (which is a means to Rājayoga) with an elaborated description of its five varieties; the process of nasal-gazing (*nāsāgradṛṣṭi*); delineation of the experiences of the person liberated while living, along with a description of some varieties of Layayoga and of *śāmbharī mudrā*; devout meditation on the attributeless *brahman*; the nature of dissolution.

CHAPTER ELEVEN

Includes an anatomical division of the body according to the yogic point of view; fourteen channels (*śirā*) and their situation and functions in the body; a remark on the channels flowing upwards (seven in number) and downwards (six in number); the *kuṇḍalinī* (coiled energy) and its deities; the vital airs; the colors of these airs; general functions of the body; some particular functions of the body; a discussion on the six vital centers.

CHAPTER TWELVE

It contains a brief account of Rāja Yoga in a few verses.

CHAPTER THIRTEEN

This Chapter mentions a few *siddhis* with the warning to *yogins* that they should not posses any attachment for these powers nor feel pride in their acquisition. The signs (i.e. portents) which indicate an approaching death are enumerated in the last section of the text.

45.SUNDARADEVA, *Haṭhatattvakaumudī*

Summary by Ram Shankar Bhattacharya

This is an unpublished text on Haṭha Yoga composed by Sundaradeva. A manuscript of the text is preserved in the Sarasvati Bhavana Library of Sampurnananda Sanskrit University, Varanasi (No. 29853). In the colophon the text is sometimes called *Haṭhakaumudī*. On the date of the author see the introduction to work number 44.

The work has been divided into nine chapters (*ullāsa*) and fifty-six sections (*uddyota*). As the text is not printed, only an outline of the text is given here.

CHAPTER ONE

I In the introductory verses the author mentions the name of his teacher (Viśvarūpa) and says that Rāja Yoga may be achieved through *haṭha* practices. It is remarked that yoga with its eight aids comes under the purview of knowledge (*jñāna*).

2 Eulogy of yoga; the characteristics of a spiritual teacher and a disciple; general rules to be followed by a disciple.

3 Means to yoga; suitable time and place for yoga-practice; the characteristic feature of a hermitage (the residing place of a practitioner of Haṭha Yoga).

4 *Āhāraśuddhi* (purity in food); moderation of diet; what is to be taken or avoided.

5 Characteristics and kinds of practitioners of yoga.

6 The six-membered yoga; the restraints and observances.

7 The technique for a variety of postures.

8 The technique for (the standard) eight cleansing acts is given.

9 The preliminaries for controlling breathing, etc.; the technique of the following acts is given here: (i) the process for moving *meru*; (ii) *cakrībandha;* (iii) *tanābhyāsa*; (iv) *jaraṇa*.

10 The nature and characteristics of the ways of stoppage

(*kumbhaka*): *sūryabheda, ujjayin, sitkārī, bhastrikā, sītalī, bhrāmarī, mūrchā* and *plāvani*; technique of some minor *kumbhakas,* namely *karṣakakumbhaka, sahajakhumbhaka, merukumbhaka.*

11 The glory of the practices enjoined in Haṭhayoga; some useful remarks on the method of practicing them.

12 The means of controlling air that cause trouble.

13 What means are generally useful for practicing Haṭha Yoga; an enumeration of some important bodily exercises with the remark that devotion can be the chief accessory to Rājayoga. A bodily exercise (*mudrā)* consists in controlling the involuntary organs connected with the channels of the body with the help of muscular and mental techniques.

14 The techniques of the *viparītakaraṇī* and *khecarī mudrās.*

15 The technique of the *bandhas--mūlabandha, uḍḍīyānabandha,* and *jālandharabandha* (with the holding of a staff)--and of the *mudrās--mahāmudrā, mahābandha* and *mahāvedha.*

16 The nature of semen (*bindu*); means of controlling its ejaculations; technique of the three exercises *vairolī, sahajolī,* and *amarolī.*

17 Praise for controlling semen.

18 Technique of *khecarī mudrā*; the *tripurabhairavī vidyā* (a particular worship).

19 Discussion of the nature of passionlessness, discriminative knowledge, and subconscious impressions.

20 Discussion of *ajapā mantra* and *haṃsa mantra*.

21 Some medicinal preparations with a few incantations. (Some lines seem to be lost in the last part of this section).

CHAPTER TWO

22 Description of *brahmapura,* that is, the human body.

23 An account of the vital airs, viz., *prāṇa, apāna*, etc.

24 Enumeration of the channels; the description and location of the navel (*nābhi*).

25 Sixteen vital centers and sixteen *ādhāras* (vital points), namely ankles, knees, big toes, perineum, etc. on which meditative fixation (*dhāraṇā*) is to be practiced.

26 Enumeration of vital centers that are helpful for the dissolution of the mind; a detailed description of the *mūlādhāra cakra* (between the anus and the genital organ at the lowest end of the *suṣumṇā* channel) and *kanda* (probably the pelvic floor).

27 A detailed description of the *svādhiṣṭhāna cakra* (near the root of the genital organ).

28 A detailed description of the *maṇipura cakra* (in the region of the navel).

29 A detailed description of the *anāhata cakra* (near the heart).

30 A detailed description of the *viśuddha cakra* (near the throat).

31 A detailed description of the *ājñā cakra* (between the eyebrows).

32 A detailed description of the thousand-petalled *cakra* situated at the *brahmarandhra.*

33 A general note on the nature of the six vital centers.

34 A description of the *yoni mudrā* which consists in cutting or piercing the six vital centers.

CHAPTER THREE

35 Importance of the purification of the channels.

36 Preliminaries to the purification of the channels.

37 The nature of the purified state of the channels.

38 The process of practicing breath-control.

39 The operations of breath-control–inhalation, exhalation and retention of breath; description of a *mātrā* (time-unit concerned in the practice of breath-control).

40 A detailed description of the state called *ārambha*; the process of piercing the vital center called *ādhāra*, i.e. the *mūlādhāra cakra.*

41 The process of conquering the ten vital airs, namely

prāṇa, apāna, samāna, udāna (vyāna is left out), *nāga, kūrma, devadatta, dhanañjaya* (*kṛkara* is left out); characteristics of a perfected person (*siddha*); description of the stages of yoga.

CHAPTER FOUR

42 Control of breathing as a helpful factor for withdrawal of the senses); proper time for practicing breath-control; an account of the *marmans* (sacrum and coccyae) as stated by Yājñavalkya; sense-withdrawal as stated by Yājñavalkya.

CHAPTER FIVE

43 A detailed description of the state called *paricaya*.

44 Description of the exercise called *śakticālana*.

45 The process of practicing the *śakticālana mudrā* and of moving the *kuṇḍalinī;* enumeration of the ten exercises.

46 The breathing called *utkarṣa* which is an accessory to the *śakticālana mudrā*.

CHAPTER SIX

47 Description of the state called *niṣpatti;* extraordinary capacities arising from comprehensive reflection (*saṃyama*).

48 Means for attaining meditative fixation, meditation and concentration; results to be achieved through these three.

49 The nature and kinds of meditative fixation and the *siddhis* arising from it.

50 The nature of meditation; the *siddhis* arising from it.

51 Description of the *saguṇa* and *nirguṇa* forms of meditation.

52 The nature of concentration (*samādhi*) and its two kinds; how a person emerges after remaining in the state of concentration for a long time.

CHAPTER SEVEN

53 Description of the breathing called *apakarṣa*.

54 Description of the breathing called *utkrānti*.

CHAPTER EIGHT

55 *Nādānusandhāna* (hearing the secret sound); the process of cutting the knots called Brahman, Rudra and Viṣṇu; the genesis or manifestation of secret sound; capacities that arise as a result of cutting the vital centers.

CHAPTER NINE

56 Description of Rājayoga.

57 Time; how to transcend time; the nature of *chāyāpuruṣa*.

46.ŚIVĀNANDA SARASVATĪ, *Yogacintāmaṇi*

Summary by Ram Shankar Bhattacharya

"E" references below are to Haridasa Vidyavagisa.

In the colophon, the author describes himself as the disciple of Rāmacandra Sāmānanda Sarasvatī. The work was composed after Vidyāraṇya (about 1360) and before Brahmānanda, the author of the *Jyotsnā* commentary on the *Haṭhayogapradīpikā*, who flourished between 1850 and 1875. Our author's date, then, is anywhere between the sixteenth and nineteenth centuries. Overall it appears to be later than earlier so that a reasonable surmise would be to place the text at the beginning of the nineteenth century.

The whole text (in four chapters) is replete with quotations from authoritative texts. Only in a few places does the author offer his own views. In fact, the work is a topical compendium of yogic texts. Only a brief summary will be given here. It should be noted, however, that this text truly attempts to integrate Pātañjala Yoga with Haṭha Yoga unlike most other Haṭha Yoga texts.

CHAPTER ONE

(E1-2) In the introductory verses the author pays homage

to the self-effulgent deity, the god Dakṣiṇāmūrti, Gaṇeśa, and says that the present work chiefly contains passages of various treatises.

(E2-6) It is the cessation of the fluctuations of awareness which is the essential nature of yoga. That cessation leads first to content-filled concentration, and the name implies that in this state there remains the distinction between cognizer, cognition, and the content of cognition. The embodied self, however becomes united with the supreme self in the seedless concentration. "Yoga" as defined by others (e.g., as the union of *prāṇa* and *apāna* or the union of the mind and the self) is a subsidiary to the principal yoga defined above. Control of breathing is not to be taken as yoga proper. The practitioners of the auxiliaries to yoga are to be regarded as desirous of attaining liberation.

In the content-filled form of yoga there exists awareness of the difference between the embodied self and *brahman*. The sense in which one experiences non-duality of the embodied self and *brahman* is called "content-free" (*asaṃprajñāta* or *nirvikalpa*) concentration. In content-filled concentration the mind persists; in content-free concentration it gets dissolved.

(E6-10) Content-filled concentration is regarded as an aid to content-free concentration. Meditative fixation, meditation and concentration are regarded as direct aids to content-filled concentration. The first five (of the eight "aids", viz., restraints, observances, etc.) are regarded as external aids, for they are helpful to the rise of concentration.

Among the final six (of the aids, viz., posture, breath-control, etc.) the following one is more helpful than the preceding one. Meditative fixation and meditation are regarded as external so far as the rise of content-free or seedless concentration is concerned. Content-filled concentration is, however, a direct of internal aid to seedless concentration.

(E10-14) According to some, yoga is of four kinds, Mantrayoga, Layayoga, Rājayoga and Haṭhayoga. Authoritative texts speak of various (other) kinds of yoga, namely

Karmayoga, Bhaktiyoga, Vairāgyayoga, and so on. In these the word "yoga" is to be taken in the sense of means of yoga (*yogasādhana*) as we find the word "*jīvana*" ("life") in the sense of means of living or a helping factor to life. It is the grace of God that brings forth perfection in yoga. In fact, recitation and the like are aids to yoga.

Rāja Yoga is said to be the same as the seedless concentration and Layayoga as the seeded concentration. The essential character of Haṭha Yoga is control of breath. The aforesaid four yogas are but the four states of what is known as Mahāyoga. Mantrayoga is the external aspect of the real yoga. Layayoga consists in dissolving the mind and the breaths in the nine vital centers.

(E14-16) The restraints and other aids are helping factors for concentration. The six purificatory acts (namely *dhautī*, etc.) and the bodily exercises are aids to Haṭha Yoga only. As these six acts eradicate phlegm, etc. they are regarded as aids to Haṭha Yoga. Some think that all the results can be achieved through breath-control. According to others, the direct result of breath-control is the eradication of blemishes (*mala*) and the bodily exercises are directly helpful in practicing the acts enjoined in Haṭha Yoga. The two exercises *viparītakaraṇī* and *khecarī* are helpful in Haṭha-practices as they purify the body.

(E16-19) The essence of Karmayoga is devotion to God. It is included among the observances. Karmayoga enables one to cultivate concentration and to attenuate afflictions. The nature of things to be discarded, the cause of those, of the state of liberation, of the means to that state, and of the union or conjunction of the seer and the seen, have all been described in accordance with the relevant *Yogasūtras*.

(E19-21) It is remarked that the word "*mātra*" ("only") in YS II.20 defining the seer simply suggests that the substance-attribute relation cannot be attributed to the seer. It does not, however, suggest that the seer is devoid of bliss. Discriminative discernment is said to be highest means to isolation (*kaivalya,* also called *hāna*) in which state the absolute identity of the embodied self and *brahman* is manifested.

(E21-28) There arises cessation of actions when the intellect becomes purified. Such a purified state arises in a person who has acquired the seedless concentration. One attains both yoga and the result of yoga practices owing to the grace of God. According to the Pātañjala school, devotion is accepted as an aid to Rāja Yoga. Hearing scriptures (*śravaṇa*) and reflecting (*manana*) are included in the observances, one of the members of the eight-membered yoga, while profound thought (*nididhyāsana*) comes under meditation connected with the conscious concentration.

(E29-34) There is no real contradiction between the two views, namely that yoga is inhibition of the vital air (*prāṇa*) and that yoga is the restriction of the mind, for the restriction of the mind implies the restriction of the vital airs. The developed stages of breath-control culminate in withdrawal of the senses. A similar relation is to be found in the last four aids of yoga. In concentration, the activity of both the vital air and the mind are dissolved, i.e. fully restricted, while in the state of liberation both are annihilated. It is held that conquering the mind depends upon conquering the vital forces. It is the subjugation of the mind which leads to liberation, the supreme goal.

(D34-38) To achieve yoga one is to maintain stability of the mind, semen, and the body. Semen should be preserved absolutely as life depends upon it. The author has given here the detailed process of restricting the movement (*parispanda*) of the vital air.

(E39-41) In the initial states one is required to cultivate faith. From faith comes firmness or zeal (*utsāha*) and memory. Gradually there arises insight as a result of faithfully following yoga-practices. Insight leads to the content-filled concentration, which in turn gives rise to the content-free concentration, the direct means to isolation. Yoga-practice largely depends upon the undisturbed calm of the mind, which comes as a result of practicing friendliness, etc. The mind may, however, reach the stable state by contemplating any desired object.

(E41-44) Effective means to be followed are described here: (i) dissolution of air (*mārutalaya*), (ii) keeping the mind bereft of thoughts (*unmanīkaraṇa*), (iii) indifference (*audāsīnya*), (iv) visions fixed to the goal (*lakṣya*), and (v) the exercise called *śāmbhavī*. The two means for practicing *unmanībhāva* have been described. It is remarked that the relation of secret sound (*nāda*), *haṭha* (the peculiar practices enjoined in Haṭha Yoga) and indifference is like that of seed, field and water.

(E45-52) Various kinds of secret sounds heard at the time of practicing yoga are mentioned. It is remarked that in this stage the three knots, namely *brahmagranthī, viṣṇugranthī* and *rudragranthī* get untied. A vivid description of the origination of secret sounds, of the means of conquering air, and of the means of hearing secret sounds, is given. The manifestation of divine bliss at the time of the rise of concentration is also mentioned.

(E52-54) There are four states of the mind, namely the emergent state, the initial stage of concentration, one-pointedness, and the suppressed state of the mental fluctuations.

(E54-70) The subdivisions of content-filled concentration, content-less concentration, engrossment and its varieties are described here. It is stated that liberation cannot be attained without the help of the seedless concentration, and that without the cessation of ignorance there can be no attainment of liberation. There are two solutions to the question as to how the inhibition (of the fluctuations of awareness), which is not of the nature of (right) cognition, can destroy ignorance (so that the self may be perceived). Some claim that the mind which is bereft of all blemishes can perceive the self directly. Others hold that a person can realize the self with the help of the great sayings (*mahāvākya*).

(E70-73) Though all persons are entitled to practice yoga, yet it is the dispassionate who are entitled to practice that particular form of yoga which directly leads to liberation.

(E73-75) One can invariably attain liberation when one's *prārabdhakarman* (karma that has already begun to bear fruit) are exhausted. The state in which actions are destroyed is called liberation while still living.

(E5-76) An account of seven goals to be reached by those yogins who die before attaining liberation as stated by the *Yogavāsiṣṭha* is given here.

(E76-78) There are two ways, called the crow and the monkey, for attaining liberation. Remarkable results are achieved even by those who belong to the initial stage of yoga.

CHAPTER TWO

(E86-87) Characteristics of a spiritual teacher; importance and exalted position of a teacher; necessity of one's own effort in achieving success in yoga-practice; the assertion that the four factors, namely learning, one's teacher, one's own experience, and restriction of the mind are essential to achieve success in the practice of yoga.

(E87-95) Instructions on (i) what is to be avoided (e.g., the company of women or the wicked), (ii) correct way of eating and recreation, (iii) performing duties, etc. (iv) the proper time for practicing yoga, and (v) eradication of the five blemishes (*doṣa*), namely lust or passion, wrath, fear, sleep, and breathing.

(E95-99) A description of proper places and times for commencing yoga practice; wrong ways of practicing yoga and their harmful results, namely deafness, blindness, etc.; yogic treatment for eradicating these results; mention of some highly suitable places (e.g., hills, temples, etc.) for practicing yoga; directions about the construction of a suitable residence for yoga practitioners, with necessary details.

(E99-100) General duties of a practitioner of yoga; an account of the vital centers, etc. to be known by yoga practitioners.

(E100-112) Purification of the channels; vital airs and their functions; the color and sacred incantations to each of these airs; description of the middle part of the body, *kanda* (it seems to be the pelvic floor) and navel; enumeration of the fourteen channels; importance of the *suṣumṇā* channel.

(E112-129) An account of the sixteen vital points (*ādhāra*), namely big toes, ankles, knees, thighs, perineum, generative organ, navel, chest, neck, throat, tongue, nose, region between the eyebrows, forehead, upper edge of the forehead, and top of the head; six vital centers and the way of piercing (i.e. transcending) them; a description of Layayoga; a description of the groups of eight and nine vital centers.

(E129-148) A detailed description of the six purificatory acts, namely (i) *dhautī* (a means for washing the heart), (ii) *basti* (a yogic method for purifying the colon, intestine, etc.), (iii) *neti* (a process of nasal cleansing), (if) *naulī* or *naulika* (an abdominal exercise by which the recti quickly change their place), (v) *kapālabhāti* (a process of internal cleansing of the forehead); a detailed description of the eight bodily exercises.

(E148-152) A general account of the eight members of yoga; definition of ten restraints and ten observances.

(E153-160) Definition and efficacy of yogic posture and description of a few important postures, namely *mṛgasvāstika, ardhacandra, añjanikā. daṇḍa, pīṭha, paryaṅka, yogapaṭṭa, prasārita, kūrma,* etc. (some of these postures are not mentioned in the current works on yoga); yogic postures to be praciced with breath-control.

CHAPTER THREE

(E160-173) A detailed process of purifying the channels is given here. It deals with (i) postures favorable to the practice of breath-control with a view to purifying the channels; (ii) the appropriate method of performing inhalation, exhalation, and suspension of breath; (iii) regions in the body on which meditation is to be fixed; (iv) signs showing the purified state of the channels; (v) proper time for practicing breath-control; (vi) varieties of breath-control to be practiced; (vii) diseases caused by wrongly practiced breath-control.

(E164-179) A detailed treatment of breath-control is given.

(E179-185) Deities to be mediated on and sacred syllables to be muttered at the time of practicing the three operations (inhalation, etc.) of breath-control; awakening the *kuṇḍalī* as a result of practicing stoppage of breath; the *sagarbha* and *vigarbha* forms of breath-control; nature of the three kinds of *sagarbha* form of breath-control, namely *sadhūma*, consisting in meditating on the three *mātrās* of *oṃ*, *sajvāla*, consisting in meditating gods associated with the *mātrās* of *oṃ*, and *praśānta*, characterized by mental recitation; process of reciting *oṃ*, of chanting the *gāyatrī* incantation with the *vyāhṛtis*, namely *bhūs*, etc.

(E186-189) Description of the four types of breath control, namely exhalation, *śūnyaka* (complete suspension of breath), inhalation, and stoppage of breath; description of the six kinds of breath control, namely *recaka, pūraka, sahita, kevala, utkarṣa* and *apakarṣa*; description of seven kinds of suspension of breath, namely *recita, pūrita, śānta, pratyāhāra, uttara, adhara,* and *sama*; exposition of *Yogasūtra* II.51 on the fourth breath-control; *udghāta* (stroke) in connection with the practice of breath control.

(E189-191) A detailed description of eight *kumbhakas*, namely *sūryabheda, ujjayī, sītalī, sītkarī, bhastrikā, bhrāmarī, mūrchā* and *sahita* (each variety consists in a particular process of stopping breath).

(E191-199) The process of conquering each of the five vital airs by means of breath control and repetition of sacred syllables; results of conquering the vital airs; the process of simultaneously conquering all the vital airs.

(E200-205) A description of general yoga practice; signs showing perfection in yoga practice; process of meditation; deities to be meditated upon; regions of the body on which meditation is to be fixed; process of leaving the body by *yogins* at the time of death.

(E206-220) The signs of conquering the vital airs; description of the four states named *ārambha, ghaṭa, paricaya* and *niṣpatti*; extraordinary capacities arising in these four states; *kāyavyūha* (creation of a body through yogic power) and the purpose of creating these bodies; awakening of the *kuṇḍalī*.

(E221-226) Withdrawal of the senses as described in the *Yogasūtras* and other works; detailed process of withdrawing the senses; maintaining air in the eighteen vital points (*marman*) in the body; withdrawal of senses to be practiced by means of stopping the breath; development in organic power as a result of practicing withdrawal.

CHAPTER FOUR

(E227-233) A detailed description of fixation in accordance with the definitions given in authoritative texts.

(E234-241) A detailed description of meditation, dealing chiefly with the definitions of meditation, derivation of the word "*dhyāna*", (and the process of practicing meditation).

(E241-244) A detailed description of concentration on the basis of *Yogasūtra* III.3 and several Purāṇic works; the results of practicing concentration.

(E244-249) A detailed account of the impediments (*antarāya) to yoga* practice,; the means of eradicating the impediments; the remark that the *siddhis* are also impediments.

(E249-254) An account of *siddhis* is given.

(E254-263) A process of gradually attaining the *siddhis* described.

(E281-282) The author remarks that he has left out some details of the practices enjoined by the former teachers of Haṭha Yoga.

47.DEVATĪRTHASVĀMIN, *Yogataraṅga*

Summary by Ram Shankar Bhattacharya

Devatīrtha Svāmin, also known as Kaṣṭhajihva Svāmin, was a disciple of Vidyāraṇyatīrtha. He was patronized by the

Mahārāja of Kāśī during his scholarly career. He died in 1852 at the age of eighty. The text called *Yogataraṅga* is a small booklet containing a few important *sūtra*s of the *Yogasūtras* with occasional observations by the author. It is a part of a series of tracts called collectively *Kāśīrājasāgara*, published in Varanasi in 1855. This is our E.

(E1-4) The word "*yoga*" is derived from the roots (i) *yuj* meaning concentration, and also from (ii) *yuj* meaning yoga, i.e. the cessation of the fluctuations. Suppression (*nirodha*) is defined as the non-rise of a fluctuation which has previously been restricted.

The author defines perception (*pratyakṣapramāṇa*) in accordance with the *Vyāsabhāṣya*. It is accepted that perception reveals both general properties (*sāmānyadharma*) like the *pṛthivītva* (earthness) in a jar, and specific properties (*viśeṣadharma*) like the jar's jarness (*ghaṭatva*).

The author remarks that the employment of the word "*abhyāsa*" in *Yogasūtra* I.1.2 as the first member of the compound *abhyāsavairāgya* is due to the particular rule of grammar Pāṇini 2.2.32, although *vairāgya* (dispassion) deserves to be treated as the first member of the compound, for it is more important than practice (*abhyāsa*).

The author further tells us that the superiority of dispassion is in accordance with the *(Yoga)Bhāṣya* (on *sūtra* I.1.2). A person is first required to cultivate dispassion, and then he can undertake the practice of discriminative knowledge. Finding fault in objects is emphasized and it is remarked that the coveting of sensual pleasure is the cause of downfall for even the gods.

(E4-6) When questioned why the *Yogasūtras* mention God and not *puruṣa* while prescribing devotion, it is state that there is a difference between these two entities. Among the three kinds of *puruṣa*s, namely *kṣara, akṣara,* and *uttama*, (perishable, imperishable, and supreme), it is the last which is the same as the God of Yoga philosophy.

Incidentally it is remarked that Āsuri, the disciple of Kapila, was the descendant of Asura.

(E6-9) There is a long discussion on the character of friendliness, etc. (mentioned in *Yogasūtra* I.33).

(E9-11) While dealing with the second Book of the *Yogasūtra*, the author remarks that the three factors of *kriyāyoga*, namely *tapas, svādhyāya* and *īśvarapraṇidhāna*, belong respectively to the fields of body, speech, and mind, and he defines the three factors in accordance with the Vyāsa *Bhāṣya*. *Svādhyāya* is given an alternative definition as "realization of the self".

It is remarked that though according to the established order "*pāyu*" (anus) is to be read after "*upastha*" (genital organ) in the Vyāsa *Bhāṣya* on II.19, yet it is placed after "*pāyu*" in accordance with a grammatical rule (Pāṇini 2.2.32). The author is in favor of taking the word "*yoga*" in "*yogāṅga*" in the sense of "the dissolution of the mind with all traces".

(E11-19) While dealing with the third Book the author quotes and explains the *sūtras* on meditative fixation and reflective meditation, though he is silent on the *sūtra* on concentration. The precise nature of comprehensive reflection has been stated here.

It is remarked that the natural power belonging to a particular species (*yoni*) becomes a supernormal power (*siddhi*) in a species different from it (for example, flying in the sky is natural power of birds; it is a supernormal power in human beings). Among other reasons, the purpose of giving an account of supernatural powers is to enable a person to judge whether he has practiced yoga properly or not.

In *Yogasūtra* III.16 on knowledge of the past and future, the word "*atīta*" ("past") also stands for the present (*vartamāna*), i.e. the uprisen mutations. While dealing elaborately with III.17 the author has explained some of the expressions used in the *Bhāṣya* on this *sūtra*. He remarks that in this *sūtra* "*śabda*" ("word"), "*artha*" ("intended object"), and "*pratyaya*" ("idea") signify *vyakti* (a particular thing or individual), *ākṛti* (a thing's form or the collocation of its parts), and *jāti* (the universal, class character, or generic attribute). He further notes that three *adhyāsas* (superimpositions) have been mentioned in this *sūtra*, namely (i) superimposition of idea (*jñāna*) on intended objects and words; (ii) superimposition of words on intended objects and ideas, and (iiii) superimposition of intended object on words and ideas. Authoritative passages have been quoted to prove the existence of these three superimpositions. The author thinks that the *sūtra* mentions three different supernatural powers, namely knowledge of words (uttered sounds), of intended objects, and of ideas concerning all creatures.

It is remarked that the word "*sūrya*" (usually meaning the sun) in III.26 means the air in the right nostril, and the word "*candra*" (the moon) in III.21 means the air in the left nostril.

The author gives a cogent reason for the appearance of supernormal powers by stating that since a powerful *yogin* becomes *sarvātman* (one who has identified himself with all) the powers existing in all species become manifested in him.

While dealing with the fourth Book the author remarks that the supernormal powers which proceed from birth are not dependent on actions, though supernormal powers that are obtained through drugs (i.e. medicinal plants, *oṣadhi*), chants, austerities, and concentration require the help of actions for their manifestation. The word "*janma*" in YS IV.1 may also be taken in the sense of species (*jāti*).

(E19-22) While explaining the last *sūtra* (IV.34) the author remarks that the name "*puruṣa*" is *anvartha* (conformable to the meaning). This means that the thing which bears the name possesses that quality which is in accordance with the literal meaning of the name. In the present case the word "*puruṣa*" is analyzed in such a way as to give the meaning that it (i.e. *puruṣa*) exists in its own form even if all things associated with it disappear.

The author holds that Māheśvarayoga has been prescribed for persons who possess emergent awarenesses (*vyutthitacitta*).

Some verses of the *Merutantra* have been quoted here to show that Rāja Yoga has been prescribed by Śiva to help even the sinful.

48.BRAHMĀNANDA, *Jyotsnā* on Svātmārāma's *Haṭhayogapradīpikā*

Summary by Ram Shankar Bhattacharya

From the introductory verses it appears that Brahmānanda was the disciple of a certain Meruśāstrin who can be dated in the mid-nineteenth century. Thus, it can be said that Brahmānanda lived in the second half of the nineteenth century. In addition to this commentary *Jyotsnā* ("moonlight") he is also the author of *Ṣaṭcakrapradīpikā* and *Śāktānandataraṅganī.*

The text as found in Iyangar 1933 has been used to prepare this summary.

CHAPTER ONE

In the introductory verses it is stated that being requested by Meruśāstrin and others the commentator, after comprehending the doctrines as taught by Gorakṣa, has composed this commentary.

I.1 Ādinātha is Śiva, who is said to have taught the science of Haṭhayoga to Devī Girijā, i.e. Pārvatī. The word "*haṭha*" is explained as a compound of the letter *ha* (signifying the sun and also *prāṇa*) and the latter *ṭha* (signifying the moon and also *cpāna*). Thus *haṭha* signifies *prāṇāyāma*, consisting in the union of *prāṇa* and *apāna*. This science (*vidyā*) was elaborately treated of in the *Mahākālayogaśāstra*, etc. Rāja Yoga is superior to the Mantra and Haṭha Yogas. it is the same as the contentless (*asamprajñāta*) yoga whose characteristic is the cessation of all the fluctuations of awareness.

I.2 The aim of Haṭha Yoga is to acquire Rāja Yoga, which

is the means to isolation (liberation).

I.3 The practice of Haṭha Yoga is especially helpful to a person with a restless mind who wants to attain Rāja Yoga which cannot be acquired by him through the practice of Mantra Yoga, etc. While explaining the meaning of the name "Svātmārāma", the commentary has given an elaborate account of the seven stages of awareness (as shown in the *Yogavāsiṣṭha*).

I.4 Like Matsyendra and Gorakṣa, Jālandhara, Bhartṛhari and Gopīcandra are said to be the teachers of Haṭha Yoga. It is stated that Hiraṇyagarbha (the creator) is the original speaker of this science (*vidyā*). It was afterwards taught to Uddhava by Kṛṣṇa. Śiva and some other deities are said to be the followers of this yoga. The refutation of yoga in *Brahmasūtra* II.1.3 is to be taken as a refutation of the doctrines like the independent existence of *prakṛti*, etc. and not of yoga itself, which is a particular kind of contemplation (*bhāvanāviśeṣa*), This yoga was cultivated by devotees like Nārada and by sages like Yājñavalkya.

I.5 Ādinātha is Śiva who is the promulgator of the Nātha tradition. The reasons for the names "Matsyendra" and "Cauraṅgī" (two Haṭhayogins) are given here. Cauraṅgī is said to be the disciple of Matsyendranātha.

I.11 Qualifications of aspirants of yoga are given here. The view of the *Yogacintāmaṇi* is that though all beings are entitled to practice yoga, yet it is the dispassionate (*virakta*) that attain to its result, i.e. liberation; this is why it is reasonable to hold that a dispassionate person is entitled to practice yoga.

I.12 The justification of the conditions (namely a pious country, etc.) for constructing a residence of a *yogin* has been aptly shown here and it is remarked that the dwelling place should not cause pain on account of heat and cold. The word "*haṭhayogin*" has been explained as a person practicing *haṭha*, i.e. union, as stated above.

I.14 The importance of a teacher in the field of yogic learning has been shown here, and some authoritative passages have been quoted.

I.15 The examples of the *niyamagraha*, namely morning bath, eating at night, and fruit-eating show that the word signifies ritual obduracy.

I.17 The practice of Haṭha Yoga consists in posture, breath-control, (*kumbhaka*), bodily exercise and hearing the internal secret sound. The aids (*aṅga*), namely withdrawal of sense-capacities, meditative fixation, meditation and concentration are included in the last practice (i.e. hearing the secret sound). Posture makes the body and mind firm by eradicating unsteadiness, a property of the *rajas guṇa*. Postures create not only lightness in the body but also hunger and the like.

I.18 Though the practice of reflection (*manana*) and union of *prāṇa* and *apāna* (*haṭha*) is common in the two groups of persons headed by Vasiṣṭha and other sages and by Matsyendra and other *yogins*, yet the separate mention of the two groups indicates that reflection was chiefly practiced by the former group while *haṭha* was chiefly performed by the latter group.

I.19 The word "*jānu*" (knee) in the verse means the shank (*jaṅghā*) near the knee.

I.20 The word "*pṛṣṭhapārśva*" (the side of the back) is traditionally taken in the sense of the lower part of the hip or waist.

I.27 *Candra* is said to be seated on the upper part of the palate (*tālu*).

I.33 It is said that out of the 8,400,000 postures (discovered by Śiva) four are the best (that is, highly suitable for yoga-practice).

I.35 *Yonisthāna* is the perineum, which is to be pressed by the left heel. *Hanu* (chin) is to be placed not on the heart (as stated in the text) but on the place four *aṅgulis* (one *aṅguli* being 3/4 of an inch) above the heart. The word "*āsana*" is derived in the sense of "that in which something sits" or "by which something is seated" (from the root *ās*, to sit).

I.37 The three other names of the *siddhāsana* are, as a matter of fact, coined from the three variations of this posture.

These chiefly consist in placing the heel in different positions.

I.38 The seven verses beginning with verse 38 praise the *siddhāsana* (this appears to be wrong, for only six verses (I.38-43) praises this posture, and verse I.44 describes the *padmāsana*).

I.44 The heart on which the chin is to be placed (as stated in the text) is to be understood as the place situated four *aṅgulis* (= 3 inches) above the heart.

I.45-46 This variation of the *padmāsana* is according to the view of Matsyendra. Both the tongue-lock (*jihvābandha*) and its natural result *mūlabandha* (contracting the anus) are to be learned from a competent teacher.

I.48 The chest on which the chin is to be placed is to be traditionally known as a place near the chest, i.e. four *aṅgulis* above the chest (a little apart from the jugular notch). The power is *kuṇḍalinī*, also called *ādhāraśakti*. If this power is awakened *prāṇa* reaches the *brāhmarandhra* through the path of *suṣumṇā*.

I.55 The *bhadrāsana* is called *gorakṣāsana*, as it was usually practiced bv Gorakṣa.

I.58 The expression *caturthāṃśāvivarjita* (leaving the fourth part) (in connection with the manner of taking food) has been explained as filling one-fourth part of the stomach with water and half of it with food, and thus keeping one-fourth part of the stomach vacant.

I.60 Acidity of any kind is to be avoided. Some authoritative passages are quoted to justify this view.

I.62 The commentator has used vernacular names of some articles of food to be eaten by *yogins*.

I.63 In the absence of cow's milk the milk of the female buffalo is to be taken. Fried food is not to be taken by a *yogin*.

CHAPTER TWO

II.1 The postures to be performed at the time of practicing breath-control are the *siddha āsana* and the like (i.e. the meditative postures) and not those that are chiefly conducive to bodily strength, namely the *kukkuṭa āsana* and the like.

II.2 The immobility to be acquired by the practice of controlling breathing is said to be either longevity or lordly powers.

II.4 Removal of toxins is essential to achieve perfection through Haṭha Yoga. The central path is said to be the *suṣumṇā*. "*Kārya*" in " *kāryasiddhi*" is explained as *kaivalya*, and *kaivalya,* isolation, may be called an effect figuratively, as it is not created by any means.

II.6 That intellect is said to be predominated by the *sattva guṇa* in which distractions, etc. (the properties of *rajas* and *tamas*) have been suppressed by devotion, etc.

II.7 "*Pūraka*" (inhalation) is defined as the taking in of the external air through a particular effort. "Stoppage of breath" (*kumbhaka*) is the suspension of breathing with the help of the *bandhas* like *jālandhara*, etc. Exhalation (*recaka*) going out of air suppressed by *kumbhaka* through a particular effort. There are, however, secondary forms of these three operations also.

II.9 Excessive restraint of air after inhalation causes perspiration and quivering of the body. Exhalation done forcibly and speedily destroys energy.

II.11 If a person becomes unable to practice breath-control in the middle of the night, he may do so three times a day in the morning, midday, and evening, eighty rounds in each sitting. The four divisions of time are defined here precisely.

II.12 The *brāhmarandhra* (an aperture in the crown of the head) is reached by practicing the highest form of controlled breathing. A large number of verses are quoted here to show the lowest, middling and best forms of breath-control. These three types of breath-control are said to have twelve, twenty-four and thirty-six *mātrās* respectively. The highest form of breath-control enables one to rise above the ground and to overcome sleep, etc. A controlled breath of twelve *mātrās* is said to constitute one, two or three strokes (*udghāta*). The measure *udghāta*, consisting of twelve *mātrās*, is explained as the upward movement of breath until it creates a stress condition for exhalation (i.e. when it returns downward). Some authoritative passages on the different definitions of the period of a *mātrā* have been quoted. Breath reaches the *brahmarandhra* if it is retained for 125 *vipalas*, which is the duration of the highest form of breath-control.

II.16 Controlled breathing is called well-poised or steadfast (*yukta*) when its practice is associated with moderation of food and with *bandhas* like *jālandhara*, etc.

II.23 *Yogins* are advised to preserve the six *karmans* (*dhautī, basti,* etc.) secretly.

II.24 The piece of cloth to be used in *dhautī* (a purificatory exercise) should be slightly warmed (by dipping it in slightly warm water).

II.25 The process of inserting a bamboo tube (with discussion on its dimension, etc.) into the anus is explained. An alternative process of *basti* (without inserting the bamboo tube) is also given. The commentator does not seem to favor this view. Both *dhautī* and *basti* are to be practiced before taking a meal.

II.29 There are variations in the length of the cord (to be inserted in the nostrils), which must be firm and without knots. The process of inserting the cord in the nostrils and of taking it out with the help of inhaling and exhaling has been clearly explained.

II.31 Matsyendra and others are said to be the teachers who taught the process of fixity of gazing (*trāṭaka*) shown here.

II.37 Yājñavalkya and others are said not to be in favor of practicing the six acts (*dhautī, basti,* etc.) but of practicing breath control.

II.40 Gazing (*dṛṣṭi*) in *bhrūvor madhyadṛṣṭi* (gazing at the middle of the two eyebrows) must be taken not in the sense of physical vision but in the sense of attending mentally to this place. Here the root *dṛś* does not mean the particular act of seeing, but the act of knowing in general.

II.42 Tranquility or steadiness (*sthairya*) of mind is the flow of the mental fluctuations having the form of the object contemplated.

II.43 The sources of the supernormal powers are said to be five, namely birth (*janma*, i.e. at the time of assuming a particular kind of body), medicinal plants or drugs (*oṣadhi*), reciting of sacred incantations, austerity (*tapas*) and yoga or concentration (*samādhi*).

II.45 The *jālandhara bandha* may be practiced even before performing the stoppage of breath (*kumbhaka*). In practicing *uḍḍiyāna* the navel region is to be drawn backwards through a particular kind of effort. It should be practiced when *kumbhaka* is still maintained and exhalation is to start.

II.46 There is a long discussion on the nature of the practice of the *uḍḍiyāna bandha*. Special case is needed for practicing contraction of the anus (*mūlabandha*). The signs indicating the right or wrong practice of this *bandha* are stated here.

II.48-49 Some authoritative verses on the method and order of yoga practice in general have been quoted, particularly on the effort of holding one's breath and on the manner of drawing in and expelling air. It is emphasized that in *kumbhaka* air must be held forcibly; if it is performed feebly, it leads to poor results.

II.50 One variety of breath-control is called "*sūryabheda*" as its first operation (i.e. inhalation) is done through the sun (i.e. the *piṅgala* channel or the right nostril).

II.53 The *ujjāyin* (also called *ujjāpin*) form of breathing may be practiced without the *bandhas*.

II.54 It is advised that in practicing the *sītkārī* breathing exhalation should not be done through the mouth as this practice causes loss of strength.

II.55 In the context of breath-control, "*prāṇa*" means the air inside the body.

II.57 At the time of drawing air with the help of the tongue, one should make the tongue resemble the beak of a bird.

II.60 In practicing *bhastrikā* breathing exhalation should be done through one nostril.

II.64 The method of closing the two nostrils (at the time of performing inhalation through the right nostril) by the thumb, ring, and little fingers is given here.

II.65 The alternative process of performing *bhastrikā* breathing especially mentioning the way and order of the operations (inhalation, etc.) is given here.

II.68 *Kumbhaka* must be performed in the practice of the *bhrāmarī* breathing though it has not been mentioned in the text. Inhalation and exhalation are especially mentioned in the verse as they are to be practiced in a particular way.

II.71 The word "*prāṇāyāma*" has been explained as the *āyāma* (meaning restriction, *nirodha*) of *prāṇa* (air flowing inside the body, i.e. breath). Each of the three (*pūraka, recaka* and *kumbhaka*) is called *prāṇāyāma*.

II.76 The word "Rājayoga" has been used here in the sense of the means to Rāja Yoga. There are fifteen or ten means to Rāja Yoga which have been described in the *Aparokṣānubhūti* and other treatises.

CHAPTER THREE

III.1 All the accessories to yoga are said to be useless if *kundalī* is not awakened.

III.8 Definitions of the eight supernormal powers are given here. It is to be noted that the commentary mentions *gariman* and not *yatrakāmāvasāyitva*, while the Vyāsa *Bhāṣya* (III.45) whose authority has been accepted by the commentator does not read *gariman* but *yatrakāmāvasāyitva.*

III.14 The word "*mahāmudrā*" (which names a bodily exercise) means that which pacifies, i.e. destroys the great afflictions (namely ignorance, etc.) and other faults.

III.15 The process of practicing *mahāmudrā* is given here. It should be practiced at first by pressing the perineum with the left heel keeping the right leg stretched and then by pressing the same with the right heel keeping the left leg stretched.

III.24 The word "*kedāra*" has been explained as the place of Śiva situated in the middle of the eyebrows.

III.28 The words "Soma", "Sūrya" and "Agni" stand for *īḍā, piṅgalā* and *suṣumṇā* respectively.

III.37 It is the cranial cavity of the forehead (*kapālakuhara*) from which these three channels are said to proceed.

III.43 *Yonimudrā* (contracting the penis) here indicates the practice of the *vajrolī mudrā*.

III.48 The word "*tālu*" is explained as referring to the upper cavity near the palate (*tālu*).

III.51 The word "*ūrdhvāsya*" ("with the face turned upwards") is suggestive of the practice of the *viparītakaraṇī mudrā*.

III.52 The word "*meru*" is explained as meaning the *suṣumṇā* channel.

III.53 The word "*śrotas*" ("stream") stands for channel. The commentary, however, does not mention all the names of the five channels beginning with *īḍā*.

III.54 Breath reaches the head directly through *suṣumṇā*.

III.64 "*Prāṇa*" is defined as the air flowing upwards, "*apāna*" as the air flowing downwards. *Nāda* is the *anāhata* sound; *bindu* is nasal sound (*anusvāra*).

III.70 The word "*hṛdaya*" is taken in the sense of "a place situated four *aṅgulis* (three inches) above the heart."

III.76 Ancient sages like Vasiṣṭha and others are said to be the followers of this school (like Matsyendra and others of modern times).

III.77-79 The moon, full of nectar, is said to be situated on the root of the palate (*tālumūla*--it appears to be the uvular region of the palate).

III.82 Yoga can check even *prārabdha* karma (i.e. that karma that has been activated to bear fruit). Some authoritative texts are quoted to justify this view.

III.84 As to why milk is required in practicing *vajrolī*, some say that drinking milk is essential to recuperate strength after the discharge of semen, while others hold that milk is required to be used as a liquid to be drawn in through the urethra. The commentator considers the latter view unjustified, for the milk drawn in through the urethra may not come out if it turns thick.

III.86 The technique of performing *vajrolī*, especially the process of inserting the tube in the urethra and the process of drawing in water, etc. through it, has been described here in detail.

III.111-112 It is advised that the methods shown in these two verses are to be learned from a competent person.

III.115 One is required to sit in the *vajra* posture while practicing *bhastrikā* breathing, which may be taken up after performing the *śakticālana mudrā*.

III.125 The verse is said to be suggestive of the fact that Haṭha Yoga is a means to Rāja Yoga.

CHAPTER FOUR

IV,1 *Nāda* is the sound similar to the resonance of the sound produced by a bell made of white copper. *Bindu* is the sound that arises after the nasal sound.

The nature of liberation in one's lifetime (*jīvanmukti*) is discussed. It is abiding in one's own immutable form. Firm ascertainment of self-knowledge is the cause of a *jīvanmukta*'s not being affected by his activities. Here the highest liberation (*paramamukti*) is defined in the same way as *kaivalya* is defined in the last *sūtra* (IV.34) of the *Yogasūtras*.

IV.10 Dissolution of breath is its complete absence of activity (*vyāpārābhāva*).

IV.11 The *sahajāvasthā* of a *yogin* is the same as the *jīvanmukti* state, which is also called the fourth state. This inactive state of breathing occurs in the *brāhmarandhra*.

IV.15 The dissolution of the mind is its assuming the form of the object contemplated. Some passages upholding the view that without yoga there can be neither knowledge nor liberation have been quoted here.

Question: While sentences like "that art thou" are capable of producing immediate (*aparokṣa*) knowledge, what is the use of practicing yoga?

Answer: Verbal knowledge cannot be accepted as

immediate. Knowledge from language is a means to immediate knowledge through yoga; it is subsidiary, while yoga is the direct means to self-knowledge.

It is not correct to hold that the self is to be known only from *śabda* (i.e. the *Upaniṣads*) for it is capable of being realized by the mind. The mind must be regarded as an organ and also an instrument for knowing the self. Realization of the self is to be regarded as a correct mental cognition (*mānasikī pramāṇa*). The self is capable of being directly realized by the mind purified by yoga.

Realization of the self is not erroneous awareness, for it is neither contradicted nor sublated nor produced by any defect. Yogic perception must not be taken as secular (*laukika*) as is accepted even by the logicians. Since *yogins* can infuse their minds with reflection on the nature of the self at the time of death, they are not born again. Janaka and others (including women like Sulalihā and others) who acquired self-knowledge without practicing yoga in their present birth, are said to have practiced yoga in their previous births, as has been stated in the *Purāṇas*, etc. There are persons who are said to be perfected from their very birth (*janmasiddha*, i.e. these persons realized the self without being instructed by others). A man who has fallen away from yoga is again born in the house of the righteous and prosperous persons. Since all are entitled to practice yoga all may attain liberation with the help of *tattvajñāna* which is the result of yoga.

IV.16 The restricted state of breathing in the *brāhmarandhra* is to be known as its dissolution, which is the cause of the dissolution of the mind.

IV.18 It is *suṣumṇā* where consciousness (*cit,* i.e. the self) is manifested. The self can be realized if it is contemplated in *suṣumṇā*.

IV.22 Decay in subconscious impressions, breath or awareness leads to the decay of the other two.

IV.31 Dissolution of the mind is its fluctuation assuming the form of the thing contemplated (*dhyeyākāra vṛtti*).

IV.39 The word "*jyotis*" means the tip of the nose (*nāsāgra*)–a meaning which is found neither in the well-known yogic texts nor in lexicons.

IV.41 "*Nāsāgra*" is defined either as the tip of the nose or as the place extending up to nine *aṅgulis*. (The latter definition seems to mean that one's gaze is to be fixed on a point 6.7 inches below the nose.)

IV.45 The interval between the eyebrows (*bhrūmadhya*), which is regarded as an aggregate of all the voids, is said to be associated with five channels.

IV.50 When the *khecarī mudrā* is accomplished, a *yogin* should abandon his fluctuations of awareness and assume the form of *brahman* with the help of supreme dispassion.

IV.55 In the last stage of yoga practice a *yogin* is required to abandon the meditation on "I am *brahman*".

IV.57 The state of liberation while living, which consists in abiding in one's own self, is manifested when the *yogin* becomes able to leave his fluctuations of awareness, having the form of his self.

IV.58 The self is said to be devoid of all conceptual constructions (*vikalpa*). A conceptual construction is explained as *viśiṣṭakalpanā*, the assuming of a non-qualified entity as qualified, e.g., taking the self as conditioned by such attributes as agency, etc.

IV.67 The secret sound (*nāda*) to be heard in the right ear is produced in the inner *suṣumṇā* channel. This sound resembles the sounds produced by bees, bamboo-trees, bells, oceans, or clouds.

IV.68 The method of closing the ears, eyes, nostrils, and mouth by placing one's fingers on them is described here.

IV.71-72 The three cavities in the heart, in the throat (*viśuddha* is the name of the center situated in the throat) and in the interval between the eyebrows are respectively called *śūnya, atiśūnya* and *mahāśūnya*. *Madhyacakra* is said to be situated in the throat.

IV.77 The expression "Rāja Yoga", which usually is used in

the sense of a means to isolation, is explained as meaning one-pointedness of mind.

IV.80 Rāja Yoga is explained as the best or highest of all yogic states; it is also known as the fourth state.

IV.94-96 The secret sound is said to posses the power of destroying distractions, of eradicating attachment, of checking the fluctuations of awareness, and of making the fluctuations have the form of *brahman* continuously or uninterruptedly.

IV.98 Here the dissolution of the mind is explained as its being characterized by *sattva* only. In this state only traces are left.

IV.101-102 That entity which after the dissolution of all fluctuations exists in its own nature is called *parabrahman, paramātman* or *parameśvara*. The content-less concentration described in IV.98-102 is another name for Rāja Yoga. In this state, which arises after a complete cessation of all fluctuations, the self abides in itself.

IV.103 The Haṭha Yoga way consists in the yogic postures, breath-controls (*kumbhaka*), and the bodily exercises, while the means prescribed in Layayoga are *nādānusandhāna* (IV.66ff.), *śāmbhavī mudrā*, etc.

IV.104 The *unmanī mudrā* is the same as content-less concentration (*vide Yogasūtra* I.18) which is caused by the supreme passionlessness. In this concentration only traces are left.

IV.107 The emergent (*vyutthāna*) state is said to have five varieties, namely the waking state, the dream state, dreamless sleep, swoon, and passing out of the body.

IV.110 Sleeping is that state in which the internal organ does not transform into objects, as in this state there is predominance of *tamas*, which covers all organs by subduing *sattva* and *rajas*. " *Mukta*" in the verse stands for *jīvanmukta*.

IV.114 Breath not running through *suṣumṇā* is called *asiddha* (not perfect). Tranquility in breathing leads to tranquility in the mind. A person is to remain in transitory existence (*saṃsāra*) until he conquers *prāṇa, bindu* and mind.

As a matter of fact it is knowledge (*jñāna*) that is the means to liberation; the conquest of breathing, etc. is to be known as a secondary cause. The means, namely knowledge (*jñāna*), action (*karman*) and devotion (*bhakti*) are included in yoga. The means, namely hearing (*śravaṇa*) and reflection (*manana*) can be included in *svādhyāya* (study of scripture). *Nididhyāsana* is included in meditation (*dhyāna*) (of the *Yogasūtra*). The performing of actions without any desire, i.e. *karmayoga*, is included in the *kriyāyoga* of *Yogasūtra* II.1, and *sādhana bhakti* (devotion of the nature of means) of nine varieties (see *Bhāgavatapurāṇa* VII.5.23) in the devotion to God (of *Yogasūtra* I.23). Resultant devotion (*phalabhūtabhakti*), that is devotion in the nature of love (*premabhakti*) is the indirect means to liberation; the direct means is self-realization.

49.AGHORĀNANDANĀTHA, *Yogakarṇikā*

This is an early twentieth-century manual on Haṭha Yoga which is largely a collection of quotations from other works. The author, Aghorānandanātha, is also known as Aghorānanda Nirvāṇin. The text was published by the Shri Ganga Prasad Asrama, Varnasi, in the Bharat Jivan Yantralaya. The work has fifteen chapters altogether. Chapter I describes rituals to be performed in the morning and gives a description of nine vital centers in the body. Chapter II focuses on meditating on parts of the body. Chapter III deals with control of breathing. Chapter IV describes the "six cleansing actions" (*ṣaṭkarmāṇi*). Chapter V deals with postures. Chapter VI describes withdrawal of the senses. Chapter VII deals with holding the breath (*kumbhaka*). Chapter XVIII discusses bodily exercises. Chapters IX, X, and XI deal respectively with *dhāraṇā, dhyāna* and *samādhi*. Chapters XII, XIII, XIV amd XV take up descriptions of Laya Yoga and unusual postures and bodily exercises.

50.SATYADEVA, *Yogarahasya* on Patañjali's *Yogasūtras*

Summary by Ram Shankar Bhattacharya

The commentary *Yogarahasya* by Satyadeva (usually with the appellation Brahmarṣi) is strictly original in the sense that he has hardly followed the fundamental views of Sāṃkhya-Yoga as expounded by such well-known commentators as Vācaspati, Gauḍapāda, Vijñānabhikṣu, Māṭhara and others. He appears to follow the Advaita point of view when treating the highest doctrines, and he also explains Yogic views accordingly. He does not follow Śaṃkarācārya in all non-essential matters and prescribes a path in which Tantric ideas are mixed with Vedic views.

The author, who was a householder, founded an institution and composed a few works in Sanskrit and in Bengali besides the *Yogarahasya*. The author died in the first quarter of this century.

The text used in preparing this summary is Y. Vandyopadhyaya, ed., *Yogarahasya of Satyadeva*, Third Edition (Calcutta: Sadhan Samar Office, 1977).

BOOK ONE

I.1 Yoga is the unity of the seer and the seen. Opposition of these two entities is apparent, not real. Absolute consciousness (*cit,* i.e. the seer) assumes the character of non-sentience. Concentration is a means to yoga and not identical with yoga (usually yoga is regarded as a particular form of concentration; this commentator does not subscribe to this traditional view.

I. The cessation of the fluctuations of awareness is called yoga in a secondary sense, because it (primarily) describes a state of awareness. Yoga as defined above is an eternally established fact. In the state of yoga the sense of difference between the seer and the seen, which is caused by ignorance, ceases and the fluctuations are restricted without any effort. In the state of liberation while living the fluctuations are partially restricted. If the fluctuations are restricted by means of withdrawal of the senses, etc. without the influence of self-knowledge, the restriction does not become perfect.

I.3 Since yoga transcends time and space, it is philosophically wrong to use the word "then" (*tadā*) in this *sūtra*. The nature of the immutable intelligent self (*cidātman*) consists of truth, knowledge, etc. Yoga, which is the unity of the seer and the seen, brings about the cessation of the fluctuations of awareness through the annihilation of ignorance. Ignorance is annihilated when the true nature of the self is realized and not vice-versa. He attains yoga who surrender himself to the self.

I.4 Fluctuations (*vṛtti*) are aspects of the self conditioned by space and time. There is no real distinction between awareness and its fluctuations. As the seer is not devoid of powers, it is called *citiśakti* (absolute an immutable knowing).

I.5-6 The afflicted (*kliṣṭa,* dominated by *rajas*) and non-afflicted (*akliṣṭa*, dominated by *sattva*) fluctuations are the same as the demonic (*āsurī*) and divine (*daivī*) natures presented in the *Bhagavadgītā* (16.3-4). All of the fluctuations are connected with the five sense-organs. These are to be known as the five mouths of Śiva who in the Tantras is described as having five faces.

I.6 The three instruments of knowledge are regarded as the three eyes of Śiva.

I.7 Error is that which is liable to be sublated afterwards; it is an indescribable (*anirvacanīya*) perception. It is called *bhrānti* and *khyāti* as well.

I.8 Though there is verbal comprehension in the fluctuation called conceptual construction, there exists in reality nothing which is denoted by words.

I.9 The fluctuation sleep *(nidrā)*, known also as dreamless sleep (*suṣupti*), has as its support (*ālambana*) awareness whose content is completely absent.

I.10 The highest form of memory is the recollection that "I am *brahman*". This knowledge is grasped by the grasper.

Memories concerning grasping (the instruments of knowing) and the grasped (external objects that are known) are of inferior character. Doubt and imagination are included in the five fluctuations.

I.12-16 The two methods of practice (*abhyāsa*, repeated effort with a view to abiding in the seer), and dispassion (*vairāgya*) arise naturally in a person who surrenders himself to the self and embraces yoga sincerely. *Abhyāsa* is the same as inquiry into *brahman* (*brahmavicāra*), which includes reciting sacred syllables, worship and the like. Though "dispassion" means absence of attachment, it also includes the absence of hatred. Since being seeable (*dṛśya*) is the distinguishing characteristic of a self, *yogins* do not feel any attachment to enjoyable things.

I.17-19 In the stage characterized by *vitarka* the existence of seer, seen, and the act of seeing is distinctly cognized. When seen and seeing are realized in the form of seer, then the stage if known as *vicāra*. A feeling of divine joy arises in the state characterized by bliss., while the feeling of "I am" exists in the stage known as egoity. Content-less concentration is the state of featureless awareness (*nirviśeṣa bodha*). In I.18 traces are those actions which are already bearing fruit (*prārabdha-karman*). The traces of accumulated karma do not cling to the *yogin*, and those of future actions get destroyed. In the content-less state ignorance ceases, though its effects (known as traces of *prārabdhakarman*) are found to exist for some time. The *videhalayas* are those who have left their gross bodies after acquiring the third state (i.e. *ānandānugata* of the content-filled concentration). Similarly, the *prakṛtilayas* are those who have acquired the fourth state (i.e. *asmitānugata*) of the content-filled concentration and have assumed causal bodies. They may attain liberation through the *devayāna* path with the help of the content-less concentration.

I.23 Devotion (*praṇidhāna*) is self-surrender. Yoga is to be known as the means of destroying disunion.

I.25 Since God himself assumes the form of a spiritual

teacher, no disciple should consider his teacher as a human being.

I.26 Though the word "*praṇava*" chiefly means the sound *oṃ*, all incantations are sometimes called "seeds" (*bīja*), for all the glories of God are denoted or suggested by it.

I.27 The reciting of sacred words or letters is called *mantracaitanya* which means the unity of the incantation, the teacher, and the intended deity.

I.28 The indirect awareness of *prāṇa* is the realization of the inner self (*pratyakcetana*).

I.30-38 *Ekatattva abhyāsa* is explained as the effort to abide in the innner self.

I.45-51 The cognitive principle (*mahat*), etc. are the objects of engrossment. The *puruṣa* is not objectified in engrossment rather, knowledge of *puruṣa* as different from *prakṛti* is the sole object. The difference between engrossment and concentration is that while the former consists in a particular kind of fluctuations, the latter consists in the cessation of undesired fluctuations. In the seedless concentration the seed of ignorance is destroyed, and nothing other than the self is perceived.

BOOK TWO

II.1 The word "*tapas*" means the realization of the self in the *ājñā cakra* (one of the six vital centers mentioned in the Tantras). *Kriyāyoga* in the *Yogasūtra* is the same as the *buddhiyoga* in the *Gītā*. Even secular duties may be regarded as *kriyāyoga* if they are deemed forms of devotion.

II.3-4 Ignorance is incomplete knowledge; it is lower than knowledge, which is the direct means of attaining the imperishable entity (*akṣara*). Ignorance, also known as *mahāmāyā*, is the cause of *vṛttisārūpya* (*puruṣa*'s appearing to assume the forms of the fluctuations of awareness). Ignorance, which may be said to be *brahman* with attributes (*saguṇa brahman*), depends upon *brahman*.

II.13 *Bhoga* means not only the actual experience (of pleasure and pain) but contact with objects also. While virtue (*puṇya*) is a helping factor for knowledge, *apuṇya* (vice) veils knowledge.

II.17-19 Contact (*saṃyoga)* is itself a form of ignorance and cannot be distinctly objectified. The assertion "I do not know myself" is based on ignorance, and gives rise to (the assumption of) internal and external objects. The seen owes its existence to the existence of a seer (*puruṣa*) and is illuminated by it. Seen things are ever-changing and not independent. They disappear for him who perceives all as different forms of self. The three *guṇas*, namely *sattva, rajas* and *tamas*, are nothing but the aspects of sportive pleasure (*līlāvilāsa*) of the seer (*puruṣa*) and are absolutely dependent on the *puruṣa* principle. They are respectively connected with the three aspects of the seer, namely existence, activity and bliss.

II.22-24 The absolute consciousness (*puruṣa*) possesses the power of ignorance (*avidyāśakti*) of ever-changing nature, which is as though opposed to its own unchanging nature. This possession or acceptance is what is known as the conjunction of *śivaśakti* (the power of property, i.e. the seen) and *svātmiśakti* (the power of proprietor, i.e. the seer). This ignorance must be regarded as a sportive faculty of *puruṣa*, because he is pure consciousness.

II.28-39 The observances of non-injury (*ahiṃsā*, etc. also have internal or mental (*ādhyātmika*) aspects. For example, non-injury is not only the act of killing an embodied being but also the absence of aversion or hatred. Similarly, contentment (*saṃtoṣa*) is not only the quality of not being disturbed by adversity, but also the cessation of the sense of want. The value of non-injury gets established in a person when he becomes devoid of attachment and aversion on account of realizing his self as the self in all beings. *Satyapratiṣṭhā* (fixity in truthfulness) means the firm conviction of the existence of the self. It is remarked that the exposition of the supernormal powers (arising from firmly practicing the restraints and observances) as found in the traditional commentaries is concerned not with liberation but with virtuousness (*dharma*).

II.46 Posture is explained as meaning the heart. Sitting in the heart the mind acquires bliss born of tranquility. *Anantasamāpatti* means engrossment with the infinite.

II.47 The first two operations of breath-control are explained as the perception of *prāṇa* in external and internal objects, and the third (i.e. *stambhavṛtti*) is the perception of *prāṇa* abiding in *prāṇa*. When controlled breathing gets established in the subtle form of space, time and number, then it is called *dīrghasūkṣma* (protracted and subtle).

II.50 Doubt or ignorance about the nature and existence of the self is known as *prakāśāvaraṇa* (the veil or covering of the light of knowledge).

BOOK THREE

III.1-7 Fixing the mind through the process of Haṭha Yoga is not a proper *yogāṅga*, because this practice has no connection with the seer (*puruṣa*). The vital centers, namely *mūlādhāra* etc. are also included in the places to which the mind is to be directed. The objects of concentration begin with the gross elements and end with egoity. The *puruṣa* principle is not an object of concentration. The external auxiliaries are the functions of the body, organs, and mind, while the internal auxiliaries are the functions of the intellect

III.9 Since cessation or restriction of fluctuations is a property of awareness, it is not yoga (defined in I.1-2). In the state of emergence awarenesses remain associated with time and space, while in the state of cessation they are only associated with time.

III.10 The three mutations called cessation, concentration and one-pointedness are connected with the *tamas, rajas,* and *sattva guṇas* respectively.

III.12 The seer (*puruṣa*) is the original property-possessor (*dharmin*) and his powers of creation, preservation, and destruction are the properties (*dharma*). The gods, namely Śiva, Viṣṇu and Prajāpati (Brahman in masculine gender) are characterized by quiescent (*śānta*), uprisen (*udita*) and indeterminable (*avyapadeśya*) attributes respectively.

III.14 When, on account of ignorance, the *puruṣa* falsely assumes a manifold form and becomes seemingly mutable, it becomes the property-possessor of the evolutes known as the *mahat*, etc.

III.16-35 The divine powers of the self are to be known as supernormal powers (*vibhūti*) and they fall under the domain of divine sport (*līlā*). Since the *vibhūtis* are aspects of the self, their cultivation gives rise to dispassion and isolation.

BOOK FOUR

IV.1 In this *sūtra* other supernormal powers born of concentration, such as hypnotism, are described in addition to those presented in the third Book. "*Samādhi*" in this *sūtra* is to be taken in the sense of a gross form of one-pointedness and not in the sense shown in *sūtra* III.3.

IV.4 The created minds (*nirmāṇacitta*) are not influenced by merit, demerit, etc.

IV.7 Though a perfect *yogin* may sometimes seem to act as if incited by anger, aversion, affection, etc. the actions of *yogins* who recognize non-duality (*advaitadarśin*) do not produce traces and as such they are not a cause of bondage.

IV.10 Though the desire for self-welfare (*āśis*) has no beginning, it gets destroyed in a person who has realized the self.

IV.15-16 Mundane existence (*jagat*) is different in different embodied beings (*jīva*), while the world projected by God is the common object of all beings. All objects are, in reality, dependent on the divine mind of God; they get dissolved when the divine mind ceases to act.

IV.20 Awareness does not transcend time. It is characterized by sequential momentary changes, and it is unable to know two things in one moment.

IV.27 Traces in this *sūtra* are those that are found in those liberated while living.

IV.33 Even the *dharmamegha* concentration is associated

with time. Only in the content-less state of awareness does a *yogin* transcend time.

51.AUTHOR UNKNOWN, *Bṛhadyogiyājñavalkya*

Summary by Ram Shankar Bhattacharya

This text is attributed to the sage Yājñavalkya (as is the *Yogayājñāvalkya* already summarized). The author and date of the text is unknown. The edition used for this summary is that of Swami Kuvalayananda and Pt. Raghunathashastri, eds. *Bṛhadyogiyajñavalkya*, second edition, Kaivalyadham, Poona 1976. It appears to be a late text concerned mainly with Incantation Yoga.

CHAPTER ONE

I.1-19 Yājñavalkya from the Mithila region was asked by sages to teach them divine knowledge as propounded in the Vedas, etc. with the necessary details so that they could transcend transitory existence (*saṃsāra*).

I.20-44 Yājñavalkya agreed to expound divine knowledge as taught in authoritative texts. A brief list of the contents of the present work is given in verses 23-44. It is remarked that while reciting a *mantra* one should keep in memory the five factors pertaining to an incantation, namely (1) *nirukta* (etymology of words), (2) *samutpatti* (origination of the incantation, (3) *prayojana* (purpose of using the incantation; (4) *pratiṣṭhāna* (foundation or basis), and (5) *stuti* (eulogy of the incantation).

CHAPTER TWO

I.1-46 The following topics are dealt with in this chapter: a eulogy of *praṇava* (i.e. *oṃ*) consisting of 3 and 1/2 *mātrās*; Agni as the deity of *oṃ*; prolonged utterance of *oṃ*; *oṃ* as uttered in sacrifices; the Vedas as aspects of *oṃ*; the various names of *oṃ*, such as *praṇava, tāra, udgītha*, etc.; the three letters of *oṃ* representing a large number of triads, namely past-present-future, pleasant-painful-stupifying, waking-dream-sleep, etc.; dissolving of the first three *mātrās* (i.e. *a*, *u*, and *m*) in the half *mātrā*; meditation on *oṃ* leading to self-knowledge; the process of attaining the ultimate goal by uttering *oṃ* at the time of death; speech pervaded by *oṃ*; God as not affected by afflictions, etc. and to be known as the lord of sacrifices; God as signified by *oṃ* and to be meditated on with the help of *oṃ*.

I.47-62 *Brahman* is said to be of two kinds, *śabdabrahman* (to be uttered by *vāc*) and *parabrahman*. *Oṃ* has five aspects, *a*, *u*, *m*, the nasal sound, and its application. With the help of the sound *oṃ* one can direct one's mind to *brahman* and can perceive one's chosen deity and can realize God hidden in him. *Oṃ* is the most powerful medium for attaining *brahman*.

I.63-99 Control of breathing can successfully be practiced with the reciting of *oṃ*, *gāyatrī* and other incantations. The three incantations of *oṃ* represent three gods, the three Vedas, the three fires, and some other triads. *Oṃ* is pronounced in different accents (*svara*) by the followers of the different recensions of the Vedas (*vide* II.78-79). Grammatically the word "*oṃ*" is neuter.

II.100-112 In the Pañcarātra system *oṃ* is accepted as the signifier of Bhagavat and as denoting three divine aspects and three divine qualities. If one leaves one's body by uttering *oṃ* at the time of death, one attains the supreme imperishable goal which transcends speech.

II.113-126 Ten names of *oṃ* are given here with their derivative meanings. The names are: *oṃ, praṇava, sarvavyāpin, ananta, tāra, śukla, vaidyuta, haṃsa, turya, and parabrahman.*

II.135-158 The process of restricting the mind and applying it to *brahman* with the help of pronouncing *oṃ* is described here in detail. At the end there are verses praising *oṃ*.

CHAPTER THREE

The whole chapter deals with the seven *vyāhṛtis* (the names/incantations of the seven realms), namely Bhūs, Bhuvas,

Svar, Mahar, Jana, Tapas and Satya. It shows their relations with the seven regions (*loka*) and the reasons for coining these seven names. At the end of the chapter the nature of the creator Brahmā and of his creations has been discussed.

CHAPTER FOUR

The Chapter deals with the Gāyatrī incantation in its various aspects. The God Savitṛ is said to be its deity, and Viśvāmitra, who is said to be identical with Prajāpati, the creator, is the *ṛṣi* (seer) of this incantation . This incantation may be uttered at the time of practicing breath-control. The expression "*oṃ apo...*", etc. is called Gāyatrī *śiras*, and may be added to this incantation while practicing breath-control, etc.

Gāyatrī, the essence of the Vedas, is called *prakṛti* while *oṃ* is called *puruṣa*. The twenty-five letters (i.e. the twenty-four letters of the Gāyatrī incantation and the one letter *oṃ*) represent the twenty-five *tattvas* (of the Sāṃkhya philosophy). *Oṃ* is to be uttered before and after the Gāyatrī incantation. This incantation is called "Gāyaṭrī" as it protects the person who chants it.

CHAPTER FIVE

The process of *nyāsa* of the Gāyatrī incantation is the topic here. "*Nyāsa*" means the mental invoking of sacred syllables or gods or holy texts for occupying certain parts of the body in order to render it faultless so that the embodied worshiper can worship his deity successfully. *Nyāsa* is said to be performed either by applying the syllables, namely *a*, *u*, and *m*, or by applying the names of the seven *vyāhṛtis* (Bhūs, etc. above) to the different parts of the body. The same process is again stated mentioning the application of the twenty-four letters of the Gāyatrī incantation to the twenty-four parts of the body. The fourth *nyāsa* of Gāyatrī is also described at the end of the Chapter (verses 11b-12).

CHAPTER SIX

The procedure of performing the *sandhyā* adoration is given here. It deals with the eulogy of *sandhyā*, the three goddesses of *sandhyā*, namely Gāyatrī, Sāvitrī, and Sarasvatī, the reason for the term "*sandhyā*", time for *sandhyā*-adoration, the repetition of the Gāyatrī incantation, etc.

CHAPTER SEVEN

This Chapter deals with the bath (*snāna*). It speaks of clay, etc. to be used, the Vedic *sūktas* and incantations to be chanted, clothes to be put on, procedure of *tarpaṇa* (the act of offering water to the sages), rules for reciting sacred syllables, etc.

CHAPTER EIGHT

VIII.1-18 Controlling breath, which is prescribed by Manu and the Vedas, is to be practiced with the reciting of the Gāyatrī incantation adding *oṃ*, the *vyāhṛtis* and the expression called *śīras (vide* Chapters III and V) with it. Breath control has three operations called inhalation, exhalation and stoppage of breath, and it also has three stages known as the low (*kanīyas*), the middling (*madhyama*), and the highest (*uttama*). These stages have 12, 24 and 36 incantations respectively. A *mātrā* (time-unit) is to be known through the process stated in verses VIII.12-13. There arise sweat, tremor, etc. in a practitioner according to the intensity of the practice of breath-control.

VIII.19-48 Clear definitions of the three operations of controlled breathing, and a description of the process of practicing them, are stated in verses 19-21. The cessation of internal function in breath-control brings about pressure in air, which brings about fire, i.e. heat (in the body), which in turn produces water. These three purify the internal aspect of the practitioner. All blemishes of organs and all sins are eradicated by breath-control, which is seen as the highest penance. Breath-control enables one to attain divine powers. In practicing breath-control air is to be drawn in and expelled slowly without shaking the body. The time-unit must always be observed.

VIII.49-53 Withdrawal of the senses is to be practiced by a person who has succeeded in practicing breath-control. Sense-withdrawal consists in withdrawing the functions of the sense-organs by the mind. Volition, etc. are also to be restricted in practicing sense-withdrawal.

CHAPTER NINE

IX.1-27 For practicing meditation successfully one is required to practice the fourth breath-control. The uttering of *oṃ* and other sacred sylables are also helpful in practicing meditation. Infinite space is one of the objects of meditation; so also is *brahman* which, having assumed the form of an embodied self, exists in the hearts of all.

IX.28-36 Both knowledge (*jñāna*) and action (*karman*) are to be applied to achieve perfection. The supreme *puruṣa* cannot be realized without devout meditation. Karmas are destroyed by yoga practice consisting of meditation, meditative fixity and control of breath. It is a mistake to think that mere verbal knowledge is also a means. One attains liberation if the self is realized with the help of eight-membered yoga. Supernormal powers like *aṇimān*, etc. are achieved through yoga.

IX.37-64 A three-fold means consisting of *vidyā* (i.e. reciting of *oṃ* and other sacred syllables), *tapas* (i.e. breath-control), and *cintā* (i.e. meditation and fixity of the mind) is also prescribed by ancient teachers.

IX.111-136 The deity existing in the sun called *īśvara, viṣṇu,* etc. is to be worshiped by sacrifices and the reciting of sacred syllables. Internal sacrifice is helpful in realizing the self residing in the heart, who is to be directly perceived through the yogic eye. The *puruṣa* (consciousness) enjoys all presented to it by the intellect.

IX.152-198 The supreme self is all-pervasive. Meditation is the most powerful means to realize the self. Among the senses, sense-objects, mind, ego, intellect, the unmanifested *prakṛti,* and *puruṣa*, the later is higher (more subtle) than the former. *Puruṣa* (consciousness) is realized through the process described in verses 187-192. It is averred that meditation is superior to mere knowledge, and renunciation is higher than meditation as peace immediately follows renunciation. The *suṣumṇā* channel is the seat of the self (i.e. the self is to be realized through the path of *suṣumṇā*). Powers such as becoming invisible, entering other's bodies, etc. are the signs of perfection in yoga.

CHAPTER TEN

The practice of performing worship of the sun with the Vedic incantations, the reciting of the Gāyatrī incantation, eulogy of the sun, etc. are described in this chapter.

CHAPTER ELEVEN

XI.1-24 The following topics are discussed: eulogy of yoga, the self, and self-knowledge; Vedic incantations on the self; study of the six aids to the Vedas; study of the Vedas; importance of good conduct and penance.

XI.25-49 Both the gross and the subtle *brahman* are described in the Vedas. The gross *brahman* is called *śabdabrahman*, i.e. the Vedas. Knowledge of the subtle *brahman* leads to liberation. Both knowledge and action are means of attaining liberation. The highest religion is to realize the self through yoga. A person who possesses *adhyātmajñāna* is the supreme authority. In the hierarchy of beings it is the knower of *brahman* who occupies the highest position. Of all the *vidyās* (traditions of learning) the science of self-knowledge is the highest.

CHAPTER TWELVE

XII.1-17 All scriptures are based on the Vedas. Sages composed various works with a view to expound obscure Vedic views. There are fourteen branches of learning (*vidyā*) by which *dharma* is to be ascertained. Kapila, Hiraṇyagarbha, Nārāyaṇa, Apāntaratamas, and Paśupati are the promulgators of Sāṃkhya, Yoga, the Pañcarātra, the Vedas, and the Pāśupata philosophy respectively. All anti-Vedic systems are to be regarded as *tāmasa* (full of ignorance) and they are said to be composed to delude the *asuras* who hold such doctrines as the non-existence of the self after death or the absence of a creator.

XII.18-33 The Naiyāyikas, however, accept God as the (efficient) cause of the world. Perception, inference, and authoritative texts are to be known correctly in order to comprehend *dharma*. The teachings of Manu are based on the Vedas. All anti-Vedic systems are full of erroneous views. The Vedas are the ultimate source of *dharma* and of divine knowledge.

52.AUTHOR UNKNOWN, *Yogatārāvalī* (attributed to Śaṃkarācārya)

Summarized by Ram Shankar Bhattacharya

This small work in twenty-nine verses is considered to be an authoritative work on Rāja Yoga and Haṭha Yoga. It is attributed to Śaṃkarācārya, but that attribution is highly unlikely. The author and date of the text are unknown. Oddly enough, verse 6 of this text has been quoted in *Yogacintāmaṇi* of Śivānanda and attributed to a work named *Nandikeśvaratārāvalī*. No commentary on this work is known. It has had a few editions, mainly in vernacular languages. The edition used for this summary is H. R. Bhagavat, ed., *Minor Works of Śaṃkara* (Ashtekar and Company: Poona, 1925, 1952), pp. 101-105.

1-2 The work begins with a eulogy to the spiritual teacher, and it is remarked that concentration on the sound within (*nādānusaṃdhāna*) is the best of all the 125,000 *layayogas* (processes of absorption of the mind).

3-4 Divine experience (*bodha*), which is a means to self-realization, emerges from the *anāhata cakra* if the channels are purified by breath-control. It is concentration on the inner sound which leads one to the region of Viṣṇu.

5-7 One can transcend time by practicing the exercises (*bandha*), namely *jālandhara* (contraction of the throat), *auḍḍiyāna* (contraction of abdominal muscles, usually called *uḍḍiyāna* in other texts), and *mūla* (contraction of the anus), since this practice awakens *kuṇḍalinī* and renders the air inside the body motionless. He is blessed who drinks nectar oozing from the moon (in the *sahasrāra cakra*)in the head) heated by the fire from the *mūlādhāra cakra.*

8-10 That form of stoppage of breath (*kumbhaka*) is best which has no connection with inhalation and exhalation and which arises as a result of constantly practicing the aforesaid *bandhas*. This stoppage of breath gets highly developed if the mind is placed in the *anāhata cakra* (in the throat). This is called *kevalakumbhaka* which is not associated with inhalation and exhalation.

11-16 Vital air gets dissolved if the void in the heart is suspended or suppressed by the practice of *kevalakumbhaka*. When the flow of air (in the body) is firmly restricted, organic functions cease. This is the state of Rāja Yoga. In the perfected state of Rāja Yoga there remains no need of fixing the mind or of restricting the air. In this state the distinction of seer and seen ceases and the absolute *saṃvit* shines.

17-20 The state in which the mind becomes devoid of will (*saṃkalpa*) and constructions (*vikalpa*) and breathing ceases is called *manonmanī*. The means of attaining this state is to perceive transitory existence with detachment and to give up formative will. The mind gets tranquil by gradually leaving supporting objects.

21-29 *Amanska mudrā* (the state of being mindless) comes into existence as a result of complete cessation of breathing. In this state the wrong identification of the self with the body gets slackened, and the *yogin* attains the state transcending the mind, and conscious sleep (*ajādvanidrā*), also known as *yoganidrā*, arises. This sleep is devoid of all conceptual constructions and is full of *saṃvit* (consciousness). In this state all actions cease and the vision of duality gets dwindled. The last verse declares that one undoubtedly attains liberation by hearing the secret sound, which is not an object of the organ of hearing.

53.AUTHOR UNKNOWN, *Pāvanavijayasvarodaya*

Summary by Jyotirmoyee Bhattacharya

This text is an example of a class of Incantation Yoga known as *svarodaya* ("the arising of breath") or *svaraśāstra* ("the science of modulation of sounds or passage of air through the nostrils"). It appears to be a sub-branch of Haṭha Yoga. The author of the text is not known. Also, the date of the text is not known. The text used for this summary is from an edition published by the Vasumati Sahitya Mandira, Calcutta. The date of publication is not given.

The text is in the form of a dialogue between Śiva and his consort Gaurī. As already mentioned, it deals with the science of breath. Two or three texts (containing a large number of identical verses) on this science are available today. There is no commentary on any of these texts. A considerable number of verses in this text are not fully intelligible. In this summary the verses have been understood in their literal meanings.

CHAPTER ONE

I.1-6 The right and the left nostrils are respectively called *piṅgalā* and *īḍā*. Some planets are said to be the lords of the *tattvas* (earth, etc.) while air flows through either of the nostrils. For example, the sun and Venus are said to be the lords of earth while air flows through the right and left nostrils respectively.

I.7-24 There are 72,000 channels in the body which are centered in the navel. Among them the left channel (i.e. īḍā associated with the moon), the right channel (i.e. *piṅgalā* associated with the sun), and the channel situated in the middle (i.e. *suṣumṇā* associated with fire) are to be regarded as the chief. The function of *iḍā* is pleasing, promoting, and strengthening; the function of *piṅgalā* is burning and absorbing. Cruel acts are to be performed while air flows in the right nostril, auspicious and virtuous acts while air flows in the left nostril. No work should be performed while air flows in both nostrils. All questions become futile if they are asked while air flows in the *suṣumṇā* channel. Planets of benevolent and evil nature rising at the time of flowing air in either of the two nostrils bring success or failure in actions according to their nature.

I.25-38 The success of a question can be indicated by observing whether the breath of the questioner flows from the nostril which corresponds to the orientation (i.e. whether the questioner stands on the left or right) of the person questioned. Generally speaking, one becomes victorious in battle if he fights towards the side corresponding to the side (left or right) of the flow of air in the nostril. As a rule, a question indicates failure if put at the time of exhalation and success if put at the time of inhalation.

I.39-40 There are signs to know the rise of the five *tattvas*, namely earth, water, fire, air, and *ākāśa* in the nostrils.

CHAPTER TWO

II.1-26 The universe (*Brahmāṇḍa*, cosmic egg) comes into existence from the *tattva* and also get dissolved in it. The taintless and formless Maheśvara is the cause of *ākāśa* which gives rise to air; from air proceeds fire; from fire, water; and from water, earth. These five *tattvas* create the cosmic egg. All these *tattvas* exist in a living organism in subtle forms.

Breath flows with the sound *haṃsa* in which *haṃ* denotes Śiva and *sa* denotes Śakti. The science of breath (*svara*) is of great importance. It should not be imparted to the wicked. All *śāstras* have their basis in this science. A knowledge of this science enables a person to achieve success in worldly pursuits.

CHAPTER THREE

III.1-11 There are 72,000 channels in the body which come together at the place between the navel and the base of the spine (*mūlādhāra*). Among these channels, ten flow upward, ten downwards, and twenty-four obliquely.

CHAPTER FOUR

IV.1-5 The ten vital airs (*vāyu*) are described.

IV.6-18 *Īḍā*, the lord of the moon, is situated on the left side; *piṅgalā*, the seat of the sun, is situated on the right side; *suṣumṇā* is the seat of Śiva, called *haṃsa*. The two sounds, *haṃ* and *sa*, which are the forms of Śiva and Śakti, are associated with exhalation and inhalation respectively. Any act or giving done while the vital air becomes associated with the sound *sa* (i.e. when it flows to the left side) brings enormous result. One should think of the five *tattvas* when both inhalation and exhalation are checked. While *īḍā* and *piṅgalā* are generally helpful in achieving success in actions, *suṣumṇā* is not so favorable. At the time of air's coming out from the left nostril and entering the right nostril, good results are achieved. *Īḍā* is regarded as a woman; its god, the moon, is yellowish red (*gaura*) in color. *Piṅgalā* is regarded as a man; its god, the sun, is white. One should perform acts favorable to perfection and release while *suṣumṇā* flows.

IV.19-25 The flow of air in the two nostrils is influenced by the appearance and disappearance of lunar days (*tithi*) and fortnights. A *yogin* is required to drive air into the right nostril in the day and into the left nostril at night.

IV.26-34 The days of the week have their respective influence on the flow of air in the nostrils. For example, if air flows in *iḍā* (i.e. in the left nostril) on Monday, Wednesday, Thursday, and Friday then good results are achieved.

CHAPTER FIVE

V.1-12 If in the morning air flows in the right nostril instead of flowing in the left nostril then eight kinds of disaster, namely loss of wealth, enmity, destruction of desired objects, anxiety, etc. happen. Generally speaking, one should move the right or left foot while air flows in the corresponding right of left nostril. There are similar rules for locomotion in connection with the days of the week. One desiring success should touch the face with the right or left hand and according as the air flows in the right or left nostril.

V.13-24 One desiring success should alternatively face towards the left or right direction as the air flows in the left or right nostril. There are some acts that should be performed when air remains held in the nostrils. Rites for eradicating poison and for subjugating women brings success if they are performed with air flowing in the left and right nostrils respectively. The practice of yoga should be taken up when air flows through the *suṣumṇā* channel. There are means for moving air from its natural place (i.e. the nostril) to other places.

CHAPTER SIX

VI.1-11 One desirous of success is required to perform the following acts while air flows in the left nostril, namely putting on ornaments, traveling great distances, entering a hermitage, constructing palaces, etc. sowing seeds, taking in medicine, commencing study, initiation, reciting sacred syllables, treating diseases, singing, dancing, practicing yoga, etc.

CHAPTER SEVEN

VII.1-10 One desiring success is required to perform the following acts while air flows in the right nostril, namely giving instructions in cruel deeds, teaching, sexual union, enjoying a harlot, killing, drinking liquor, applying poison to an enemy, learning the method of using weapons, mountaineering, playing dice, stealing, taking physical exercise, crossing a river, buying, selling, donating, fighting, etc. All cruel acts are to be performed while air flows in the right nostril.

CHAPTER EIGHT

VIII.1-12 The *suṣumṇā* channel becomes active when breath moves from one nostril to another in each moment (*kṣaṇa*).

CHAPTER NINE

IX.1-10 Creation proceeds from the five *tattvas*, namely (1) earth, water, fire, air, and *ākāśa*. The taintless (i.e. *brahman*) transcends the *tattvas*. All beings residing in the seven worlds, namely *satya*, etc. are associated with these *tattvas*. The *tattvas* arise in the left or right nostril (i.e. the air in the nostrils shows the predominance of a *tattva* in the body). One should observe daily the rise of these *tattvas* with reference to the following factors, namely number, conjunction of breaths, the type of breath, place, color, the vital energy, taste, and motion.

IX.20-35 A detailed account of actions to be performed during the rise of the five *tattvas* is given in these verses, with the mention of favorable and unfavorable times for performing actions.

CHAPTER TEN

X.1-15 The rise of the *tattvas* brings about contentment, nourishment, pleasure or delight, sport, victory, laughter, sleep, fever, tremor, diminution of the duration of life, and death.

X.15-21 Some constellations are said to be the lords of the *tattvas*. Victory in war can be ascertained by observing the rise of the *tattvas*. Arjuna becomes victorious (in the Bhārata war) while the Kauravas were defeated as the *tattvas* were favorable to the former and unfavorable to the latter.

CHAPTER ELEVEN

XI.1-8 The process of meditating on the *tattvas* is stated here with necessary details.

CHAPTER TWELVE

XII.1-14 The science of *svara* helps one to ascertain the happening of victory, defeat, etc. It is respiration which is the highest helper of beings. It resides in a body in two forms, inhalation and exhalation. The length of breath used in inhalation and exhalation varies in various activities.

XII.15-33 There are fixed periods of the flow of air in the nostrils. The flow of air in nostrils indicates profit or loss, victory or defeat, and success or failure in activities.

CHAPTER THIRTEEN

XIII.1-18 The right (*piṅgalā*) and left (*īḍā*) channels are favorable to men and women respectively. The functions of the *īḍā, piṅgalā*, and *suṣumṇā* channels should be checked when fighting with others. Questions regarding victory or defeat may be answered by observing the flow of air in the two nostrils. Flow of air in the right nostril of the inquirer standing behind the astrologer indicates death of the enemy.

CHAPTER FOURTEEN

XIV.1-12 A person, failing to perceive the rise of a *tattva*, may perform a particular rite in order to ascertain the rise of a *tattva*. The practice of breath-control while the air *tattva* rises enables one to achieve success in gambling. A person well versed in the science of breathing (*svara*) acquirers enormous strength. By practicing meditation combined with the stoppage of breath and by performing *homa* (the act of offering oblation to fire) one achieves vast gain and victory. Knowing that his visible existence has emanated from the formless (i.e. *brahman*) one accepts this existence as a transformation of *brahman*.

CHAPTER FIFTEEN

XV.1-8 This chapter deals with the process of winning over or subjection (*vaśīkaraṇa*). Some of the processes are to interchange the place of the *īḍā* and *piṅgalā* channels, to restrict the functions of some of the channels, and to inhale air through some particular processes. By applying these processes one can keep women under control, can achieve a long span of life, or can check aging.

CHAPTER SIXTEEN

XVI.1-7 A detailed procedure for keeping all kinds of women under control is shown here. The procedure consists in reciting certain incantations and engaging in certain esoteric practices associated with *īḍā* and other channels.

CHAPTER SEVENTEEN

XVII.1-7 This chapter deals with conception and childbirth. Particular drugs favorable to the birth of different kinds of children are prescribed here. The rise of the *tattvas* has its effect on pregnancy and also on the sex of the child. Some fruitful means for impregnation have been stated here. For example, if at the time of sexual union air flows in the left nostril of the woman and in the right nostril of the man, then conception must occur.

XVII.8-15 Some signs of ascertaining the birth of a boy, girl, or an impotent person have been enumerated here. An account of different kinds of conception (based on the time of the rise of the *tattvas*) and their effect on the birth of children of various types (e.g., rich, fortunate, etc.) is given here. It is advised that all processes stated here are to be learnt from a *guru*.

CHAPTER EIGHTEEN

XVIII.1-15 One should observe the rise of the *tattvas* while air flows in the left nostril on the first day of the bright half of the month of Caitra, or on the first day of the winter and summer solstice (*uttarāyaṇa* and *dakṣiṇāyaṇa*). The rise of the *tattvas* indicates various results. The rise of the earth *tattva* indicates prosperity and an abundant crop. If the *suṣumṇā* channel flows in the aforesaid days there arise revolution, disaster, etc. Similar results are indicated by the flow of air in different nostrils in the day on which the sun enters Aries (the first sign of the zodiac).

CHAPTER NINETEEN

XIX.1-12 It is advised that one should perform rites for eradicating diseases which get developed as a result of taking food at the time of rising of some *tattvas*. For example, if food causing wind is taken at the time of the rise of the air *tattva*, then the diseases caused by wind get developed.

XIX.13-31 By observing the flowing of air in the nostrils one can ascertain the time of death.

CHAPTER TWENTY

XX.1-14 The three operations (inhalation, etc.) of breath-control are to be practiced daily for achieving specific results. Breath-control should be practiced according to one's strength. Both inhalation and exhalation may be practiced alternatively through both the nostrils. Through the process described here one should try to know the rise of the *tattvas* with their color, motion, etc. A *yogin* transcends time by forsaking his subconscious impressions. He can move in the whole universe. The span of his life is lengthened.

CHAPTER TWENTY-ONE

The final chapter praises the science called *svara* which deals with the following nine subjects: breath, incantation, *tattva* (earth, etc.), war, the act of subjugating women, conception, year, diseases, and auspicious or inauspicious times. One desirous of attaining unfailing speech should meditate on the supreme self and should be moderate in eating and sleep.

54.AUTHOR UNKNOWN, *Uttaragītā*

Summarized by Ram Shankar Bhattacharya

This short text in three chapters in dialogue form between Bhāgavat (Kṛṣṇa) and Arjuna is regarded as an authoritative text on yoga. Although its language is similar to the

Bhagavadgītā, in some places it uses esoteric and enigmatic expressions. The author and date of the work are unknown. In Bengal it is usually regarded as belonging to the *Brahmāṇḍapurāṇa*, but the printed editions of this Purāṇa do not contain these three chapters. In some of it manuscripts it is said to belong to the *Bhāgavatapurāṇa* or the *Mahābhārata*, although, again, no edition of these works contains these three chapters.

For this summary an old edition prepared by Mahādeva Śarman has been used, published by the Gujarati Printing Press, 1912. This edition includes a commentary on the text by a certain Gauḍapāda, and this commentary has been used in preparing the present summary. Whether the Gauḍapāda of the commentary is the same as the Vedāntin Gauḍapāda or the Gauḍapāda of the *Bhāṣya* on the *Sāṃkhyakārikās* cannot be determined. Also, the date of the commentary cannot be determined.

The ideas in the text represent a simplified Vedānta monism together with the theory and practice of Haṭha Yoga not unlike the point of view found in many of the so-called Yoga Upaniṣads, summarized later in this Volume. This may well provide an important clue for dating this text, that is, roughly the same time as the composition of the Yoga Upaniṣads.

The text as explained by Gauḍapāda is summarized here.

CHAPTER ONE

I.1-18 On attaining the unconditioned and imperishable supreme self, one is separated from transmigratory existence. The way to realize unity with the supreme self is described in verse 7 in an enigmatic way. At the time of realizing the self, which is devoid of all mental fluctuations and states, the vital air ceases. One realizing the self becomes identified with God, who is denoted by the subtlest aspect of the sound *oṃ*.

I.19-36 After the realization of reality all means, including the study of the Vedas, become useless. A perfected being is not required to perform any duty enjoined by scriptures. The reality of the self, which is to be perceived with the help of meditation and the reciting of *oṃ*, has neither agency, activity, nor enjoyership. It is self-effulgent (*svayamprakāśa*) and is present in all embodied beings. it exists in the mind as the witnessing principle (*sākṣin*). In the initial state, practice of the restraints is absolutely necessary; in the last stage, by fixing the mind on the absolute reality which is not conditioned by space, etc. a *yogin* transcends both virtue and vice.

I.37-57 The self is realized in its purest form in the state of concentration. A divine luster shines in the subtlest aspect of the *anāhata* sound (a sound produced otherwise than by the heart's beating). If the mind is fixed on this luster, it gets dissolved in the highest abode of the lord Viṣṇu. Merit, demerit, etc., remain existent until the realization of the imperishable *brahman*. External actions, if properly performed, are also helpful in acquiring knowledge of reality.

CHAPTER TWO

II.1-34 The knots (*bandha*) of actions get destroyed by the knowledge of *brahman*, and an embodied self, provided his ignorance is annihilated, becomes non-different from *brahman*. The supreme self is devoid of agency and the like. There are two paths, namely the *devayāna* (directly leading to liberation) which is connected with the *piṅgalā* channel, and the *pitṛyāṇa* (leading to liberation through successive states) which is connected with the *īḍā* channel The *kuṇḍalinī śākti* is identified with all deities. A *yogin* by closing the nine gates through breath-control becomes endowed with divine knowledge. The all-pervading nature of *kuṇḍalinī* has been described in verses 22-26. In verses 27-34 it is shown that different regions of the *brahmāṇḍa* (cosmic egg) are situated in different parts of the body.

II.35-48 The gradual process of dissolution, beginning with the earth, has been shown here. All evolutes get dissolved in the *kṣetrajña* (the knower of the field), who in turn gets dissolved or becomes absorbed in the supreme self. The unity of the embodied self with the supreme self is the same as the unity of the *ghaṭākāśa* (the space in the jar) with infinite space when the jar is broken. This unity is realized through the practice of *jñānayoga*. Duties enjoined in scriptures are to be performed until *brahman* is realized. Attachment and non-attachment are the causes of bondage and liberation respectively. When the mind attains *unmanībhāva* (absence of all distractions, egoism, etc.) it attains the highest goal.

CHAPTER THREE

III.1-18 Only the essential teachings of scripture need be known. All external activities are to be known as impediments to yoga-practice. The whole world becomes meaningless to him who can control the sense of taste and sexual desire. A *yogin* perceives everything as forms of *brahman*. A *yogin* is advised to take as much as is required to maintain his body and to realize that possession of mundane things for future prosperity is useless. He should remain undisturbed or contented by acquiring things for the present time.

APPENDIX: SOME ADDITIONAL TEXTS

55.AUTHOR UNKNOWN, YOGAVĀSIṢṬHARĀMĀYAṆA (attributed to Vālmikī)

This is a huge poetic work of some 30,000 verses, attributed to Vālmikī, author of the great epic *Rāmāyaṇa*. The text appears in the form of a dialogue between Rāma and his teacher Vāsiṣtha. The authorship and date of the text cannot easily be determined. It probably reached its current form some time between the tenth and thirteenth centuries.

Obviously it is not possible to summarize such an enormous work. Suffice it to say that in terms of theoretical perspective, the text overall, as Feuerstein has aptly put it, is "radically nondualist".[169] That is to say, it is very much in the tradition of non-dual Vedānta. In terms of practice, yoga is taught as a discipline made up of seven stages (*bhūmi*), including (1) desiring what is good, (2) careful reflection, (3) expansion of thinking, (4) attaining authentic truth, (5) detachment, (6) reflecting upon the transience of external things, and (7) abiding in ultimate truth.

YOGA UPANIṢADS

The class of texts known as Upaniṣads was originally linked with various traditions of Vedic ritual and interpretation. Various Upaniṣads were associated with the *Ṛg Veda*, the *Sāma Veda,* the *Yajur Veda*, and eventually the *Atharva Veda*. For example, such major Upaniṣads as the *Bṛhadāraṇyaka* and the *Chāndogya* were linked respectively with the *Yajur Veda* and the *Sāma Veda,* and so forth. Altogether there are over one hundred Upaniṣads, and, according to some, over two hundred. Apart from the thirteen to fifteen major Upaniṣads, almost all of the others are post-Vedic and linked with the *Atharva Veda.*

At the end of the nineteenth and the beginning of the twentieth century, Paul Deussen attempted to sort out these many minor Upaniṣads linked to the *Atharva Veda* into thematic groupings.[170] He detected five basic groupings. There was, first, a group focusing largely on the old Vedānta notions of *ātman* and *brahman*. Second, he identified a group especially focused on the practice of yoga of one kind or another. Third, he distinguished a group focusing on the life of *saṃnyāsa*. Fourth, he recognized a group that appeared to be clearly sectarian Śaivite. Finally, he pinpointed a group that appeared to be clearly sectarian Vaiṣṇava. To some extent, of course, there was considerable overlapping among the various categories, but Deussen's categorization has continued to have at least heuristic value even down to the present.

In any case, the Adyar Library over the years, largely following Deussen's classification, has published a series of volumes of these minor Upaniṣads, one of which is the group known as the Yoga Upaniṣads. Our E is the Sanskrit edition, edited by A. Mahadeva Sastri, and entitled *The Yoga Upaniṣads*, first published in 1920, and reprinted in 1968, by the Adyar Library and Research Centre, Madras. It should perhaps be noted that this is not a critical edition of these texts. An English translation was published in 1938 by T. R. Srinivasa Ayyangar in another volume of the Adyar Libaray and Research Centre, Madras. This is our T.

As the brief summaries that follow indicate, these Yoga Upaniṣads are uniformly late. That is to say, they reflect primarily traditions of Haṭha Yoga and, thus, are all texts that are probably post-tenth century or later. In terms of philosophical orientation, they reflect a non-technical and/or simplified non-dualist Vedānta in a Haṭha Yoga practical framework of *kuṇḍalinī yoga*. There are also elements of Tantra as well.

The following summaries are in the order that they are of published in the edition and translation cited above. The sequential numbering corresponds to the arrangement of the texts in E. Not all of these texts are translated in T.

56.AUTHOR UNKNOWN, *Advayatāraka Upaniṣad*

Summarized by K. N. Misra

1 (E 1-10; T1-16) The work is meant for ascetics (*yati*).

2 (E 2) Conceiving oneself as of the nature of consciousness (*citsvarūpa*), seeing through introspection the transcendent *brahman* as the peak of effulgence of existence, consciousness and bliss above the middle of the eyebrows, one becomes of the nature of that (*brahman*).

3 (E2-3) *Tāraka* is called so because it enables one to cross the great fear of the cycle of birth and death, etc. It is called non-dual *brahman* , since it is that which remains after the self and God have been realized to be illusory.

4 (E3)To attain it, one should meditate on the three objects of concentration, namely internal, external and intermediate.

5 (E 3-4) An aspirant for liberation (*mumukṣu*) should practice meditation on an internal object of concentration like *kuṇḍalinī*, an effulgence in the specific region in the forehead, a blue radiant space between the eyes, or an effulgence in the heart.

6 (E 4) The external object of concentration is like the space seen at a certain distance in front of one's nose, or like beans seen in front of one's eyes, of like radiant rays seen at the end of the outer corner of the eyes, or as a halo seen over one's head.

7 (E 4-5) The intermediate object of concentration is the five-fold space. Seeing these, one becomes like them. It is only the concentration on *tāraka* which bears the fruit of non-mindedness.

8 (E 5) *Tāraka* is of two kinds: the earlier is known as *tāraka* and the later as *amanaska.*

9 (E 5-6) One should realize only *tāraka* through introspection.

10 (E 6-7) That *tāraka* is of two kinds, namely *amūrtitāraka,* which is knowable through the senses, and

mūrtitāraka, which transcends concentration on the eyebrows. It is introspection accompanied by mind which makes realization of this two-fold *tāraka* possible.

11 (E 7) The earlier kind consists in the manifestation of an effulgence as a result of concentration on the crevice between the eyebrows, and the later kind is meditation on the radiant rays above the root of the palate.

12 (E 7-8) Then there occurs what is known as *śāmbhāvī mudrā*. The presence of one who has attained it sanctifies the earth and the people. Whosoever worships such a *yogin* gets liberated.

13 (E 8) The internal object of concentration is of the nature of burning effulgence. Through the instruction of a great teacher it is conceived in various forms, seen through the grace of a good preceptor.

14-16 (E 9) A preceptor (*ācārya*) is one who is well-trained in the Vedas, is a devotee of Viṣṇu, who knows and is well-versed in yoga. Being devoted to his teacher and having realized the *puruṣa*, he is called *guru*. The syllable *gu* stands for darkness and *ru* for its dispeller, and a teacher, therefore, is called *guru* because he dispels darkness.

17-18 (E 9) Such a teacher is the transcendent *brahman*, supreme knowledge, highest resort and the best wealth. He is greater than all, because he teaches *that*.

19 (E 9) One who reads this work even once gets rid of the cycle of rebirth and achieves all the ends of human life.

57.AUTHOR UNKNOWN, *Amṛtanāda Upaniṣad*

Summary by N. S. S. Raman

(E 11-25) *Amṛtanāda* consists of 39 verses, yogic rather than Vedāntic in character. It opens with a stress on the need to realize God. It refers to the six limbs of yoga (in contrast to Patañjali who mentions eight): withdrawal of the senses, meditation, breath-control, fixation of mind, reason (*tarka*) and concentration. There follows a description of breath-control. Various chants like *oṃ* are referred to as preconditions for breath-control. The technique of breath-control is then described. Definitions of fixation of mind and concentration are also given as means to achieve equanimity in order to realize God. Some yogic postures are mentioned. Other yogic techniques are also described, along with the stress on the need to desist from passions, dreaming, overeating, excessive fasting, etc. which are all criticized. Chanting of various incantations is regarded as beneficial. The various places where life-breath (*prāṇa*) resides are mentioned to be the heart, rectum, navel, etc. Life-breath is described as having red color and other breaths of different colors are also mentioned. Rebirth does not occur if all the breaths (*vāyu*) break through their encirclement in the abdomen and reach the region of the brain.

58.AUTHOR UNKNOWN, *Amṛtabindu Upaniṣad*

Summary by K. N. Misra

1-2 (E 26-27; T17-21) Mind (*manas*) is of two kinds, viz., pure or devoid of desire and impure or associated with desire. It leads to liberation if it is not attached to or does not have an object of desire, and otherwise to bondage.

3-6 (E 27-28) The aspirant for peace must, therefore, render his mind free from attachment to the objects of desire.

When the mind, freed from the attachment to the objects of desire and inhibited (*saṃniruddha*) in the heart reaches the state of self-effacement–in which it becomes defunct–one attains to the highest state.

Wisdom and meditation consist in inhibiting the mind in the heart until it gets effaced and one realizes *brahman*.

7-10 (E 28-30) One should first concentrate on the mystic syllable (*svara*) and then on that which is beyond it (*asvara*).

The "beyond the syllable" alone is the non-qualified *brahman*, realizing which one becomes that and gets liberated.

11-12 (E 30) One should concentrate on the self as that which is one and the same in the waking, dreaming and sleeping states. One who transcends these three and reaches the fourth (*turīya*) state is not born again.

One and the same self (*bhūtātman*) is seen–like the moon reflected in water–in various beings.

13-14 (E 31) The space in a pot is not carried from place to place when the pot is carried, nor does it perish when the pot disintegrates. It assumes various forms similar to pots, but when they disintegrate it is comprehended not as destroyed but as expansive space. So also is the self eternal and ubiquitous like space.

15 (E 31-32) Enveloped by the illusory world of words or name and form, one does not see the self, but when the darkness is dispelled, realizes its oneness.

16-18 (E 32-33) An aspirant for peace should meditate on the non-decaying reality (*akṣara*) underlying the non-decaying syllable (*śabdākṣara*).

Two sciences are to be known, namely of *brahman* in the form of word (*śabdabrahman*) and the transcendent (*para*) *brahman*. One who is well-established in the former aims for the latter.

The wise man after having studied the books (Vedas), intent on acquisition of knowledge and realization, should abandon the books, like a seeker after grain who discards the straw.

19-20 (E 33-34) Wise men look upon the self as milk–which is of the same white color in cows of various colors.

21-22 (E 34-35) The self abides hidden in all beings and one, therefore, should churn constantly wth the churning-stick of mind, and using one's eye of knowledge extract the transcendental *brahman* regarded as one's own self.

I am the Vāsudeva who, though the support of all beings, with a view to bless them is dwelling (*vasati*) in all beings.

59.AUTHOR UNKNOWN, *Kṣurikā Upaniṣad*

Summary by N. S. S. Raman

(E 36-44; T22-26) *Kṣurikā* (which means "knife") is a short work of twenty-five verses. It stresses fixation of the mind which, if practiced thoroughly, is capable of cutting through bondage, thus eliminating rebirth. There are references to various yogic postures and to exercises capable of arousing the serpent power (*kuṇḍalinī*). There are also descriptions of how to control the life-breath (*prāṇa vāyu*). The *yogin* is said to accumulate all channels in the region of the throat. Of all the channels, 101 are regarded as the most important, but the Upaniṣad does not name or place these. The subtle channels (*sūkṣmanāḍī*) are supposed to number 72,000. Through penance one can overcome the various empirical manifestations of awareness. Arousing the so-called *suṣumṇā* channel can destroy rebirth. Stress is laid on renunciation and attachment in order to overcome bondage (*saṃsāra*) and to achieve destruction of all merits and demerits (karma), of fetters of passion that bind man to the world, through the practice of breath-control and attainment of immortality through the elimination of all desires.

60.AUTHOR UNKNOWON, *Tejobindu Upaniṣad*

Summary by N. S. S. Raman

(E 44-64; T27-87) *Tejobindu* is one of the longer Yoga Upaniṣads, consisting of six chapters of varying lengths and 463 verses in all. The topics dealt with in these chapters are: explanation and description of the chant *oṃ*; description of the nature of consciousness (*cit*); the nature of the experience of the higher self; the power of the incantation "I am *brahman*"; the character of the self liberated while living; the nature of release from bodily existence; and the nature of the ultimate reality. There is often a great deal of repetition and some portions, especially in Chapter Six, are quite obscure.

The work opens with a description of the nature of ultimate reality, *brahman*, which is described as atomic, peaceful, subtle, free from determinations and limitations, shapeless, formless, incorporeal, non-dual, blissful, immobile, indestructible and fit for contemplation by those who are unhappy and face hardships of life and are desirous of conquering the mind and the senses. This ultimate reality is also identified with Viṣṇu, with universal consciousness, and is regarded as free from all passions and desires, from fear, from joys and sorrows, and is identical with *oṃ*. Further descriptions of this ultimate state continue till verse 50. The emphasis is on contemplation of ultimate reality by yogic means.

The second chapter introduces a dialogue between Kumāra and his father, Śiva, which continues till Chapter Five, where another dialogue is introduced between Nidāgha and Ṛbhu.

The second chapter deals with the nature of the Whole (*akhaṇḍa*) and its identity with consciousness. The Whole is regarded as a vision in totality of the various aspects of the empirical world-cosmos, passions, scripture, knowledge, life, bodily existence, God, etc. But the Whole is spiritual in character, being in essence consciousness. The immanent as well as the transcendental character of the Whole is emphasized. There is nothing apart from consciousness (*cinmātra*). If reality is not understood in its spiritual character there is no possibility of liberation.

The third chapter deals with the nature of the experience of the transcendental self, which is also described as *parabrahman,* infinite, eternal, embracing the whole cosmos and possessing the character of truth, consciousness and bliss. It is pure and eternal and is identical with the knowledge of God, who is formless, bodiless, speechless and free from the limiting conditions of consciousness. The great self is indeterminate and yet determines all existence, all knowledge and all scripture. As self, it is also unqualified (*nirguṇa*). Other descriptions of the self in this section follow the same characterizations found in the major Vedānta Upaniṣads. All that which belongs to the empirical world has nothing to do with ultimate reality. The importance of the great saying "I am Brahman" which is raised to the status of an incantation here, is emphasized in verses 60-73. This incantation appears in every verse in this portion of the work.

The fourth chapter describes the nature of the liberated self. But apart from its positive description as bodily release, bliss, pure consciousness and as identical with the formless and non-qualified *brahman*, the description is negative, i.e. what the liberated self is not. The description of the self also follows the familiar pattern of the principal Upaniṣads. It is beyond thought and speech, beyond sense and feeling. It is on this self that Śiva asks Kumāra to contemplate.

The fifth chapter (which opens the dialogue between Nidāgha and Ṛbhu) asserts the theory of the existence of the self as against that of its nonexistence. Here the same doctrines are repeated.

The sixth chapter similarly opens with a description of the ultimate state rather negatively by showing what it is not. Then follows a description of the nature of *brahman*, with which we are familiar in our reading the principal Upaniṣads. The rest of the verses are somewhat obscure.

Chapters Five and Six seem to bear no relation with the earlier chapters and are possibly later additions.

61.AUTHOR UNKNOWN, *Triśikhībrāhmaṇa Upaniṣad*

Summary by N. S. S. Raman

(E116-151; T88-116) This work consists of 164 verses, though the introductory passages are in prose. Its ideas pertain more to Yoga than to Vedānta. Triśikhī Brāhmaṇa is a mythical figure who travels to the world of the Ādityas and poses four basic questions regarding the nature of the body, of life, of the cause and of the self. Only the first of these questions appears to have been answered in detail in this work. The various aspects of the bodily self and its evolution are described. As in Sāṃkhya-Yoga, evolution takes place from the unmanifest *prakṛti* to intellect (*mahat*), ego, the five subtle elements, the five gross elements, etc. Then follows a classification of the various foundations of the body and mind.

10-14 (E 123-124) Mention is also made of the four states of awareness–waking, dreaming, deep sleep and the "fourth", and of the sheaths (*kośa*).

19-27 (E 126-128) The importance of yogic practice and knowledge is emphasized. The two paths of the discipline of knowledge and of action are mentioned, as also the eight-limbed yoga.

28-52 (E 128-132) A description of the various postures follows: *padmāsana, vīrāsana*, etc.

64-99 (E 134-140) *Kuṇḍalinī yoga* is then referred to and the various vital centers, channels and breaths are explained. The importance and the benefits of performing various yogic exercises are explained. All sins are destroyed, many diseases are cured and victory is attained over the senses.

100-144 (E 140-146) The importance and technique of breath control, of meditative fixation, recitation and penance are highlighted.

145-165 (E 146-151) The rest of the work emphasizes the importance of reflective meditation and the attainment of the highest state of beatitude (*sākṣātkāra*). Only by the sincere and faithful performance of yogic practices is the grace of God attained.

Realization of the meaning of the chant "I am indeed the highest *brahman*" is regarded as identical with the attainment of yogic concentration.

62.AUTHOR UNKNOWN, *Darśana Upaniṣad*

Summary by N. S. S. Raman

This work consists of ten sections and can be called a paraphrase on Haṭha Yoga and to some extent Pātañjala Yoga (or *aṣṭāṅgayoga*). It also synthesizes Yoga with the ideas of the Vedānta as is the case with most of the Yoga Upaniṣads,

(E 152-156; T116-150) The first section describes the means of attaining liberation while alive. Restraints of ten kinds (non-violence, truthfulness, abstinence from stealing, celibacy, etc.) are described; the self is identified with *brahman* and is said to be realized on practicing these moral precepts.

(E 156-159) In Section Two the ten observances (penance, contentment, faith in supreme truth, etc.) are described again almost in the manner Pātañjala Yoga describes them.

(E159-161) Section Three describes those yogic postures which are regarded as the foremost.

(E161-170) Section Four describes the dimensions of the body and enumerates the various channels, which are fourteen in number. The most important of the channels is regarded as the *brahmanāḍī*. *Kuṇḍalinī* or serpent power is then mentioned as occupying a place two digits below the navel, and its functions are described. The vital airs and their relation to the channels are then dealt with in detail and these is nothing new here. Śiva, Hari, Varuṇa and other deities are said to preside over the various channels. So also the sun and the moon are said to move in the various channels. Various places of pilgrimage (*tīrtha*) like Vārāṇasi and Kurukṣetra are associated with parts of the body. But what this Upaniṣad calls the internal place of pilgrimage, awareness (*citta*), if contaminated, cannot be purified by any water from any place of external pilgrimage. The place of pilgrimage of the self is the greatest. Śiva can be realized within man, rather than in stone images at various place of pilgrimage, which are for ignorant people. One sees *brahman* in one's own self by becoming this "cluster of channels".

(E 170-172) Section Five deals with the purification of channels by devout action and by yogic practices.

(E 172-179) Section Six deals with various aspects of breath-control. It is said to consist in forms representing *a*, *u*, and *m* (=*oṃ*). Each of these is explained with reference to the benefits to be derived from this practice.

Varieties of breath-control are then described. Conquest of vital airs will result in gnosis and other benefits like curing bodily diseases.

(E 179-181) Section Seven describes retention of breath, and Section Eight fixation of mind in the manner of Pātañjala Yoga.

(E 182-183) Section Nine deals with two kinds of meditation on Brahman–*saviśeṣa* (on qualified *brahman* as God) and *nirviśeṣa* (on non-qualified *brahman* as the self)–which one has to practice in order to attain liberation.

(E 183-185) The last Section deals with concentration and explains it in familiar yogic as well as Vedāntic terms. Attainment of *brahman* is the last stage of Yoga and Vedānta.

63.AUTHOR UNKNOWN, *Dhyānabindu Upaniṣad*

Summary by R. N. Mukerji

1-8 (E 186-213; T150-171) All sins are destroyed by *dhyānayoga* alone. The seed letter is the *bindu* (as the origin of all letters), and the *nāda* is above it. When the *yogin* attains what is beyond even what is above unstruck (*anāhata*) sound, all his doubts are dispelled, and *nirañjana* (supreme reality untouched by ignorance) remains, beyond even the very subtle. Just as fragrance, butter, etc. respectively pervade the whole of flower, milk, etc., the supremely subtle reality, *brahman*, pervades all things. It holds them together like the spring that holds precious stones together in a necklace.

9-18 (E 189-191) All aspirants for liberation have to concentrate on *brahman* as *oṃ*, which breaks down into *a* and *u* (the dissimilation of the diphthong *o*) and *m*. *Bhūr*, fire, the *Ṛgveda*, earth and Brahmā merge in *a*, which is the first part of *oṃ*. The horizon, *Yajurveda*, *bhūvar* and Viṣṇu merge with *u*, which is the second part of *oṃ*. And space, sun, *Sāmaveda*, *svar* and Maheśvara merge in the third part of *oṃ*, which is *m*. *A* is yellow in color, as it emanates *rajas*. *U* is white and *sāttvika*, and *n* is black and dark. He who does not know the eight limbs, four steps, three locations, and five deities of *oṃ* is no *brāhmaṇa*. The target of *brahman* is to be aimed at, with concentrated mind, with *oṃ* as the bow, and the self as the arrow. *Praṇava* is the origin of all things, remover of all sins, and giver of liberation. The beginning of *praṇava* is continuous like the flow of oil or the resonance of a gong.

19-21 (E 191-192) At the pericarp of the heart-lotus, one should concentrate on the God of *oṃkāra*, of the size of a thumb like an unshaking (non-flickering) flame of a lamp. Having inhaled air by *īḍā* (and retaining it in the stomach) one should contemplate *oṃkāra* in the middle of the body. Brahmā (in inhaling), Viṣṇu (in retention) and Rudra (in exhaling) are the deities of breath-control.

22-24 (E 192) With the sound of *oṃkāra* he engages in inhaling and exhaling as long as possible, until in this to-and-fro process the *nāda* is merged in motionless and bright *oṃkāra*. He who perceives the *haṃsa*-like *praṇava*, which resides in the heart of all, sheds all impurities.

25-29 (E 192-193) Where mind (*manas*), which is the cause of the creation, maintenance, and destruction of the world, vanishes, that is the supreme abode of Viṣṇu. The heart-lotus is of eight petals and thirty-two filaments. In its middle is the sun with the moon within it. This moon again has fire within carrying light in turn. Within this light is the jeweled throne of Vāsudeva (Viṣṇu), who is to be meditated upon.

30-32 (E 193) While controlling breath one should meditate on Viṣṇu, yellow and four-armed at the navel; while inhaling, Brahmā, red and four-faced at the heart during retention of the breath; and Rudra (Śiva), three-eyed and shining like a crystal at the forehead, during exhaling.

33-37 (E 194-195) In the heart is the lotus with one hundred petals (for one hundred years of life), with flower turned downwards, and the stalk above like that of the plantain. (Through one-pointed attention, having turned this lotus upwards) one should see the sun, moon, and fire, one above the other. By grasping their seeds stability of the self is attained.

38-40 (E 195-196) Just as man sucks up water through a stem of lotus, *yogins* engage in *yogasādhanā* by drawing up the mind. The mind is attracted along the *suṣumṇā* and through the vital centers to get merged at the *ājñā cakra* at the forehead, between the brows, where is located the immortal abode of *brahman*.

41 (E 196) The six limbs of yoga, i.e. postures, breath-control, etc.

42-43 (E 196-197) There are as many postures as there are forms of animals; the four important ones are *siddha, bhadra, siṃha* and *padma*.

Five of the well-known six vital centers of Yoga, viz., *mūlādhāra, svādhiṣṭhāna, maṇipūraka, anāhata, (viśuddhi)* and *ājñā* are mentioned. In the *ādhāra cakra (mūlādhāra)* there is a lotus of four petals. In its middle is *yoni kāmākhyā* adored by realized selves. In this *yoni* there is a *liṅga* facing west. The brilliant light at its top is known only to *yogins*. Between the private parts there is the sonorous *prāṇa* like molten gold in color and bright like lightning, based on the *svādhiṣṭhāna cakra* of six petals. *Maṇipūraka cakra* of ten petals is said to be made up of fibers of *maṇi* filled with wind, and located at the navel. The *anāhata* center of twelve petals is also mentioned as determiner of sins and merits. Above it are located the *viśuddha cakra* of sixteen petals, *ājñā cakra* of two petals, the region of sun and moon, and finally *sahasrāra cakra*.

50-55 (E 198-199) Seventy-two thousand channels

emanating from the egg-like region close to *svādhiṣṭhāna cakra* are mentioned. of these ten are named, while the functions of the following three are specified.

Along the centers breath moves through three main channels, *īḍā* to the left, *piṅgalā* to the right, and *suṣumṇā* in the middle established by sun, moon and fire.

56-60 (E 199-200) Internal bodily processes are held to be regulated by ten breaths. *Prāṇa* is supposed to move upwards, and *apāna* downwards. In this up-and-down and to-and-fro process, the self is also supposed to be shuttled around. For the stability of the self the equilibrium of *prāṇa* and *apāna* is prescribed. This is to be achieved by control of the breath.

66-68 (E 201-202) The divine *śakti* has kept the path of realization (through *suṣumṇā*) covered by her mouth. When by fire-yoga she is wakened, she unlocks the door of realization, and entering *suṣumṇā*, goes upwards, carrying the breath and the mind like a needle carrying thread.

75-77 (E 203-204) *Uḍḍīyāna, jālandhara, khecarī* are all described.

91-93 (E 206-207) *Mahāmudrā* is for purifying the vital fluids. The breast is to be pressed by the chin, the *yoni*-spot is to be pressed by the left ankle, and the right foot is to be outstretched. In this posture one should slowly exhale from full lungs. As the lotus of eight petals at the heart, the individual self resides as an atom of light. Everything is located in this self, and it knows and does everything.

101-106 (E 211-213) One should constrict the throat and the sex organ, and also the *suṣumṇā*, which latter emerges from the *mūlādhāra* like a stalk of lotus. Then he will hear unexpressed (*amūrta*) *nāda*, like that of a *vīṇā*, with the sound of the conch-shell in it. In the orifice of the forehead, there is the middle of the four doorways. *Nāda* traversing from there to *ākāśarandhra* (the highest point in the space at the top of the head of the *yogin*) is like the voice of a peacock. Like the sun in space, here the self resides, and between two brows of the *brahmarandhra* there is *śakti.* Having merged his mind here, the *yogin* should perceive his self, for here *nādabindu,* of the luster of precious stones, is the abode of the great God (*Maheśvara).*

64.AUTHOR UNKNOWN, *Nādabindu Upaniṣad*

Summary by R. N. Mukerji

1-6 (E 214-226; T 172-180) The syllable *oṃ* (=*a, u, m*) has the form of a swan with the *a-mātrā* as its right wing, the *u-mātrā* as the left one, the *m-mātrā* as the tail, and *ardhamātrā*, that is, the sign of the nasalization, as its head. *Guṇas* are its feet, and *tattva* is its body. Its right and left eyes are *dharma* and *adharma*. At its feet, knees, waist, navel, heart, neck and between its eyes are located the seven regions (*loka*): *bhūḥ, bhuvaḥ, svaḥ, mahaḥ, jana, tapaḥ* and *satya*. This incantation with one thousand aspects has been exhibited above. The *haṃsayogin*, riding astride it, is not pierced by sin.

6-11 (E 216-217) The first *mātrā* is fiery. The second is of the air. The third is like the orb of the sun, and the fourth is the half-syllable and watery.

17-20 (E218-219) Beyond the above states there is pure, pervasive, undefiled blessedness, from which all effulgence emanates. When the mind merges in that reality which is beyond sense and *guṇas*, and which is matchless, blessed and peaceful, it is said to be united in *yoga.* When man is entirely devoted to this (reality) he gradually gives up (attachment) to the body and the company of others. Thus purified and having shed all his fetters, as *brahman* and Lord he attains supreme bliss.

21-41 (E 219-220) The fruits of past actions (*prārabdha-karman*) continue even after self-knowledge, but become ineffective like last night's dreams or the illusory serpent on the perception of the rope. To reduce *prārabdha* to such ineffectiveness, one should concentrate on *nāda* for the sake of insight into ultimate reality.

When *prārabdhas* are thus extinguished, on searching for lustrous and auspicious *nāda*, as *brahmapraṇava*, the self reveals itself like the sun when clouds are dispelled. The *yogin* should sit at *siddhāsana* in *vaiṣṇava mudrā*, and listen to the internal unstruck *oṃ (anāhatanāda)* in his right ear. When thus he concentrates on *nāda*, it suppresses the external sounds, and by mastering both the wings of *praṇava* he attains the fourth state. At first he starts with loud notes, and with practice he proceeds to subtler and subtler sounds. First he hears the sounds of the ocean, clouds, *bheri* (a type of drum) and fountain. In this way he proceeds to ever more subtle sounds in the course of concentration. When listening to loud notes, he should look for subtler nuances within them. Thus he should let his mind roam from loud notes to subtle ones, and from subtle notes to loud ones, instead of getting distracted by any other subject. When the mind gets concentrated on any *nāda* it gets merged there. Having forgotten everything external and having merged in *nāda*, like water and milk the mind merges in *cidākāśa* (the space of consciousness). In this state, having become indifferent to the world, ever self-controlled, and earnest in yogic practice, he quietly attains the state of no-mind, with sole concentration on *nāda*. Having given up all thoughts and efforts, only looking for *nāda*, his mind merges in *nāda*.

42-45 (E 223-224) Next certain popular illustrations are given to show how concentration on *nāda* weans the mind from attachment to the world.

46-50 (E 224-225) When *nāda* merges in *praṇava*, it becomes bright and effulgent, and the mind attains the supreme state of Viṣṇu. In the mind the idea of space continues only as long as sounds (words) are there; when sounds terminate the mind has the experience of the supreme self. As long as there is *nāda*, there is also mind; when *nādas* end, mind becomes no-mind. When all sounds vanish there remains the silent ultimate. When due to constant seeking after *nāda* desires are extinguished, mind merges in reality. Millions of *nādas* and *bindus* merge in *brahmapraṇava*.

51-56 (E 225-226) When released from all states and worries the *yogin* continues as dead (to worldly life) he attains liberation (*mokṣa*). In this condition of no-mind the body becomes insensitive like a log, and he no longer hears the *nādas*. He is immune to heat or cold, joy or sorrow, respect or disrespect. He does not seek the three states of waking, dreaming and dreamless sleep, but established in his own true nature, he gets released from waking and sleeping. When the vision becomes steadfast without any object of vision, wind becomes steady without any effort, and the mind gets concentrated without any support, that is the ultimate state of *brahmapraṇava*.

65.AUTHOR UNKNOWN, *Pāśupatabrahma Upaniṣad*

Summary by N. S. S. Raman

(E 227-248; T191-197) This is a short *upaniṣad* divided into two sections. The earlier, *pūrvakāṇḍa*, in thirty-two verses, deals with such varied questions as the nature of knowledge, God, time, sacrifice, etc. The latter section, *uttarakāṇḍa*, in forty-six verses, concerns itself with the attainment of *brahman*.

The text begins by asking some questions and answering them. What is the nature of knowledge (*vidyā*)? What is the nature of God who rules over the waking and the ultimate ("fourth") state of consciousness? What is the duration of time? Under whose control are the stars and planets? Whose greatness is manifested in the vast reaches of *ākāśa*? The answers to these are given by Svayambhū, who regards the alphabet (*mātṛkā*) as the basis of all speech. The three letters constituting the *oṃkāra–a*, *u*, and *m*–themselves constitute the deity (*devatā*), which is the very life of the individual self, which rules over all the worlds. The ego controls all ages, all worlds and the expanse of the skies. Verse 10, which speaks of the three deities Rudra, Viṣṇu and Brahmā as identical with the embodiment of *māyā* of the three qualities of dullness (*tamas*), light (*sattva*) and activity (*rajas*), appears to be somewhat unconnected with the other verses.

There follows a description of the performer (*kartṛ*) of all sacrifices as Paśupati or Rudra, Viṣṇu being the *yāgadeva* or the subject to whom sacrifices are offered, Adhvaryu being their protector, and Indra the conductor of the sacrifices. Brahmā is the witness of all. The manifestation of *brahman* as the witness consists in the realization of the meaning of the saying "I am he, I am he" (*haṃsa-so'ham*). To realize this identity is indeed all sacrifice (*yajña*) performed. This ultimate self (*haṃsa*), which moves to and fro in the body, thus encompasses everything. Inside the body it kills the enemies in serpent-form–lust, anger, greed, self-deception, infatuation and hatred, and all desires of the senses.

Then there is fanciful comparison of the sacred thread (*yajñasūtra*) and the *Brahmasūtra*, the great Vedānta text. The *brāhmaṇa* is regarded as the only one possessing all qualifications to perform the great sacrifice to *brahman* (*brahmayajña*). His sacrificial thread represents the *haṃsa* or supreme self, which also represents the *Brahmasūtras*. The spiritual yoga (*manoyoga*) consists in the performance of the daily sacrifices of a *brāhmaṇa* (*sandhyā*). The sacred thread is identified also with the chant *oṃ* or *a-u-m* (*praṇava*) which is the same as *haṃsa* or the supreme self. It is of the same form as the radiant sun of the inner self, internal sacrifice consisting in the meditation on the three letters *a*, *u*, and *m* and on the *brahman* revealed by them.

The *haṃsa*-threads of the internal sun (*hṛdāditya*) are said to be ninety-six in number. Knowledge of the supreme self is regarded as leading to liberation and immortality of the self. In any case the internal sacrifice is regarded as superior to external sacrifice. The Upaniṣads dealing with *brahman* are *brahman* itself and *brāhmaṇas* steeped in learning can therefore attain *brahman*. *Brahmayajña* is compared to the horse (*aśvamedha*) sacrifice.

The latter half of this Upaniṣad is an explanation of some of the fundamental concepts of Vedānta–*brahman, māyā, īśvara*, etc. At the outset there is an identification of *brahman* with the supreme self (*paramātman, haṃsa*), God (*īśvara*), and highest consciousness (*puruṣa*). Knowledge of the self is regarded as identical with the being of *brahman*, the partless form–which is also identified with the conjoined Śiva and Śakti, revealed as bliss which is the fulness of consciousness (*cinmayānanda*). The three eyes of Śiva are characterized as nasal vibrations (*nāda*), the spot on the forehead (*bindu*), and digit of the moon (*kalā*), the three bodies of Śiva being the gross, the subtle and the causal and the three tufts (*śikhā*) being the waking, dreaming, and sleeping states of consciousness. Procedure is laid down for meditation on this supreme *brahman*. Śiva or Paśupati or God is the witness of all functions of the mind. He directs them, moves the vital breath as well as speech, and the functions of other senses. Yet he himself remains unknown. God regulates the functions of all organs of sense, but himself is beyond the reach of these organs. *Brahman* is beyond all action, all reason and all testimony.

The self is described as radiance and *māyā* as darkness. Hence *māyā* is totally incompatible with the self. From the point of view of ultimate reality there is no *māyā*. Knowledge (*vidyā*) and ignorance (*avidyā*) belong to the everyday empirical world. From the point of view of ultimate truth everything empirical is an appearance (*mithyā*) and the ultimate is non-dual. Silence is the best course to adopt on matters of ultimate truth. Ultimate knowledge does not admit of differences like caste, stage in life, injunction, prohibition, etc. There is no misery of any kind. For the knower of ultimate consciousness there is only *brahman*. Even the distinction between substance and non-substance is of no importance for *brahman*, which transcends all mind and speech and which cannot be seen or grasped, which is formless and immortal.

Transcendental knowledge (*parāvidyā*) is attained through truthfulness, meditation and celibacy. Only people who are free from impurities can attain this state of self-luminous *brahman*. For the *yogin* there is no other goal to aim at than the attainment of this supreme state.

One should therefore avoid eating inferior food, as the only proper food for the *yogin* is the knowledge of *brahman*. Indeed for the knower of *brahman* all differences between prohibited and permitted food vanish. *Brahman* or ultimate being is the only existence. The world as *māyā* is a creature of the self. Ths *yogin* conceives it so, and in him *brahman* as witness-consciousness shines forth. *Māyā* is not seen by him at all once he attains knowledge of *brahman*.

This Upaniṣad may be said to incorporate many of the tenets of Advaita doctrine.

66.AUTHOR UNKNOWN, *Brahmavidyā Upaniṣad*

Summary by N. S. S. Raman

(E249; T198-216) This Upaniṣad consists of about 110 verses and deals with a variety of topics like the nature of knowledge of Brahman (*brahmavidyā*), of *oṃ*, of the nature of the self and its bondage and liberation. It is more mythical and symbolic than philosophical in character.

(E 249-251) The first ten stanzas deal with the secret of the *praṇava* (*oṃ*) chant. The three letters are identified with the three Vedas, the three worlds, the three forms of sun, moon and fire. Then comes a description of the middle channel in the body (*suṣumṇā*) as being similar to the brilliance of the sun and dominating over all the 72,000 channels. *Oṃ* enables the *yogin* to dissolve his being into that of *brahman* as the ringing of all bells merge into one sound of peace. The delusion of individual existence is thus eliminated. The individual self is described as of three kinds–air, vital breath, and *ākāśa*. The emission of the sound *so'ham* ("I am that") is the same as the chanting of *oṃ*. Reciting this chant will enable the self to realize its identity with the supreme self, even as clarified butter is identical at the source with milk. The mention of the channels, of the vital centers in the body, and of reciting reminds us of Kuṇḍalinī Yoga. The supreme self (*haṃsa*) is described as the great bird which takes its residence within the heart and as soon as its knowledge is realized, the self is released from bondage.

(E 251-252) In verses 21-26 are described the yogic technique of arousing marvelous powers by bringing into control the vital airs. Knowledge of the supreme self is attained by devotion to the commands of the preceptor and consists in the realization of the unity of the self and *brahman* in the renunciation of all relationship with the body, of castes, stages in life, Veda, sciences (*śāstra*), etc. The preceptor alone can help us to attain this state. He is verily the Lord himself and the supreme self can be attained through his good offices and through the Vedas.

(E 256) Then follows in verses 33-35 a familiar description of the nature of the supreme self and its identity with Brahmā, Viṣṇu, Śiva and *puruṣa*.

(E 256-258) Verses 36 to 42 describe the difference between the finite and infinite self (between *jīva* and *brahman*). The five selves are regarded as identical with the five deities–Brahmā, Viṣṇu, Rudra, Maheśvara and Sadāśiva–with their seats in the heart, throat, palate, forehead, and tip of the nose respectively.

49-51 (E 259) Yoga as the secret doctrine should not be revealed to everybody but only to those who are qualified to receive it. The preceptor should bestow it only on the deserving and devoted pupil. Attainment of yogic knowledge frees one from vice and virtue and from merit and demerit of actions and enables him to attain eternal bliss.

(E 260-261) Then in verses 53-57 there is a sudden exhortation to Gautama to understand the significance of sacrifice in order to realize the supreme being. The references to several yoga practices leading to attainment of the supreme being reminds us once again of Kuṇḍalinī Yoga and Tantra. The yoga of the supreme self (*haṃsayoga*) as meditation on the *haṃsa* chant (*haṃsa-so'ham*) enables us to realize the supreme being.

(E 262) Several verses (60-63) glorify the supreme self. The practice of concentration should be preceded by regular chanting of the *haṃsa*-chant, seeking protection of God, Maheśvara. The yoga of the supreme self is described along with physical posture, which is drawn from *kuṇḍalinīyoga*.

81-111 (E 267-272) The rest of the Upaniṣad is a description of the various forms of the self to be contemplated upon by the so-called *haṃsayogin* in the form of chants–I am the imperishable, I am the unthinkable, I am the originless, etc. One who realizes the truth in this manner indeed attains the highest spiritual being (*puruṣa*).

67.AUTHOR UNKNOWN, *Maṇḍalabrāhmaṇa Upaniṣad*

Summary by N. S. S. Raman

(E273-300; T217-245) This is one of the longer Yoga Upaniṣads, consisting of five chapters (of which the first is the longest). These deal respectively with (1) the nature of the self and the relevance of the eight-limbed yoga to the doctrine of the self; (2) methods of accomplishing or attaining the self or *brahman* or liberation (*kaivalya*); (3) attainment of a state of destruction of the mind (*amanaska*); (4) knowledge of the five-fold space (*vyoman*); (5) nature of the ultimate state and attainment of extraordinary capacities. Chapter Four is somewhat obscure though short. This Upaniṣad is in prose in the form of dialogues. The influence of the Tantras is very obvious throughout.

(E 273-282) The first chapter consists of a description of

the eightfold yoga largely in keeping with Pātañjala Yoga. The five inherent defects of the body are then sought to be explained (lust, anger, lack of breath-control, fear, and sleep) and the need to root them out is stressed. The liberating object (*tāraka*) is then described as *brahman*–a boat which takes us to the realm of being, consciousness, and bliss. Three kinds of reflection are mentioned–in terms of Kuṇḍalinī Yoga–internal reflection, reflection on the external object, intermediary reflection on the ethereal space. Yoga is said to be of two kinds: the yoga dependent on means either physical (*mūrtitāraka*) or non-physical, and the yoga of the non-mental (*amanaska*). The position of the fingers is described and influence of the Tantra is here evident. The object of internal reflection, the Upaniṣad recognizes, is a matter of controversy among *yogins*, Vaiṣṇavas, Śaivas and others but all these objects refer to one and the same self or *brahman*. The self attains *brahman*hood and becomes liberated by conquering the twenty-four forms of creation. These forms of creation are the same as described by Sāṃkhya-Yoga–the five senses, the five gross elements, and so forth.

(E 283-293) The second chapter describes the radiant self (*jyotirātman*) as the basis of all existence and the prime cause of the universe. The description is a synthesis of the Sāṃkhya doctrine of the ultimate spirit (*puruṣa*) and the Upaniṣadic doctrine of the self, with elements of Tantra thrown in here and there, e.g., description of the positions of fingers. Inner radiance is described in terms of vibration or *nāda* (identified with intellect), point or *bindu* (identified with mind), and the digits of the moon or cosmic reason (*kalā*), and its relation with *oṃ* is shown. Merit or demerit (*karman*) does not affect one who knows the truth of the *praṇava*. Attainment of the state of mindlessness (*unmanī*) is preliminary to the realization of the ultimate, which is the highest state of all. Liberation is attained by contemplation of *brahman*. Although deep sleep and concentration are apparently similar, they are vastly different–the form has the character of darkness (*tāmasa*) whereas the latter involves the dissolution of the world of appearances. The knower of *brahman* becomes *brahman*, knowledge becoming identical with giving rise to bliss. To attain this state, all acts of volition have to be given up. This Upaniṣad mentions the four states described in other Upaniṣads (waking, dreaming, sleeping and *turīya*) but adds a fifth state of consciousness, called the state beyond the fourth (the *turīyātīta*). These states reflect the gradual transition of the self to liberation. Worldly life (*pravṛtti*) is distinguished from transcendental life (*nivṛtti*). The ocean of worldly bondage has to be crossed by performing all rules of spiritual practice (*sādhanā*). Mind being the cause of all bondage ḥas to be emptied of all content in order to transcend this phenomenal world. Then only is the self conscious of its identity with *brahman*. This is described as yogic slumber (*yoganidrā*), by which mind is dissolved of its content and attains the state known as the construction-free concentration (*nirvikalpakasamādhi*). The *yogin* who has attained this state is characterized as the supreme *yogin* and knower of the best *brahman*.

(E 294-296) The third chapter is somewhat sketchy and describes the mindless state .

(E 297-298) The fourth chapter talks of five kinds of space (*ākāśa, parākāśa, mahākāśa, sūryākāśa, paramākāśa*)–much of which is untranslatable and mythical. The highest of these is supreme space (*paramākāśa*), which is identical with the state of bliss.

(E 298-300) The fifth and last chapter describes the rules relating to the attainment of the supreme state (*paramātman*) and of the state of construction-free coṇcentration. The *yogin* who attains this state is characterized as a supreme self, a great ascetic (*avadhūta*), who in attaining this state also liberates his progeny from bondage.

68.AUTHOR UNKNOWN, *Mahāvākya Upaniṣad*

Summary by N. S. S. Raman

(E 301-306; T216-250) A short work dealing mainly with the attainment of the nature of *brahman*, the nature of knowledge and ignorance, and the knowledge of the supreme self.

The highest state can be achieved only by one well-initiated into yogic practices. The secret of this Upaniṣad can be realized by one with a rational temperament and who is eager to get instruction. We perceive the phenomenal world through a vision characterized by observing darkness. The entire phenomenal world including the great macrocosm (*brahmāṇḍa*) is darkness and is characterized by fulfilment of sensual desires (*kāma*) even in the observance of Vedic rituals. This world is destroyed by the dawn of new knowledge.

The self is light; it is the radiant sun of absolute knowledge, truth and consciousness. This is the goal of the chanting of the *gāyatrī* as well as of *haṃsa(-so'ham)*. Falsity is annihilated by contemplation on the threefold aspect of the self–waking, dreaming, and deep sleep. Then the supreme self manifests itself as truth, consciousness and bliss. This Upaniṣad draws a distinction between realization of the ultimate state of the self and yogic concentration (*samādhi*). There is no alternative to the realization of the supreme self, which leads to immortality. Gods are also said to have attained the state of supreme selves as knowers of *brahman*.

This Upaniṣad proclaims: I am that radiant sun of absolute knowledge. I am Śiva, the sun and the brilliant white radiance. This knowledge about the radiance should be studied at dawn and dusk to destroy the sins committed during night and day respectively. If one studies at mid-day, it could destroy all the great sins; the merit desired is equal to that flowing from the study of the entire Veda. One would attain union with the great god Mahāviṣṇu.

69.AUTHOR UNKNOWN, *Yogakuṇḍalī Upaniṣad*

Summary by N. S. S. Raman

(E307-336; T251-278) This medium-sized Upaniṣad shows the influence of Haṭha Yoga and Mantra Yoga. It is divided into three chapters, the first dealing with some basic concepts of the yoga of serpent power (*kuṇḍalinī*) and the second and third with the yoga of the chants (Mantra Yoga). The account closes with identification of *brahman* with the goal of all yoga.

(E 307-321) Chapter One opens with an account of the three expedients essential for the conquest of vital breath (*prāṇa*), these being self-control in the consumption of food, performance of yogic postures, and arousing the inner serpent power. Two kinds of yogic postures are particularly emphasized, the lotus posture (*padmāsana*) and the diamond posture (*vajrāsana*). For arousing the *kuṇḍalinī* two essential steps are mentioned: arousing the *sarasvatī*-channel, in the description of which there is nothing new, and the control of vital breath. Two kinds of breath-control are described: to direct the breathing through the body (*prāṇāyāma*) and holding the breath (*kumbhaka*).

Next, the three postures (*bandha*) of Kuṇḍalinī Yoga are described. Several obstacles to the practice of yoga are mentioned, viz., sleeping during the day, excessive sex, the obstruction to movement of the bowels and the bladder, etc. One should have faith in yoga and should never doubt its efficacy. Confusion, sloth, sleep, indifference, delusion, concern with worldly affairs, incapacity to explain and ineptitude in the understanding of yoga are other obstacles.

The rest of the first chapter is devoted to a description of the concepts and procedures of Kuṇḍalinī Yoga, including that of concentration in that yoga.

(E 321-328) Chapter Two begins by eulogizing the practice of the so-called *khecarīvidyā* which consists of chanting esoteric *khecarī* incantations (*hrim, bham, sam, mam, pam, ksam*). It should be recited as a chant 50,000 times daily for about twelve days in order to attain *khecarīyoga*. Methods for practicing this through physical posture are described as in the texts on Kuṇḍalinī Yoga.

70.AUTHOR UNKNOWN, *Yogacūḍāmaṇi Upaniṣad*

Summary by N. S. S.Raman

(E337-362; T279-300) The work consists of 121 verses and shows the obvious influence of the Kuṇḍalinī and Haṭha Yoga systems.

1-3 (E 337-338) The text begins by a mention of the six stages of Yoga (in contrast to Patañjali's eight)–posture, breath-control, etc. Two postures–the perfect and the lotus–are specially mentioned.

Then follows an archaic description of the human body by reference to six vital centers, sixteen supports (*ādhāra*), three views (*lakṣya*), and five *ākāśas*. The description of energy centers is metaphorical and obscure; the familiar metaphor of the roses to describe the heart, the navel, the *yoni*, etc. is used. Similarly, the channels (which are 72,000 in number) are also described as taking their origin in embryo, which resembles the egg of a bird.

18-21 (E 341) Ten channels are regarded as important: the *īḍā*, the *piṅgalā*, the *suṣumṇā*, the *gandhāri*, the *hastijihvā,* the *pusā*, the *yaśavin*, the *alambuṣā*, the *kuhū*, and the *śaṅkhinī* (most of these are untranslatable and obscure). These have definite positions in the human body.

22-26 (E 341-342) The various vital airs are also described as having definite positions and functions in the body. The movement of the self is related to the movement of the vital airs.

This Upaniṣad then describes the meditation on the *haṃsa*-chant which releases one from sin and bondage. This chant is said to be based on the power of the serpent, which is described in eloquent terms as essential for the yogin to attain liberation. The students of Kuṇḍalinī Yoga are familiar with the mode of working of this serpent-power and its movement upwards, which is described in this text.

45-51 (E 345-346) The position of fingers are then described.

65-70 (E 349-350) *Yoni mudrā* or constriction of the semen) is then described followed by an account of the great *mudrā (mahāmudrā)*, its practice, and the clinical effects of such practice.

74-81 (E 352-354) The chanting of *oṃ* is then described by reference to the significance of the incantation in the attainment of *brahman* (this portion of the Upaniṣad is in prose form). Then the meaning of each letter of the chant (*a, u, m*) is described, and *brahman* becomes radiant at its chanting.

82-84 (E 354-355) Then follows an account of the significance of the *haṃsa*-chant.

85-99 (E 355-357)The self is revealed by the *oṃ*-chant, but breath-control by the *yogin* is a necessary adjunct to this chant as channels are purified by it. The mode and posture for breath-control are then described.

100-108 (E 357-359) The twelve units of measurement (*mātrā*) of breath and the varieties of breath-control are mentioned, but in an obscure manner. Its practice is said to lead the yogin to liberation from bondage and to eliminate all his sins.

109-113 (E 359-360) The benefits of the practice of other aspects of yoga–withdrawal of sense, fixation of mind, meditation and concentration are then briefly explained.

114-115 (E 360) The accomplishment of a great sound like that of the bell, produced by the attainment of the *ākāśa* in the body, namely the heart, is possible by adopting the position of fingers called *ṣaṇmukhi mudrā*, which is described.

116-119 (E 361) A great many diseases like hiccups, bronchitis, asthma, etc. could be cured by breath-control. But it should be accompanied by withdrawal of the senses.

71.AUTHOR UNKNOWN, *Yogatattva Upaniṣad*

Summary by N. S. S. Raman

(E363-359; T301-325) This is a typical Yoga Upaniṣad, showing the influence of the various forms of Yoga, including Patañjali's Yoga, Haṭha Yoga and Kuṇḍalinī Yoga.

(E 363-389) The opening verses serve as an invocation to Viṣṇu, called the great sage, the great *yogin*, the supreme spirit (*puruṣa*). Then he begins Hṛṣīkeśa's exposition of the various yogas, in answer to the request of the *pitāmaha* to explain them. It is pointed out that all selves have been ensnared into appearances (*māyā*) and they can be saved and led into the path of liberation by helping them to acquired the knowledge of *brahman*. The sciences (*śāstra*) are of no help. *Brahman* is self-manifested and therefore is inexpressible by words and their meanings. The state of the self is only apparent and is assumed by the supreme self by transforming himself into various states–the ego, five subtle and gross elements, eggs (*piṇḍa*), the seven humors conditioned by the three qualities. Pleasure and pain accompany these states and the various selves come into being. When a self is rid of its defects like lust, anger, fear, self-deception, greed, etc. then it becomes identical with the supreme self. For liberation both yoga and knowledge are essential. Knowledge is release from ignorance. *Brahman* is then described as pure and formless in familiar Vedānta terms and knowledge of that state is knowledge and liberation.

Yoga, however, is said to be of four kinds: Mantra Yoga of the chants, Laya Yoga of deep concentration, Haṭha Yoga of exertion, and simple meditative Rāja Yoga. The stages of yoga are enumerated. Yoga chant is described as the chanting of the various letters of the alphabet. This is an inferior form of yoga. Yoga of deep concentration (Laya Yoga) is gradual elimination of the mind by meditation in order to attain union with the Lord (*īśvara*). Then the two kinds of yoga–the eight-limbed and Haṭha Yoga--are described. The eight divisions of the former and the twelve divisions of the latter are mentioned. Then each of the divisions is described in detail.

The focus overall is especially on Haṭha Yoga. Rāja Yoga is hardly mentioned. The various obstacles to be overcome in the practice of the various stages of yoga and the diet to be observed are stressed. The various yoga powers (*siddhi*) are described. The importance of the various chants are emphasized. Meditation on the qualified (*saguṇadhyāna*) is distinguished from meditation on unqualified reality (*nirguṇadhyāna*). Concentration as the last stage is identical with the state of liberation.

The twelve stages of Haṭha Yoga are then described. The practice of these two yogas together form twenty states and is characterized as Rāja Yoga (but is really Haṭha Yoga). The cycle of births and deaths is the cause of attachment. The three worlds, the three Vedas, the three parts of the day, the three sacred letters (*a, u, m*)), the three *guṇas*, all rest on the three stages of consciousness. In the fourth stage (*turīya*) one embraces all things and transcends them all in the attainment of *brahman.* Verses 137-139 refer to the lotus in the region of the heart, in the middle of which is mind (identical with *a*). The lotus blooms in dreaming state and the *yogin* attains the *nāda* or truth at the second letter *u*, with *m* becoming deep sleep at the last stage. The gradual cessation of all bodily functions is implicit in the various stages of Haṭha Yoga and hence the last stage is also known as liberation from the body (*videhamukti*).

72.AUTHOR UNKNOWN, *Yogaśikhā Upaniṣad*

Summary by N. S. S. Raman

(E390-463; T326-396) This is one of the longest of the Yoga Upaniṣads and represents a blending of Yoga and Vedānta. It consists of six chapters of unequal length, the first, partly dealing with the path of knowledge, being the longest.

1-4 (E 390-391) The Upaniṣad begins by declaring that all selves are affected by delusion (*māyā*) and suffer happiness or misery and this Upaniṣad seeks to destroy it, enabling the self to escape from the chain of births and deaths and to attain liberation.

5-11 (E 391-393) The sciences alone are inadequate to attain this goal. The problem is: How does the ultimate self, which is beyond all knowledge, beyond all fruits of action, attain the state of the embodied self? The answer to this question is that the supreme self, which in the beginning is suspended as it were in an unattached manner, passes through the five stages of existence, attaining first of all self-awareness and later acquiring the seven constituents (blood, flesh, fat, bone, etc.) and the three qualities, thus becoming embodied self. But the self becomes in the process susceptible to many defects like lust, anger, greed, etc. A self devoid of these defects is called the pure being (*śiva*).

The defects of the self are eliminated by knowledge and yoga, a happy blending of both of which is necessary for liberation. The seeker after liberation should realize that knowledge alone can lead us to *brahman*. Knowledge should be distinguished from awarenesses of the spurious kind. The self and knowledge are all-comprehensive and free from all defects of attachment to worldly life. Even conduct is of no relevance to one who attains knowledge. *Brahman* is described as being the complete whole (*paripūrṇa*). *Brahman* is as all-pervasive as the sky and has acquired the character of worldly existence. The ignorant man as well as one who is in possession of delusive awareness fall into the way of worldly life, and to such people there is no question of liberation except through yoga.

24-25 (E 396) Even the man who has achieved ultimate knowledge by his own efforts or has divided knowledge cannot attain liberation without the help of yoga. Corporeal beings become ripe (*pakva*) only by practice of yoga. Even the already ripe beings become mellowed and purified by the yogic fire and become devoid of misery. False awarenesses make the misery of man endless; he does not know how to control his senses and is subject to physical torment and mental pain of various kinds. To prevent such torments it is necessary to overcome all obstacles to the knowledge of the ultimate. Even if egoism is lost by meditation and knowledge, one's body is not lost and becomes subject to all diseases and torments. The bodily impediments can be vanquished only by *yogins* who have conquered the senses, mind, intellect and emotions. The yogic fire consumes all the seven bodily constituents (*dhātu*). The *yogin* can attain and withdraw from various forms with perfect ease.

47 (E 400) Death does not mean anything to him, for he has conquered it by becoming liberated while living, being pure and free from all blemishes.The man who has knowledge without yoga can fall prey to rebirth, whereas a *yogin* is not reborn again. One should associate oneself with perfect beings in order to liberate oneself from the cycle of births and deaths. Therefore it may be said that knowledge and yoga are inseparably related to each other. Liberation is not possible without the aid of both of them, for while knowledge bestows on one mental peace and prowess, yoga frees one from bondage to the body and to rebirth. Knowledge of the self is possible only by one who has conquered the body by breath-control. The vital air should be conquered first for attaining liberation with the help of yoga.

69-74 (E404-405) *Yogaśikhā* is then described. This consists in contemplating *oṃ* in the lotus posture. The body should never be identified with the self.

117 (E 413) At this point this Upaniṣad takes several ideas of the yoga of serpent power and incorporates them into its account of yoga. The aim is achievement of a transcendent state similar to the union of Śiva with Śakti.

129-138 (E 416-417) The importance of *kuṇḍalinī yoga* is recognized in attaining liberation. There is less reference to eight-limbed yoga, although great yoga (*mahāyoga*) is referred to in terms of the four yogas– Mantrayoga, Layayoga, Haṭhayoga, and Rājayoga, each of which is defined.

All these four yogas lead to the common goal of liberation, besides curing diseases and eliminating dullness. The need to preserve extraordinary capacities (*siddhi*) is emphasized. The pyschic powers acquired by artificial means (by drugs, herbs and spells) are transient. On the contrary, natural psychical powers are permanent and successful in releasing one from this world. The *yogin* can indeed attain liberation even with the possession of a body, which becomes free from passions and from death. The body is described as a city with ten gates, with ten channels, ten kinds of airs, bound by ten organs of perception and motor action with six inner centers of energy. This description tallies with that of Haṭha Yoga. Ṭhe boḍy is described as the abode of Śiva. The vital centers of energy are then described at the end of the chapter.

(E 426-431) The second chapter deals with the glory of the basic chant (*mūlamantra*), also called the *praṇava*. It is called *mūlamantra* because it emanates from the main center of the body. *Oṃ* is regarded as the root of all chants and is said to have the form of a thread (*sūtra*). The *oṃ*-chant is again said to be creative in nature (*prakṛti*) and various goddesses are associated with it. The rest of the chapter deals with the means of acquiring what is characterized as *praṇavabrahman*, with the nature of *brahman* and the greatness of *nāda* (the vibration of *oṃ*).

The third chapter (E 432-436) is an elaboration of the forms of vibratory *brahman (nādabrahman)*, namely word-*brahman (śabdabrahman)*, etc. The letter (*akṣara*) corresponds to the formless, immeasurable, dimensionless, limitless, flawless *brahman.* The Upaniṣad also speaks of word-*brahman* as identical with the omniscient and omnipotent supreme power.

The fourth chapter (E 437-441) deals with such familiar themes as the falsity of the self, *brahman* as the cause of the phenomenal world, which is itself false though imperishable apart from *brahman*. Ignorance is the root cause for our ascribing reality even to false things. Only through ignorance do we regard the self as having a body.

The fifth chapter (E 441-449) is obviously influenced by the yoga of the serpent power (*kuṇḍalinīyoga*). The body is regarded as a temple of Viṣṇu; other metaphors–body as a city with ten gateways and ten highways (channels), a great forest fit for performance of all six yogas provided with lamps of the four Vedas--are also found here. A detailed account of the vital centers and channels follows, and the whole chapter ends with rhetoric praising the preceptor and extolling the profound secret of yoga.

The last chapter (E 450-463) speaks of modes of cultivating serpent power, the importance of the central channel (*suṣumṇā*), and the ultimate power (*parāśakti*). The importance of meditation *(dhyāna)* on the highest self is emphasized. The way of attaining liberation through *kuṇḍalinīyoga* is also described, and there is nothing here with which we are not already familiar. Similarly, this Upaniṣad talks about the greatness of the *haṃsa* chant and the *oṃ*-chant. The Upaniṣad closes with an explanation of the process of the dissolution of the mind and the dawning of knowledge through yoga.

73.AUTHOR UNKNOWN, *Varāha Upaniṣad*

Summary by N. S. S. Raman

(E464-517; T397-447) The work consists of five chapters devoted to (1) the various truths (*tattva*); (2) the means of achieving excellence and liberation from bondage; (3) the nature of the ultimate state of release; (4) the nature of the liberated self, and (5) the discipline of the body through the various types of yoga.

Chapter One (E 464-468) describes the various truths, sometimes described as twenty-four, at other times as thirty-six or ninety-six in number These relate to organs, senses and functions of the body and mind. God transcends all these truths, which can all be subsumed under one head–under *māyā*.

Chapter Two (E 468-485) speaks of the fourfold means of achieving a state of readiness for liberation–that is to say, (i) the ability to distinguish between the eternal and the non-eternal, (ii) detachment from the objects of this phenomenal world, (iii) successful attainment of the six gifts of body and mind, such as control of the sense-organs, etc. and (iv) desire for release (*mokṣa*). Then there is the familiar Vedānta description of the nature of ultimate bliss, of the nature of the identity of the self with *brahman*, the distinction of the self from *māyā*. The distinction between the wise one and the ignorant one is given in terms of the capacity of the former to know the resplendent *brahman*, the absolute consciousness which is all-pervading, eternal and the whole. In the self there is no bondage or liberation, as there is no body in the state of self or *brahman*. Consequently there is no merit or demerit to bind the self, which as a pure being is free from all attachment to the phenomenal world. Even the mere thought of God or *brahman* in the form of the self has the capacity to liberate one from bondage. Attachment is like a snake. One who is devoid of lust should look upon a beautiful damsel as a carrion and sensual pleasures as poison. Then he would be a supreme self (*paramahaṃsa*) who would become a Lord Vāsudeva. Mere fasting (*upavāsa*) cannot take us nearer to *brahman*. Proper fasting consists in emancipation from the body. The means to liberation consists in the direct knowledge of *brahman*, in giving up the sense of mineness, and in eliminating all passion. Scripture gives us knowledge of *brahman*. The self as it occurs in the phenomenal world is bound by *māyā*. So iS the conception of God based on delusion. And schools of thought from the Lokāyata to Sāṃkhya are based on delusions about the reality of the self. All these do not understand the nature of *brahman* and, hence, of what meaning are liberation and happiness for them?

The rest of this chapter is a reaffirmation of the Advaita standpoint about *brahman* transcending all empirical states and about knowledge and being of *brahman* being identical. It also emphasizes the futility of actions and affirms *brahman's* being the essence of consciousness. The chapter ends by refering to the concept of vibration (*nāda*) as *brahman* (in Kuṇḍalinī Yoga), which should be meditated upon in order to realize the Yoga-empire (*yogasāmrājya*).

Chapter Three (E 485-491) comes back to the Vedānta themes about the nature of the supreme self, the means of attaining truth, consciousness and bliss, and the value of devotion (*bhakti*), the phenomenal character of the world, and the need to purify mind and to realize the self in its pure state.

Chapter Four (E 491-501) opens with a statement about the seven stages of knowledge (desire to know, investigation, functions of the pure mind, attainment of rhythm, detachment, right conception of reality, and the *turīya* state) and the fourfold nature of the *oṃ*-chant with the four "syllables" (*a, u, m* and the half-syllable, the last representing the *turīya* state) corresponding to the four states of consciousness–waking, dreaming, sleeping and the *turīya*. Four kinds of liberated selves are described (seeker after liberation, knower of *brahman,* a more exalted knower of *brahman*, and the most exalted knower of *brahman*). The second part of this chapter is called a *mantra.*

Chapter Five (E 501-517) relates to the knowledge of the body essential to the *yogin*. It explains the various yoga practices including the yoga of deep concentration (Layayoga), yoga of chants (Mantrayoga), Haṭha Yoga and the eight-limbed yoga. The last of these finds an elaborate description. The rest of the chapter is devoted to the concepts of *kuṇḍalinī yoga*. Breath-control and *oṃ*-chant are also re-emphasized.

74.AUTHOR UNKNOWN, *Śāṇḍilya Upaniṣad*

Summary by N. S. S. Raman

(E518-558; T448-491) This work is divided into three chapters with several sections in each chapter. Its main theme is yoga of various types; it is one of the most detailed statements of that which can be found among the Upaniṣads.

Chapter One (E 418-449) (consisting of eleven sections) deals with yoga of various types. Sections 1-3 enunciate the eight-fold yoga of Patañjali. Ten kinds of rules of restraint are described in the way Patañjali describes them. Similarly, ten rules of observance and eight postures are described. Rules of restraint, observance and postures together with breath-control are essential for the purification of channels.

Channels are then explained in Section 4. Measure of the vital air in the human body, the place of fire in the triangle in the center of the human body and the circling of the center of the navel by the self are then explained. The serpent power, the fourteen channels (in particular the central or *suṣumṇā* channel) are then described, followed by detailed explanation of the ten vital airs (as mentioned in the works on Kuṇḍalinī Yoga).

Section Five describes the qualification of a *yogin* (possessed of self-control, devoid of attachment, proficient in theory and practice of yoga, devoted to righteous conduct, etc.) and the ideal place for the practice of yoga (abounding in fruits, roots and water-courses, temple, river bank, neither too high nor too low, etc.) The manner of performing breath-control is then laid down, along with the procedure of purifying channels.

Section Six speaks of breath-control and its relation to *oṃ* and of the mode of meditation on the letters *a, u,* and *m* identical with the mythical goddess Gāyatrī riding the swan, Sāvitrī riding the eagle, and Sarasvatī riding the bull. The one imperishable transcendental *brahman* embraces all letters of the *oṃ*-chant.

Section Seven explains how the practice of breath-control can purify the central channel (*suṣumṇā nāḍī*) and describes the procedure for its performance. In the beginning one may start by performing breath-control four times a day, gradually increasing it to eighty-four times a day. Although tiresome in the beginning, it will produce strength in the limbs and the body will become light. The type of food to be taken during this period consisting of milk and melted butter is prescribed. Due care is to be taken of this practice of breath-control with the same caution as in the taming of a lion, elephant or tiger. When all this is done an ecstatic state of mind is the result. The entire procedure of breath-control, of the yogic postures, and purification of the channels is similar to the ones prescribed by treatises on Kuṇḍalinī Yoga. So also the kinds of breath-control and the position of fingers, etc. are familiar to those acquainted with Kuṇḍalinī Yoga. The practice of yoga enlightens the *yogin* with the truth of *brahman* and enables him to differentiate it from delusion. Meditation (*pūraka* and *dhyāna*) is mentioned as a necessary adjunct of breath-control and the *oṃ*-chant. Vibration (*spanda*) is explained at length along with the procedure of breaking through the central channel (*suṣumṇā nāḍī*), giving up the left (*īḍā*) channel and the right (*piṅgalā*) channel is reminiscent of the procedure laid down in texts on Kuṇḍalinī Yoga. The procedure for fixation of mind and attaining of many psychic powers is explained at the end of this chapter.

Chapter Two (E 550-552) of the *Śāṇḍilya* is a short explanation of the familiar Vedānta position regarding the nature of unqualified (*nirguṇa*) *brahman* which is beyond the range of thought and speech and identical with truth, consciousness and bliss, and with the unity of all things in the ultimate self.

Chapter Three (E 552-558), Section One explains the coming into being of the phenomenal world from *brahman* and the three forms of *brahman*: (1) the divisible, (2) the indivisible, (3) the partly divisible and partly indivisible *brahman*. From the divisible *brahman* evolves *māyā,* ignorance and creative energy (*prakṛti*). The third form of *brahman* represents God in various forms (Brahmā, Rudra and Viṣṇu); the three castes, the three sacrificial fires, the three letters of *oṃ*, the three Vedas and finally Lord Dattātreya.

Section Two defines absolute reality as (1) the highest self (*parabrahman*), (2) the self, (3) as Lord Maheśvara, (4) as Lord Dattātrreya. These names are to be known and meditated upon The name of the lord of lords, "Dattātreya" is mentioned in particular as leading to liberation and eternal bliss.

75.AUTHOR UNKNOWN, *Haṃsa Upaniṣad*

Summary by N. S. S. Raman

(E559=570; T492-502) This is a very short work in the form of a dialogue between Gautama and Sanatkumāra. The former asks the latter as to how knowledge of *brahman* is awakened. The reply of Sanatkumāra extends to the whole Upaniṣad.

(E 559-570) The highly esoteric character of the knowledge of *brahman (brahmavidyā)* is first emphasized. This knowledge is not meant for everybody. The details of the nature of *haṃsa* (the universal self) is like a treasure obtainable by one who reaches the state of self. Only a celibate person possessed of self-control can reach the fourth state, which is as resplendent as a million suns, and realize *haṃsa*; the supreme self pervades all beings as fire pervades fuel or as oil pervaded all sesamum seeds. Even a blade of grass is pervaded by *brahman*. The method of realizing *brahman* prescribed by this Upaniṣad is the same as prescribed by Kuṇḍalinī Yoga, to some of the basic concepts of which (e.g., centers, channels, lotus of the heart, etc.) references have already been made. But the Upaniṣad, being short, is also very sketchy and obscure. Meditation on the three letters *a, u,* and *m* is particularly emphasized, to realize the ultimate state of the self. The self can be entered from various directions, as the center of the lotus can be entered from different petals. These directions (which are like eight petals of the lotus) determine also the character of the attainment. The method of offering a salutation by chant (*haṃsa*) is mentioned.

Prayer is said to induce ten different kinds of sacred sound (*nāda*). These include the following: (1) *cini*-sound, (2) *cini-cini* sound, (3) sound of a bell, (4) blast of a conch-shell, (5) sound of a string of a lute, (6) sound of cymbals, (7) sound of a flute, (8) sound of a drum, (9) sound of a trumpet, and (10)sound of thunder. The tenth alone is important, as the fruit attained by it is of the nature of the highest self (*paramātman*). The mind is dissolved in that state. Merits and demerits are destroyed. All volitions are also eliminated and the *haṃsa* attains the character of Lord Sadāśiva or of Śakti, the character of the creator of all things, self-luminous, pure, enlightened and having the character of knowledge, eternal, devoid of *māyā* and shining forth as a state of peace.

ENDNOTES

1 Larson and Bhattacharya 1987, pp.18-29.
2 Eliade 1958, p. 101.
3 Larson 1979, pp. 108-134.
4 Eliade 1958, pp. 128-134
5 For the Pāśupatas see Lorenzen pp. 1-71. For the Hiraṇyagarbha tradition of the Ahirbudhnya Saṃhitā, see Schrader, pp. 94-146, and for the Sanskrit text regarding the Hiraṇyagarbha Vaiṣṇava Yoga, see Ramanujacharya, Volume I, pp. 108-109.
6 See Eliade 1958, *passim* and Lorenzen, *passim*. For the most recent discussion of these later traditions, see White 1996, pp. 123-170, 335-352.
7 Ibid.
8 See Katre, p. 188 for IV.68 and p. 1193 for VII.7.
9 Cited in Feuerstein 1979, p. 25. Hauer's comment in German, "...statt die echte Yoga-Philosophie zu bieten, die Sāṃkhya-Philosophie dem Yoga untergeschoben", is perhaps even stronger than "foists upon". The verb "unterschieben" also means "falsely attributed". See Hauer, p. 265.
10 Bronkhorst 1981, p. 310.
11 Ibid., p. 311. Matilal, p. 77, concurs with this assessment.
12 Ibid., pp. 316-317.
13 See Larson 1979, pp. 75-153; Larson-Bhattacharya 1987, pp. 3-41; and Larson 1995a, pp. 75-101.
14 Edgerton 1924, pp. 1-46.
15 For a full discussion of this history see Larson 1979, pp. 95-134.
16 Brockington 1999, pp. 473-490. See also the treatment of Sāṃkhya and Yoga in Brockington 1998, pp. 302-312. See also Schreiner, pp. 755-777.
17 Brockington 1999, p. 490.
18 Schreiner, pp. 774-775
19 Larson 1979, p. 122.
20 Poussin 1937, pp. 226-227, says as follows: "Yoga 'pur' ou 'vierge de métaphysique', avons-nous dit. Pour préciser, le Yoga

est bien une méthode à l'usage de diverses eschatologies commandées par diverses métaphysiques. Mais le Yoga peut être à lui-meme sa propre fin: lorsque l'ascete definit le bien suprême et definitif, l'immortalité, en termes d'êxtase. Tels, semble-t-il, Arāḍa et Udraka, et tous les infideles qui identifient le Nirvāṇa avec le recueillements d'inconscience". In other words, the "Yogas" at the time of the Buddha were a loose and diffuse set of traditions in search of ecstatic immortality and clearly not the Pātañjala-yoga-śāstra of later times.

21 Van Buitenen 1957, pp. 101-102.

22 Any of the standard histories of Indian philosophy may be consulted for details, and Dasgupta HIP is still useful in this regard for a comprehensive overview. The various volumes of the Encyclopedia of Indian Philosophies provide, of course, much more detailed up-to-date treatments. Regarding the dates of the various *sūtra*-collections Jacobi pp. 1-9 is still essential reading.

23 Here I am simply following Frauwallner, Volume One, pp. 275 ff.

24 Larson-Bhattacharya 1987, pp. 3-14 and 125-163.

25 Ibid., pp. 107-123.

26 Ibid., 1987, pp. 149 ff.

27 Ibid., pp. 131-140 and 142-146.

28 The most useful current work on the rise of Buddhist philosophy is to be found in EnIndP Volume 7, especially pp. 73-133 (on the *Mahāvibhāṣā*), and Volume 8, especially pp. 3-75 and pp. 483-565 (Vasubandhu's *Abhidharmakośa* and *Bhāṣya*).

29 Stefan Anacker describes the historical context of the famous clash in Anacker pp. 20-21. Anacker notes in a footnote (see p. 27) that Hsüan-tsang's account of the debate differs somewhat, though it agrees that the debate took place in the presence of the Emperor and that Vasubandhu was not present.

30 See Larson-Bhattacharya 1987, pp. 145-146 for the views of Frauwallner and Chakravarti. Ashok Aklujkar expressed a similar view in an unpublished paper entitled "Yoga, *vyākaraṇa* and the chronology and works of some early *śāstra* authors", read at an International Seminar on Concepts of Knowledge East and West, January 1995.

31 See also Larson-Bhattacharya 1987, pp. 141-146.

32 I have discussed these historical issues in Larson 1989 and in Larson1995b, pp. 723-732.

33 Larson 1989, p. 138.

34 For a full listing of the sixty topics, see ibid., p. 137.

35 For detailed discussions of the philosophy of Sāṃkhya, see Larson 1979, pp. 154-208 and Larson-Bhattacharya 1987, pp. 43-103.

36 For a discussion of what I call "Pātañjala Sāṃkhya" see Larson-Bhattacharya 1979, pp. 27-29.

37 For a detailed discussion of the history of Yoga (and Sāṃkhya) in the older textual traditions, see Larson 1979, pp. 75-153.

38 For references to the many discussions of *antarābhava* in the *Abhidharmakośa* and *Bhāṣya* see Pruden, Volume IV, p. 1383.

39 See Larson-Bhattacharya 1987, pp. 95-103.

40 For an excellent discussion of the so-called "Hiraṇyagarbha Śāstra", and its relation to the Vaiṣṇava Pāñcarātra tradition as articulated in the *Ahirbudhnya Saṃhitā*, as well as to Śaiva references and to the many references in the *Purāṇas*, see RSB 1985, pp. 16-24.

41 Ibid.

42 Woods, pp. xv-xvii.

43 Wezler n.d. pp. 1-33.

44 Dasgupta HIP, Volume I, 1963, p. 232.

45 RSB 1985, pp. 85-89.

46 Ibid., p. 86.

47 Ibid., pp. 85-106.

48 Ibid., p. 94.

49 Staal, pp. 86-91.

50 A fascinating capsule history of German Indology may be found in Stache-Rosen.

51 Feuerstein 1979, pp. 36-37.

52 Deussen 1922, Volume One, Part Three, pp. 507-578.
53 Hauer, pp. 239-258. Hauer considers IV,1 to be a later interpolation and, thus, does not include it in his analysis of the various texts included in the YS.
54 Ibid., pp. 221 ff.
55 Frauwallner, Band I, pp. 408-445.
56 Feuerstein 1979, pp. 36-89
57 Ibid., pp. 39-40.
58 For the Sanskrit text of the YS, the Vyāsa *Bhāṣya* and the *Tattvavaiśāradī* I have used RSB on YS. See pp. 1-3 for the characterization of Book One, *Samādhi Pāda*. For English translation, references will be to Woods. For Book one, see Woods, pp. 3-8.
59 RSB on YS, p. 51, and Woods, p. 103.
60 RSB on YS, p. 104, and Woods, pp. 203-204.
61 RSB on YS, pp. 156-157, and Woods, pp. 299-300.
62 "*Yogāṅgānuṣṭhānād aśuddhikṣaye jñānadiptir āvivekakhyāteḥ.*"
63 For traditions of medical learning and their relations to Sāṃkhya and Yoga see Larson 1987, pp. 245-259.
64 See Edgerton 1965, pp. 58 and 60.
65 Ibid., pp. 69, 96 and 121.
66 RSB on YS, p. 2. Vācaspatimiśra explains that that is the reason for the term "*anuśāsana*" in YS I.1, meaning a teaching that can be traced back in tradition instead of simply "*śāsana*", which would imply a totally new teaching.
67 See RSB 1985, pp. 16-24 for a detailed account of Hiraṇyagarbha traditions and Yoga. See there his excellent discussion of the *Hiraṇyagarbhaśāṣtra* as set forth in the *Ahirbudhnya Saṃhitā* of the Pāñcarātra Vaiṣṇavas.
68 RSB on YS, pp. 1-2 of Vācaspatimiśra's commentary.
69 See Larson 1983. I presented the same argument in Larson-Bhattacharya 1987, pp. 73 ff.
70 I have argued that Yoga is an "eliminative materialism" and an "eliminative dualism" in Larson 1995b, pp. 36-51 (pp. 132-151 of the Indian version).

71 Woods pp. 3 ff.
72 The terms "*dharmamegha*" (perhaps something like "truth-cloud") and supreme "*prasaṃkhyāna*" ("reflection") are undoubtedly technical terms, or perhaps better, proper names for certain high states of yogic realization.
73 For a full discussion see Larson-Bhattacharya 1987, pp. 65-73.
74 See Larson 1997, pp. 248-258.
75 See Larson-Bhattacharya 1987, pp. 83-103.
76 RSB on YS, Vyāsa's *Bhāṣya*, pp. 9-10.
77 Ibid., pp. 5-6.
78 See Larson 1992 and K. C. Bhattacharya, p. 195.
79 Churchland 1988, p. 21.
80 Churchland 1979, p. 108.
81 See Hauer p. 465 and p. 226, and RSB 1985, pp. 163-169.
82 For the Sanskrit text see RSB on YS, p. 51, and for the English rendering see Woods, p. 103.
83 See Wezler 1984.
84 RSB 1985, pp. 58-59, and the reference to Pāṇini III.3.2.46 in Katre, p. 235.
85 See Monier-William p. 1132.
86 For a discussion of the traditional *siddhis* and the Sāṃkhya philosophical reinterpretation of the *siddhis* see Larson-Bhattacharya 1987, pp. 56-57, 187 and 368.
87 RSB 1985, pp. 94-96 and p. 123.
88 RSB 1985, p. 13 and p. 137.
89 Ibid.
90 Ibid.
91 Ibid., p. 137n.
92 Missing, of course, is any reference to *kuṇḍalinīśakti* in Pātañjala Yoga.
93 RSB 1985, p. 134.
94 Regarding these first six *sūtras*, I am following the interpretation favored by J. W. Hauer and Georg Feuerstein. See Feuerstein 1979, p. 128. The reference to "alchemy" (*rasāyana*) is in Vyāsa's *Bhāṣya* on YS IV.1. For the current

discussion of the state of research on *rasāyana* see White 1996, *passim.*

95 The best recent translation and discussion of the *Gītā* is Van Buitenen 1981. The translation is one of the few based on a critical edition of the text.

96 Cf. Mahadeva Sastri; the *Yogatattva* may be found on pp. 363-389. For good recent English translations of the Upaniṣads see Olivelle 1996 and Olivelle 1992.

97 The subject of Tantra is vast and complex and is only in the earliest stages of being properly researched. A useful survey of the literature on the Tantra is P. C. Bagchi, "Evolution of the Tantras" in Lokeshwarananda. The articles by A. Padoux ("Tantrism") and A. Sanderson ("Śaivism; Krama Śaivism", "Śaivism: Śaivism in Kashmir" and "Śaivism, Trika Śaivism" in Eliade 1986, Volume 14, pp. 272-276 (for Padoux) and Volume 13, pp. 14-17 (for Sanderson) also provide useful overviews. For more comprehensive studies see Dyczkowski, *passim*, White 1996 and White 2003. David Gordon White's essay "Yoga in early Hindu tantra" in Whicher/Carpenter, pp. 143-161 is a useful brief treatment of the early history of the Hindu Tantra. Finally, I should perhaps make clear that I am not including a discussion of Buddhist or Jaina Tantra.

98 Cited in White 2003, p. 15. See also Padoux, "Tantrism", ibid.

99 See, for example, Bagchi's interesting remarks in the section "Foreign influence on the Tantra" in his article in Lokeshwarananda cited in the previous endnote.

100 Kane 5, p. 1427.

101 For the most recent and useful discussion of Matsyendranātha and Gorakṣanātha, the *siddhas*, the Nātha Yoga tradition, and so forth, see the two books of David Gordon White, White 1996 and White 2003. Also, for Haṭha Yoga generally see Feuerstein 2002, pp. 505-566. Also useful is Burley. There is also the dated but still interesting Bernard.

102 Essential for serious research on the origins of Haṭha Yoga and the tradition of Matsyendranātha is Bagchi/Magee, and see

especially the masterful Introduction by Bagchi, pp. 1-94 (including a useful summary of each chapter of the text).
103 In my view Briggs is still the best treatment of the Kānphaṭas.
104 *Yogatattva Upaniṣad* vss. 24-27.
105 Ibid., vss. 126-127.
106 White, "Yoga in early Hindu Tantra", in Whicher/Carpenter, pp. 145-146.
107 Schrader, pp. 109-111. See the Sanskrit text in Ramanujacharya, pp. 106-109.
108 See RSB 1985, pp. 16-24. Ram Shankar Bhattacharya distinguishes between a *Hiraṇyagarbhaśāstra*, now lost, and the Vaiṣṇava redaction as found in the *Ahirbudhnya*.
109 Feuerstein 2002, pp. 344-346. See also the dated but still interesting account in Bhandarkar, pp. 121-128.
110 Feuerstein, ibid. See also the chapter entitled "Lakulīśa and the Paśupatas" (Chapter VI) in Lorenzen, pp. 173-192.
111 Feuerstein 2002, p. 349.
112 Eliade 1958, pp. 96-301.
113 Lorenzen, p. 97-172.
114 Ibid., p. 81.
115 Hauer p. 74.
116 White 199, p. 2
117 Ibid., p. 99.
118 Sjoman, *passim*.
119 Ibid., p. 54.
120 Ibid., p. 61.
121 See Sell.
122 See Scott.
123 See Choudhury.
124 See Satchidananda.
125 See Iyengar.
126 See Bhajan.
127 See Desai
128 See Birch.
129 See Yogananda.

130 See Brooks/Sabharathnam.
131 See Desikachar.
132 See Swenson.
133 Cf. Dowson, p. 214, for the story of Nahuṣa.
134 Rukmani 2001, and see Introduction, pp. ix-xxxi.
135 Ibid., pp. xxv-xxix.
136 Kaviraj, pp. 133-136.
137 See Gelblum and Arya.
138 Massignon, p. 97.
139 See Ritter.
140 See Pines-Gelblum 1966, 1977
141 Hyd, p. 6. Cf. Sachau: "I have already translated two books into Arabic, one about the *origines* and a description of all created beings, called *Saṃkhya*, and another about the emancipation of the soul from the fetters of the body, called *Patañjali* (Pātañjala?)".
142 Sachau, Index 1, s.v. Patañjali.
143 Sachau, p. 264 (annotations).
144 Dasgupta 1930, p. 64.
145 Garbe 1896, p. 41.
146 Garbe 1894, p. 63.
147 Garbe 1896, p. 41.
148 Dasgupta 1930, pp. 63-64.
149 Pines/Gelblum 1966, p. 308.
150 Ibid., p. 302.
151 Ibid., n. 51.
152 Ritter 199, (line 1); 197 (line 20). Cf. Hyd pp. 61, 66, 102. Cf. Pines/Gelblum 1966, p. 305.
153 Dasgupta 1930, p. 63.
154 Pines/Gelblum 1966, p. 305.
155 Ibid., p. 310.
156 Ibid., p. 312.
157 Ibid., pp. 313-314.
158 For a full discussion of this point see Pines/Gelblum 1977, p. 530, note 15.
159 See Pines/Gelblum 1977, p. 540, n. 92.

160 For an interesting discussion of Bhoja's reign, see Keay pp. 226-230.
161 White 1996, p. 102.
162 Abhyankar pp. 331-388.
163 See Kaviraj.
164 See Endo.
165 Bib I, pp. 693-694.
166 The text of Nāgeśa's *Yogasūtravṛtti* may be found in Dundhiraja Sastri 1982. See also Arya 1986, Volume I, p. 10.
167 Bagchi/Magee pp. 1-120.
168 Ibid., pp. 83-94.
169 Feuerstein 2002, pp. 402-403.
170 Deussen 1980, Volume II, pp. 555-568.

LIST OF WORKS CITED

Abhyankar = V. S. Abhyankar, *Sarva-Darśana-Saṃgraha of Śāyaṇa Mādhava* (Poona: Bhandarkar Oriental Research Institute, 1978)

Alter = Joseph S. Alter, *Yoga in Modern India:* The Body between Science and Philosophy (Princeton: Princeton University Press, 2004)

Anacker = Stefan Anacker, *Seven Works of Vasubandhu, the Buddhist Psychological Doctor* (Delhi: Motilal Banarsidass, 1984)

Arya = Ushabudh Arya, tr., *Yoga-Sūtras of Patañjali with the Exposition of Vyāsa* (Honesdale, Pa.: The Himalayan International Institute, 1986)

Avalon = Arthur Avalon (Sir John Woodroffe), *The Serpent Power* (Madras: Ganesh and Co., 1964)

Ayyangar = T. R. S. Ayyangar, trans., *The Yoga Upaniṣads* (Adyar: Vasanta Press, 1952)

Bagchi/Magee = P. C. Bagchi, ed., *Kaulajñānanirṇaya of the School of Matsyendranātha*. Michael Magee, trans. Tantra Granthamala No. 12 (Varanasi: Prachya Prakashan, 1986)

Bernard = Theos Bernard, *Haṭha Yoga: The Report of a Personal Experience* (London: Rider and Co., 1974)

Bhajan = Yogi Bhajan, *The Teachings of Yogi Bhajan* (New York: Hawthorne Press, 1977)

Bhandarkar = R. G. Bhandarkar, *Vaiṣṇavism, Śaivism and Minor Religous Systems* (Varanasi: The Indological Bookhouse, 1965)

Bhattacharya = R. K. Bhattacharya, ed. *Maṇiprabhā on Pātañjaladarśana by Rāmānanda Sarasvatī* (Akhil Vandhu Bhattacharya Publishing Sanskrit Pustkalaya, n.d.)

Bib = K. H. Potter ed., *Bibliography of Indian Philosophies.* Third Edition. Two volumes (Delhi: Motilal Banarsidass, 19

Birch = Beryl Binder Birch, *Power Yoga: Total Strength and Flexibility Workout* (New Y ork: Fireside, 1995)

B. K. S Iyengar = B. K. S. Iyengar, *Light on Yoga* (New York: George Allen and Unwin (Publishers) Ltd., 1966)

Briggs = George Weston Briggs, *Gorakhnāth and the Kānpaṭha Yogis* (Delhi: Motilal Banarsidass reprint, 1982)

Brockington 1998 = John Brockington, *The Sanskrit Epics* (Leiden: E. J. Brill, 1998)

Brockington 1999 = John Brockington, "Epic Sāṃkhya: texts, teachers, terminology", Asiatische Studien/Etudes Asiatiques 53.3, 1999, pp. 473-490

Bronkhorst 1981 = Johannes Bronkhorst, "Yoga and *śeṣvara* Sāṃkhya", Journal of Indian Philosophy 9, 1981, pp. 309-320

Bronokhorst 1993 = Johannes Bronkhorst, *The Two Sources of Indian Asceticism* (Bern: Peter Lang, 1993)

Brooks/Sabharathnan = Douglas R. Brooks and S, P. Sabharathnan, eds., *Meditation Revolution: A History and Theology of the Siddha Yoga Lineage* (South Fallsburg: Agama Press, 1997)

Burley = Mikel Burley, *Haṭha Yoga: Its Context, Theory and Practice* (Delhi: Motilal Banarsidass, 2000)

Chalmers = David J. Chalmers, *The Conscious Mind* (New Y ork: Oxford University Press, 1996)

Chapple/Kelly = Chris Chapple and Eugene Kelly, trans., *The Yoga Sūtras of Patañjali* (Delhi: Sri Satguru Publications, 1990)

Choudhury = Bikram Choudhury, *Bikram's Beginning Yoga Class* (New Y ork: Putnam Boks, 2000)

Churchland 1979 = Paul Churchland, *Scientific Realism and the Plasticity of Mind* (Cambridge: Cambridge University Press, 1979)

Churchland 1988 = Paul Churchland, *Matter and Consciousness: A Contemporary Introduction to the Philosophy of Mind.* Revised Edition (Cambridge, Mass.: MIT Press, 1988)

Conze = Edward Conze, *Buddhist Meditation* (*London: George Allen and Unwin, 1956)

Coward = Harold Coward, *Yoga and Psychology* (Albany: State University of New York Press, 2002)

Dasgupta HIP = Surendranath Dasgupta, *History of Indian Philosophy*. Five Volumes (Cambridge: Cambridge University Press, 1922-1955)

Dasgupta 1930 = S. N. Dasgupta, *Yoga Philosophy in relation to other systems of Indian thought* (Calcutta, 1930; reprint Delhi 1974)

De Michelis = De Michelis, *A History of Modern India* (London: Continuum 2001)

Dennett = Daniel C. Dennett, *Consciousness Explained* (Boston: Little, Brown and Co., 1991)

Desai = Amrit Desai, *Kripalu Yoga: Meditation in Motion*. Book I (Lenox, Mass.: Kripalu Publications, 1985)

Desikachar = T. K. V. Desikachar, *The Heart of Yoga: Developing a Personal Practice* (Bombay: Inner Traditions, 1995)

Deussen 1897 = Paul Deussen, transl., *Sechzig Upanisads des Veda* (Leipzig: F. A. Brockhaus 1897, 1905)

Deussen 1922 = Paul Deussen, *Allgemeine Geschichte des Philosophie*. Two Volumes in Six Parts (Leipzig: V. A. Brockhaus, 1922)

Deussen 1980 = Deussen 1897 translated into English by V. M. Bedekar and B. B. Palsule as *Sixty Upaniṣads of the Veda*. Two Volumes (Delhi: Motilal Banarsidass, 1980)

Digambara Svami = Digambara Svami, ed., *Vasiṣṭha-saṃhitā* (Lonavla, Poona, Maharashtra: Kaivalyadham: S. M. Y. M. Samiti, 1969)

Dowson = Dowson, *A Classical Dictionary of Hindu Mythology* (London, 1957)

Dundhiraja Sastri 1931 = Dundhiraja Sastri, ed., *Yogasūtra* with *Bāladeva Miśra's Yogapradīpikā*. Kashi Sanskrit Series 85 (Varanasi: Chaukhamba Sanskrit Samsthan, 1931)

Dundhiraja Sastri 1982 = Dundhiraja Sastri, ed., *Yogasūtram with Six Commentaries* (Varanasi: Chaukhamba Sanskrit Samsthan, 1982)

Dyczkowski = M. Dyczkowski, *The Canon of the Śaivāgama and the Kubjikā Tantras of the Western Kaula Tradition* (Albany: State University of New York Press, 1988

Eccles/Robinson = Sir John Eccles and Daniel N. Robinson, *The Wonder of Being Human* (Boston: Shambala Publications, 1985)

Edgerton 1924 = Franklin Edgerton, "The meaning of Sāṃkhya and Yoga", American Journal of Philology 45.1, 1924

Edgerton 1965 = Franklin Edgerton, *The Beginnings of Indian Philosophy* (Cambridge: Harvard University Press, 1965)

Eliade 1958 = Mircea Eliade, *Yoga: Immortality and Freedom.* Translated by Willard R. Trask. Bollingen Series 56 (New York: Pantheon Books, 1958)

Eliade 1986 = M. Eliade (ed.), *Encyclopedia of Religions* (New York: Macmillan 1986)

Endo = Ko Endo, "The works and flourishing period of Nārāyaṇa Tīrtha, the author of the Yogasiddhāntacandrikā", Sambhāṣā: Nagoya Studies in Indian Culture and Buddhism 14, 1993, pp. 41-60

EnIndP 7 = Karl H. Potter, Robert E. Buswell, Jr., Padmanath S. Jaini and Noble Ross Reat, eds., *Abhidharma Buddhism to 150 A.D.* Encyclopedia of Indian Philosophies, Volume Seven (Delhi: Motilal Banarsidass, 1996)

EnIndP 8 = Karl H. Potter, ed., *Buddhist Philosophy from 100 to 350 A.D.* Encyclopedia of Indian Philosophies, Volume Eight (Delhi: Motilal Banarsidass, 1999)

Feuerstein 1979 = Georg Feuerstein, *The Yoga Sūtras: an Exercise in the Methodology of Textual Analysis* (New Delhi: Arnold Heinemann, 1979; also Folkestone, Kent, England: Dowson & Sons Ltd., 1979)

Feuerstein 1990 = Georg Feuerstein, *Encyclopedic Dictionary of Yoga* (New York: Paragon House, 1990)

Feuerstein 2002 = Georg Feuerstein, *The Yoga Tradition* (Delhi: Motilal Banarsidass, 2002

Frauwallner = Erich Frauwallner, *Geschichte der indischen philosophie*, Two Volumes (Salzburg: Otto Muller, 1953)

Garbe 1894 = R. Garbe, *Die Sāṃkhya-Philosophie* (Leipzig, 1894)

Garbe 1896 = R. Garbe, *Sāṃkhya und Yoga* (Strassburg 1896)

Gimello = Robert Gimello, "Mysticism and meditation" in S. Katz, (ed.), *Mysticism and Philosophical Analysis* (New York: Oxford University Press, 1975)

Gelblum = Tuvia Gelblum, "Notes on an English translation of the Yogasūtrabhāṣyavivaraṇa", Bulletin of the School of Oriental and African Studies, Volume LV, Part One, 1992, pp. 76-89

Gregory = Richard L. Gregoary, ed., *The Oxford Companion to the Mind* (Oxford: Oxford University Press, 1987)

Hacker = Paul Hacker, "Śaṇkara der Yogin and Śaṇkara der Advaitin", Wiener Zeitschrift fur die Kunde Sudasiens 12-13, 1968-69, pp. 119-148

Halbfass = Wilhelm Halbfass, *Studies in Kumārila and Śaṃkara* (Reinbek, 1983)

Haridasa Vidyavagisa = Jarodāsa Vidyāvāgīśa, ed., *Yogacintāmaṇi of Śivānanda* (Calcutta: Calcutta Oriental Press, n.d.)

Hariharananda Aranya = Harihārānanda Āraṇya, *Śivoktayogayukti* (West Bengal: Kapilasrama, Hooghly, 1914)

Hauer = J. W. Hauer, *Der Yoga* (Stuttgart: W. Kohlhammer, 1958)

Horshe = Cidghanānandanātha, *Ṣaṭkarasaṃgraha*, ed. R. G. Horshe (Yoga Mimamsa Prakashan, Kaivalydham, Lonavla, Poona, Maharashtra, n.d.)

Hyd = *Kitāb tī taḥgīg mā li' l-Hind or al-Bīrūnī's India* (Arabic text) (Hyderabad, 1958)

Iyangar = *Haṭha-yoga-pradīpikā of Svātmārāma Svāmin*, edited and translated by Yogī Śrīnivāsa Iyaṅgar, B. A. Second edition (Adyar, Madras: Theosophical Publising House, 1933). (First published T. P. H:, Oriental Series No. 15, 1893)

Jacobi = Hermann Jacobi, "The dates of the philosophical *sūtras* of the Brahmans" Journal of the American Oriental Society 31, 1911, pp. 1-9

Janacek = Adolf Janacek, "The 'voluntaristic' type of Yoga in

Patañjali's Yogasūtras", Archiv Orientalni 22, 1952, 69-87

Jha = *An English Translation of Yoga-sāra-saṅgraha of Vijñāna Bhikṣu* by Gaṅgānātha Jha. Theosophical Publishing House, Series No. 10 (Adyar, Madras, 1933)

Johnston = E. H. Johnston, tr., *The Buddhacarita, or, Acts of the Buddha.* Part II (Calcutta: Baptist Mission Press, 1936)

Kane 5 = P. V. Kane, *History of Dharmaśāstra* Volume V, Part II (Poona: Bhandrakar Oriental Research Institute, 1977)

Karnatak = *Yogasiddhantācandrikā of Śrīnārāyaṇatīrtha*, edited by Vimal Karnatak. Chowkhamba Sanskrit Series 108 (Varnasi 2000)

Katre = S. M. Katre, trans., *Aṣṭādhyāyī of Pāṇini* (Delhi: Motilal Banarsidass, 1980)

Kaviraj = Gopinath Kaviraj, "Mīmāṃsā manuscripts" in *Catalogue of Sanskrit Manuscripts in the Sanskrit College Library*, Volume VI, Banaras (Allahabad, n.d.)

K. C. Bhattacharya = K. C. Bhattacharya, "Studies in Sāṃkhya philosophy" in Gopinath Bhattacharya, ed., *Studies in Philosophy,* volume I (Calcutta: Progressive Publishers, 1956)

Keay = John Keay, *India: A History* (New York: Atlantic Monthly Press, 2000)

Keith = A. B. Keith, *The Sāṃkhya System.* Second Edition (Calcutta: YMCA Publishing Co., 1949)

Kenghe = C. T. Kenghe, ed., *Rājayogabhāṣya by Śaṃkarācārya* (Poona: Swami Basant Ananda Gadgil, Sarada Office, 1967)

Koelman = Gaspar M. Koelman, *Pātañjala Yoga: From Related Ego to Absolute Self* (Poona: Papal Athenaeum, n.d.)

Larson 1979 = Gerald James Larson, *Classical Sāṃkhya.* Second Edition (Delhi: Motilal Banarsidass, 1979)

Larson 1981 = Gerald James Larson, "Yoga", Abingdon Dictionary of Living Religions (Nashville: Abingdon, 1981)

Larson 1983 = Gerald James Larson, "An eccentric ghost in the machine: formal and qualitative aspects of the Sāṃkhya-Yoga dualism", Philosophy East and West 33, 1983, pp. 9-

233
Larson 1987 = Gerald James Larson, "Ayurveda and the Hindu philosophical systems", Philosophy East and West 37.3, 1987, pp. 245-250
Larson-Bhattacharya = Gerald James Larson and Ram Shankar Bhattacharya, eds., *Sāṃkhya: A Dualist Tradition in Indian Philosophy*. Encyclopedia of Indian Philosophies Volume Four (Delhi: Motilal Banarsidass, 1987)
Larson 1989 = Gerald James Larson, "An old problem revisited: the relation between Sāṃkhya, Yoga and Buddhism", Studien zur Indologie und Iranistik 15, 1989, pp. 129-146
Larson 1992 = Gerald James Larson, "K. C. Bhattacharya and the plurality of *puruṣas* (*puruṣabahutva*) in Sāṃkhya", Journal of the Indian Council for Philosophical Research 10.1, 1992, pp.93-104.
Larson 1995a = Gerald James Larson, *India's Agony over Religion* (Albany, N.Y.: State University of New York Press, 1995)
Larson 1995b = Gerald James Larson, "Classical Yoga philosophy and some issues in the philosophy of mind", Religious Studies and Theology 13-14, 1998, pp. 36-51. Reprinted in Susan Walters and J. L. Shaw, eds., *Concepts of Knowledge East and West* (Calcutta: The Ramakrishna Institute of Culture, 2000), pp. 132-151.
Larson 1997 = Gerald James Larson, "Indian conceptions of reality and divinity" in E. Deutsch and R. Bontekoe, eds., *A Companion to World Philosophies* (Oxford: Blackwell Publishers, Let., 1997), pp. 248-258
Larson 1999 = Gerald J. Larson, "Classical Yoga as Neo-Sāṃkhya: a chapter in the history of Indian philosophy", Asiatische Studien/Etudes Asiatique 53.3, 1999
Larson 2004 = Gerald J. Larson, "The aesthetic ascetic: Abhinavagupta's perspective as poetry, religion and visual art" , Marg: A Magazine of the Arts 56.2, December 2004, pp. 54-61
Leggett = Trevor Leggett (trans.), *The Complete Commentary by*

Śaṃkara on the Yoga-Sūtras (London: Kegan Paul, 1990)

Lokeshwarananda = Swami Lokeshwarananda, ed., *Studies on the Tantras* (Calcutta; The Ramakrishna Institute of Culture, 1975)

Lorenzen = D. N. Lorenzen, *The Kāpālikas and Kālamukhas* (Berkeley: University of California Press, 1972)

Mahadeva Sastri = A. Mahadeva Sastri, ed., *The Yoga Upaniṣads* (Adyar: Adyar Library and Research Center, 1968)

M. Sarma = Mahidhara Sarma, ed., *Gorakṣa Paddhati* (Bombay: Khemaraja Srikrishnadas, 1983)

Mallik = *Gorakṣanātha's Siddhasiddhāntapaddhati*, ed. Kalyani Mallik (Poona: Poona Oriental Book House, 1954)

Massignon = L. Massignon, *Essai sur les origines du lexique technique de la mystique musulmans* (Paris, 1922; second edition Paris, 1954), p. 97

Matilal = B. K. Matilal, *Nyāya-Vaiśeṣika* (Wiesbaden: Otto Harrassowitz, 1977)

Monier-Williams = M. Monier-Williams, *Sanskrit-English Dictionary* (Oxford: Oxford University Press, 1889; current reprint, 1998)

Miller = Barbara Stoler Miller, trans., *Yoga: Discipline of Freedom*, The Yoga Sūtra attributed to Patañjali (Berkeley: University of Callifornia Press, 1996)

Mukerji = Hariharānanda Āraṇya, *Yoga Philosophy of Patañjali*, translated by P. N. Mukerji (Albany: State University of New York Press, 1963)

Muller-Ortega = Paul Muller-Ortega, *The Triadic Heart of Śiva* (Albany: State University of New York Press, 1989)

Nakamura = Hajime Nakamura, *A History of Early Vedānta Philosophy* (New Delhi: Motilal Banarsidass, 2004.) Reprint of multi-vlume work, first published 1950-1956

Naraharinatha = Naraharinātha, ed., *Yogabīja of Gorakṣanātha* (Varnasi: Raja Candranatha, 1959)

Nowotny = Karl A. Nowotny, ed., *Das Gorakṣaśataka* (Bonn: Richard Schwarzbold, 1976)

Oberhammer = G. Oberhammer, *Strukturen Yogischer Meditation* (Wien: Osterreichische Akademie der Wissenschaften, 1977)

Olivelle 1992 = Patrick Olivelle, trans., *Saṃnyāsa Upaniṣads* (Oxford and New York: Oxford University Press, 1992)

Olivelle 1996 = Patrick Olivelle, trans., *Upaniṣads* (Oxford and New York. Oxford University Press, 1996)

Padoux = André Padoux, *Vāc: The Concept of the Word in Selected Hindu Tantras*, trans. J. Gontier (Albany: State University of New York Press, 1990)

Pandeya = Janardana Sastri Pandey, ed., *Gorakṣasiddhāntasaṃgraha*. Saraswati Bhavan Granthamala 110 (Varanasi: Varanaseya Sanskrta Vidyavidyodaya, 1973)

Pensa = Corrado Pensa, "On the purification concept in Indian tradition, with special regard to Yoga", East and West 19, 1969, 194-228

Phillips = Stephen H. Phillips, "The conflict of voluntarism and dualism in the Yogasūtra", Journal of Indian Philosophy 13, 1985, 399-414

Pines/Gelblum 1966 = Shlomo Pines and Tuvia Gelblum, "Al-Bīrūnī's Arabic version of Patañjali's *Yogasūtra*: a translation of his first chapter and a comparison with related texts", Bulletin of the School of Oriental and African Studies, University of London 29.2, 1966, pp. 302-325

Pines/Gelblum 1977 = Shlomo Pines, and Tuvia Gelblum, "Al-Bīrūnī's version of Patañjalis *Yogasūtra*: a translation of the second chapter and a comparison with related texts", Bulletin of the School of Oriental and African Studies, University of London 40, 1977, pp. 522-549

Popper/Eccles = Karl R. Popper and John C. Eccles, *The Self and the Brain* (London: Routledge and Kegan Paul, 1977)

Poussin = Louis de la Vallée Poussin, "Le bouddhisme et la yoga des Patāñjali", Mélanges chinois et bouddhiques 5, 1926-37 (Bruxelles 1937)

Priest = Stephen Priest, *Theories of the Mind* (Boston: Houghton

Mifflin Co., 1991)

Pruden = Leo M. Pruden, transl., *Abhidharmakośabhāṣyam by Louis de la Vallee Poussin*. Four Volumes (Berkeley: Asian Humanitis Press, 1990)

Putnam = Hilary Putnam, "The nature of mental states" in D. M. Rosenthal, ed., *The Nature of Mind* (Oxford: Oxford University Press, 1991)

Raghavan = K. Raghavan, ed. and transl., *The Vākyapadīya: Critical Text of Cantos I and II* (Delhi: Motilal Banarsidass, 1971)

Ramanujacharya = *Ahirbudhnya-Saṃhitā of the Pāñcarātrāgama*, ed. M. D. Ramanujacharya. Volume I (Madras: Adyar Library, 1916)

Reddy = Śrīnivāsa Bhaṭṭa, *Haṭharatnāvalī,* edited and translated by M. Venkata Reddy (Sri M. Ramakrishna Reddy, Andhra Pradesh, 1982)

Ritter = H. Ritter, "Al-Bīrūnī's ubersetzung der Yoga-Sūtra des Patañjali", in H. Ritter, Oriens, tr. E. C. Sachau, Alberuni's India, London 1910; reprinted Delhi 1964.

Rorty = Richard Rorty, *Objectivity, Relativism and Truth: Philosophical Papers.* Volume One (Cambridge: Cambridge University Press, 1991)

RSB 1985 = Ram Shankar Bhattacharya, *An Introdouction to the Yogasūtra* (Delhi: Bharatiya Vidya Prakashan, 1985)

RSB on YS = Ram Shankar Bhattacharya, ed., *Pātañjala-Yogadarśanam with Vyāsabhāṣya and Tattvavaiśāradī of Vācaspati Miśra* (Varanasi: Bharatiya Vidya Prakasana, 1963)

Rukmani 1981, 1983, 1987, 1989 = T. S. Rukmani, trans., *The Yogavārttika of Vijñānabhikṣu.* Four Volumes (Delhi: Munshiram Manoharlal) Volume I (1891); Volume II (1983), Volume III (1987), Volume IV (1989).

Rukmani 2001 = T. S. Rukmani, trans., *Yogasūtrabhāṣya-vivaraṇa*. Two Volumes (Delhi: Munshi Ram Manoharlal, 2001)

Sachau = E. W. Sachau (tr.), *Alberuni's India* (London 1910,

reprinted Delhi 1964)
Sanderson = Alexis Sanderson, "Śaivism: Krama Śaivism", "Śaivism: Śaivism in Kashmir", and "Śaivism: Trika Śaivism", in Encyclopedia of Religion, Mircea Eliade, ed., Volume 13, pp. 14-17
Sarbacker = Stuart Ray Sarbacker, *Samādhi: The Numinous and Cessative in Indo-Tibetan Yoga* (Albany: State University of New York Press, 2005)
Sarman = Pūrṇānanda, *Ṣaṭcakranirūpaṇa*, ed. Jyestharama Mukundaji Sarman (Bombay 1899)
Sastri and Sastri = S. Sastri and N. S. Sastri (eds.), *Yogasūtra with Vyāsa's Bhāṣya, Bhojadeva's Rājamārtaṇḍa and Kṛṣṇavallabhācārya's Kiraṇā* (Varanasi 1939)
Satchidananda = Swami Satchidananda, *Integral Yoga Haṭha*. (Buckingham, Va.: Satchidananda Ashram-Yoga-ville, 1971)
Schrader = F. Otto Schrader, *Introduction to the Pāñcarātra and the Ahirbudhnya Saṃhitā* (Madras: Adyar Library, 1916)
Schreiner = Peter Schreiner, "What comes first (in the Mahābhārata): Sāṃkhya or Yoga?", Asiatische Studien/Etudes Asiatique 55.3, 1999, pp. 755-777
Scott = John Scott, *Ashtanga Yoga: The Definitive Step by Step Guide to Dynamic Yoga* (New York: Three Rivers Press, 2000)
Searle 1984 = John Searle, *Minds, Brains and Science* (Cambridge, Mass.: Harvard University Press, 1984)
Searle 2004 = John R. Searle, *Mind: A Brief Introduction* (Oxford: Oxford University Press, 2004)
Sell = Christina Sell, *Yoga from the Inside out. Making Peace with Your Body through Yoga.* (Prescott, Ariz.: Hoh Press, 2003)
Sinh = Pancham Sinh, tr., *The Haṭha Yoga Pradīpikā* (Allahabad: Panini Office, 1914-15. Third Edition Delhi: Oriental Books Reprint Corporation, 1980)
Sjoman = N. E. Sjoman, *The Yoga Traditions of the Mysore Palace* (New Delhi: Ahinav Publisher, 1995)

Smith = Anthony Smith, *The Mind* (Harmonsworth, England: Penguin Books, 1984)

Staal = J. F. Staal, *Exploring Mysticism* (Berkeley: University of California Press, 1975)

Stache-Rosen = Valentina Stache-Rosen, *German Indologists: Biographies of Scholars in Indian Studies Writing in German* (New Delhi: Max Mueller Bhavan, 1981)

Swenson = Doug Swenson, *Mastering the Secrets of Yoga Flow* (New York: Berkeley Publishing Group, 2004)

Van Buitenen 1957 = J. A. B. Van Buitenen, "Studies in Sāṃkhya (III)", Journal of the American Oriental Society 77, 1957.

Van Buitenen 1981 = J. A. B. Van Buitenen, trans., *The Bhagavadgītā in the Mahābhārata* (Chicago: University of Chicago Press, 1981)

Vasu = *The Gheraṇḍa Saṃhitā.* Edited and translated by Rai Bahadur Srisa Chandra Vasu. Sacred Books of the Hindus, Volume Fifteen, Part Two. Allahabad 1914

V. Sarma = Pt. V. Sarma (ed.), *The Yogasārasaṃgraha of Vijñānabhikṣu* (Madras: Theosophical Publishing House, 1933

Vasu = S. C. Vasu, *The Śiva Saṃhitā* (Allahabad; Panini Ofice, 1914; Delhi: Oriental Books Reprint Corporation, 1979)

Wezler, n.d. = Albrecht Wezler, "A note on *Mahābhāṣya* II. 366-26: *guṇasaṃdrāva dravyam*" in *Studies in Mallavādin's Dvādaśāranayacakra II,* published in *Buddhism and Its Relation to Other Religions: Essays in Honor of Dr. Shozen Kumoi on his Seventieth Birthday*, n.d., pp. 1-33

Wezler 1983 = A. Wezler, "Philological observations on the so-called Pātañjalayogasūtrabhāṣyavivaraṇa", Indo-Iranian Journal 25, 1983

Wezler 1984a = A. Wezler, "On the quadruple division of the Yogaśāṣtra, the *caturvyūhatva* of the Cikitsāśāstra , and the four noble truths of the Buddha", Indologica Taurinensia 12, 1984, 289-337

Wezler 1984b = A. Wezler, "Further references to the Vaiśeṣikasūtras in the Pātañjalayogaśāstravivaraṇa" in S. D. Joshi (ed.), *Amṛtabhara: Dandekar Felicitation Volume* (Delhi: Ajanta Books Internationl, 1984)

Wezler 1986 = A. Wezler, "On the *varṇa* system as conceived by the author of the Pātañjala-Yoga-Śāstra-Vivaraṇa" in *Dr. B. R. Sharma Felicitation Volume* (Tirupati: Kendriya Sanskrit Vidyapitha, 1986)

Whicher = Ian Whicher, *The Integrity of the Yoga Darśana* (Albany: State University of New York Press, 1998

Whicher/Carpenter = I. Whicher and D. Carpenter (eds.), *Yoga: The Indian Tradition* (London and New York: Routledge Curzon, 2003)

White 1996 = David Gordon White, *The Alchemical Body* (Chicago: University of Chicago Press, 1996)

White 2003 = David Gordon White, *Kiss of the Yoginī: 'Tantric Sex' in its South Asian Contexts* (Chicago: University of Chicago Press, 2003)

Woods = J. H. Woods, *The Yoga-System of Patañjali.* Harvard Oriental Series 12 (Cambridge, Mass.: Harvard University Press, 1914. Second Edition 1927; reprinted Delhi, Motilal Banarsidass, 1966

Yogananda = Paramahamsa Yogananda, *Autobiography of a Yogi.* (1946; reprinted Los Angeles: Self-Realization Fellowship, 1993)

Zimmer = Heinrich Zimmer, *Artistic Form and Yoga in the Sacred Images of India,* transl. Gerald Chapple and James B. Lawson (Princeton: Princeton University Pres, 1984

GLOSSARY-INDEX

abdomen (*naulī*) - 141, 462, 493, 500, 513, 523, 593
-contraction (*uḍḍiyāna*) - 494, 496, 510, 512-514, 527, 532, 553, 575, 603
abhāva, see absence
abheda, see identity
Abhidharma Buddhism - 39, 42-44, 53, 68, 644, 655
Abhidharmakośa (Vasubandhu) - 38, 43-44, 47, 53, 632-633, 650, 655
-*Bhāṣya* (Vasubandhu) - 38, 43, 47, 632-633, 650
abhighāta, see tormented
abhimāna, see self-awareness
abhimata - see pleasing
Abhinavabhāratī (Abhinavagupta) - 40
Abhinavagupta - 40, 114, 647
abhiniveśa, see clinging to (one's own) conventional life
bhyankara, B. S. - 641
abhyāsa, see practice
absence (*abhāva*) - 82-83, 162, 170, 250, 279, 300, 322, 338, 358
absorption, complete (*samarasa*) - 307, 497
abstinence, see restraint
ācāra, see ritual
ācārya, see teacher
accent (*svara*)
acquisition (*prāpti*) - 210, 234, 277, 422, 443
action (*karman, kriyā*) (see also karma) - to many occurrences to list)
capable of fulfilling a purpose (*kāmya*-) - 399
cessation of (*nivṛtti*) - 136, 258, 297, 463, 472
, internal, see mind
-lessness, God's - 188, 303, 326, 412
, organ of (-*indriya*) - 46, 80, 112, 169, 197, 289, 382, 419, 462, 511, 622
, (six)purification(s) of (*ṣaṭ*-) - 457, 461-462, 503-504, 522-523, 537, 541, 552, 560

antardṛṣṭi, see introspection
aṇu, see atom
anubhūta, see experienced
anumāna, see inference
anupalabdhi, see non-perception
anus (*bhū; guhya; pāyu*) - 444-445, 448, 458, 461, 480, 495, 513, 533, 552-553, 604
    , cleaning the (*cakrī-*) - 522-523
    -contraction (*mūlabandha*) - 493, 495-496, 513, 527-528, 532, 550, 553
Anusāra Yoga - 151
anuśāsana - 74, 334, 396, 634
anuśrāvaka, see content, scriptural
anuṣṭhāna, see practice, systematic
anusvāra - 269, 556, 569
anuvyavasāya, see after-cognition
anvaya, see agreement; relation
anxiety (*tāpa*) - 210, 271, 368, 418, 579
anyathā, see other(wise)ness
    -lhyāti, see error, theory of as positive mistaking
anyonyāśraya, see dependence, mutual
apakarṣa, apāna, see breath(-control), exhalation
Apāntaratamas - 574
aparā piṇḍa, s.v.
aparāntajñāna, see death, knowing the time of one's own
aparigraha, see non-avarice
Aparokṣānubhūti - 554
apavāda, see superimposition, removal of
apavarga, see liberation
aperture in the cranium, see *brāhmarandhra*
aphorism, see *sūtra*
apparent (*vivarta*) - 233
appearance (*mithyā*), see error
application (*viniyoga*), see distribution
appropriating (-ed, -ion), see stealing
apramāda, see insanity, temporary

avayava, see part
avayavin, see whole
aversion (*dveṣa*) - 117, 196, 214, 220, 228, 232, 251, 270, 284, 289, 308, 319, 326, 375, 387, 416, 565, 567
Avīci - 93, 207
avidyā, see ignorance
, the word - 228, 250, 308, 312, 387
avirati, see worldliness
avyakta, see unmanifest
avyapadeśya, see indeterminate
awareness (*citta, darśana, jñāna*) (many entries)
, aesthetic (*ānanda*) - 75, 100-104, 108, 112-114, 163
, all-pervasive (*sarvārtha*) - 202, 214, 236, 392
, altered state of, see concentration
, changingness of, s.v.
, correct, see knowledge
, consciousness of, s.v.
, content- or construction-filled or seeded (*samprajñāta-, sabīja-, savikalpa-*) - 52, 62, 66, 75, 77, 100, 103, 105, 115, 184, 186, 283, 297, 319,
, content- or construction-free or seedless (*asamprajñāta-, nirbīja-, nirvikalpa-*) - 49, 52, 62, 66, 75, 77, 100, 108, 112-113, 115, 238, 319, 325, 344, 411, 606
, depressed (*mūḍha*) - 29, 75, 100, 184, 218, 283, 290, 407
, discriminative, see discrimination
, distracted (*kṣipta*) - 29, 75, 100, 184, 219, 267, 271, 283, 296, 389, 397, 407
, emergent state of, s.v.
, empirical (*vitarka*) - 75, 100-104, 108, 110, 112, 115-116, 163, 166, 238, 246-247, 323-325, 335, 339, 343-344
, false, see error
, fluctuations or transformations of (*-vṛtti*) (many entries
, individual (*nirmāṇa-*) 62-63, 126, 134, 180
, (non)intentional, see awareness, content-free/-filled

celibacy (*brahmacarya*) - 118, 170-171, 199-200, 347, 354, 409, 454, 450-460, 471, 477-478, 491, 599, 609, 628
center, vital (*cakra*) - 120, 127-128, 141, 176, 255, 305, 343, 351, 366, 427-428, 437-439, 445-446, 457-458, 463, 468, 477, 480-481, 493, 503, 512, 515-516, 519-521, 523, 528-530, 533, 535, 537, 541, 560, 566, 598, 602, 610, 616, 623, 628
, *ājñā-* - 342, 458-459, 515, 520, 533, 564, 602,
, *amṛta-* - 446
, *anāhata-* - 458, 515, 518-519, 533, 575, 602
, basal (*mūlādhāra*) - 141-142, 343, 364, 446, 458-459, 447, 497, 505, 509, 515, 517, 521, 525, 528-529, 566, 578, 603
, *kanda-* - 533
, lotus-petalled (*sahasrāra-*), see lotus, thousand-petalled
, *madhya-* - 559
, *maṇipūraka-* - 458, 515, 518-519, 530, 533, 602
, *nāḍī-* - 351, 525
, navel (*nābhi-*) - 120, 127, 351, 360, 446, 480
, *nirvāṇa-* - 446
, *svādhiṣṭhāna-* - 446, 458, 515, 518, 528, 533, 602-603
, *tālu-* - 446, 515
, *viśuddhi-* or *kaṇṭha-*- 446, 458, 515, 518-520, 533, 602
cessation (*nirodha, nivṛtti, śānti*) of the fluctuations of awareness - 27, 43, 62-63, 75, 77, 82, 86, 95, 99, 106, 116-117, 122, 133, 143, 162-163, 174, 267, 280, 283-284, 286, 291, 297, 300, 315, 322-323, 326, 328, 330-331, 339, 353, 359-360, 369, 371, 373-374, 379-380, 382, 386-389, 397, 500, 523, 536, 538, 544, 548, 561-562, 566, 619
ceṣṭā, see gesture
cetana, the word - 272
-ścaitanya, see consciousness of consciousness
Chakravarti, Pullinbehari - 40, 633
Chalmers, David - 72
Chāndogya Upaniṣad - 337, 348, 589

compassion (*karuṇā*) - 165, 188-189, 220, 224, 245, 303-304, 368, 413
-ate Yoga, see Kripalu Yoga
, God's 188, 224
competence (*adhikāra*) - 88, 131
compound - 547
, *prasajyapratiṣedha*, s.v.
, *paryudāsa*, s.v.
, *tatpuruṣa*, s.v.
concealing (*āvaraṇa*) - 508
concentration (*samādhi*) (many entries)
, accompanied by deliberation (*savitarka*) - 108, 110, 397, 404, 407-408, 410, 424-425, 539
, accompanied by reflection (*savicāra*) - 108, 111, 301, 382, 397, 404, 410
, conscious (*bhāvanā*) (see also engrossment) - 323-324
-filled or seeded (*samprajñāta-*) - 29, 100, 132, 163-164, 166, 184, 187, 192, 240-241, 243, 246, 264-268, 283, 290, 297, 301, 305-306, 321-322, 344, 349, 356, 358, 373-374, 382, 384, 386, 389, 397, 404, 407-408, 410, 424-425, 539, 536-537, 539, 563
-free or -less or restricted (*asamprajñāta-*) - 27, 29, 51, 66, 76-77, 94-95, 106, 116, 133, 163, 167, 185, 187, 202, 241, 243, 248, 255, 302, 304, 307, 309, 321-322, 339, 353, 356, 358, 373-374, 380, 384, 386, 389, 397-398, 400, 405, 407-408, 410-413, 415, 424, 428, 433, 536-539, 559, 563-564
, object of (*lakṣya*) - 445, 447, 457
, obstacle to (*upasarga*) - 130, 177, 208, 411
, spontaneous (*sahaja avasthā*) - 452, 498, 506
, unaccompanied by deliberation (*nirvitarka*)- 108, 111, 247, 397, 404
, unaccompanied by reflection (*nirvicāra*) - 111, 166-167, 301, 397, 404, 414
, unconscious - 323, 328
conception (mental)- 50, 404, 447, 474, 625, 647

dormant state - 214, 375
doṣa, see blemish; fault
doubt (*saṃśaya*) - 164, 165, 189-190, 264, 267, 269, 275, 299, 304, 359, 403-404, 409, 563, 566, 600, 615
douche, nasal - 141
Dowson - 638
draṣṭṛ, see consciousness
, the word - 262
dravya, see substance
dream(ing) (*svapna*) - 165, 186, 215, 221, 225, 246, 270, 285, 298, 300, 305, 319, 393, 342, 350, 353, 360, 365, 414, 444, 559, 569, 593-594, 598, 604, 606, 613-614, 618-619, 625
drink - 249, 526, 579
dṛśi, see seer
, the word - 272
dṛṣṭa, see content, perceptible
drugs (*oṣadhi*) - 278, 429, 546, 553, 582, 622
drum (*bheri, mardala*) - 500-501, 605, 629
dualism - 44, 72-73, 77, 79, 85-86, 90-91, 635
, epiphenomenal(ist), s.v.
duality (*dvandva*) - 172, 474
, subject/object - 424, 473
duḥkha, see frustration; pain; suffering
dullness (*styāna*) - 164-165, 189, 462, 622
(*tamas*), s.v.
Dundhiraja Sastri - 639, 643
Durgā - 14, 508
duty (*dharma*) - 288, 312, 330, 466, 477, 482, 484, 486-487, 510, 549-541, 564, 585
Dvaita Vedānta - 295
dvandva, see duality
dvāra, see entrance; gate
dveṣa, see aversion; hatred
dvīpa, see island
Dyczkowski, Mark - 636, 643-644

epistemology - 17, 33, 44, 48, 257, 263
equanimity, see peace
equilibrium of the *guṇas*, s.v.
erotic - 138, 435-436, 437
error (*bhrānti, viparyaya*) - 41, 43, 47, 81, 83, 114, 162, 164-165, 185-186, 189, 191-194, 198-199, 205, 219-221, 226, 228-229, 232, 243, 249, 264, 267, 275, 285, 290, 299, 304-305, 307-308, 337-337, 345-346, 353-354, 359, 373, 375, 386-388, 395, 397, 403-404, 409, 411, 415-418, 420-421, 424, 507-508, 510, 557, 562, 574, 608, 614, 621
, *anyathākhyāti* theory of - 299, 308
, *sadasadanirvacanīya* theory of, s.v.
, *sadasatkhyāti* theory of, s.v.
escape (*hāna*), see liberation
essential nature, s.v.
eternal (*ananta, nitya, śāśvata*) - 86, 102, 133, 147, 188, 231, 252, 259, 288, 293, 333, 380, 400, 507, 566, 624
excellence, s.v.
etymology (*nirukti*) - 28, 51, 59, 75, 106, 120, 142, 308, 473, 568
eulogy (*stuti*) - 362, 526, 531, 568, 570, 573-574, 615
Europe - 67, 151-158
evening - 492, 551
even-toned (*ekatānatā*) awareness, s.v.
evil (see also karma, bad) - 135, 186, 206, 246, 264, 306, 347, 407-408, 577
evolute - 312, 363, 376, 419, 567, 586
(*piṇḍa*), see organism
evolution, see change
(filling in) of *prakṛti* - 233, 352-355, 442
excellence (*utkarṣa, bhaga*) - 111, 136, 188, 224, 244, 294, 303, 307, 379, 475, 623
, eternal (*śāśvatika*) - 50, 97-99, 244
of intellect, s.v.
excitement, sexual, s.v.
exclusion (in inference) - 243

43. *Haṭharatnāvalī* (Śrīnivāsa Bhaṭṭa - **522-526**
44. *Haṭhasaṃkeṭacandrikā* (Sundaradeva) - **526-531**
45. *Haṭha(tattva)kaumudī* (Sundaradeva) - **531-535**
Haṭha Yoga (many)
37. *Haṭhayogapradīpikā* (Svātmarāma) - 140, 456, 476, **489-502**, 503, 522-524
48. *Jyotsnā* (Brahmāṇanda) - 140, 535, **547-560**
hatred (*dveśa*) - 43, 83, 167-168, 193-194, 221, 249, 271, 303, 327, 399, 418, 449, 563, 566, 608
Hauer, J. W. - 26, 30-31, 62-63, 68, 72, 99, 100-102, 145, 631, 634-635, 637, 645
head (*mūrdhan, mūrdhni*) - 105, 142, 208, 330, 343, 365, 454, 461, 481-482, 484, 487, 489-490, 496, 514-515, 517, 556, 575, 592
, light at the top of the (*jyotiṣmati*), see *brāhmarandhara*
health - 76, 140, 153, 155, 158, 406, 444, 512
hearing (*śravaṇa, śrotra*) - 104-106, 113, 129, 177-178, 215, 277, 492, 501, 538, 560
heart (*hṛdaya*) - 92, 105, 128, 141, 176-177, 201, 208, 291, 330-331, 349, 401, 428, 446, 458, 480-481, 485-486, 488-489, 501, 505, 610-512, 515, 519, 521, 533, 549-550, 555, 558, 567, 572, 575, 585, 593, 602-604, 610, 616-617
, knot of the, see egoity
, lotus of the (*-puṇḍārīka*) - 120, 128, 601
heat (*tejas*) (see also fire) - 119, 153, 200, 209, 288, 328, 344, 348, 362, 423, 452, 466, 489, 529, 549, 572, 575, 606
heaven (*svar, svarga*) - 93, 207, 236, 329, 351, 364, 371, 400, 410, 449, 461, 474
heavy, heaviness - 189
, becoming (*gariman*) - *277, 351,* 358, 360, 402, 429, *555*
heedlessness (*pramāda*) - 164, 189, 211
heel - 230, 496, 550, 555
hell (*naraka*) - 93, 96, 207, 329, 422, 427, 449, 461
herb - 212, 257, 622
, medicinal (*oṣadhi, auṣadha*) - 470, 629
hermit (*vānaprastha*) - 478

inhalation, see breath(-control), inhaling
inherence cause, s.v.
inhibition (*saṃniruddha*) - 291, 321, 359, 397, 522, 538-539, 593
initiation - 157, 455, 579
injunction - 357, 465, 472, 608
injury - 224, 311
insanity - 105
, temporary (*apramāda)* - 443
insight (*prajñā*) - 68, 95, 116-117, 164, 167, 170, 191-192, 199, 201, 210-212, 216, 222, 227, 240, 242, 248-249, 254-255, 257-258, 300-302, 305, 307-308, 310, 312-313, 317, 320, 326, 349, 357, 369, 397, 399, 409-410, 539
, authentic, "the light of" (*-āloka*) - 121, 130, 173, 315, 358
, discriminative, see discernment
, truth-bearing (*ṛtambharā-*) - 43, 106, 114-116, 121, 128, 130, 167, 192, 211, 248, 287, 306, 308, 317, 320, 325, 358, 360
instrument (*karaṇa*) - 46-47, 80, 84, 112, 242, 308, 358
, cognitive, see knowledge, instrument of
Integral Yoga - 153-154
intellect (*buddhi, manas, mahat*) (many entries)
, excellence of (*cittasattva*) - 76, 85-86, 97-98, 100, 114, 122, 133, 135-136, 199, 379
, fluctuations of, see awareness, fluctuations of
, purification of (*-śuddhi*) - 277, 291, 489
's *sattva* (*buddhisattva*) - 103, 114-115, 133, 135
intensity, change in, s.v.
intensity, degrees of - 95, 99, 123, 127, 164, 171, 188, 287, 369, 401, 411-412, 421, 514
intentional (*samprajñāta*)
awareness or consciousness, see awareness, content-filled/free
, the word - 51, 87
intercourse, sexual, s.v.

Kaniṣka - 37, 41
Kannada - 149, 150
Kānphata - 140, 145, 436, 637
kaṇṭaka, see thorn
kaṇṭha, see throat
  -bandha, see bond, *kantha*
  -cakra, see center (,vital), *kantha-*
  -mudrā, s.v.
kapāla, see skull
  -bhāti, see phlegm, removing
  -kuhara, see forehead, cavity of the
Kāpālika - 144, 146-147
Kapila - 38, 49, 58-59, 99, 142, 188, 278, 367, 379, 429, 544, 573
  Maṭha - 367
Kapilāśramīyapatañjalīyadarśana (Hariharānanda Āraṇya) - 367
karaṇa, see instrument; organ
  , the term 110
kāraṇa, see cause
karman, karma (see also action) - 49, 75, 93, 143, 164, 184, 193, 205-206, 209, 217, 229-232, 243, 249, 257, 298, 320, 323, 345-346, 353, 399, 431, 477-478, 508, 595, 612
  , accumulated for subsequent lives (*sañcita-*), see trace
  , bad - 195, 230, 257, 309, 341, 347-348, 354, 368, 407-408, 417, 421, 472, 483, 502, 510, 512, 572, 577, 598, 600, 602, 604, 614, 616
  , being earned in this life (*vartamāna-*) - 84, 251, 309, 426, 430
  , black - 134, 180, 213, 257, 430
  , black and white - 134, 180, 213, 257, 430
  , good - 230, 258, 309, 417, 448, 510, 626
  , neither black nor white - 134, 180, 213, 257, 402, 430
  , ripening or fruition of (*-vipāka*) - 49, 84, 93, 95, 164, 168, 171, 180-181, 185, 188, 193, 195, 212-213, 220, 230-231, 249, 251-252, 270-271, 275, 288, 307, 309-

mūla
  ādhāra, see center, basal; genital organ; perineum
  -bandha, see anus-contraction
  -mudrā, s.v.
  prakṛti, see *prakṛti*, primordial
Muller-Orteva, Paul - 648
mumukṣu, see aspirant; seeker
muni, see sage
mūrdhā, see head
music, musician - 111-114, 154-155, 449
Muslim - 263
mutation, see change
muttering, see recitation
Mysore - 148-152, 154, 652
mystic(ism) - 30, 32, 74, 110, 341
nābhi, see navel
  cakra, s.v.
nāda, see sound, secret
  -bindu - 438, 475, 496, 498, 512, 555-556, 570604
  -śakti, see God
  , the word - 471
64. *Nādabindu Upaniṣad* (A.U.) - **604-606**
nāḍī, see channel
  -cakra, see center, (vital), *nāḍī*
  -turīya, s.v.
nāga, see snake
  -prāṇa, see breath(-control), *nāga*
Nāgas, Daśanāmī - 146
Nāgārjuna - 37-38
Nāgeśa or Nāgojī Bhaṭṭa - 22, 355-356, 639
Nahuṣa - 230, 638
Nakamura, Hajime - 53, 239, 648
nāma, see name
namaskāra, see obeisance

observance (purificatory, ritual) (*caryā, niyama*) - 68, 117, 170-172, 286, 290, 307, 313, 330, 357, 362, 389, 421-422, 452, 457, 479, 482, 486, 490, 522, 524, 527, 531, 537-538, 541, 549, 556, 599, 626-527
obstacle (*antarāya*) - 164-165, 245, 326, 400, 402, 412-413, 250, 304, 426, 514, 615, 619
to concentration, s.v.
obstruction (*āvaraṇa*) - 180, 183, 213, 238, 259, 429-430, 615
ocean (*samudra*) - 93, 207, 296, 448, 501, 558, 605, 613
old age, s.v.
olfactory organ, see nose
Olivelle, Patrick - 25, 626
oṃ, praṇava, the sacred syllable - 96, 98-100, 164, 188, 193, 200, 245, 259, 269, 287-288, 303, 305, 326, 328, 340-341, 349, 375, 386, 413, 416, 444, 447, 461, 470, 472-474, 482-483, 486, 489, 505, 512, 520-521, 529, 542, 564, 569-570, 585, 593, 595-596, 601, 604-612, 617, 622-627
omnipotence (*śaktimān*) - 129, 245, 340, 404, 450, 470, 486, 518, 623
, God's - 188, 224, 303, 326, 341, 384, 404, 412
omniscience (*sarvajña*) - 96, 98, 129, 164, 179, 188, 224-225, 237, 258, 275, 303, 317, 326, 332, 368, 393, 404, 426, 452, 469, 520, 623
, God's, s.v.
one-pointedness, see awareness, one-pointed
opposites (*pratipakṣa*) - 200, 421, 502
, cultivation of, s.v.
or (*vā*), the word - 99-100, 224, 287
organ (*grahaṇa, karaṇa*) - 363, 372, 387, 398-399, 402, 405, 466, 498, 511, 566, 572, 624
, action-, s.v.
, genital, s.v.
, internal, s.v.
, sense-, s.v.
orgasm - 28, 435, 459

penis (*meḍhra*) - 459, 463, 509, 517
, contracting the (*yonimudrā*) - 555
Pensa, Corrado - 26, 649
perception, direct or sense- (*pratyakṣa, sākṣātkāra*) - 37, 44, 72, 81, 104, 113, 162, 167, 169, 185, 189, 192, 215, 219, 223, 229, 234, 242, 248, 263, 275, 285, 298, 304, 313, 315-317, 322-324, 331, 336-337, 377, 381, 409, 415, 444, 474, 539-540, 544, 572, 574, 622
, extrasensory - 422
, higher, see engrossment, *nirvicāra*
incorrect or erroneous, see error
, joyful, see bliss
, *sāmānyalakṣaṇa* - 338
, yogic (*yogipratyakṣa*) - 324, 557
perfected being, see *siddha*
perfection (*siddhi*) - 420, 424, 428, 458-459, 474-476, 491, 497-498, 511-512, 516, 527, 537, 543, 551, 557, 572-573, 575, 578, 585
of the body, s.v.
, regress from - 467
perineum (*mūlādhāra, yoni*) - 495, 513, 515, 525, 533, 541, 549, 554
permanence, -t (*nitya, sthiti*) - 168, 181, 194, 203, 231-232, 250, 254, 256, 308, 320, 316, 318, 375, 402-403
person (*puruṣa*)
, great (*mahā-*) - 370, 443
, trustworthy (*āpta*), s.v.
pervaded, pervader - 227, 316, 481, 488, 507, 569, 601, 629
pervasion (*vyāpti*) - 243, 275, 285, 315, 337, 340, 370, 507
petal - 343-344, 458, 486-487, 515, 518-520, 602-603, 629
phala), see effect; purpose; result
phase (*bhūmikā*) - 270, 469
Phillips, Stephen H. - 26, 649
phlegm - 486, 493, 537
, removing (*kapāla-* or *mastaka-bhāti*) - 141, 463, 523, 541
physicalism - 44-45, 73, 90-91

quality (*guṇa, viśeṣaṇa*) - 237, 275, 316, 323, 325, 390, 400-401, 443, 474, 569, 618, 620
, change of (*-pariṇāma*) - 48, 77, 79, 125, 156, 202-203, 270, 279, 293, 311, 349-350, 398, 426
quarrel - 337, 443, 455
questions
/answers - 261
, futile - 577
, philosophical - 433
quiescence (*śānta*) - 192, 217, 567
, afflicted state of, see affliction, dormant
quivering, bodily - 483, 512, 551
race - 448
, aboriginal - 449
radiance - 208, 276, 608, 615
, inner - 612
rāga, see attachment; passion
Raghavan, K. - 650
Rāghavānanda Sarasvatī - 294
Raghu - 521
Raghunāthashastri - 568
rāja, see king
rajas - 29, 50, 76, 79-80, 85-86, 96-97, 100, 122, 133, 136, 207, 217-218, 232, 258-259, 265, 272, 274, 279, 283, 286-287, 291, 296, 335, 358, 369, 382, 397, 407, 415, 420, 425, 432, 443, 460, 481, 508-509, 549, 551, 560, 562, 601, 607
, a secretion - 514
Rāja Yoga - 137-139, 153, 330, 334, 339, 347, 361, 364-366, 435, 469, 493, 498, 501-503, 506, 514, 516, 523, 525-526, 529-532, 535, 537-538, 547-548, 556, 574-575, 618-619, 622
, the word - 362, 490, 554, 559
19. *Rājayogabhāṣya* (Śamkārācārya) - 361
Rajput - 266
Rākinī - 518

Śarman, Mahādeva - 584
Sarma, Mahidhara - 648
Sarman, Jyestharama Mukundaji - 517
Sarman, Purnananda - 516, 651
Sarman, V. - 321
sārūpya, see conformity
7. *Sarvadarśanasaṃgraha* (Mādhava) - 54, **282**
Sarvāstivāda - 38-39, 42, 44, 47-48, 53, 124
Ṣaṣṭitantra - 38, 41, 43-45, 47, 53, 67, 142
sarvaviṣaya, see all-encompassing
śāstra, see scripture; tradition
Sastri, A Mahadeva - 590, 636, 648
Sastri, Dundhiraja - 266, 333, 356, 359, 396
Sastri, K. S. - 477
Sastri, N. S. - 403, 651
Sastri, S. - 403, 651
Sastrin, Ananta Kṛṣṇa - 361
Śastrin, Rāmamiśra - 366
śāśvata, *-ika*, see eternal(ity)
sat, see existence
40. *Ṣaṭcakranirūpaṇa* (Pūrṇānanda) - **516-521**
Ṣaṭcakrapradīpikā (Brahmānanda) - 547
Satchidananda - 153, 637, 651
satisfaction (*sukha*) - 78, 187, 196
42. *Ṣaṭkarmasaṃgraha* (Cidghanānandanātha) - **522**
satkāryavāda - 315, 349-351
sattā, see being
sattva (see also being)
, *buddhi*, s.v.
, *citī-* - 89, 133, 280
, *citta-*, s.v.
, (the)-*guṇa* - 29, 76-80, 86, 122, 133, 177, 179, 184, 188, 217, 219, 232, 234, 259, 265, 267, 275-277, 283, 324, 337, 344, 350, 352, 354, 363, 382, 397, 402, 407-408, 420, 432, 443, 508, 551, 559-560, 562, 607
-*mātra*, see being, pure

spinal
cord (*meru*) - 445, 448, 458, 516
column - 444, 509
spine - 525
, base of the - 142, 155, 364, 578
spirit - 152, 343, 422, 427
, evil (*bhūta*) - 449
spirituality - 24, 27, 151
spontaneous, see effortless
concentration, s.v.
intuition, s.v.
sport (*līlā*) - 340, 565, 580
, divine (*cidvilāsa*) - 449, 453, 567
śraddhā, see faith
śrāvana, see hearing
, the word - 276
śreyas, see prosperity
śrī, see beauty
Śrīdhara - 40
Śrīkaṇṭha - 443
Śrīnivāsa Bhaṭṭa (17th c.) - 522-526
Śrītattvacintāmaṇi (Pūrṇānanda) - 516
Śrītattvanidhi (M. K. Wodeyar) - 149-150
śrotas, see stream
, the word - 555
śrotra, see hearing
śruta, see authority, reliable; knowledge, scriptural
śruti, see knowledge, scriptural; scripture
texts - 306
Staal, J. Frits - 26, 62, 633, 651
stability (*sthiti*) - 75, 85, 165, 187, 189-190, 215, 219, 225, 237, 268, 274, 286, 311, 338, 350, 373, 498, 538, 602-603
, failure to attain (*ālabdha*) - 164, 189
, mental, see steadiness
, non-, see instability
Stache-Rosen - 633, 652

stambhavṛtti, see stoppage of breath
star (*nakṣatra, tārā*) - 93, 244, 427, 449, 580
, -light - 355
, pole- (*dhruva*) - 92-93, 127, 176, 207
s' arrangements and movements, knowledge of the - 127, 176, 358
state (*avasthā*) - 363
, dream, s.v.
,= government - 407
, sleep, deep, s.v.
, waking, s.v.
steadiness, mental (*sthairya, sthira, sthiti*) - 118, 165-166, 172, 177, 190, 220, 242, 245-246, 248-249, 268, 274, 286-287, 290, 304-305, 311, 328, 338, 350, 362, 374, 382, 385, 389, 413, 417, 422-423, 428, 460, 474, 492, 499-500, 503, 506, 516, 523-524, 553, 602
stealing - 79, 443, 511, 580, 599
stem, verbal - 206, 312
sthairya, see steadiness
sthira, sthiti, see objectification; permanence; stability; steadiness; sustenance
sthūla, see element, gross; materiality, gross
body, see body, gross
stick - 144, 454
stillness (*niścalatva*) - 274
stomach - 225, 319, 461-462, 491, 527, 550, 601
stone
, philosopher's (*cintāmaṇi*) - 467
, precious, see jewel
, *śālagrām* - 336
stoppage, see suspension
storehouse - 83
consciousness (*ālayavijñāna*) - 246
straightforwardness (*ārjava*) - 479
stream (*śrotas*) - 220, 242, 420, 448, 464, 495, 555
, causal - 213

, devotion or service to or worship of the (*gurubhakti*) - 157, 238, 362, 440, 453, 468, 511
, God as teacher of teachers - 95-96, 164, 326, 328, 339-341, 412
-s, transmission of (*-paramparā*) - 37, 131
tears - 371, 462
tejas, see fire; heat
60. *Tejobindu Upaniṣad* (A.U.) - **595-597**
Telugu - 334
temple - 438, 452, 540, 623, 626
tendency, latent, see trace
term, naming or technical (*pratibhāṣika, saṃjñā*) - 120, 127, 130-132, 201, 235, 255, 315, 440
testimony - 608
, reliable (*āgama*) - 162, 185
, verbal (*śabda*) - 219, 248, 285, 337, 384-385, 409
texts,
, authoritative or sacred - 200, 333, 428, 574
, vernacular - 138-139
theism - 73, 81-100, 126-127
, devotional, see *bhakti*
, eliminative - 74
theology - 33, 49, 74, 98, 137, 141, 147, 152, 435, 642
Theravāda - 47
thing, existing (*bhūtārtha*) - 186, 215
, actual, see real (thing)
thinking, see thought
(*cintā*), see fixity, meditative
, right (*vicāra*) - 474-475
thirst (*pipāsā*) (see also desire) - 196, 249, 265, 288, 344, 349, 410, 452, 465, 468, 510, 512
, cessation of (*-nivṛtti*) - 176, 452, 514
Thomism - 116
thorn (*kaṇṭaka*) - 177-178

ūrdhvāsya, see face turned upward
urethra - 141, 555-556
urine - 448, 460, 513-514
, drinking one's - 141, 496
usage, conventional (*saṃketa*) - 188, 205, 225
usefulness - 194
uselessness- 194, 233, 327
utkarṣa. see breath(-control), inhalation; excellence
54. *Uttaragītā* (A.U.) - **584-586**
utthānakūrma āsana, see posture, *utthānakūrma*
vā, see or
Vācaspati Miśra (9th c.) - 15, 22, 28, 30, 43, 49-50, 54, 60, 66-67, 69-72, 85, 107, 109, 112, 116, 118-119, 125, 131-132, 218-240, 244, 254, 294-296, 298-301, 304-306, 308-309, 311-312, 314, 316-317, 320, 398, 406, 561, 634,-635
vacuum - 495, 499
Vādirāja Sūri - 40
vahinī, see fire
vāhita, see flow
Vaidika, see Veda
vaidya(ka), see medicine; physician
, the word - 569
Vaināśika, see Buddhism
vaira, see hostililty
vairāgya, see detachment; dispassion; non-attachment; renunciation
Yoga - 537
vaiśāradya, see elarness, great; cultivation; skill
Vaiśeṣika (see also Nyāya-Vaiśeṣika) - 211, 218, 240, 299, 343-455
Vaiśeṣikasūtras - 37
Vaiṣṇava, Vaiṣṇavism - 26, 30, 137-138, 142-143, 146-147, 436, 454-455, 590, 612, 633-634, 637
-*mudrā*, s.v.
Yoga - 631
vaiśya - 448, 454, 478

astral or celestial or internalist (*antarikṣa-*) - 93, 207, 427
, cause of the - 345, 500, 612, 623
, creation of the, s.v.
, destruction of the, s.v.
, empirical or phenomenal - 442, 608, 614, 624-625
, external (*bhūta-*) - 122, 169, 174
, intermediate, s.v.
, internal or subjective (*-indriya*) - 174, 177
, lower or nether, see hell
of truth, s.v.
worldliness (*avirati*) - 164, 189
worship - 265, 342, 365, 371, 401, 438, 440, 451, 455, 464, 514, 519, 532, 563, 570, 592
of God, s.v.
, sun, s.v.
wrath - 194, 229, 465-466, 518, 540
wrestling - 149-150
wrinkle(s) - 494, 496
yāga, see sacrifice
Yājñavalkya - 352, 477-478, 480, 482, 489, 534, 548, 552, 568
Yajurveda - 473-474, 589, 601
yama, see restraint
Yamunā - 343, 448
yāna, see path
yantra, see diagram, magical
yaśasvinī nāḍi, see channel, *yaśasvinī*
yatamāna, see dispassion
ṣaṃjñā, see striving, awareness of
yati, see ascetic(ism)
yatrakāmāvasāyatva, see wish-fulfilment
yawn(ing) - 458, 510
yellow - 447, 519, 601-602
yoga (*yoga*) (the whole volume!)
, aids or auxiliaries of - 347, 354, 357, 362, 369, 377, 400, 524, 531, 536-537, 549, 554, 566
, eight-limbed (*āṣṭāṅga-*) 62-65, 95, 139-140, 148, 152,

CORRIGENDA

[Some final corrections in the Camera Ready Copy were not in-corporated in the final printing of this volume. The most important of these are the following.]

Page references in the Table of Contents to be corrected:

Sanskrit citations in asterisk footnote references to be corrected:

p. 55 Asterisk footnote:

śabdānām anuśāsanaṃ vididhatā pātañjale kurvatā vṛttṃ
rājamṛgānka-saṃjñakam api vyātanvatā vaidyake/
vāk-ceto-vapuṣāṃ malaḥ phaṇibhṛtāṃ bhartrā iva yena uddhṛtas tasya
śrī-raṇarangamalla-nṛpater vāco jayanty ujjvalāḥ//

p.56 First asterisk footnote:

Pātañjala-Mahābhāṣya-Carakapratisamskṛtaiḥ
mano-vāk-kāya-doṣāṇāṃ hantre 'hipataye namaḥ

p. 56 Second asterisk footnote:

yogena cittasya, padena vācāṃ malaṃ śarīrasya tu vaidyakena
yo 'pākarot, taṃ pravaraṃ munīnāṃ Patañjaliṃ prāñjalir ānato 'smi.

p. 57 Asterisk footnote:

kāya-vāg-buddhi-viṣayā ye malāḥ samavathitāḥ,
cikitsā-lakṣaṇa-adhyātma-śāstrais teṣāṃ viśuddhayaḥ

ENCYCLOPEDIA OF INDIAN PHILOSOPHIES (27 Vols.)

General Editor ***Karl H. Potter***

The aim of this series is to present the contents of different streams of Indian Philosophical texts to make more and more people aware about Indian Philosophical thought, citing experts on the points that seem debatable. So far, **thirteen** volumes have been brought out.

Vol. I: Bibliography (Sections I and II) indicates the scope of the project and provides a list of sources which will be surveyed in the subsequent volumes, as well as provides a guide to secondary literature for further study of Indian Philosophy.

Vol. II: Indian Metaphysics and Epistemology provides a detailed résumé of current knowledge about the classical Indian philosophical system of Nyāya-Vaiśeṣika in its earlier stages. It covers the literature from the beginning, i.e., the *sūtra* of Gautama and Kaṇāda up to the time of Gaṅgeśa (about 1350 A.D.). Herein are included summaries of the major works of the school.

Vol. III: Advaita Vedānta (Part I) summarizes early Advaita Vedānta upto Śaṅkara's pupils. An introduction introduces to the concepts utilized by Gauḍapāda, Śaṅkarācārya and Maṇḍanamiśra in expounding and defending the Advaita views. This is followed by summaries of all the authentic works of these authors together with those of Sureśvara and Padmapāda.

Vol. IV: Sāṁkhya includes lengthy introduction (by G. J. Larson) which discusses the history of the system and its philosophical contours overall. The remainder of the volume includes summaries in English of all extant Sanskrit texts of the Sāṁkhya system.

Vol. V: The Philosophy of the Grammarians summarizes the main sources concentrating on the philosophical ideas contained therein. An exhaustive bibliography of original and secondary writings on the philosophy of grammar is also appended.

Vol. VI: Indian Philosophical Analysis takes up the history of Nyāya-Vaiśeṣika where Volume Two left off, i.e., from Gaṅgeśa to Raghunātha Śiromaṇi, in the 14th century. It also reconstructs the development of Nyāya-Vaiśeṣika through the next two centuries.

Vol. VII: Abhidharma Buddhism to 150 A.D. summarizes as the gist of Buddhist philosophical teachings, termed Abhidharma, from the first texts that developed after the Buddha. All the texts summarized here originated in a period from no earlier than 350 B.C. through no later than 150 A.D.

Vol. VIII: Buddhist Philosophy from 100 to 350 A.D. limits itself to chronologically summarize texts of philosophical interest with all its polemics well expounded in a context where defence of one view among alternatives is appropriate.

Vol. IX: Buddhist Philosophy from 350 to 600 A.D. The most important author treated here is clearly Dignaga, who is almost entirely responsible for turning Indian Buddhism toward an exhaustive analysis of epistemic considerations and in particular of inferential reasoning. Among other authors whose works are summarized here include Yogacara commentators, Buddapalita and Bhavya.

Vol. X: Jain Philosophy (Part-1) explores the basic questions and their possible answers regarding the position which lead to evident problems in assessing any of the philosophical thesis broached by a Jain.

Vol. XI: Advaita Vedānta from 800 to 1200 A.D. takes up the history of that movement from where Volume Three of this Encyclopedia left off, and covers the literature from Vācaspati Miśra in the tenth century to Citsukha in the thirteenth.

Vol. XII: Yoga volume traces the intellectual history of Pātañjala Yoga philosophy from the early centuries of the Common Era through the twentieth century and provides a systematic discussion of the philosophy of classical Yoga. Altogether the volume contains summaries and or notations for some seventy-five Sanskrit texts.

Vol. XIII : Nyāya-Vaiśeṣika philosophy from 1515 to 1660 A.D.(2010) resumes the history of Nyāya-Vaiśeṣika from Volume Six of the series and brought up to the time of Gadādhara (ca. 1660). This is the period of the great sub-commentators (Jagadīśa, Mathurānātha, Gadādhara) on Raghunātha Śiromaṇi's *Tattvacintāmaṇididhiti*, the culmination of some of the most intricate philosophical analysis the world has ever known.